A C H S

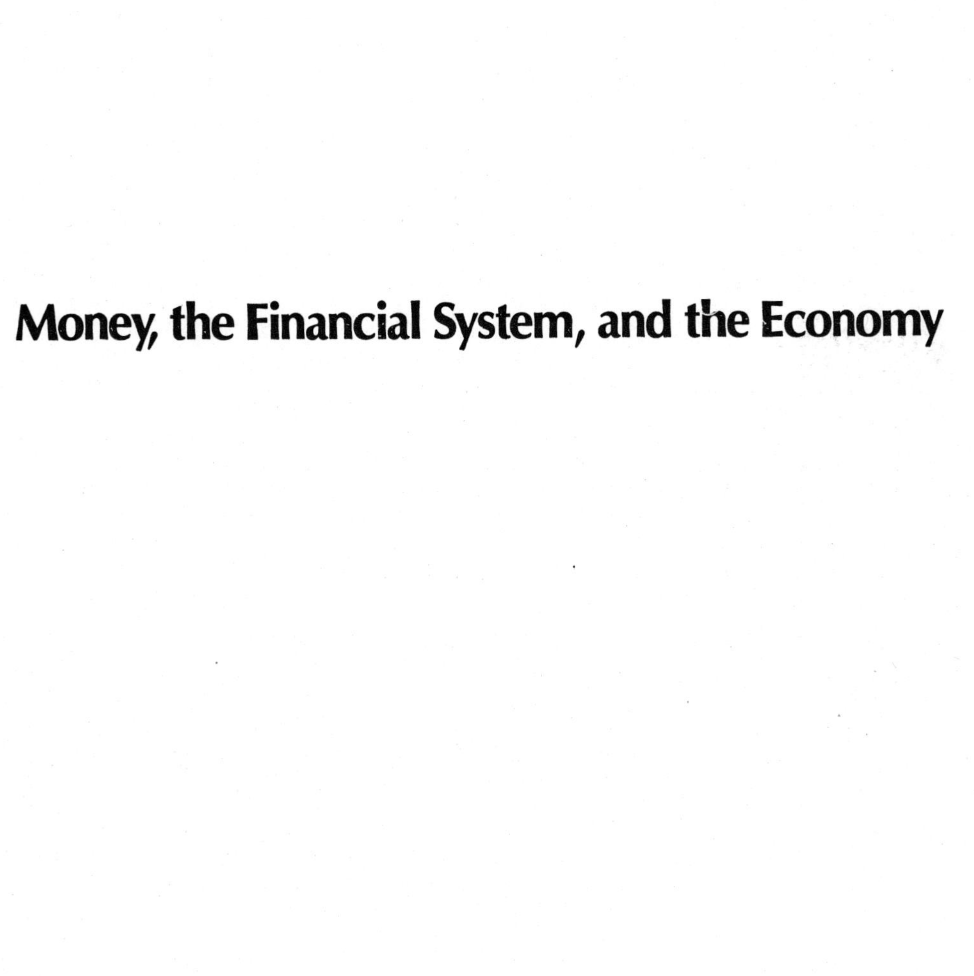

Money, the Financial System, and the Economy

Money, the Financial System, and the Economy

George G. Kaufman
University of Oregon

Rand McNally & Company
Chicago • New York • San Francisco • London

Rand McNally Economics and Business Series
Ralph E. Beals, *Advisory Editor*

Second Printing, 1973

Printed in U.S.A. by Rand McNally & Company
Library of Congress Catalog Card Number 72-9418

The first requisite for constructive work in modern science, and indeed for any work of inquiry that shall bring enduring results, is a skeptical frame of mind. The enterprising skeptic alone can be counted on to further the increase of knowledge in any substantial fashion.

—Thorstein Veblen

Preface

This book is designed primarily as an introductory text on the financial system and its relationship with the other sectors of the economy. Thus, the book is intended for courses in money and banking. It may also serve in courses on money markets and in macroeconomics in which the major emphasis is on money and economic policy. The book may be used both in departments of economics and in schools of business administration at both the undergraduate and the first-year graduate levels. Although an introductory text, at least one previous course in economics and some familiarity with economic terms is assumed.

This book is both traditional and innovative. It is traditional in its emphasis on the institutions of the financial sector. Without a solid understanding of the institutions, theory and policy cannot be properly evaluated. It is innovative in its emphasis on recent advances in theory and analysis. Theory is introduced not for its own sake, but for purposes of explaining observed behavior and is used both to understand and to evaluate policy strategy. Money is viewed as an important, but not the sole, policy variable affecting economic activity. Components of the newer monetarist theory are grafted onto the more traditional neo-Keynesian income-expenditure theory to provide a model explaining a wider spectrum of behavior and policy. Differences among competing theories are identified and illustrated with examples from the FRB-MIT and Federal Reserve Bank of St. Louis econometric models. Simple policy simulation experiments are conducted on these models. Where possible, empirical tests are brought to bear to evaluate competing hypotheses. Current issues in both theory and policy are discussed evenly from all sides.

The book differs in a number of significant ways from competing texts and includes several unique features. Equal weight is given to the examination of institutions (Chapters 1-7), the development of theory (Chapters 8, 9, 12-15, 17, and 18), and the formulation, execution, and evaluation of monetary policy (Chapters 10, 11, 16, and 19-21). While the primary focus of the book is on the financial sector, this sector is fully integrated into the behavior of the economy as a whole. Financial variables are examined not only in the context of the financial sector, but also in the broader context of the overall economy. Thus, money is examined both in its role in facilitating exchange and as an instrument of economic policy. Interest rates are considered in their role of allocating financial claims and as determinants of consumption and capital spending. Financial institutions are analyzed as ongoing business firms and as transmitters of monetary policy. Monetary policy is discussed both from the technical point of view and in relation to the performance of the economy.

The development of monetary theory is traced from the beginning of the quantity theory to the present and is viewed as modifications on a continuum rather than a series of abrupt, unrelated changes. The contributions of the monetarists are described, evaluated, and in part integrated into the more traditional analyses. Likewise, the traditional views are held up to scrutiny by empirical test. The transmission mechanism linking the financial and real sectors is carefully delineated. The traditional interest rate channel is supplemented by the more recently developed wealth and credit rationing channels. A simple four-sector model of the economy encompassing the financial, consumption, investment, and government sectors is constructed and is employed as the underlying framework for the subsequent analysis. To increase the clarity and also to provide current relevance, the analysis is reinforced by illustrations drawn from current econometric models. In the process, the linkages incorporated in the monetarist Federal Reserve Bank of St. Louis model and the larger-scale neo-Keynesian FRB-MIT model are contrasted. The uses and limitations of econometric models are clearly delineated. The different implications of each model for analysis and policy are discussed. The models are further used to simulate the implications of alternative policy strategies.

Recent developments are applied to analyzing a number of important ongoi issues and controversies in theory and policy. Two chapters are devoted to discu ing topics such as indicators, targets, and objectives of monetary policy; lags in the transmission of policy; incidence of policy on industry sectors and income distribution; financing of government budget deficits; the interrelationship between monetary and fiscal policies; inflation; and incomes policy. The final chapter reviews and evaluates postwar economic policy through the New Economic Policy, in light of the preceding analysis. Upon completion, the student should be in a position to describe, appreciate, and evaluate monetary policy independently.

Because of the great importance of interest rates in the operation of the financial system, two chapters are devoted to exploring their characteristics and behavior. Chapter 8 considers theories of the level of interest rates, including the effect of price expectations, and the mechanics of bond prices. Chapter 9 examines the reasons why interest rates on different debt securities differ—term to maturity, risk of default, tax treatment, and marketability—and whether these differences may be systematically explained.

An unusually large number of tables and diagrams are included to assist the reader in understanding and evaluating the analyses. The book also includes a large number of equations. However, most are simple functional notations and do not require knowledge of mathematics beyond college algebra. In addition, they are explained verbally. A small number of equations are more complicated, but for the most part these are introduced to acquaint the reader with representative equations actually used by analysts. The most complex of these equations are not an integral part of the text and may be omitted without loss of continuity.

A word should be said about another unique feature, one of deliberate omission. Years of teaching and analysis have convinced me that the now traditional IS-LM cross entails greater costs than benefits. While simple and, in contrast to the Keynesian 45-degree cross, explicitly introducing the role of money, important differences in the elasticities of the demand for money, supply of money, marginal efficiency of investment, and consumption functions are disguised in the reduced form IS-LM equations and cannot be analyzed. In addition, feedback from the real sector, the accelerator effect on investment, and the recently emphasized interest rate–wealth effects on consumption, for example, are difficult to incorporate into this framework. Instead, the major schedules in each of the four sections of the model are specified individually. Although this increases the number of diagrams from one to four, it results in a more robust model. The linkages in the transmission process from the taking of a monetary policy action to the impact on aggregate income are clearly identifiable and the implications of alternative assumptions in each sector can be clearly traced.

I have made minimum use of footnotes. I feel that they make an elementary text less readable and are almost always passed over by the student. As few, if any, of the ideas in this book are original, this procedure risks the danger of failing to provide proper credit when due. On such occasions, I apologize in advance to those slighted. However, except for possible oversights, the author of credit is cited among the references at the end of each chapter.

The book is designed to include all topics typically covered in a one-semester course on monetary economics, institutions, and policy. A basic quarter course may be constructed from Chapters 1 through 7, sections of Chapters 8 and 9, 10 through 15, and 21. The sections and chapters omitted may be used in a second quarter sequence focusing on macroeconomics, interest rate theory, international finance, and problems in monetary theory and policy.

Like any book, this book reflects the personality, beliefs, hopes, and anguish of the author. It represents the sum of my experiences as a teacher, researcher, and policy adviser. The ideas presented cannot help but have been shaped, for good or for bad, by my ten years in the "hectic" atmosphere of policy decision-making at the Federal Reserve Bank of Chicago, followed by two years as an outside observer from the "calm" of academe.

I am indebted to a large number of persons, both for helping me to understand economics and the financial system and for encouraging and assisting me in completing this book. Particular mention must be made of Dorothy Nichols and Larry Mote of the Federal Reserve Bank of Chicago, Burton Zwick of UCLA, and my colleagues Michael Hopewell and Henry Goldstein at the University of Oregon, all of whom have reviewed, criticized, and improved one or more chapters. The major typing chores were successfully completed by Virginia Nasholm. Stella Jenks of Rand McNally provided editorial assistance and supervised the production process. The art work was done by the Graphic Arts Service at the University of Oregon under the supervision of Helen Spiller. The Federal Reserve Bank of St. Louis provided more than its share of the diagrams. Mary Korns prepared the index. I only wish I could hold these individuals responsible for the bad as well as the good. Unfortunately, if, after their careful review, errors of fact or judgment remain, the fault is mine alone.

George G. Kaufman

Eugene, Oregon
November, 1972

Contents

Tables

Figures

PART I

Money

Introduction and Overview 1

Money is one of the most familiar and at the same time one of the most puzzling things we handle. We know we need money to buy the goods and services we want and that we basically work to earn money to spend. What and how much we buy is related to how much money we have. As money is nothing more than paper and is almost without cost to produce, why, then, not print enough to permit everyone to buy all he needs or wants? We understand that we are employed and paid only if we produce things others want to buy with their money. Why, then, not print enough money to provide sufficient purchasing power to keep everyone employed? How is it that at times there appears to be too much money in circulation so it has only little value and prices are high, and at other times there appears to be not enough so that its value is high and prices are low? It is evident that money affects not only the individual but the economy as a whole and that monetary problems are of widespread importance and concern.

Money is what this book is about. It considers how money is created, how its worth is determined, how ownership of it is transferred, and how it affects the economic well-being of households, business firms, and governments. In the process, the book describes and discusses the sector of the economy dealing primarily in money and money-like, or financial, assets, including the institutions trading such instruments and the markets in which they are traded. We will see that what happens in the financial sector has important implications for what happens in other sectors of the economy in terms of income, employment, and prices; and what happens in the other sectors, in turn, has important implications for the financial sector in terms of the cost and availability of money. As a result, the book emphasizes the interface of the financial and real sectors; in particular, the implications of government-induced changes in the financial sector in order to affect economic activity in other sectors of the economy.

Because of the importance and all-pervasive nature of money, it behooves us to analyze money from the perspective of the economy as a whole. Thus, we begin our journey with a brief discussion of the nature and objectives of the economy.

Goals of the Economy

Although man does not live by bread alone, pursuit of material satisfaction represents a significant aspect of man's life. Economics may be defined as the study of how mankind fulfills its material wants. Economics is important because man's wants usually are insatiable while the material resources available to accommodate these wants are limited. Thus, decisions or choices must be made as to *what* goods and services are to be produced, *how* these goods are to be produced, and *for whom* these goods and services are to be produced. These decisions must be made by society as a whole. Economists are no more or no less qualified to make them than anyone else. Their primary contribution is to calculate the costs and benefits associated with each alternative. That is, economists can provide the background information necessary to permit the members of a society to make the most knowledgeable decision.

From a purely economic point of view, economists can determine the combination of land, labor, and capital inputs that would permit the maximum amount of goods and services to be produced. This solution of what, how, and for whom goods and services are produced may be called the efficient solution. But efficiency is not the only goal a society may wish to attain. A society has goals for many of the same reasons individuals have goals—to give it a sense of direction and to permit it to evaluate where it is and where it has been with respect to where it wishes to go. Socially and politically these goals, at least in Western democracies, are to attain the maximum amount of individual freedom and equality of opportunity consistent with minimum interference with the rights of others. Economically, the goal is generally to attain the highest overall level of material well-being both for society as a whole and for each member of the society. The responsibility of the federal government in achieving the economic goals of the society in this country was acknowledged in the Employment Act of 1946:

> The Congress hereby declares that it is the continuing policy and responsibility of the Federal Government to use all practicable means consistent with its needs and obligations and other essential considerations of national policy, with the assistance

> and cooperation of industry, agriculture, labor, and State and local governments, to coordinate and utilize all its plans, functions, and resources for the purpose of creating and maintaining, in a manner calculated to foster and promote free competitive enterprise and the general welfare, conditions under which there will be afforded useful employment opportunities, including self-employment, for those able, willing, and seeking to work, and to promote maximum employment, production, and purchasing power.

More specifically, these goals are generally stated in terms of:

1. full employment
2. economic growth
3. stable prices
4. equilibrium in the international balance of payments
5. efficient production
6. equitable distribution of income.

We will briefly examine each of these.

Full Employment. The production of goods and services in the economy will be greatest when the largest numbers of persons in the labor force are employed. Society generally determines who is to be in the labor force and the number of hours to be worked. In this country, we generally exclude children under 16 and adults over 65 years of age from the labor force and currently consider 40 hours a week as the normal workweek. Within these limits, all members of society would be better off and none would be worse off if all individuals seeking work were employed. This would be so for two reasons. First, the larger the number of persons employed, the greater is the total output to be divided among all members of the economy. The total output of the economy is referred to as Gross National Product (GNP). Thus, by maximizing employment, society maximizes GNP. Second, because we do not permit persons to starve, the greater the number unemployed, the more the employed have to share part of their output with the unemployed. Thus, full employment both increases the amount of total output and everyone's average share of that output.

Economic Growth. Economic growth is a fancy term for a rising standard of living which, in turn, implies expanding output for a constant or decreasing input. It is economic growth that permits us to enjoy far greater material wealth today working an average of 40 hours a week than our grandparents enjoyed working more than 50 hours a week and their grandparents before them working even longer hours. Growth arises from increased productivity of both labor and capital. This is achieved by transferring resources from producing goods and services for current consumption to producing for investment use. That is, to provide greater future consumption than otherwise, it is necessary to increase both the education and quality of the labor force and the amount of efficient plant and equipment. The faster the target rate of growth, the greater is the amount of resources that must be transferred from consumption to investment use.

Economic growth may be analyzed in two parts. The first part considers the rate of growth necessary to provide employment opportunities for natural increases in the labor force. This part is related to the full employment goal and its achievement benefits all members of the economy. If employment opportunities expand more slowly than the natural growth of the labor force, unemployment results. The second part considers any rate of growth in excess of the minimum rate necessary to absorb additions to the labor force and assure full employment. As noted above, the faster the rate of economic growth, the greater is the amount of investment required and the smaller is the current income that can be consumed; that is, the higher is savings.

Growth, thus, effectively involves a tradeoff between less consumption today and greater consumption tomorrow. The proportion of income individuals wish to consume and save may reasonably be expected to differ from person to person. Thus, unlike the attainment of the minimum rate of growth necessary to maintain full employment, attainment of a growth target in excess of that rate would not necessarily benefit everyone. Those, primarily older persons, who prefer to consume much and save little will be worse off with a growth rate that requires greater savings, while others who prefer to consume little and save much may find a particular rate of growth slower than the one they would most prefer. As a result, it is often argued that in a democratic society the rate of economic growth in excess of the full employment rate should not be determined by the government but by the summation of the consumption-saving preferences of the individual members as indicated in the marketplace. That is, economic growth in excess of the full employment rate should not be a goal of government policy.

In recent years, increased emphasis has been focused on some disadvantages of material growth; namely, noise, air, and water pollution; increased psychological strain; and reduced interpersonal relationships. These undesirable factors are not really the consequence of growth per se but rather of how growth has been measured. Growth is currently measured by the increase in GNP or the gross output of goods and services that are priced on the market. Both the costs of generating the output and the production of goods that are not priced on the market are omitted. While some of the omitted goods have positive values and, if included, would increase the rate of growth, for example, increased comfort, longer life expectancy, housework, child care, and self-shaving in the mornings; others have negative values and are costs that should be deducted against the output, for example, the air pollution, originating from, say, steel mills, that dirties clothing or increases lung diseases in the surrounding community should be deducted from the value of the output of the steel.

Moreover, the value of the output of goods and services required to offset undesirable side effects of generating pollution output are included in the measure of growth thereby effectively giving a positive weight to these negative value outputs. Thus, pollution is given double weight in the national accounts, once when produced and again when combated. At least some laundry and medical expenses can be considered a direct consequence of air pollution and therefore a deduction from, not an addition to, national product. It appears likely that under a more welfare or socially oriented accounting system, the rate of economic growth of the United States and most other countries would have been considerably slower.[1] In this light, increased pollution can be considered a by-product of change, but not necessarily of growth. While all growth is change, all change is not growth.

Price Stability. Changes in the price level affect members of the economy differently. We all have expectations about future price changes when we enter into contracts concerning future income payments or expenses. Contracts are typically stated in nominal dollar terms. If prices rise faster than anticipated, the purchasing power associated with a particular income agreement is less than expected. At the same time, the purchasing power cost of a contracted expense is less. The results are just the opposite when prices rise less than expected. Individuals with fixed-income contracts gain and individuals with fixed-cost contracts lose. Thus, unexpected price changes redistribute income benefiting some and harming others.

All persons are not equally good at forming accurate expectations and, even if they were, the time and energy devoted to such a project may not be the most productive use of the person's time. If this is so, society as a whole is best off when prices remain relatively stable through time, obviating the need to make adjustments for price changes. Because the value of money is affected by price changes and price changes, in turn, are affected by changes in the supply of money, we shall examine the implications of price changes, in particular, of rising prices or inflation, in greater detail in a later chapter.

It should be emphasized at this point, however, that stable prices need not imply that the price of each and every good or service should not change. On the contrary, individual prices must be free to fluctuate if the economy is to attain its other objectives. It is only through changes in relative prices that consumers in a market-oriented economy are able to notify producers what they want them to produce and producers, in turn, are able to notify employees and suppliers what

1. Such an accounting system would be analogous in part to that used by business firms which distinguish between gross income from sales and net income after all costs of attaining the sales. In addition, the system may include measures of noneconomic well-being, such as health, quality of life, etc.

they require. By bidding up the prices of goods and resources in demand, the supply of these goods and services is increased. By bidding down the prices of goods and services not in demand, the supply of these goods is reduced. In addition, as techniques of production change, the implications of these changes should be reflected in the prices charged. Some goods in great demand are lower in price today than earlier because of technological improvements in production. Price stability then implies stability in an average of all goods and services purchased, that is, in the purchasing power of the dollar.

Balance of Payments Equilibrium. This is a more difficult goal to envision than the others. The balance of international payments is the accounting record of a nation's transactions with all other nations. If a nation sells more to others or invests less in them than it buys from them or invests in them, that nation gains claims on the other countries and its balance of payment is said to be in surplus. If it does just the opposite, foreign countries gain claims on it, and its balance of payments is in deficit. Eventually the claims must be paid off in goods and services. A country that perpetuates a deficit in its balance of payments effectively postpones its payment date at three costs. First, the claims carry interest so that future payments will be greater than current payments. Second, the larger the payment, the greater is the loss of income at the time of repayment, and the harder is the adjustment to this loss. Third, it is likely that after a time creditor (surplus) countries will accept additional claims only at a lower value (a depreciation in the value of the deficit country's currency in relation to that of the surplus country's), and the eventual payment will involve greater physical transfers of goods and services. A country that perpetuates a surplus is foregoing enjoyment of current material rewards for its labors. Equilibrium in the balance of payments so that neither deficits nor surpluses are perpetuated generates the greatest net benefit both to a country and to all trading partners as a whole. The mechanics and implications of the balance of payments and the interrelation of domestic and international finance will be discussed in later chapters of the book.

Efficiency. Efficiency may be defined as the maximum output for a given amount and mix of resources. Inefficient production implies that the existing inputs could be used to generate a greater output of goods and services than is being produced. Resources are being wasted. The greater the efficiency, the greater the output, and the greater the overall material welfare of the economy is.

Equitable Distribution of Income. Most economies attempt to provide for some minimum level of income for their members that permits everyone to participate in the productive wealth of the economy. This may require some redistribution of income from wealthier to less wealthy members. Because the value of a dollar to an individual is considered to decrease as his income becomes greater, the gain to a less wealthy recipient from a redistribution of income is believed to exceed the loss to the wealthier payer. To the extent that this is true, more equitable income distribution increases the welfare of the economy as a whole. On the other hand, excessive redistribution may reduce the incentives of the higher income earners to produce efficiently, and thereby reduce total output. Determination of the optimum distribution of incomes in an economy is as much a social issue as an economic issue, and as such should be decided upon by all members of the economy through the ballot box.

Economic Policy

Unfortunately, nearly all countries have found that they have not been able to attain all these goals at all times. This is true of economies such as ours, which can be described as basically a market-oriented capitalistic (or free-enterprise) economy, as well as alternative economies, which may be described as market-oriented socialistic economies, planned capitalistic economies, or planned socialistic economies.[2]

Moreover, the goals may be mutually inconsistent, particularly in the short run. Efforts to achieve full employment frequently generate inflation; strict maintenance of full employment may reduce the rate of economic growth and encourage deficits in the balance of payments; and an income distribution consistent with the most efficient production may not be acceptable on the basis of a sense of equity. If these goals are mutually unattainable, choices must be made and priorities assigned.

For as long as governments have remained in power, they have had the responsibility for attaining satisfactory economic performance. Economic policy involves the attempts of governments to direct their economies toward the target levels of economic performance when they are not operating at these levels. Modern governments have a number of different types of economic-policy instruments at their disposal. These operate through different channels and may affect different sectors of the economy. Some instruments are superior to others for particular objectives. The major economic policies in use in developed countries include:

Monetary policy—Monetary policy is predicated on a direct relationship between the amount of money in circulation and aggregate levels of income, production, and prices. By changing the amount of money in circulation, the government can affect the levels of employment, growth, and prices. Increases in money exert upward pressure on these goal variables, while decreases exert downward pressure.

Fiscal policy—Fiscal policy involves the spending and taxing decisions of the federal government. When the government increases its expenditures, it injects

---

2. The first term applied to each economy describes the type of distribution organization, and the second term the type of ownership of the factors of production, particularly capital. *Capitalistic* indicates private ownership of capital and *socialistic*, public ownership.

purchasing power into the economy, and vice versa. When the government increases its taxes, it withdraws purchasing power, and vice versa. Fiscal policy affects income, employment, and prices through changing the income of spending units. In addition, both expenditures and taxes can be readily directed by the government at specific sectors to affect income distribution.

Debt management—Debt management involves changing the maturity structure of the federal government's debt. Generally, the shorter the term to maturity of the debt, the closer the debt resembles money, and the greater the impact of any given amount of debt on private spending. Thus, the government can affect aggregate levels of economic activity by lengthening or shortening the maturity structure of its debt.

Incomes policy—Incomes policies involve direct price, wage, and profit controls. Such controls impose fixed or adjustable ceilings on prices, wages, and the profits of business firms. They are primarily directed at attaining price stability but, since they generally start from the prices, wages, and profits in existence at a particular moment of time, they tend to maintain the status quo and have important and secondary implications for income distribution and efficiency.

Antitrust policy—Antitrust policies attempt to promote efficiency by promoting competition. Low levels of competition and high levels of business concentration tend to result in reduced output, slower growth, and higher prices, all of which are inconsistent with the goals of economic policy. In many economies, excessive reductions in competition have led to the introduction of governmental regulations to achieve the beneficial results of competition without competition itself. Antitrust policy may be viewed as an alternative to the need for government controls and/or ownership.

Definitions

In this book we consider primarily monetary policy. Before starting on our examination of money, the financial system, and the economy, it is necessary to define a few terms.

Market—A market is any place trade occurs. Markets may be classified in a number of ways according to their major characteristics—financial or nonfinancial, central or local, retail or wholesale, new or used, specialized or general. Financial markets trade financial claims, that is, direct or indirect claims against tangible goods and services. Some of these claims are traded in a large number of local markets, such as at individual commercial banks and savings and loan associations, while others are traded at a single centralized location in the country, such as the New York Stock Exchange.[3] Primary financial markets trade only in newly

3. Approximately one-half of the outstanding dollar amount of corporate stocks are listed on the New York Stock Exchange. While large in dollar amount, the New York Stock Exchange is only one of a number of financial markets.

issued financial claims, while secondary markets trade in existing claims. Some financial markets trade in only a single type of financial claim, for example, the market for U.S. Treasury bills, while other markets trade in a variety of financial instruments. Lastly, some markets deal in claims of all dollar denominations while others trade in only very large (wholesale) or very small (retail) denominations. We shall see examples of all these markets in later chapters.

Trading in the markets is ordered by prices. Sellers sell their wares to the highest bidders while buyers buy at the lowest prices. The equilibrium price at which trading occurs is determined by the intersection of the supply schedule, identifying the quantities potential suppliers of particular goods and services are willing to provide at different prices, and the demand schedule, identifying the quantities of the same items potential buyers are willing to purchase at these prices. If there are large numbers of buyers and sellers in the market, competition and the ability to do business with alternative traders guarantees that neither side will be able to take advantage of the other and that the resulting price will exclude any excessive profits or costs.

Real and financial variables—A variable is a quantity whose value can change. Economic variables describe material and financial wealth such as production, employment, automobiles, prices, and money supply. Variables that describe tangible items are called real variables and the sector of the economy that encompasses them the real sector. Variables that describe financial claims, institutions, and markets are called financial variables and the sector that encompasses them the financial sector.

References

Denison, Edward F., "Welfare Measurement and the GNP," *Survey of Current Business*, 51 (1), January, 1971, 13-16.

Mishan, Edward J., *The Cost of Economic Growth* (New York: Praeger, 1967).

President's Commission on National Goals, *Goals for Americans* (Englewood Cliffs, N.J.: Prentice-Hall, 1960).

Schultze, Charles L., Edward R. Fried, Alice M. Ravlin, and Nancy H. Teeters, *Setting National Priorities, The 1973 Budget* (Washington, D.C.: The Brookings Institution, 1972).

2 The Role of Money

Money has always been a fascinating subject. Money has been claimed, alternatively, to be the root of all evil, the source of all power, the provider of all happiness, and the cause of all sorrow. Some have warned that money is worthless, that it corrupts, and that man cannot live by bread alone—although cynics have argued that it could be used to purchase the missing items.

Fascination has been accompanied by bewilderment about what gives money its unique properties. Unlike almost all other items, its value greatly exceeds its costs of production and it generally is demanded for all reasons but its own sake. Not infrequently, social and political reformers have focused their diagnoses of the evils of society on money and have vowed to operate without it. Revolutions and social, political, and economic systems have come and gone, but the use of money is more widespread than ever. Writing some 125 years ago, the great English economist and scholar, John Stuart Mill, noted that

> confusion . . . envelopes the whole matter; partly from a lingering remnant of . . . misleading associations, and partly from the mass of vapoury and baseless speculation with which this, more than any other topic of political economy, has in latter times become surrounded.

Only a little, if any, of the mystery enveloping money in the public image has been clarified in the intervening years.

Why We Have Money

Money is the product of a specialized economy in which few, if any, participants are self-sufficient and a person's labors are not directly transferable into satisfaction of his wants. Money is an invention. It expedites the transfer of goods and services among persons. In the early days of world history, money did not exist. Man was totally self-sufficient. He raised his own food, prepared his own clothing, constructed his own shelter, and provided for his own security. He engaged in no trade and had no use for money.

In time, self-sufficient man discovered that he was not equally good at all tasks and neither were his neighbors. He observed that he consistently outperformed others at some types of work but was, in turn, outperformed by others at different tasks. He soon realized that he and everyone else in his community would be better off in terms of greater output if everyone concentrated on doing that at which he was best and pooled their resources. The sum of the outputs generated by specialists exceed the sum of the outputs generated by generalists.

In small groups, the distribution of the goods in the pool among the pool participants did not present formidable problems. However, as the size of the group expanded and relationships became more impersonal, the problems of distribution became more complex. Pooling arrangements gave way to direct barter among participants in which each individual traded the output of his comparative advantage for the output of the comparative advantage of others for which he had a need. Although such trade increased everyone's welfare, it was highly inefficient and absorbed time and energy that could well have been put to better use. Not only did traders have to find others who wanted what they had to offer and who, in turn, had to offer what the first person wanted, but they had to find individuals who had the correct quantities of the particular items.

Money was invented to overcome the limitations of a barter system. Primitive forms of money differed considerably from its present form. But in at least one way early forms resembled modern money: money was demanded not only for its own sake, but for its exchange value or value in current or future trade. Under barter, the price of each good had to be specified in terms of every other good. This resulted in a very large number of prices. The overall number of prices in such a system is given by the following equation:

$$N = \frac{n(n-1)}{2},$$

where:

N = number of total prices
n = number of goods.

In an economy with 500 goods, the total number of prices would be 124,750.

Transactors would require a great amount of information to trade efficiently and maximize their profits. By introducing money as a common denominator, or numerairé, the price of each good needs to be specified only in terms of money and the overall number of prices is reduced to the number of goods. Thus, in the economy above, the number of prices would be reduced to 500.

The introduction of money increased the welfare of both the user and the community in two ways. First, the use of money decreased the time and effort involved in trade and thereby increased the time that could be directed toward additional production or leisure. Second, the use of money encouraged further specialization of resources and trade, and thereby increased efficiency.

History of Money

Primitive monies consisted of items for which the exchange or monetary value was shared with the intrinsic or market value of the commodity for its own sake. This provided holders with protection against deep declines in exchange value. The intrinsic value served as a floor for the exchange value. If at times the exchange value threatened to decline below the intrinsic value, the commodity could always be sold for its own sake. On the other hand, at times the intrinsic value climbed above the exchange value, the commodity stopped serving as money, and was used for its own sake. Early societies used grain, cattle (the word *pecuniary* is derived from the Latin word for cattle), salt, and various metals as monies. As recently as the early American colonial period, shells and tobacco functioned as money. Even though many items have served as money at different times, commodities that had a number of important properties eventually began to dominate. These properties included:

1. *Scarcity*—Scarcity limits the items serving as money to those whose supply is restricted and which have barriers against abrupt increases. Scarcity acts to maintain the exchange value of money. Failure to satisfy this condition led to the demise of many types of commodity monies, such as grains, since the supply of such monies could readily be increased by additional planting with a consequent decline in their exchange value and usefulness.

2. *Durability*—Durability permits purchasing power to be stored through time. By maintaining its value through time, money permits the separation of sales, or the receipt of funds, from purchases, or the expenditure of funds. This greatly increases the usefulness of money to the extent that, without durability, a particular form of money would soon be replaced.

3. *Divisibility*—This property permits money to be used in financing transactions of all denominations and increases its general acceptability.

Early societies found that metal coins possessed these properties best. Most metals, particularly gold, silver, and copper, were in limited supply, costly to mine, durable, and divisible in almost any amount. Governments increased the usefulness of metal monies further by standardizing the amounts; that is, by minting coins in standard denominations. In the process, the governments discovered a tidy source of revenue. By setting the monetary or exchange value of the metal coin above the value of the metal in alternative uses, they were able to sell the coins for more than the value of the metallic contents. This difference, called seigniorage, served as a major source of revenue for many early governments. To maintain an exchange value greater than the metallic value of the coin, it was generally necessary for the government to accept the coins at this rate in payment of taxes and other charges. To protect this source of income, governments typically assumed a monopoly over minting money and prohibited others from this practice without license. This restriction has been carried down to modern times. The United States Constitution specifically gives the Congress the sole power to mint money. Congress, in turn, as we shall see later, effectively transferred this authority to the Federal Reserve System.

Metal coins served as the primary form of money throughout the larger part of recorded history. Coins from the ancient Roman, Greek, Persian, Hebrew, and even older societies have been unearthed in substantial quantities and may be seen on display at many museums. As trade and specialization increased, accelerated by the commercial revolution in the 1600s and the industrial revolution a century later, coins served progressively less well as an efficient form of money. Their weight and size made them clumsy to transport and the ever-larger scale of transactions made them difficult to store and protect. In addition, not infrequently the intrinsic value rose above their monetary value and the coins were withdrawn from circulation, melted down, and sold for their metallic content. At such times, money shortages developed.[1]

By means discussed in later chapters, coins were supplemented by paper notes and currency issued first by private parties and later by governments. At first, these notes only substituted for coins and could be exchanged for coins or their metal content at a fixed exchange rate upon demand. Through time, however, the link with metallic value was broken and notes and currency were accepted for their own exchange value. Today coins also have little meaningful metallic value.

The continued expansion of commerce and the scale of business soon outpaced the ability of notes and currency to serve as efficient modes of finance for large transactions, and man invented another form of money, the check. Checking accounts, or technically demand deposits, are deposits at commercial banks that can be transferred immediately by the written order of the depositor to a designated second party in any denomination less than the amount of the writer's

1. As recently as the mid-1960s, sharply increasing demands for silver by industry and the arts caused its market price to rise above its monetary value established many years earlier. As a result, some coins were melted down by the public for their silver content and a number of denominations became scarce. To prevent a shortage of these coins, their silver content was reduced.

deposit balance. Demand deposits provided greater transferability and safety than alternative forms of money and replaced the other forms as the most frequently used form of financing. Although no one can vouch for their accuracy, some studies have estimated that currently more than 90 percent of the dollar volume of all transactions in the United States are financed by check. The proportion of the total number of transactions financed by check may be expected to be smaller.

Properties of Money

In recent years, items other than coins, currency, and checks have also been used to finance transactions; for example, traveler's checks, consumer credit cards, and business trade credit. Should these items also be included in the definition of money? It appears clear that, while money may be an artifact, what we consider money changes through time. Items that commonly serve as money are generally considered to possess three properties:

1. Be a commonly accepted medium of exchange.
2. Serve as a store of value.
3. Serve as a standard of value.

Service as a commonly accepted medium of exchange appears to be a self-evident property of money. It is the principal reason money came into existence. Yet everything we implicitly consider money may not perform this function equally well at all times. A hundred-dollar bill will hardly be accepted in payment for a daily newspaper, while a personal check may not be accepted by a seller unfamiliar with the identity of the purchaser. Moreover, some items that are clearly not media of exchange, such as time deposits at commercial banks, are often considered "money" by their holders since it requires only a letter or trip to the bank to convert a passbook savings account into currency or a demand deposit. Likewise, loans on the cash value of life insurance policies may be quickly arranged.

Money must serve as a store of value in order to continue to remain in use in its existing form. If money declines rapidly in value, then it cannot properly perform one of its more important functions, that of permitting the separation of the acts of receiving and spending income. As a store of value, money serves as a temporary abode of purchasing power. Since the value of money is computed by what can be bought with it, the goal of stable prices, discussed in Chapter 1, can now be seen as a prerequisite for saving and providing for the production of future consumption goods. Many items that do not serve as good media of exchange serve as good stores of value. These would include time and savings deposits at commercial banks, deposits at mutual savings banks and savings and loan associations, U.S. Treasury savings bonds, and even some very liquid types of marketable securities.

By being exchangeable into all other commodities, money effectively values all goods and services in its own image. That is what is meant by a standard of value. In this country we price everything in terms of dollars, in England in terms of the pound sterling, in France in terms of francs, and in Japan in terms of yen. This property permits persons in the same country to maintain uniform accounts of the values of different items.

Contemporary Money

Definition of Money

It is obvious that no single item uniquely possesses all of these three properties and that many items possess some of each property in varying degrees. The items that are selected to be included in the definition of money are somewhat arbitrary and depend to some extent upon the use to which the particular definition of money is to be put. Most economists in the United States place greatest emphasis on the medium-of-exchange property and define the stock of money to include private nonbank holdings of coin, currency, and demand deposits. Others prefer to define money on the basis of the degree of substitutability among financial assets, and include as money those assets the public views as close substitutes for currency and demand deposits. Still others define money on the basis of the correlation between groupings of financial assets and aggregate income, including as money those assets that, as a group, generate the highest correlation. However, none of these approaches delineates clearly defined or unique sets of financial assets.

Financial assets excluded by any of these definitions are referred to as liquid assets or near-monies. The dollar amounts of the major forms of money and near-monies outstanding in each year of the twentieth century to date are shown in Table 2-1.

The rapid increase in demand deposits at the beginning of the century reflects a great expansion in the number of commercial banks and deposit banking and the substitution of deposits for currency, the previous primary medium of exchange. The sharp decline in demand deposits and slight increase in currency in the early 1930s reflect the large number of bank failures of that period and loss of faith in demand deposits as money by the public. This induced widespread substitution of currency for deposits. The considerably faster rise in the quantities of near-monies throughout most of the post–World War II period reflects the rising interest returns that could be earned on these assets but not on money. Holders substituted near-monies for money and used their money balances more intensively. The sharp growth of savings and loan associations, spurred by aggressive mortgage lending, is particularly noticeable in this period. After being only half as large as mutual savings banks at the end of World War II, savings and

Table 2-1 **Money and Selected Near-Monies, 1900-71**
(Seasonally adjusted, billion dollars)

Year-end	Currency	Demand Deposits†	Time Deposits, Commercial Banks	Deposits, Mutual Savings Banks	Deposits, Savings & Loan Associations	Deposits, Postal Savings	U.S. Savings Bonds
1900*	1.2	4.4	0.9	2.1	0.4		
1901*	1.3	5.2	1.1	2.3	0.4		
1902*	1.3	5.7	1.2	2.4	0.4		
1903*	1.4	6.0	1.3	2.5	0.4		
1904*	1.4	6.3	1.4	2.6	0.4		
1905*	1.5	7.1	1.7	2.7	0.4		
1906*	1.6	7.5	1.9	2.9	0.4		
1907*	1.9	7.9	2.3	3.1	0.5		
1908*	1.7	7.4	2.4	3.1	0.5		
1909*	1.7	7.8	3.2	3.1	0.6		
1910*	1.8	8.3	3.6	3.3	0.6		
1911*	1.7	8.7	3.9	3.4	0.7		
1912*	1.8	9.2	4.3	3.6	0.8		
1913*	1.9	9.1	4.6	3.7	0.9		
1914	1.9	9.9	4.8	3.9	0.9	0.1	
1915	2.0	11.6	5.7	4.0	1.0	0.1	
1916	2.3	13.6	7.0	4.3	1.1	0.1	
1917	3.2	15.4	7.6	4.4	1.2	0.1	
1918	4.1	16.9	8.3	4.5	1.3	0.2	
1919	4.2	19.5	10.2	4.9	1.5	0.2	
1920	4.5	18.9	11.5	5.4	1.7	0.2	
1921	3.8	17.1	11.3	5.6	2.0	0.1	
1922	3.8	19.3	12.9	5.9	2.2	0.1	
1923	4.0	19.2	14.2	6.4	2.6	0.1	
1924	3.9	20.7	15.7	6.8	3.2	0.1	
1925	4.0	22.3	17.0	7.2	3.8	0.1	
1926	4.1	21.7	17.7	7.7	4.3	0.1	
1927	3.9	22.1	19.3	8.3	5.0	0.2	
1928	3.9	22.8	20.3	8.8	5.8	0.2	
1929	3.8	22.9	19.6	8.8	6.2	0.2	
1930	3.8	21.4	19.4	9.4	6.3	0.2	
1931	4.7	17.7	15.9	10.0	5.9	0.6	
1932	4.9	15.9	14.5	9.9	5.3	0.9	
1933	4.9	15.3	11.9	9.5	4.8	1.2	
1934	4.6	18.7	12.8	9.7	4.5	1.2	
1935	4.9	22.6	13.6	9.8	4.3	1.2	0.2
1936	5.5	25.9	14.3	10.0	4.2	1.3	0.5

Table 2-1 (Continued)

Year-end	Currency	Demand Deposits†	Time Deposits, Commercial Banks	Deposits, Mutual Savings Banks	Deposits, Savings & Loan Associations	Deposits, Postal Savings	U.S. Savings Bonds
1937	5.6	24.1	15.0	10.1	4.1	1.3	1.0
1938	5.7	26.7	14.9	10.2	4.1	1.3	1.4
1939	6.3	30.6	15.3	10.5	4.1	1.3	2.2
1940	7.4	35.5	15.8	10.6	4.3	1.3	3.2
1941	9.6	39.4	16.0	10.5	4.7	1.3	6.1
1942	13.8	49.5	16.3	10.6	4.9	1.4	15.0
1943	18.7	61.8	19.2	11.7	5.5	1.8	27.4
1944	23.4	67.9	24.2	13.3	6.3	2.3	40.4
1945	26.3	76.8	30.3	15.3	7.4	2.9	48.2
1946	26.4	82.0	33.9	16.8	8.6	3.3	49.8
1947	26.4	86.7	35.4	17.7	9.8	3.4	52.1
1948	25.8	85.8	36.0	18.4	11.0	3.3	55.1
1949	25.1	86.0	36.4	19.3	12.5	3.2	56.7
1950	25.0	91.2	36.7	20.0	14.0	2.9	58.0
1951	26.1	96.5	38.2	20.8	16.1	2.7	57.6
1952	27.3	100.1	41.1	22.6	19.1	2.5	57.9
1953	27.7	101.1	44.5	24.3	22.8	2.4	57.7
1954	27.4	104.9	48.3	26.2	27.1	2.1	57.7
1955	27.8	107.4	50.0	28.0	31.8	1.9	57.9
1956	28.2	108.7	51.9	29.9	36.8	1.6	56.3
1957	28.3	107.6	57.4	31.6	41.5	1.3	52.5
1958	28.6	112.6	65.4	33.9	47.5	1.1	51.2
1959	28.9	113.1	67.4	34.9	54.1	1.0	48.2
1960	28.9	112.1	72.9	36.2	61.6	0.8	47.2
1961	29.6	115.9	82.7	38.4	70.3	0.7	47.5
1962	30.6	116.8	97.8	41.4	79.6	0.5	47.5
1963	32.5	120.5	112.4	44.6	90.6	0.5	48.8
1964	34.2	125.1	126.6	48.8	101.3	0.4	49.7
1965	36.3	130.4	146.7	52.6	109.8	0.3	50.3
1966	38.3	132.1	158.5	55.1	113.4	0.1	50.8
1967	40.4	142.7	183.7	60.1	124.0		51.7
1968	43.4	154.0	204.9	64.6	131.6		52.3
1969	46.0	157.7	194.1	67.0	135.5		52.2
1970	49.0	165.8	228.9	71.6	146.4		52.5
1971	52.5	175.7	269.9	81.4	174.5		54.9

* June, not seasonally adjusted.

† Other than interbank and U.S. Government, less cash items in process of collection.

Sources: Friedman and Schwartz, *Monetary Statistics of the United States*, pp. 4-53; Board of Governors of the Federal Reserve System, *Banking and Monetary Statistics* (Washington, D.C.: 1943); *Federal Reserve Bulletin*, various issues; Council of Economic Advisers, *Annual Report*, various issues.

loan associations surpassed these banks in 1954 and by the end of 1971 were more than twice as large. Deposits at savings and loans also gained in relation to time deposits at commercial banks, but have remained at a lower level. Time deposits at commercial banks also expanded rapidly and have surpassed demand deposits as the major source of funds for commercial banks.

Importance of Money

Why is money more important than any other good or service and worthy of special consideration? Money is uniquely important because a substantial body of evidence generated over the course of history indicates that money is related to aggregate levels of spending, prices, income, production, and employment more importantly than any other single economic variable. While economists may differ about the precise nature of the relationships between money and aggregate economic activity, there is no disagreement that an insufficient amount of money will hamper commerce and induce a slowing of spending and income and a decline in employment. On the other hand, too large a quantity of money will induce a decline in the transactions value of money and result in a move away from money and into goods and services. Such a substitution would push up prices and may increase employment and production, to a point. About a century ago, Walter Bagehot, a careful observer of the British economic scene, concluded that "money does not manage itself." Modern economies have the choice of either managing money in the public interest or being themselves managed by money. History provides ample evidence that the absence of official monetary management has resulted in periodic economic crises as money was alternately too plentiful and too scarce. Many of these fluctuations reflected changes in the relationship between the intrinsic and exchange values of commodity monies, and were frequently the result of discoveries of new metal sources and exhaustion of old sources as well as changing nonmoney uses of the metals serving as money. As a result, all contemporary governments consider monetary management an important part of their economic responsibilities.

Credit

One final word about the difference between money and credit. The two terms are often incorrectly used interchangeably, and it is important to differentiate between them. Money is an asset of the user, credit is a liability of the user. In a modern economy the two are closely interrelated. The greater part of what performs as money is the liability or credit of someone else, primarily the commercial banks. Indeed, as will be seen in a later chapter, the provision of demand deposits by a commercial bank is frequently directly associated with a credit extension by the bank. Money, however, can exist without credit as is evidenced by metal coins. Credit, on the other hand, cannot exist separately from money. Indeed, credit arises from the renting of money. Money is rented because the user may not be interested in money per se as an asset, but only in the purchasing-power services it renders. The initial holder of the money is not willing to surrender it as an asset—otherwise he would have purchased goods and services with it—but he is willing to surrender temporary use of its purchasing-power services at an interest return. This he does by loaning the money.

As the same dollars can be rented a large number of times when not in use, money can give rise to a much larger quantity of credit. Interest, as we will see later, is the cost of renting money or the cost of obtaining credit. Although money and credit generally change in the same direction, they need not always do so and may not have equal effects on the economy. Some economists consider money effects to be the more important and predictable, while others consider credit to be more closely associated with changes in economic activity. These differences will be examined in later chapters.

References

Brunner, Karl, and Allan H. Meltzer, "The Uses of Money: Money in the Theory of an Exchange Economy," *American Economic Review*, 61 (5), December, 1971, 784–805.

Friedman, Milton, and Anna J. Schwartz, *A Monetary History of the United States, 1867–1960* (Princeton: National Bureau of Economic Research, 1963).

———, *Monetary Statistics of the United States* (New York: National Bureau of Economic Research, 1970).

Kaufman, George G., *The Demand for Currency* (Washington, D.C.: Board of Governors of the Federal Reserve System, 1966).

Laidler, David, "The Definition of Money," *Journal of Money, Credit, and Banking*, 1 (3), August, 1969, 508–524. Reprinted in William E. Gibson and George G. Kaufman, *Monetary Economics: Readings on Current Issues* (New York: McGraw-Hill, 1971).

Nussbaum, Arthur, *A History of the Dollar* (New York: Columbia University Press, 1957).

3 Prices and the Value of Money

Money is worth what one can buy with it. The value of money changes through time as what can be bought with it changes. Thus, if in one period one dollar buys two pounds of meat and in a subsequent period it buys only one pound, the value of the dollar has fallen by one-half. Of course, we value the dollar in terms of more than one item. At the same time the purchasing value of the dollar was declining with respect to meat, it may have been increasing with respect to, say, vegetables or automobiles. The value of any currency is measured with respect to a broad spectrum of goods and services traded in the economy. The value of money and the prices of goods and services vary inversely. The higher prices are, the lower the value of money, and vice versa. Knowledge of one permits computation of the other.

Index Numbers

Prices and the value of the dollar are of interest not so much for their absolute values but for their value in relation to both past and future purchasing power. We are not so much interested in whether prices are high, but in whether they are rising, steady, or falling. This type of information is an important input for economic decision-making with respect to expenditures and savings. Changes in values over a period of time are easiest to interpret by converting the observed values into index numbers. Index numbers are constructed by dividing each observation by the value of the observation in the period selected as a base. Such a conversion changes the observations from absolute numbers to relative numbers. The base value is established at 100. Values smaller than the base value are less than 100 and values larger, greater than 100. Changes from the base period are automatically shown as percentage changes. Thus, a value of 134 indicates a level 34 percent greater than in the base period. For comparison with periods other than the base period, percentage change must be calculated. A value of 134 in a period represents four percentage points increase from 130 in, say, the previous period, but only a 3 percent increase.

The average price of a collection of goods and services can change between two periods for two reasons: (1) changes in the prices of the individual items in the collection, and (2) changes in the composition or mix of the individual items in the collection. The latter change could cause a change in the average price even though the price of each and every item in the collection remained the same. For example, with unchanged prices, an increase in the use of more expensive goods and services, such as driving a Cadillac relative to driving a Chevrolet, would result in an increase in the average price of the collection. Two types of price indexes are commonly computed:

$$I_1 = \frac{\Sigma p_{i2} q_{i1}}{\Sigma p_{i1} q_{i1}}; \; I_2 = \frac{\Sigma p_{i2} q_{i2}}{\Sigma p_{i1} q_{i2}},$$

where:

p_{i1} = price of item i in period 1
p_{i2} = price of item i in period 2
q_{i1} = quantity of item i in period 1
q_{i2} = quantity of item i in period 2.

I_1, named the Laspeyres Index, measures the change in the price of a constant collection of items. To the extent that the types and quantities of items included change through time so that the collection currently purchased differs from the base collection, this index may measure the price of an increasingly less meaningful set of items.

I_2, named the Paasche Index, measures the change in the price of the current collection of goods and services from the base period. Unlike I_1, the base period applies to prices, not quantities. Through time, this index reflects changes in the price of differing collections of items. These differences reflect both changes in buyer preferences and changes in purchasing patterns in response to relative price changes on individual items. Thus I_2 provides historical price information on the collection of items actually purchased in each period regardless of whether these items were purchased previously in the same combinations. The differences between the two indexes are shown below:

Index	Time Period 1	2	3	4
I_1	$\frac{\Sigma p_1 q_1}{\Sigma p_1 q_1}$	$\frac{\Sigma p_2 q_1}{\Sigma p_1 q_1}$	$\frac{\Sigma p_3 q_1}{\Sigma p_1 q_1}$	$\frac{\Sigma p_4 q_1}{\Sigma p_1 q_1}$
I_2	$\frac{\Sigma p_1 q_1}{\Sigma p_1 q_1}$	$\frac{\Sigma p_2 q_2}{\Sigma p_1 q_2}$	$\frac{\Sigma p_3 q_3}{\Sigma p_1 q_3}$	$\frac{\Sigma p_4 q_4}{\Sigma p_1 q_4}$

Popular price indexes in the United States include both types.

Consumer Price Index

Perhaps the best known of the different price indexes regularly compiled and published for the United States is the consumer price index, frequently abbreviated CPI. Price data for this index are collected monthly by the Bureau of Labor Statistics of the U.S. Department of Labor. The index is of the I_1 type. Retail prices are recorded for some 400 different goods and services that previous surveys have indicated are included in the market basket of purchases made by urban wage earners and salaried clerical workers with families. The individual prices are aggregated into an average price by weighting the price of each particular item by how important the item is in the budget of the consumers surveyed. Thus, the cost of the same market basket is determined at different periods through time. The items and weights included are changed periodically on the basis of new survey information to maintain the relevancy of the market basket. The major items and accompanying weights included in the index are shown in Table 3–1. Since, strictly defined, the CPI is representative only of the retail cost of purchasing a group of items purchased on the average by a particular segment of the population, it is not a universally accurate measure of the value of the dollar. But because many of these items also appear in the budget of most consumers, although in different degrees, and because of the lack of other equally comprehensive price data, the CPI is frequently used as a general cost of living index for almost all groups.

In 1971, the CPI was 121.3 on a base of 100 for 1967. Thus, prices were 21 percent higher than four years earlier. The index was also five percentage points, or 4.1 percent, higher than in 1970 when the index was 116.3. The purchasing power value of the dollar is computed by the reciprocal of the CPI. Hence, the

Table 3-1 **Relative Importance of Major Goods and Services and Number of Items Priced in Consumer Price Index, 1965**

	Percent of Total		No. of Items	
All Items	100.00		398	
Food	22.43		105	
Meat, fish, poultry		5.63		29
Restaurant service		4.54		9
Housing	33.23		81	
Shelter		20.15		18
Fuel and utilities		5.26		10
Household furnishings		7.82		53
Apparel	10.63		77	
Transportation	13.88		34	
Private automobile		12.64		29
Health and Recreation	19.45		101	
Medical care		5.70		38
Tobacco		1.89		5
Alcoholic beverages		2.64		9
Recreation		4.36		27
Miscellaneous	0.38			

Source: Bureau of Labor Statistics.

value of the dollar in 1971 was 1/121.3 or $.82 compared to $1.00 in 1967 and $1.95 in 1929 when the CPI was 51.3. That is, a dollar in 1971 purchased only 82 percent of the same goods and services it purchased in 1967 and less than one-half of what it had purchased in 1929. Values of the CPI since 1800 are shown in Figure 3–1.

Wholesale Price Index

Another common price index of a fixed basket of goods is the wholesale price index or WPI. This index, also prepared by the U.S. Department of Labor, is a monthly measure of changes in the prices of some 2,500 commodities sold on primary markets to producers. Each commodity is weighted by its importance in total industrial shipments in designated base years. Because price movements on primary markets tend to be more volatile than price movements on retail markets, the WPI should be a more sensitive measure of price pressures than the CPI. As many of the commodities priced in the WPI are used in the production of items priced in the CPI, changes in the WPI often precede changes in the CPI and are used as a leading indicator of coming changes in retail prices. On the other side, because service items, which have been increasing in price faster than other items, are not included in the WPI, the index should show smaller long-run

Figure 3-1 Wholesale Price Index, 1720-1971, and Consumer Price Index, 1800-1971

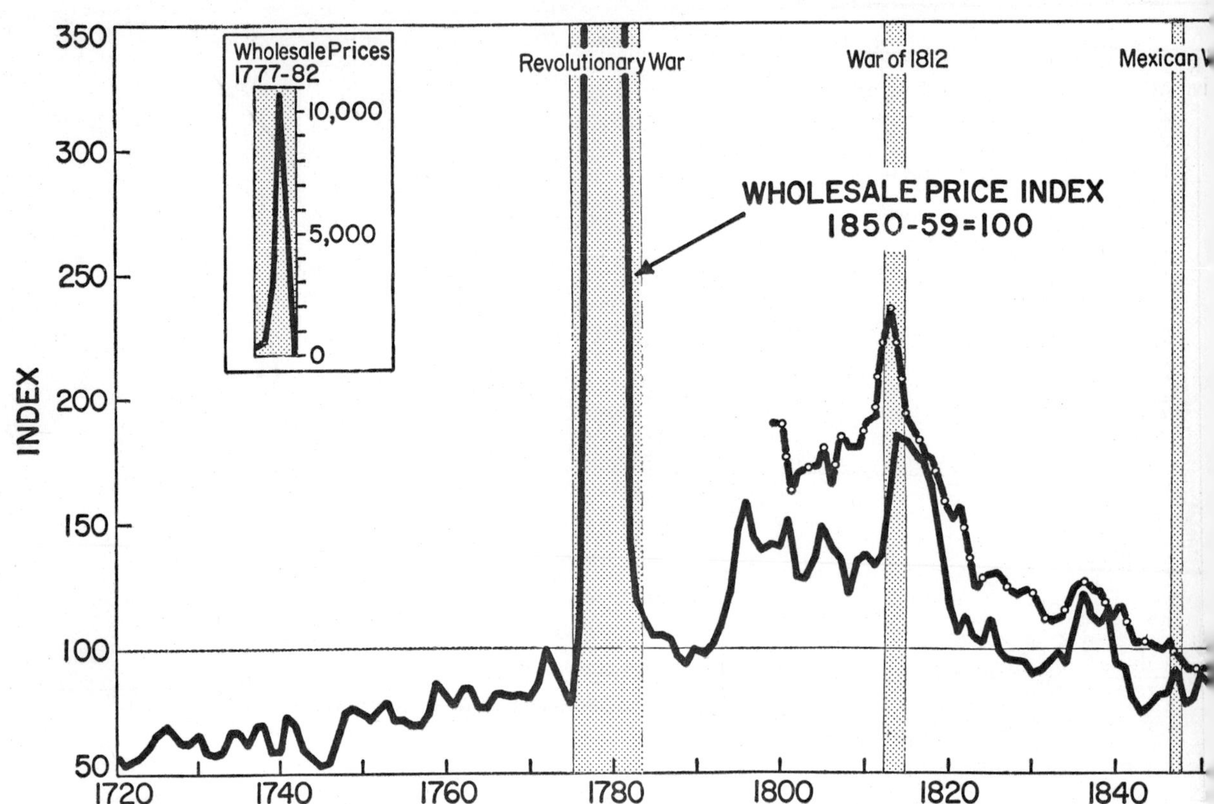

Sources: 1720–1958, U.S. Congress, Joint Economic Committee, *Hearings, Employment Growth and Price Levels, Part 2, Historical and Comparative Rates of Production, Productivity and Prices* (86th Congress, April, 1959), pp. 394–398; 1959–71, Council of Economic Advisers, *Annual Report, 1972*, pp. 248–250.

increases than the CPI. The usefulness of this index has been questioned recently because of the use of published prices posted by sellers, which tend to be changed very slowly, rather than of the prices at which transactions were actually consummated.

Estimates of wholesale prices are available back to the American colonial period. These data are plotted in Figure 3-1. While interesting, the meaningfulness of such a lengthy series is open to some question as the demand for many of the items included has changed drastically over time. The very sharp runups in prices during the earlier war periods reflect the heavy reliance of the United States on imports in those days, the supply of which was reduced greatly by embargos.

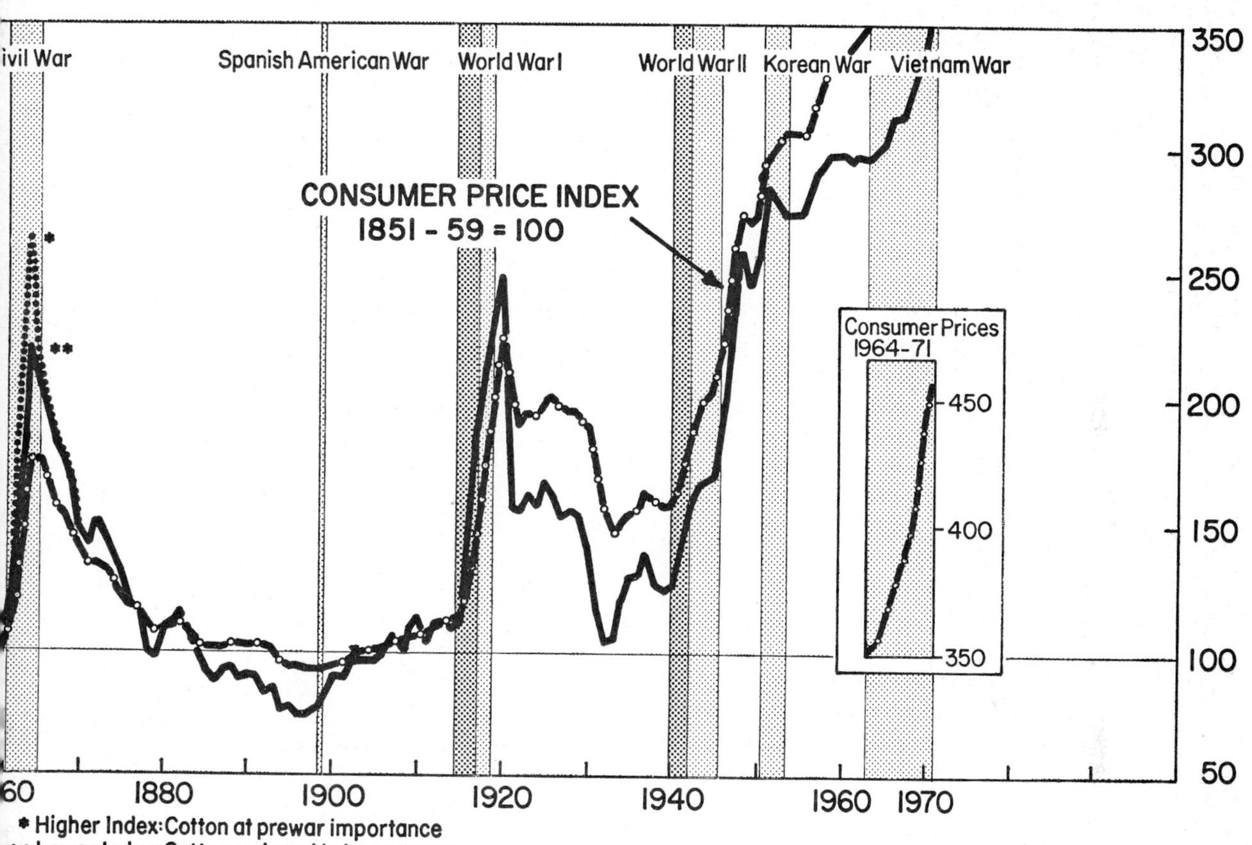

Commodity Price Index

Another sensitive price index of the I_1 type is the commodity price index. This index measures prices of a number of widely used raw and semiraw materials for which supply and demand are highly volatile. As a result, the index is very sensitive to changes in supply and demand conditions and is frequently used as a forerunner of other price changes. However, as the items included in this index make up only a small part of the value of most finished products, the commodity price index does not provide a representative measure of price changes.

Gross National Product Deflator

The gross national product deflator (GNPD) is of the I_2 type. It measures changes in the prices of the total quantity of goods and services produced in a period from a given base period. Because the composition of goods and services changes through time, the deflator reflects price changes for a changing collection of items. The substitution of a lower priced good for a higher priced good, for example, can result in a decline in the GNPD. The deflator is computed quarterly by the U.S. Department of Commerce in the process of preparing the nation's national income accounts.

Because it includes all items produced, the GNPD includes many items that are not consumed directly and is a poor indicator of the cost of living. On the other hand, its comprehensiveness, in contrast to the limited sample of the CPI, may make it more representative of overall price changes in the economy. In addition, by including changes in the mix of output, the deflator may better reflect the public's awareness of price changes, which is based on items actually purchased and not necessarily only those in a fixed market basket, and consequently, it may be a good gauge of their reactions to such price changes.

History of Prices

Over the longer run, most price indexes show similar movements. The history of price movements is dominated by few abrupt increases generally followed by abrupt decreases of about the same magnitude. An examination of the timing of these abrupt increases in Figure 3-1 reveals that they are associated with war years. Thus, for the United States, there were dramatic price increases starting in 1777, concurrent with the Revolutionary War; in 1862, concurrent with the Civil War; and in 1917, concurrent with World War I. Less dramatic but substantial price increases were recorded near the outbreak of the War of 1812, World War II, the Korean war, and the Vietnam war. The price increase associated with World War II is, in part, disguised in the longer price upswing starting at the depths of the Great Depression in 1933. With the exception of the post–World War II period, the sharp war-related price increases were followed by equally sharp price declines upon cessation of hostilities.

During nonwar periods, price declines were sharper and more numerous than price increases. Prices declined sharply from 1837 through 1843, following a smaller runup; from about 1880 almost through 1900, continuing the post–Civil War deflation that started in 1865; and from 1929 through 1932, at the onset of the Great Depression. If war periods were omitted, one recent study showed that the current consumer price index would be below that of both 150 years ago and the turn of the twentieth century. Nonetheless, the overall trend of prices is dominated by war-associated price increases.

Since World War II, prices have increased almost continuously, but the rate of increase has varied considerably. Similar to the earlier periods, the sharpest increases were associated with armed conflicts. Unlike the earlier periods, however, prices did not fall at the termination of the hostilities, although the rate of increase did slow. The failure of prices to decline significantly in this period and the slow rate at which prices decelerated after runups suggest that prices may have become less flexible in a downward direction. This would have important implications for the achievement of price stability.

A number of reasons may explain this increased price rigidity. First, in part attributable to successful economic policies, the economy has operated closer to full employment for longer periods of time in the post–World War II period than in any earlier periods and has also avoided more severe economic slumps, periods in which prices are most likely to recede. Second, besides operating closer to capacity, welfare and unemployment benefits have been expanded and have helped to attenuate declines in consumer purchasing power during periods of economic slump.

Lastly, changes in consumer tastes have diverted sales increasingly to the service sector from the goods sector of the economy. In 1950, services accounted for about one-third of the total consumption expenditures. Twenty years later, in 1970, they accounted for more than 40 percent. The provision of many services is highly labor-intensive and, on the average, subject to only slow gains in labor or capital productivity. In these areas, wage increases are passed on to the consumer in an almost one-to-one relationship. In contrast, productivity has increased substantially in manufacturing and agriculture. Employment in manufacturing was 25 percent greater in 1970 than 20 years earlier, while production had increased more than twofold. Employment in agriculture actually fell by more than one-half in this period, although the output of agricultural commodities increased almost 50 percent. In such a setting, a significant portion of wage increases are absorbed by the increased efficiencies in production and not reflected in final prices. The prices for durable goods included in the CPI increased 25 percent between 1950 and 1970, and for agricultural products, 55 percent. In contrast, the price of services included in the market basket of consumer items more than doubled. Moreover, the trend toward services and away from manufactured and agricultural goods may be expected to continue. It should, however, be noted that the price rise in services may be overstated. The computational adjustments necessary to maintain consistency in the quality of products priced are more difficult to apply in this sector than in others. While medical and hospitalization costs have risen faster than other service costs, the increase in the quality of these services has also been very great but exceedingly difficult to measure precisely.

For all three reasons, price stability may need to be defined as a slow 1 or 2 percent annual rate of increase rather than as a zero rate of price increase. Such a rate would reflect a change in consumer tastes more than inflation symptomatic of demand greater than full employment can supply. Prices increased less than 2 percent annually throughout most of the first half of the 1960s. In contrast, prices increased almost three times as quickly in the second half of the decade, a clear reflection of excessive demand pressures.

Inflation

Inflation is a rise in the price level. Inflation occurs when more prices rise, adjusted for quality improvements and for relative importance in the budget, than fall. Inflation has dominated price movements in the United States in the last 100 years. There are many reasons for inflation but, without fail, price increases are greatest when the economy is operating at, or rapidly approaching, full utilization of labor and capital. The reasons prices accelerate at these times will be examined in later chapters. It is important, however, to distinguish between inflation and the causes of inflation. Inflation refers only to the symptom of price increases. The causes can be many—too rapid a growth in the money supply, too large a deficit in the federal government budget, a poor food harvest, war, etc. But none of these forces are by themselves always associated with inflation and need not by themselves indicate inflation.

The Incidence of Inflation

We noted in Chapter 1 that price stability is a goal of the economy primarily because lack of stability is injurious to a significant proportion of the population, although it may be beneficial to some segments. When prices rise, the real (or purchasing-power) value of fixed nominal-value-income contracts falls and of fixed nominal-value-expense contracts rises. Vice versa, when prices decline, the real value of fixed-income contracts rises and of fixed-expense contracts declines. Those for whom the real value of income contracts declines lose purchasing power relative to those for whom the real value of income contracts rises. An individual's economic welfare is measured in real, not nominal, terms. If everyone correctly anticipated a change in prices, they would adjust their contract terms to avoid losses. In the adjustment process, gains from price changes would also be eliminated. It follows that injury to economic units does not result from changes in the price level per se, but from those price changes that are unanticipated.[1]

It appears reasonable that all economic units do not adjust equally quickly or equally skillfully to price-level changes. Those who adjust most slowly will suffer the greatest relative injury. To evaluate the extent of injury from price changes, it is necessary to identify those groups that adjust most slowly. For the purposes of the analysis, we will consider only price increases or inflation. Price declines, as noted earlier, have been infrequent in the postwar period and may reasonably be expected not to become more frequent in the immediate future.[2]

1. This argument abstracts from balance of payments considerations and pertains only to a closed economy. International implications of inflation are discussed in a later chapter. Moreover, the analysis assumes that levels of employment are not affected by price changes.

2. An analysis of the incidence of deflation during the prolonged period of price decline from 1870 to 1895 appears in Friedman and Schwartz, *A Monetary History of the United States, 1867–1960*, Chapter 3.

The differential impact of inflation on economic units may be divided into two parts, an income effect and a wealth effect. The income effect considers gains and losses attributed to differences between nominal and constant purchasing power, or real income, flows. The wealth effect considers gains and losses in real net worth attributed to differences in the composition of items on the balance sheets of different economic units.

Income Effects

In this country, economic decisions are, in the first instance, generally based on nominal values. That is, we accept or reject employment on the basis of the dollar amount of the contract offered, we purchase or decline to purchase an item on the basis of the dollar amount of the price, and we borrow or decline to borrow on the basis of the percentage interest rate charged on a loan. If prices are changing, however, the nominal value will differ from the real value. An increase in prices will lower the real value of a given dollar value of an employment contract, a purchase price, or an interest payment. For example, a $500 salary increase on a base salary of $10,000 may not represent any increase at all in real income if prices are increasing at more than 5 percent annually. Such an increase with a price rise of 7 percent would represent a decrease in real income.

If economic decision-makers are aware of price increases, they will attempt to adjust nominal values for the increases and base their decisions on deflated or real values. If inflation were anticipated correctly and the appropriate adjustments could be made, changes in nominal income included in a contract would exceed changes in desired real income by the rate of inflation. If inflation is not anticipated or is anticipated to be slower than actually occurs, the contracted changes in nominal income may be greater than the desired changes in real income but not by enough to attain the intended or targeted amount of real income. In the above salary example, for instance, real income could be decreasing at the same time nominal income is increasing. Units who base decisions on nominal values without regard to concomitant price changes are said to be operating under "money illusion."

Money illusion is not uncommon in our society. Some persons may operate under money illusion because they have insufficient knowledge of price trends and/or the benefits of adjusting nominal values for price changes. Other persons may operate under money illusion with full knowledge of price trends and the costs of such behavior because they have calculated that the costs associated with adjusting for price changes are greater than the benefits to be derived. Converting from nominal to real values is not costless. One needs to obtain the necessary price data for the items in his budget, estimate future price patterns, and make the necessary computations. This involves considerable time, effort, and possibly even out-of-pocket expenses. If the price rise is expected to be small, the costs of basing decisions on nominal values may be smaller than the costs of adjusting to real values. As the costs of adjusting are generally independent of the amount of the price rise, the greater the price rise, the greater are the costs of not adjusting relative to the costs of adjusting and the greater is the incentive to adjust.

Not only is converting nominal values to real values costly, but the cost may differ among economic units. It appears reasonable that awareness of price trends and the knowledge and ability to adjust nominal values for price changes is related to levels of both education and income. The more educated or the higher the income, the more likely an economic unit will make this adjustment. If this is so, and because education level and income level are highly correlated, price increases would, at first, tend to redistribute real income from lower- to higher-income groups until all groups adjust equally.

Wealth Effects

The wealth of an economic unit is measured by the real net worth of his balance sheet. Price changes will affect the real value of the various items on the balance sheet differently. An economic unit's balance sheet can be summarized as follows:

Assets	Liabilities
Fixed-value assets	Fixed-value liabilities
Variable-value assets	Variable-value liabilities
	Net worth

Net worth is equal to total assets less total liabilities. Increases in the real value of net worth (increases in the real value of assets or decreases in the real value of liabilities) indicate increases in wealth, and decreases, decreases in wealth. Fixed-value assets and liabilities are those assets whose principal or maturity values are denominated in nominal terms and do not change automatically in response to changes in commodity prices. (We use the term *commodity prices* to distinguish the prices of goods and services from the prices of financial instruments.) On the whole, fixed-value assets and liabilities are financial instruments. Such assets include money, savings deposits, most life insurance policies, and bonds. Such liabilities include consumer and mortgage debt. As commodity prices rise, the real value of fixed-value instruments declines. This would increase the real net worth of households to whom the instrument is a liability (debt) at the expense of households to whom the instrument is an asset.

Variable-value assets and liabilities automatically change in nominal value more or less in line with changes in commodity prices. They may be either real (tangible) or financial. Real assets encompass durable goods, machinery, houses, etc. Variable-value financial assets are primarily ownership claims on real assets, e.g., common stocks. Variable-value liabilities involve the promise to deliver an asset in the future at its market price at the time of delivery. As commodity prices rise, the nominal market values of variable-value assets and liabilities rise more or less proportionately so that the real values remain more or less constant. Owners of such assets are thereby protected, and benefit at the expense of wealth holders whose assets are fixed in value; while owners of such liabilities have disadvantages with respect to owners of fixed-value liabilities. Overall, during periods of rising prices, the greater the proportion of the total assets on the balance sheet invested in variable-value assets and the greater the proportion of total liabilities in the form of fixed-value liabilities, the greater the increase in real net worth.

As the composition of balance sheets differs among income groups, some general impressions of the potential impact of inflation on the wealth of different income groups can be obtained by examining their balance sheets. Data on the composition of assets are available from a Federal Reserve Board survey of consumers in 1962.[3] This survey shows that the proportion of fixed-value assets to total wealth decreases with increases in income. For example, liquid assets, which comprise the great majority of fixed-value assets, account for about 17 percent of the total wealth of consumer units with income in 1962 of $3,000 to $5,000, and only 6 percent of the total wealth of units with income of $50,000 to $100,000 (Table 3–2). In addition, fewer low-income households possess non-fixed-value assets relative to higher-income households than possess fixed-value assets relative to the higher-income groups.

Analysis of the liability side of the balance sheets of different income groups is somewhat more complex. To the extent that taxpayers bear the ultimate liability for government debt and shareholders for corporate debt, it is necessary to allocate this debt to individuals. Estimates of the effective liability side of the balance sheet by income group were made by Professors Brownlee and Conrad for 1957.[4] Liability for the federal debt was allocated to taxpayers in proportion to their federal income tax liability on the assumption that tax revenues are used to finance the interest payments on the debt and, if the occasion ever arises, would also be used to retire the debt. Because of the moderately progressive nature of the federal tax structure, higher-income groups pay proportionately higher taxes, and proportionately larger shares of the debt liability are allocated to these groups. State and local debt, likewise, was allocated among income groups proportionately to state and local tax liabilities. Corporate debt was allocated in proportion to both

3. Dorothy S. Projector, and Gertrude S. Weiss, *Survey of Financial Characteristics of Consumers* (Washington, D.C.: Board of Governors of the Federal Reserve System, 1966).

4. Brownlee and Conrad, "Effects Upon the Distribution of Income of a Tight Money Policy," pp. 499–558.

Table 3-2 **Composition of Wealth by Income Group, 1962**

Income (Thousand Dollars)	Wealth Component								
	Own Home		Liquid Assets[a]		Investment Assets		Assets in Business or Profession		Miscellaneous
	Percent of Group	Percent of Wealth	Percent of Group	Percent of Wealth	Percent of Group	Percent of Wealth	Percent of Group	Percent of Wealth	Percent of Wealth
0 - 3	40	42	56	19	15	17	12	19	3
3 - 5	45	34	74	17	20	32	12	13	4
5 - 7.5	60	34	86	14	30	21	17	17	14
7.5- 10	73	37	96	14	41	31	18	12	6
10 - 15	80	34	96	16	56	28	22	15	7
15 - 25	86	24	100	14	73	37	26	16	9
25 - 50	92	11	99	7	93	42	64	21	19
50 -100	94	6	100	6	96	43	70	42	3
100 and over	96	5	99	3	99	69	35	17	6

[a]Checking accounts, savings accounts, and U.S. savings bonds.

Source: Projector and Weiss, *Survey of Financial Characteristics of Consumers*, p. 110.

dividend receipts and consumer expenditures. Overall, the estimates indicated that the ratio of liabilities, most of which are fixed value, to assets increased with income.

This evidence suggests that, ceteris paribus, inflation would benefit the higher-income groups on both the asset and liability sides of the balance sheet and redistribute real wealth from lower- to higher-income units. This conclusion is valid only if price changes are not accompanied by changes in unemployment, a condition examined in later chapters.

Evidence from the Inflation of the 1960s

Prices rose throughout the decade of the 1960s, but increased considerably faster in the second half of the decade than the first. From 1960 through 1965, consumer prices rose at an annual rate of 1.3 percent. From 1965 through 1970, the annual rate of increase was 4.2 percent, or three times as rapid. By comparing the relative performance of different income groups in the two periods, information can be generated to show the income incidence of inflation. Such a study was conducted by Albert Burger of the Federal Reserve Bank of St. Louis.[5]

The impact of inflation was measured by both income and wealth effects. On the whole, Burger found that the earnings of professional workers, such as engineers, accountants, chemists, and lawyers, increased more in real terms in the period of faster price growth than both in the earlier period of slower price growth and in relation to the real earnings of unskilled and blue-collar workers. For the latter groups, real income rose less in the second period than in the first, although nominal income increased faster in the second period. These groups benefited in the earlier period by a sharp decline in unemployment, which did not occur in the later period. As professional workers may be assumed to be more educated and better paid than nonprofessionals, this evidence is consistent with our earlier theoretical conjecture that inflation distributes income from lower- to higher-income groups. Contrary to popular belief, Burger also found that Social Security payments increased considerably faster than prices in the more inflationary period after increasing at about the same rate as prices in the earlier period. Recent actions by Congress provide evidence of determination to continue a policy of increasing such payments faster than the cost of living. As a result, inflation may no longer bear heaviest on older and retired citizens, as was once strongly believed.

With respect to wealth, Burger found that, as prices accelerated, the greatest increase in real values was recorded for such real assets as land and houses. Losses in real value were recorded for fixed-value assets, such as savings accounts at

5. Burger, "The Effects of Inflation, 1960–68," pp. 25–36.

commercial banks and thrift institutions, and, particularly, for marketable debt securities. The economic units that benefited most from the acceleration in inflation were those who had the largest proportion of variable-value assets and the largest proportion of fixed-value liabilities on their balance sheets. As noted, such a mix is found more frequently among higher- than lower-income groups. Thus the wealth effect, similar to the income effect, appears to redirect real income during periods of inflation from lower- to higher-income groups.

The conclusion that, ceteris paribus, inflation redistributes income regressively is not accepted by all. Another recent study has reported finding effects too modest to support any contention that inflation redistributes either income or wealth. Thus it appears that the substantial redistribution effects frequently attributed to inflation are, at minimum, grossly exaggerated.

References

Alchian, Armen, and Reuben Kessel, "Effects of Inflation," *Journal of Political Economy*, 70, December, 1962, 527–537.

Brownlee, Oswald, and Alfred Conrad, "Effects Upon the Distribution of Income of a Tight Money Policy," in *Stabilization Policies*, Commission on Money and Credit (Englewood Cliffs, N.J.: Prentice-Hall, 1963).

Budd, Edward C., and David F. Seiders, "The Impact of Inflation on the Distribution of Income and Wealth," *American Economic Review*, 61 (2), May, 1971, 128–138.

Burger, Albert E., "The Effects of Inflation, 1960–68," *Review* (Federal Reserve Bank of St. Louis), 51, November, 1969, 25–36.

Moore, Geoffrey H., *The Anatomy of Inflation*, U.S. Department of Labor, Bureau of Labor Statistics, Report 373 (Washington, D.C.: 1969).

Morley, Samuel A., *The Economics of Inflation* (Hinsdale, Ill.: Dryden Press, 1971).

Stigler, George J., and James K. Kindahl, *The Behavior of Industrial Prices* (New York: National Bureau of Economic Research, 1970).

Wallace, William H., *Measuring Price Changes: A Study of the Price Indexes* (Richmond: Federal Reserve Bank of Richmond, 1970).

PART II

The Financial System

The Financial Sector—An Overview

4

The financial sector of the economy encompasses financial instruments, financial institutions, and financial markets. Financial instruments are traded on financial markets by financial institutions. The financial sector performs the important function of collecting savings from individual savers, or surplus spending units, and directing the funds to individual borrowers, or deficit spending units. Such a transfer is necessary in an economy in which savers and investors are, in most instances, not the same individuals. The more efficient the transfer is, the larger the flow, the greater the accommodation of individual preferences, and the greater the welfare gain to the economy. This chapter examines the nature of surplus and deficit spending units, describes the characteristics of financial claims, identifies the distinguishing features of major financial institutions, and delineates the operations of financial markets.

Surplus and Deficit Spending Units

A surplus spending unit (SSU) may be defined as *a spending unit who prefers to spend on current consumption and/or investment goods less than his current income at current market rates of interest.* A deficit spending unit (DSU) may be defined as *a spending unit who prefers to spend on current consumption and/or investment goods more than his current income at current market rates of interest.* The division of spending units between surplus and deficit is dependent upon a large number of factors. These include current income, expected income, wealth, age, health, education, family status, tastes, and current interest rates. As interest rates vary, individual spending units may shift from surplus to deficit or vice versa.

The relationship between age and spending unit characteristics appears to be well documented. Throughout his early years of formal schooling, the average person is a deficit spending unit, borrowing primarily from his family. A person continues to be a DSU upon marriage and through the start-up expenses of a new household. Thereafter, he becomes an SSU until his children attain college age when he may temporarily revert to DSU status. Upon the completion of his children's schooling, he continues as an SSU until retirement. At this point he again becomes a DSU. Over his entire life span, the average person tends to be a moderate SSU, with his unspent savings bequeathed to his children. However, unless interrupted by actuarially premature death, he begins and ends life as a DSU.

Surplus spending units have three options. They may hold their surplus income as money balances, they may repurchase and retire their own outstanding financial claims sold at times they were DSUs, or they may temporarily rent out purchasing power to current DSUs by purchasing financial claims issued by them. Deficit spending units also have three options. They may reduce their money balances, sell claims on others acquired when they were SSUs, or sell new claims on themselves to current SSUs.

Financial Claims

Financial claims are future claims on real resources. Until maturity, they transfer purchasing power from spending units purchasing the claims (SSUs) to spending units selling the claims (DSUs). Financial claims are created by DSUs and sold to SSUs. At the time of the transaction, claims are transferred from the DSU to the SSU and money from the SSU to the DSU. Once outstanding, some financial claims may be traded among SSUs so that the maturity of the claim and the time preference of the SSU need not coincide. An SSU may purchase claims with longer terms to maturity than his preferred savings horizon if he can sell the claim to another SSU at the appropriate time. Likewise, an SSU may purchase claims with shorter terms to maturity than his savings horizon if he can purchase additional claims, either new or outstanding, upon the maturity of the original claim.

Until the claim is converted into real goods and services, it typically generates interest. This is to reward the claim holder for the temporary use of his purchasing power and for abstaining from using it himself. The primary exception to interest-bearing financial claims is money. Currency does not yield interest in any country. At least in the United States, commercial banks are prohibited by law from paying explicit interest on demand deposits. This is not to suggest that money yields no interest return at all. On the contrary, it yields an important implicit return in terms of convenience, efficiency, protection against decreases in the price level, and, for demand deposits, safety against theft. In addition, commercial banks often provide safekeeping and bookkeeping services below cost for their demand deposit customers in payment for the use of their funds.

There is a wide variety of financial claims in this country. Claims are tailored to the preferences of both lenders and borrowers. Basically, claims differ among themselves according to term to maturity, marketability prior to maturity, and risk of default. Default is defined as a failure by the issuer of the claim to return to the holder of the claim the full nominal amount of the purchasing power at maturity plus the full interest payments at the scheduled intervals. Different securities will command different interest rates. The longer the term to maturity, generally, the higher the interest rate demanded by the purchaser of the claim. The greater the marketability of a claim prior to its maturity in terms of both lower transactions costs and ability to obtain quickly the purchase price or close to purchase price, the lower the interest rate demanded. Lastly, the greater the risk of default, the higher the interest rate demanded by the purchaser to compensate him for the greater probability of temporary or permanent loss of all or part of his nominal purchasing power. While important, these three factors are not the only forces explaining differences in interest rates on different financial claims. A more detailed examination is postponed until Chapter 9.

Moneyness of Claims

Because financial claims vary widely in their characteristics, it simplifies their examination if they can be classified in a meaningful framework. One such classification scheme is to rank the claims by their liquidity or "moneyness." This concept considers both the cost of converting the claims into money and the price at which they can be converted. The lower the conversion cost is and the nearer the conversion price to the purchase price, that is, the lower the price risk or risk of obtaining less than the purchase price of the asset, the greater the moneyness of the claim. The major financial claims are ranked in Table 4-1 in descending order by their approximate moneyness. The dollar amounts of each outstanding at year-end 1971 are also shown.

While money is a financial claim, it is the claim against which all other claims are exchanged, at least initially, and serves as a standard of comparison for all other claims. Money possesses neither transactions costs nor price risk. Savings deposits at major financial institutions can be readily, quickly, and cheaply converted into either currency or demand deposits at their par value during normal working hours. The cash surrender value of a life insurance policy is not marketable but can be readily realized at par through either cancellation of the policy or borrowing against the policy. Short-term securities of the U.S. Treasury, such as 90-day bills, are readily marketable at low cost prior to maturity, but may be

Table 4-1 **Major Financial Claims Ranked by Moneyness**
(Not seasonally adjusted)

Claim	Amount Outstanding December 31, 1971 (billion dollars)
Currency[a]	53.5
Demand deposits[a]	182.5
Savings deposits at commercial banks[b]	235.1
Savings deposits at mutual savings banks	81.4
Savings deposits at savings and loan associations	174.5
Savings deposits at credit unions	18.3
Certificates of deposit at commercial banks	33.9
Reserves of life insurance companies	129.5
U.S. Treasury savings bonds (nonmarketable)	54.9
U.S. Treasury bills (marketable)	97.5
U.S. Treasury notes and bonds (marketable)	164.6
Bankers' acceptances	7.9
Short-term corporate debt (commercial paper)	29.9
Municipal government debt	166.5
Long-term corporate debt	231.6
Corporate equity	1,085.5

[a]Components of money supply.
[b]All time deposits except large CDs.
Source: *Federal Reserve Bulletin*, 58 (6), June, 1972.

traded at less than (also at more than) their purchase price. Claims further down the list have higher transactions costs and/or are more likely to be traded before maturity at prices further from their purchase price. Generally, the less money-like the financial claim, the higher the interest return to compensate the holder for the additional conversion costs and risks.

Financial Institutions

Financial institutions expedite the transfer of funds from SSUs to DSUs. In their absence, SSUs and DSUs may incur substantial outlays of time and money locating each other. Not only do they need to locate each other, but they also need to locate a member of the opposite type of spending unit who has precisely the same preferences in maturity, risk, and marketability. Upon locating each other, DSUs exchange their claims for money. SSUs gain direct claims on DSUs. Financial institutions expedite the exchange of claims for money. These institutions may be grouped into two classes: those that help DSUs and SSUs locate each other to exchange claims and funds directly, and those that bring the two together indirectly by substituting their own claims, which have broader appeal, for the primary claims offered by ultimate DSUs.

Savers and lenders are brought together on the private-capital market by brokers and dealers, sometimes called investment bankers. The two differ in their operations. Brokers provide a pure search service; they do not take legal possession of the claims traded. They locate the participants in a pending trade before the trade occurs and receive a commission from both parties for this service upon consummation of the trade. In contrast, dealers take legal possession of the claims by buying the claims from DSUs for their own inventory and subsequently selling the claims to SSUs from this inventory. Their income is derived from the spread between the buying and selling price of the claim; the greater the spread, the greater the earnings of the dealer. Because the dealer may not sell a claim immediately after purchasing it, the claim may remain in his inventory for some time. During this period the dealer incurs a risk of unfavorable price changes that may depress the price of the claim below its purchase price. In such a case, the dealer's profit from trading is threatened. On the other hand, prices may rise during the time a claim is held in inventory, enhancing the dealer's profits. In all transactions conducted on the private-capital market, with or without the aid of a broker or a dealer, the SSUs hold the primary claim issued by the DSUs.

Financial intermediaries provide an alternative channel to the private market for funds to be transferred from SSUs to DSUs. An intermediary issues and sells claims on itself. With the proceeds of the sale of these claims to SSUs, it purchases primary claims from DSUs. The claims an intermediary issues are called secondary claims. Secondary claims represent indirect ownership of the primary claims. Unlike the direct flow of funds and claims between SSUs and DSUs on the private-capital market, flows on the intermediation market are indirect in two nearly simultaneous transactions. Funds flow from SSUs to the intermediaries and then to the DSUs. This process is called intermediation. In all transactions conducted through the intermediation market, the SSUs hold the secondary claims issued by the financial institutions rather than the primary claims issued by the ultimate DSUs. The channels through which funds are transferred from SSUs to DSUs are shown in Figure 4-1.

The secondary claims issued by the financial intermediaries differ in a number of significant ways from the primary claims purchased by these institutions in order to make them more desirable to SSUs. To the extent that they are successful in marketing their claims, financial intermediaries both increase the flow of funds from SSUs to DSUs and decrease the effective cost of engaging in financial transactions and thereby the net interest rate to both SSUs and DSUs.

Financial intermediaries issue secondary securities, generally called by other names such as deposits, that stimulate savings by SSUs in four ways:

1. The securities have a wider range of maturities than those in which primary securities are typically issued. Intermediaries accept (borrow) funds for as short as overnight or as long as many years.

Figure 4-1 Channels for Transfer of Funds

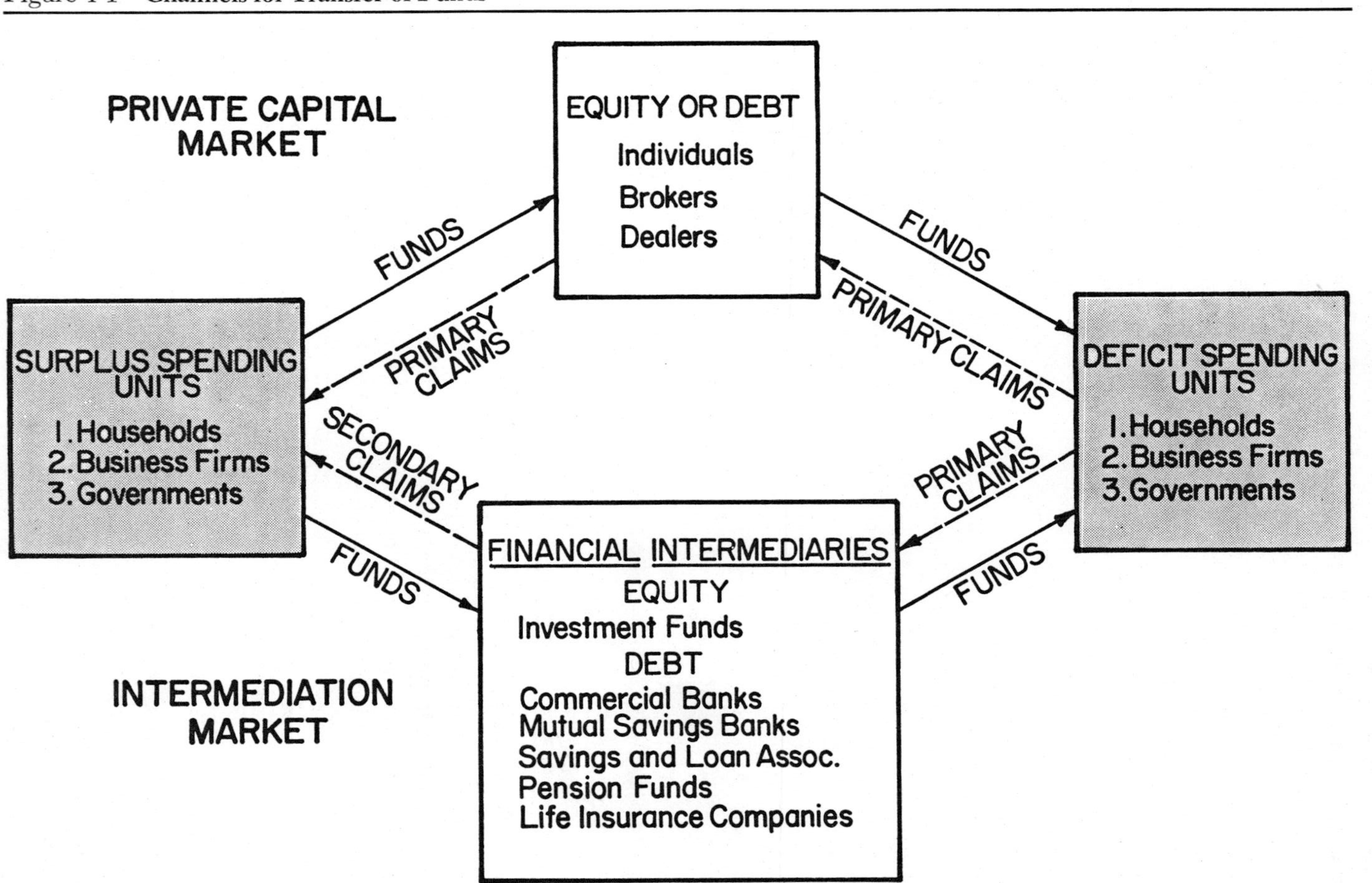

2. The securities have a wider range of denominations than those in which primary securities are typically issued. Financial intermediaries sell securities and accept funds in almost any amount from $1 up.

3. The securities carry smaller effective risks of default for the SSUs than primary securities. Intermediaries are able to reduce risk by investing the proceeds from the sale of their secondary securities in a wider range of different primary securities than is practical for most single SSUs. In this way the secondary security holders benefit from reduced risk resulting from diversification. In addition, intermediaries are generally also better equipped to evaluate creditworthiness of borrowers and screen out the higher risks.

4. The securities have a higher net interest yield than is available on comparable primary securities. Through the ready availability of many offices and intensive advertising, the intermediaries have reduced the search costs of SSUs in locating appropriate securities. Search costs must be deducted from the gross interest yields of both primary and secondary securities to accurately measure the net return to the holder. The lower the search costs are, the higher the net interest yield for any given gross yield.

Financial intermediaries simultaneously stimulate borrowing by DSUs for four reasons:

1. They buy primary securities from DSUs in a wider range of maturities than most other buyers. Intermediaries loan funds from overnight to long-term mortgages.

2. They buy primary securities in a wider range of denominations than most other buyers. Intermediaries loan funds in almost any amount.

3. They pay a higher net price—charge a lower net interest rate—for the securities than most other buyers. The lower net rates arise both from the lower search costs DSUs pay in placing their new claims and from the lower costs of evaluating creditworthiness resulting from the greater expertise of these institutions.

4. In addition to providing financing, the institutions often provide valuable advice to borrowers with respect to maximizing the return on the item purchased with the loan, and/or additional services related to the operation of the financed item. Thus, the interest charge covers more than the pure financing most SSUs provide DSUs on the private-capital market.

Intermediaries Reduce Interest Rates

It is stated above that financial intermediaries both raise the net interest return to SSUs and lower the net interest cost to DSUs. How this can occur is depicted in a numerical example in Table 4-2.

Assume that the gross interest rate in the private capital market on one year

Table 4-2 **How Intermediaries Reduce Interest Rates**

		Interest Rate (Percent)
Private-Capital Market		
Equilibrium Gross Rate		8
Lenders		
Risk Premium	−2	
Search costs	−2	
Net Rate		4
Borrowers		
Search Costs	+2	
Net Rate		10
Intermediation Market		
Equilibrium Gross Rate		8
Financial Intermediary		
Risk Premium	−1	
Search Costs	−1	
Profits	−1	
Net Savings Rate		5
Lenders		
Risk Premium	−¼	
Search Costs	−¼	
Net Rate		4½
Borrowers		
Search Costs	+¼	
Net Rate		8¼

securities is 8 percent. This is the observed rate at which primary claims are traded. The effective return to the SSU lender is this rate minus any costs associated with finding the appropriate claim and costs of insuring against risk of default. The effective cost to the DSU borrower is 8 percent plus search costs in locating the appropriate SSU. Assuming equal search costs of 2 percent to both borrower and lender and a risk premium of 2 percent to the lender to actuarially compensate him for loss from default, the net return to the lender is reduced to 4 percent while the net interest cost to the borrower is raised to 10 percent.

Assume an equal gross equilibrium rate of 8 percent in the intermediation market. This is the observed rate at which financial intermediaries purchase primary claims. Because of their ability to evaluate creditworthiness more carefully than individuals, to pool risks over a larger number of primary claims, and to search for primary claims more effectively, financial intermediaries may be expected to have both lower search costs and lower risk premiums, say, 1 percent each. Because they are private profit-motivated business firms, financial intermediaries expect to generate profits from their activities. Assuming a profit margin of 1 percent, the intermediary can pay savers a return of 5 percent. From this rate the SSUs must deduct search costs and risk premiums, which may be expected to be minimal for secondary securities, say, ¼ percent each. The net return to savers is thus 4½ percent, or ½ percent greater than the 4 percent return on the private market. The search cost to DSUs in locating the intermediary is also quite small and the net interest cost is thus only slightly greater than the gross equilibrium rate. This is considerably below the net loan cost in the private-capital market. As both parties in this example are better off, funds may be expected to flow from SSUs to DSUs through the intermediation market rather than through the private market.

Keep in mind that this is only a numerical example. While financial intermediaries can lower the loan cost to borrowers and increase the savings return to savers, they may not always be able to do so. If at times the institutions cannot offer SSUs higher net yields or DSUs lower net interest rates, funds would be routed through the private market.

The long-run trend in the United States has been for funds to increasingly flow through the intermediation market. In the 1920s, one-half of the gross flow of funds from SSUs to DSUs was channeled through the intermediation market. The other half was channeled through the private market. In the 1950s, the proportion of funds channeled through the intermediation market increased to 80 percent, and by the 1960s this proportion exceeded 90 percent. While the overall trend has been in favor of the intermediation market, the proportions channeled through each market can vary significantly from year to year. For example, in the first half of the 1960s, less than 5 percent of the funds from SSUs to DSUs flowed through the private market. In the second half of the decade, attributable both to rapidly rising market rates of interest and to direct government intervention with the maximum interest rates financial intermediaries were permitted to pay on savings, many intermediaries were unable to offer rates on most of their secondary securities competitive with those available on primary securities on the private market. As a result, the share of funds channeled through the private-capital market more than doubled to 10 percent.

By making saving both easier and, on net, more rewarding, financial intermediaries have tended to increase the proportion of income saved and to lower interest rates relative to where they would have been in the absence of these institutions. Personal acquisition of financial assets as a percent of disposable (after federal income tax) personal income increased slightly from 10 to 11 percent between the 1920s and 1960s. But this increase understates the true increase in personal savings. The introduction of Social Security and other retirement programs in this period should have reduced slightly the incentive to save for old age.

Figure 4-2 **Effects of Financial Intermediaries on Flow of Funds**

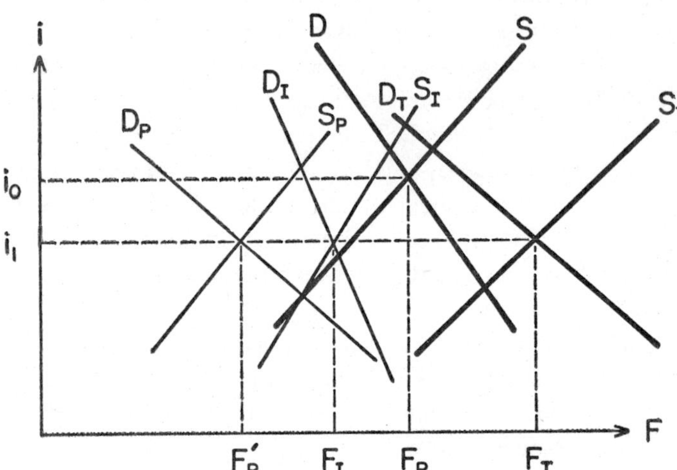

Diagrammatical Representation of Intermediation

The effects of the introduction of financial intermediaries on the flow of funds can be seen in Figure 4-2. Before intermediation, funds were channeled from SSUs to DSUs entirely through the direct private-capital market. The demand for funds by DSUs is shown by schedule *D* and the supply of funds by SSUs by schedule S. Both supply of and demand for funds are sensitive to the interest rate. The demand for funds decreases as interest rates rise, while the supply of funds increases. The equilibrium interest rate is that rate which equates the demand for funds with the supply of funds. This rate is shown as the intersection of the *D* and S schedules at gross interest rate i_0. (In reality, the net interest rate should be measured on the vertical axis. However, as this rate both varies from person to person and cannot be easily obtained, the gross rate is used instead.) The accompanying equilibrium flow of funds is at F_P. Now introduce intermediation. Because of reductions in net interest rates (as shown in Table 4-2), some of the funds will be diverted from the private market to the new intermediation market. In addition, for reasons discussed earlier, as intermediaries provide profitable savings opportunities for a broader range of income groups, the flow through the intermediaries will be greater than the reduction in the private market and the total flow of funds through both markets will exceed the previous flow through only the private market. Because of its characteristics, intermediation may increase the supply of funds more rapidly than it stimulates demand and the equilibrium interest rate will be reduced.

After intermediation, the overall supply schedule is S_T and the overall demand schedule is D_T. The new equilibrium flow of funds from SSUs to DSUs is F_T at

i_1. The funds channeled through the private and intermediation markets are F'_P and F_I, respectively, where $F_T = F'_P + F_I$. Although $F_P > F'_P$, $F_T > F_P$. In equilibrium, the interest rate in both markets must be equal. Otherwise, DSUs or SSUs will shift funds or claims from one market to the other until the rates in each are equalized. As it is likely that the elasticities of the demand and supply schedules in each of the markets differ, shifts in the overall demand for or supply of funds may be expected to change the proportion of funds being channeled through each market.

Types of Financial Intermediaries

For reasons closely associated with the development of the United States, a large number of different financial intermediaries coexist. The institutions differ from one another in the characteristics of the secondary securities they sell and the primary securities they buy. The differences can be categorized in a number of ways, but the most important difference is whether the securities are debt or equity instruments. Debt instruments represent a first and fixed claim on the earnings of the borrower, while equity represents a residual claim on these earnings. The institutions can be classified further by the riskiness of the securities they buy or sell, the maturity of the debt securities, the size or denomination of the securities, and whether the secondary securities are a deposit or contractual type of liability. The more important financial intermediaries are classified in Table 4-3 according to the characteristics of their primary and secondary securities. The differences among institutions on both sides of the balance sheet are immediately evident. Many of the differences reflect historical or legal constraints. On the other hand, there are considerable similarities. To the extent of the similarities, the intermediaries compete with each other.

Although for any one institution the two sides of the balance sheet may not have the same characteristics, the two are not unrelated. With only few exceptions, primary and secondary securities for a particular type of intermediary are both either debt or equity. Most intermediaries deal in debt. On the whole, the secondary securities are shorter term, less risky, and of smaller denomination than the primary securities. As noted earlier, this is to make the securities attractive to as many SSUs as possible and is particularly evident for deposit-type intermediaries.

The asset side of the balance sheet of the major types of financial institutions at year-end 1968 is shown in Table 4-4, and the growth between 1950 and 1968 in Table 4-5.

The next sections will review the salient characteristics of the major types of intermediaries. The institutions are discussed in order of size.

Commercial Banks. Commercial banks are the largest, most important, and most diversified of all financial intermediaries. They are commonly referred to as the

Table 4-3 **Characteristics of Major Financial Intermediaries**

Intermediary	Assets (Primary securities)					Liabilities (Secondary securities)				
	Equity or debt	Features			Major security	Equity or debt	Features			Major security
		Mat	Risk	Den			Mat	Risk	Den	
Commercial Banks	D[t]	A	S	A	Business loans	D	T	S	A	Demand deposit
Savings and Loan Associations	D	L	S	S-M	Residential mortgages	D	T	S	S	Savings deposit
Mutual Savings Banks	D	L	S	S-M	Residential mortgages	D	T	S	S	Savings deposit
Credit Unions	D	T	M	S	Consumer loans	D	T	M	S	Savings deposit
Life Insurance Firms	D	L	S	R	Corporate bonds	D*	L	S	A	Life insurance policy
Casualty Insurance Firms	D-E	T-L	S-H	R	Corporate stock	D*	T	M	A	Property insurance policy
Pension Funds	E	L	M-H	R	Corporate stock	D*	L	S	S	Pension rights
Mutual Funds	E	L	M-H	A	Corporate stock	E	T	M-H	A	Stock
Sales Finance Companies	D	M	S	A	Consumer loans	D	T-L	S	R	Bonds
Consumer Finance Companies	D	T	H	S	Consumer loans	D	L	S-H	S-M	Bonds

Key
D–Debt
E–Equity
A–All

L–Long Term
T–Short Term
M–Medium

S–Small
H–High
R–Large

* Contractual
t–Excludes Trust Departments

Mat–Maturity
Risk–Risk of Default
Den–Denomination

Table 4-4 Asset Size and Composition of Major Financial Intermediaries
December 31, 1968 (billion dollars)

	Total Assets	Business Loans	Corporate Bonds	Corporate Equity	Mortgages	Treasury Sec.	Municipal Sec.	Consumer Loans
Commercial Banks	440	137			65	75	59	45
Life Insurance Companies	183		71	13	70	5	3	12
Savings and Loan Associations	153				131	11		2
Private Pension Funds	98		25	60	4	3		
Mutual Savings Banks	71		7	2	53	5		
Mutual Funds	53		3	46		1		
Finance Companies	50	13			5			29
Casualty Insurance Companies	48		5	18		5	15	
Credit Unions	12				1			10
Total	1,108	150	111	139	329	125	77	99
Total Outstanding			168	1,036	398	312	124	113
Omitted Sectors								
Federal Government					13			
Municipal Retirement Funds			25		38			
Households[*]			20	873		92	37	

[*] Includes commercial bank trust departments.

Source: Board of Governors of the Federal Reserve System, *Flow of Funds Accounts, 1945-68*, pp. 58-65.

Table 4-5 Growth of Financial Intermediaries, 1950-68

	Total Assets				Change in Assets 1950-1968		
	December, 1950		December, 1968				
	Billion Dollars	Percent of Total	Billion Dollars	Percent of Total	Billion Dollars	Percent	% of $ Change
Commercial Banks	148	52	440	40	292	197	35
Life Insurance Companies	63	22	183	17	120	190	15
Savings and Loan Associations	17	6	153	14	136	800	16
Private Pension Funds	7	2	98	9	91	1,362	11
Mutual Savings Banks	22	8	71	6	49	222	6
Mutual Funds	3	1	53	5	50	1,506	6
Finance Companies	9	3	50	5	41	437	5
Casualty Insurance Companies	13	5	48	4	35	269	4
Credit Unions	1	*	12	1	11	1,233	1
Total	283	100	1,108	100	825	292	100
GNP	285		865			201	

[*] Less than 0.5.

Source: *Ibid.*

department store of finance. With only rare exceptions, they are the only intermediary legally permitted to offer demand deposits or deposits subject to transfer by check by the depositor. As noted, these deposits are a widely accepted medium of exchange and account for about three-fourths of the country's money supply. Their other major source of funds is time and savings deposits. For the most part, bank deposits are available in all denominations and carry a minimum of risk of default. Up to $20,000 of each depositor's account is insured against loss by the Federal Deposit Insurance Corporation, an agency of the federal government.

On the asset side, commercial banks invest in a greater variety of primary securities than any other intermediary. For their own account, banks are permitted to invest only in debt securities. Banks are the largest single granters of loans to business firms, the federal treasury, municipal governments, and consumers. They are also important makers of mortgage loans. They make short- as well as medium- and long-term loans in all possible denominations. Through their trust departments, commercial banks also trade in corporate equities in a trustee or fiduciary capacity for their household, business, and municipal government customers. The operating characteristics of banks are discussed in greater detail in the next chapter.

Life Insurance Companies. Life insurance companies raise funds by selling protection against the loss of income from actuarially premature death or retirement. In the first instance, payments are made to the deceased's living beneficiaries who relied on his income during his life, and in the second to the insured himself. Besides pure risk protection, most insurance policies involve some savings.

Insurance companies offer additional savings opportunities in the form of annuity or endowment policies. Premiums charged on policies are related to both the amount of risk protection purchased and the amount of savings or the present value of the guaranteed future income. Because their sources of funds are primarily long term and their outflows highly predictable actuarially, life insurance companies can invest primarily in longer-term assets. Approximately two-thirds of their assets are invested in mortgages and corporate bonds in about equal proportions. The greater the earnings on the investments, the lower the premiums charged for a given insurance policy. Despite their large size, life insurance companies have experienced the slowest growth in the postwar period of any major type of financial institution.

Savings and Loan Associations. Savings and loan associations are primarily personal-savings and mortgage-lending institutions. They effectively borrow short term through passbook savings, in which they compete with commercial banks, and lend long term on real estate collateral. Savings and loans are the most specialized of the major intermediaries. As a result, at times when the demand for residential mortgages weakens, they cannot shift their new investments into other outlets and experience difficulty generating sufficient current earnings to pay competitive savings rates and maintain inflows. In the first 20 years of the postwar period, the demand for residential construction was strong and savings and loan associations expanded rapidly. When the demand for mortgages slackened in the second half of the 1960s, their growth rate slowed temporarily.

Private Pension Funds. Pension funds collect contributions from either or both the employee and/or his employer during an employee's working years and make monthly payments upon his retirement. They ease the process of saving for retirement. Pension funds are now common among employers, both business firms and governments. A fund for almost all employees in the United States, operated by the federal government, is the Old Age and Survivors Insurance Fund, better known as Social Security.

The monies collected are invested by the pension fund until payment to enlarge the payments or reduce future collections. Pension funds may be managed by the employer, the employees, a life insurance company, the trust department of a commercial bank, or a trustee. Private noninsured pension funds—all private funds not managed by a life insurance company—tend to invest heavily in corporate equities. Similar to life insurance companies, inflows into pension funds are long term and outflows highly predictable. This lessens the need for short-term liquid investments. By emphasizing equities, private pension funds expect to increase earnings and reduce the amount of monthly contributions necessary to finance a given income stream at retirement. Private pension funds have grown very rapidly in the postwar period, increasing by some 1,400 percent between 1950 and 1968, second only in growth to mutual funds.

Mutual Savings Banks. Mutual savings banks are similar to savings and loan associations. They gather funds primarily through passbook savings accounts and invest primarily in residential mortgages. In most states, their lending authority is somewhat broader than that for savings and loan associations. However, they have, on the average, expanded considerably slower than savings and loan associations in the postwar period. By state laws, they are restricted to a limited number of states, primarily on the north Atlantic seaboard. This area has experienced slower growth in residential mortgage demand than most other areas of the country in which savings and loans are located.

Mutual Funds. Mutual funds differ from other financial intermediaries in that both the secondary securities they sell and the primary securities they purchase are equity securities. In effect, mutual funds permit individuals to participate in equity investments in any denomination, with reduced risk resulting from diversification and the assistance of professional management and counsel. Mutual funds stand ready to sell their secondary securities, primarily through salesmen, in any amounts demanded at the current net value of their asset portfolio and repurchase the securities upon demand at the net asset value at that time. These funds may pursue a range of investment strategies. Some funds prefer to purchase primary equities of a wide spectrum of different firms in different industries with different risks, while others may concentrate on a particular industry or a particular risk category. The characteristics of the primary securities purchased are reflected in the price and risk characteristics of the secondary securities sold. Mutual funds have experienced the most rapid growth of the institutions summarized in Table 4-5.

Mutual funds are only one of two intermediaries that specialize in equity securities on both sides of their balance sheets, although they are by far the largest and most rapidly growing. The other intermediary is closed-end investment companies. These firms differ from mutual funds primarily by selling only a fixed number of secondary securities, which are then traded in secondary markets. Mutual funds and closed-end investment companies are both generally classified as investment companies.

Finance Companies. Finance companies make loans to business firms and households. Business finance companies specialize in lending to firms, sales finance companies specialize in lending to households to finance the purchase of automobiles and large consumer durables, and personal finance companies specialize in financing small consumer purchases and extending small personal loans to reasonably high-risk borrowers. Sales finance companies are frequently subsidiaries of large manufacturing firms, such as General Motors and General Electric, or large merchandising firms, such as Sears, Roebuck and Montgomery Ward. They are established to help finance purchases of their parent's products or merchandise. Finance companies raise funds by selling both short- and long-term secondary securities to commercial banks, other financial intermediaries, and individuals.

Casualty Insurance Companies. Casualty insurance companies sell protection against the loss of property resulting from accident, fire, theft, negligence, and other predictable reasons. The companies sell secondary securities in the form of premiums whose prices are related to the actuarial probability of the occurrence of the event triggering the loss. Until insured losses are realized, the casualty companies invest the funds in primary securities. Because the probabilities of events resulting in property losses are more difficult to calculate accurately than the probabilities of human death, the payments or outflows of casualty insurance companies are more uncertain than those from life insurance companies, and casualty companies invest more heavily in short-term, highly marketable securities. To offset the lower income generated by such securities, casualty companies also invest substantially in corporate equities.

Credit Unions. Credit unions are small consumer-oriented savings and lending institutions. They are typically organized by members of the same employees' group, profession, or geographical neighborhood to gather savings from members of the group and extend loans to members of the group. Their liabilities are primarily passbook savings deposits and their investments almost entirely consumer loans.

Financial Markets

Financial institutions buy and sell their securities on financial markets. An efficient economy that maximizes economic welfare requires an efficient market mechanism for financial claims to permit quick, large, and smooth transfers of funds from SSUs to DSUs. Market efficiency implies an ordering of trade according to price, low costs of physical transfer, search and information, and a large availability of offers to buy and sell at close to the prevailing market price. The smaller the brokers' commissions and spreads between dealers' bid (buying) or offer (selling) prices, the smaller the fluctuations in price from trade to trade, and the larger the volume of trade either in dollar amount or relative to the amount outstanding, the more efficient a particular market is. For purposes of description, financial markets may be categorized by the age of the claims traded, by the number of intermediaries between ultimate DSUs and SSUs, by the term to maturity of the claims traded, by the unit size of trade, and by location.

Primary and Secondary Markets

Primary markets trade in newly created claims. All financial claims, whether debt or equity, primary or secondary, have primary markets. A security can only be traded on the primary market once—at the time it is issued. All financial intermediaries and almost all brokers and dealers operate on the primary market. The efficiency of the primary market varies from claim to claim. The size of the primary market has both a stock and a flow dimension. The stock dimension measures the size of the market by the aggregate dollar amount of all claims outstanding. The flow dimension incorporates time. It measures the size of the market by the dollar volume of new issues sold in a particular period of time, say, one month or one year. As securities with shorter maturities are more likely to be refinanced more frequently, this measure gives greater weight to short-term securities. Thus, a primary market that sells $10 million of one-month securities every month or $120 million in one year may be considered larger than a market that sells a single issue of $100 million one-year securities once a year, although at any one time more of the one-year securities are outstanding than of the one-month securities.

The secondary market trades in outstanding securities. To be traded on the secondary market, a security needs to be legally negotiable. As all securities are not legally negotiable, the number of different securities traded on the secondary market is less than the number traded on the primary market. However, a security can be traded any number of times on the secondary market.

The volume of trading on the secondary market is directly related to transactions costs. While a security needs to be legally negotiable to be eligible for trade on the secondary market, negotiability does not insure marketability. The higher the costs of physical trade, search, and information are, the smaller the volume of trading and the less marketable the security. Only a fraction of negotiable financial claims are actively traded on secondary markets. Conventional residential mortgages, while legally negotiable, trade only infrequently on the secondary market because of high transaction costs arising from their odd denominations, nonstandardized loan contracts, and limited information on the creditworthiness of the ultimate DSU. On the other hand, securities of the U.S. Treasury and major business corporations trade frequently as transactions costs are low, reflecting large and common denominations, standardized loan contracts, and more readily available information on the creditworthiness of the borrower. The daily average dollar of trade and the turnover (dollar amount traded divided by dollar amount outstanding) of major securities traded on the secondary markets are shown in Table 4-6.

By far the most actively traded securities are federal funds. These transactions involve overnight interbank trading of balances on deposit at Federal Reserve Banks. Technically, it may be argued that since ownership does not change before maturity, federal funds are traded on the primary, not the secondary, market. But their extremely short-term maturity causes a rapid turnover of ownership and makes their behavior more comparable to that of securities traded on the secondary market. Daily trading in federal funds is four times greater than the dollar volume of trading in Treasury securities, the next most active security, and more than 20 times greater than trading on the much publicized New York Stock Exchange. In terms of turnover, the spread is even larger. Over 40 percent of all member-bank reserves, the total amount of potential federal funds, are traded every day. In contrast, turnover is only 2.2 percent for Treasury bills, 0.4 percent for Treasury securities maturing in over one year, and 0.1 percent for stocks listed on the New York Stock Exchange.

In general, trading costs to the buyer are somewhat lower on the primary markets where the seller usually pays the total cost. On the secondary market the buyer and seller split the trading costs.

Table 4-6 **Trading on the Secondary Market, 1970**

Security	Market	Amount Outstanding[a] (Billion $)	Trading Volume (Daily Avg. Billion $)	Turnover (Daily Percent)
Federal Funds	M	24	10	42.5
Treasury Securities (marketable)	M-C	248	2.5	1.0
Bills	M	88	1.9	2.2
Notes	C	101	0.6	0.4
Bonds	C	59		
U.S. Agencies	M-C	50	0.5	1.0
Certificates of Deposit	M	26	0.1	0.4
Corporate Bonds	C	206	NA	NA
Municipal Bonds	C	143	NA	NA
Mortgages	C	451	NA	NA
Corporate Stock	C	912	NA	NA
New York Stock Exchange	C	636	0.4	0.1

[a]December 31, 1970.
M—Money Market.
C—Capital Market.
NA—Not Available.

Private and Intermediation Markets

As noted, funds may be routed from SSUs to DSUs either through the private or direct financial market or through the indirect or intermediation market (see Figure 4-1). Funds that flow directly from SSUs to the ultimate DSUs so that the SSU holds a primary claim on the ultimate DSU are said to be directed through the private financial market whether or not the transaction involves a dealer or broker.

As discussed earlier, high transaction costs for many securities on the primary markets encouraged the development of financial intermediaries. By purchasing primary securities on the primary and secondary markets and issuing secondary securities with a different set of properties, they are able to reduce transactions costs and increase the efficiency of the financial markets, particularly of the primary market. Funds that are directed from SSUs to DSUs through an intermediary so that the SSU does not hold a primary claim on the ultimate DSU are said to be directed through the intermediation market. All secondary claims of financial intermediaries trade on the intermediation market.

Money and Capital Markets

Financial markets are sometimes classified by the term to maturity of the claims traded. Short-term securities are traded on the money market and long-term securities on the capital market. The dividing line between short- and long-term is arbitrary and not universally accepted. Most participants in financial markets divide these two markets by whether the security has more or less than one year to maturity. Those securities with less than one year to maturity are said to be traded on the money market; those with more, on the capital market. It is quite common for long-term securities to be traded on both markets during their life. In their early years they trade on the capital market. In their last year before maturity, they trade on the money market. Equities have no designated maturity and trade on the capital market.

Centralized and Decentralized Markets

Financial markets may be centralized or decentralized. The markets for securities that typically trade in large units, say, of $1 million or more, tend to be centralized in a limited number of major cities called financial centers, while those for smaller trading units exist in almost every city throughout the country. There are a number of reasons primary and secondary markets for large trading units are highly centralized:

1. The securities traded have standardized contracts and need not be personally inspected by the trading partners. The value of the security is read from the financial statements of the ultimate DSU and does not require a personal investigation of the issuer. This permits the physical trading to be conducted at a distance from the location of the buyers and sellers.

2. Although physically easy to transport, securities are costly to transport safely the farther the distance. Moreover, the farther the distance, the longer the delivery and the slower the transfer of funds. For this reason, most securities are stored close to the location of the trading. Recent advances in transferring securities by telegraph and in replacing physical securities with book entries in computer memory cores have reduced the need for centralization to minimize transportation costs.

3. Much security trading is undertaken on the basis of new or differently interpreted information. Because the cost of collecting and transmitting information varies with the distance from the source of the information, participants in the financial markets prefer to locate close to each other.

4. Many financial trades require immediate, very large, and highly specialized financing. This suggests a clustering of financial markets near financial institutions, particularly near large commercial banks.

The major financial center in the United States is New York City. The majority of major financial institutions are headquartered in New York, including six of the country's ten largest banks, the four largest life insurance companies, nine of the ten largest mutual savings banks, the two largest organized stock exchanges, all large security dealers, and all large security brokers. In addition, almost all other major financial institutions headquartered elsewhere, either in the U.S. or overseas, have offices in New York and many large nonfinancial firms maintain their finance offices there. The next largest domestic financial centers are Chicago, San Francisco, Los Angeles, and Boston. Worldwide, the largest financial centers outside the United States are London, Zurich, and Hong Kong.

Markets for small-denomination secondary securities exist wherever there is a financial institution. Markets for passbook savings exist at every commercial bank, savings and loan association, and mutual savings bank in the country, of which there are more than 20,000 operating about twice as many branches.

Organized and Over-the-Counter Markets

A financial market is said to be organized if a large volume of trading in many securities is conducted at a central location under a specific set of rules and regulations. An organized market is commonly referred to as an exchange. Buyers and sellers frequently trade through agents of the exchange, not with each other. The exchange matches the orders and establishes the equilibrium price. The largest organized exchange in the United States is the New York Stock Exchange on which the equity and debt securities of most corporations are traded. Smaller organized markets include the American Stock Exchange (New York), the Midwest Stock Exchange (Chicago), and the Pacific Coast Stock Exchange (San Francisco). Organized exchanges are considerably more important in the trading of equity than debt securities.

Over-the-counter markets exist wherever financial claims are sold under conditions different from those for an organized exchange. Every dealer and intermediary operates an over-the-counter market in his shop when he buys or sells claims for his own account. Buyers and sellers trade directly with each other. One party generally specifies volume and the other price. If agreement is reached, the transaction is consummated. An important proportion of all equity instruments and the large majority of all marketable debt instruments are traded "over-the-counter" by security dealers. Banks, savings and loan associations, and life insurance companies raise their funds over-the-counter at their offices. The rules and regulations vary from market to market. Prices and terms may also vary. The same security can be traded in a large number of different locations simultaneously. Prices in the different markets are "kept in line" by arbitrators who simultaneously buy in cheap markets and sell in dear markets. Customers may also shop around.

Almost all the securities listed in Table 4-6, except equity listed on the New York Stock Exchange, are traded over-the-counter. Obviously, volume on this market dwarfs the volume on organized markets.

References

Bankers Trust Company, *The Investment Outlook for 1971* (New York: 1971).

Black, Robert P., and Doris E. Harless, *Nonbank Financial Institutions* (Richmond: Federal Reserve Bank of Richmond, 1969).

Board of Governors of the Federal Reserve System, *Flow of Funds Accounts, 1945-68* (Washington, D.C.: 1970).

——, *Joint Treasury–Federal Reserve Study of the U.S. Government Securities Market; Report* (Washington, D.C.: 1969); *Staff Studies, Part I* (Washington, D.C.: 1970); *Staff Studies, Part 2* (Washington, D.C.: 1971).

Brill, Daniel H., and Ann P. Ulrey, "The Role of Financial Intermediaries in U.S. Capital Markets," *Federal Reserve Bulletin,* January, 1967, 18-31.

Dougall, Herbert E., *Capital Markets and Institutions* (Englewood Cliffs, N.J.: Prentice-Hall, 1970).

Grebler, Leo, *The Future of Thrift Institutions* (Danville, Ill.: Joint Savings and Loan and Mutual Savings Bank Exchange Group, 1969).

Jacobs, Donald P., Loring C. Farwell, and Edwin Neave, *Financial Institutions* (Homewood, Ill.: Irwin, 1972).

Krooss, Herman E., and Martin R. Blyn, *A History of Financial Intermediaries* (New York: Random House, 1971).

Madden, Carl H., *The Money Side of "The Street"* (New York: Federal Reserve Bank of New York, 1959).

Polakoff, Murray E., et al., *Financial Institutions and Markets* (Boston: Houghton Mifflin, 1970).

Scott, Ira O., *Government Securities Market* (New York: McGraw-Hill, 1965).

Silber, William L., *Portfolio Behavior of Financial Institutions* (New York: Holt, Rinehart & Winston, 1970).

Van Horne, James C., *Function and Analysis of Capital Market Rates* (Englewood Cliffs, N.J.: Prentice-Hall, 1970).

Commercial Banks as Financial Firms

5

Commercial banks are the dominant institution in the financial sector of the economy and one of the most important institutions in the overall economy. They are by far the largest financial institution, purchase the widest variety of primary claims, and are effectively the only private institution to offer demand deposits, which not only serve as money but account for the largest part of the country's money stock. Like all other financial intermediaries, banks provide for the transfer of funds from SSUs to DSUs but, in the process, unlike other intermediaries, also provide the nation's payments mechanism. This chapter considers commercial banks as profit-maximizing private business firms and describes their operations.

History of Commercial Banking

The history of commercial banks is long and colorful. Our purpose in tracing their history is to consider how and why the banks attained their important position in the economy. This objective may be achieved most efficiently by providing a somewhat fictionalized account of their development.

As discussed in Chapter 3, full-bodied coins valued only slightly above the market worth of their metallic content of gold, silver, or copper served as the primary form of money through the beginning of the commercial and industrial revolutions. As the denominations of transactions increased, secure storage and transfer of coins became a problem. Enterprising goldsmiths, who had vaults on their premises, agreed to deposit customers' coins for safekeeping for a fee. As proof of ownership, customers were provided with deposit receipts. Whenever a customer engaged in a purchase, he would redeem his receipt and physically transfer the appropriate amount of coins to the seller. The latter, in turn, would most likely redeposit the coins with a goldsmith, possibly even the same one.

Through time, it became apparent to both the goldsmiths and their customers that everyone would benefit if, rather than redeeming the receipts and physically transferring the coins, the buyer would only transfer his receipt to the seller. The transaction could be further expedited if receipts were issued in common denominations, say, in units of 1, 10, or 100. Gradually the goldsmiths standardized the denominations, color, and form of their deposit receipts. Receipt holders could convert their receipts into coin at any time. Mostly, however, the receipts were not redeemed and they became increasingly used as a medium of exchange. In recognition of their use as money, the receipts were renamed *notes* and served as early currency.

Sometime during the development of the note, goldsmiths noticed that all notes were not simultaneously redeemed for coins. It was possible to estimate statistically the probabilities of any amount of notes being offered for redemption at any one goldsmith on any one day. Under normal circumstances, the probabilities indicated that only a small fraction of coins would be needed to satisfy regular note redemptions. Why not, mused some more enterprising goldsmith, issue additional notes to persons in temporary need of purchasing power? The borrower would pay interest on the loan and back it with his IOU or more valuable collateral. After a note issue, the balance sheet of the goldsmith would show the value of coins to be less than the value of note liabilities by the amount of IOUs or loans. This is shown in T-account form below:

(a)

Assets	Liabilities
Coins $1,000	Notes $1,000

(b)

Assets	Liabilities
Coins $1,000	Notes $2,000
Loans $1,000	

In this example, total note liabilities are doubled by the note issue from $1,000 to $2,000 and coins now provide a reserve to accommodate note withdrawals of only 50 percent rather than of 100 percent. In the jargon of bankers, this represented a change from 100 percent reserve banking to fractional reserve banking.

Before long such "note creation" became more profitable for some goldsmiths than their gold fabricating and safekeeping business and they concentrated increasingly on it, eventually even changing their identification from goldsmith to bank. Many older European banks can trace their beginnings back to goldsmiths and have maintained or incorporated the crest of their former trade.

As long as banks maintained sufficient reserves in the form of coins to accommodate note redemptions, banking was a profitable venture. Interest charges on the notes loaned needed only to exceed the costs of safekeeping the coins, extending the loan, and covering occasional defaults. Periodically, however, for a variety of reasons, more noteholders than usual attempted to convert their notes into coins. At such times, unless the bank was able to quickly convert its IOUs into coins at about face value, all noteholders were not satisfied and the value of the remaining notes declined sharply. Because noteholders recognized that banks held insufficient reserves to satisfy all of them, the slightest rumor of a bank's inability to convert its notes into coins precipitated a run on the bank by noteholders in order to be the first to convert into the available coin. While any one bank may have maintained free and unlimited convertibility under such circumstances by calling in or selling its IOUs, all banks together were unable to maintain convertibility in the face of a run on all of them simultaneously. On these occasions, the market value of notes declined relative to coins, and notes no longer served as money at par value. The resulting decline in the stock of money contributed to a decline in trade, economic activity, employment, and general welfare.

In the United States private banks supplied almost all of the note issue until 1913 when Congress authorized the Federal Reserve to issue notes. Until 1863, all notes were issued by state-chartered banks. From 1863 to 1913, note issue was conducted by federally chartered national banks. National bank notes were not withdrawn from circulation until 1935.

Bank notes replaced coin and served as the primary form of money in both the United States and England until close to the turn of the twentieth century. At that time, the continual increase in the scale of transactions made notes subject to the same limitations as coin had experienced some time earlier. Bank customers found it more desirable to transfer ownership of the appropriate amount of deposit by written order to the bank rather than by note. This led to the development of the check and the eventual emergence of demand deposits as the dominant part of the money supply.

Commercial Bank Operations

Commercial banks like any other privately operated business firm aim to maximize their long-run profits. Banks do so by attempting to earn more interest income on their loans and investments than the combined cost of the interest expense on deposits and the cost of servicing both loans and deposits. In attempting to maximize profits, commercial banks are subject to a number of constraints some of which are similar to constraints impinging on other types of firms and some

Table 5-1 Balance Sheet, All Insured Commercial Banks
December 31, 1971

	All Banks		New York City Member Banks		Nonmember Banks	
	Billion $	Percent	Billion $	Percent	Billion $	Percent
Assets						
Loans	345	54	47	52	70	56
Commercial and Industrial	118	19	27	30	17	13
Agricultural	12	2	°	—	5	4
Security	11	2	5	5	1	1
Financial Institutions	41	6	6	7	6	5
Real Estate	81	13	4	4	21	17
Consumer	74	12	4	4	19	15
Other	8	1	2	2	1	1
Investments	170	27	15	16	42	33
U.S. Treasury	65	10	6	7	17	13
Municipal Securities	82	13	8	9	17	13
Other	22	3	1	1	8	6
Cash Assets	98	15	22	24	12	10
Reserves at FRB	27	4	5	5	—	—
Vault Cash	8	1	1	1	2	2
Due from Banks	25	4	2	2	9	7
Cash Items in Process of Collection	39	6	14	15	1	1
Miscellaneous	23	4	7	8	2	2
Total	636	100	91	100	126	100

of which are unique to commercial banks. Among the more important constraints are:

1. The need to accommodate withdrawals of deposits immediately upon demand for demand deposits, and at maturity for time deposits. Failure to satisfy such demands would result in insolvency and immediate bank closing.
2. Minimum capital requirements established by law.
3. Minimum reserve requirements established by law.
4. Legal upper limits on interest rates that may be paid on deposits.
5. Legal upper limits on interest rates that may be charged on some loans.
6. Legal restrictions on the type of loans and investments that may be made.
7. Legal restrictions on the dollar amount that may be loaned to any one borrower.
8. Legal restrictions on merging or consolidating with another bank or banking system.
9. Legal restrictions on entry into the banking industry.
10. Legal restrictions on the establishment of additional offices.

	All Banks		New York City Member Banks		Nonmember Banks	
	Billion $	Percent	Billion $	Percent	Billion $	Percent
Liabilities and Capital						
Demand Deposits	261	41	46	51	49	39
Private	191	30	26	29	39	31
Due to Banks	32	5	14	15	2	2
U.S. Treasury	10	2	2	2	2	2
Municipal Gov'ts.	18	3	1	1	5	4
Certified Checks	10	2	4	4	1	1
Time Deposits	275	43	25	27	63	50
Passbook Savings	111	17	6	7	26	21
Consumer Certificates and Misc.	130	20	8	9	37	29
Negotiable Certificates of Deposit	34	5	11	12	—	—
Borrowed Funds	26	4	5	5	1	1
Federal Reserve Banks	*	—	—	—	—	—
Other Banks	24	4	5	5	1	1
Eurodollars	1	—	*	—	—	—
Capital Account	47	7	7	8	10	7
Miscellaneous	27	4	8	9	3	2
Total	636	100	91	100	126	100

*Less than $1 billion.

Source: Federal Deposit Insurance Corporation, *Assets and Liabilities, Commercial and Mutual Savings Banks, December 31, 1971.*

The first constraint is purely operational and can be examined in isolation from the others. The legal and regulatory constraints will be examined later.

The Bank Balance Sheet

The major items on both sides of the balance sheet of all federally insured commercial banks are shown in Table 5-1. The same items are also shown for New York City banks that are members of the Federal Reserve System and for nonmember banks. The former can be assumed to be very large banks, while the latter are mostly smaller banks.

Liabilities and Capital

The major liabilities of commercial banks are deposits. Economically, deposits are difficult to distinguish from borrowed funds and may be considered as such. Legally, deposits take precedence in case of bank liquidation over most, although not all, types of borrowed funds.

Demand Deposits. Demand deposits account for almost one-half of all sources of funds of commercial banks. Being a medium of exchange, demand deposits are closely associated with transactions and are relatively more important as a source of funds at larger commercial banks, which typically have a larger proportion of business customers, than at smaller banks. Demand deposits are owned by almost everyone. The largest holder of demand deposits is the private sector—individuals, partnerships, and business corporations. The next largest holders are other commercial banks who for a number of reasons find it advantageous to hold deposits at other, primarily larger, banks. Smaller balances are held by federal, state, city, and local governments.

By law, banks may not pay explicit interest on demand deposits. However, they are able to reward depositors by providing deposit-related services, such as safe-keeping and accounting, at below cost. To the bank, the cost of demand deposits is the cost of providing these services in addition to the cost of check processing.

Time Deposits. Unlike demand deposits, time deposits are not legally convertible into currency or demand deposits at the demand of the depositor. Time deposits either have a specific maturity date, at least 30 days from day of deposit, or may require 30-day notification of desire to withdraw at the discretion of the bank. Ownership cannot be transferred by check. Rather time deposits must first be converted into currency or demand deposits. To compensate depositors for the reduced liquidity of time deposits, banks pay explicit interest rates. Time deposits account for 43 percent of total bank funds and are considerably more important at small banks than at large banks. Time deposits are almost entirely owned by the private sector. There are three basic types of time deposits:

Passbook savings—Passbook savings are deposits evidenced by entries in a passbook savings account book. Deposits may be made in any amount. Although a depositor may be requested to furnish 30-day advance notice of withdrawal, this practice has not been used with any frequency since the era of massive bank failures during the Great Depression of the early 1930s and withdrawals effectively can be made at any time. In addition, these funds are available at their face value at all times. Thus, passbook savings provide almost instant liquidity during bank working hours. Reflecting this high degree of liquidity, interest rates on passbook savings are generally somewhat lower than on other types of deposits. Interest is typically paid quarterly on funds on deposit either from day of deposit to day of withdrawal, or continuously on deposit from day of deposit to the end of the quarter. Because of the difficulties of differentiating among funds, all passbook savings are paid the same interest rate. Banks can change the rate at any time for the remainder of the quarter.

Consumer certificates of deposit—Consumer certificates of deposit are issued in designated denominations, have fixed maturity dates, and bear fixed rates of interest to maturity. They can be redeemed prior to maturity only in emergency and at a penalty. Interest rates are generally somewhat higher than on passbook accounts and, because the bank can distinguish the funds, may vary from certificate to certificate depending upon the bank's need for funds at the time of issue. Thus, they provide a more flexible source of funds to the banks than do passbook savings.

Negotiable certificates of deposit—These, commonly referred to as CDs, are very large certificates of deposit usually issued in denominations of $1 million to business firms and government units. Similar to consumer certificates, they have fixed maturity dates and interest rates. Because of their large size, they are issued primarily by the largest banks. Large banks are generally well known in the financial markets and their CDs are traded on a secondary market. By selling a CD, its holders can effectively redeem their deposit before maturity without loss of funds to the bank. The marketability feature makes CDs attractive to temporary holders of large funds and permits large banks to tap the national money market for funds. Interest rates on CDs must be competitive with market rates on comparable money-market instruments. As funds flow quickly in this market, a bank can increase its deposits quickly and substantially by offering a slightly higher rate of interest. CDs are a relatively new form of deposit, having been introduced only in 1961. In their brief existence they have expanded rapidly to where they account for more than one-half of total time deposits at some large banks.

Borrowed Funds. Borrowed funds are, for all economic purposes, similar to deposits. Banks borrow funds primarily from three sources:

Other banks—As noted earlier, banks have to hold cash reserves equal to a percentage of their deposits. At times banks may have more or less than this amount. Banks that have more may lend (sell) the reserves to banks that have less. Bank reserves on deposit at Federal Reserve Banks are called federal funds. The usual maturity of federal fund loans is just overnight and units of trade tend to be very large, generally $1 million.

Federal Reserve Banks—Banks that belong to the Federal Reserve System may borrow for short periods of time from their district Federal Reserve Bank. Such borrowing is considered only temporary until the banks can obtain funds in the necessary amounts elsewhere. The interest rate charged by the Federal Reserve for such borrowing is the discount rate.

Eurodollars—These are short-term dollar borrowings from foreign banks or overseas branches of U.S. banks. Eurodollars are discussed in greater detail in Chapter 18.

Borrowing from other commercial banks is more important at the larger banks, and borrowing from the Federal Reserve Banks at the smaller banks.

Capital. Bank capital consists of equity, or ownership funds, and subordinated long-term debt. Although banks have stepped up sales of long-term debt in recent years, such debt still represents only a small portion of bank capital. Overall, capital accounts for less than 10 percent of total bank resources; the remainder is borrowed funds. This low percentage of capital makes banks particularly vulnerable to declines in earnings and is one of the reasons for the substantial degree of government regulation of banking including the imposition of minimum capital requirements. Capital protects depositors by providing a buffer against which losses on assets can be charged. If losses were to be charged against deposits, the bank would be unable to repay the full value of the amount of deposits and might be forced to close. The larger the proportion of capital to deposits is, the greater the protection to depositors.

Assets

Banks invest in a wide variety of primary claims of different sectors, risks, and maturities. Bank earning assets are commonly classified as either loans or investments. Loans are credit extensions involving an ongoing personal relationship between the lending bank and the borrower. The amount, repayment, and other features of the loan are tailored to the particular needs of the customer. Loans typically involve personal evaluation of creditworthiness and frequently involve deposit, advisory, and other services, in addition to the credit service. In contrast, investments are credit extensions in common denominations on an impersonal basis to large and well-known borrowers evidenced by a standardized loan contract. Investments represent pure financing. Because of the standardized contract, reputation of the borrower, and large denomination, investments are frequently marketable and can be traded on active secondary markets. Reflecting these differences, loans generally yield higher gross interest rates than investments of comparable maturity and, although involving higher costs, generally also tend to yield higher net returns to the bank.

Loans.

Business loans—Commercial banks are the largest provider of credit to business firms. Commercial and industrial loans comprise the largest single category of the earning assets of banks. Most business loans are short term, maturing within one year, but an increasing proportion are longer or "term" loans. The interest charged the largest and best customers is called the prime rate. Rates for other customers are scaled up from this floor. Business loan customers are frequently required to maintain compensating demand deposit balances at the lending bank. To the extent that these balances exceed the amount of working balance the firm would usually hold in its demand deposit account, compensating balances add to the cost of the loan and are used as a competitive instrument by the banks. Reflecting the differences in the types of business the banks conduct, business loans are considerably more important at large city banks than at smaller rural banks.

Agricultural loans—Banks provide credit to farmers to finance the purchase of seed, feed, livestock, equipment, and land. (Loans for buildings are classified under mortgages.) As might be expected, agricultural loans are far more important at smaller banks than at larger banks, accounting for an insignificant proportion of the assets of New York City banks, for example. At some small banks, agricultural loans represent the most important loan category and heavily influence the operation of the bank.

Security loans—These loans finance the purchase and carrying of equity and debt securities by individuals, dealers, brokers, and brokers' customers. The loans are collateralized by the securities purchased. Loans to individuals account for somewhat less than half of the total loans and are subject to margin requirements (Federal Reserve Regulation U), which specify the maximum percentage a lender can lend on the purchase price of an equity-type security. As of year-end 1971, the margin requirement on common stock was 55 percent. That is, a lender could lend only a maximum of 45 percent of the purchase price of a stock. The remaining 55 percent must be financed by the purchaser from his own resources. Dealers use the proceeds of the loan primarily to finance their inventories. Brokers use the proceeds to relend to their customers subject to the same margin requirements as banks. Security loans tend to be relatively more important at larger banks.

Financial institution loans—Loans to financial institutions include primarily loans to other banks and to finance companies. Loans to other banks are loans (sales) of federal funds. Such loans involve minimal transactions costs and risks of default so that the net return to the lending banks is almost equivalent to the gross interest rate. Although they are short-term loans, federal funds may be turned over every day and can serve as an effective longer-term investment outlet. Finance companies use the proceeds of bank loans to relend to their business and consumer customers. Loans to both these borrowers are generally in large denominations so that loans to financial institutions are made primarily by larger banks.

Real estate loans—These are mortgage loans collateralized by real estate. Commercial banks are the third most important extenders of mortgage loans, a substantial distance behind savings and loan associations, which specialize in this type of lending, but only slightly behind life insurance companies. Mortgage loans are made to finance purchases of both new and existing commercial and residential structures. Mortgages are long-term loans, generally at a fixed interest rate, that have regular installment-type repayment schedules. They are extended in a wide variety of denominations related to the appraised value of the real estate collateral. Mortgage loans are extended to both households and business firms in all and any denominations. A number of mortgage insurance programs exist to make mortgage lending more attractive to the lender. Mortgages insured by the Federal Housing Administration (FHA) and guaranteed by the Veterans Administration (VA) have lower down payments and longer maturities than noninsured conventional mortgages and have stimulated residential construction.

Mortgage loans account for 13 percent of the total assets of banks and about one-fourth of their total loans. This represents the second most important lending activity for banks after business loans. Slightly less than two-thirds of the mortgage loans are for residential housing, slightly less than one-third for commercial structures, and the remainder for farm buildings. Mortgage loans are considerably more important at small than at large banks. About one-fourth of the residential mortgages are insured by the FHA or VA.

In December, 1970, the average conventional residential mortgage on a new home extended by a commercial bank had a maturity of 22.4 years and covered about 65 percent of the value of the home. This was somewhat shorter than the maturity of mortgages extended by savings and loan associations and covered a somewhat lower percentage of the value. Federally chartered commercial banks are limited by law on conventional mortgages to loans of no more than 30 years in maturity with minimum initial down payment of 10 percent. Other mortgage lenders generally operate under somewhat more liberal restrictions.

Consumer loans—Banks loan funds to consumers to help finance a large variety of purchases other than housing. The denominations and maturities of these loans vary with the item purchased from, say, one month for small-ticket items to more than three years for automobiles. On longer loans, installment or amortized repayment schedules are most common; on shorter loans, single repayments are the rule. Although consumer loans account for only 12 percent of bank assets, banks are the largest supplier of installment credit to consumers, providing about 40 percent of the total. Automobile loans account for almost one-half of all bank consumer installment loans. Personal loans account for another fourth and loans to purchase consumer durable goods absorb most of the rest. Similar to mortgage loans, consumer loans are more important at smaller banks.

A rapidly expanding but a still small part of bank consumer loans is bank charge-card loans. Credit cards permit eligible consumers to make purchases at merchants who have entered into an agreement with a bank (or other institution for nonbank cards) operating a particular credit card and postpone payment until a later date. If payment is made within a specified number of days after the purchase, the consumer pays no interest. Thereafter, the bank charges interest, generally at a rate somewhat above that charged on other consumer loans. Participating merchants receive immediate payment from their banks upon presentation of the credit receipts. For this service, the banks charge the merchants a rate computed as a discount on the amount of credit receipts.

At year-end 1970, credit extended on bank credit cards totaled $4 billion. This amounted to 6 percent of total consumer loans and only 1 percent of total bank loans. Moreover, this amount includes the credit outstanding before the expiration of the grace period and on which interest is not charged. While there are some 50 million card-holder accounts throughout the country, only about one-third of these accounts are considered active. The average amount of credit outstanding per active bank credit card was $207.

Investments.

U.S. Treasury securities—Securities issued by the U.S. Treasury Department are considered to be free of risk of default. Unless replaced by a government which repudiates debts incurred by its predecessor, the power to print money gives the Treasury the ability to redeem its debt obligations at maturity at all times. Because of the risk-free feature, Treasury securities yield the lowest interest rates of any securities of the particular maturity. There are four different types of securities issued by the Treasury.

Treasury bills are issued with a term to maturity of one year or less. Bills bear no coupon interest rate. Rather they are sold at a discount from maturity value and the interest return is equivalent to the amount of the discount divided by the price of the bill adjusted for the number of days held. This feature makes the effective interest rate on these instruments simple to calculate and serves to enhance their value as a trading instrument on the secondary market. The Treasury sells bills at auction at regular intervals through competitive bidding. The largest amount of bills outstanding are initially issued with 91 days, or three months, to maturity. These bills are auctioned weekly. As a result, a wide variety of different maturities are available at all times, another feature that adds to the attractiveness of bills on the secondary market. Of the $250 million of marketable Treasury securities outstanding, $90 million or 35 percent are bills.

Certificates of indebtedness or certificates, as these securities are known, are sold with initial maturities of one year or less. Unlike bills, however, certificates carry a coupon interest rate. In recent years certificates have tended to be replaced by bills, and, when sold, are available only in relatively small amounts. At year-end 1971, there were no certificates outstanding.

Treasury notes are coupon issues sold with from one to seven years to maturity. Unlike bills, notes are not sold on a regular schedule but at times when new funds have to be raised to finance a federal budget deficit or maturing issues need to be refinanced.

Treasury bonds are the longest-term securities issued by the Treasury. They have original terms to maturity of seven years or more. Similar to notes, bonds carry a coupon rate of interest. Except for initial term to maturity, Treasury notes and bonds are identical. At year-end 1971, the longest issue outstanding matures in 1998. It was sold originally in 1960. A listing of all Treasury notes and bonds by issue including the coupon rate, maturity date, amount outstanding, and market price as of year-end 1970 is shown in Table 5-2.

At year-end 1970, Treasury securities of all types accounted for 10 percent of bank assets. Treasury securities are relatively more important at smaller banks. Some larger banks hold Treasury securities only to amounts necessary to serve as collateral for public deposits (deposits of federal and local governments), the only type of deposits eligible for such special treatment.

Municipal securities—One of the more rapidly expanding items in the banks' portfolios of earning assets is municipal securities. These debt securities are sold by state, city, and other local governments. They are collateralized either by the full taxing powers of the issuing municipality (general obligation bonds) or by revenues derived from the particular project the bonds financed (revenue bonds). Maturities vary from a few weeks to 20 or more years. All coupon interest payments are exempt from federal income taxes. For larger banks, whose federal income tax liability is close to 50 percent of income, the effective interest return on municipal securities is almost twice the nominal rate in comparison to bonds on which the coupon payments are fully taxed. Similar to Treasury securities, municipal securities are relatively more important in the asset portfolio of smaller banks.

Cash Assets.

Reserves at Federal Reserve Banks—Member banks hold balances at their district Federal Reserve Banks or branches in order to satisfy legal reserve requirements. These deposits also serve as check-clearing balances to which the dollar amount of checks deposited at other banks is credited and the dollar amount of checks written on other banks is debited. Balances at the Federal Reserve Bank do not yield interest income. Banks may transfer these balances to other banks in much the same fashion individuals and firms can transfer amounts from their demand deposit balances at commercial banks to other accounts. Both because reserve requirements are greater for larger banks and because smaller banks tend not to be members of the Federal Reserve System, balances at Federal Reserve Banks are more important for larger banks.

Vault cash—Banks hold coin and currency in their own vaults both to accommodate demands to convert deposits and to satisfy legal reserve requirements. Because costs of security and transfer are both greater for balances maintained on bank premises than at Federal Reserve Banks, banks typically maintain only minimum amounts of vault cash. Vault cash may be included in computing legal reserves.

Balances due from other banks—Banks may hold demand deposit balances at

Table 5-2 **Characteristics of Outstanding Treasury Notes and Bonds**
December 31, 1970

Issue %	Issue Maturity	Initial Date Issued	Amount Outstanding[a]	Market Price[b]	Market Yield to Maturity
5⅜	2/15/71	8/30/67	2,509	100.11	1.14
7¾	2/15/71	8/15/69	2,924	100.17	1.80
2½	3/15/66–71	12/1/44	1,219	99.25	2.96
5¼	5/15/71	8/15/66	4,265	100.8	4.16
8	5/15/71	10/1/69	4,176	101.6	4.24
4	8/15/71	3/1/62	2,805	99.16	4.63
8¼	8/15/71	2/15/70	2,257	102.5	4.43
3⅞	11/15/71	5/15/62	2,760	99.7	4.66
5⅜	11/15/71	11/15/66	1,734	100.14	4.70
7¾	11/15/71	5/15/70	10,743	102.14	4.68
4	2/15/72	11/15/62	2,344	98.21	5.02
4¾	2/15/72	2/15/67	2,006	99.14	5.16
7½	2/15/72	8/15/70	3,362	102.13	5.13
4¾	5/15/72	5/15/67	5,310	99.9	5.11
6¾	5/15/72	8/15/70	2,038	101.29	5.18
2½	6/15/67–72	6/1/45	1,236	96.2	5.19
4	8/15/72	9/15/62	2,578	97.25	5.29
2½	9/15/67–72	10/20/41	1,951	95.6	5.36
2½	12/15/67–72	11/15/45	2,569	94.15	5.40
7¾	5/15/73	10/1/69	5,842	104.24	5.46
4	8/15/73	9/15/63	3,894	95.24	5.67
8⅛	8/15/73	2/15/70	1,839	106.0	5.52
4⅛	11/15/73	7/22/64	4,345	95.20	5.71
4⅛	2/15/74	1/15/65	3,127	94.28	5.86
7¾	2/15/74	8/15/70	3,140	105.6	5.82
4¼	5/15/74	5/15/64	3,581	94.27	5.88
7¼	5/15/74	1/15/70	4,511	104.4	5.80
5⅝	8/15/74	8/15/68	10,284	98.26	5.92
3⅞	11/15/74	12/2/57	2,239	92.26	5.91
5¾	11/15/74	11/15/67	3,981	99.16	5.82
5¾	2/15/75	2/15/68	5,148	99.12	5.85
6	5/15/75	5/15/68	6,760	100.11	5.84
6¼	2/15/76	2/15/69	3,737	101.0	5.96
6½	5/15/76	5/15/69	2,697	102.2	5.99
7½	8/15/76	10/1/69	4,195	106.8	6.11
8	2/15/77	2/15/70	5,163	109.5	6.3
7¾	8/15/77	8/5/70	2,263	108.12	6.14
4	2/15/80	1/23/59	2,593	83.8	6.30
3½	11/15/80	10/3/60	1,905	78.4	6.39
3¼	6/15/78–83	5/1/53	1,543	71.16	6.51
3¼	5/15/85	6/3/58	1,075	69.28	6.38
4¼	5/15/75–85	4/5/60	1,213	79.4	6.38

Table 5-2 (Continued)

%	Issue Maturity	Initial Date Issued	Amount Outstanding[a]	Market Price[b]	Market Yield to Maturity
3½	2/15/90	2/14/58	4,735	68.28	6.22
4¼	8/15/87–92	8/15/62	3,810	73.22	6.43
4	2/15/88–93	1/17/63	248	72.24	6.20
4⅛	5/15/89–94	4/18/63	1,554	72.28	6.27
3	2/15/95	2/15/55	1,262	68.18	5.24
3½	11/15/98	10/30/60	4,027	68.16	5.70

[a] Million dollars.

[b] Decimals in thirty-seconds of a dollar.

Sources: Federal Reserve Bank of New York; U.S. Treasury Department.

other banks for a number of reasons. In most states, banks that are not members of the Federal Reserve System may include balances at larger banks as legal reserves. Many smaller banks have larger correspondent banks collect payment on the checks deposited with them and maintain clearing accounts at these banks. Smaller banks may also make use of some larger bank services that they cannot provide economically either to themselves, as investment advice, or to their customers, as foreign currency transfers, because of specialized personnel needed or infrequent demand. Often payment for these services is made in the form of balances at the selling bank rather than as an explicit payment. Because of the large number of small banks in the United States, the purchase of services from large city correspondent banks is common practice. As a result, due-from balances loom large on the balance sheet of smaller banks and are insignificant for larger banks.

Cash items in the process of collection—This account, generally referred to as CIPC, arises from the collection of checks for payment. After a check written on another bank is deposited, the receiving bank has to collect the funds. This is done by shipping the check to the bank on which it is drawn and presenting it for payment. Until the check is collected, the bank does not have the funds to invest. Funds in the process of collection are debited to the CIPC account. At the time of receipt of payment, this account is credited and reserves are increased by a like amount. The check-clearing process is examined in the next chapter.

Because CIPC are nonearning assets, banks attempt to keep the amount as low as possible. The amount of CIPC a bank has is dependent on the type of business it conducts. The larger the number and dollar amounts of checks deposited per dollar of bank deposits and the more distant the bank on which the checks are drawn, the larger the relative amount of CIPC. As both of these factors tend to be positively related to bank size, CIPC tends to be proportionately greater at large banks. For example, CIPC amount to around 15 percent of the assets of New York City member banks and for less than 1 percent of the assets of nonmember banks.

Bank Liquidity

A commercial bank requires liquidity in order to accommodate deposit withdrawals. Individual banks experience deposit losses due to conversions into currency and adverse check clearings. If a bank has insufficient funds available to meet these demands, it is forced to close its doors. Payment of deposit withdrawals can only be made from assets. Moreover, these assets have to be in a form amenable to immediate payment at or near face or purchase value. This property is satisfied by currency on hand, deposits at the Federal Reserve Bank, deposits at other commercial banks, and, to a somewhat lesser degree, by highly marketable assets. These assets must either be on hand in the bank's portfolio or be able to be acquired quickly by attracting the necessary funds. Bank strategy to maintain sufficient liquidity to remain solvent within a framework of maximizing overall profits may be pursued on either or both sides of the balance sheet. Strategy that involves the asset side is called asset management, that which involves the liability side is called liability management.

Asset Management

Cash assets, except for CIPC, are available for payment at no cost. All other assets must first be converted into cash assets. This involves costs of exchange and risk of obtaining less than the purchase price of the asset. The longer the time period available for conversion, the better the probability of obtaining a higher selling price for the asset. The liquidity of a particular asset may be defined as the overall costs of converting a noncash asset into a cash asset quickly at close to its purchase price. The lower the costs are, the greater the liquidity. Marketability and maturity are two dimensions of liquidity. The more marketable an asset on the secondary market, the lower are transactions costs and the shorter is the time required to obtain its maximum selling price. Nevertheless, highly marketable assets at times may sell at considerably below their purchase price. The shorter the maturity of a debt asset, the closer the selling price will be to the maturity value. For reasons discussed earlier, investments are, on the average, more liquid than loans, and short-term investments more liquid than longer-term investments.

Liquid assets of a bank are often divided into two groups:

Primary (cash) reserves—These are assets immediately available at no cost to accommodate deposit withdrawals. Primary reserves include vault cash, deposits at correspondent banks, and deposits at Federal Reserve Banks. They yield no interest.

Secondary reserves—These are assets that can be converted quickly at low cost into cash at close to their purchase price. They yield an interest return lower than less liquid assets but higher than primary reserves. Secondary reserves include federal funds sold, short-term Treasury securities, and short-term securities of financial institutions and other business firms, e.g., commercial paper and bankers' acceptances.

Bank asset liquidity may be measured by the proportion of completely and highly liquid assets to total assets. The greater the proportion of assets in primary and secondary reserves is, the greater the liquidity of the bank's portfolio. The lower the liquidity of an asset is, the higher the interest return to compensate the holder for the sacrifice of liquidity. In the absence of liquidity constraints, a bank can maximize profits by investing all of its assets in nonliquid securities. The necessity of meeting deposit losses, however, requires some liquid assets and some corresponding sacrifice of income. Bank asset strategy maximizes income by holding the least amount of primary and secondary reserves, that is, minimum liquidity, consistent with solvency.

The amount of primary and secondary reserves a bank holds is related to the character of its deposit variability. The greater the probability of deposit withdrawals, the more necessary is liquidity in the portfolio. In the absence of additional information, the probabilities of deposit losses are best estimated by careful study of past deposit behavior, particularly deposit variability, which measures changes in the relationship of deposit inflows and outflows. The greater the variability, the more likely are deposit outflows. Variability differs considerably among different types of deposits. A recent study of deposit variability at large banks in the Chicago Federal Reserve district indicated that day-to-day percentage changes in demand deposits of the U.S. Treasury are more than one hundred and fifty times as great as daily percentage changes in savings deposits (Table 5-3). It follows that the greater the proportion of U.S. Treasury demand to total deposits, the greater the liquidity needs of the bank are.

Variability may be divided into two types, predictable and unpredictable. Predictable variability is primarily seasonal, recurring every year at about the same time. Unpredictable variability has no systematic pattern. In a world of complete certainty, banks would have to maintain liquidity in order to accommodate predictable deposit drains. If we introduce uncertainty and unpredictable variability, the need for liquidity increases. In sum, the greater the total deposit variability, the greater the asset liquidity requirements of a bank are, and the greater the proportion of unpredictable to total variability, the still greater the need for primary and secondary reserves.

Table 5-3 Deposit Variability at Large Banks in Chicago Federal Reserve District, 1967-69

Type of Deposit	Deposit Item as Percent of Total Deposits	Average Absolute Percent Change	
		Daily	Monthly
Demand Deposits			
U.S. Treasury	1.3	31.2	39.1
Commercial Banks	5.4	12.4	11.4
Other	40.0	3.1	2.9
Savings Deposits	26.7	0.2	0.9
Other Time Deposits	26.5	0.3	2.9
Total Deposits	100.0	1.6	1.6

Liability Management

Asset management assumes a given asset and liability size and a given mix of deposits and, therefore, deposit variability. Liability management is predicated on the assumption that an important portion of bank deposit and nondeposit sources of funds is sensitive to interest rate changes. By raising interest rates above market rates for, say, CDs or federal funds, a bank may obtain additional funds and, therefore, cash assets quickly. By lowering rates below market, a bank may permit funds to run off.

Liability management is useful to a bank in a number of ways. It can be used to smooth out deposit inflows and outflows and reduce their variability. Reduced deposit variability requires less asset liquidity and permits greater investments in higher yielding assets. If available returns on assets exceed the market cost of funds plus the additional cost of bank operations, banks can increase both their earning assets and their income by acquiring the additional funds through liability management. Lastly, deposit drains may be offset through the inflow of other deposits rather than financed through the reduction of earning assets. Liability management supplements, but does not replace, asset management. If used properly, it permits banks to operate with lower levels of asset liquidity and thus generate greater income. The broadening of the federal funds market and the increased sensitivity of depositors to interest rates greatly increased the importance of liability management in the 1960s, particularly to larger banks.

Required Reserves

As discussed before, banks that are members of the Federal Reserve System are required to maintain minimum cash reserves equivalent to a percentage of their deposit and designated nondeposit liabilities either on deposit at their district

Federal Reserve Bank or in their own vaults. The percentages are related to the deposit size of the bank and the type of its deposits and nondeposits. Reserve requirements in effect at year-end 1972 are shown in Table 5-4. Balances due foreign branches are Eurodollar borrowings by domestic banks. Reserve requirements may be changed by the Board of Governors of the Federal Reserve System within the range established by Congress.

The amount of reserves a member bank is required to maintain is computed each week by applying the appropriate percentage reserve requirements against the dollar amounts in each deposit and nondeposit category two weeks earlier. The bank must hold deposits at the Federal Reserve Bank equal to or greater than this amount less the amount of the vault cash on hand during the earlier period. The requirement does not have to be met every day. Banks may average both the requirement and their legal reserves over the reserve week, which begins Thursday and ends Wednesday. Thus, banks may be above their weekly requirement on some days of the reserve period and below it on others. In addition, because of their deposit characteristics, some banks may find it necessary to hold larger cash reserves than required by law. Reserves held in excess of the legal requirement are called excess reserves. When a bank fails to meet its requirements, it is said to be deficient. Deficient banks are required to pay a fee on the amount of the deficit equal to two percentage points above the prevailing discount rate.

In addition to averaging reserves through the reserve week, banks are permitted to apply excess reserves in an amount not to exceed 2 percent of required reserves against deficiencies in either the preceding or succeeding reserve week without penalty. This permits the banks to average a small portion of their legal reserves over a two-week period.

At the start of any reserve week, a bank knows precisely the amount of deposits required at the Federal Reserve Bank for that period based on its deposits and vault cash two weeks earlier. It can focus all its attention on satisfying this requirement. Before 1968, reserves were required to be maintained in the same period as the deposits against which the requirements were applied. Under this system, the bank was uncertain until the last day of the reserve period about its required amount of reserves, in addition to being uncertain about the source and cost of the reserves. The present system eliminates the first uncertainty.

Reserve requirements for banks that are not members of the Federal Reserve System are established by the respective states. In most instances, these requirements are either below those of the Federal Reserve or may be satisfied to some degree by designated secondary reserves.

Liquidity Implications of Required Reserves

Cash reserves permit immediate accommodation of deposit withdrawals at zero

Table 5-4 Reserve Requirements for Federal Reserve Member Banks, December 31, 1972
(Percent)

	Net Demand Deposits[a,b]					Time Deposits[b]			Nondeposits
	Country Banks				Reserve City Banks	Savings Deposits	Other Time Deposits		Balances Due Foreign Branches
	First $2 or less	Next $2-10	Next $10-100	Next $100-400	Over $400		Under $5	Over $5	
	8	10	12	13	17½	3	3	5	20[c]
Legal Limits									
Minimum	7				10	3			
Maximum	14				22	10			

[a] Gross demand deposits minus cash items in process of collection and demand balances due from domestic banks.

[b] Million dollars.

[c] On balances in excess of a specified base amount.

conversion costs. If all reserves were held voluntarily by the bank in accord with past deposit behavior and the bank is willing to operate at times below its preferred reserve percentage, reserves provide almost perfect liquidity. Assume bank A prefers to hold cash reserves equal to 10 percent of its deposits (see *a* below).

(a)

	Assets	Liabilities
R	100	1,000 D
EA	900	

(b)

	Assets	Liabilities
R	50	950 D
EA	900	

(c)

	Assets	Liabilities
R	95	950 D
EA	855	

Introduce a deposit drain of $50. The bank can fully accommodate this amount out of its reserves and leave earning assets unaffected (*b*). However the bank is now out of equilibrium and will attempt to return to a 10 percent reserve level. The speed of its adjustment is a decision of the bank and is probably dependent upon the characteristics of its earning assets. The less liquid the earning assets, the longer the time of adjustment is. Eventually, the bank will arrive at its new equilibrium position (*c*). Reserves provide time for liquidating high-yielding assets that are not very liquid.

Assume now that a 10 percent legal reserve requirement is imposed and that it must be satisfied at all times. Unless the bank has excess reserves, a $50 deposit loss can now be fully financed out of reserves only for, at most, less than a day without experiencing a deficiency. It must immediately sell $45 of earning assets (required reserves decline by $5 = 10% of $50). The less liquid the portfolio of earning assets, the more costly this adjustment is to the bank. The bank may be forced to sell the necessary assets at a loss. The liquidity property of reserves had been reduced substantially. As before, the bank regains the equilibrium shown in *c*, but this time more rapidly. Surprising as it seems, transforming voluntary reserves into legally required reserves reduces the liquidity of the reserves by permitting only a portion of reserves to be used to finance deposit withdrawals. To compensate, the bank must hold proportionately more liquid earning assets. By permitting banks to average reserves over a week, the Federal Reserve increases the liquidity property of reserves somewhat, but not to the degree inherent under fully voluntary requirements. As will be discussed later, the primary contemporary function of reserves and reserve requirements is as a fulcrum for Federal Reserve monetary control, not liquidity.

References

American Bankers Association, *The Commercial Banking Industry* (Englewood Cliffs, N.J.: Prentice-Hall, 1962).

Baughn, William H., and Charls E. Walker, eds., *The Bankers' Handbook* (Homewood, Ill.: Dow Jones–Irwin, 1966).

Cohen, Kalman J., and Frederick S. Hammer, *Analytical Methods in Banking* (Homewood, Ill.: Irwin, 1966).

Crosse, Howard D., *Management Policies for Commercial Banks* (New York: Prentice-Hall, 1962).

Federal Reserve Bank of Chicago, *Midwest Banking in the Sixties* (Chicago: 1970).

Hodgman, Donald, *Commercial Bank Loan and Investment Policy* (Urbana: University of Illinois Press, 1963).

Jessup, Paul E., *Innovations in Bank Management* (New York: Holt, Rinehart & Winston, 1969).

Nadler, Paul S., *Commercial Banking in the Economy* (New York: Random House, 1968).

Reed, Edward W., *Commercial Bank Management* (New York: Harper & Row, 1963).

Woodworth, Walter G., *The Management of Cyclical Liquidity of Commercial Liquidity of Commercial Banks* (Boston: Bankers Publishing Co., 1967).

6 Commercial Banks and the Payments System: Regulation, Structure, and Performance

Banks are constrained in their pursuit of maximizing profits by a number of legal and regulatory constraints, as discussed in the preceding chapter. These constraints are imposed because banks are considered too vital to the welfare of the economy to be permitted to operate freely under the laws of supply and demand. Among their more important functions:

1. Banks provide three-fourths of the country's money supply.
2. Banks participate importantly in the operation of the national payments mechanism.
3. Banks are the key link in the transmission of monetary policy from the Federal Reserve System to the economy.
4. Banks safekeep a significant proportion of total financial wealth, most of which is viewed as riskless by the wealth-holder.
5. Banks furnish a large proportion of credit to the economy and importantly affect the allocation of credit among sectors.

Because of their unique importance:

1. Excessive concentration in banking may have important undesirable implications for both local and national economies, and
2. Bank failures may be far more detrimental to the community than the failure of other types of businesses.

Bank Failures

Most of the current constraints on banks are due to the fear of bank failures and to the particular vulnerability of banks to mismanagement as a result of their usually low capital-to-asset ratio. The failure of any firm has unfortunate implications for its owners and employees and to a lesser extent to its creditors and customers. The failure of a bank, however, has equally serious implications for all four groups. Moreover, the number of bank creditors and customers is typically far greater than the number of bank owners and employees. In addition, unlike the creditors of other business firms, most of the creditors of banks do not consider themselves creditors. Rather, they view banks as basically performing a riskless safekeeping function. Only the largest depositors will examine the financial statement of their banks.

Bank failures arise because losses on assets exceed the amount of capital and must be charged against deposits so that the bank is unable to repay depositors in full. This can occur for two reasons: bad loans or simultaneous attempts by a large number of depositors to withdraw their deposits. Until the 1930s, the majority of domestic bank failures reflected the latter reason. As banks maintain only fractional reserves, they are unable to accommodate unexpectedly large deposit withdrawals. Even if their earning assets were good before the "run" on the bank, the banks might not have sufficient time to convert noncash assets into cash assets quickly enough. Unlike the failure of other types of business, bank failures:

1. Induce fears about the solvency of other banks. As depositors realize that only the first deposit withdrawals can be accommodated in full, they attempt to be the first to be accommodated. Better cautious than sorry! The greater the number of banks experiencing deposit withdrawals, the less they are able to sell their assets to other banks and the less willing depositors are to accept deposits at other banks. Eventually, as bank failures accumulate, depositors will accept only currency, and banks as a whole will have no effective market for their assets, good or bad.

2. Reduce the money supply in the community, thereby dampening spending and igniting declines in employment and income production.

3. Reduce time deposits, next to the money supply the most liquid part of financial wealth, further reducing spending, employment, production, and income.

4. Break ongoing credit relationships, leaving debtors without sufficient financing to conduct their operations. This also will result in reductions in employment, production, and income.

Bank Regulation

United States history records frequent periods of bank failures. Many business crises, culminating in the major economic depression of 1929–33, were either started or prolonged by bank failures on a large scale. Between 1929 and 1933, the number of commercial banks declined by more than 40 percent, mostly attributable to bank failures. In many cities, the reduction in the number of banks was proportionately far greater. In Chicago, for example, the number of banks declined by more than three-fourths, from 224 to 50. Deposits at suspended banks throughout the country totaled nearly $7 billion, or 15 percent of total deposits at all banks in 1929. Of this amount, losses borne by depositors have been estimated at nearly $1.5 billion. As a result of this and preceding crises, federal and state governments took a number of actions to reduce the possibilities of future large-scale bank failures. Among other actions, the governments:

1. Limited entry. Banks requesting new charters had to demonstrate a need for the new bank facilities before the chartering agency would grant the request and the newly established Federal Deposit Insurance Corporation (FDIC) would grant deposit insurance. A study in the early 1960s found that the number of banks then in operation was some 10 percent smaller than the number that would have existed in the absence of restrictions to entry of new banks.

2. Separated commercial and investment banking. Investment banking involves the underwriting and distribution of new securities. Before separation, some banks were tempted to place slow-moving securities in the bank's own portfolio or in their trust departments. Separation of these two activities removed an important source of temptation involving potential conflicts of interest. Banks are permitted to underwrite securities of the federal government and selected securities of municipalities.

3. Established federal deposit insurance. The primary cause of cumulative bank failures is the attempt of depositors to be the first to convert deposits into currency. All cannot be accommodated. By insuring deposits, the incentive of depositors to protect their funds by converting their deposits into currency is reduced by at least up to an amount equal to the insurance. The amount of insurance has been steadily increased from $2,500 per individual deposit account in 1933 to a present ceiling of $20,000. In 1970, 99 percent of all bank accounts had deposits of under $20,000. In addition, similar insurance has been extended to deposits at savings and loan associations and mutual savings banks. The Federal Deposit Insurance Corporation, an instrumentality of the federal government, provides deposit insurance to commercial banks. The Federal Savings and Loan Insurance Corporation, also an instrumentality of the federal government, provides similar protection to depositors at savings and loan associations.

4. Established ceilings on interest rates banks may pay on deposits. It was widely believed immediately after the Great Depression that a major cause of the numerous bank failures was excessive interbank competition. The argument was that in their competition for funds, banks bid up the interest rates they paid on deposits. To afford these high rates, banks would invest in higher-yielding, but riskier, assets. As business activity slowed, the riskier assets declined in value and

contributed to the inability of the banks to accommodate deposit losses. In response, federal and local governments both imposed controls on the interest rates banks may pay on deposits. Federal law forbids banks to pay any interest at all on demand deposits. Interest payments on time and savings deposits are subject to ceilings imposed by the regulatory agencies. In more recent years, interest rate ceilings have been extended from banks to savings and loan associations and mutual savings banks.

Subsequent research has provided little evidence that the bank failures in the early 1930s could be attributed to excessively high interest rates paid on bank deposits. In the meantime, however, additional justifications have been introduced to support the necessity of maintaining restrictions on interest rates banks may pay for funds. The newer reasons for, and the consequences of, these restrictions are explained later in this chapter.

In addition to these constraints, banks are subject to a large number of other constraints imposed in earlier or later years. The necessity of satisfying solvency and legal-reserve requirements have already been discussed.

Other constraints imposed include:

1. Restrictions on the number of offices. Banks are restricted by state law as to branch offices. In some states, banks are prohibited from having any office whatsoever besides their main office. In other states, banks may organize branch offices, either statewide or within limited geographical or political boundaries, e.g., within a city or county. National banks are subject to state law on branching. Approximately one-third of the states, including Illinois, do not permit any branching (unit banking); another third, including New York, permit limited branching; and the last third, including California, permit statewide branching. In all states, banks require authorization from the appropriate federal or state regulatory agency before establishing a new branch.

2. Consolidation with other banks, either through merger or affiliation by a holding company, must receive prior approval from one or more regulatory agencies and is subject to review by the Department of Justice under antitrust legislation. The Bank Merger Act of 1966 prohibits any bank merger

> which would result in a monopoly . . . [or] whose effect in any section of the country may be substantially to lessen competition, or to tend to create a monopoly . . . unless . . . the anticompetitive effects of the proposed transaction are clearly outweighed in the public interest by the probable effect of the transaction in meeting the convenience and needs of the community to be served.

3. Bank consolidation with nonbanking business firms is severely restricted. A bank may not have non-bank-related subsidiaries. A holding company that owns one or more banks may not also own non-bank-related business. However, a holding company that owns only one bank may retain ownership of most nonbank

firms it owned before mid-1968, but may not acquire additional non-bank-related firms. The definition of bank-related activity is the responsibility of the Board of Governors of the Federal Reserve System.

4. Banks are prohibited from investing in equity securities for their own portfolios. This reflects a long-standing tradition in American banking intended to lessen potential conflicts arising from combining the owner and creditor functions. Commercial banks are permitted to trade in equities through their trust departments in a trustee or fiduciary relationship for their customers.

5. Banks are required to satisfy minimum capital requirements at their time of organization. The amount of capital required depends on the size of the city in which the bank is chartered.

6. Banks are restricted in their maximum investment in particular areas in order to increase safety through diversification. For example, a national bank may not extend loans to any single private borrower in excess of an amount equal to 10 percent of its capital and surplus, extend mortgage loans with maturities in excess of 30 years, or hold aggregate mortgage loans in excess of capital and surplus or 70 percent of time and savings deposits, whichever is the greater.

7. Banks are examined regularly by one or more regulatory authorities. These examinations are unannounced. Although not a complete audit, the examination inspects the quality of the loan portfolio, appraises the market value of investments, evaluates the adequacy of capital, verifies cash assets, records practices not in accord with accepted procedures, and assesses the overall capabilities of management.

8. Although not restricting the size of individual banks, the size of the banking industry is restricted by the Federal Reserve System in its execution of monetary policy through the amount of reserves provided and the level of legal reserve requirements. This constraint is discussed in considerable detail in later chapters.

Bank Regulatory Agencies

In the United States, commercial banks are regulated and supervised by up to three federal agencies plus one state agency. In addition, bank practices and consolidations, similar to practices and consolidations of nonbank firms, are subject to antitrust prosecution by the Department of Justice. The major regulatory agencies are:

Comptroller of the Currency—The Comptroller is the oldest bank regulatory authority. It was established by the National Banking Act of 1863 to charter and supervise the operations of national banks.

Federal Reserve System—The Fed, as it is commonly referred to, has substantial regulatory responsibilities, in addition to its better-known monetary policy responsibilities. It was established in 1913 primarily to prevent economic crises originating in the financial sector.

Federal Deposit Insurance Corporation—The FDIC was established by Congress in 1935 to provide deposit insurance for banks. Its regulatory responsibilities are derived from its interest, as an insurance seller, in the financial condition of the insured.

The major responsibilities of each agency are:

Bank Charter:
- National Banks—Comptroller of the Currency
- State Banks—state banking agency

Branch Office (if permitted by state law):
- National Banks—Comptroller of the Currency, Federal Deposit Insurance Corporation
- State Banks—state agency, Federal Deposit Insurance Corporation

Bank Merger:
- National Banks—Comptroller of the Currency, Department of Justice
- State Banks—state agency, Federal Reserve System,* Federal Deposit Insurance Corporation, Department of Justice

Bank and Nonbank Acquisition by Bank Holding Company:
- National Banks—Federal Reserve System, Department of Justice
- State Banks—state agency, Federal Reserve System, Department of Justice

Bank Examination:
- National Banks—Comptroller of the Currency, Federal Reserve System,* Federal Deposit Insurance Corporation
- State Banks—state agency, Federal Reserve System,* Federal Deposit Insurance Corporation

The responsibilities of the regulatory agencies overlap substantially, as is obvious from the above listing. To reduce both the costs of duplication and the burden on the banks, the three federal agencies established a working arrangement to divide the operations. The Comptroller of the Currency has primary responsibility for national banks, the Federal Reserve System for state-chartered member banks, and the Federal Deposit Insurance Corporation for state-chartered insured banks that are not members of the Federal Reserve System. The three agencies freely exchange information with each other and also with the state banking agencies. The granting of bank charters by both the federal and state governments and the sharing of supervisory and regulatory authority by agencies of the two governments is referred to as the dual banking system.

---

*If bank is a member of the Federal Reserve System.

Evaluation of Regulation

The thrust of government regulation of banking is to maintain the solvency of banks. In the process, regulation, of necessity, acts to reduce interbank competition, aggressiveness, and the riskiness of the asset portfolios. Evaluated on the basis of the small number of bank failures since 1933, bank regulation must be considered highly successful. During the 1960s fewer than 10 banks a year closed their doors due to financial difficulties. In contrast, almost 4,000 banks failed in 1933 alone, more than 1,000 annually in each of the three preceding years, and an annual average of more than 500 during the 1920s. To date, no business downturn in the post–World War II period was either started or prolonged by bank failures.

However, regulation is not a one-sided blessing. The advantages must be weighed against some possible disadvantages. By reducing the number of banking firms and increasing barriers to both entry and exit, regulation reduces the number of competitors. While numbers do not guarantee competition, competition cannot exist without numbers. In a free market, competition acts as an automatic regulator promoting efficiency, maximizing output, encouraging responsiveness to market forces, and inducing the lowest prices. Insufficient competition can result in inefficiency, reduced output, unresponsiveness, and higher prices. In the absence of the threat of new firms and loss of markets, existing firms may be slow both to provide optimal services and to respond to changes in market forces. Restrictions on investments may also reduce bank aggressiveness. Overregulation may result in the protection of competitors rather than of competition and the public interest. Some observers have argued that the costs of a somewhat higher incidence of bank failures attributable to fewer restrictions on bank aggressiveness are smaller than the benefits derived from lower loan rates, higher deposit rates, and a higher quality of bank services.

Banking Structure

At year-end 1971, there were nearly 14,000 commercial banks in the United States. While this number may seem large, this was only half as many as there were in the 1920s, the era of the largest number of banks (Table 6-1). Following the sharp decline in the number of banks during the Great Depression, the number of banks continued to decline slowly through the 1950s. Since 1960, the number of banks has increased slightly. The net change in the number of banks understates the number of new banks organized by the number of banks disappearing through mergers or failures. In 1969, the total number of commercial banks declined by 17 from 13,698 to 13,681. However, 135 new banks were established during the year. This number was more than offset by 147 bank mergers, four bank failures, and one voluntary liquidation.

Table 6-1 **Number of Banks, Branches, Offices, and Deposits, 1920–70**

Year	Banks	Branches (Number)	Total Offices	Total Deposits (Billion dollars)
1920[a]	30,909	1,281	32,190	43
1929[a]	25,568	3,353	28,921	60
1933[a]	14,771	2,784	17,555	42
1950[b]	14,693	5,158	19,851	155
1960[b]	13,484	10,619	24,103	230
1970[b]	13,688	21,424	35,112	481

[a]June.
[b]December.
Sources: Federal Reserve System; Federal Deposit Insurance Corporation.

Number and Location of Banks

Although the number of banks has declined sharply in the past 50 years, the number of banking offices has increased because of a sharp rise in the number of branch offices. At year-end 1971, there were some 23,000 branch offices or almost twice the number of banks. In contrast, in 1929 there were only 3,353 branches of 25,568 banks. The number of branches did not begin to expand rapidly until after World War II, then it doubled during the 1950s, and again during the 1960s. The number of branches did not surpass the number of banks until 1964. The rapid growth of branch banking in the postwar period is attributed to the strategy of banks of pursuing their customers from the cities out to the suburbs and to liberalization in state branching restrictions. In all, there are currently a record 36,000 banking offices in the United States.

As is to be expected, there are proportionately more banks in unit-banking states than in branch-banking states. With only rare exceptions, banks can operate full-service offices only in the state in which their main office is located. The major exception is the Bank of California, headquartered in San Francisco, which has two offices in Washington and one in Oregon besides its California offices. However, at present, it may establish additional branch offices only in California. Although unit-banking states account for less than one-third of all states and have only one-fourth of the population, they possess more than one-half of the banks in the country (Table 6-2). States in which statewide branching is prevalent are about as numerous as unit-banking states and account for only a slightly smaller proportion of the country's population. However, they contain only 8 percent of all banks. Total banking offices are more evenly distributed. The number of banking offices is distributed among unit banking, limited branch banking, and

Table 6-2 **Number of Banks and Banking Offices by Prevailing State Banking Structure, 1964**

Prevailing Structure	No. of States	Population Million	Population Percent	Banks Number	Banks Percent	Total Offices Number	Total Offices Percent
Statewide Branching	18	43.8	23	1,087	8	6,660	24
Limited Branching	17	95.1	50	5,500	40	13,698	49
Unit Banking	16	51.5	27	7,173	52	7,740	27
Total	51*	190.4	100	13,760	100	28,098	100

*Includes District of Columbia.

Figure 6-1 **Structure of Banking by States, 1970**

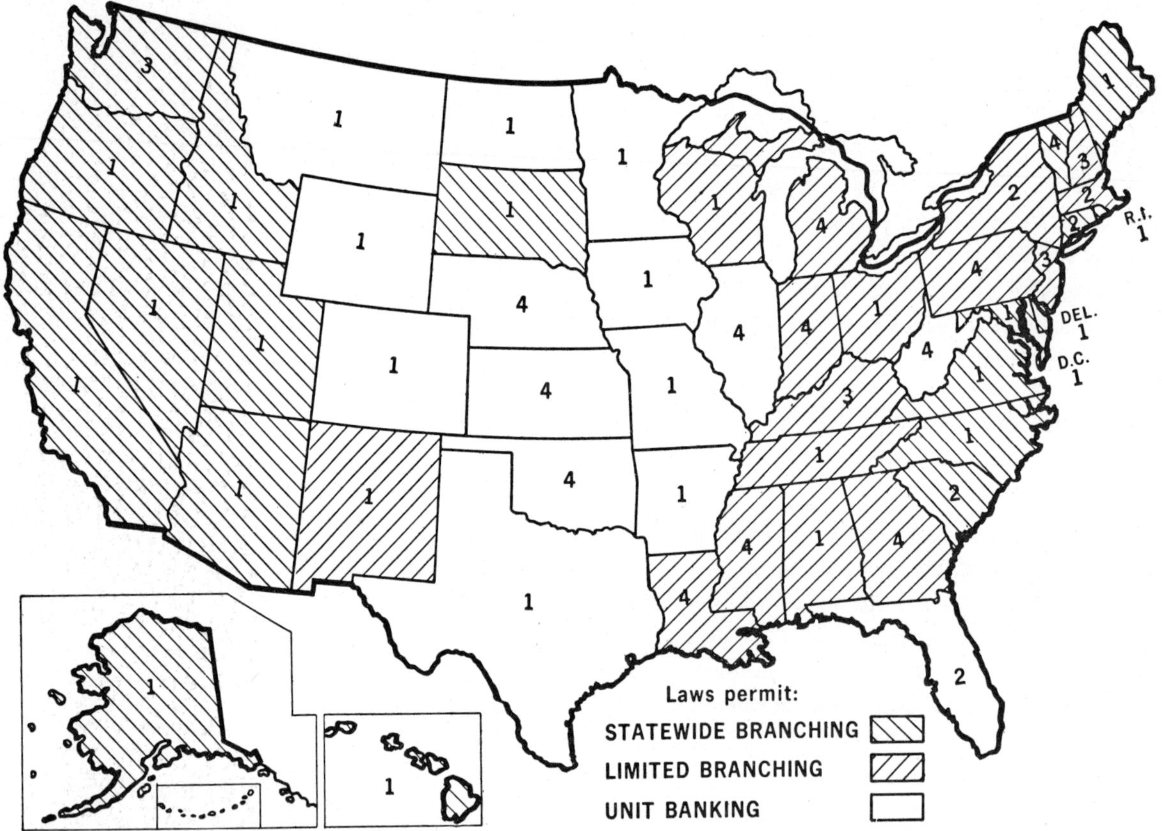

Numbers indicate the following for each state: 1—no explicit holding company law; 2—law permits holding companies but requires state approval; 3—law permits holding companies but restricts operations; 4—law prohibits holding companies.

Source: "Recent Changes in the Structure of Commercial Banking," *Federal Reserve Bulletin*, March, 1970, p. 201.

statewide branch banking in almost exact proportion to the distribution of population. The prevailing structure of banking by state is shown in Figure 6-1. States with similar branch structures are closely bunched. Unit banking predominates in the Midwest, limited branch banking in the East, and statewide branch banking in the West. In large part, this pattern reflects the financial history of the United States. Unit banking in the Midwest is an outgrowth of past deep-rooted distrust of banks by farmers and their fear of financial concentration. Statewide branch banking in the Western states was necessitated at the time banking legislation was adopted by these states by the need to serve a relatively small population scattered thinly over a large territory.

Slightly more than one-third of all commercial banks are chartered by the federal government (Figure 6-2). These banks are required to have the word *national* in their titles. Although a minority of the number of banks, national banks tend to be the larger banks and account for about 60 percent of all bank deposits. All national banks are required to be members of the Federal Reserve System.

State banks may be accepted as members of the Federal Reserve System upon application, but only a minority apply. Overall, less than one-half of all banks are members of the Federal Reserve System. Similar to national banks, state member banks tend to be the larger banks. Federal Reserve member banks hold more than 75 percent of total bank deposits.

Almost all banks are insured by the Federal Deposit Insurance Corporation. All banks that are members of the Federal Reserve System are required to be members of the FDIC. Most other banks prefer to join. Only 1 percent of all banks, accounting for less than 1 percent of all deposits, are not insured by the FDIC.

Bank Size

Bank size varies greatly among the 14,000 banks. At year-end 1969, the average deposit size of all banks was $32 million. Yet almost 90 percent of all banks had total deposits less than this amount. Banks with deposits of less than $10 million accounted for 60 percent of the number of all banks, but only 10 percent of all deposits (Table 6-3). In contrast, 110 banks with deposits in excess of $500 million, less than 1 percent of all banks, accounted for almost 45 percent of all bank deposits.

The largest bank in deposit size in the United States is the Bank of America, headquartered in San Francisco. At year-end 1970, it had total deposits of $26 billion. The second and third largest banks are the First National City Bank and the Chase-Manhattan National Bank, both headquartered in New York City, each having total deposits of $21 billion. The largest fifteen banks are listed in Table 6-4. As may be expected, large banks are located in major states. Of the fifteen

Figure 6-2 **Structure of Banks, December 31, 1971**

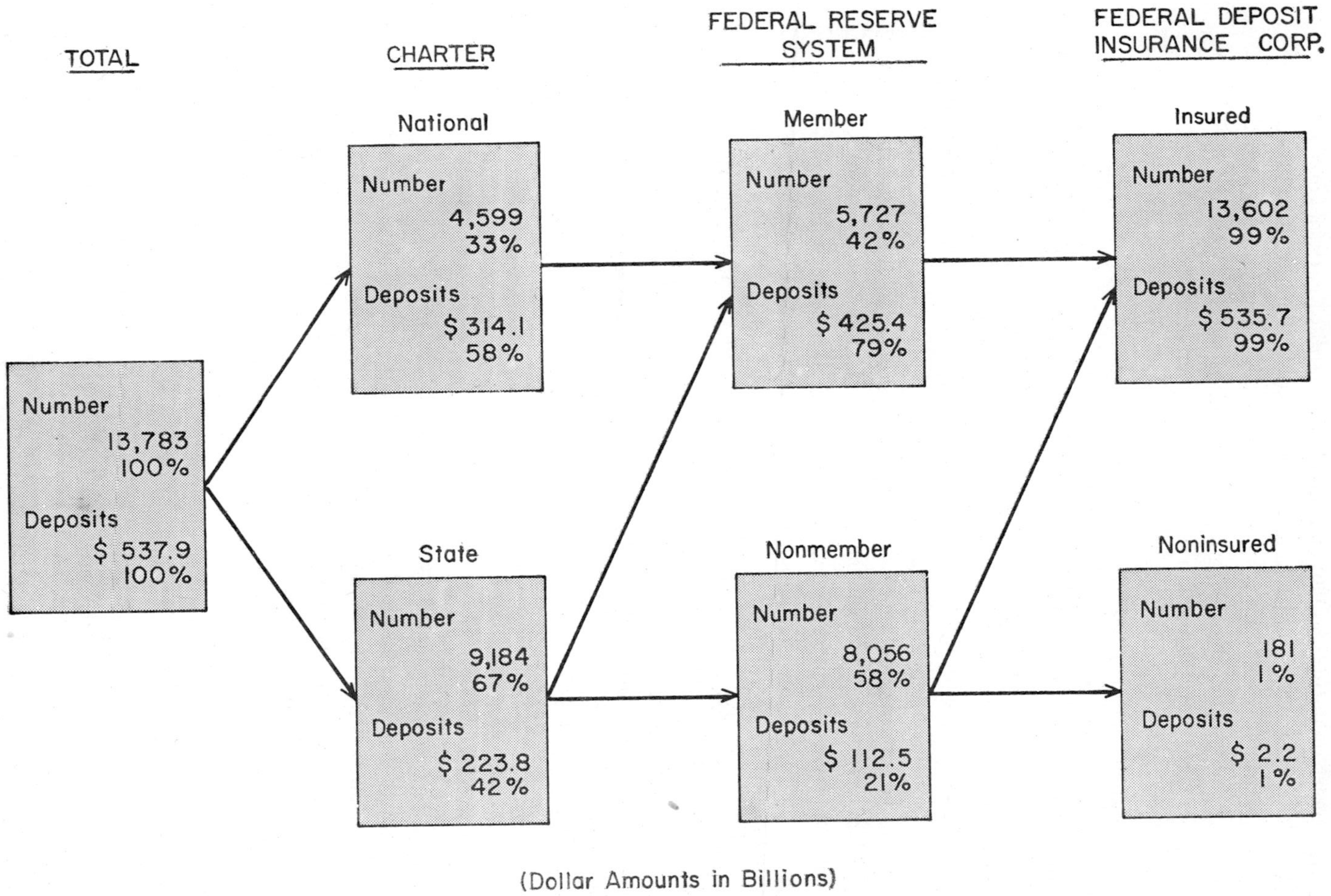

TOTAL

Number 13,783 100%
Deposits $ 537.9 100%

CHARTER

National
Number 4,599 33%
Deposits $ 314.1 58%

State
Number 9,184 67%
Deposits $ 223.8 42%

FEDERAL RESERVE SYSTEM

Member
Number 5,727 42%
Deposits $ 425.4 79%

Nonmember
Number 8,056 58%
Deposits $ 112.5 21%

FEDERAL DEPOSIT INSURANCE CORP.

Insured
Number 13,602 99%
Deposits $ 535.7 99%

Noninsured
Number 181 1%
Deposits $ 2.2 1%

(Dollar Amounts in Billions)

Source: *Federal Reserve Bulletin*, July, 1972, pp. A 20-23.

Table 6-3 Size Distribution of All Commercial Banks
December 31, 1969

Bank Deposit Size (Million dollars)	Number of Banks		Total Deposits	
	Number	Percent	Billion dollars	Percent
Under 2	1,314	10	1.9	0.4
2-5	3,516	26	12.0	3
5-10	3,448	25	24.9	6
10-25	3,194	23	49.1	11
25-50	1,104	8	38.1	9
50-100	484	4	32.5	7
100-500	413	3	87.0	20
500-1,000	59	0.4	41.7	9
1,000 or more	49	0.4	151.9	35
Total	13,681	100.0	440.0	100.0

Source: Federal Deposit Insurance Corporation.

Table 6-4 Fifteen Largest Banks Ranked by Deposit Size
December 31, 1970

Bank	Deposits (Billion dollars)	Trust Assets (Billion dollars)
1. Bank of America National, San Francisco	25.6	4.2
2. Chase-Manhattan National, New York	21.2	14.2
3. First National City, New York	21.1	11.7
4. Manufacturers Hanover Trust, New York	11.1	8.1
5. Morgan Guaranty Trust, New York	9.6	19.0
6. Chemical Bank, New York	9.0	5.0
7. Bankers Trust, New York	8.1	16.5
8. Continental Illinois National, Chicago	7.2	6.5
9. Security Pacific National, Los Angeles	7.0	2.8
10. First National, Chicago	6.3	6.1
11. Wells Fargo National, San Francisco	5.2	2.5
12. Crocker National, San Francisco	4.9	2.4
13. Mellon National, Pittsburgh	4.8	7.7
14. Irving Trust, New York	4.6	2.2
15. United California, Los Angeles	4.3	3.1

Source: *American Banker.*

banks, seven are headquartered in New York, five in California, two in Illinois, and one in Pennsylvania.

Banks may also be joined together under common ownership through holding companies. At year-end 1969, there were almost 100 holding companies that held controlling interest in two or more banks. These holding companies operated a total of 723 banks having 2,674 branch offices. Deposits at these banks amounted to 15 percent of total bank deposits. The importance of multibank-holding-company banks varied considerably from state to state. Twenty states do not permit multibank holding companies. In three states—Minnesota, Montana, and Nevada—banks owned by multibank holding companies accounted for more than 50 percent of all deposits in the state.

In more recent years, banks have used holding companies to affiliate with nonbanking rather than with banking firms. In order to prevent undue economic concentration, the Bank Holding Company Act of 1956 prohibited multibank holding companies from operating firms other than those engaged in activities "closely related" to banking. In 1970, amendments to this act extended these provisions to one-bank holding companies. These companies were given a choice of becoming bank or nonbank holding companies. If they preferred the former, they could not increase their nonbank holdings and could be forced to divest themselves of some incongruous nonbank activities if so required by the Federal Reserve. Those that wished to become nonbank holding companies and to be free to extend their activities in these fields must divest themselves of their bank affiliates.

Although not permitted to own equity securities for their own portfolios, commercial banks engage in equity transactions as trustees and fiduciary agents for their customers. Equity investments account for two-thirds of the total assets of bank trust departments. The bank functions as administrator of these securities, rather than as owner. In 1968, about one-fourth of all banks operated trust departments. The market value of assets managed by these departments totaled almost $300 billion, an amount equivalent to 70 percent of the owned banking assets of the banks. Trust operations tend to be both larger and relatively more important at large banks than at small banks. Seven of the ten largest banks by deposit size also ranked among the ten largest banks in trust department assets. Of the three banks ranked among the ten highest in trust assets but not in deposits, two ranked among the twenty largest in deposit size, and one did not actively engage in commercial banking.

The largest trust department was operated by J. P. Morgan and Company, the holding company for the Morgan Guaranty Bank, the fifth largest bank in the country. Trust assets at this bank, as well as at the Bankers Trust, the next largest trust department and seventh largest bank, were each twice the size of the banks' own assets. In contrast, trust assets at the Bank of America, the country's largest bank, were equivalent to less than 20 percent of its own assets but were still sufficiently large to rank sixteenth in dollar size. The asset size of trust departments for the fifteen largest banks in the country is shown in Table 6-4.

The importance to the bank of income derived from trust operations varies with

Table 6-5 **Size Distribution of Bank Trust Departments, 1968**

Trust Asset Size* (Billion dollars)	Number of Banks		Trust Assets*		Bank Assets	
	Number	Percent	Billion dollars	Percent	Billion dollars	Percent
Under 10	2,413	73	4	1	60	15
10-25	331	10	5	2	24	6
25-100	304	9	15	5	42	11
100-500	186	6	38	14	69	17
500-1,000	32	1	22	7	28	7
1,000 and more	51	2	198	70	180	45
Total	3,317	100	283	100	405	100

*Market value of assets in all trust accounts.

Source: Federal Deposit Insurance Corporation, *Trust Assets of Insured Commercial Banks—1968.*

the size of the department relative to the bank's other activities. Trust operations generated 11 percent of the total operating income of the Morgan Guaranty Bank in 1970 and only 2 percent of the operating income of the Bank of America.

Bank trust operations are more concentrated than bank deposit operations. Although 50 percent of total bank assets are held by only 3 percent of the largest banks, fully 70 percent of total trust assets are held by only 2 percent of the banks with the largest trust departments (Table 6-5). These banks hold only 45 percent of all bank assets of banks with trust departments. Banks with 73 percent of all bank trust departments have only 1 percent of all bank trust assets, but 15 percent of all banking assets.

A complete description of bank structure needs also to consider the structure of financial institutions that compete with banks in any of a number of service lines. This would include a large number of different financial institutions, but primarily savings and loan associations and mutual savings banks, which compete with banks for savings deposits and mortgage loans. A description of the market structure of these institutions is outside the scope of this book.

Bank Performance

The private and social performance of a business firm may be evaluated in terms of the prices it charges, the quality of its product, its responsiveness to market changes, and its profits. Unlike private performance, which considers the welfare of the firm, social performance considers the welfare of the community. For example, lowest possible prices for a firm's products may not contribute as much to the welfare of the firm as to that of the community. Private performance is a concern of bank management, while social performance is a concern of public policy.

Because banks are financial intermediaries, measurement of their performance has an additional dimension. Banks can be evaluated not only on the loan rates they charge but also on the deposit rates they pay. In addition, because entry is not free and because banks are chartered by the government, which, among other things, directs them to provide for the financial needs and convenience of the communities they serve, the amount of loans extended is frequently used to gauge bank performance. In this view, local loans are considered more productive than investments in, say, Treasury securities, which most likely will result in the funds being spent outside the bank's community.

The economic performance of banks may be expected to be related to a large number of economic and noneconomic factors. This relation may be summarized in a functional notation as follows:

$$P=f(R, L, S, E, M, X),$$

where:

P = performance
R = regulation
L = legislation
S = structure
E = economic forces
M = bank management
X = other forces.

Regulation, legislation, and structure can all be changed in the public interest to affect the performance of banks. If regulation and legislation are to be changed in a manner consistent with the desired effect on performance, the relationship between structure and performance needs to be known. Although a number of studies have investigated this relationship in recent years, the evidence is fragmentary at best.

Most studies have found the structure of banks in a market area to have a weak, but statistically significant, effect on bank performance. The effect is weak in relation to the total of the other forces also affecting performance. On the whole, the larger the number of banks in an area or the lower the concentration of deposits at a few banks, the lower are loan rates, the higher are deposit rates, the lower are service charges on demand deposits, and the higher is the ratio of time to total deposits. The evidence also suggests that loans account for a larger proportion of earning assets at branch banks than at unit banks, and at holding company banks than at independent banks. Profits do not appear to be higher the fewer the number of banks, or to be affected by whether the bank is a branch system or a unit bank or whether it is owned by a holding company. This may indicate either that these factors do not affect profits or more likely that, in the absence of competition, banks do not operate as efficiently as possible and that the higher revenues from more loans are absorbed by the higher costs of making the loans.

Another important structural characteristic generally believed to affect bank performance is bank size. Larger banks are considered to be able to provide the same services more cheaply than smaller banks. Economists call this relationship *economies of scale.* Such economies exist if a doubling of output increases costs by less than twofold. Economies of scale are difficult to measure empirically in any industry, but they have been particularly difficult to quantify in banking. To measure these effects accurately, firms of different sizes must provide precisely the same services. But the type and number of services are generally related to the size of the firm. Much as supermarkets rarely provide the same package of groceries and service as the corner neighborhood grocer, large banks offer a wider variety of differentiated services than do small banks. As a result, it is difficult to distinguish between changes in bank costs resulting from differences in the mix of services from changes in costs associated with differences in size of the same services. The evidence available suggests moderate economies of scale in banking, except for smaller banks where the cost savings are more pronounced. The studies also suggest, however, that these savings can be wiped out if expansion is pursued through branching. The ability of small and large, unit and branch, and holding company and independent banks to coexist peacefully lends support to the finding that economies of scale are not overwhelming.

Some critics of the social performance of banks prefer to blame any below-par performance on legislation and regulation rather than on structure. They do not foresee great improvement in the performance of banks until both legislation and regulation are changed. Because many of the laws and regulations were introduced during or immediately after the greatest financial disaster in American history in the 1930s and the structure and needs of the economy have changed greatly since then, there is considerable sympathy for overhauling the entire regulatory framework. Many favor giving the banks greater freedom of action. A number of diverse studies and commissions have reviewed the existing legislation and regulation and have recommended considerable, but quite similar, changes. At year-end 1971, the President's Commission on Financial Structure and Regulation, the latest of a number of official and quasi-official commissions to survey the financial system, published its findings and recommendations. Very generally, the Commission recommended that depository institutions be permitted to engage in a wider range of financial services, that legal differences among competing institutions eventually be removed, that all similar institutions operate under similar regulations, and that restrictive and protective regulations be liberalized. Whether these proposals, many of which have been recommended before, or other significant changes will be made remains to be seen. Unfortunately, this country has a predilection for leaving sleeping dogs lie and making major overhauls only after crises have appeared.

Regulation Q

As discussed earlier, ceilings were initially imposed on deposit rates in 1933 in response to the large-scale bank failures. Although subsequent evidence provides little support for the need for such ceilings to prevent bank failures, the ceilings have not only not been removed but in 1966 were extended to savings and loan associations and mutual savings banks. Because these ceilings have had an increasingly important effect on the economy, it is worthwhile to examine more closely the reasons for their use and their effects.

In the Banking Acts of 1933 and 1935, Congress authorized the Federal Reserve System and the Federal Deposit Insurance Corporation to specify maximum rates commercial banks may pay on time and savings deposits for three reasons:

1. to protect against bank failures by reducing the need for banks to acquire high yielding, risky assets in order to finance high interest rates on deposits;
2. to reduce the flow of funds from country to city banks; and
3. to reduce interest costs to borrowers by reducing the return paid to savers.

Although Regulation Q has been in effect since the 1930s, it did not have an important effect until almost 30 years later in the mid-1960s. Until the 1950s, market rates of interest were low and the interest rates banks paid on time and savings deposits were below the ceiling rates. As interest rates increased through the 1950s and early 1960s, the regulatory agencies raised ceiling rates whenever they threatened to prevent banks from attracting deposits. However, Regulation Q policy changed drastically in the middle part of the 1960s. Ceiling rates were not increased concommitantly with increases in market rates and were extended to savings and loan associations and mutual savings banks. These steps were introduced to:

1. protect the solvency of thrift institutions,
2. maintain a high flow of funds into the mortgage market and residential construction,
3. dampen competition between large and small banks, and
4. reduce the growth of bank credit.

The first reason reflected the increasing financial pressures on savings and loan associations and mutual savings banks from sharp increases in interest rates. As noted, these institutions borrow short, primarily through passbook savings, and lend long, primarily in residential mortgages. Such intermediation is profitable if the institution correctly predicts short-term interest rates over the maturity of the loan and charges the appropriate loan rate. In the postwar period, many institutions underestimated the sharp increase in interest rates that occurred in the second half of the 1960s. As a result, they charged lower rates on their long-term loans than were required, in retrospect, to break even. As short-term rates climbed faster than expected, the institutions, to remain competitive, found it necessary to pay higher than expected rates on almost all their funds but, because only a fraction of mortgages mature each year, they earned higher rates only on their new mortgages. Thus, expenses outran revenues, and profits came under pressure. Ceilings on interest paid on deposits were imposed to slow the rise in expenses. The subsequent inability of thrift institutions to compete effectively for funds during periods of rising interest rates with investment outlets not subject to such ceilings, combined with a temporary reluctance of households to finance housing at the higher rates, reduced the flow of funds into mortgages and dampened residential construction. This generated considerable concern among policy-makers as housing is not only an important economic sector, but also is a high-priority social sector.

The introduction of large CDs in the early 1960s greatly increased the mobility of large deposits and provided the rationale for the last two reasons. Banks could attract these deposits from other banks by paying slightly higher interest rates. Because large banks extend a relatively larger proportion of higher-yielding business loans, it was argued that they had an advantage over smaller banks in competing for funds during periods of heavy business-loan demand. Reducing the ability of large banks to compete for CDs through the use of rate ceilings was also considered an effective supplement to other monetary controls in restraining the flow of funds to large business corporations during a period of restrictive monetary policy.

The economic impact of Regulation Q can be evaluated in terms of the costs of compliance and costs of avoidance.

Costs of Compliance

1. To the extent that Regulation Q reduces the rates banks and thrift institutions pay on deposits relative to market interest rates on alternative investments, it reduces both the inflow of funds into these institutions and the loans extended by these institutions relative to what they would have been without this regulation.

2. To the extent that Regulation Q causes deposit rates to be lower than otherwise, it has the greatest impact on lower-income depositors at the institutions. Transfers of funds to alternative investments, which are not subject to Regulation Q, involve costs that are, for the most part, independent of the size of transfer. Thus, the relative cost of transfer is greatest for small deposits and these funds are less likely to be shifted as market rates climb above savings rates. Small deposits belong proportionately more to lower-income groups. Large deposits held primarily by higher-income groups are more likely to be shifted to investment outlets not subject to Regulation Q ceilings.

3. To the extent that Regulation Q lowers deposit rates and this is reflected

in lower mortgage rates, mortgage borrowers were assisted. Studies show that home ownership is proportionately greater among higher- than lower-income groups and it appears reasonable that benefits of lower mortgage costs would be apportioned similarly. This would result in a redistribution of income from lower- to higher-income groups.

4. To the extent that Regulation Q is effective in causing lower than market-determined interest rates in some sectors, it interferes with the flow of funds to where they can be used most productively by the market test, e.g., large business corporations, large banks, large cities, etc., and reduces the efficiency of the economy.

5. To the extent that Regulation Q is effective in equalizing deposit rates paid by all comparable financial institutions at levels lower than they might otherwise be, it protects the inefficient institutions and reduces the rewards and incentives for efficiency.

Costs of Avoidance

1. To the extent that financial institutions subject to Regulation Q wish to outbid others for funds, they are forced to offer savers either nonmonetary payments, such as gifts, or reduced prices on other services (tied pricing). Such inducements limit the savers' choices and are more costly to both the institution and the saver, reducing everyone's welfare. To restrict avoidance, the regulations must be applied to a progressively broader range of institutions and modes of interest payments.

2. To the extent that savers maximize profits, they are forced either to divert savings to alternative outlets not subject to Q or to accept nonmonetary payments. Both processes involve considerable cost and reduce efficiency.

3. To the extent that financial institutions and/or savers are able to circumvent the controls, Regulation Q has achieved none of its objectives, but has increased costs considerably.

The Evidence

The evidence from the latter half of the 1960s suggests that Regulation Q was partially effective. To this extent, it involved both costs of compliance and costs of avoidance. Inflows of savings to both commercial banks and thrift institutions were greatly reduced with a consequent reduction in mortgage flows. Large deposits were affected less than small deposits leading to a regressive transfer of income. Funds were diverted from their most productive uses and inefficient financial institutions kept alive. On the other hand, both savers and financial institutions tried hard to circumvent the ceilings, and they were partially successful. Banks and thrift institutions offered a variety of gifts, free checking accounts,

Figure 6-3 **Outstanding Volume and Rates on Certificates of Deposit, Commercial Paper, and Eurodollars**

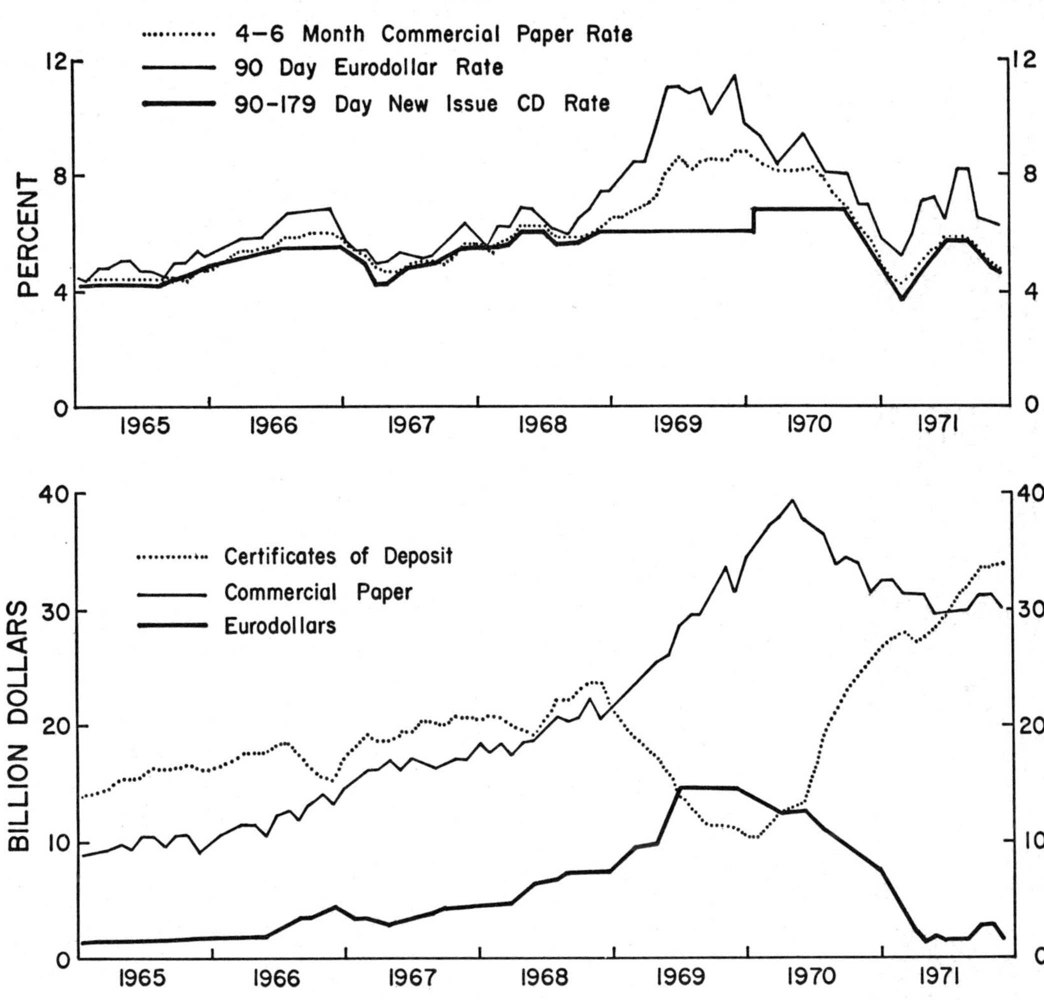

Sources: Federal Reserve Banks of New York and St. Louis; *Federal Reserve Bulletin.*

free safe-deposit boxes, and other inducements. Large savers were so successful in transferring funds to Treasury bills that the federal government was forced to sharply increase transactions costs on such transfers by raising the minimum denomination on new issues of bills from $1,000 to $10,000 and by accepting only certified checks in payment. These actions served to discriminate further against small savers.

The ability of both large financial institutions and large depositors to circumvent Regulation Q is clearly evident from Figure 6-3 and Table 6-6. The top half

Table 6-6 **Changes in Bank Use of Selected Short-Term Sources of Funds, 1968–70**

		(Billion Dollars)	
	1968	1969	1970
Certificates of Deposit	2.9	−12.8	14.8
Eurodollar Borrowing	2.6	6.8	− 6.0
Bank-Related Commercial Paper		5.9	− 2.4

Source: Board of Governors of the Federal Reserve System, *Annual Report, 1970,* p. 21.

of the figure traces interest rates on large CDs, commercial paper, and Eurodollars of comparable maturities. Starting at the end of 1968, market rates of interest climbed above the ceiling rates commercial banks were permitted to pay on CDs. As a result, the banks were unable to sell new CDs to replace maturing issues. To offset the decline in deposits, banks turned to alternative sources of funds not subject to Q ceilings. One source was borrowing from a parent holding company. Many banks had recently become affiliated with a one-bank holding company and were able to use this path. The holding companies, in turn, acquired funds by issuing commercial paper. Another source of funds was to sell some of the loans in the banks' portfolios, particularly to parent holding companies. A third, and, at least for large banks, the most popular way of circumventing Q was to borrow from their overseas branches. These borrowings were not subject to Regulation Q ceilings. In many instances the overseas branches had obtained the funds by offering U.S. banks and depositors higher rates than those permitted by Q, to which they were not subject. It is evident from the table that banks matched the runoff in CDs in 1969 almost to the dollar by increasing Eurodollar borrowings and selling commercial paper. In 1970, after ceilings were suspended on CDs with 30–89 days in maturity, banks rebuilt their CD holdings and reduced their reliance on the costlier alternatives.

Bank customers who were unable to obtain bank financing because of the deposit rundown also tapped alternative sources. Large corporations stepped up their borrowings through commercial paper on the private capital market. As these securities yielded higher returns than CDs, they were eagerly purchased by holders of maturing CDs. The sharp increase in the volume of Eurodollars and commercial paper outstanding as CDs declined dominates the lower panel of the chart. The subsequent decline in these securities after the Federal Reserve suspended the ceilings on some CD maturities, in response to potential disorder in the commercial-paper market following the failure of the Penn Central Railroad to redeem their paper at maturity, and market rates of interest again declined below Q ceilings, suggests that these alternative sources of funds are more costly and less efficient than traditional modes of bank intermediation.

In sum, even if the objectives of Regulation Q were economically desirable and the regulation effective, the high cost of compliance suggests that alternative strategies be considered for achieving these objectives. Alternative strategies to safeguard the solvency of thrift institutions would include better overall economic policies reducing abrupt interest-rate increases, broader deposit insurance, and structural changes in the institutions emphasizing greater diversification of assets and liabilities. Moreover, outright explicit subsidies are preferable to hidden subsidies to channel credit into mortgages and other socially desirable channels. Governments and controls may come and go, but the market and the drive of market participants to optimize, like death and taxes, are forever.

The Payments Mechanism

Because demand deposits serve as the primary medium of exchange in the United States, commercial banks effectively operate the national payments mechanism. As discussed earlier, the more efficient the payment mechanism is, the higher the economic welfare of the community. The efficiency of the bank payments mechanism is reflected in the speed and cost at which funds are transferred through the banking system in response to the use of demand deposits.

Checks are orders to banks to transfer a given amount of funds from the account of the writer at that bank to a designated party. Typically, checks are not deposited at the same bank on which they are drawn. When a bank credits the account of a depositor for the amount of a check deposited, it credits funds it does not yet have. The bank must collect the funds from the bank on which the check is drawn. To do so, it must physically present the check for payment. As there are nearly 14,000 banks in the country, the process of check sorting, transporting, and payment is complex and costly.

In the earlier days of commercial banking, this process was even more difficult. Transportation and communication were slower. Standards for payment were common in only some parts of the country, and it was to the advantage of the bank on which the check was drawn to delay payment to the receiving bank for as long as possible. As the cost and time of collection varies with distance between banks, many banks did not grant depositors full credit for the amount of checks deposited until they had collected the funds. Many sellers were reluctant to accept payment by checks drawn on distant banks regardless of the financial integrity of the buyer. The payments system was neither national nor efficient.

It was to the advantage of both the banks and the general public to reduce the cost and time of check collection or check clearing. Smaller banks arranged for larger banks to collect their checks for them in return for maintaining clearing balances at these banks. Many banks in the same city arranged for a common clearing. Instead of each bank sending checks on all other banks in the same city directly to the banks for collection, the banks delivered the checks to a common clearing location, called the clearinghouse. The amounts each bank owed all other banks were tallied and only the net differences paid. As banks typically receive checks drawn on the same banks as have checks drawn on them and both banks have checks drawn on and owe payments to third banks, the costs of payment are reduced substantially by offsetting the gross payments and receipts of all banks with all other banks participating in the clearing arrangement. Clearinghouses greatly facilitated local check payments, but did not fundamentally affect the national system.

One of the major responsibilities assigned the newly established Federal Reserve System in 1914 was to provide the benefits of local clearing arrangements to the national scene. The Federal Reserve has developed an efficient national clearing system centered on the 12 Federal Reserve Banks and 24 branch offices. Each member bank remits checks to and receives payment from its district bank or branch. The remaining clearing is conducted among the Reserve banks and branches themselves. To reduce the effects of transportation delays and uncertainties on the transfer of funds, the Federal Reserve Banks credit the reserve accounts of member banks for checks delivered according to a fixed schedule based on distance between banks rather than time of collection. Frequently, credit is granted one bank before payment is received from the other. In this instance, both banks claim the same deposits and the Federal Reserve temporarily provides the necessary reserves.

The additional reserves so provided are called *Federal Reserve float*, which is defined as *the difference between the asset entry Cash Items in the Process of Collection (CIPC) on the Federal Reserve balance sheet and the liability item Deferred Availability of Cash Items (DACI).* Until a commercial bank collects the funds on the checks it has sent for collection, it debits the amount of the checks to CIPC on its own books. This entry is called *bank float.*

A clearer picture of check collection can be obtained by tracing the journey of a check through the clearing process. Assume a check for $100 drawn on Bank S in San Francisco is deposited by a customer in Bank C in Chicago (Table 6-7).

1. Bank C credits the deposit account of the depositor and debits CIPC both by $100.

2. Bank C sends the check to the Federal Reserve Bank of Chicago for payment. The Chicago Fed debits CIPC and credits DACI by $100 on its statements. Because the check is drawn on a San Francisco bank, the Chicago Fed forwards the check to the San Francisco Federal Reserve Bank and schedules to credit Bank C with the amount of the check in two days, the maximum time delay on the Federal Reserve schedule.

3. Upon receipt of the check, say two days later, the San Francisco Fed debits its CIPC and credits an inter–Federal Reserve Bank clearing account, the Interdistrict Settlement Fund (ISF), for the amount of its debt to the Chicago Fed. At that time, the Chicago Fed credits CIPC and debits ISF.

Table 6-7 **Steps in Check Collection between Banks in Different Federal Reserve Districts**

Bank C

R	$1,000	$1,000	D
① CIPC +	100	+ 100	D
④ CIPC −	100		
R +	100		
⑥ R	1,100	1,100	D

FRB Chicago

GC	$1,000	$1,000	R
② CIPC +	100	+ 100	DACI
③ CIPC −	100		
ISF +	100		
④		− 100	DACI
		+ 100	R (Bank C)
⑤ ISF −	100		
GC +	100		
⑥ GC	1,100	1,100	R

FRB San Francisco

GC	$1,000	$1,000	R
③ CIPC +	100	+ 100	ISF
⑤ CIPC −	100	− 100	R (Bank S)
GC −	100	− 100	ISF
⑥ GC	900	900	R

Bank S

R	$1,000	$1,000	D
⑤ R	− 100	− 100	D
⑥ R	900	900	D

4. At the same time, the Fed of Chicago credits the reserve deposit account of Bank C and debits DACI by an equivalent amount. Bank C credits CIPC and debits its reserve account. It now has collected payment and can transform the reserves into earning assets. Note that at this time both Bank C and Bank S carry the same deposit on their books and the Federal Reserve System has effectively provided the necessary reserves through a higher float to support the duplication.

5. The San Francisco Fed transmits the check to Bank S for verification and the next day credits CIPC and debits that bank's reserve account. The funds are transferred to the Chicago Fed. This is recorded by a debit to ISF. To execute the transfer, the Fed of San Francisco transfers ownership of an equivalent amount of gold certificates (GC) to the Federal Reserve Bank of Chicago. The Fed of Chicago records the collection of the debt by crediting ISF and the receipt of the gold certificates by debiting this account. Bank S debits the check writer's account and credits its reserve balance at the San Francisco Federal Reserve Bank to complete the transfer of funds. By crediting CIPC upon payment, the San Francisco Federal Reserve Bank has eliminated the Federal Reserve float.

6. At the end of the process, Bank C and the Federal Reserve Bank of Chicago have both gained funds and Bank S and the Federal Reserve Bank of San Francisco have both lost an equivalent amount of funds.

Recently, the Federal Reserve has acted to reduce the amount of its float outstanding by further reducing the time it takes to complete the clearing of checks. To implement this policy, additional regional clearinghouses have been established and banks have been required to make payments on checks to the Federal Reserve Banks more quickly. In addition, a number of experiments are under way in different parts of the country utilizing on-line remote computer units to process payments simultaneously with transactions. By synchronizing payments and receipts, neither bank nor Federal Reserve float is created.

References

Bell, Frederick W., and Neil B. Murphy, *Costs in Commercial Banking: A Quantitative Analysis of Bank Behavior and Its Relation to Bank Regulation* (Boston: Federal Reserve Bank of Boston, 1968).

Board of Governors of the Federal Reserve System, *The Federal Reserve System: Purposes and Functions,* Fifth edition (Washington, D.C.: 1963).

Comptroller of the Currency, *Studies in Banking Competition and The Banking Structure* (Washington, D.C.: 1966).

Federal Reserve Bank of Chicago, *Commercial Banking: Structure, Competition and Performance* (Chicago: 1967).

———, *Proceedings of a Conference on Bank Structure and Competition* (Chicago: 1967, 1968, 1969, 1970, 1971).

Federal Reserve Bank of St. Louis, *Bank Supervision* (St. Louis: 1963).

Fischer, Gerald C., *American Banking Structure* (New York: Columbia University Press, 1968).

Friedman, Milton, "Controls on Interest Rates Paid by Banks," *Journal of Money, Credit, and Banking,* 2 (1), February, 1970, 15-32.

Friend, Irwin, ed., *Study of the Savings and Loan Industry* (Washington, D.C.: Federal Home Loan Bank Board, 1969).

Gies, Thomas G., and Vincent P. Apilado, eds., *Banking Markets and Financial Institutions* (Homewood, Ill.: Irwin, 1971).

Guttentag, Jack M., and Edward S. Herman, "Banking Structure and Performance," *The Bulletin* (New York University, Institute of Finance), Nos. 41-43, February, 1967.

Lindsay, Robert, "The Economics of Interest Rate Ceilings," *The Bulletin* (New York University, Institute of Finance), Nos. 68-69, December, 1970.

Luttrell, Clifton B., "Interest Rate Controls—Perspective, Purpose and Problems," *Review* (Federal Reserve Bank of St. Louis), 50 (9), September, 1968, 6-14.

President's Commission on Financial Structure and Regulation, *Report* (Washington, D.C.: U.S. Government Printing Office, 1971).

Bank Deposit Expansion and the Supply of Money

7

Under a fractional reserve banking system, banks maintain cash reserves equal to only a percentage of their deposit liabilities. As a result, changes in the dollar amount of reserves, holding the reserve percentage constant, generate larger changes in the same direction in the dollar amount of deposits. Likewise, changes in the reserve percentage, holding the dollar amount of reserves constant, generate changes in the opposite direction in the dollar amount of deposits. This chapter analyzes the relationship between bank reserves and bank deposits and considers the implications for the dollar amount of bank deposits of dollar changes in reserves, changes in the reserve to deposit ratio, changes in the mix of deposits, changes in bank behavior, and changes in the behavior of depositors. In any period, banks are required to hold cash reserves equal to or greater than an amount determined by multiplying the relevant reserve requirement percentage by the dollar amount of deposits. This may be expressed in equation form:

$$R \geq RR = (r_D DD) + (r_T TD),$$

where:

R = total bank reserves
RR = required reserves
DD = demand deposits
TD = time deposits
r_D = percent reserve requirement on demand deposits
r_T = percent reserve requirement on time deposits.

Demand Deposit Expansion

The consequences of changes in reserves and reserve ratios on bank deposits can be traced step by step by means of T-accounting statements. We start with a simple, highly constrained example and then relax the assumptions one at a time.

Initial Assumptions:

1. There is only one bank in the banking system. As a result there are neither adverse nor favorable check clearings.
2. There are no changes in the public's currency holdings after the initial change.
3. Banks desire to hold zero excess reserves; that is, the amount of reserves they wish to hold against deposits is exactly equal to the amount they are legally required to hold. The banking system is assumed to be in equilibrium only when its actual excess reserves are equal to its desired excess reserves.
4. There is only one type of bank liability—demand deposits—and no net worth or capital.
5. There is only one type of bank earning asset—loans.
6. All banks are subject to the same reserve requirements.
7. Reserves are required to be held against deposits in the same reserve period.

Initial Conditions:

1. The reserve requirement on demand deposits is 20 percent.
2. The banking system's initial balance sheet shows total reserves of $2,000, loans of $8,000, and demand deposits of $10,000. As all reserves are required, excess reserves are zero, and the system is in equilibrium.

Assets			Liabilities	
R		2,000	10,000	DD
	RR	2,000		
	ER	0		
L		8,000		
		10,000	10,000	

3. Inject reserves of $1,000 into the banking system through an inflow of an equal dollar amount of currency exchanged for demand deposits.

In the analyses which follow, these notations will be used:

D = total bank deposits
DD = demand deposits
TD = time deposits
R = total bank reserves
RR = required reserves
ER = excess reserves
L = total bank loans

C = currency held by the public
r_D = percent reserve requirement on demand deposits (20%)
r_T = percent reserve requirement on time deposits (10%)
$\bar{r}$ = average percent reserve requirement on total deposits.

Case 1. The Monopoly Bank

The inflow of $1,000 into the banking system (represented by The First Monopoly Bank of the United States) in exchange for deposits increases reserves by the same amount. The bank now has demand deposits of $11,000, total reserves of $3,000, and loans of $8,000. The balance sheet balances. However, required reserves are only $2,200 (.20 × $11,000), and the bank has excess reserves of $800 on which it is not earning income.

The First Monopoly Bank of the United States

Assets			Liabilities
R +		1,000	+ 1,000 DD
R		3,000	11,000 DD
	RR	2,200	
	ER	800	
L		8,000	
		11,000	11,000

To increase its income, the bank will lend this amount by lowering its lending rates or liberalizing its lending terms slightly. The borrower receives a demand deposit of $800. This increases the bank's deposits to $11,800 and ups its required reserves to $2,360. Borrowers borrow funds to spend, not to hold, and quickly pass ownership of the deposits to sellers. As there is only one bank, however,

The First Monopoly Bank of the United States

Assets			Liabilities
L +		800	+ 800 DD
R		3,000	11,800 DD
	RR	2,360	
	ER	640	
L		8,800	
		11,800	11,800

all deposits remain at the same bank, and a deposit transfer changes only the ownership and not the total amount of deposits at either the bank or in the banking system.

After the credit extension, the bank still has $3,000 minus $2,360, or $640, of excess reserves to loan. Although the balance sheet balances, the banking system is not in equilibrium as it is holding more excess reserves than it wishes. Thus, it will extend an additional $640 of loans. As a result of this loan, the bank increases demand deposits to $12,440, and the process repeats itself.

The First Monopoly Bank of the United States

Assets			Liabilities
L	+	640	+ 640 DD
R		3,000	12,440 DD
	RR	2,488	
	ER	512	
L		9,440	
		12,440	12,440

However, as deposits expand, an increasing percentage of total reserves are absorbed as required reserves. The deposit expansion stops when all reserves are required. At this point, excess reserves are zero and the banking system is in equilibrium. The full expansion process is summarized on the balance sheet in Table 7-1. After the last step, total deposits have been expanded to $15,000, loans to $12,000, and total reserves are equal to required reserves.

Table 7-1 **Step Summary of Balance Sheet Deposit Expansion The First Monopoly Bank of the United States**

Step	Assets				Liabilities	Deposit Inflow
	Reserves			Loans	Demand Deposits	
	Total	Required	Excess			
1.	$2,000	$2,000	$ 0	$8,000	$10,000	
2.	3,000	2,200	800	8,000	11,000	+$1,000
3.	3,000	2,360	640	8,800	11,800	
4.	3,000	2,488	512	9.440	12,400	
.						
.						
.						
$n-1$	3,000	2,999	1	11,999	14,999	
n	3,000	3,000	0	12,000	15,000	

A number of important observations can be drawn from this example:

1. Deposits have expanded by a multiple of the initial reserve inflow. Both the initial and final relationships between total reserves and demand deposits are given by the following equation:[1]

$$DD = kR, \tag{7-1}$$

where:

$k = 1/r_D$.

The reciprocal of the reserve requirement ratio is called the deposit multiplier and is designated by k. If $R = \$3{,}000$ and $r_D = .20$, then by equation 7-1, $k = 5$ and demand deposits $= \$15{,}000$. Initially, when reserves were only \$2,000, equation 7-1 predicted demand deposits of \$10,000. The value of k varies inversely with r_D. If r_D is reduced from .20 to .10, k increases from 5 to 10.

2. Equilibrium *changes* in deposits are related to *changes* in reserves by an equation derived from equation 7-1:

Period t	$DD_t = kR_t$,
Period $t + 1$	$DD_{t+1} = kR_{t+1}$.

Subtracting deposits in t from deposits in $t+1$:

$$DD_{t+1} - DD_t = kR_{t+1} - kR_t = k(R_{t+1} - R_t),$$

and letting Δ represent the change from period t to period $t+1$:

$$\Delta DD = k\Delta R. \tag{7-2}$$

If $\Delta R = \$1{,}000$ and $k = 5$, $\Delta DD = \$5{,}000$.

---

1. This equation is the sum of a geometric progression in which a constant term, R, is progressively multiplied by consecutively increasing powers of a factor, p:

$$DD = R + Rp + Rp^2 + Rp^3 + \cdots + Rp^{n-1} - R(1 - p^n)/(1 - p).$$

If $p^2 < 1$, then as n approaches infinity,

$$DD = R/(1 - p).$$

From the demand deposit column of Table 7-1, it is obvious that $p = (1 - r_D)$, so that $(1 - p) = r_D$. Thus $DD = R / r_D$. And letting $k = 1 / r_D$; $DD = kR$.

Somewhat simpler, this equation can be derived by relating required reserves to demand deposits and the required reserve ratio:

$$R = r_D DD,$$
$$DD = R/r_D = kR.$$

3. Changes in reserves affect loans in a systematic fashion as well as deposits. The loan-reserve relationships are summarized by the following equations derived from the balance sheet identity $R + L = DD$. Transposing this equation to solve for L and substituting kR for DD from equation 7-1 yields:

$$L = kR - R,$$

and

$$L = (k-1)R, \qquad (7\text{-}3)$$

$$\Delta L = (k-1)\Delta R. \qquad (7\text{-}4)$$

If $\Delta R = \$1{,}000$ and $k = 5$, $\Delta L = \$4{,}000$.

Case 2. The Case of Many Banks

In this example, the assumption of only a single bank is relaxed and many different banks introduced. As was seen in Chapter 6, this conforms with the market structure of banks in the United States. Individual banks now may experience gains from and losses of deposits to other banks. As before, assume that \$1,000 of demand deposits and reserves are injected into the banking system from without, this time into Bank A, as shown in Table 7-2 (*a*). Bank A requires only \$200 of additional required reserves to support these deposits and will lend the remaining \$800 of excess reserves. After making the loan, Bank A has deposits of \$11,800, reserves of \$3,000, and loans of \$8,800. Up to this point, the analysis is the same as for the case of the monopoly bank.

But after the transfer of ownership of the newly created \$800 of deposits from the borrowers to the sellers, it is unlikely that the funds will be redeposited in Bank A. In a world of many banks, it is more likely that the sellers patronize other banks. These banks may all be designated as Bank B. Upon deposit of \$800, Bank B credits the accounts of the depositors and after debiting cash items in the process of collection sends the checks to Bank A for payment. Upon receipt of the borrowers' checks on their accounts at A, Bank A simultaneously reduces deposits by \$800 and transfers \$800 of reserves, say, on deposit at its district Federal Reserve Bank, to Bank B. After this transaction, Bank A has \$11,000 of deposits, \$2,200 of reserves and \$8,800 of loans. The balance sheet balances and total reserves are exactly equal to required reserves. The bank is in equilibrium. Its deposits are \$1,000 greater than before, loans \$800 greater, and reserves \$200 greater.

Upon receiving payment, Bank B has deposits of \$800 and reserves of \$800. But its required reserves are only \$160. It has \$640 to lend, as shown in (*b*) of Table 7-2. Upon lending this amount, its deposits temporarily rise to \$1,440. If

Table 7-2 Balance Sheets Showing Deposit Expansion, Many Banks

(a) Bank A Assets		Bank A Liabilities	(b) Bank B Assets		Bank B Liabilities	To Bank C
R	2,000	10,000 DD				
RR	2,000					
ER	0					
L	8,000					
R	+1,000	+1,000 DD	R	+800	+800 DD	
R	3,000	11,000 DD	R	800	800 DD	
RR	2,200		RR	160		
ER	800		ER	640		
L	8,000		L	0		
L	+800	+ 800 DD	L	+640	+640 DD	
R	3,000	11,800 DD	R	800	1,440 DD	
RR	2,360		RR	288		
ER	640		ER	512		
L	8,800		L	640		
R	−800	−800 DD	R	−640	−640 DD	
R	2,200	11,000 DD	R	160	800 DD	
RR	2,200		RR	160		
ER	0		ER	0		
L	8,800		L	640		
	11,000	11,000		800	800	

the sellers of goods and services to borrowers from Bank B patronize Bank C, deposits at Bank B will soon return to $800. At this point, its loans total $640, required reserves $160, and excess reserves are zero. The balance sheet is in balance and the bank is in equilibrium.

The process is repeated involving Banks D, E, and so on until, as with the monopoly bank, all reserves are absorbed by required reserves and excess reserves are zero both for each bank individually and for the banking system as a whole. The expansion process resembles that shown in Table 7-1 except that a different bank is represented at each step. At the new equilibrium, deposits and loans have expanded by the same amounts as with a monopoly bank and as predicted by equations 7-1 through 7-4. Individual banks, however, have performed differently. Because of the loss of deposits to other banks, each bank has expanded deposits only by the amount of its original reserve inflow; Bank A by $1,000, Bank B by $800, and so on. Thus, individual banks cannot do what all banks together can. They cannot expand deposits by a multiple of the initial reserve inflow.[2]

Note that total reserves in the banking system did not change during the expansion process. What did change was the mix of reserves between required and excess reserves and the ownership of the reserves among the banks. Except for short-term borrowing from the Federal Reserve, neither individual banks nor the banking system can change the amount of aggregate reserves. With the above exception, all changes in total reserves originate outside the commercial banking system.

Case 3. Excess Reserves Greater Than Zero

Banks may desire to hold reserves in excess of the amount legally required for a number of reasons. Some banks may feel that the amount of required reserves is insufficient to accommodate potential deposit losses and desire to possess greater liquidity. Others may feel that the return on investing the last dollar of excess reserves is not worth the cost. Bank demand for excess reserves can be summarized in functional notation as follows:

$$ER = f(\overset{-}{i_S}, \overset{+}{V}, X), \tag{7-5}$$

where:

i_S = market rate of interest on securities
V = deposit variability
X = all other factors, such as the economic outlook.

Given the cost of extending loans, the higher the rate of interest on securities, the less profitable it is to hold excess reserves. The greater the variability of deposits is, the greater the need to accommodate deposit drains and the greater the inducement to hold excess reserves.

The greater the amount of excess reserves banks demand, the less they will lend and the smaller the resulting deposit expansion on a given reserve inflow. Excess reserves may be considered a "leakage" in the deposit expansion process. If banks demand excess reserves in some fixed proportion, e, of their demand deposits, that is, $ER = eDD$, the deposit expansion equation can be derived from dividing a change in total reserves into either required reserves or excess reserves:

$$\Delta R = \Delta RR + \Delta ER.$$

2. To the extent that deposits resulting from new loans are not transferred to other banks, individual banks can, to an extent, expand deposits by a multiple of the initial deposit inflow.

As

$$\Delta RR = r_D \Delta DD,$$

and

$$\Delta ER = e\Delta DD,$$

then, by substitution:

$$\Delta R = r_D \Delta DD + e\Delta DD = \Delta DD\,(r_D + e),$$

or:

$$\Delta DD = k'\Delta R, \qquad (7\text{-}6)$$

where:

$$k' = \frac{1}{r_D + e}.$$

If $\Delta R = \$1{,}000$, $r_D = .20$, and $e = .02$; $k' = 1/.22 = 4.55$, and $\Delta DD = \$4{,}550$. This is smaller than the previous expansion of \$5,000 in deposits on a \$1,000 inflow of reserves in the absence of positive excess reserves.

In reality, banks hold very few excess reserves. In December, 1971, total excess reserves at all Federal Reserve member banks were less than \$200 million, or one-half of 1 percent of total reserves and less than one-tenth of 1 percent of total demand deposits. By far the largest amount of excess reserves were held by smaller banks.

Case 4. Currency Changes

As currency and demand deposits are close substitutes, it appears reasonable that the public will change its demand for currency at those times when its demand for demand deposits changes. We shall now relax the restriction of no changes in the public's holdings of currency. Assume for the sake of simplicity, that the public desires to hold currency in a fixed proportion (c) to its demand deposits. That is, $C = cDD$. Thus, as demand deposits expand, currency increases proportionately. Because banks can obtain currency to accommodate an exchange of deposits for currency only from their own holdings of vault cash or by purchasing the amount from the Federal Reserve, an increase in currency holdings by the public absorbs bank reserves by an equal dollar amount and reduces the reserves available to support deposits. Like excess reserves, currency is a leakage in the deposit expansion process.

An increase in reserves may now be absorbed by increases in required reserves, excess reserves, or currency. The deposit expansion equation incorporating currency changes may be derived as follows:

$$\begin{aligned}\Delta R &= \Delta RR + \Delta ER + \Delta C\\ &= r_D \Delta DD + e\Delta DD + c\Delta DD\\ &= \Delta DD\,(r_D + e + c).\end{aligned}$$

And

$$\Delta DD = k''\Delta R, \qquad (7\text{-}7)$$

where:

$$k'' = \frac{1}{r_D + e + c}.$$

If $\Delta R = \$1{,}000$, $r_D = .20$, $e = .02$, and $c = .10$; $k'' = 1/.32 = 3.1$; and $\Delta DD = \$3{,}100$. The greater the public's demand for currency is, the smaller the deposit expansion for a given inflow of reserves.

Case 5. Time Deposits

Finally, we relax the last restriction that banks offer only demand deposits. In this case, banks are assumed to offer both demand and time deposits. However, as is usually the case, reserve requirements are assumed to be lower on time deposits; $r_T < r_D$. (If reserve requirements were the same on demand as time deposits, the composition of deposits would be less interesting.) Assume the public demands time deposits in some fixed proportion, t, of their holdings of demand deposits, that is, $t = TD/DD$. Time deposits absorb reserves that could otherwise support demand deposits in an amount equal to $r_T(t)\ DD$. Thus, time deposits represent another leakage in the demand deposit expansion process. The complete demand deposit expansion equation can be derived as before:

$$\begin{aligned}\Delta R &= \Delta RR_{DD} + \Delta RR_{TD} + \Delta ER + \Delta C\\ &= r_D \Delta DD + r_T(t)\Delta DD + e\Delta DD + c\Delta DD\\ &= \Delta DD(r_D + r_T + e + c).\end{aligned}$$

And

$$\Delta DD = k'''\Delta R, \tag{7-8}$$

where:

$$k''' = \frac{1}{r_D + e + c + r_T t}.$$

If $\Delta R = \$1{,}000$, $r_D = .20$, $e = .02$, $c = .10$, $r_T = .10$, and $t = .50$; $k''' = 1/.37 = 2.7$, and $\Delta DD = \$2{,}700$. From above, it can be seen that k''' is related to its determinants or leakages as follows:

$$k''' = f(\bar{r}_D, \bar{e}, \bar{c}, \bar{t}, \bar{r}_T).$$

The smaller any of the leakages is, the larger the expansion of demand deposits for a given increase in total reserves. For example, if, in the last example, c declines from .1 to .05, k''' increases from 2.7 to 3.1. A summary of the effects on changes in demand deposits resulting from the introduction of each of the leakages appears in Table 7-3.

Total Deposit Expansion

If banks can offer both demand and time deposits, it is important to examine the implications of changes in reserves on total bank deposits as well as on demand deposits. As noted earlier, some definitions of money include all bank deposits. Moreover, changes in bank loans are related to changes in total deposits, not to changes in demand or time deposits separately. If e and c are both assumed to be zero, total deposits are related to total reserves by the reciprocal of the average reserve requirement ratio in which the requirement on each type of deposit is weighted by the proportion of that type of deposit to total deposits.

$$\Delta D = \bar{k}\Delta R, \tag{7-9}$$

where:

$$\bar{k} = \frac{1}{\bar{r}} = \frac{1}{r_D\left(\frac{DD}{DD+TD}\right) + r_T\left(\frac{TD}{DD+TD}\right)}.$$

If $\Delta R = \$1{,}000$, $r_D = .2$, $r_T = .1$, $t = .5$, and $DD = \$1{,}000$, $TD = tDD = .5(\$1{,}000) = \$500$, and

$$\bar{r} = .2\left(\frac{1}{1.5}\right) + .1\left(\frac{0.5}{1.5}\right) = .2\,(.67) + .1(.33) = .167,$$

$$\bar{k} = 1/\bar{r} = 1/.167 = 6.0.$$

Table 7-3 Summary of Effects on Demand Deposits of Changes in Reserves

(a) Values of Demand Deposit Multiplier under Alternative Restrictions

Restriction 1: Only *DD*; *ER*, *C*, *TD* = 0; $r_D = .20$.

$$k = \frac{1}{r_D} = \frac{1}{.20} = 5.$$

Restriction 2: Only *DD*, *ER*>0; *C*, *TD*=0; $r_D = .20$, $e = .02$.

$$k' = \frac{1}{r_D + e} = \frac{1}{.20 + .02} = 4.55.$$

Restriction 3: Only *DD*, *ER*>0, *C* >0; *TD*=0; $r_D = .20$, $e = .02$, $c = .10$.

$$k'' = \frac{1}{r_D + e + c} = \frac{1}{.20 + .02 + .10} = 3.1.$$

Restriction 4: Both *DD* and *TD*; $r_D = .20$, $e = .02$, $c = .10$, $t = .50$, $r_T = .10$.

$$k''' = \frac{1}{r_D + e + c + r_T(t)} = \frac{1}{.20 + .02 + .10 + .10(.50)} = 2.7.$$

(b) Expansion in Demand Deposits after $1,000 Increase in Reserves under Alternative Restrictions

Restriction	ΔDD
1	$5,000
2	4,550
3	3,100
4	2,700

Thus,

$$\Delta D = \$6{,}000.$$

Likewise:

$$\Delta L = (\bar{k} - 1)\Delta R, \tag{7-10}$$

$$\Delta L = \$5{,}000.$$

The mix of the increase in total deposits between demand and time deposits may be determined by the equations derived earlier.

$$\Delta DD = k'''\Delta R,$$

where:

$$k''' = \frac{1}{r_D + e + c + r_T t}.$$

In our example,

$$k''' = \frac{1}{.2+.5(.1)} = \frac{1}{.25} = 4,$$

and

$$\Delta DD = \$4{,}000.$$

Time deposits are obtained from the balance sheet identity,

$$\begin{aligned}\Delta TD &= \Delta D - \Delta DD \\ &= \$6{,}000 - \$4{,}000 = \$2{,}000.\end{aligned}$$

Proof:

$$\Delta R_D = r_D(\Delta DD) = .2(\$4{,}000) = \$800.$$

$$\Delta R_T = r_T(\Delta TD) = .1(\$2{,}000) = \$200.$$

$$\Delta R = \Delta R_D + \Delta R_T = \$800 + \$200 = \$1{,}000.$$

This is the amount of reserves initially injected.

Note that if reserve requirements on time deposits are below those on demand deposits, a given increase in reserves will generate a larger dollar increase in total deposits than in demand deposits. Likewise, the greater the ratio of time deposits to total deposits, the smaller is the amount of demand deposits, but the greater is the amount of total deposits a given reserve base is able to support. The total deposit multiplier is largest in the extreme case in which all deposits are held in the form of time deposits.

Deposit Contraction

When reserves are withdrawn from a fractional reserve banking system, deposits are contracted by a multiple of the reserve reduction. This occurs because the initial reduction in reserves, although matched by an equal dollar reduction in deposits, leaves the banks with insufficient reserves to satisfy the legal reserve requirement on the remaining deposits. The banks are in a deficit position, that is, they have negative excess reserves. Thus, they have to contract deposits until required reserves are reduced to the level that can be satisfied by the amount of reserves available in the banking system and not demanded as excess reserves.

Individual banks can reduce deposits to levels consistent with their reserves by either not renewing maturing loans or by selling loans to other banks. The banking

Table 7-4 **Step Summary of Balance Sheet Deposit Contraction The First Monopoly Bank of the United States**

Step	Assets				Liabilities	Deposit
	Reserves			Loans	Demand Deposits	Outflow
	Total	Required	Excess			
1.	$3,000	$3,000	$ 0	$12,000	$15,000	
2.	2,000	2,800	−800	12,000	14,000	−$1,000
3	2,000	2,640	−640	11,200	13,200	
4.	2,000	2,502	−502	10,560	12,560	
.						
.						
.						
$n-1$	2,000	2,001	−1	8,001	10,001	
n	2,000	2,000	0	8,000	10,000	

system as a whole can contract deposits by not renewing maturing loans or by selling loans to the nonbank public. In the process, loan rates will rise and loan terms will become more restrictive. The deposit contraction stops when the reserve deficit is eliminated and banks are again holding their desired level of excess reserves.

The deposit contraction process is precisely the reverse of the deposit expansion process. The process is traced in stepwise fashion in Table 7-4. Under the restrictions applicable to a monopoly bank with e, c, and $t=0$, a $1,000 initial reduction in reserves contracts demand deposits by $5,000 and loans by $4,000. The deposit contraction equation is:

$$-\Delta D = k(-\Delta R). \tag{7-11}$$

Similar to the deposit expansion example, the restrictions can be relaxed to incorporate bank demands for excess reserves, changes in the public's holdings of currency, and bank time deposits. It can be seen from equation 7-8 that the larger e, c, t, or r_T, the smaller the contraction in demand deposits for a given dollar decline in reserves. Likewise, an increase in any of these variables, ceteris paribus, generates a deposit contraction. For example, an autonomous increase in the demand of banks for excess reserves from $e=.02$ to .1 would reduce k''' in the earlier example from 2.7 to 2.2 and initiate a contraction in deposits. It is of interest to note that although currency and demand deposits are both components of the money supply, a shift in preference by the public from demand deposits to an equal amount of currency will induce a reduction in the stock of money.

Demand for Financial Assets

The previous examples of deposit expansion and contraction make it appear that the process is pretty mechanical. Nothing can be further from the truth. The public must want to hold the demand deposits, time deposits, and currency, and the banks, the excess reserves. The factors underlying the demand for each of these financial assets may be collected in a demand function. Similar to the demand functions for any other good, the demand functions for financial assets include a budget constraint and a menu of prices or interest rates. The interest rate variables determine both (1) the overall dollar amount of financial asset holdings, and (2) the distribution of the overall holdings among the various types of financial assets. Generally, the higher the level of all interest rates, the greater the overall amount of financial assets demanded, and the higher any specific interest rate in relation to other rates, the greater the demand for that particular financial asset. The aggregate demand for the financial assets introduced in the earlier half of this chapter may be written in functional notations as:

$$C_p = f(\overset{+}{y}, \overset{+}{P}, Z). \quad (7\text{-}12)$$

$$DD_p = f(\overset{+}{y}, \overset{+}{P}, \overset{+}{w}, \overset{-}{i_T}, \overset{-}{i_S}, \overset{-}{sc}). \quad (7\text{-}13)$$

$$TD_p = f(\overset{+}{y}, \overset{+}{P}, \overset{+}{w}, \overset{+}{i_T}, \overset{-}{i_S}, \overset{+}{sc}). \quad (7\text{-}14)$$

$$ER_b = f(\overset{-}{i_S}, \overset{+}{V}, X). \quad (7\text{-}15)$$

Where:

p = private nonbank sector
y = aggregate income in constant dollars
P = commodity price level
Z = other factors affecting the demand for currency, e.g., volume of small ticket purchases, safety, etc.
w = aggregate wealth in constant dollars
i_T = interest rate on bank time deposits
i_S = interest rate on market securities
sc = bank service charges on demand deposits
b = commercial banks
V = deposit variability
X = all other factors affecting bank demand for excess reserves.

Thus, the ability of the banking system to successfully expand deposits is dependent on the willingness of the public to hold the additional deposits. The public will do so only if the return on these deposits is made more favorable relative to the return on alternative assets.

The above demand functions indicate that the public views demand deposits and time deposits as substitutes for each other, and both as substitutes for market securities. In economics, two goods are considered substitutes when, if the price of one rises (i.e., the interest rate declines), the quantity demanded of the other increases, and vice versa. Thus, the higher the interest rate on time deposits, for example, the higher the public's demand for time deposits and the lower the public's demand for demand deposits and market securities (S). In notational form the relationships between the financial assets and interest rates on time deposits can be written:

$$\frac{\Delta TD}{\Delta i_T} > 0, \; \frac{\Delta DD}{\Delta i_T} < 0, \; \frac{\Delta S}{\Delta i_T} < 0.$$

The relationship between these assets and interest rates on market securities and service charges on demand deposits can be similarly summarized.

Consider an increase in reserves, supplying the banks with greater than desired excess reserves. As these represent nonearning assets, the banks will loan or invest the surplus excess reserves. This will bid up the price of securities and lower their market yields. The reduction in security rates will increase the attractiveness of demand and time deposits relative to securities, and some members of the public will change the composition of their financial assets in favor of bank deposits. Likewise, in consequence of a decline in bank reserves, banks will sell securities, bidding up the yields and reducing the relative attractiveness of bank deposits. If banks wish to increase their time deposits, they can do so by raising rates on these deposits. This will induce a shift into time deposits from both demand deposits and securities. To the extent that time deposits absorb fewer required reserves than demand deposits, increasing interest rates on time deposits can generate an increase in total bank deposits and bank loans on a given reserve base.

Predictability of Deposit Response

Because demand deposits account for three-fourths of the money supply, the Federal Reserve influences the money supply primarily by acting on bank reserves in accordance with the deposit demand expansion equation (equation 7-2) $\Delta DD = k\Delta R$. To be able to predict the outcome of its actions, the Federal Reserve must be able to predict k. As discussed, if all the leakages are taken into account, $k = f(r_D, e, c, r_T, t)$. Only two of these variables, r_D and r_T, are under the control of the Federal Reserve. The remainder are determined by the public and the banks, and are subject to considerable variation through time. As a result, k may fluctuate and it is necessary to consider the implications of such fluctuations for the ability of the Federal Reserve to control the money supply.

Investigations into the predictability of k need to distinguish between two factors: (1) stability, and (2) constancy. Stability refers to the nature of the relationship between the variable being predicted (the dependent variable) and the variables to which it is considered related and whose values are known or controllable (independent variables). If the relationship between the two sets of variables is rigid through time, the relationship is said to be stable. Constancy refers only to the variability of a variable. It does not consider the nature of its relationship to other variables. Although a dependent variable may fluctuate considerably, this change may still be predictable if it bears a known and reasonably fixed relationship with variables whose values are known. Stability, not constancy, is the key to predictability. It follows that predictability of k does not require constant values of e, c, and t, but only that the demand functions for C, TD, and ER (equations 7-12, 7-14, and 7-15) are known and stable.

A number of recent empirical studies have concluded that, for time periods of three months or longer, the demand functions for most financial assets are sufficiently stable to permit reasonably accurate predictions. If these studies are correct, the reserve-deposit multiplier (k) can also be predicted. Thus, the simplified expansion and contraction processes described in this chapter serve as an adequate representation of the actual processes by which the Federal Reserve, the commercial banks, and the public affect deposits and thereby the stock of money, and they can be helpful in identifying the implications of changes in reserves and reserve requirements. As we will see in later chapters, these relationships underlie the ability of the Federal Reserve to conduct monetary policy.

References

Anderson, Jane, and Thomas M. Humphrey, "Determinants of Change in the Money Stock: 1960–70," *Monthly Review* (Federal Reserve Bank of Richmond), 58 (3), March, 1972, 3-8.

Burger, Albert E., *The Money Supply Process* (Belmont, Calif.: Wadsworth, 1971).

Cagan, Phillip, *Determinants in Effects of Changes in the Stock of Money 1875–1960* (New York: National Bureau of Economic Research, 1965).

Federal Reserve Bank of Chicago, *Modern Money Mechanics: A Workbook* (Chicago: 1971).

Jordan, Jerry L., "Elements of Money Stock Determination," *Review* (Federal Reserve Bank of St. Louis), 51 (10), October, 1969, 10-19.

Kalish, Lionel, III, "A Study of Money Supply Control," *Journal of Finance*, 25 (4), September, 1970, 761-776.

Rasche, Robert H., "A Review of Empirical Studies of the Money Supply Mechanism," *Review* (Federal Reserve Bank of St. Louis), 54 (7), July, 1972, 11-19.

Tobin, James, "Commercial Banks as Creators of 'Money,'" in *Banking and Monetary Studies*, Deane Carson, ed. (Homewood, Ill.: Irwin, 1963).

PART III

Interest Rates

The Level of Interest Rates

8

Interest rates are the price of borrowing or renting money as an asset for the use of its flow of purchasing power services. As the renting of money creates credit, interest is the price of credit. Interest is not the price of money. Money is sold when it is used to buy a good or service. The price of money is thus the cost of what is bought with it. Changes in the price of money may be measured by changes in the reciprocal of the price level.

To the borrower, interest is the cost of advancing consumption before income is received. To the lender, interest is the reward for postponing consumption until the maturity of the loan. At the maturity of a loan contract, the same nominal amount of money is repaid the lender. During the life of the contract, the borrower must also pay the lender periodic interest, typically stated at an annual rate. Because there is a possibility that the borrower may default on repaying the full amount of either the loan principal or the interest, the lender will charge additional interest to compensate himself actuarially against the risk of such losses. The greater the risk of default is, the higher the interest rate. In addition, loan contracts are specified for varying terms to maturity and the interest rates may differ for each term. At any one time there exists a wide range of interest rates on the marketplace corresponding to an even wider range of debt contracts with different risks of default, different terms to maturity, and different other characteristics.

As prices, interest rates have a dual allocative function. They allocate income between spending and saving, and they allocate financial claims on the financial markets. Ceteris paribus, the higher the rate of interest is, the greater the reward for postponing consumption and the greater savings. Similarly, the higher the interest rate is on any particular type of security, the greater the demand for that security and the smaller the supply. That is, SSUs buy financial claims that yield the highest returns while DSUs sell claims at the lowest rates. This chapter investigates the determinants of the level of interest rates, the fluctuations of interest rates over the business cycle, and the relationship between the market rate of interest on a security and its market price. The next chapter examines the reasons for differences in interest rates on different securities.

The Level of Interest Rates

Similar to all prices, interest rates are determined by the supply of and demand for the item in question, in this instance financial claims. Because there are many interest rates, it is useful in describing the forces impinging on interest rates to select one rate to serve as more or less representative of all rates. The fewer the unique features of a particular financial claim, the greater are the number of forces affecting its behavior that are common to the forces affecting other securities and the more representative it is. Short-term default-free securities are generally considered to possess the fewest unique features and their rates are commonly used as proxies for the "pure" or "the" rate of interest. On the market place, this is best approximated by the three-month U.S. Treasury bill rate.

The determinants of the level of interest rates can be analyzed in either stock or flow dimensions. The stock dimension—liquidity preference—considers the demand for and supply of the stock of money as an asset at any moment of time, while the flow dimension—loanable funds—considers the renting of money or the demand for and supply of financial claims over a period of time.

Liquidity Preference

The demand for and supply of money, defined conventionally as currency and demand deposits, can each be specified as a function of a number of important variables. For the moment neglecting changes in the ratio of currency to demand deposits, the supply of money is jointly determined by the Federal Reserve and the commercial banks. The Federal Reserve provides bank reserves in response to the performance of the economy in relation to its target levels. The greater the amount of total reserves provided, the greater the supply of money. Given legal reserve ratios, the commercial banks can affect the value of the reserve-deposit multiplier by changing their amount of excess reserves.[1] Ceteris paribus, the greater the bank holdings of excess reserves are, the smaller the multiplier and the smaller the amount of money a given amount of reserves can support. As discussed earlier, bank demand for excess reserves is inversely related to the interest rate. Since excess reserves are inversely related to the money supply, the supply of money is directly related to the interest rate. The supply function for money can be written:

$$SM = f(\overset{+}{R}, \overset{+}{i}). \tag{8-1}$$

The relationship, ceteris paribus, between the supply of money and interest rates for a given dollar amount of reserves is plotted in (*a*) of Figure 8-1. The money–interest rate schedule slopes upward and to the right. At higher interest rates, excess reserves are lower, and a greater amount of money is supplied. Increases in reserves provided by the Federal Reserve shift the schedule outward to the right, from R_0 to R_1, and decreases shift it inward to the left. Some economists, as we shall see later, believe that, by offsetting bank changes in excess reserves, the Federal Reserve has complete control of the supply of money and they prefer to draw the money supply schedule perfectly interest inelastic (that is, the money stock does not vary at all in response to changes in the rate of interest), as shown by schedule R' in (*a*).

The demand for money balances by the public was discussed in Chapter 7 and can be summarized in functional form as:

$$DM = f(\overset{+}{y}, \overset{+}{P}, \overset{+}{w}, \overset{-}{i}, \overset{-}{i}_T). \tag{8-2}$$

For the purposes at hand, this relationship can be simplified by transforming y and P into Y (total output in current prices) and temporarily omitting w and i_T. Thus:

$$DM = f(\overset{+}{Y}, \overset{-}{i}). \tag{8-3}$$

The demand for money with respect to interest rates is shown by line Y_0 in Figure 8-1 (*b*). The higher the interest rate, the greater is the opportunity cost of holding non-interest-bearing money balances instead of alternative financial claims, that is, instead of renting money out. In addition, as will be seen later, the higher the

1. The banking system can also attempt to change the total amount of its reserves by changing borrowed reserves. In this analysis, such changes are assumed offsetable by the Federal Reserve and are, thereby, included in changes in total reserves and considered no different than changes in any of the other factors affecting total reserves, which will be discussed in Chapter 10.

Figure 8-1 Interest Rate Determination: The Liquidity Preference Theory

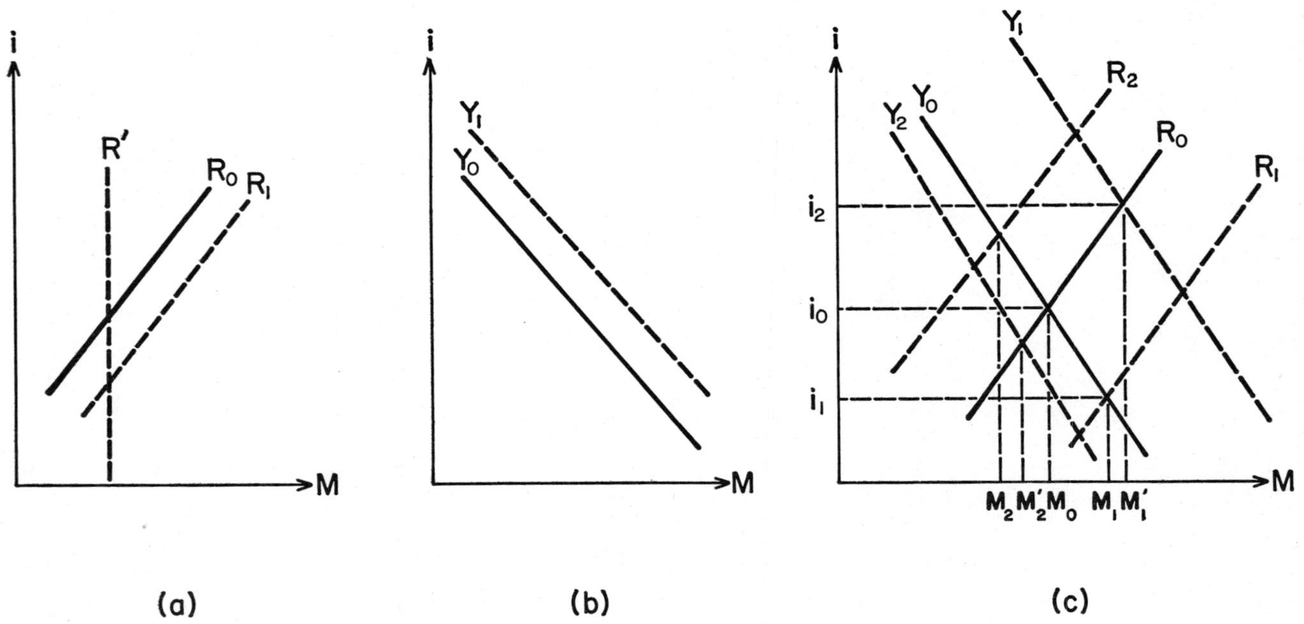

(a)

(b)

(c)

interest rate, the lower is the effective or holding-period yield on money. For both reasons, the higher the interest rate, the smaller is the demand for money by the public at every level of income. Changes in the level of income shift the schedule outward when income increases (Y_1) and inward when income decreases.

In equilibrium $DM = SM$, and equations 8-1 and 8-3 can be solved for the market-clearing interest rate:

$$i = f(\overset{-}{R}, \overset{+}{Y}). \tag{8-4}$$

The equilibrium rate is shown in Figure 8-1 *(c)* by the intersection of demand schedule Y_0 and supply schedule R_0 at i_0 with money stock M_0. An increase in the Federal Reserve supply of reserves from R_0 to R_1 increases the stock of money from M_0 to M_1 and lowers the equilibrium interest rate from i_0 to i_1. An increase in income from Y_0 to Y_1 increases the demand for money and raises the interest rate from i_0 to i_2. At the same time, the amount of money is increased from M_0 to M'_1 as banks respond by reducing excess reserves. The implications for interest rates of decreases in income from Y_0 to Y_2, or decreases in reserves provided by the Fed from R_0 to R_2 can be analyzed similarly.

Loanable Funds

Alternatively, the level of interest rates is determined by the demand for and supply of credit generated by renting money, or the demand for and supply of financial claims on the primary and secondary markets in a particular period of time. This approach is referred to as the *loanable funds theory.* The supply of claims (demand for credit)—both new claims and already outstanding claims—originates with household, business, and government DSUs. These sectors raise funds to finance business investments (*BI*), consumer investments in durable goods (*CI*), consumer nondurable credit purchases (*CN*), and deficits in federal government (*FD*) and local government (*LD*) budgets. The demand for claims (supply of credit) originates with the same or different decision units in these sectors. Business firms generate loanable funds through depreciation and retained earnings (*BS*), consumers through personal savings (*CS*) and reducing their money balances (*CM*), and federal (–*FD*) and local governments (*LS*) through generating greater tax revenues than expenditures. In addition, the Federal Reserve can provide additional reserves to increase the stock of money (ΔM). The supply of claims in a period, both individually and in the aggregate, is inversely related to interest rates; the demand for claims is positively related.

To be consistent with the previous analysis, the relationships are plotted in

Figure 8-2 **Interest Rate Determination: The Loanable Funds Theory**

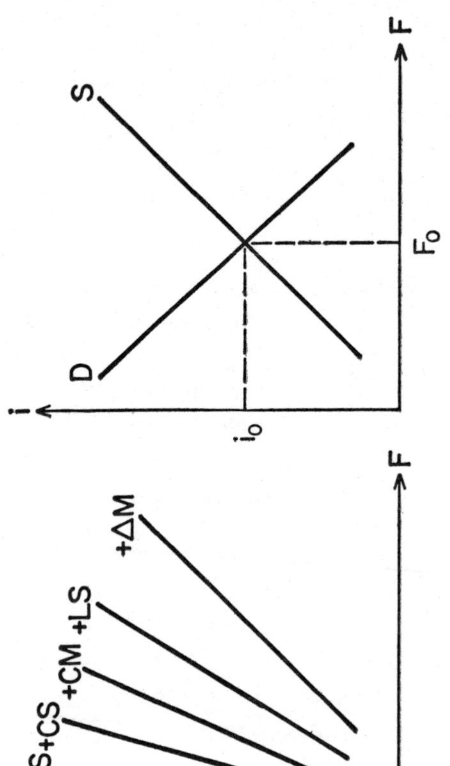

Figure 8-2 as demand and supply schedules for credit funds, not for claims. Thus, the supply schedule for claims is shown as the demand schedule for funds and the demand schedule for claims as the supply of funds. Figure 8-2 (*a*) shows the demand for funds as an inverse function of interest rates assuming that the interest elasticities for all sectors are equal. The schedules are progressively added so that each one farther out to the right shows the total demand for funds from the sectors specified to the left. The schedule farthest to the right shows the overall demand for funds. Likewise, the supply of funds is shown in (*b*). Again the schedule farthest to the right shows the overall supply of additional funds at each interest rate. Equilibrium exists where the total demand for funds is equal to the total supply of funds:

Demand for Funds (Supply of Claims)	Supply of Funds (Demand for Claims)

$$BI + CI + CN + FD + LD = BS + CS + CM + LS + \Delta M. \qquad (8\text{-}5)$$

In (*c*) the equilibrium interest rate is shown by the intersection of the aggregate demand schedule for funds and the aggregate supply schedule of funds at i_0. An increase in the demand for funds by any sector not offset by a decline in another would cause interest rates to rise. An increase in the supply of new funds in any sector not offset by an increase in another would cause interest rates to decline. The Federal Reserve influences the level of interest rates by adding to or subtracting from already outstanding reserves.

Participants in the financial markets generally prefer the loanable funds theory to the liquidity preference theory. Through their daily operations in the market, these participants gain insights into the demands for funds by various sectors and the locations of sources of funds. Frequently, use is made of matrix tables tracing the flows of funds from sources to uses by major sectors and through major channels. One such flow of funds table is prepared and published by the Federal Reserve System and reproduced in part in Table 8-1. These tables serve to identify not only overall pressures on interest rates, but also pressures in individual sectors.

The equilibrium interest rates derived from both the liquidity preference and loanable funds theories are, of necessity, equal. This can be seen by remembering that claims are sold only for money. Money, of course, can be turned over quickly so that a given dollar stock can, over a period of time, generate a multiple amount of credit funds to purchase a larger dollar amount of claims. The amount of funds so created, however, is related to the stock of money at any moment of time in the period. Hence, the two theories represent alternative approaches to analyzing the same phenomenon and generate the same answer.

Table 8-1 **Summary of Flow of Funds Accounts for Year 1970**
(Seasonally adjusted annual rates; in billions of dollars)

	Sector	Private domestic nonfinancial sectors								U.S. Govt.	
		Households		Business		State and local govts.		Total			
	Transaction category	U[2]	S[2]	U	S	U	S	U	S	U	S
1	Gross saving		160.5		82.4		−4.9		238.0		−13.2
2	Capital consumption		91.2		71.9				163.1		
3	Net saving (1–2)		69.3		10.5		−4.9		74.9		−13.2
4	Gross investment (5+10)	159.8		79.6		−4.9		234.5		−10.3	
5	Private capital expenditures	113.4		109.9				223.3			
6	Consumer durables	89.4						89.4			
7	Residential construction	18.6		11.1				29.7			
8	Plant and equipment	5.5		95.2				100.7			
9	Inventory change			3.6				3.6			
10	Net financial investment (11−12)	46.4		−30.3		−4.9		11.2		−10.3	
11	Financial uses	66.8		23.8		7.7		98.3		5.1	
12	Financial sources		20.4		54.1		12.7		87.2		15.4
13	Gold, SDR's, and official fgn. exchange									−2.0	
14	Treasury currency and SDR ctfs.										.6
15	Demand deposits and currency										
16	Private domestic	3.3		1.1		.9		5.3			
17	U.S. Government									2.5	
18	Foreign										
19	Time and savings accounts	34.5						56.4			
20	At commercial banks	17.9		12.8		9.1		39.8		.2	
21	At savings institutions	16.6						16.6			
22	Life insurance reserves	4.9						4.9			.1
23	Pension fund reserves	17.5						17.5			2.3
24	Interbank items										
25	Corporate shares	−1.1			6.7			−1.1	6.7		
26	Other credit market instru.	8.2	21.3	1.9	39.7	−2.7	12.2	7.4	73.1	3.3	12.7
27	U.S. Government securities	−5.3		1.7		−3.1		−6.8		.1	12.7
28	State and local obligations	−1.5		.4		.3	11.8	−.9	11.8		
29	Corporate and foreign bonds	12.6			21.3	.2		12.7	21.3		
30	Home mortgages	.5	12.6		.1	°		.5	12.7	−.1	°
31	Other mortgages	2.0	1.4		10.5			2.0	11.9	.4	
32	Consumer credit		4.3	1.9				1.9	4.3		
33	Bank loans n.e.c.		.3		.9				1.2		
34	Other loans		2.7	−2.0	6.9		.4	−2.0	10.0	2.9	
35	Security credit	−.6	−1.8					−.6	−1.8		
36	To brokers and dealers	−.6						−.6			
37	To others		−1.8						−1.8		

Financial sectors										Rest of the world		All sectors		Discrep-ancy	Natl. savings and invest-ment	
Total		Sponsored credit agencies		Mone-tary auth.		Coml.[1] banks		Pvt. nonbank finance								
U	S	U	S	U	S	U	S	U	S	U	S	U	S	U		
	3.7		.1		.1		3.0		.5		−.7		227.8		228.5	1
	1.6						.9		.7				164.7		164.7	2
	2.1		.1		.1		2.2		−.2		−.7		63.1		63.8	3
3.4		*		.1		3.2		.2		.8		228.4		−.6	224.5	4
1.9						1.1		.8				225.2		2.6	225.2	5
												89.4			89.4	6
												29.7			29.7	7
1.9						1.1		.8				102.6			102.6	8
												3.6			3.6	9
1.5		*		.1		2.1		−.7		.8		3.2		−3.2	−.8	10
107.8		9.9		5.2		41.9		50.9		6.1		217.4			5.4	11
	106.3		9.8		5.1		39.8		51.6		5.4		214.2		6.1	12
−1.4				−1.4						.8	−2.5	−2.5	−2.5			13
.7				.7								.7	.6	−.1		14
	8.9				2.5		6.4					9.0	8.9			15
.9	6.4	*			2.9		3.4	.9				6.2	6.4	.1		16
	2.3				−.4		2.7					2.5	2.3	−.3		17
	.3				*		.3			.3			.3			18
.7	55.4							.7					55.4			19
	38.0						38.0			−1.9			38.0			20
.7	17.3							.7	17.3				17.3			21
	4.8								4.8				4.9			22
	15.2								15.2				17.5			23
3.0	3.0			.9	2.2	2.1	.7					3.0	3.0			24
10.3	3.2						*	10.3	3.2	.7	*		9.8			25
78.1	9.5	8.8	7.6	5.0		27.5	−1.8	36.8	3.7	9.4	2.9		98.2			26
18.6	7.6	1.5	7.6	5.0		8.2		3.9		8.4			20.3			27
12.7						11.2		1.5					11.8			28
11.3	2.1					.5	*	10.7	2.1	.5	1.1		24.5			29
12.9	.6	4.2				.9		7.8	.6				13.3			30
9.5		.8				1.0		7.7					11.9			31
2.5						1.9		.6					4.3			32
.6	−.2					.6			−.2		−.4		.6			33
10.1	−.7	2.3		*		3.2	−1.9	4.6	1.2	.5	2.2		11.5			34
.4	1.5					1.8		−1.4	1.5	−.2	−.1		−.4			35
2.3	1.5					2.3			1.5	−.2			1.5			36
−1.9						−.5		−1.4			−.1		−1.9			37

Table 8-1 (Continued)

Transaction category / Sector	Households[1]		Business		State and local govts.		Total		U.S. Govt.	
	Private domestic nonfinancial sectors									
	U[2]	S[2]	U	S	U	S	U	S	U	S
38 Taxes payable				1.6	.3		.3	1.6	1.4	
39 Trade credit		.6	6.9	7.1		.5	6.9	8.1	−.7	−.9
40 Equity in noncorporate business	−2.3			−2.3			−2.3	−2.3		
41 Miscellaneous claims	2.5	.4	1.1	1.3			3.6	1.7	.4	.5
42 Sector discrepancies (1−4)	.6		2.8		*		3.5		−2.9	

[1]Commercial banks and unconsolidated affiliates.

[2]U stands for Uses; S for Sources.

*Less than .1.

Source: *Federal Reserve Bulletin*, March, 1971, p. A 70.

Price Expectations

While the liquidity preference and the loanable funds theories both generate the same equilibrium interest rate, they both also fail to include a determinant that has become increasingly important in recent years. Loan contracts are typically denominated in nominal terms. At maturity, the borrower promises to repay the lender the same nominal amount of dollars he borrowed earlier. However, as he has loaned command over purchasing power, the lender is interested not so much in receiving back the same amount of dollars as he is in receiving back control over the same amount of purchasing power. Likewise, the borrower secured a sum of money generating a given amount of purchasing power and is prepared to return to the lender control over the same amount of purchasing power.

If commodity prices do not change between the origination and maturity of the loan, the same amount of dollars will generate the same amount of purchasing power at maturity as at origination. However, if the price level changes during the loan contract, the same amount of dollars will generate a different amount of purchasing power. An increase in prices during the life of the loan will decrease the purchasing power of the dollars, while a decrease in prices will increase the purchasing power. It is in the interests of both parties to the loan contract to protect themselves against either repaying or being repaid purchasing power in a different amount than was initially transferred. Protection against such a risk can be incorporated in the interest rate on the loan.[2] If prices rise, interest rates can be increased by an amount corresponding to the percentage of depreciation

2. Although not analyzed in this book, an alternative form of protection against changes in purchasing power is the purchasing power bond. The maturity value of this bond varies directly with the commodity price level.

Financial sectors										Rest of the world		All sectors		Discrep-ancy	Natl. savings and invest-ment	
Total		Sponsored credit agencies		Mone-tary auth.		Coml.[1] banks		Pvt. nonbank finance								
U	S	U	S	U	S	U	S	U	S	U	S	U	S	U		
	.1				*		.1		*			1.7	1.7	*		38
.4								.4		1.0	.7	7.6	7.9	.3		39
													−2.3			40
14.7	4.8	1.1	.6		.4	10.5	−3.7	3.2	5.9	−4.0	4.4	14.7	11.4	−3.3		41
.3						−.1		.4		−1.5		−.6		−.6	4.0	42

in the purchasing power value of the nominal dollars. If prices fall, interest rates can be reduced by an amount equal to the percentage of appreciation in the value of money. If purchasing power protection is sought through interest rates, the observed or market interest rate will reflect accurately the reward for postponing consumption only during periods of no change in prices. We shall designate the equilibrium interest rate during periods of no change in prices as the *real interest rate.*

The effectiveness of interest rates in protecting against purchasing power changes during the life of a loan can be best demonstrated through a simple numerical example. Assume an equilibrium interest rate of 5 percent. At the maturity of a one-year loan, the lender receives $105 for every $100 lent. If prices did not change during the year, this represents an increase of $5 in purchasing power, which is his reward for abstaining from consumption during the period. Now, let prices rise by 3 percent in the next year. If the interest rate were unchanged, the lender would still receive $105 at maturity. However, the purchasing power of this amount, in terms of the dollars loaned, would be only about $102 ($105.00 − .03 × $105.00 = $101.85) and the effective interest rate only about 2 percent. The borrower would have experienced a windfall equivalent to the lender's loss. The lender can guard against such a loss in purchasing power by adding to the interest rate he charges an amount approximately equal to the percent increase in prices during the period, in this instance 3 percent. More precisely, the increase in interest rate should compensate for the loss in purchasing power of both the principal ($100.00 × .03 = $3.00) and the interest ($5.00 × .03 = $0.15) and would be equal to 3.15 percent. As long as the price change is small, the adjustment for the interest payment is small in relation to that for the principal and is commonly neglected. At the new 8 percent rate of interest, the lender would receive \$108 at maturity which, however, would have a purchasing power equal to only about \$105 in terms of the purchasing power of dollars at the origination of the loan.

Alternatively, let prices fall by 3 percent during the year. The \$105 repaid at maturity now represents purchasing power of about \$108 in terms of dollars at the beginning of the year. This would be a purchasing power gain to the lender of some \$3 more than he had expected and a loss to the borrower of the same amount. In this case, the borrower would be willing to borrow only at an interest rate that adjusts for the gain in purchasing power. This rate would be approximately equivalent to the real rate of interest less the percent decrease in prices, or 5% − 3% = 2%. The borrower would repay only \$102 which, however, would be equivalent to \$105 in constant purchasing power. Although it would appear from this analysis that if the price decline were greater than 5 percent, the interest rate would turn negative, this will not be the case. A lender would always be better off holding on to his dollars at 0 percent interest than lending them at a negative rate.

The above analysis indicates that complete protection against price changes is achieved when the observed nominal, or market, interest rate charged is equivalent to the sum of the real rate of interest, or the rate that would exist in the absence of any price changes, and the percent change in prices. This can be written:[3]

$$i = r + \dot{P}, \qquad (8\text{-}6)$$

where:

i = observed nominal rate of interest
r = real rate of interest
$\dot{P}$ = percentage change in commodity prices $= \dfrac{P_{t+1} - P_t}{P_t}$.

Note that this equation relates the nominal interest rate to the percentage rate of price change, not to the level of prices. Thus, in the previous example with a real interest rate of 5 percent, an increase in the rate of price change from 0 to 3 percent increases the equilibrium nominal rate from 5 to 8 percent. If prices

3. This equation is an approximation derived from:

$$\begin{aligned}(1 + i) &= (1 + r)(1 + \dot{P}) \\ &= 1 + r + r\dot{P} + \dot{P} \\ i &= r + \dot{P} + r\dot{P}.\end{aligned}$$

If either or both r and P are small, rP is very small and approximates 0 and

$$i = r + \dot{P}.$$

Table 8-2 Price Changes and Nominal Rates of Interest
(Percent)

Time Period	Real Rate	Price Change	Nominal Rate
1	5	0	5
2	5	3	8
3	5	3	8
4	5	6	11
5	5	3	8
6	5	1	6
7	5	0	5
8	5	−3	2
9	5	−6	0

continue to rise at 3 percent annually, the nominal interest rate will not increase further unless the real rate changes. The 8 percent annual rate of interest will provide for a 5 percent real rate and protection against a continued annual 3 percent decline in purchasing power because in each case the new loan is made with dollars which include the previous change in purchasing power. If prices continue to rise, but at a slower annual rate, say 1 percent, the nominal interest rate in the next period will decline from 8 to 6 percent. The nominal interest rate will become greater only if the rate of price increases becomes greater. Equilibrium changes in nominal interest rates consistent with changes in the rate of price change in a period are shown in Table 8-2. Note that if prices decline, the nominal rate will be below the real rate by the rate of price decline. However, the nominal rate will never decline below zero regardless of the rate of price decline.

Expected Price Changes

To this point, we have assumed that we knew what the actual rate of price change would be in the loan period. But this is not known at the time a loan contract originates. Lenders and borrowers only have expectations of price changes in the period covered by the loan. The negotiated interest rate is based on expected price changes. To predict interest rates, it is therefore necessary to first predict price changes. Like expectations of any kind, individuals' expectations of prices cannot be observed directly. One method of measuring expectations is to survey market participants. However, the results of such surveys have not proven very reliable for price changes.

At the turn of the twentieth century, Professor Irving Fisher, one of the first American economists to gain a worldwide reputation, speculated that if, as appears reasonable, decision-making units base their predictions or expectations in large measure on past observations, one should be able to measure predictions by simulating this process. He assumed that expectations of price changes were based with declining importance on past observations of price changes, thusly:

$$\dot{P}_{E_t} = a_1\dot{P}_{t-1} + a_2\dot{P}_{t-2} + \cdots + a_n\dot{P}_{t-n}, \tag{8-7}$$

where:

$\dot{P}_E$ = expectations of percent rate of price change
$\dot{P}$ = actual percent rate of price change
a = weight given each price change.

The a's would decline, the more distant the price observation. While all the price values ($\dot{P}$) on the right side of the equation can be observed, the a's cannot. Summing the right side of the equation yields:

$$\dot{P}_{E_t} = \sum_{m=1}^{n} a_m\dot{P}_{t-m}. \tag{8-8}$$

To solve for $\dot{P}_E$, it is first necessary to obtain values for the a's. Fisher did this by assuming the following interest rate equation:

$$i = r + \dot{P}_E, \tag{8-9}$$

in which the ex post or actual rate of change in price in equation 8-6 is replaced by the expected rate of change. Substituting equation 8-8 into 8-9 yields:

$$i = r + \sum_{m=1}^{n} a_m\dot{P}_{t-m}. \tag{8-10}$$

If one assumes that the real rate of interest does not change greatly in the short run, it can be replaced by a constant term (b). The resulting equation can be written in linear form as:

$$i = b + \sum_{m=1}^{n} a_m\dot{P}_{t-m}. \tag{8-11}$$

Fisher experimented with a number of variations of equation 8-11 for long-term interest rates in the United States and the United Kingdom and estimated values of a that declined only slowly over a long period of time. He found that observations as distant as 30 years earlier entered into the process of formulating long-term price expectations. As a result, one-half of the ultimate adjustment in interest rates to changes in price expectations occurred only after 10 years. This suggests that for all practical purposes nominal interest rates never fully adjust to changes in price expectations as suggested in our example.

However, some more recent studies conducted at the Federal Reserve Bank of St. Louis for the post–World War II period have generated evidence of shorter lags, with one-half of the ultimate adjustment in interest rates occurring in less than two years. Evidence of quicker, although still partial, adjustment of interest rates to price expectations has also recently been generated from studies using data on price expectations obtained from a survey of a panel of financial officers. The recent evidence suggests that expectations of price increases may need to exceed some minimum threshold level for investors to incorporate these expectations in interest rates fully and promptly. In addition, equation 8-11 may generate inaccurate measures of the speed and the degree of adjustment at times expectations are based to a considerable extent on forces other than past price changes.

The Real Rate of Interest

As will be discussed in later chapters, in the longer run, investment decisions of both households and business firms are based primarily on real rates of interest, not on market rates. Thus, knowledge of this rate is important. However, except at times when prices are not expected to change so price expectations are zero, this rate cannot be observed directly. The rate of interest that is observed in the market is the nominal rate. As a result, values of the real rate must be obtained indirectly.

One procedure for estimating the real rate is to compute the price-expectations adjustment and subtract it from the observed interest rate. By equation 8-9, the remainder is the real rate. Estimates of the real rate for the decade of the 1960s were derived by the researchers at the Federal Reserve Bank of St. Louis using a procedure for generating the price-expectations effect based on the Fisher equation. The observed nominal and estimated real rates are reproduced in Figure 8-3. This figure shows that the major variations in observed interest rates during the 1960s are attributed to changes in price expectations and only little to other changes in demand and supply. As is evident from the behavior of the real rate, the reward for postponing consumption remained relatively constant during this period.

These estimates, however, assume both that expectations are measured correctly and that they were realized. The difficulties in measuring expectations have already been noted. As all of us are aware from personal experience, expectations are not always realized. Thus, even if expectations were measured accurately, the computed ex post real rate may differ from the ex ante real rate or the real rate that decision-makers thought existed at the time. Assuming that interest rates

Figure 8-3 **Nominal and Estimated Real Long-Term Rates of Interest on High Grade Corporate Bonds**

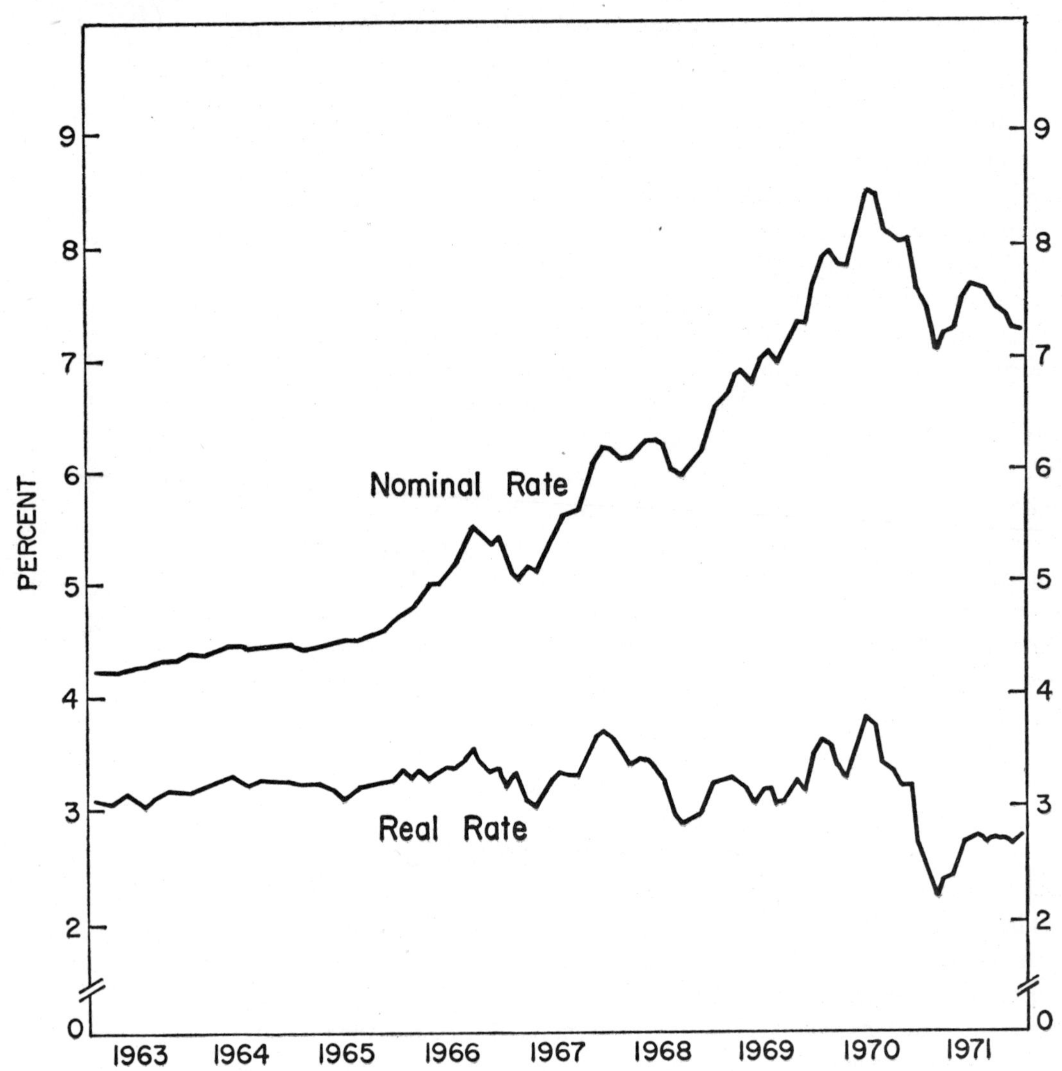

Source: Federal Reserve Bank of St. Louis.

adjust fully and promptly to price expectations, if decision-makers expected prices to rise 5 percent this year, or 2 percent faster than last year when the observed interest rate was 6 percent, they would have predicted an interest rate of 8 percent. At the same time, they would have predicted a real rate of 3 percent and based their actions on this expected rate. Assume that the predicted 8 percent rate of interest actually occurred, but that prices increased 6 percent, rather than 5 percent, during the year. The computed ex post real rate would then be only 2 percent and would probably not help others to explain greatly the observed actions of decision-makers. They may wonder why businessmen did not invest more than they did. Nevertheless, estimates of price expectations are useful in predicting nominal interest rate changes.

Thus, the specifications derived earlier for both the liquidity preference and loanable funds theories are incomplete. They are valid only when market participants do not expect changes in commodity prices, that is, when their price expectations are zero. At these times, the nominal and real rates of interest are one and the same. At times when price expectations are not zero, the two rates are not equal and any theory of market rates must include information on price expectations. This information can be incorporated in the liquidity preference theory by expanding equation 8-4 to read:

$$i = f(\overset{-}{R}, \overset{+}{Y}, \overset{+}{\dot{P}_E}). \tag{8-12}$$

Behavior of Interest Rates Over the Business Cycle

Movements in interest rates on short- and long-term securities are plotted for the postwar period in Figure 8-4. Superimposed on the figure is the business cycle. Periods in which economic activity contracted are shaded. Movements in interest rates closely follow the business cycle, rising during periods in which economic activity expands and declining during periods in which economic activity contracts. (The decline in interest rates in 1967 accompanied a slowing in economic activity, which is not considered sufficiently severe to officially classify as a recession.) This pattern is predicted by equation 8-12. During periods of business expansion, the Federal Reserve may reasonably be expected to slow the rate of reserve provision, the demand for funds to increase, and price expectations to be revised upwards. All three forces act to exert upward pressure on interest rates. During periods of business contraction, the opposite forces dominate. Interest rates decline as the Federal Reserve accelerates its provision of reserves, credit demands deteriorate with falling income, and prices are expected to increase at a slower pace if at all.

The cyclical movements of interest rates are not smooth. A great number of short-run forces, particularly seasonal forces, are superimposed on the cyclical forces and contribute to the irregular movements in rates. Nevertheless, over time the cyclical forces dominate the more temporary factors. For reasons to be discussed in the next section, short-term rates are more volatile over the cycle than long-term rates, rising more in periods of expansion and declining further in recessions.

Figure 8-4 Movements in Interest Rates Over the Business Cycle

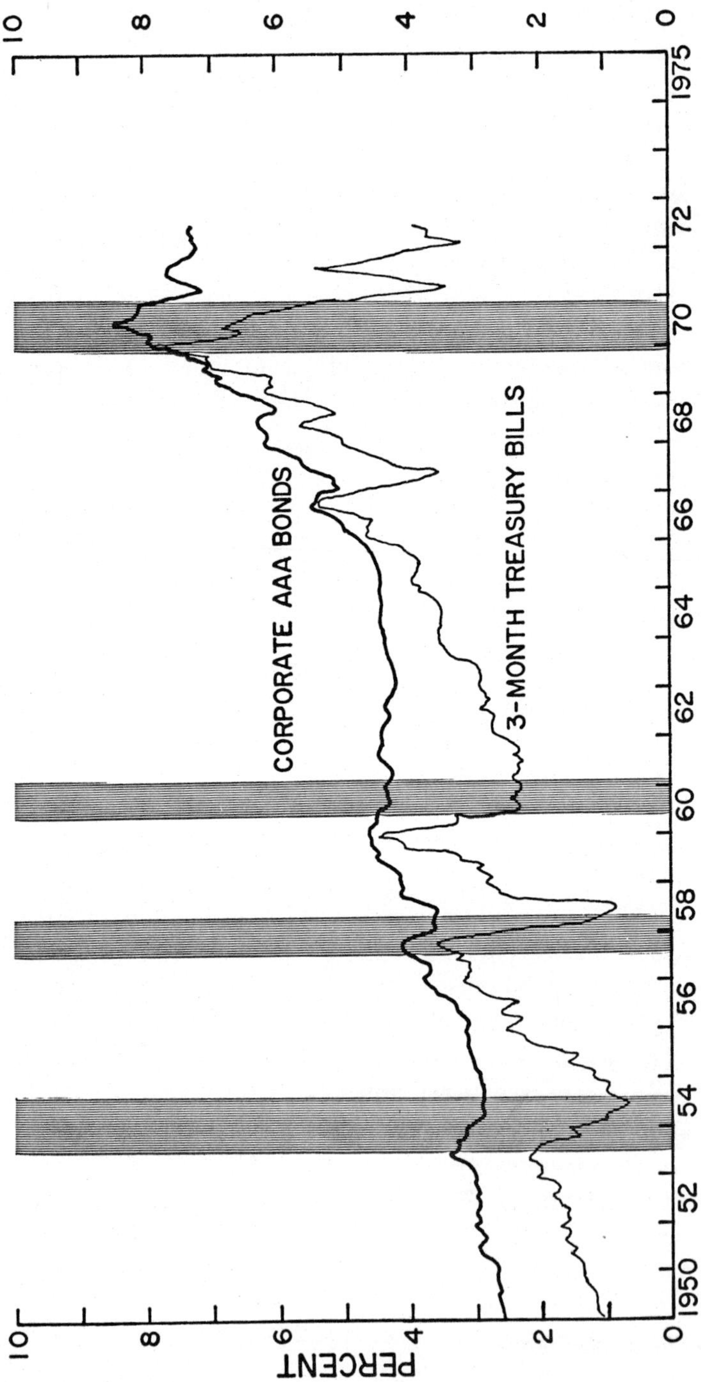

Shaded areas indicate periods of business recession.

Source: Federal Reserve Bank of St. Louis.

The Mathematics of Interest Rates and Bond Prices

Debt securities are typically issued with a promised, fixed par or maturity value and a promised, fixed periodic coupon payment. The coupon rate is computed by:

$$c = C/A, \tag{8-13}$$

where:

c = coupon interest rate
C = annual dollar coupon payment
A = par or maturity value of the bond.

At the time of issue, the coupon rate on a bond sold at par must approximate the market rate of interest in order for the bond to be marketed successfully at the lowest cost to the DSU. As market rates of interest change through time, so does the market price of the outstanding bond. For all marketable bonds, a strict relationship exists between coupon rate, market interest rate, and market price. This relationship is easiest to analyze for a bond that does not have a maturity date. Perpetual bonds, called *consols*, are similar in nature to a continuous income annuity and common in a number of European countries. For a consol, the following relationship exists:

$$PB = C/i, \tag{8-14}$$

where:

PB = market price of the bond
i = market or nominal rate of interest.

Likewise:

$$i = C/PB. \tag{8-15}$$

Equations 8-14 and 8-15 indicate that market price and market interest rate vary inversely. When market interest rates rise, market prices fall, and vice versa. Consider a \$100 default-free consol with a 4 percent coupon rate. If issued at par, the market interest rate must also have been 4 percent. If, subsequently, market interest rates increase to 5 percent, the market price of the bond declines to \$80. By equation 8-14:

$$PB = C/i = \$4/.05 = \$80.$$

This is the correct market price because an investor would only buy the bond at the same interest rate he could obtain on new bonds. To obtain a 5 percent yield on a bond generating $4.00 annually, he would be willing to pay only $80. If market interest rates declined to 3 percent, the market price of the consol would climb to $133.33. If the market interest rate is above the coupon rate, the bond sells at a *discount* from par value. If the market interest rate is below the coupon rate, the market price of the bond is above its par value and it sells at a *premium.*

In this country bonds typically have maturity dates. While this does not change the general relationship between coupon rate, market interest rate, and market price determined above, it does complicate the computation of the relationship somewhat. Consider a bond with 20 years remaining to maturity, an annual coupon payment of $4.00, and selling at $88. What is its market interest rate, now defined as the promised yield to maturity? It is not given by equation 8-15 because at maturity the investor receives $100, or $12 above his purchase price. Accepted accounting practice amortizes this gain over the remaining 20-year life of the bond at approximately $.60 per year. Thus, the effective or accounting annual dollar return would be increased from $4.00 to $4.60, although the $.60 would not be received until the maturity or sale of the bond. To compute the return on the investment, it is necessary to consider the average value of the investment during the holding period, not just its purchase price. If held to maturity, this would be approximated by the average of the buying and maturity prices, or $94.00. The resulting yield on the bond, if held to maturity, is $4.60/$94.00, or close to 5 percent (4.89 percent). This series of computations can be summarized in equation form as:

$$i=\frac{C+\frac{A-PB}{n}}{\frac{A+PB}{2}}, \qquad (8\text{-}16)$$

where:

n = number of years to maturity
PB = market price at time of purchase
A = maturity (selling) price.

Equation 8-15 for consols is a special case of equation 8-16 in which n approaches infinity and A is effectively equal to PB.

Equation 8-16 can be solved for PB:

$$PB=\frac{A(1-\frac{ni}{2})+Cn}{1+\frac{ni}{2}}. \qquad (8\text{-}17)$$

Thus, if the market interest rate on a 20-year-to-maturity $100 bond with a 4 percent coupon were 5 percent, its market price according to equation 8-17 would be $86.67. The difference between this price and our original $88.00 results from the use of 5 percent as the market interest rate rather than 4.89 percent.

Equations 8-16 and 8-17 only approximate the true relationship between coupon rate, maturity, market interest rate, and market price. As bonds involve promises to make future payments, the exact relationship considers the present value of these payments. Bonds generate two future payments: (1) the final maturity payment, and (2) a continuous stream of coupon payments. The present value of any future payment is equal to an amount, which, if invested today at current interest rates, would expand to the amount of the future payment. Present values are the prices one would pay today for promised payments in the future, and are computed by discounting the amount of the future payments by the current or expected market rate of interest:

$$PV = \frac{Q}{(1+i)^n}, \tag{8-18}$$

where:

PV = present value
Q = amount of payment
n = number of periods to payment.

The present value of the par value (A) of a bond is:

$$PV_A = \frac{A}{(1+i)^m}, \tag{8-19}$$

where:

m = number of periods to maturity.

Diagrammatically, this can be shown as a linear scale on which the present value of A dollars paid in future period m is reduced by $(1+i)$ for each period closer to the present period (0). On the scale, each space represents a period. The present period is designated as zero and the period of payment as m. The present value in each period of the A dollars paid in period m is shown at the top of the scale and the periods are identified at the bottom.

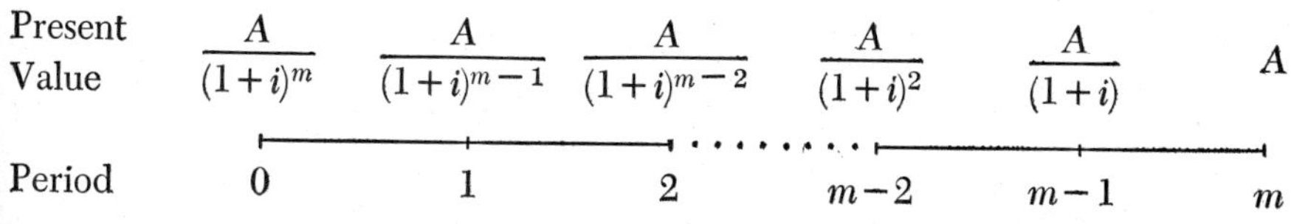

Present Value	$\frac{A}{(1+i)^m}$	$\frac{A}{(1+i)^{m-1}}$	$\frac{A}{(1+i)^{m-2}}$	$\frac{A}{(1+i)^2}$	$\frac{A}{(1+i)}$	A
Period	0	1	2	$m-2$	$m-1$	m

It follows that the shorter the number of periods to maturity or the lower the interest rate, the greater the present value of a given future amount.

The present value of the coupon payments is equivalent to the present value of an annuity yielding C dollars each period until period m. Diagrammatically, this can be shown as a series of scales similar to the one for the maturity payment but viewing each coupon payment received in periods 1 through m separately:

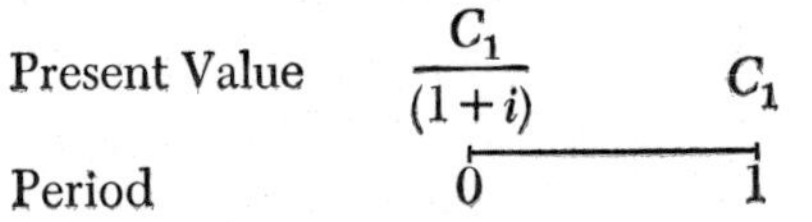

Present Value	$\frac{C_1}{(1+i)}$	C_1			
Period	0	1			

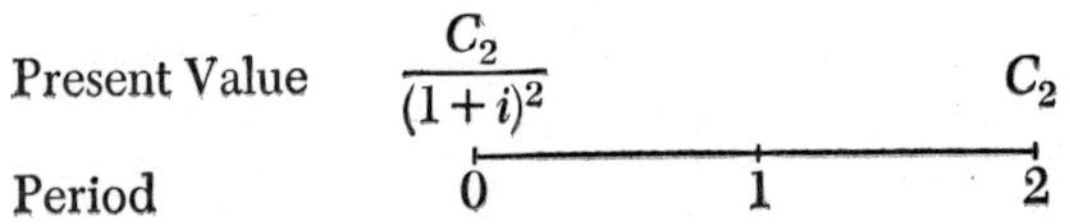

Present Value	$\frac{C_2}{(1+i)^2}$		C_2		
Period	0	1	2		

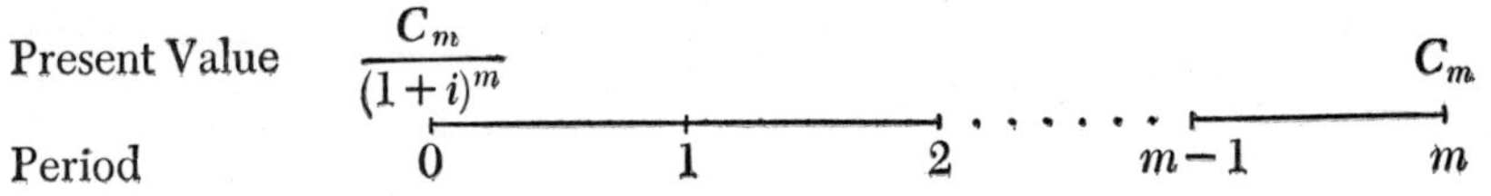

Present Value	$\frac{C_m}{(1+i)^m}$				C_m
Period	0	1	2	$m-1$	m

and arithmetically:

$$PV_C = \frac{C_1}{(1+i)} + \frac{C_2}{(1+i)^2} + \cdots + \frac{C_n}{(1+i)^m}. \tag{8-20}$$

If

$$C_1 = C_2 = \cdots = C_m,$$

equation 8-20 can be summarized as:

$$PV_C = \sum_{n=1}^{m} PV_{C_n}. \tag{8-21}$$

The present value of the total payments (PV_B), which is the price of the bond, is the sum of the present value of the maturity payment and the present value of the coupon payments:

$$PB = PV_B = \frac{C_1}{(1+i)} + \frac{C_2}{(1+i)^2} + \cdots + \frac{C_n}{(1+i)^m} + \frac{A}{(1+i)^m}, \tag{8-22}$$

or

$$PB = PV_A + \sum_{n=1}^{m} PV_{C_n} = PV_A + PV_C. \tag{8-23}$$

This is the price one would pay to buy an *n* period bond of par value *A* with annual coupon payments of *C* at current market interest rates *i*. In the above example of a 20-year bond with a par value of $100 and annual coupon payments of $4.00, a market interest rate of 5 percent would generate a present value of $87.54. From equation 8-19, the present value of $100 paid in 20 years discounted at the market interest rate of 5 percent is $37.69. From equation 8-20, the present value of annual $4.00 payments for 20 years discounted at 5 percent is $49.85. Thus:

$$PB = \$37.69 + \$49.85 = \$87.54.$$

This is not too greatly different from the price computed earlier by the approximate method. The price one would pay for the promise of a sum of $180.00 in the future is thus less than one-half of the ultimate payments. The higher the market rate of interest is, the lower the present value, and thus the lower the market price of an outstanding bond.

It may be noted that this method of computation assumes both that all coupon payments are reinvested and that they are reinvested at a rate of interest equal to the rate in effect when the bond was purchased. If the coupon payments are spent for other purposes, the effective yield of the bond is reduced as the interest on the reinvestment, the compound interest, is withdrawn. If the payments are reinvested but, because of a change in interest rates, at a rate different from the initial rate, the yield realized on the security will be either greater or less than the computed promised yield.

Equation 8-22 can, of course, be transposed to solve for *i* knowing *P*. Fortunately, it is not necessary to use either the exact or the approximate method of computing the market price of a bond. These computations are all available from published bond tables generated by the precise method. If one knows four of the five necessary features of a bond, *C*, *i*, *A*, *m*, or *PB*, one can read the remaining feature from the bond table. A page of a bond table pertinent to the bond in our example is reproduced as Table 8-3. The page applies to all bonds with 4 percent coupon rates. The price of our bond is obtained by going down the 20-year column to the 5 percent market yield row. The price is shown as $87.45 per $100.00. This is slightly less than the price computed above. The difference arises because interest on bonds is typically compounded semiannually, not annually as in the previous example, and this practice is incorporated in the bond tables.

Table 8-3 Bond Table

4% **YEARS** and MONTHS

Yield	18·6	19·0	19·6	20·0	20·6	21·0	21·6	22·0
2.00	130.80	131.48	132.16	132.83	133.50	134.16	134.81	135.46
2.20	127.24	127.83	128.42	129.00	129.57	130.14	130.70	131.26
2.40	123.79	124.30	124.80	125.30	125.79	126.27	126.75	127.22
2.60	120.46	120.89	121.31	121.73	122.14	122.55	122.95	123.34
2.80	117.23	117.59	117.94	118.28	118.62	118.96	119.29	119.61
3.00	114.12	114.40	114.68	114.96	115.23	115.50	115.76	116.02
3.20	111.10	111.32	111.54	111.75	111.96	112.16	112.37	112.57
3.40	108.19	108.35	108.50	108.66	108.81	108.95	109.10	109.24
3.60	105.37	105.47	105.57	105.67	105.76	105.86	105.95	106.04
3.80	102.64	102.69	102.74	102.78	102.83	102.88	102.92	102.96
4.00	100.00	100.00	100.00	100.00	100.00	100.00	100.00	100.00
4.20	97.45	97.40	97.36	97.31	97.27	97.23	97.19	97.15
4.40	94.97	94.89	94.80	94.72	94.63	94.55	94.48	94.40
4.60	92.58	92.45	92.33	92.21	92.09	91.98	91.86	91.75
4.80	90.26	90.10	89.94	89.79	89.64	89.49	89.34	89.20
5.00	88.02	87.83	87.63	87.45	87.27	87.09	86.92	86.75
5.10	86.93	86.72	86.51	86.31	86.11	85.92	85.74	85.55
5.20	85.85	85.62	85.40	85.19	84.98	84.78	84.58	84.38
5.30	84.79	84.55	84.32	84.09	83.87	83.65	83.44	83.23
5.40	83.75	83.49	83.25	83.01	82.77	82.54	82.32	82.10
5.50	82.72	82.46	82.19	81.94	81.69	81.45	81.22	80.99
5.60	81.71	81.43	81.16	80.90	80.64	80.39	80.14	79.91
5.70	80.72	80.43	80.14	79.87	79.60	79.34	79.08	78.84
5.80	79.74	79.44	79.14	78.86	78.58	78.31	78.04	77.79
5.90	78.78	78.47	78.16	77.86	77.57	77.29	77.02	76.76
6.00	77.83	77.51	77.19	76.89	76.59	76.30	76.02	75.75
6.10	76.90	76.57	76.24	75.92	75.62	75.32	75.03	74.75
6.20	75.98	75.64	75.30	74.98	74.67	74.36	74.06	73.78
6.30	75.08	74.73	74.38	74.05	73.73	73.42	73.11	72.82
6.40	74.19	73.83	73.48	73.14	72.81	72.49	72.18	71.88
6.50	73.32	72.95	72.59	72.24	71.90	71.58	71.26	70.95
6.60	72.46	72.08	71.71	71.36	71.01	70.68	70.36	70.05
6.70	71.61	71.22	70.85	70.49	70.14	69.80	69.47	69.16
6.80	70.77	70.38	70.00	69.63	69.28	68.93	68.60	68.28
6.90	69.95	69.55	69.17	68.79	68.43	68.08	67.75	67.42
7.00	69.14	68.74	68.35	67.97	67.60	67.25	66.91	66.58
7.10	68.35	67.94	67.54	67.15	66.78	66.43	66.08	65.75
7.20	67.56	67.15	66.74	66.36	65.98	65.62	65.27	64.93
7.30	66.79	66.37	65.96	65.57	65.19	64.82	64.47	64.13
7.40	66.03	65.61	65.19	64.80	64.41	64.04	63.69	63.34
7.50	65.29	64.85	64.44	64.04	63.65	63.28	62.92	62.57
7.60	64.55	64.11	63.69	63.29	62.90	62.52	62.16	61.81
7.70	63.82	63.38	62.96	62.55	62.16	61.78	61.42	61.06
7.80	63.11	62.67	62.24	61.83	61.43	61.05	60.68	60.33
7.90	62.41	61.96	61.53	61.12	60.72	60.33	59.97	59.61
8.00	61.71	61.26	60.83	60.41	60.01	59.63	59.26	58.90
8.10	61.03	60.58	60.14	59.72	59.32	58.94	58.56	58.21
8.20	60.36	59.91	59.47	59.05	58.64	58.25	57.88	57.52
8.30	59.70	59.24	58.80	58.38	57.97	57.58	57.21	56.85
8.40	59.05	58.59	58.15	57.72	57.32	56.92	56.55	56.19
8.50	58.41	57.95	57.50	57.08	56.67	56.28	55.90	55.54
8.60	57.78	57.31	56.87	56.44	56.03	55.64	55.26	54.90
8.70	57.15	56.69	56.24	55.81	55.40	55.01	54.63	54.27
8.80	56.54	56.07	55.63	55.20	54.79	54.39	54.02	53.66
8.90	55.94	55.47	55.02	54.59	54.18	53.79	53.41	53.05
9.00	55.34	54.88	54.43	54.00	53.58	53.19	52.81	52.45
9.20	54.18	53.71	53.26	52.83	52.42	52.03	51.65	51.29
9.40	53.05	52.58	52.13	51.70	51.29	50.90	50.53	50.17
9.60	51.96	51.49	51.04	50.61	50.20	49.81	49.44	49.08
9.80	50.90	50.43	49.98	49.55	49.14	48.75	48.38	48.03
10.00	49.87	49.40	48.95	48.52	48.12	47.73	47.36	47.01

Source: *Expanded Bond Values Tables,* Boston: Financial Publishing Co., 1970, p. 304. Reproduced with permission from Financial Publishing Company.

Short- and Long-Term Interest Rates

The preceding bond price equations have interesting implications for the relationship between short- and long-term rates. For a consol, interest rates and prices vary inversely in close to a one-to-one relationship. A 1 percent increase in interest rates results in approximately a 1 percent decline in price.[4] As the term to maturity is shortened, the percentage change in prices for a given change in interest rates becomes smaller.[5] In the foregoing examples, the market price of a 4 percent coupon consol when market interest rates were 5 percent was computed to be $80, or 20 percent below par. When the maturity was shortened to 20 years, the price increased to $87.45, or only 13 percent lower. The shorter the term to maturity, the closer the market price of the bond fluctuates about the maturity value for a given change in interest rates. Similarly, a given change in the price of a bond, say $20, will generate a greater change in interest rates, the shorter the term to maturity of the bond.

As a general rule, the longer the term to maturity, the wider the price swings and the narrower the interest rate swings. The shorter the term to maturity, the wider the interest rate swings and the narrower the price swings. This explains the greater movements in short-term rates over the business cycle relative to long-term rates shown in Figure 8-4. If prices were plotted, prices on long-term issues would fluctuate more over the cycle than prices on short-term issues.

References

Cagan, Phillip, and Jack M. Guttentag, *Essays on Interest Rates, Volume 1* (New York: National Bureau of Economic Research, 1969).

Conard, Joseph W., *Introduction to the Theory of Interest Rates* (Berkeley: University of California Press, 1963).

First Boston Corporation, *Handbook of the United States Government and Federal Agencies and Related Money Market Instruments* (Boston: 1970).

Fisher, Irving, *The Theory of Interest Rates* (New York: Macmillan, 1930).

Gibson, William E., "Interest Rates and Monetary Policy," *The Journal of Political Economy,* 78 (3), May/June, 1970, 431-455.

Homer, Sidney, *A History of Interest Rates* (New Brunswick, N.J.: Rutgers University Press, 1963).

Van Horne, James C., *Function and Analysis of Capital Market Rates* (Englewood Cliffs, N.J.: Prentice-Hall, 1970).

Yohe, William P., and Denis S. Karnosky, "Interest Rates and Price Level Changes," *Review* (Federal Reserve Bank of St. Louis), 51 (12), December, 1969, 18-38.

---

4. The relationship between changes in interest rates and prices is not strictly one-to-one because of the mathematics of percentages. The same absolute change represents a larger percentage change when it is an increase than a decrease. For example, a $10 change in the price of a bond represents a 10 percent decline in price from $100 to $90 but an 11 percent increase in price from $90 to $100. Because interest rates and bond prices are inversely related, a given percentage increase in interest rates will yield a smaller percentage decline in price, and a given percentage decline in interest rates a larger percentage increase in price.

5. This relationship may not hold for bonds selling at a discount with long terms to maturity.

9 The Structure of Interest Rates

Examination of any newspaper listing of daily market quotations on debt securities indicates that a large number of different interest rates coexist on the financial markets at any one time. The previous chapter identified the determinants of the level of and changes in "the" rate of interest. This chapter examines the differences in interest rates. In particular, this chapter will consider whether these differences can be explained in a systematic fashion or whether they reflect only random forces. If the former, then economic analysis can be used to predict individual interest rates as well as to choose the most profitable opportunities among alternatives.

Differences in interest rates are attributed to differences in the characteristics of their underlying securities. Four factors have been isolated by analysts as being primarily responsible for interest rate differences:

1. term to maturity,
2. risk of default,
3. tax treatment, and
4. marketability.

Each factor will be considered individually.

Term to Maturity

The pattern of interest rates on securities that are identical in all respects but term to maturity is referred to as the *term structure of rates.* Interest rates on Treasury securities on June 30, 1969 are plotted according to the maturity of the

Figure 9-1 **Yields of Treasury Securities, June 30, 1969**

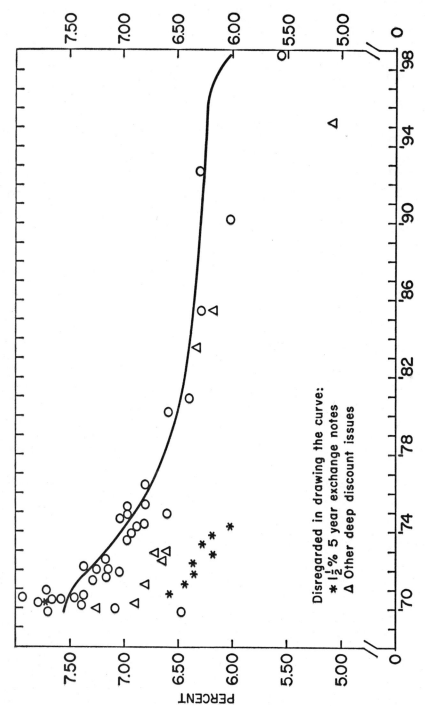

Note: The smooth curve is fitted by eye. Market yields on coupon issues due in less than 3 months are excluded.

Source: U.S. Treasury Department, *Treasury Bulletin*, July, 1969, p. 80.

Figure 9-2 **Yield Curves Vary Through Time**
Yields on United States Government Securities

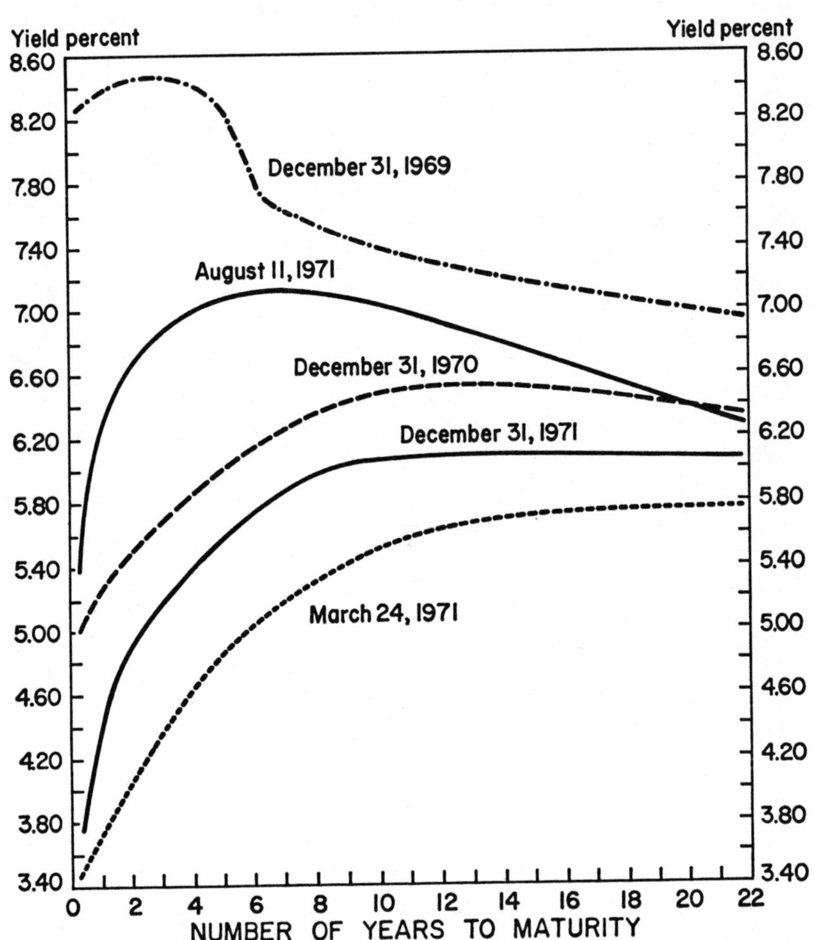

Source: Federal Reserve Bank of New York, *Monthly Review*, 54 (1), January, 1972, p. 11.

security in Figure 9-1. Market rates of interest are measured along the vertical axis and year of maturity along the horizontal axis. A line drawn through the center of these points is called the *yield curve* or *term pattern*. At midyear 1969, interest rates on short-term securities were higher than on long-term securities and the yield curve slopes downward to the right.

The yield curve does not remain constant through time. Yield curves with different slopes are shown in Figure 9-2 for five selected dates in recent years. As can be observed, a year and a half after the downward-sloping yield curve of

Figure 9-1, short-term rates had declined below long-term rates and the curve slopes upward. Three alternative theories attempt to explain both the structure of the yield curve at any time and the changes in the curve through time. These are the unbiased expectations theory, the liquidity premium theory, and the market segmentation theory.

Unbiased Expectations Theory

The unbiased expectations theory postulates that long-term rates reflect the expectations of decision-makers about the future course of short-term interest rates. If all interest payments are reinvested until maturity, the interest return on a long-term security may be viewed as being equal to the return on a series of consecutive short-term securities, whose maturities sum to the maturity of the long-term security. Of course, only the long-term and initial short-term security actually exist. The remaining short-term securities may be viewed as *forward securities*, or contracts to purchase or sell short-term securities at specified dates in the future. Interest rates on forward securities are called *forward rates.*

The reinvestment of all coupon payments upon receipt generates compound interest and involves computing interest on interest. This requires that the interest rate in each period be applied to the sum of the principal and all previous interest payments. For every unit of principal at the beginning of a period, A, an interest rate of R percent generates a sum at the end of the period of $A(1+R)$. In the next period, the ending sum is $[A(1+R)](1+R)$, or $A(1+R)^2$. Unlike simple interest, the compound-interest rate relationship through time is multiplicative rather than additive.

The relationship at time period t between the actual interest rate on a long-term security and the actual and forward interest rates on a consecutive series of current and forward short-term securities summing to the same maturity may be written:

$$(1+{}_tR_n)^n = (1+{}_tR_1)(1+{}_{t+1}r_1)(1+{}_{t+2}r_1)\cdots(1+{}_{t+n-1}r_1), \qquad \textbf{(9-1)}$$

where:

R = observed rate of interest
r = forward rate of interest.

The presubscript identifies the time period in which the security originates, e.g., this period, t, or the next period, $t+1$. The postsubscript identifies the maturity of the security. Thus ${}_tR_n$ denotes the observed interest rate in period t on an existing security with n periods to maturity, and ${}_{t+n}r_1$ denotes the forward interest rate in period t on a security originating in period $t+n$ with one period to maturity. By taking the nth root of both sides of equation 9-1, the long-term rate becomes the geometric average of the current short-term rate and the forward short-term rates:

$$ {}_tR_n = \sqrt[n]{(1+{}_tR_1)(1+{}_{t+1}r_1)(1+{}_{t+2}r_1)\cdots(1+{}_{t+n-1}r_1)} - 1. \quad (9\text{-}2) $$

As a market for forward securities does not exist, the forward interest rate cannot be observed directly. It is possible, however, to compute a forward interest rate that satisfies equation 9-1. Solving equation 9-1 for the forward interest rate in the last period $({}_{t+n-1}r_1)$:

$$ {}_{t+n-1}r_1 = \frac{(1+{}_tR_n)^n}{(1+{}_tR_1)(1+{}_{t+1}r_1)\cdots(1+{}_{t+n-2}r_1)} - 1. \quad (9\text{-}3) $$

It follows from equation 9-1 that:

$$ (1+{}_tR_{n-1})^{n-1} = (1+{}_tR_1)(1+{}_{t+1}r_1)\cdots(1+{}_{t+n-2}r_1). \quad (9\text{-}4) $$

The right side of this equation is equivalent to the denominator of equation 9-3. Substituting the left side of equation 9-4 for the right side in equation 9-3 yields:

$$ {}_{t+n-1}r_1 = \frac{(1+{}_tR_n)^n}{(1+{}_tR_{n-1})^{n-1}} - 1. \quad (9\text{-}5) $$

The forward rate is now computable as the quotient of two observable rates. For the two-period case ($t=1$, $n=2$), this simplifies to:

$$ {}_2r_1 = \frac{(1+{}_1R_2)^2}{(1+{}_1R_1)} - 1. $$

(These equations may be approximated in simpler form by using arithmetic averages. This is done later in equations 9-8 and 9-9.)

Equation 9-5 is a mathematical tautology. By itself, it transmits little meaningful information. At best, the computed forward rate can be interpreted as the forward rate one would accept now on a one-period security originating at $t+n-1$, given ${}_tR_{n-1}$ and ${}_tR_n$. The unbiased expectations theory instills the computed forward interest rate with behavioral properties. This rate is assumed to be the best or unbiased estimate of the rate of interest that the consensus of the market believes will actually exist in the particular future period, m. That is:

$$ {}_{t+m}r_1 = {}_{t+m}\rho_1, \quad (9\text{-}6) $$

where:

$_{t+m}\rho_1$ = unbiased estimate of the one-period rate that will exist in period $t+m$ (the future rate).

Thus, ρ can be substituted for r in equation 9-1.

In addition, the unbiased expectations theory postulates that market participants are motivated only by profit maximization. From this, it follows that, without considering transactions costs, SSUs and DSUs are indifferent to the maturity of the financial claims they buy and sell. SSUs will purchase the combination of securities they expect will generate the highest return over their planned investment or holding period regardless of the composition of the individual maturities. DSUs, on the other hand, will sell the combination of securities they expect will provide the lowest cost over the life of their overall borrowing period regardless of the composite maturities. That is, an investor with funds to invest for two years would be indifferent to buying two successive one-year securities, a two-year security, or a longer-term security which he can sell at the end of two years. Likewise, a borrower who wishes to borrow for a two-year period would be indifferent to selling two successive one-year securities, a two-year security, or a longer security which he can repurchase after two years. The participants would be sensitive only to differences in expected interest rates for the two-year holding period. If one alternative were more profitable than the others, it would be selected. Funds would flow freely through the maturity structure to the most favorable maturity sector. In the process of choosing the most profitable alternative and neglecting the others, the participants would alter the relative prices of the securities and act to equalize the interest returns on all the options for the same holding period. In equilibrium, the expected holding-period yields on all alternative combinations of maturities summing to a given holding period would be equal, where the holding-period yield for holding-period n is defined as:

$$i_n = \frac{\sum_{t=1}^{n} C_t + \sum_{j=1}^{m} \Delta PB_j}{PB_t}, \tag{9-7}$$

where:

C = coupon payment

PB_t = purchase price of the initial security

ΔPB = difference between the purchase and selling prices of the m securities held during the period.

Because the price at which a security will be sold prior to maturity is not known with certainty at the time of purchase, holding-period yields at the time of purchase are only expected returns. In contrast, the observed interest rate on the security is the yield promised at the time of purchase, if the security is held to maturity and all the coupons are reinvested. This rate is referred to as the *yield to maturity.*

The implications of the unbiased expectations theory for the interrelationship of interest rates on securities with different terms to maturity may be seen from a simple two-period example.

Assume: ${}_tR_1 = 2\%$
${}_tR_2 = 3\%$.

Both these rates are observable on the market. We can calculate the expected future one-year rate for the second year from equation 9-5:

$${}_2r_1 = \frac{(1.03)^2}{1.02} - 1 = \frac{1.0609}{1.02} - 1 = 1.0401 - 1 = 4.01\%.$$

This is the rate for the second year that would yield an investor an annual compound return of 3 percent for the two years regardless of whether he invests in one two-year security at 3 percent annually or in two successive one-year securities, the first one yielding 2 percent and the second 4.01 percent. The equality of return on the two investment strategies may be seen from computing the respective expected two-year holding period yields. Assuming that all securities are purchased and sold at par value, so that no capital gains or losses accrue ($\Delta PB = 0$), and remembering that all coupon interest payments are reinvested, equation 9-7 may be rewritten:

$$i_2 = \frac{\sum_{t=1}^{2} C_t}{PB_1} = \frac{\sum_{t=1}^{2} c_t PB_t}{PB_1} = \frac{c_1 PB_1 + c_2 PB_2}{PB_1} = \frac{c_1 PB_1 + c_2(PB_1 + c_1 PB_1)}{PB_1}.$$

For the one two-year bond:

$$i_2 = \frac{.03(100) + .03(103)}{100} = \frac{3.0 + 3.09}{100} = .0609 = 6.09\%.$$

For the two one-year bonds:

$$i_2 = \frac{.02(100) + .0401(102)}{100} = \frac{2.0 + 4.09}{100} = .0609 = 6.09\%.$$

Thus both strategies generate the same return over the two-year holding period.

If an investor's expectations of future rates differed from the computed forward rates, which may be expected to reflect the consensus of expectations of all market participants, his expected holding-period yields on all alternatives would not be equal and he would choose the alternative combination of investments generating the highest yield for the holding period. If sufficient investors accepted this new set of expectations, the market yields on the most profitable maturity combinations would gradually be bid down to the point where they fully reflected the new market expectations and yield no advantage over alternative investment strategies for the holding period. For example, if, in the above example, investors suddenly expected the future one-year interest rate one year hence to be 3½ percent rather than 4 percent, they would purchase the two-year security generating an annual 3 percent yield over the two-year holding period. The alternative of purchasing two successive one-year securities would be expected to yield only about 2¾ percent annually over the two years. In time, sufficient purchases of the two-year securities will reduce their yield to 2¾ percent. This rate will fully reflect current expectations, and expected holding-period yields will again be equal for all alternative investment combinations.

For purposes of exposition, the geometric average of equation 9-5 can be replaced by a simple arithmetic average. This simplifies the relation between the long- and short-term rates. For the two-period case:

$$ {}_tR_2 = \frac{{}_tR_1 + {}_{t+1}r_1}{2}, $$

or

$$ {}_{t+1}r_1 = 2({}_tR_2) - {}_tR_1. \tag{9-8} $$

More generally:

$$ {}_{t+n-1}r_1 = n_t R_n - \left({}_tR_1 + \sum_{m=1}^{n-2} {}_{t+m}r_1\right). \tag{9-9} $$

For the two-period example above, the forward rate one year hence from the current period ($t=1$), or at the beginning of year two, is:

$$ {}_2r_1 = 2(3) - 2 = 4\%. $$

Assume additionally that the current observed interest rate on three-year securities

Figure 9-3 **Yield Curve for Expected Increases in Short-Term Interest Rates**

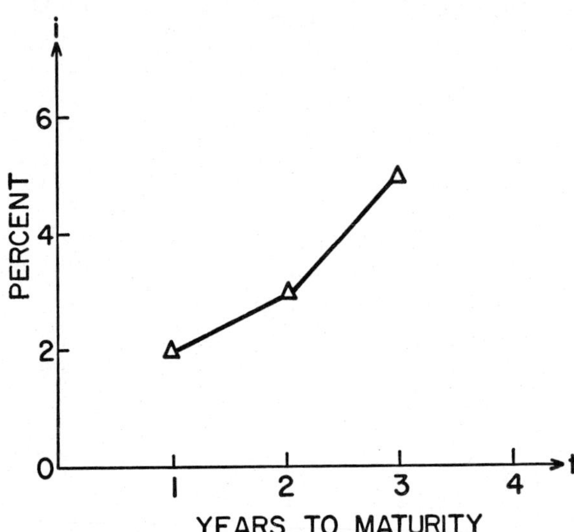

is 5 percent. This implies that the one-year rate expected two years hence at the beginning of year three is:

$$_{3}r_{1}=3(5)-(2+4)=9\%.$$

Proof:

$$_{t}R_{3}=\frac{_{t}R_{1}+{_{t+1}r_{1}}+{_{t+2}r_{1}}}{n}=\frac{2+4+9}{3}=5\%.$$

It follows that the unbiased expectations theory relates the shape of the yield curve to expectations of future interest rates. If short-term rates in the future are expected to be above current short-term rates, the long-term rates (which are averages of these short-term rates) will be above current short-term rates, and the yield curve will slope upward to the right. In the example above, one-year rates in future periods are expected to rise from 2 to 4 to 9 percent. As a result, the current two-year rate exceeds the current one-year rate and is itself exceeded by the current three-year rate. This pattern is plotted in Figure 9-3. Vice versa, if future short-term rates are expected to decline below current short-term rates, long-term rates will be below the current short-term rate and the curve will slope downward to the right. If short-term rates are expected to remain unchanged, the yield curve will be horizontal.

Liquidity Premium Theory

The liquidity premium explanation of the term structure differs in only one major respect from the unbiased expectations theory. Similar to the unbiased expectations theory, it postulates that the forward rate computed from equation 9-5 represents an estimate of the rate the market expects will exist in the particular future period. However, unlike the unbiased expectations theory, the liquidity premium theory postulates that this forward rate is a biased estimate of the future rate. It is biased upward by an amount equal to a liquidity premium. That is, the long-term rate is the geometric average of current and expected future short-term rates plus a liquidity premium.

The liquidity premium arises because SSUs and DSUs are postulated to possess different market preferences. SSUs or lenders are risk averters and prefer capital certainty, that is, they give greater weight to securing the principal of the loan at any time than to stabilizing the interest rate through time. In the absence of differences in risk of default, the principal value of securities of different terms to maturity can be threatened only by declines in market price resulting from increases in the overall level of interest rates. The risk of not being able to obtain the purchase price of a security prior to maturity due to a decline in its market price is called *price risk*. This risk can be represented by a measure of the variability of price around its average value. Using the standard deviation as the measure of variability:

$$PR = \sum_{n=1}^{m} \frac{(PB_n - \overline{PB})^2}{m-1}, \qquad (9\text{-}10)$$

where:

PB = market price
$\overline{PB}$ = average market price.

As discussed in Chapter 8, the longer the term to maturity of a security, generally the greater are its price fluctuations. Thus, with rare exceptions, the greater the term to maturity is, the greater the price risk and the lower the capital certainty, or the certainty of recovering the purchase price at any time. That is, capital certainty decreases with time to maturity. Although greater price variability implies an increased probability of selling the security at above its purchase price as well as an increased probability of a loss, the theory assumes that investors are more sensitive to the risk of loss.

DSUs or borrowers, on the other hand, are hypothesized to give greater weight to assuring a steady source of financing at a known constant interest rate than to protecting the value of the principal. As a result, lenders prefer to lend short and borrowers prefer to borrow long. To obtain long-term loans, borrowers must effectively bribe lenders to lend long by offering a premium, called *the liquidity premium,* to offset the risk of capital uncertainty. As capital uncertainty increases with term to maturity, the liquidity premium increases in magnitude, although at a decreasing rate, with term to maturity.

In equation form, the liquidity premium theory modifies equation 9-1 to read:

$$(1+{}_tR_n)^n = (1+{}_tR_1)(1+{}_{t+1}\rho_1+{}_{t+1}L_1)(1+{}_{t+2}\rho_1+{}_{t+2}L_1)\cdots(1+{}_{t+n-1}\rho_1+{}_{t+n-1}L_1), \tag{9-11}$$

where:

L = liquidity premium, and ${}_{t+1}L_1 < {}_{t+2}L_1 < \cdots < {}_{t+n-1}L_1$.

In contrast to equation 9-6:

$${}_{t+m}r_1 = {}_{t+m}\rho_1 + {}_{t+m}L_1. \tag{9-12}$$

That is, the computed forward rate includes not only the expected future rate, but also the liquidity premium. Thus, for a given pattern of observed interest rates, the estimate of the future rate generated by the liquidity premium theory is always lower than that generated by the unbiased expectations theory by an amount equal to the liquidity premium. Unlike the unbiased expectations theory, the liquidity premium theory does not predict equal expected holding-period yields. For any given holding period, a strategy involving longer composite maturities will always yield a higher expected return than one involving shorter composite maturities, but it would not be more desirable because the extra yield would just compensate the holder for the risk associated with the greater degree of uncertainty he accepts.

Because of the liquidity premium, the liquidity premium theory postulates that the yield curve will generally slope upward, so long-term rates will generally exceed short-term rates. Only in periods when short-term interest rates are expected to decline sharply by an average amount greater than the liquidity premium will the yield curve slope downward. As shown in Figure 9-4, for every yield curve generated by the unbiased expectations theory for a particular set of future rates, the liquidity premium theory generates one sloping more steeply upward or less steeply downward.

Market Segmentation Theory

The market segmentation theory emphasizes transactions costs and the risk of not realizing the expected interest yield. It is based on the assumption that both borrowers and lenders have preferred markets for financial claims and that, in

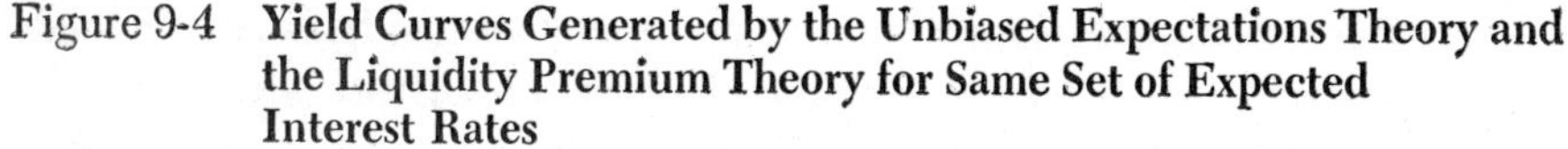

Figure 9-4 **Yield Curves Generated by the Unbiased Expectations Theory and the Liquidity Premium Theory for Same Set of Expected Interest Rates**

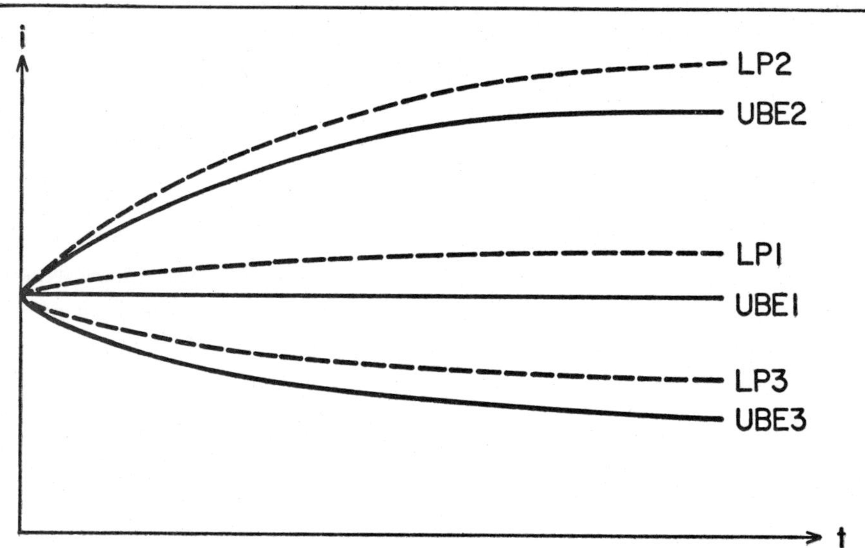

the absence of very large interest-rate differentials, they will buy or sell securities with maturities consistent with these preferences. This theory views transactions costs in the broadest sense as incorporating not only costs of trade, search, physical transfer, and information, but also costs of generating accurate interest-rate forecasts on a wide spectrum of maturities, which is implied by the alternative theories. The greater these costs, the more market participants will maximize their utilities by reducing the number of transactions and synchronizing the maturities of their assets and liabilities.

In addition, the greater the number of security transactions during the holding period because of the use of securities with maturities shorter than the expected holding period, the greater the probability of interest-rate changes affecting the rate on the new securities, and the greater the probability of not realizing the expected return. Likewise, the longer the maturity of a security is beyond the expected holding period, the greater is the likelihood of selling the security at the end of the holding period at below the expected selling price. Both lenders and borrowers can protect themselves against the risk of not realizing their expected return by operating only in securities whose maturities correspond to the planned period of participation in the financial markets. However, even for such securities, the expected holding-period return is guaranteed only if the coupons can be reinvested at the expected interest rates.

As a result, the market segmentation theory postulates that lenders with funds available for a particular period of time will purchase securities with maturities corresponding to this period rather than a series of shorter-term securities or a longer-term security. Likewise, borrowers with a demand for funds for a particular period of time will not borrow for either shorter or longer periods. Commercial banks, which have a large proportion of short-term liabilities, will prefer to invest short, while life insurance companies, whose liabilities are long term, will prefer to invest long. Interest rates in each maturity sector are determined by conditions of demand and supply in that sector and only slightly affect or are affected by interest rates in other maturity sectors. Funds do not flow freely through the maturity spectrum to the most profitable maturity. Participants concentrate their activities pretty much in a limited number of maturity sectors. The shape of the yield curve at any time reflects primarily the underlying demand and supply forces in each sector at the time. If demand forces are relatively greater than supply forces in the short-term sectors as compared with the long-term sectors, market interest rates will be higher for short-term maturities than for long-term maturities. Similar to the liquidity premium theory, holding-period yields reflect the composite maturities but, unlike the liquidity premium theory, the effect of maturity mix is not the same at all times. That is, for any given holding period, different combinations of securities will generate different expected holding-period yields, which are not related systematically to the maturity mix of the composite securities.

In its emphasis, the market segmentation theory differs significantly from the unbiased expectations theory, which postulates both that market participants are insensitive to maturity and that holding-period yields are equal regardless of the combination of composite maturities summing to the holding period, and also from the liquidity premium theory, which postulates that participants are increasingly sensitive to term to maturity so that the longer the maturities of the securities for a given holding period, the higher the premium over rates on shorter-term securities in that period and the higher the holding period yields.

Cyclical Changes in the Yield Curve

As noted in the previous chapter, while interest rates on all maturities fluctuate with the business cycle, short-term rates fluctuate more than long-term rates. Near cyclical peaks, short-term rates tend to exceed long-term rates; near cyclical troughs, they tend to be below long-term rates (Figure 9-5). This pattern implies a downward-sloping yield curve in periods when economic expansions are ending and an upward-sloping yield curve in periods when economic expansions are beginning. In midexpansion, short- and long-term rates are about the same and the yield curve is close to horizontal (Figure 9-6). All three term-structure theories generate yield curves consistent with such a pattern.

Figure 9-5 **Interest Rates on Treasury Securities, 1950-71**

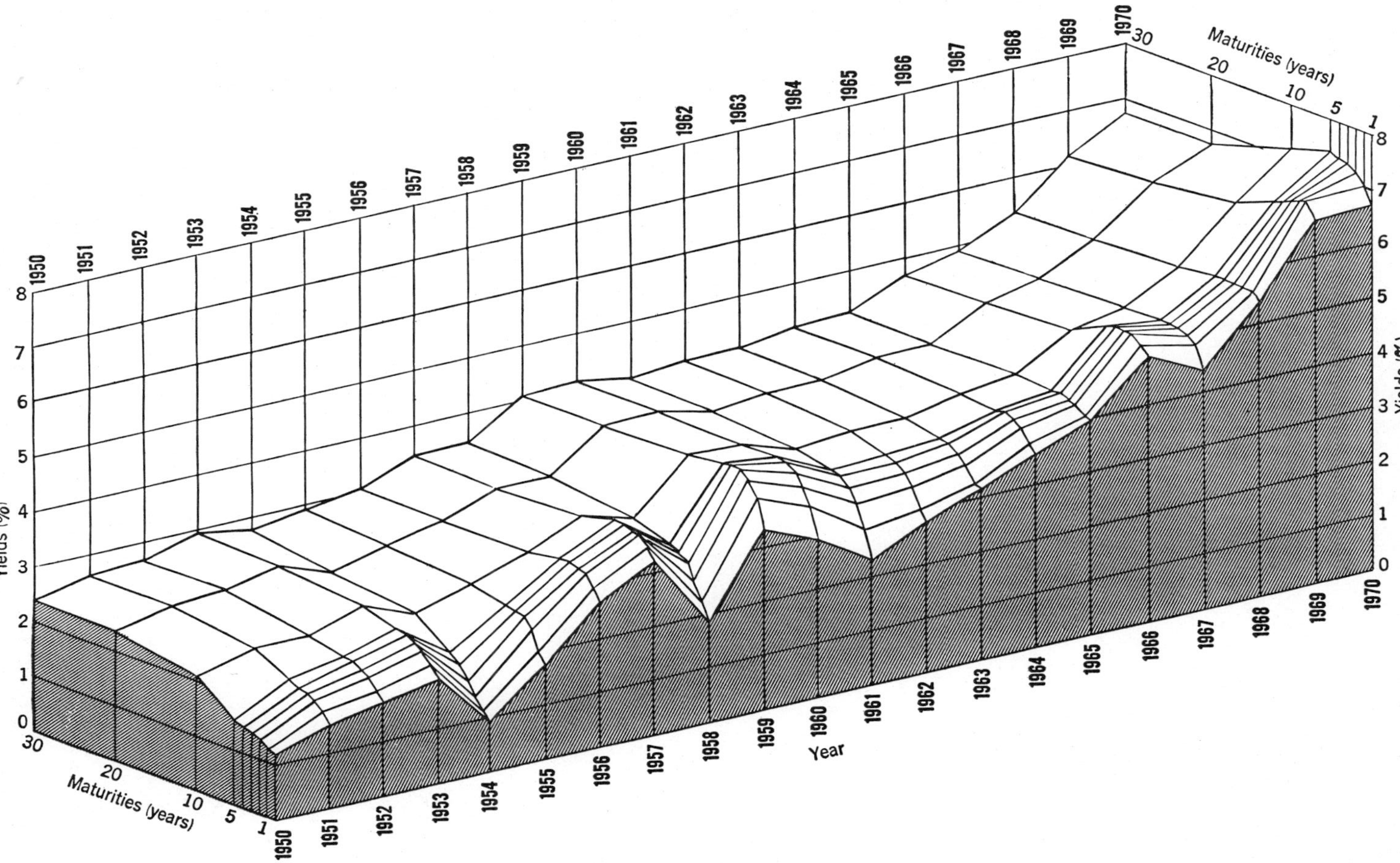

Source: Salomon Brothers, *An Analytical Record of Yields and Yield Spreads* (New York: 1972), p. 25, reprinted with permission.

Figure 9-6 **The Yield Curve Over the Business Cycle**

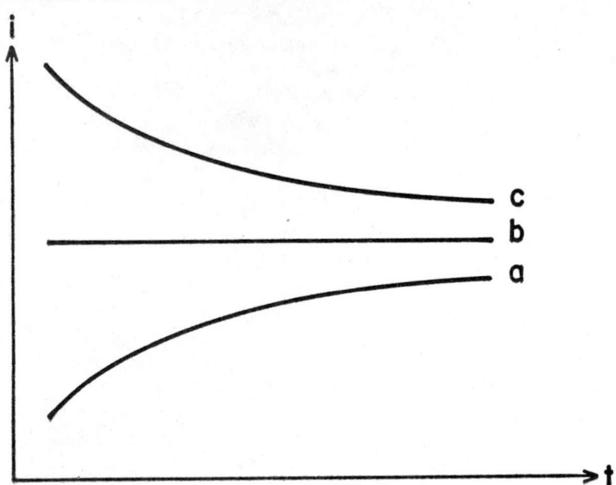

a Near trough of economic expansion.
b At midexpansion.
c Near peak of economic expansion.

Consider the start of an economic expansion. At such times, short-term interest rates are expected to increase from their current levels. The unbiased expectations theory would predict long-term rates to exceed current short-term levels because of the expected increase in short-term rates. The liquidity premium theory accepts the same reasoning but enlarges the spread by which long-term rates exceed current short-term rates by an amount equal to the liquidity premium (Figure 9-4). The market segmentation theory postulates that the demands for short-term funds increase in this period by less in relation to the supplies of such funds than do the demands for long-term funds in relation to their supply. As a consequence, short-term rates are lower than long-term rates. The supply of short-term funds is augmented near troughs in economic activity by increased Federal Reserve injection of reserves, large inflows of funds into commercial banks, and high levels of household and business savings. The demand for short-term funds is relatively strong only by the federal government, reflecting its need to finance contracyclical budget deficits.

In contrast, at periods close to cyclical peaks in economic activity, all three theories postulate downward-sloping yield curves. Reflecting the anticipated decline in short-term rates, both the unbiased expectations theory and the liquidity premium theory predict long-term rate levels below short-term levels, although a narrower spread is predicted by the liquidity premium hypothesis. Short-term rates above long-term rates are also predicted by the market segmentation theory on the basis of unusually heavy demands for short-term funds relative to their availability. Business firms tend to finance expanding inventory at these times and consumers, increased purchases of durable goods. Concurrently, inflows into commercial banks are restricted, in no small measure as a consequence of reduced reserve injection by the Federal Reserve, and corporation and household savings are absorbed in financing their own expenditures. Long-term investments and savings are less affected by cyclical changes.

The Evidence for Each Theory

As with many economic issues, the available evidence is not sufficiently persuasive to differentiate clearly among the alternative theories of the term structure. Rather, the observed phenomena appear to be explained by a little of each theory. Short-run changes in the term structure reveal patterns more consistent with the market segmentation hypothesis, while changes over periods of one quarter or longer appear to be more consistent with either the unbiased expectations or liquidity preference theory.

Strong evidence for the expectations theory is of relatively recent origin. For some years observers had noted a tendency for changes in longer short-term securities, say, three months, to precede changes in shorter-term maturities of, say, one month. This was consistent with market anticipation of well-recognized seasonal patterns. For example, three-month Treasury bill rates regularly started to climb in the fall of each year, in anticipation of the usual, heavy Christmas credit demands, some time before one-month Treasury bill rates rose. But longer-term rates generated little evidence of changes in patterns consistent with the expectations hypotheses. In no small measure, these results were foredoomed by the tests applied. Forward rates were computed and compared with the actual rates later observed for the same period. The relationship between the two rates may be expressed in functional notation:

$$ {}_{t}R_{nt} = f({}_{t+1}r_{n\,(t-1)}). \qquad \textbf{(9-13)} $$

The second postsubscript identifies the period in which the rate was forecast or observed. With perfect foresight, the correlations between the forward or predicted rates and the observed rates should be 1. However, the computed correlations were small, indicating the actual rates differed substantially from those predicted in earlier periods. By itself, this is insufficient evidence to reject the importance of expectations. The low correlations may just reflect poor forecasting. After all, perfect foresight is a rather heroic assumption in economics.

In the early 1960s, Professor David Meiselman devised a technique for separating evidence of incorrect forecasts of interest rates by market participants from evidence of the use of forecasts of short-term rates in estimating interest rates for longer maturities. Meiselman recognized that expectations are not always realized and that market participants continually revise their forecasts in the light of ongoing experience. Evidence of the use of expectations would not necessarily require a close correlation between the expected and actual outcomes, but only a close correlation between changes in information and expected interest rates. If forward rates computed from observed longer-term rates represent expectations of future rates, changes should be related systematically to changes in information.

One important source of new information is the errors made in past forecasts. Revisions in expected rates should reflect adjustments for such past errors. An error-learning hypothesis for interest rate forecasting can be written as follows:

$$_{t+n}r_{nt} - {}_{t+n}r_{n\,(t-1)} = f\left({}_tR_{nt} - {}_tr_{n\,(t-1)}\right) = f(E), \tag{9-14}$$

where:

E = error in predicting the interest rate.

Equation 9-14 states that market participants revise their expectations of future rates in response to differences between the observed rate and the rate that they had predicted in the previous period. The center term of equation 9-14 represents the effective error in predicting the current rate. A high correlation between changes in forward rates and past prediction errors would indicate that these rates are revised systematically and, to the extent the forward rates reflect expected future rates, that observed long rates incorporate expectations of briefer rates.

Tests of equation 9-14 generated strong evidence in favor of the expectations theory. The coefficient of correlation between forward-rate revisions and forecasting errors varied from more than +0.90 for near-term forecasts to about +0.60 as forecasts were progressively lengthened.

On the other hand, considerable skepticism surrounds the meaningfulness of four important implications of the unbiased expectations theory: (1) zero transactions costs, (2) that market participants are both willing and able to predict short-term interest rates over the entire maturity of long-term securities, (3) that such rate predictions are firmly held without allowance for error, and (4) that expectations of the holding period are held with certainty, again without allowance for error. If expectations of either rates or holding periods are not realized, the alternative composite maturity strategies will not yield equal holding-period returns. Risk averters who do not hold rate or holding-period expectations with complete certainty would then consider some maturity strategies superior to others.

The evidence also suggests that liquidity premiums exist. Experiments have shown that short-term interest rates exceed long-term rates at cyclical peaks by less than they fall short of long-term rates at cyclical troughs. This would be consistent with a liquidity premium on long-term securities. Similar asymmetrical results are obtained when interest rate spreads are examined for standardized symmetrical business cycles. The unbiased expectations hypothesis postulates symmetrical differences in rate spreads at these times. Moreover, the results from the error-learning experiments are consistent with the liquidity premium theory as well as the unbiased expectations theory.

Support for the market segmentation theory has stemmed primarily from its intuitive appeal, observations that many market participants are vitally concerned with minimizing the risk of not realizing the expected rate of return for an expected holding period (because of either a change in rates or a change in holding period), the failure of perfect foresight models to generate strong evidence in favor of alternative explanations, and survey results indicating that a number of financial institutions require substantial interest rate thresholds to change the maturity structure of their portfolios. This support has been eroded somewhat in recent years, at least for quarterly or longer-rate observations, by the success of the error-learning model in generating evidence in favor of the importance of rate expectations and the realization that holding-period yields can be equalized by a sufficiently large number of arbitragers operating at the margin without involving every market participant. Every housewife does not have to visit every grocery store in order to equalize grocery prices in a neighborhood. In addition, a number of recent tests have failed to find evidence of lasting changes in the term structure of rates when changes in the amounts of securities in different maturity sectors were added to expectations variables.

Nevertheless, visual evidence indicates that abrupt jumps and declines in daily and weekly interest rates in different maturity sectors frequently occur at times when large new issues are marketed or existing issues mature and are either not refinanced or refinanced in another maturity sector. This suggests that funds do not flow immediately among maturity categories in response to differences in supply and demand conditions in the different maturity sectors. In contrast to longer-run changes, short-run changes in term structure appear to be explained jointly by market segmentation and by expectations.

Thus, it appears likely that the term structure is explained most completely by a general theory incorporating parts of all three partial theories. Rates on securities differing only in term to maturity are interrelated in the first instance both by market participants' expectations of rates for various subperiods encompassed by the maturity of the securities and by the potential use of these securities as substitutes for each other in pursuing an investment or borrowing strategy for a given holding period. If one set of maturities summing to the holding period promises to generate a more favorable return than alternative sets of securities, the profit incentive of market participants will induce flows of funds throughout the maturity spectrum to the most favorable opportunity set. However, the flows will fall short of the amount necessary to equalize completely the return on all alternative combinations of maturities. For any holding period, differences in rates on securities of different maturities will exist in relation to differences in the costs of trade and in risk aversion among borrowers and lenders. The greater the costs of trade or the greater risk aversion in terms of increasing the likelihood of obtaining the expected rate of return over the expected holding period, the greater is the incentive to synchronize the maturity of a security to the expected holding period and the smaller the equilibrating flows.

Economic Forecasting from the Term Structure

To the extent that expectations of future interest rates are incorporated in the term structure and interest rates are correlated with levels of economic activity and the rate of change in prices, analysis of the term structure generates information on the consensus of market participants with respect to the future course of business. If long-term rates, adjusted for any liquidity premiums, are above short-term rates, the market expects economic expansion and/or acceleration in the rate of price increase. If adjusted long-term rates are below short-term rates, the market expects economic contraction and/or reduced price pressures. Additional information can be obtained from observing whether the spread between long- and short-term rates is widening or narrowing. A narrowing of the adjusted spread when long-term rates exceed short-term rates, for example, indicates a consensus that the rate of economic expansion or inflation will be slowing.

While the yield curve may reveal information about market expectations, these expectations may not be realized. Thus, short-term rates may exceed long-term rates for a considerable period of time before the economy turns down, if indeed it does. Nevertheless, knowledge of the expectations of the market is useful in making one's own predictions about the course of interest rates and overall economic activity.

Risk of Default

Debt securities include a promise by the borrower to make coupon and final payments to the holder according to a prearranged schedule. At times, the borrower is unable to meet these payments on schedule and defaults on the agreement.

To compensate for potential losses from default on some or all of a loan's principal or interest payments, lenders charge higher interest rates the greater they evaluate the risk of default. Market rates of interest at year-end 1970 are shown in Table 9-1 for a large number of marketable securities with different terms to maturity, risks of default, marketability, and tax considerations. The degree of default risk the market considers a particular security to possess can be gauged by the difference between the market yield on that security and that on a default-free security of the same term to maturity with equal tax treatment and marketability. This difference is called *risk premium* and can be written:

Table 9-1 **Market Rates of Interest, January 2, 1971**

Security	Interest Rate (Percent)
Treasury Bill: 3 months	4.87*
Treasury Bill: 6 months	4.88*
Bankers Acceptances: 3 months	5.25*
Commercial Paper (Finance companies): 3–6 months	5.44*
Commercial Paper (Nonfinance companies): 4–6 months	5.75*
Treasury Securities: 3–5 years	5.94
Treasury Bonds	6.16
Corporate Bonds: Aaa	7.48
Corporate Bonds: Baa	8.97
Corporate Bonds: industrial	7.75
Corporate Bonds: utility	8.31
Corporate Bonds: railroad	8.86
Municipal Bonds: Aaa	5.25†
Municipal Bonds: Baa	5.75†

*Discount basis.

†Interest not subject to federal income tax.

Source: *Federal Reserve Bulletin*, 57 (2), February, 1971, p. A 33-34.

$$RP = {}_tR_n - {}_tR'_n, \tag{9-15}$$

where R' refers to the market rate of interest on a default-free security. The larger the risk premium, the greater the market's evaluation of the probability of default.

Risk premiums have been computed for a number of highly marketable short- and long-term securities subject to similar federal income tax treatment at year-end 1970. Because the federal government has the power to print money and, therefore, is always able to meet nominal coupon and maturity payments, securities issued by the U.S. Treasury are considered free of the risk of default. Three-month Treasury bills may thus be specified as a default-free, short-term security and long-term Treasury bonds as a default-free, long-term security. In these examples, small differences in term to maturity and in marketability are disregarded. The computed risk premiums are shown in Table 9-2. It is readily apparent that the market assigns greatly different probabilities of default to the different securities. Railroad bonds, for example, are viewed as considerably more risky than industrial bonds of the same term to maturity.

From Tables 9-1 and 9-2, it appears that the higher the risk, the higher the interest rate. But, this is not necessarily true. At year-end 1969, for example, the market interest rate on 4-6-month nonfinance company prime commercial paper was 8.84 percent, slightly higher than the yield of 8.65 percent on long-term corporate Baa bonds. Yet the market gauged the corporate bonds to be riskier; the risk premium was 1.03 percentage points on the commercial paper compared

Table 9-2 **Risk Premiums for Selected Securities**
(Year-end 1970)

	$_tR_n$		$_tR'_n$		Risk Premium
Short term			(Percent)		
Bankers acceptances	5.25	−	4.87	=	0.38
Finance company paper	5.44	−	4.87	=	0.57
Nonfinance company paper	5.75	−	4.87	=	0.88
Long term					
Corporate bonds: Aaa	7.48	−	6.16	=	1.32
Corporate bonds: Baa	8.97	−	6.16	=	2.81
Corporate bonds: industrial	7.75	−	6.16	=	1.59
Corporate bonds: utility	8.31	−	6.16	=	2.15
Corporate bonds: railroad	8.86	−	6.16	=	2.70

Short-term securities are compared with three-month Treasury bills, and long-term securities with long-term Treasury bonds.

to 1.84 percentage points on the corporate bonds. The rate pattern reflects the downward-sloping nature of the underlying yield curve at the time. As a comparison of the risk premiums for year-end 1969 and 1970 suggests, evaluations of risk of default need not be constant through time.

Similar to the forward rates computed from observed market rates, the computed risk premiums reflect the consensus of the market. They may disguise a wide range of different risk evaluations held by individual investors. If the risk premium on a particular security computed by an individual investor on the basis of his analysis of the borrower's financial integrity is less than the risk premium charged by the market, the security would be a good investment for the investor. A number of empirical studies have developed evidence that the risk premiums imposed by the market appear to be somewhat greater than necessary to compensate for actual loss experience on the securities. This suggests that the market as a whole acts as a risk averter, charging proportionately higher risk premiums as risk of default increases.

The cost to individual investors of evaluating the probabilities of default on the large number of different corporate and municipal bonds available to him for purchase is great. To reduce this cost, a number of private firms conduct thorough analyses both of the financial position of each major borrower and of the particular characteristics of the securities issued. On this basis they evaluate the risk of default of major issues. The two principal bond-rating services are Moody's and Standard and Poor's. Both firms group securities into nine risk classifications identified by letters. While the coding schemes differ somewhat between the two rating agencies, both assign multiples of the first letter of the

Table 9-3 **Key to Bond Ratings by Moody's Investors Service**

Rating	Explanation
Aaa	Best quality
Aa	High quality
A	Upper medium grade
Baa	Medium grade
Ba	Speculative elements
B	Undesirable
Caa	Poor
Ca	Highly speculative
C	Extremely poor

Source: Moody's Investors Service, Inc., *Municipal and Government Manual, 1972* (New York: 1972), p. vi.

alphabet to the securities with the least risk of default and lower letters to securities with higher risks. The rating codes used by Moody's and their accompanying explanations are shown in Table 9-3. The agencies continue to evaluate the risk of default during the life of a security and periodically may change the risk designation of a security on the basis of additional information.

The risk ratings of the two services are widely accepted and have a significant effect on market interest rates. As can be seen from Table 9-2, bonds rated Baa by Moody's carry noticeably higher risk premiums than bonds rated Aaa. Through their ability to affect interest rates on individual securities, the rating agencies possess considerable influence on the financial markets. It is not surprising that both the firms and their methods of risk evaluation periodically become centers of controversy.

Tax Treatment

In general, investors are interested in after-tax returns on their investments. To the extent that interest income from different securities is subject to different tax rates, pretax market yields are not a good indicator of after-tax returns. Basically, like all income, interest income is subject to federal, state, and local income taxes, where applicable. But there are exemptions. Traditionally, governments have not taxed the property or income of other domestic governmental units. This has been extended to interest payments on their obligations. The federal government exempts coupon interest earnings on municipal bonds from federal income taxation, and state and local governments typically exempt coupon interest earnings on Treasury securities from their income taxation.

Even when subject to income taxation, different rates may apply to different portions of interest earnings. The market yield on securities is composed of two parts: the coupon yield, and the amortized difference between the market and maturity value. The second part represents income from a change in the capital value of property. The federal government and most state and local governments apply a lower rate of tax to capital gains, if the asset is held for at least six months, than they apply to income from the sale of goods and services. Thus, the market yield on a taxable security is subject to two rates—the regular rate on the coupon payments, and the capital gains rate on the remainder—and the relationship between the before- and after-tax yield is dependent upon the relation between the coupon and market rates of interest. The higher the market rate is above the coupon rate, the lower the market value of the security, the smaller the proportion of the total yield accounted for by coupon payments, the greater the proportion accounted for by amortization of the discount from maturity value, the greater the proportion of the return subject to the lower capital gains rate, and the higher is the after-tax yield for the same pretax yield. If the market rate is below the coupon rate, the bond is selling at a premium and the amortization of the premium represents a capital loss, which has no widespread tax advantage. Thus, the entire interest return is subject to full income tax rates and the lower is the after-tax yield for the same pretax yield.

Because all investors are not in the same federal and state income tax brackets, the after-tax yield on a given security differs from investor to investor. For purposes of measuring after-tax returns on different securities, it is common practice to apply the rates applicable to the largest single group of investors, namely corporations. The importance of differences in tax rates on after-tax returns can be seen from the simple example below. Assume a 50 percent federal income tax rate on regular corporate income, a 30 percent rate on corporate capital gains, and a zero rate on interest earnings from municipal securities. State and local taxes are disregarded. Consider the following three bonds:

Corporate Bond A: coupon 5%, market yield 5%

Corporate Bond B: coupon 4%, market yield 5%

Municipal Bond C: coupon 3%, market yield 3%.

On the basis of pretax yields, Bonds A and B are both preferred to Bond C. However, this is not true on an after-tax basis. Interest on both corporate securities are subject to federal income tax but at differing rates. Interest on the municipal security is tax exempt. The after-tax yield for each security is shown in Table 9-4. Bond C which had the lowest pretax yield has the highest after-tax yield. Bond B has a higher after-tax yield than Bond A because the lower capital gains rate is applied to part of the return. Only Bond A is subject to the full income tax rate and becomes the least attractive alternative.

Because of differences in investor income tax brackets, the full exemption of coupon interest on municipal securities has different value to different investors.

Table 9-4 **Pre- and After-Tax Yields on Different Bonds**
(Percent)

	Bond A		Bond B		Bond C	
	Pretax Yield	After-tax Yield	Pretax Yield	After-tax Yield	Pretax Yield	After-tax Yield
Coupon	5	2.5	4	2.0	3	3
Discount	0	0	1	0.7	0	0
Total	5	2.5	5	2.7	3	3

In the example above, the investor would have to select a fully taxed security yielding at least 6 percent to match the after-tax income on the municipal bond. If the investor's marginal federal income tax bracket were 25 percent, the after-tax rate of 3 percent is equivalent to a before-tax yield of 4 percent. For an investor in the 70 percent marginal federal income tax bracket, the highest prevailing tax rate, the 3 percent after-tax yield is equivalent to a 10 percent pretax rate.

Because of the relatively greater tax advantage, municipal bonds are purchased primarily by investors in the higher income tax brackets. Table 9-1 shows that at year-end 1970 the pretax yield on municipal Aaa bonds was almost one hundred percentage points below Treasury bonds and two hundred twenty-five percentage points below corporate bonds of equal risk rating. By permitting municipalities to sell their debt at lower costs, the exemption from federal income taxation effectively serves as a subsidy to municipalities and their taxpayers for debt financing, paid by all federal taxpayers through higher taxes. Municipal securities are subject to most state and local income taxes. Because state and local income tax rates are considerably below those of the federal government, exemption from these taxes imposes only a small benefit to holders of Treasury securities.

The effect of income tax differences on market rates of interest can also be seen from the yield curve for Treasury securities. Figure 9-1 shows a number of yields falling substantially below the curve. This does not so much reflect failure of arbitrage as differences in tax treatment. The securities yielding below-average pretax returns are low coupon bonds issued at earlier times when market rates were lower. As market rates increased, the price of these bonds dropped to substantial discounts, subjecting their market yields to lower effective tax rates. A plotting of after-tax yields would show them to be closer to the curve. Low pretax yields are particularly common for longer-term Treasury bonds. This reflects both the limited ability of the Treasury to sell significant amounts of bonds in recent years because of a federal statutory prohibition against a coupon rate in excess of 4¼ percent, which has resulted in outstanding earlier-issued, low-coupon, long-term bonds selling at discounts; and the eligibility of these bonds to satisfy federal estate taxes at par value, regardless of market price at the time. As a result, because almost all bonds in the long-term sector are subject to lower effective tax rates, the pretax yield curve in this sector is lower than it would be otherwise in comparison to short-term issues.

Marketability

Interest rates on different securities also vary with differences in the marketability of the security on the secondary market. The more marketable an issue is, the lower its interest rate, ceteris paribus. Marketability refers to the costs of trade, physical transfer, search, and information, and is greater the lower these costs. The marketability of a security can be gauged by its volume on the secondary market. As was discussed in Chapter 4, short-term Treasury bills have the most active secondary markets and are much demanded as a trading instrument. This permits them to be sold quickly at a lower net interest return than a similar, but less marketable, security. In general, short-term securities are more marketable than longer-term issues.

Cross-Section Interest Rate Patterns

The preceding discussion indicates that, although interest rates on various securities differ, they are interrelated to some extent. This section will explore how much. As noted earlier, short- and long-term Treasury securities tend to move together, although short-term rates fluctuate more widely than long-term rates. The degree and rapidity at which interest rate changes in one sector are transmitted throughout the market depends upon the "linkages" connecting the sector. The tighter the linkages are, the greater and more quickly changes in the supply and demand for funds in one sector will affect other sectors.

Table 9-5 shows simple correlation coefficients computed between monthly changes in the market yields on three-month Treasury bills and monthly changes in yields on 13 other groups of securities differing in term to maturity, risk of default, tax treatment, and marketability. The correlations were computed both for changes in yields in the same month and for changes in the three-month Treasury bill yield with changes in yields on the other securities one and two months later.

Changes in Treasury bill yields are more closely related to changes in yield on other short-term securities than to yields on longer-term securities. Holding other factors constant, the correlation of bill yields with yields on other Treasury securities declines as term to maturity increases. Thus, while the coefficient of correlation between monthly changes in yields on three-month and nine-to-twelve-month bills is 0.87, the correlation of three-month bill yields with long-term bond yields is only 0.53. Holding term to maturity constant, the greater the risk of default, the lower the correlation is between Treasury bill yields and the yields on other securities. The correlation between three-month Treasury bill yields and long-

Table 9-5 Simple Correlation Coefficients of Monthly Changes in Market Yields on Three-Month Treasury Bills and Other Securities, 1955–70

Other Security	Correlation Coefficient Change in Yield on Other Security in		
	Same Month	One Month Later	Two Months Later
Bankers Acceptances	.79	.43	.17
Finance Company Paper	.75	.27	.18
Nonfinance Company Paper	.75	.35	.20
Treasury Bills: 9–12 months	.87	.50	.16
Treasury Securities: 3–5 years	.72	.44	.21
Treasury Bonds: Long term	.53	.35	.16
State and Local Bonds: Aaa	.46	.33	.13
State and Local Bonds: Baa	.50	.33	.12
Corporate Bonds: Aaa	.47	.28	.14
Corporate Bonds: Baa	.49	.21	−.02
Corporate Bonds—Public utility	.49	.29	.11
Corporate Bonds—Industrial	.49	.25	.05
Corporate Bonds—Railroad	.44	.24	.01

term bond yields declines from 0.53 to 0.47 when corporate Aaa bonds are substituted for Treasury bonds. However, the correlation coefficients do not distinguish greatly between differences in risks of default among non-default-free securities. Indeed, monthly changes in Treasury bill yields appear to be somewhat more closely correlated with concurrent monthly changes in yields on Baa bonds than on the corresponding Aaa bonds.

Changes in yields on three-month Treasury bills that are transmitted to other sectors are transmitted quickly. The correlations between contemporaneous changes in yields are substantially higher in all sectors than they are between changes in three-month bill yields and yields on the other securities one or two months later. This evidence suggests that all sectors of the market respond quickly to the forces causing changes in short-term Treasury bill yields, although not to the same extent as the changes in bills. The greater the similarities are in both maturity and risk, the more closely and quickly do changes in other rates approximate those in bills.

This evidence supports the implications of the analysis earlier in this chapter that interest rates on different securities are related in a systematic fashion to the characteristics of the securities. If these characteristics are accurately identified, knowledge of any one rate would permit reasonable estimation of all other interest rates and be useful in designing optimal investment and borrowing strategies.

References

Cagan, Phillip, and Jack M. Guttentag, *Essays on Interest Rates, Volume 1* (New York: National Bureau of Economic Research, 1969).

———, *Essays on Interest Rates, Volume 2* (New York: National Bureau of Economic Research, 1971).

Kessel, Reuben A., *The Cyclical Behavior of the Term Structure of Interest Rates* (New York: National Bureau of Economic Research, 1965).

Malkiel, Burton G., *The Term Structure of Interest Rates* (Princeton: Princeton University Press, 1966).

———, *The Term Structure of Interest Rates: Theory, Empirical Evidence, and Applications* (New York: McCaleb-Seiler Publishing Co., 1970).

Meiselman, David, *The Term Structure of Interest Rates* (Englewood Cliffs, N.J.: Prentice-Hall, 1962).

Struble, Frederick M., "Current Debate on the Term Structure of Interest Rates," *Monthly Review* (Federal Reserve Bank of Kansas City), January-February, 1966, 10-16.

Van Horne, James C., *Function and Analysis of Capital Market Rates* (Englewood Cliffs, N.J.: Prentice-Hall, 1970).

PART IV

The Federal Reserve System

The Federal Reserve System: Purposes, Organization, Functions, and Operations

10

The Federal Reserve System is the central bank of the United States. Its primary function is to foster an efficient financial system and to promote financial conditions conducive to the achievement of the goals of the economy.

American Financial History Before 1913

Developments in the financial system do not always contribute to economic stability. The economic history of the United States records numerous occasions during which instability in the financial system was transmitted to other sectors. In the last years of the nineteenth century, gold discoveries in South Africa and Alaska generated rapid expansions in the money supply and sharp increases in prices. But most often, disturbances in the financial sector ignited or reinforced downturns in economic activity. Until recently such crises occurred with painful regularity in the United States once in almost every decade. Major financial panics and business recessions were recorded in 1819, 1837, 1857, 1873, 1884, 1907, 1921, and 1929. With the exception of 1921, the panics all had a common feature—a sudden attempt by the public to exchange one form of money for another. In the earlier panics, this was manifested by a desire to convert bank notes into gold specie and in the later panics by a desire to exchange bank deposits for currency.

In 1837, for example, the end of a speculative land boom depressing land prices and reducing the value of bank loan collateral in the form of land, coupled with a policy of the federal government to increase public use of gold specie, brought about a run on the banks to convert bank notes into gold. The banks were unable to accommodate the demands and suspended gold payments, producing a fall in the value of their notes, a reduction in the money supply, and a major economic recession.

Following the Civil War, smaller banks were encouraged to hold reserves with large city banks, primarily in New York City. As the smaller banks were serving primarily agricultural areas, they generated wide seasonal movements of funds into and out of New York City and other large financial centers. The flow was accompanied by a liquidation of bank assets in the areas losing reserves and an expansion of bank credit in areas gaining reserves. In this period, communications and transportation were slow and financial markets tended to be geographically segmented. Banks gaining reserves did not necessarily trade in the same securities as banks losing reserves and pressures in one part of the banking system were not quickly relieved by surpluses in other parts.

In 1873, unusually large seasonal flows out of the major financial centers coincided with severe difficulties in the railroad industry. The railroads had entered into an era of rapid expansion, following the end of the Civil War, financed by large bond flotations. These bonds were in large part purchased by banks and bank customers who used them as collateral for bank loans. However, by 1873 overexpansion and intense competition forced an increasing number of rail lines to default on their interest payments and this exerted additional pressures on city banks already liquidating assets to meet the larger than anticipated outflow of funds to country banks. The subsequent failure of a number of important New York City banks was followed by bank failures nationwide and amplified a slowing of business activity into a severe and prolonged economic downturn.

A decade later in 1884, the same set of circumstances interrupted the recovery from the 1873 recession and led to a less severe downturn. In 1893, a run on the banks caused by overexpansion of currency convertible into silver in relation to domestic and international demands for gold resulted in attempts to convert currency into gold, another wave of bank failures, and another severe business contraction.

Fourteen years later in 1907, the cycle repeated, this time as a consequence of an abrupt collapse in stock prices following a speculative upsurge. Again bank customers defaulted on loans and a run on banks developed. Although this run did not involve gold to the extent of previous runs, the desire to acquire currency was more severe. Sellers accepted bank checks only at a 4 percent discount with respect to currency. In their attempts to liquidate assets, banks bid up the daily interest rate on call loans to over 100 percent.

Attempts to prevent financial disorders date to the early years of the country's independence. In 1791, Congress chartered the first Bank of the United States.

Although primarily privately owned, the bank was authorized to perform many duties today delegated the Federal Reserve System. It issued uniform notes which circulated freely throughout the country. It served as the fiscal agent and largest depository for the Treasury. It was able to shift funds to banks facing temporary reserve pressure, thereby staving off individual bank failures. However, for a number of reasons, including displeasure with a developing pattern of foreign ownership, fear of centralized national power, and concern over the competitive effects on state banks, Congress did not renew the bank's 20-year charter upon expiration.

The next few years witnessed a rapid expansion in note issue by state banks, in part generated by the need to finance the War of 1812, and eventual inability of these banks to redeem their notes for gold. At that time, the supply of money decreased sharply. Concurrently, the replacement of standardized notes by sundry notes of various and distant banks discouraged the acceptance of the notes in areas geographically removed from the bank of issue and further weakened the national payments mechanism.

In response, Congress in 1816 chartered the second Bank of the United States. The bank reintroduced a standard currency acceptable throughout the country at par and curbed excessive expansion of notes by state banks by collecting these notes upon receipt and presenting them at randomly spaced intervals to the banks of issue for redemption. In the process, the bank effectively regulated the nation's money supply. These activities did not endear the bank to those who preferred a more rapid growth in money, a larger role for state banks, and more widely distributed financial power. Although Congress voted to renew the bank's charter, President Jackson vetoed the measure for many of the same reasons used against the first bank. Shortly thereafter, the state banks suspended specie payments renewing the cycle of financial and business crises. Despite a number of attempts to charter another central bank, corrective actions were singularly unsuccessful until the Civil War, some 30 years later.

In 1863, at the height of the Civil War, Congress enacted the National Bank Act. This act provided for the chartering of national banks subject to minimum capital and reserve requirements with the power to issue new standardized national bank notes. At the same time, Congress levied a tax on note issues of state banks encouraging most of these banks to convert to national charters, at least until the beginning of the rapid expansion in demand deposit banking in the 1880s. The new national bank notes were effectively liabilities of the Treasury through a provision requiring banks to collateralize their notes with Treasury securities. If the bank failed, the Treasury could sell the securities to redeem the notes. The fact that the government was issuing large amounts of new debt to finance the war and the new national banks would provide a captive market lessened congressional opposition to the banking act.

Although the National Bank Act reintroduced a national currency, it did not solve the problem of abrupt changes in the public demands between now specie and national bank notes on the one hand and bank deposits on the other. Nor did the act provide means of controlling the money supply in response to economic developments. Thus, the periodic crises continued. Finally, in response to the Panic of 1907, Congress passed the Currency (Aldridge-Vreeland) Act of 1908 which, among other things, established a National Monetary Commission to inquire into the causes of the periodic panics and make recommendations for improvements in the financial structure. The commission issued its findings and recommendations, including the establishment of a central bank, in 1912. In December, 1913, after considerable debate, Congress passed and President Wilson signed the Federal Reserve Act establishing the Federal Reserve System "to furnish an elastic currency, to afford means of rediscounting commercial paper [and] to establish a more effective supervision of banking."

Organization of the Federal Reserve System

The organization of the Federal Reserve System reflected the political and economic differences of the early twentieth century. Agriculture, labor, and the newer Western states harbored a long-standing distrust of the banking community and the established Eastern commercial interests. Reflecting their primarily debtor status, these sectors also preferred rapid monetary expansion, earlier manifested in the Populist and silver movements of the late 1800s. In response to the pressures from these groups, authority in the Federal Reserve System was decentralized among 12 regional reserve banks and a board in Washington, whose members were appointed by the president, and the power to issue currency was transferred from the commercial banks to the new System. The banking and commercial communities, on the other hand, favored slower monetary growth, stable prices, and a central bank owned and managed by the commercial banks. To placate this group, ownership of the regional reserve banks was vested in the member commercial banks, bankers and businessmen were given strong representation on the boards of these banks, and the System's ability to expand Federal Reserve notes was restricted. Through the years the organization of the System has changed in response to the changing economic environment. Major modifications were introduced by the Banking Acts of 1933 and 1935 as a consequence of the apparent inability of the System to counteract the depression. More authority was shifted to a reorganized Board of Governors in Washington and its powers to engage in active stabilization measures were strengthened.

The present organization remains a product of the legacy of American financial history. It is highly doubtful whether a newly established central bank would be similarly organized. In a study for the Commission of Money and Credit, a private committee organized in 1958 to examine changes in the financial system and make recommendations for improvement, Michael Reagan likened the organization of

Figure 10-1 **Structure of the Federal Reserve System**

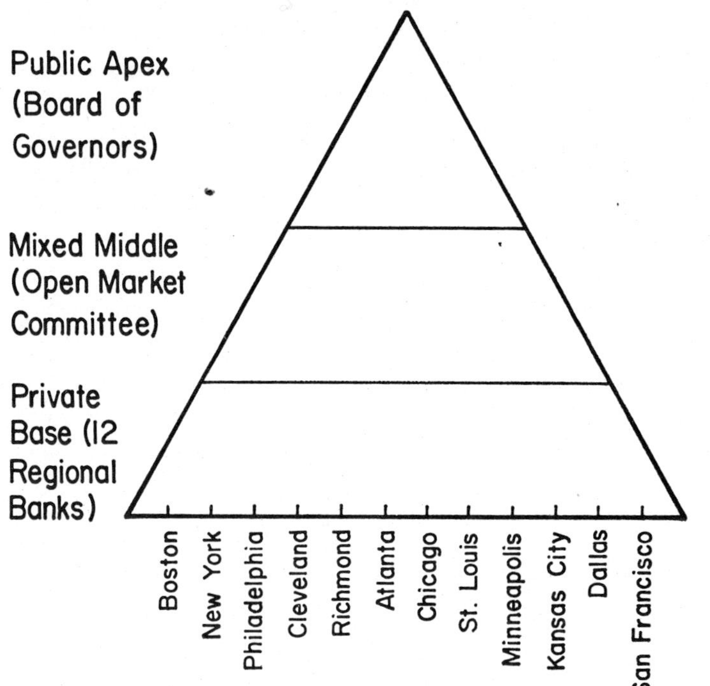

the Federal Reserve System to a triangle having "a private base, a mixed middle and a public apex" (Figure 10-1).

Board of Governors

The Board of Governors represents the public apex of the organizational triangle and is the most important policy group in the system. The Board consists of seven members appointed for 14-year terms by the president of the United States subject to the approval of the U.S. Senate. The terms are staggered in such a fashion that one expires every two years. A governor cannot be reappointed to another term if he has already served one complete term. One of the seven Board members is appointed by the president to serve as chairman for an unlimited number of four-year terms within the boundaries of his term on the Board. The governors reside in Washington and generally meet daily at the Board of Governors Building. Their major responsibilities are to:

1. determine reserve requirements for member banks within the limits established by Congress.
2. make final review and determination of the discount rate established by each

regional reserve bank. In recent years, the Board has actively assumed this power, in effect determining the rate.

3. serve on the Federal Open Market Committee.
4. establish ceilings on interest rates member banks may pay on time deposits (Regulation Q).
5. evaluate applications for bank mergers where the resulting bank is a state member bank.
6. evaluate applications for acquisition of banks and other firms by bank holding companies.
7. establish bank supervision and examination policies.
8. approve the appointment of the presidents of the regional reserve banks, appoint a minority of the directors of the banks, and audit the operations of the banks.

Many of the actions of the Board are announced publicly at the time they are taken with an accompanying explanation. Additional information on their actions is published in their *Annual Report.*

Federal Open Market Committee (FOMC)

The FOMC is the mixed middle of the triangle. It is comprised of the seven members of the Board of Governors and the five presidents of the 12 regional reserve banks. The presidents serve one-year terms in an established rotational order. The president of the Federal Reserve Bank of New York is a permanent member of the committee and serves as vice-chairman. The chairman of the Board of Governors also serves as chairman of the FOMC. As the name suggests, the FOMC has the responsibility for formulating open market policy. These operations, to be discussed in the next chapter, involve changing the dollar amount of bank reserves by buying Treasury securities from the public and selling Treasury securities to the public.

The committee meets every three or four weeks in Washington for an entire day. Although only five presidents of the regional reserve banks are voting members, all 12 presidents attend the meetings. Also attending are the senior staffs of the reserve banks, the senior staff of the Board of Governors, and the officers in direct charge of domestic and international securities operations. At the meetings, the committee members receive briefings on past, current, and projected domestic and international economic activity, analyses of the execution and impact of past and current policies, and forecasts of the implications of alternative policy strategies. The members then discuss aspects of economic developments and policy before voting on a policy strategy to guide open market operations until the next meeting of the committee. The policy statement is in the form of a directive delivered to the Manager of the Open Market Account, who has daily responsibility for the execution of domestic securities transactions.

Figure 10-2 The Organization of the Federal Reserve System

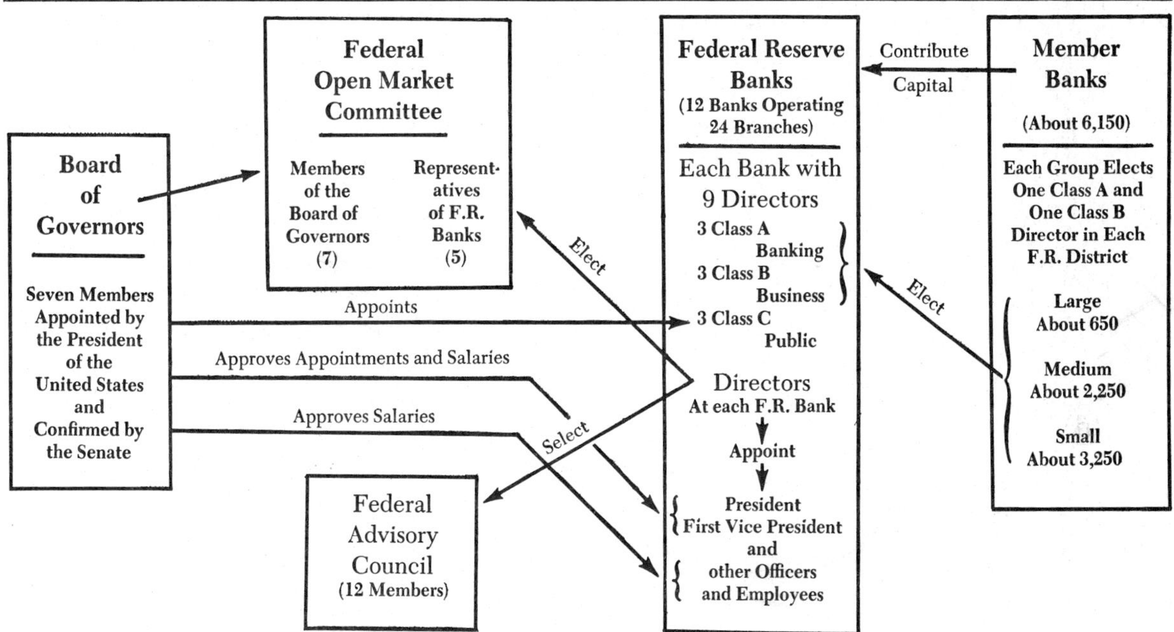

Source: Board of Governors, *The Federal Reserve System: Purposes and Functions*, p. 23.

The policy directive is in two paragraphs. The first paragraph details the committee's evaluation of current economic developments at home and abroad and specifies the committee's immediate policy objectives. The second paragraph delineates the conditions in the financial sector the FOMC believes to be consistent with the achievement of these objectives and which the manager of the account is instructed to attain in his daily operations. The directive below was unanimously adopted by the FOMC on March 21, 1972.

> The information reviewed at this meeting suggests that real output of goods and services is increasing in the current quarter at about the stepped-up rate attained in the fourth quarter of 1971. Several measures of business activity have strengthened recently and demands for labor have improved somewhat, but the unemployment rate remains high. Wholesale prices continued to rise rapidly in January and February, in part because of large increases in prices of foods. However, the advance in wage rates slowed markedly after the post-freeze surge in December. Following a period of sluggish growth, the narrowly defined money stock increased sharply in February, partly reflecting a substantial reduction in U.S. Government deposits. Inflows of time and savings funds at bank and nonbank thrift institutions continued rapid in February, although below January's extraordinary pace. Short-term interest rates have risen considerably in recent weeks while yields on long-term securities have changed little on balance. Exchange rates for most major foreign currencies against the dollar appreciated further in February and early March, as recurrent speculative outflows of capital added to the U.S. balance of payments deficit. In light of the foregoing develop-

> ments, it is the policy of the Federal Open Market Committee to foster financial conditions conducive to sustainable real economic growth and increased employment, abatement of inflationary pressures, and attainment of reasonable equilibrium in the country's balance of payments.
>
> To implement this policy, while taking account of international developments and possible Treasury financing, the Committee seeks to achieve bank reserve and money market conditions that will support moderate growth in monetary aggregates over the months ahead.

The sessions of the FOMC are private and confidential. Unlike the policy actions of the Board alone, the actions of the committee with respect to operations for the coming period are not publicly announced at the time. The policy directive and a summary of the meeting are published 90 days after each meeting. Additional background material appears in the *Annual Report* of the Board of Governors. The complete minutes of the meetings are generally published with a lag of several years.

Regional Reserve Banks

The 12 regional reserve banks represent the private base of the Federal Reserve triangle. In the early years of the System, the banks enjoyed considerable policy powers and autonomy, but through the years the power has gradually been centralized in the Board of Governors as a result of both legal reorganizations and changes in personalities. Technically, the 12 district banks and their 24 branches continue to be owned by the member banks. But unlike most forms of ownership, member bank ownership of the reserve banks does not include many of the usual rights of proprietorship. (The location of the district reserve banks and branches and the boundaries of their regions are mapped in Figure 10-3.)

Although the ownership is evidenced by stock certificates, the stock cannot be bought or sold freely. Each member bank is required to subscribe to an amount of stock in its district reserve bank equal to 3 percent of its capital and surplus. This stock is not marketable and must be redeemed upon leaving membership. Member banks are eligible to receive a maximum dividend return of 6 percent on the par value of the stock. In the postwar period the Federal Reserve has generated earnings far in excess of this amount but transfers these earnings to the U.S. Treasury. In 1971, the 12 Federal Reserve Banks generated current earnings of almost $4 billion. Operation of the banks absorbed about 10 percent of this amount and dividends 1 percent. Approximately 90 percent was transferred to the Treasury. As about the same percentage of the System's total current earnings are derived from interest on its portfolio of Treasury securities, this represents only a return transfer.

The member banks elect the majority of the directors at their respective reserve bank or branch. Each bank has nine directors. Six are elected by the member banks,

Figure 10-3 Boundaries of Federal Reserve Districts and Their Branch Territories

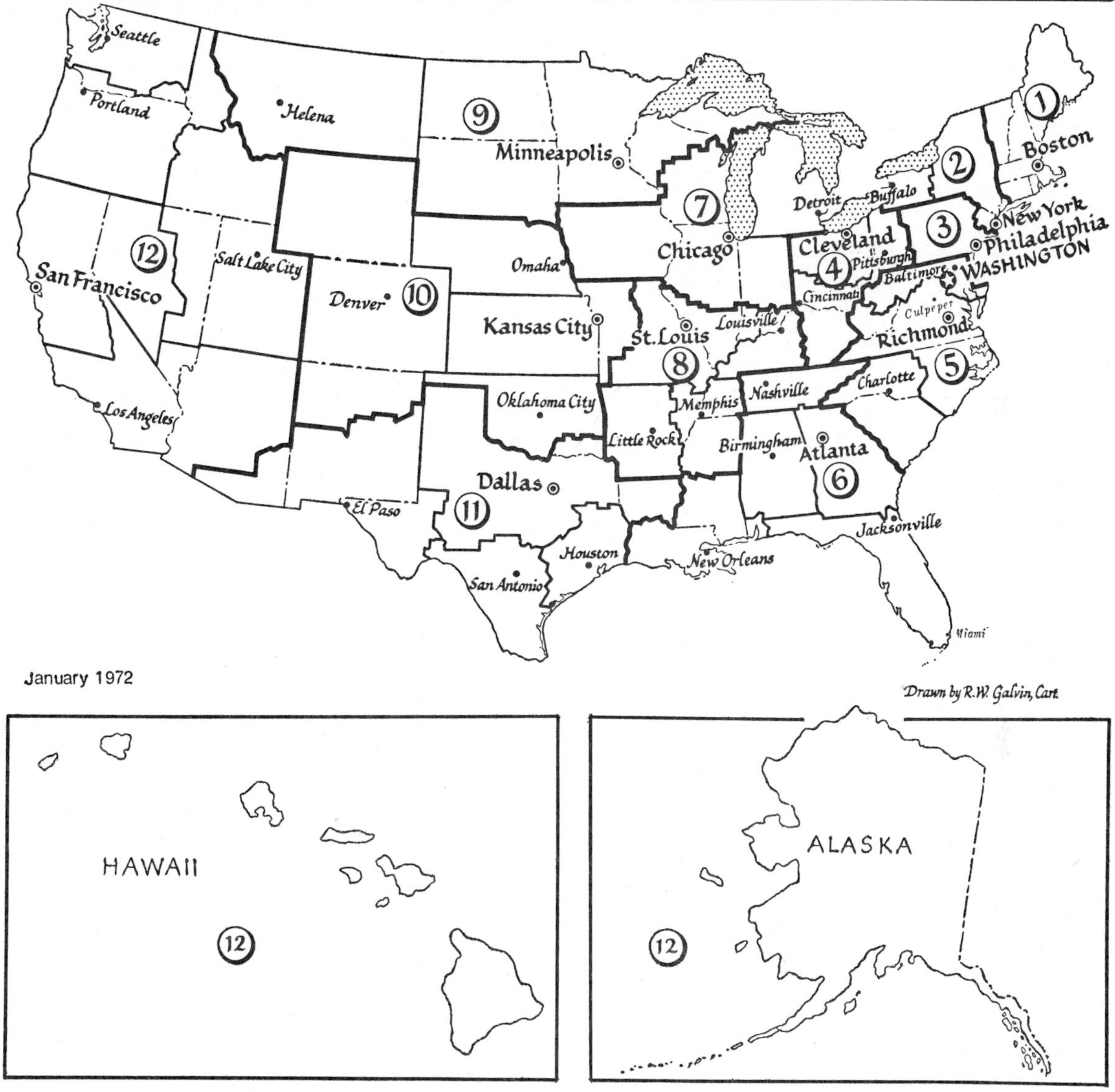

January 1972

Drawn by R.W. Galvin, Cart.

Legend

- Boundaries of Federal Reserve Districts
- Boundaries of Federal Reserve Branch Territories
- Board of Governors of the Federal Reserve System
- Federal Reserve Bank Cities
- Federal Reserve Branch Cities
- Federal Reserve Bank Facilities

Source: *Federal Reserve Bulletin.*

three from among bankers representing member banks of different sizes and three from among nonbankers, typically businessmen. The remaining three members are appointed by the Board of Governors and are considered public members. One of these three public members is designated chairman and another deputy chairman. The Board of Directors of each bank performs four basic functions:

1. It elects the president of the reserve bank subject to approval by the Board of Governors. As a member of the FOMC, the president serves as a policy-maker.
2. It oversees the day-to-day operations of the reserve bank.
3. It establishes the discount rate charged by the reserve bank, subject to review and final determination by the Board of Governors.
4. It provides a channel of communications between the business community and the reserve banks and, thereby, to the Board of Governors and the FOMC.

The Board of Directors meets periodically at its respective reserve bank or branch. The meetings are devoted to a review of the nonpolicy operations of the bank or branch, a review and approval of the discounts and advances to member banks, a review of the discount rate, a briefing on the state of the economy by economists at the reserve bank, and a two-way discussion with the senior staff of the bank on economic developments and economic policy, particularly as they apply to the region. This discussion supplements the economic intelligence available to the System from economic-data series. To minimize potential conflicts of interest, the bank directors are not permitted to receive confidential information before it is released to the general public.

Member Banks

Banks derive a number of benefits from being members of the Federal Reserve System. Besides the limited proprietory rights of ownership and an effectively guaranteed 6 percent return on their stock, member banks have access to the discount window for temporary borrowings, can use the check-clearing facilities of the System, can obtain currency shipments, and have access to its research facilities. On the other hand, there are a number of costs of membership. Reserve requirements on member banks are generally considerably higher than the requirements that states impose on nonmember banks. Member banks also must agree to accept all checks presented for payment at par value. Nonpar clearing is a remnant of earlier years when uncertainties and delays in the collection process led many banks to accept checks written on distant banks only at a discount.

For many banks the costs of membership appear to outweigh the benefits. Large city-correspondent banks frequently offer to provide smaller banks with check-clearing and borrowing services, in addition to services such as investment and credit advice, foreign collection, and loan participation, which the Federal Reserve Banks are prohibited from offering by law. For many banks the cost of these services from correspondents is less than the cost of the income foregone by holding greater amounts of nonearning assets as required reserves than they would otherwise. As a result, less than 15 percent of state banks prefer to belong to the Federal Reserve System and the number of state member banks has declined steadily, decreasing by 25 percent during the 1960s. National banks are required to be members of the System.

Independence of the Federal Reserve

Probably the most controversial aspect of the organization of the Federal Reserve System is its so-called independence. Although the System is a prime formulator of economic policy in the public interest, it is not directly under the authority of either Congress or the administration. In part, this reflects historical legacies and, in part, general satisfaction with operations under this organizational structure. The independence of the System applies only to the short run and is derived both from the long 14-year terms of the governors, which insulate them from day-to-day political pressures, and from its large portfolio of Treasury securities, which relieves the System of having to obtain annual appropriations from Congress, thereby becoming subject to the congressional power of the purse. The long terms of the governors also make it difficult for an incoming president to appoint a majority of the Board. Assuming no resignations, he can appoint only two governors in his first four-year term and a majority of the Board only late in his second term.

In the longer run, the System's freedom is considerably more restricted. The Federal Reserve System was created by an act of Congress (The Federal Reserve Act, 1913), can be modified by Congress (the Banking Acts of 1933 and 1935), and can even be terminated by Congress (the first and second Banks of the United States). The Federal Reserve is subject to all the laws of the United States including the Employment Act of 1946, which gives explicit recognition to the economic responsibilities of the government and specifies the goals of the economy in general terms. Moreover, the record indicates that the Board of Governors, like the Supreme Court, is not immune to the desires of the electorate, as reflected in the ballot box, and has been receptive to the policies and objectives of the contemporaneous administration and Congress. It is, thereby, more accurate to describe the Federal Reserve as independent within, rather than independent of, the government.

Functions of the Federal Reserve System

Monetary Functions

Because money does not manage itself, Congress has delegated to the Federal Reserve System the responsibility of managing money in the public interest. The management of money has undergone a number of changes in emphasis since the inception of the Federal Reserve. The Federal Reserve Act directed the Fed only "to furnish an elastic currency [and] to afford means of discounting commercial paper." This charged the Federal Reserve with accommodating the needs of business, a policy that, by promoting monetary changes in the same direction as business changes, in effect served to reinforce rather than offset business cycles. In the 1920s, the primary emphasis of Federal Reserve policy was directed at achieving price stability and influencing capital flows among countries in order to maintain international parity between the price of gold and the value of national currencies. In the 1930s, Federal Reserve operations concentrated on achieving a gradual recovery from the Great Depression.

In the first half of the 1940s, monetary policy accommodated the need to finance World War II at low interest rates. In the second half of the decade, policy was concerned with promoting a smooth transition to a peacetime economy by supporting the market value of the large federal government debt contracted during the war. This involved resisting any tendency for interest rates to rise and bond prices to fall. Since the 1950s, Federal Reserve policy has been coordinated with fiscal policy in guiding the economy toward the multiple goals of full employment, stable prices, and equilibrium in the balance of payments. In the 1960s, the Federal Reserve also became engaged in conducting operations in the foreign exchange markets designed to stabilize international capital flows and the exchange value of the dollar.

Nonmonetary Functions

In addition to the monetary policy functions, the Federal Reserve has a large number of important regulatory, supervisory, research, and housekeeping functions.

Maintenance of a National Payments System. The Federal Reserve is charged with promoting an efficient and effective national payments system. It implements this responsibility by providing sufficient amounts of currency (excess currency returns to the banks for exchange into deposits), almost all of which, with the exception of coin, is issued by the Federal Reserve, requiring par clearings, and maintaining efficient check-collection and check-clearing facilities. In 1971, about 23 billion checks, or some 62 million a day, were written for more than $16 trillion. Of these, the Federal Reserve cleared 8.5 billion checks, totaling somewhat more than $4 trillion (Table 10-1). Most of the checks handled represent out-of-city clearings; in-city clearings are generally conducted through clearinghouses or other interbank clearing arrangements. Federal Reserve clearings in 1971 were double the number of checks handled ten years earlier and are expected to double again in the next decade. As checks involve costly paper transfers, the Federal Reserve is actively reviewing alternative payment systems, such as on-line computer clearings and various forms of gyro transfers, which eliminate at least some of the check-handling steps in the clearing process.

Table 10-1 **Volume of Operations in Principal Departments of Federal Reserve Banks, 1968-71**
(Number in thousands; amounts in thousands of dollars)

Operation	1971	1970	1969	1968
NUMBER OF PIECES HANDLED[1]				
Loans	7	13	23	11
Currency received and counted	6,270,732	r6,029,373	5,720,499	5,561,500
Currency verified and destroyed	2,446,244	2,174,444	2,115,564	2,057,607
Coin received and counted	13,736,840	r13,402,165	12,873,277	10,957,259
Checks handled:				
U.S. Govt. checks	628,602	622,144	575,118	554,813
Postal money orders	181,054	183,574	187,123	195,871
All other[2]	7,704,732	r7,158,441	6,503,449	5,904,929
Collection items handled:				
U.S. Govt. coupons paid	13,523	r14,210	13,118	13,255
All other	26,994	r27,364	27,895	26,299
Issues, redemptions, and exchanges of U.S. Govt. securities	258,174	r276,172	283,175	267,826
Transfers of funds	8,148	r27,364	6,662	5,894
Food stamps redeemed	1,842,026	r1,277,007	519,595	384,763
AMOUNTS HANDLED				
Loans	85,254,860	129,578,588	154,305,388	84,525,110
Currency received and counted	48,783,022	45,718,990	43,273,577	40,585,320
Currency verified and destroyed	13,261,100	12,092,137	11,832,628	10,548,073
Coin received and counted	1,602,994	1,533,972	1,432,623	1,173,761
Checks handled:				
U.S. Govt. checks	211,996,633	208,858,062	208,155,031	190,653,523
Postal money orders	4,806,963	4,736,564	4,603,938	4,640,992
All other[2]	3,822,111,968	r3,330,673,690	2,774,422,163	2,350,761,951
Collection items handled:				
U.S. Govt. coupons paid	6,239,761	5,702,894	6,849,373	6,765,295
All other	22,103,954	21,022,409	19,782,240	19,865,950
Issues, redemptions, and exchanges on U.S. Govt. securities	1,951,122,313	r1,433,118,703	1,151,579,538	1,055,426,914
Transfers of funds	14,858,172,824	12,332,001,386	9,800,324,538	7,727,430,821
Food stamps redeemed	3,116,904	1,840,100	694,394	513,618

r Revised.
[1] Packaged items handled as a single item are counted as one piece.
[2] Exclusive of checks drawn on the F.R. Banks.

Source: Board of Governors of the Federal Reserve System, *Annual Report, 1971*, p. 256.

Fiscal Agent for the U.S. Treasury. As fiscal agent for the federal government, the Federal Reserve Banks perform four main functions:

1. They maintain the working balances of the Treasury from which all payments are made.

2. They safekeep the collateral commercial banks are required to maintain against U.S. Treasury deposits at their banks.
3. They process Treasury debt transactions with the public. This involves receiving and processing applications for new securities, allocating and delivering the securities to purchasers, receiving and processing payments, transferring securities, and redeeming the securities at maturity. These services are provided for both marketable securities and savings bonds.
4. The Federal Reserve Bank of New York acts as transfer agent for official gold transactions with foreign governments and international institutions.

Bank Supervision. The Federal Reserve has the responsibility of examining every member bank. To avoid unnecessary duplication, the Fed delegates the function of examining national banks to the Comptroller of the Currency and receives examination reports from him. All banks are examined at least once a year. The examinations are conducted by the staffs of the regional reserve banks. The St. Louis Federal Reserve Bank describes the objective of bank examination as the "appraisal of individual banks . . . by the technique of verifying that the books show all assets and liabilities at correct, or at least prudent, valuation, checking compliance with applicable laws [and] assessing the adequacy of capital and managerial ability and capacity." As noted earlier, bank examinations are not audits, although surprise examinations occasionally unearth defalcations. Bank management is required to correct any unsatisfactory conditions discovered in the examination process.

Bank Regulation. The Board of Governors is charged with regulating the structure of commercial banking in order to achieve satisfactory performance. In the process, the Board has the responsibility of evaluating applications for bank mergers where the resulting bank is a state member bank, and advising the appropriate regulatory agency—the Comptroller of the Currency or the FDIC—on applications where the resulting bank is not a state member. The Board also has responsibility for approving acquisitions of any banks and nonbanking firms by bank holding companies, and for determining what activities are sufficiently closely related to commercial banking to be permitted to be conducted by banks and bank holding companies. The collection and evaluation of evidence pertinent to merger and holding-company applications are conducted jointly by the staffs of the regional reserve banks and the Board of Governors. Decisions by the Board, which must comply with federal antitrust statutes, are subject to challenge by the U.S. Department of Justice and to final determination by the federal courts.

Economic Research. In the performance of its functions, the Federal Reserve participates in a wide range of research activities. These studies are conducted by economic research staffs of both the Board of Governors and the regional reserve banks. The major research functions include:

1. The collection of economic intelligence. The major portion of financial-data series, including the money supply, interest rates, and the balance sheet items of commercial banks, are collected by the Federal Reserve. In addition, the Federal Reserve compiles a number of important nonfinancial series, such as the widely used index of industrial production in manufacturing, mining, and the utilities. Almost all of the data collected are disseminated to the public in a number of forms, most noticeably in the *Federal Reserve Bulletin*, published monthly by the Board of Governors.

2. The analysis and evaluation of the economic intelligence collected by themselves and others to identify where the economy is, where it has been, and where it is going. Economic activity in foreign countries that may affect the United States through the balance of payments is also studied. These studies provide the base for policy decisions. Much of the analyses is shared with the public through publication in the *Bulletin* and the monthly reviews published by each regional bank, and through speeches and congressional testimony of high officials in the System.

3. Research into the functioning of the economy; in particular, the operation of the financial sector, the interrelationships between the financial and real sectors, and the implications of alternative policy strategies. Increased knowledge of the linkages between these sectors increases the precision of monetary policy. The research varies from intensive analyses of specific sectors to the construction of large econometric models of the entire economy that can be used both for prediction and for identifying the implications of simulated alternative policy strategies.

4. Research into the interrelationships between alternative structures of commercial banking, the conduct of bank supervision and regulation, and the economic performance of banks. The output of these studies helps the System evaluate applications for mergers and holding-company acquisitions and make recommendations with respect to the desirabilities of unit versus branch banking, independent versus holding-company banking, and the benefits of size and the number of competitors in a market area.

The Federal Reserve Balance Sheet

To understand how the Federal Reserve affects the financial sector, it is first necessary to analyze the balance sheets of the Federal Reserve Banks. As we have seen, bank reserves are the major policy determinant of both the money stock and interest rates. Except for changes in vault cash and a few minor Treasury accounts, all changes in bank reserves originate in changes in items on the Fed balance sheet. The major items on the consolidated statement of position of the 12 regional reserve banks are shown in Table 10-2 for year-end 1971. Before considering the causes of change in these items and analyzing the implications

Table 10-2 **Consolidated Statement of Condition of All Federal Reserve Banks, December 31, 1971**

	(Million Dollars)
Assets	
Gold certificates	9,875
Discounts and advances	39
U.S. Government securities	
Bought outright	68,996
Under repurchase agreements	1,222
Cash items in process of collection	11,906
Other assets	2,576
Total	94,614
Liabilities and Capital	
Federal Reserve notes	53,819
Deposits	
Member banks	27,780
U.S. Treasury	2,020
Foreign	294
Other	1,018
Deferred availability of cash items	7,552
Other liabilities	647
Capital account	1,484
Total	94,614

Source: *Federal Reserve Bulletin*, January, 1972, p. A 12.

for bank reserves, money supply, and interest rates, the individual accounts are described.

Asset Accounts

Gold Certificates. The gold account is a legacy of the days when currency and deposits were convertible into gold specie and the Federal Reserve Banks needed to be prepared to accommodate conversion demands. Gold reserve requirements on Federal Reserve note and deposit liabilities were incorporated in the Federal Reserve Act. In 1933, Congress prohibited private residents from owning gold and limited gold ownership for uses other than industry and the arts to the Treasury. The Federal Reserve sold its gold to the Treasury in exchange for an equal dollar amount of gold certificates, which were permitted to satisfy the reserve requirement. Through time whenever the requirement threatened to interfere with the ability of the Federal Reserve to expand the money supply, the requirement was reduced, and it was finally eliminated altogether in the 1960s. As a matter of practice, the Federal Reserve, as an agent for the Treasury, conducts most of the country's gold transactions with foreign governments, and changes in the gold certificates effectively mirror changes in the Treasury stock of gold.

Treasury Securities. The Federal Reserve holds a large portfolio of marketable Treasury securities acquired in the course of its monetary policy operations. A significant portion of the portfolio was acquired during war periods when the federal debt was greatly enlarged. The large majority of securities is held outright and a small amount is held under repurchase agreement with security dealers. These latter securities are required to be repurchased by the seller, in these instances nonbank security dealers, within an agreed period of up to 15 days or sooner at the option of either party. Treasury securities represent the System's main source of income. More importantly, they are also the ammunition with which the Federal Reserve conducts open market operations. In recent years, Congress has authorized the Federal Reserve to also purchase the securities of federal agencies, such as the Federal National Mortgage Association.

Discounts and Advances (Loans). This account represents short-term borrowing by member banks from the Federal Reserve Banks. The borrowings are required to be collateralized by Treasury securities or other eligible negotiable paper. The rate charged by the Federal Reserve Bank for such borrowing is the discount rate.

Cash Items in the Process of Collection. As described earlier in Chapter 6, this account arises from the Federal Reserve's check-clearing operations and represents the dollar amount of checks in the process of collection. It varies with changes in payment patterns and transportation conditions. When the liability item, Deferred Availability of Cash Items, is subtracted from CIPC, the remainder is Federal Reserve float. As CIPC is almost always larger than DACI, float is considered an asset item.

Liability and Capital Accounts

Federal Reserve Notes. These notes account for almost all the currency in circulation, except for coins.

Deposits.

a. *Member banks*—Deposits by member banks account for the lion's share of deposits at the Federal Reserve Banks and, except for vault cash, represent total member bank reserves.
b. *U.S. Treasury*—This is the working balance of the Treasury. As all payments are made from this account, which is typically kept at minimum levels, the balance is continuously replenished from the Treasury's considerably larger tax and loan accounts (*TT* and *L*) at commercial banks.
c. *Foreign and other*—Many foreign governments maintain working balances at the Federal Reserve for settling international accounts. A few nonmember commercial banks use some of the clearing facilities of the System and are

required to hold minimum clearing balances. Private parties may not have deposits with the Federal Reserve.

Deferred Availability of Cash Items. This represents the delay in crediting payment to banks which have presented checks for collection. Payment is made according to a time schedule related to the geographical distance between banks. In no instance is the delay more than two days whether or not the Federal Reserve has collected the funds from the paying bank.

The Reserve Equation

By the balance sheet identity, the total of the asset accounts equals the total of the liability accounts:

$$TA = TL. \tag{10-1}$$

Because we are interested in member bank reserves, this account can be broken out of total liabilities. Abstracting from vault cash at banks:

$$R = TL - OL, \tag{10-2}$$

where:

OL = liabilities and capital other than member bank deposits.

Substituting for TL from equation 10-1,

$$R = TA - OL. \tag{10-3}$$

This equation can be expanded to specify the individual asset and liability accounts:

$$R = G + TS + D + F - C - TRD - FD, \tag{10-4}$$

where:

R = member bank reserves
G = gold certificates
TS = Treasury securities
D = discounts and advances
F = float (CIPC–DACI)
C = currency
TRD = Treasury deposits
FD = foreign deposits.

This equation shows that reserves vary directly in a one-to-one relationship with assets and inversely with other liabilities. Thus, reserves vary directly with changes in *G, TS, D,* and *F* and inversely with changes in *C, TRD,* and *FD.* An increase of $1,000 in the Fed's portfolio of Treasury securities, ceteris paribus, increases reserves by $1,000, while an increase of $1,000 in the public's holdings of currency decreases reserves by the same amount.

The mechanics of these changes can be traced through T-accounts. Consider a payment of $1,000 by the Treasury from its account at the Federal Reserve Bank to Mr. Jones for overpayment of his income taxes. Mr. Jones deposits the check in his bank which credits his demand deposit account by the amount and presents the check to its Federal Reserve for payment.

Bank A

Assets		Liabilities
Reserves	+$1,000	+$1,000 Deposit Mr. Jones
Required	+200	
Excess	+800	

Federal Reserve Bank

Assets	Liabilities
	−$1,000 Treasury Deposits
	+ 1,000 Bank A Deposits

All Treasury checks are paid the same day in federal funds and the district Federal Reserve Bank credits the reserve account of Bank A and debits the Treasury's balance. Assuming a reserve requirement of 20 percent on demand deposits, no leakages, and only demand deposits, Bank A now has $800 of excess reserves and can initiate a demand deposit expansion of up to another $4,000. To minimize the impact of its operations on bank reserves, the Treasury would most likely transfer to the Federal Reserve $1,000 from its *TT* and *L* accounts at commercial banks built up through receipts from tax payments and sales of new securities. This would offset the reserve and deposit increase.

Federal Reserve Control of Reserves

While, in the absence of changes in vault cash and minor Treasury accounts, member bank reserves can only change if another account on the Federal Reserve balance sheet changes, this does not indicate that the Fed has control over bank reserves. Most of the accounts on the Federal Reserve balance sheet are not under its control. For example, Treasury balances are under the control of the Treasury, while float changes with changes in weather conditions affecting transportation and the physical transfer of checks. The major determinants of each asset and liability account are:

$$\Delta G = f(\Delta \overset{+}{B}). \tag{10-5}$$

$$\Delta TS = f(FED). \tag{10-6}$$

$$\Delta D = f(\Delta \overset{-}{i_D}, \Delta \overset{+}{i_S}). \tag{10-7}$$

$$\Delta F = f(\Delta W, \Delta P). \tag{10-8}$$

$$\Delta C = f(\Delta \overset{+}{Y}). \tag{10-9}$$

$$\Delta TRD = f(TRE). \tag{10-10}$$

$$\Delta FD = f(\Delta X). \tag{10-11}$$

where:

B = U.S. balance of payments surplus
FED = Federal Reserve System
i_D = discount rate
i_S = market rate of interest on securities
W = weather
P = payment patterns
Y = gross national product
TRE = Treasury
X = foreign central banks.

Signs for the relationships are now shown where unambiguous. Thus, the Federal Reserve has complete control only over its own portfolio of Treasury securities and partial control through the discount rate over member bank borrowing. Substituting equations 10-5 through 10-11 into equation 10-4 and recognizing that the Federal Reserve establishes the discount rate shows that changes in reserves of a large number of diverse forces:

$$\Delta R = f(\Delta \overset{+}{B}, \Delta \overset{+}{i_S}, \Delta W, \Delta P, \Delta \overset{-}{Y}, \Delta X, TRE, FED). \tag{10-12}$$

Although the Federal Reserve is only one factor affecting reserves, it is a unique factor. Through its operations, the Federal Reserve can offset, if it so wishes, the effects of changes in the other factors on reserves. Thus, total member bank reserves can be considered effectively under Federal Reserve control.

The impact of Federal Reserve control of reserves is readily evident. During the 1960s, gold certificates declined by almost \$7 billion and currency in circulation increased by about \$24 billion. The sum effect of these two forces was to decrease reserves by some \$30 billion. Yet reserves increased by some \$10 billion in this period. The increase is in large measure attributed to an increase of \$34 billion in Federal Reserve holdings of Treasury securities. It follows that changes in the Fed's portfolio of Treasury securities is a poor indicator of changes ir reserves. This is true in the short run as well as in the long run. In the first quarter

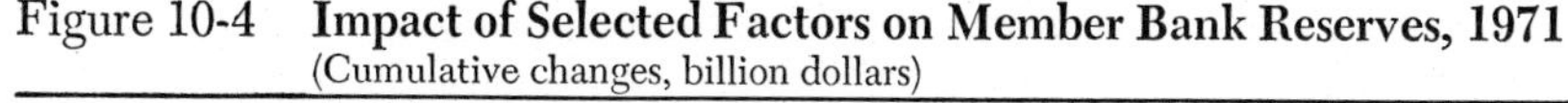

Figure 10-4 **Impact of Selected Factors on Member Bank Reserves, 1971**
(Cumulative changes, billion dollars)

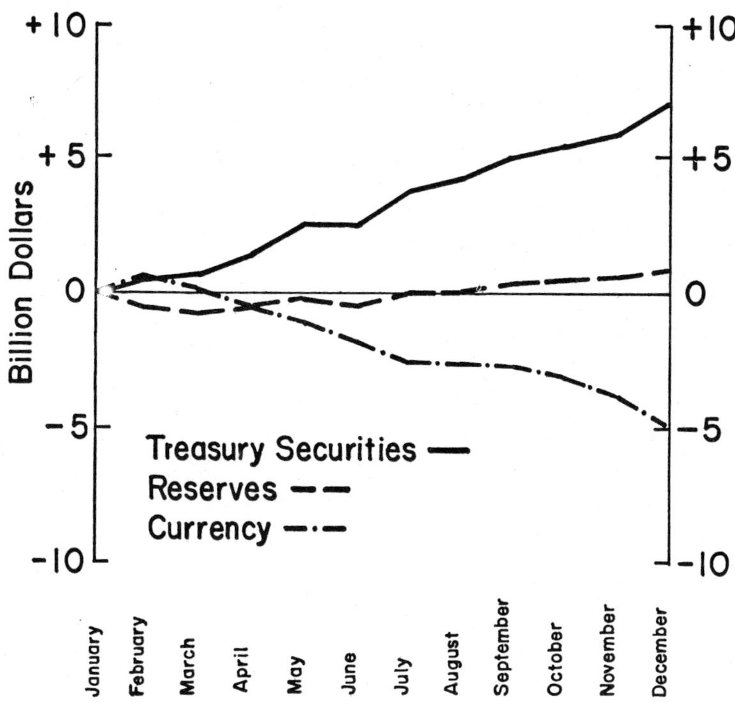

Source: *Federal Reserve Bulletin,* February, 1972, pp. A 4, A 5.

of 1971, the Federal Reserve purchased $700 million of Treasury securities. However, member bank reserves declined by $800 million in the period. For 1971 as a whole, Fed purchases of Treasury securities totaled $7 billion, while reserves increased less than $1 billion. To a large extent, the security purchases offset reserve losses generated by large increases in the public's demand for currency, which increased $5 billion. These changes are plotted in Figure 10-4. Thus, it is possible to have no change in reserves simultaneous with large changes in either direction in the Fed's portfolio or large changes in reserves with no Fed purchases or sales of Treasury securities.

For purposes of monetary analysis, changes in total reserves, not changes in any particular asset or liability accounts, are important in gauging the implications of Federal Reserve actions on money, interest rates, and aggregate income. Changes in the other accounts are of importance primarily in explaining the reasons for Federal Reserve operations during the period.

Every Thursday afternoon the Federal Reserve publishes a balance sheet for the close of business Wednesday. This report is carefully scrutinized by the participants in the financial markets for clues to past and pending Federal Reserve operations. Because the report encompasses a period of only one week, it is generally insufficient in itself to provide much guidance regarding Federal Reserve intentions. However, if analyzed over longer periods of time, these reports provide more accurate information about the thrust of Federal Reserve stabilization operations. Nevertheless, total reserves are not the only monetary variable used by financial analysts to gauge Federal Reserve actions or intent. The selection and interpretation of indicators of Federal Reserve policy is one of the more controversial areas in monetary economics and will be discussed in greater detail in Chapter 20.

References

Board of Governors of the Federal Reserve System, *The Federal Reserve System: Purposes and Functions,* Fifth edition (Washington, D.C.: 1963).

Committee on Banking and Currency, *The Federal Reserve After Fifty Years: Hearings,* Volumes 1–3 (88th U.S. Congress, Second session, 1964).

——, *Federal Reserve Structure and the Development of Monetary Policy: 1915–1935* (92nd U.S. Congress, First session, 1971).

Federal Reserve Bank of St. Louis, *Bank Supervision* (St. Louis: 1963).

Friedman, Milton, and Anna J. Schwartz, *A Monetary History of the United States, 1867–1960* (Princeton: National Bureau of Economic Research, 1963).

Lenhart, Harry, Jr., "Agency Study: The Federal Reserve System," *National Journal,* 2 (44), October 31, 1970, 2375-2392, and 2 (45), November 7, 1970, 2447-2462.

Reagan, Michael D., "The Internal Structure of the Federal Reserve: A Political Analysis," in *Monetary Management,* Commission on Money and Credit (Englewood Cliffs, N.J.: Prentice-Hall, 1963).

Studenski, Paul, and Herman E. Krooss, *Financial History of the United States* (New York: McGraw-Hill, 1963).

Instruments of Monetary Policy

11

The basic deposit-reserve equation developed in Chapter 7,

$$\Delta D = k\Delta R, \tag{11-1}$$

shows that the Federal Reserve can affect the quantity of bank deposits (D), and thereby the money stock, in two ways, by changing the dollar amount of total reserves (R) and by changing the reserve multiplier (k). The instruments available to the Federal Reserve to generate changes in the stock of money are called *quantitative instruments of monetary control.* At times, the Federal Reserve may also wish to affect the ownership composition of the money supply or bank credit. This requires a different set of instruments referred to as *qualitative tools.* This chapter describes the instruments available to the Federal Reserve in implementing its policy strategies and discusses the ways these instruments are employed.

Quantitative Instruments

Quantitative instruments permit the Federal Reserve to change the overall dollar quantities of money and bank credit. To the extent total funds and credit in the economy are positively linked to these measures, the quantitative tools also permit the System to affect total credit and flows of funds.

Changing the Deposit-Reserve Multiplier

Reserve Requirements. The bank deposit-reserve multiplier (k) was defined in Chapter 7 as:

$$k = \frac{1}{\bar{r} + e + c},$$

where:

$\bar{r}$ = average reserve requirement on demand and time deposits.

The Federal Reserve has control only over $\bar{r}$. The banks determine e and the public c. The value of the multiplier is inversely related to the values of the individual reserve requirements on different types of deposits. As discussed earlier, the Federal Reserve has the authority to vary these requirements within limits established by Congress. Increases in reserve requirements reduce the dollar amount of deposits a given dollar amount of reserves can support. Decreases in requirements increase the deposits supportable by a given reserve base. For example, a reduction in reserve requirements on demand deposits from 20 percent to 10 percent will, in the absence of leakages and other types of deposits, double the amount of demand deposits that $1,000 of reserves can support from $5,000 to $10,000.

The mechanics of this process involve two steps. In the first step, the reduction in reserve requirements on the existing $5,000 deposits lowers the amount of required reserves by $500 and increases excess reserves by the same amount. In the second step, the banking system expands deposits to the point where all the excess reserves are again absorbed as required reserves (Table 11-1).

If leakages and other deposits are introduced, the deposit impact of reductions in reserve requirements is more difficult to calculate but the direction of the effect remains unchanged. Thus, the Fed can expand the dollar amount of bank deposits by lowering reserve requirements on either demand or time deposits and cut back on deposit expansion by raising requirements.

To minimize the burden on banks of computing required reserves accurately, requirements are rarely changed in amounts of less than one-half of a percentage point. As a result, changes in reserve requirements generate large potential effects on deposits and are used only infrequently. An across-the-board increase in 1969 of one-half of a percentage point on all demand deposits absorbed some $650 million of reserves on a reserve base of $26 billion, or an amount equal to 2½ percent of total reserves. As Table 11-2 shows, between 1966 and the major restructuring of reserve requirements in 1972, there have been effectively only two changes in reserve requirements on demand deposits and a like number on time deposits. This is far fewer than the number of changes in other policy instruments during the same period.

Table 11-1 **Effect of Reduction in Reserve Requirements**

Initial Condition

Assets		Liabilities	
Reserves	$1,000	$5,000	Demand Deposits
Required	1,000		
Excess	0		
Loans	4,000		
	$5,000	$5,000	

Reduction in Requirement

Assets		Liabilities	
Reserves	$1,000	$5,000	Demand Deposits
Required	500		
Excess	500		
Loans	4,000		
	$5,000	$5,000	

New Equilibrium

Assets		Liabilities	
Reserves	$1,000	$10,000	Demand Deposits
Required	1,000		
Excess	0		
Loans	9,000		
	$10,000	$10,000	

Changes in reserve requirements are, of necessity, public knowledge and are accompanied by a statement summarizing the reasons for the change. Such changes thus provide the Federal Reserve with an opportunity to communicate its intentions to the public. However, as is discussed in the next section, public announcements may, on occasion, be interpreted differently than intended and generate a perverse response. This possibility has reinforced Federal Reserve reluctance to make frequent changes in reserve requirements.

Changing Reserves

The Discount Rate. The Federal Reserve Banks maintain facilities to finance short-term borrowing needs of their member banks. The member banks may discount eligible commercial paper with, or receive advances on eligible collateral (primarily Treasury securities valued at par) from, the Federal Reserve Banks. Most loans are now in the form of advances, but the facility retains the name *discount window* reflecting its earlier mode of operations.

The discount window is not intended to provide either unlimited or long-term funds to the banks but to help them accommodate, at a reasonable cost, short-run

Table 11-2 Reserve Requirements of Member Banks
(Percent of deposits)

Effective date[1]	Net demand deposits [2,3]				Time deposits [3] (all classes of banks)		
	Reserve city banks		Country banks		Savings deposits	Other time deposits	
	Under $5 million	Over $5 million	Under $5 million	Over $5 million		Under $5 million	Over $5 million
1966—July 14, 21	16½		12		4	4	5
Sept. 8, 15							6
1967—Mar. 2					3½	3½	
Mar. 16					3	3	
1968—Jan. 11, 18	16½	17	12	12½			
1969—Apr. 17	17	17½	12½	13			
1970—Oct. 1							5

Effective Date[1]	Net demand deposits[2,3] (Million dollars)					Time deposits [3] (all classes of banks)		
						Savings deposits	Other time deposits	
	$2 or less	$2 to $10	$10 to $100	$100 to $400	Over $400		Under $5 million	Over $5 million
1972—Nov. 16	8	10	12	13	17½	3	3	5
In effect—Dec. 31, 1972	8	10	12	13	17½	3	3	5

[1] When two dates are shown, the first applies to the change at central reserve or reserve city banks and the second to the change at country banks. For changes prior to 1966 see Board's Annual Reports.

[2] Demand deposits subject to reserve requirements are gross demand deposits minus cash items in process of collection and demand balances due from domestic banks.

[3] Since Oct. 16, 1969, member banks have been required under Regulation M to maintain reserves against balances above a specified base due from domestic offices to their foreign branches. Effective Jan. 7, 1971, the applicable reserve percentage was increased from the original 10 per cent to 20 per cent. Regulation D imposes a similar reserve requirement on borrowings above a specified base from foreign banks by domestic offices of a member bank. For details concerning these requirements, see Regulations D and M.

Source: *Federal Reserve Bulletin*, July, 1972, pp. A 10, 679–681; Federal Reserve Press Release, October 24, 1972.

and unexpected outflows in deposits or increases in local loan demands until the bank is able to obtain the necessary reserves elsewhere. Federal Reserve regulations prohibit borrowing from the Federal Reserve Banks for "profiting from rate differentials and . . . extending an undue amount of credit for the speculative carrying of or trading in securities, real estate, or commodities, or otherwise."

Table 11-3 Effect of Increase in Member Bank Discounting

Initial Condition

Assets		Liabilities	
Reserves	$1,000	$5,000	Demand Deposits
Required	1,000		
Excess	0		
Loans	4,000		
	$5,000	$5,000	

Increase in Discounting

Assets		Liabilities	
Reserves	$2,000	$5,000	Demand Deposits
Required	1,000		
Excess	1,000	1,000	Borrowing from Fed.
Loans	4,000		
	$6,000	$6,000	

New Equilibrium

Assets		Liabilities	
Reserves	$2,000	$10,000	Demand Deposits
Required	2,000		
Excess	0	1,000	Borrowing from Fed.
Loans	9,000		
	$11,000	$11,000	

Ceteris paribus, when a bank borrows from the Federal Reserve not only its but the entire banking system's reserves increase by a like amount and a multiple expansion of deposits can ensue. When a bank repays such borrowings, reserves in the entire banking system decline and a multiple deposit contraction results. As reserves are not required to be held against borrowing at the discount window, changes in borrowing generate bank credit expansions and contractions larger by the amount of borrowing than an equal dollar change in reserves accompanying changes in deposits, as shown in the example (Table 11-3). Loans expand by $5,000 to $9,000 rather than by $4,000 to $8,000 as would have been the case had the additional $1,000 in reserves been provided through an inflow of deposits.

The discount window is not a policy instrument per se. It is always open to accommodate "legitimate" borrowing needs. The Fed influences the amount of borrowing through the discount rate and through discount administration. Banks can be expected to favor the discount window as a source of reserves more when the costs of these funds are low relative to costs on alternative funds than when they are high. Ceteris paribus, the lower the discount rate is, the higher the level of member bank borrowing from Federal Reserve Banks, and vice versa. Thus, the impact on reserves of changes in the discount rate is determined jointly by the willingness of commercial banks to borrow from the Federal Reserve and the Federal Reserve's aggressiveness with respect to establishing the relation of the discount rate to market rates of interest. On the whole, the Federal Reserve prefers to maintain the discount rate in line with market rates on alternative sources of short-term funds.

But the discount rate is not the total effective cost to individual banks of borrowing at the window. The Federal Reserve Banks police the window to insure that the funds are being used by the banks in ways consistent with the intent of the discount window. Banks which employ the funds inappropriately are "disciplined" to search for alternative sources. In addition, the longer a bank borrows continuously at the window, the more it is encouraged by the reserve bank to make its reserve adjustment by other means. These policies are reinforced by the reluctance of a number of banks to be in debt to the Federal Reserve and, thereby, open their operations to the scrutiny of the System. Thus, the amounts borrowed and the number of times a bank may tap the window per period of time are limited either by the Fed or by self-imposed preferences, raising the effective discount rate above the nominal rate.

The Federal Reserve may change the discount rate in order to encourage or discourage banks from borrowing. However, when the rates on alternative sources of short-term funds change, the discount rate may be changed only to maintain the same relative degree of encouragement. Because the discount rate is a highly visible interest rate and completely under the control of the Federal Reserve, market participants scrutinize any changes for signs of Federal Reserve policy intentions. Experience has indicated that the effects of the announcement of changes in the rate tend to be ambiguous and not a satisfactory transmitter of policy intent. An increase in the discount rate, for example, is interpreted by some market participants as an indication of Federal Reserve intent to curtail business activity and discourages them from additional borrowing. Others, however, interpret the increase as a confirmation that business activity is strong and that one might as well borrow while the funds are available at the existing market rate.

In addition to the ambiguity in interpretation of the direction of the impact, the discount rate is believed by some to signal not only the longer-run policy intent of the Federal Reserve but also shorter-run interest rate intent as well. Thus, to them, an increase in the discount rate also indicates that the Fed is raising interest rates across-the-board. For all these reasons, in recent years the Federal Reserve has been reluctant to change the discount rate in harmony with changes in market yields, particularly during periods of rapidly rising interest rates. Figure 11-1 shows that in these periods the discount rate "loses touch" with market rates.

Figure 11-1 The Discount Rate, Federal Funds Rate, and Member Bank Borrowings, 1966–72

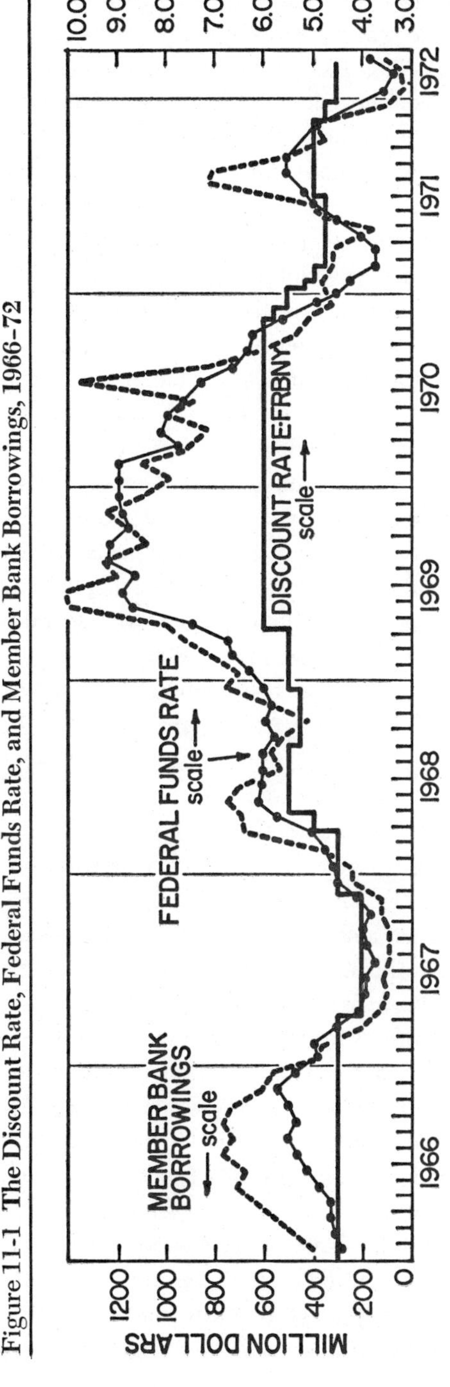

Source: Federal Reserve Bank of New York, *Annual Report, 1971*, p. 24; and *Monthly Review*, May, 1972, p. 117.

Because bank demands for funds tend to be procyclical, the Federal Reserve has, in the absence of corresponding increases in the discount rate, relied on increasingly tighter policing of the window to raise the effective cost of funds to the banks, discouraging greater-than-desired borrowings.

Nonetheless, the amount of borrowing at the discount window varies procyclically. In 1961, at a trough of business activity, about 10 percent of all member banks borrowed at the discount window an amount equal to less than one-half of 1 percent of total reserves in the banking system. In 1966, during a period of rapid business expansion, twice as many banks borrowed 3 percent of total reserves. On the average, member bank borrowings from the Federal Reserve account for only 2 percent of total reserves. This suggests that changes in the discount rate are more symbolic than representative of important changes in the cost of reserves to the banks and are not a major factor affecting rates of interest banks charge or pay.

The discount rate and discount window have assumed some additional policy importance in consequence of the introduction of the lagged-reserve accounting system in 1968. As requirements in any weekly reserve period are based on deposits two weeks earlier, banks not only know their requirements with certainty in each reserve period but cannot do anything to alter the amount. Thus, because the Federal Reserve does not pursue a deliberate policy of generating reserve deficiency, the Fed must provide all the reserves necessary to satisfy the requirements either through open market operations or through the discount window. To introduce restraint, the Federal Reserve must signal its intentions to the banks in advance. This it may do by increasing the discount rate, which would indicate higher reserve costs in the future to support deposits, and by forcing the banks increasingly to the window through reducing the reserves provided through open market operations. Because the reserve banks exert pressure on the borrowing banks to repay quickly, the Federal Reserve considers borrowed reserves more restrictive than an equal dollar amount of reserves provided through open market operations, and increases in the amount of borrowed reserves as inducements to the banks to curtail deposit expansion.

In view of the many problems in the operation of both the discount window and the discount rate, the Board of Governors commissioned a thorough reappraisal of the discount mechanism. The study was conducted by a committee of high Federal Reserve officials from the Board of Governors and the reserve banks. The committee recommended that the discount function be broadened to encompass three types of credit. An automatic basic credit line, limited in both amount and frequency of use, would be granted to all member banks. This credit would be subject to only minimum scrutiny by the reserve banks. Banks would also be granted a seasonal borrowing privilege to accommodate a portion of their predicted seasonal needs for reserves arising from regularly recurring seasonal changes in deposits and local loans. Lastly, banks could borrow for other adjust-

Table 11-4 **Effect of Open Market Purchase**

Federal Reserve Bank

Assets		Liabilities	
Treasury Securities	+$1,000	+$1,000	Bank A Deposit

Bank A

Assets		Liabilities	
Reserves	+$1,000	+$1,000	Dealer A
Required	200		
Excess	800		

ment or emergency purposes, which would be subject to much the same administration and scrutiny by the district reserve bank as at present. The committee also recommended that the discount rate be changed more frequently and in smaller quantum steps in harmony with changes in market rates of interest in order to reduce the emphasis market participants put on the rate. Implementation of some of these recommendations may be expected. Federal Reserve discount policy during the sharp decline in interest rates near year-end 1970 suggests that smaller and more frequent changes in the discount rate may be anticipated.

Open Market Operations. These operations are the most frequently used of the three quantitative instruments of monetary control. Open market operations inject and withdraw reserves into and out of the banking system through Federal Reserve purchases and sales, respectively, of Treasury securities. As noted earlier, ownership of Treasury securities is widespread and the securities are traded on a broad secondary market. Thus, Federal Reserve operations in these securities have a broad impact with only minimum disturbance to the market.

When the Fed wishes to inject reserves into the banking system, it purchases Treasury securities for its portfolio from security dealers at the lowest market price. Bank reserves are increased when the dealers deposit the checks from the sales at their banks and the banks present them to the Federal Reserve for payment. These payments are frequently made in federal funds, which are transferred by telephone order almost immediately, and the transactions are completed within one day. The transaction leaves the banks with excess reserves and the banking system can then expand deposits by a multiple of the reserve injection (Table 11-4).

Likewise, the Federal Reserve can absorb reserves by selling Treasury securities to security dealers at the highest prices. Reserves are withdrawn from the banks when the Federal Reserve presents the sellers' checks to the banks for collection. To the extent that this causes banks to become deficient in their required reserves, a multiple contraction in deposits results. All open market operations are conducted through competitive bidding with security dealers. At some price, dealers are willing to either buy or sell securities. As the dealers act to restore their inventories to desired levels, the effects of the transactions are transmitted through the financial system.

Open market operations have a number of advantages over the other two quantitative instruments. Unlike reserve requirements, they can be used in any strength. Unlike the discount rate, the effect on reserves is entirely at the initiative of the Federal Reserve. Open market operations are also flexible and can be reinforced or reversed quickly. If it appears that too many reserves were injected into the banking system as a result of security purchases in the morning or at the beginning of a reserve period, the reserves may be absorbed later the same day or later in the reserve period through security sales. Open market operations are conducted daily without public announcement so that the possibilities of speculation and misinterpretation are reduced. However, at the times when large operations are undertaken, the curiosity of the financial community is aroused.

Open market operations may be divided into two types, dynamic and defensive. *Dynamic operations* are designed to affect reserves in order to pursue the longer-run cyclical and secular stabilization goals of the economy. These would include operations such as providing reserves to increase the rate of expansion of the money stock in order to accelerate economic activity. Although dynamic operations are important and the primary subject of the remainder of this book, they represent only a small fraction of overall open market operations. In 1969, a year of monetary restraint, the Open Market Desk purchased almost $35 billion of Treasury securities and entered into repurchase agreements for another $24 billion. Yet, for the year as a whole, the Fed's holdings of Treasury securities increased by only $4 billion and total bank reserves increased less than $1 billion. In that year, less than 2 percent of the total open market operations could be considered dynamic operations. Even in years of monetary expansion, the percentage of dynamic operations is only slightly greater, rarely accounting for more than 10 percent of overall open market operations.

The large majority of all open market operations are *defensive operations* undertaken to offset short-run and primarily temporary, self-reversing forces that affect the supply and demand for reserves. In the absence of offsetting operations, these forces may be expected to generate abrupt short-run changes in the supply and cost of credit. For example, Federal Reserve float follows a very distinct intramonthly cycle rising to a peak near midmonth and declining thereafter. If not offset, this pattern would alternately inject and withdraw some three-fourths of a billion dollars of reserves into the financial system and produce wide intramonthly swings in short-term interest rates. Likewise, demands for credit are not smoothly spaced throughout the year, tending to rise abruptly at times of large new security issues and to decline between offerings. Left alone, interest rates would be expected to move in sympathy. Defensive operations are undertaken to reduce such swings in the cost of credit, which, by introducing additional uncertainty in the markets, are believed to reduce market participation and generate lower flows of funds than would otherwise be expected. Thus, open market operations may offset a potential temporary increase in interest rates in consequence of, say, a new Treasury financing (a policy referred to as *even keeling*), or of regular seasonal increases in credit demands every fall, which will reverse after Christmas.

Most, although not all, open market operations are conducted in the short-term sector to minimize their effects on interest rates and bond prices. In 1971, 95 percent of all outright purchases and sales were in Treasury bills. The $45 billion of Treasury bill transactions by the System accounted for only some 10 percent of all dealer transactions in bills on the secondary market.

At times, the Open Market Desk may wish to provide or withdraw bank reserves for only brief periods of time. In order to minimize any market impact of such transactions, the desk can effectively signal the fleeting nature of its operations. Rather than provide reserves temporarily through outright security purchases closely followed by offsetting sales, the desk may enter into agreements with security dealers to purchase securities subject to dealer repurchase within a specified time period. The dealer repurchases the securities at the same price at which he sold them, but is charged interest for the duration of the desk's ownership approximating the discount rate. When the desk wishes to absorb reserves briefly, it may, at its initiative, simultaneously sell and repurchase securities for future delivery. Under such matched sale-purchase operations, the desk conducts business with the dealers who buy the securities at the highest price and resell them at the lowest price.

Although open market policy is determined by the FOMC in Washington, all open market operations are conducted at the Open Market Trading Desk at the Federal Reserve Bank of New York to be closer to the financial markets. The day-to-day operations are directed by the manager of the Open Market Account who is an officer of both the FOMC and the New York Federal Reserve Bank. Changes in the portfolio of Treasury securities resulting from open market operations are allocated daily among the 12 Federal Reserve Banks according to their size.

The manager conducts daily operations in accordance with the policy directive drafted by the FOMC at its preceding meeting. The second paragraph of the directive contains the instructions to the manager. As the directive quoted in Chapter 10 shows, the instructions are not worded in terms of the amounts and time pattern of security purchases or sales. Rather, the paragraph specifies the conditions in the money market and/or growth rates in monetary and credit aggregates that the manager is to achieve. The determination of a trading strategy that will generate these conditions is assigned to the manager.

The manager formulates his daily trading strategy on the basis of the most recent information about the current values of the financial variables he is trying to affect, of short-term projections of the demand and supply forces affecting these variables, and of consideration of the target levels of these variables he has been directed to achieve. Although the manager plans his strategy daily, his time horizon depends on the target variable. While he may attempt to achieve daily targets in the federal funds rate or dealer loan rates (for which readings are immediately and accurately available), he may aim at weekly targets of borrowed or free reserves and monthly or quarterly targets of money supply and bank credit (for which accurate readings are not available until some time later and daily observations are not economically meaningful). Free reserves are the algebraic difference between aggregate excess and borrowed reserves. Their significance is discussed later in this chapter.

Although delegating the conduct of daily operations to the manager, the responsibility for the operations remains with the FOMC. Before undertaking each day's operations, the manager submits his strategy via a conference telephone call to a representative of the Board of Governors in Washington and to one of the four voting Federal Reserve Bank presidents, other than New York, for approval. A telegram summarizing the contents of this conversation is immediately sent to all reserve bank presidents. After the close of business each day, a complete report is prepared on the day's operations and is circulated to all members of the Board of Governors and to all reserve banks. At each meeting of the FOMC, the manager also reviews and defends his operations during the previous period.

Coordination of the Three Instruments

The three instruments of quantitative controls are generally used to reinforce each other. In periods of increasing monetary restraint, reserve requirements and the discount rate tend to be raised and dynamic open market operations directed at providing fewer reserves. However, all three instruments may not be deployed in these directions at all times during monetary restraint. The instruments are often used to cushion the effects of large changes in one of them and to spread the impact smoothly over a longer period. Open market operations are frequently used in this way to restructure the abrupt effects of changes in reserve requirements. For example, while reserve requirements were increased one-half of one percentage point on all demand deposits in April, 1969, absorbing $650 million of reserves, member bank reserves (adjusted for the increase in reserve requirements) actually increased during the month, indicating that open market operations not only offset all of the restrictive impact of the increase but injected some additional reserves into the economy. Total reserves did decline in subsequent months, implementing the increase in restraint. Likewise, when reserve requirements are reduced, open market operations generally distribute the increase in excess reserves evenly over a period consistent with stability in the money and credit markets.

Open market operations are also frequently used to offset large changes in member bank borrowing at the discount window so that total reserves do not change abruptly. On the other hand, unexpected changes in reserves, in consequence of open market operations, may cause banks to increase or decrease their borrowings at the discount window.

As a result of the coordinated use of the three instruments, changes in any one instrument alone are insufficient to describe Federal Reserve actions. It is necessary to combine changes in all three instruments. This can be accomplished in a single measure by adjusting observed reserves for reserves released or absorbed by changes in reserve requirements. One method to derive such a series is to multiply the dollar amount of actual deposits in the period considered by a constant set of reserve requirements, say, those in effect at the end of the period. Decreases in reserve requirements accompanied by increases in deposits are observed as increases in effective reserves, and increases in requirements as decreases in effective reserves. Such a series of effective reserves was, until recently, prepared monthly by the Federal Reserve and published in the *Federal Reserve Bulletin.*

Qualitative Instruments

Unlike the three quantitative instruments, which affect the aggregate amounts of deposits and credit and let the distribution among alternative uses be determined by market forces, qualitative tools are directed at affecting the ownership mix of deposits and credit. The use of qualitative tools reflects dissatisfaction with the credit allocation generated by market demand and supply. Such dissatisfaction may arise both because market imperfections are believed to interfere with the efficient accommodation of market forces and because the free market distribution generated is inconsistent with social priorities or equity. Qualitative monetary controls redirect credit by affecting cost differentials either to the lender in extending credit among particular sectors or to the borrower in acquiring different types of credit.

Cost differentials affecting lenders usually take the form of asset reserve requirements, that is, requiring lenders to hold designated percentages of particular types of credit in their portfolios. This increases the attractiveness of the favored types of credit at the expense of other credit and induces lenders to bid down the interest rate on the former type of credit and bid up the interest rates on other credit. Cost differentials affecting borrowers usually involve changing the terms of the credit, primarily the percentage of down payment and the term to maturity. While leaving the nominal cost unchanged, this alters the effective cost of the credit to the borrower. Increases in the minimum required down payment and decreases in the allowable term to maturity both increase the effective interest rate above the nominal rate and, as financial claims are ordered on the basis of effective rates and not nominal rates, alter the distribution of credit.

Because the total amount of all credit is not greatly affected by these measures, qualitative instruments reorder the recipients of the existing amount of credit, increasing the credit to some sectors and reducing it to others.

Wartime Controls. In this country, qualitative credit controls have been used most frequently during war years. In these periods, the government has typically preferred to finance a substantial portion of its increased war-related expenditures through the sale of debt rather than by raising taxes. At the same time, it has not wished to generate inflation, thus ruling out rapid monetary expansions to absorb the debt, nor to sell the debt at much higher interest rates, raising its expenditures even further. The strategy pursued was to discourage the demand for private credit and, thereby, also private spending by raising the effective cost of such credit without increasing its nominal cost. To achieve these ends, the Federal Reserve was directed to impose appropriate minimum down-payment requirements and maximum terms to maturity on consumer and real estate credit. With credit demands from these sectors reduced, banks invested heavily in newly issued Treasury securities. These controls were not popular and generally were quickly removed once peace returned and the high social importance of financing the government sector at low interest rates diminished.

Regulations G, T, and U. These controls establish minimum down payments or margins investors must make when borrowing to finance the purchase of equity securities and convertible bonds and when using these securities as collateral. The Federal Reserve was first authorized to impose margin requirements by the Securities Exchange Act of 1934 "for the purpose of preventing the excessive use of credit for the purchase or carrying of securities." Undue use of credit was believed responsible for the sharp runup in stock prices in the late 1920s and to have contributed significantly to the severity of the subsequent decline by forcing the sale of securities as their market prices declined beneath the necessary collateral value for the loans. In addition, it was felt that the use of credit for the purpose of purchasing stocks was economically unproductive and socially undesirable, absorbing credit that could be used more beneficially in other sectors. Initially, margin requirements applied only to loans extended by commercial banks and security dealers and brokers on equity securities listed on major stock exchanges. In recent years, the regulations have been broadened to encompass additional lenders and securities to reduce public avoidance through borrowing amounts greater than permitted by margin requirements from exempt lenders or on exempt securities.

The act also granted the Board of Governors the authority to change the margin requirements. Increases in margin requirements discourage the use of stock market credit by increasing the down payment, while decreases in margin requirements encourage the use of credit in purchasing stock. Changes in margin requirements

Table 11-5 **Margin Requirements**
(Percent of market value)

Period		For credit extended under Regulations T (brokers and dealers), U (banks), and G (others than brokers, dealers, or banks)						
Beginning date	Ending date	On margin stocks			On convertible bonds			On short sales (T)
		T	U	G	T	U	G	
1937–Nov. 1	1945–Feb. 4	40						50
1945–Feb. 5	July 4	50						50
July 5	1946–Jan. 20	75						75
1946–Jan. 21	1947–Jan. 31	100						100
1947–Feb. 1	1949–Mar. 29	75						75
1949–Mar. 30	1951–Jan. 16	50						50
1951–Jan. 17	1953–Feb. 19	75						75
1953–Feb. 20	1955–Jan. 3	50						50
1955–Jan. 4	Apr. 22	60						60
Apr. 23	1958–Jan. 15	70						70
1958–Jan. 16	Aug. 4	50						50
Aug. 5	Oct. 15	70						70
Oct. 16	1960–July 27	90						90
1960–July 28	1962–July 9	70						70
1962–July 10	1963–Nov. 5	50						50
1963–Nov. 6	1968–Mar. 10	70						70
1968–Mar. 11	June 7	70			50			70
June 8	1970–May 5	80			60			80
1970–May 6	1971–Dec. 3	65			50			65
In effect Sept. 30, 1972		55			50			55

NOTE.—Regulations G, T, and U, prescribed in accordance with the Securities Exchange Act of 1934, limit the amount of credit to purchase and carry margin stocks that may be extended on securities as collateral by prescribing a maximum loan value, which is a specified percentage of the market value of the collateral at the time the credit is extended; margin requirements are the difference between the market value (100 per cent) and the maximum loan value. The term margin stocks is defined in the corresponding regulation.

Regulation G and special margin requirements for bonds convertible into stocks were adopted by the Board of Governors effective Mar. 11, 1968.

Source: *Ibid.*, p. A 10.

are shown in Table 11-5. At midyear 1972, the requirement on stocks was 55 percent. That is, buyers of stock on credit who also used the stock to collateralize the loan were required to make minimum down payments equal to 55 percent of the purchase price and could borrow, at most, 45 percent. On occasion, the requirement has been 100 percent, preventing any stock purchases whatsoever on credit.

Regulation Q. This regulation has already been discussed in earlier chapters as a constraint on bank management in its daily operations and as reducing interbank competition. But it also has important implications for affecting the distribution of credit. As noted earlier, by maintaining lower interest rate ceilings on commercial banks than on thrift institutions, Regulation Q and its analogous regulations on nonmember banks and thrift institutions, to the extent they are effective, induce larger credit flows into residential mortgages than otherwise.

In recent years, the Federal Reserve has also used Regulation Q to attempt to redirect credit away from large corporate borrowers at times of inflationary pressures. As market interest rates increased at such times, the maximum rates banks were permitted to pay on large CDs were not raised correspondingly. This had the greatest impact on the largest banks, which tend, on the average, to acquire a greater proportion of their deposits through CDs than do smaller banks. The largest banks are also the most important lenders to large business corporations. The Federal Reserve believed the large business corporations contributed in a major way to the inflationary pressures of the later 1960s by continuing to increase their capital expenditures, financed to a considerable extent by bank credit. By slowing the deposit growth and thereby the lending capacity of large banks, the main source of bank financing to these corporations was curtailed. To the extent that this was effective, credit was diverted to smaller banks and smaller firms.

Regulation Q was also employed by the Board of Governors in the late 1960s to curtail the overall increase in bank credit. This policy was preferred to retarding credit expansion by slowing the overall provision of reserves to the banking system because it diverted fewer funds from the smaller banks and their loan customers. If credit had been curtailed solely by a slowing in reserve provision without effective interest ceilings, the larger banks might have been able to outbid the smaller banks for the reserves through their ability to tap the national money market. As a quantitative control, Regulation Q, unlike open market operations, does not permit fine gradations in executing policy and, as discussed earlier, encourages avoidance by the institutions whose operations are restricted. Changes in Regulation Q during the 1960s are shown in Table 11-6.

Moral Suasion. At times, the Federal Reserve and other government agencies attempt to affect both the total and the mix of credit by appeal and voluntary response rather than by regulation and authority. These programs have tended to be most effective in the short run and in periods in which the basis for the appeal was both visible and meaningful to the institutions involved, such as during wars, when the appeal was closely tied to patriotism. In the longer run and at times when the reason for appeal is less apparent or meaningful, compliance is reduced. In large measure, this reflects the pressures of competition. While each institution individually may claim to be willing to comply with the appeal, it is not certain that its competitors are equally "public-spirited" and may not attempt to invade its markets. The Federal Reserve has frequently found it necessary either to replace voluntary compliance with enforced compliance or to introduce threats

Table 11-6 Maximum Interest Rates Payable on Time and Savings Deposits
(Percent per annum)

Rates Jan. 1, 1962–July 19, 1966

Type of deposit	Effective date: Jan. 1, 1962	July 17, 1963	Nov. 24, 1964	Dec. 6, 1965
Savings deposits:				
12 months or more	4	4	4	4
Less than 12 months	3½	3½		
Other time deposits:				
12 months or more	4			
6 months to 12 months	3½	4	4½	
90 days to 6 months	2½			5½
Less than 90 days (30–89 days)	1	1	4	

Rates beginning July 20, 1966

Type of deposit	Effective date: July 20, 1966	Sept. 26, 1966	Apr. 19, 1968	Jan. 21, 1970
Savings deposits	4	4	4	4½
Other time deposits:				
Multiple maturity:				
30–89 days	4	4	4	4½
90 days–1 year				5
1 year to 2 years	5	5	5	5½
2 years and over				5¾
Single-maturity:				
Less than $100,000:				
30 days to 1 year				5
1 year to 2 years	5½	5	5	5½
2 years and over				5¾
$100,000 and over:				
30–59 days			5½	–
60–89 days			5¾	–
90–179 days	5½	5½	6	6¾
180 days to 1 yr.			6¼	7
1 year or more				7½

Source: *Ibid.*, p. A 11.

of retaliation for failure to comply. Two recent examples which demonstrate this sequence are the discount letter of 1966 and the voluntary foreign credit restraint program.

In mid-1966 the Federal Reserve was pursuing a policy of monetary restraint. Partially as a consequence of this policy, interest rates had risen to high levels and a number of high social-priority sectors, such as state and local governments and residential construction, were forced to pay higher rates for smaller amounts of credit. At the same time, business loans continued to expand sharply. After a number of apparently fruitless verbal requests by the Board of Governors to the banks to reconsider their loan priorities, a formal letter was sent to each member bank by the Board over the signature of the district reserve bank president. Although the Board denied that the letter represented a change in policy, the letter impressed many banks with the enforcement potentials available to the Federal Reserve. It read in part:

> The System believes that the national economic interest would be better served by a slower rate of expansion of bank loans to business within the context of moderate overall money and credit growth. Further substantial adjustments through bank liquidation of municipal securities or other investments would add to pressures on financial markets. Hence, the System believes that a greater share of member bank adjustments should take the form of moderation in the rate of expansion of loans, and particularly business loans.
>
> Accordingly, this objective will be kept in mind by the Federal Reserve Banks in their extensions of credit to member banks through the discount window. Member banks will be expected to cooperate in the System's efforts to hold down the rate of business loan expansion—apart from normal seasonal needs—and to use the discount facilities of the Reserve Banks in a manner consistent with these efforts.[1]

In response to continued deterioration in the balance of payments, the president requested the Federal Reserve System in 1965 to establish a voluntary program to curtail overseas lending by American banks and other financial institutions. The Federal Reserve issued guidelines suggesting that each bank limit its foreign lending in 1965 to a designated percentage over 1964. Similar guidelines were established for nonbank financial institutions. The formal nature of the guidelines issued, the limited number of large banks effectively affected, under 200, and the detailed reporting procedures adopted convinced the banks that compliance was the better part of valor. Although continued on a voluntary basis, subsequent modifications in the program permitted the Board of Governors to shift noncomplying institutions from the voluntary program to a nonvoluntary program that specified penalties for failure to comply. At year-end 1971, foreign bank loans subject to the voluntary ceiling were at about the same dollar level as they were at the time the program was introduced and well under the imposed ceilings. At the same time, the program had been expanded and exceptional cases incorporated to the extent that the guidelines for 1971 occupied ten pages in the January, 1971, issue of the *Federal Reserve Bulletin.*

Because of the difficulties of achieving truly voluntary compliance, moral suasion has not been a major instrument of Federal Reserve control. Considerably greater emphasis is placed on such suasion by foreign central banks. However, the banking structure is greatly different in these countries. Instead of 14,000 competing commercial banks, they generally have only a handful of banks, less than 15 in many countries. The effectiveness of moral suasion is inversely related to the number of banks.

Selective Open Market Operations. A number of proposals have been made to broaden Federal Reserve open market purchases to include not only Treasury

1. Board of Governors of the Federal Reserve System, *Fifty-third Annual Report, 1966* (Washington, D.C.: 1967), p. 103.

securities but also securities issued by such high social-priority sectors as municipal governments, agriculture, and housing. It is argued that such purchases would expand the market for these securities and lower their interest rates. The Federal Reserve has resisted such proposals for a number of reasons, including the narrowness of the secondary market for many of these instruments, which would cause Federal Reserve operations to have significant price effects, and the potentiality for public dissatisfaction developing at such times as the Federal Reserve might find it necessary to sell the securities, exerting downward price pressures. In addition, it is likely that, in the process of bidding up the prices of the affected securities and lowering their yields, the Federal Reserve would reduce the participation of other buyers to an extent that the market would not be enlarged by much, if at all, and final levels of interest rates would not be much lower than they were in the absence of such operations.

Nevertheless, in 1966, Congress authorized the Federal Reserve to include securities issued by federal agencies in their open market operations and the Federal Open Market Committee changed its operating regulations to permit these securities to be used both in outright transactions and in repurchase agreements. Since then, the manager has conducted limited operations in federal agency obligations. In 1971, operations in these securities represented only a small fraction of all open market operations. However, such operations promise to be more important in coming years.

Effectiveness of Qualitative Controls. Qualitative controls tend to be more difficult to enforce than quantitative controls. Because these controls attempt to subvert individual self-interest, unless all participants and types of credit in the financial markets are subject to the controls, prolonged compliance is difficult to enforce. Moreover, even if compliance were high, effectiveness may still be small as those affected search out new means of satisfying their needs. In addition, the costs of administration and enforcement frequently become sufficiently great to reduce substantially any benefits of the controls. Nevertheless, both because of their strong intuitive appeal and because they project a sense of action, a quality much desired in times of difficulty, qualitative controls continue to be recommended.

Intermediate Targets

The Federal Reserve employs its instruments of monetary control in order to execute its policy intent. In formulating its strategy, the Federal Reserve must determine which instrument or set of instruments to use, and when and by how much each should be changed. As will be discussed in following chapters, the chain of causation from monetary policy action to the ultimate objectives of policy is long and the transmission of policy along this chain is slow. In addition, accurate observations of the ultimate targets are available only monthly, at best, and frequently only with a significant time lag. For both reasons, the Federal Reserve may not be able to quickly identify or evaluate the impact of changes in its instruments. To reduce the area of uncertainty within which it operates, the Fed finds it useful to aim its policy actions at variables along the chain of causation that are more quickly affected by its actions and for which accurate readings are both more continuous and more quickly available. By directing their dynamic actions at such variables, referred to as *intermediate policy targets,* the policy-makers can obtain quicker evaluations of their strategies and, if necessary, modify the use of their instruments accordingly.

The Federal Reserve employs both money-market conditions and monetary aggregates as intermediate targets. Ceteris paribus, the firmer the conditions in the money market and/or the slower the growth of monetary aggregates, the greater the restraint monetary policy exerts on aggregate economic activity. Money-market conditions and monetary aggregates can be translated into more specific variables. Generally, accurate observations of measures of money-market conditions are more continuously available with less, if any, time lag than are measures of monetary aggregates. Accurate observations of a number of yields of important money-market instruments are available continuously throughout the day and thereby permit continuous monitoring of operations. On the other hand, readings of monetary aggregates are available, at best, only daily and then with a lag of a few days, are subject to substantial revision and, because of great day-to-day variability, are meaningful only for periods of a reserve week or considerably longer.

In more recent years, the Federal Reserve has directed its dynamic operations at money-market conditions as much to affect monetary aggregates as for their own sake. Defensive operations are directed primarily at money-market conditions as an ultimate target to promote a financial environment the Federal Reserve considers necessary for achieving its dynamic objectives. The more frequently used intermediate targets of monetary policy, the nature of their linkage with variables further out in the policy transmission mechanism, and the availability of accurate and timely observations of them are described below. The arguments for and against each of these variables as intermediate targets are discussed in Chapter 20.

Federal Funds Rate. This is the most sensitive of all interest rates and is an indicator of the pressure on commercial bank activities in the money market. By exerting upward pressure on this rate through affecting bank reserves, the Federal Reserve forces the banks to reevaluate their asset portfolio and curtail credit and deposits. Accurate readings of the federal funds rate are available throughout the day. The rate on these overnight interbank loans is highly volatile and it is not unusual for it to fluctuate 25 percent on either side of its average level for the day.

Dealer Loan Rate. This is the rate large financial-center banks charge securities dealers for overnight loans to finance their inventories. By exerting upward pressures on this rate through bank reserves, the Federal Reserve encourages dealers to reduce inventories, transmitting the higher rates through the money and capital markets. At the same time, the dealers will reduce their credit at banks. The dealer loan rate is typically established by the banks every morning and maintained through the day.

Treasury Bill Rates. This is the broadest money-market rate and the rate most directly affected by Federal Reserve open market operations. Changes in the bill rate are noted in all financial sectors. By exerting upward pressure on bill rates, the Federal Reserve transmits its restrictive actions broadly. Continuous accurate readings of rates on all Treasury bills are available throughout the day.

Bank Borrowing at the Discount Window. Under the lagged reserve system, the Federal Reserve can determine aggregate bank borrowings at the discount window almost to the dollar. It cannot, of course, determine which banks will borrow, as individual banks have alternative sources of adjustment funds, primarily the federal funds market. It follows, however, that Federal Reserve actions to drive banks into the discount window exert pressure on the federal funds rate through the attempts of some banks to avoid the window. Because borrowing banks are under pressure to repay quickly, the Fed considers reserves provided through the discount window more restrictive than an equal dollar of reserves provided through open market operations. To them, an increase in borrowed reserves indicates a firmer money market and portends credit curtailment. Accurate readings of daily borrowings are available to the Federal Reserve the following day, but, because banks have the entire reserve period to satisfy their reserve requirements, borrowings are meaningful as a target value only on a weekly average basis.

Free Reserves. These are the algebraic difference between bank excess reserves and bank borrowings at the discount window. When excess reserves exceed borrowings, free reserves are positive. When excess reserves are less than borrowings, free reserves are negative, and are sometimes referred to as *net borrowed reserves.* The greater the positive free reserves, the greater the expansion potential of the banking system is and the easier the money market, and vice versa. However, to the extent that banks have a stable demand for excess reserves, potential deposit expansion is not equivalent to actual deposit expansion. It should also be recognized that the banks that hold excess reserves and those that borrow are not simultaneously the same banks and may be motivated differently. Unlike borrowings, which approach zero during recessions and are not an effective target at those times, free reserves may be used as a target over the entire cycle.

Data on excess reserves are less reliable than data on borrowings and, while estimates of daily free reserves are available to the Federal Reserve the next day, they are subject to considerable revision. In addition, the ability of banks to carry some excess reserves back into the preceding reserve period or forward into the subsequent period reduces somewhat the reliability of free reserves estimates as a measure of the current position of banks and the money market. Similar to borrowings, free reserves are meaningful only for the reserve period.

Conventional Money Supply (M1). This definition of money includes currency and gross demand deposits less cash items in the process of collection, U.S. Treasury deposits, and deposits due to other banks. By cushioning the money market from short-run swings, Federal Reserve defensive operations often introduce additional short-run shocks or "noise" into an already volatile money supply, and daily and even weekly measurements are not very meaningful targets by themselves. Figure 11-2 shows weekly, monthly, and three-months' changes in the money supply during 1970. The longer the time period, the smoother the money supply series is. Over the longer run, the greater the money supply is, the greater the stimulus to economic activity.

Estimates of daily money supply are available internally to the manager with a one- to two-day lag and every Thursday afternoon the Federal Reserve releases preliminary estimates of the daily average money supply for the reserve week ending one week ago Wednesday. These estimates are subject to considerable revision for reporting omissions and errors, changes in seasonal adjustments, and changes in definition.

Broad Money Supply (M2). This definition encompasses M1 plus time and savings deposits at commercial banks, other than large CDs. Because of changes in the public's demand for different financial assets, changes in M2 need not parallel changes in M1 in the short run. Over longer periods of time, the two series tend to move in harmony (Figure 11-3). Estimates of M2 are available with the same lags and caveats as for M1. Also similar to M1, the greater the desired stimulus, the greater the growth rate of M2.

Broad Money Supply (M3). This is an even broader definition of money and encompasses the assets included in M2 plus deposits at savings and loan associations and mutual savings banks. This measure reflects the public's holding of almost all fixed-value liquid assets. Thus, it washes out many of the public's shifts among different liquid financial assets, say, from demand deposits to savings and loan association accounts, and is generally less volatile in the short run than narrower definitions. However, the Federal Reserve is able to affect deposits at thrift institutions less directly than deposits at commercial banks so this is a more difficult target to control.

Figure 11-2 **Changes in the Money Supply Are Less Volatile the Longer the Period**
(Percentage changes at annual rates. Calculated from averages of daily figures, seasonally adjusted.)

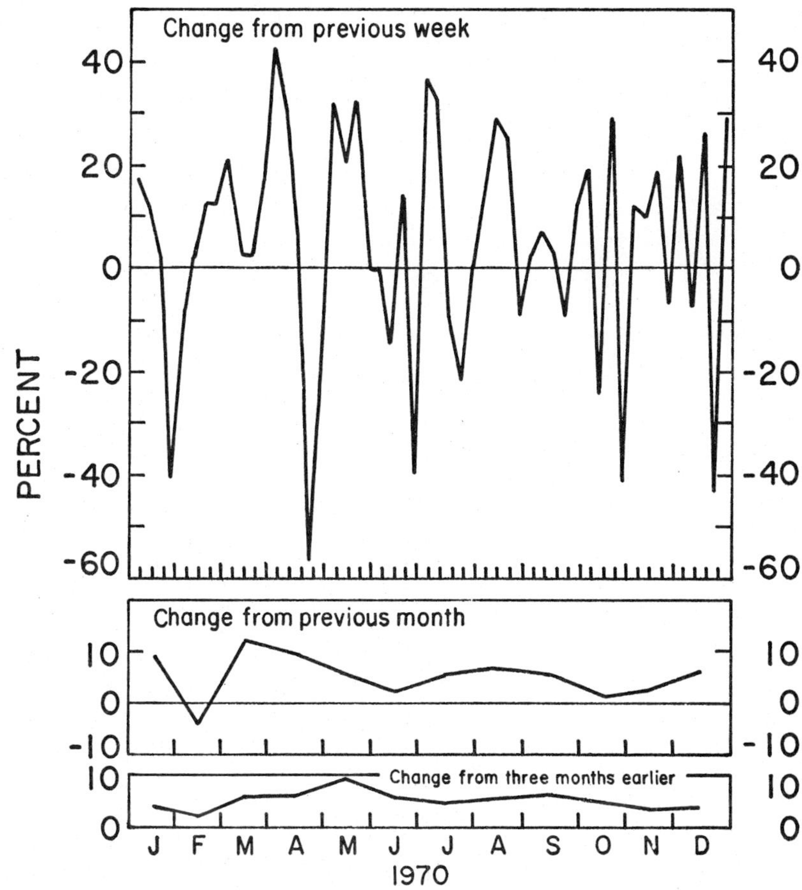

Source: *Monthly Review* (Federal Reserve Bank of New York), April, 1971, p. 87.

Bank Credit. This is the sum of all bank earning assets. To some, bank credit is more directly linked to economic activity than is money supply, although in the same direction, and thus is a better target. The greater bank credit is, the greater the stimulus to economic activity provided by monetary policy. Some economists prefer to partition total bank credit into loans and investments, and put greater significance on the former as a target for affecting economic conditions to come. Estimates of total bank credit and its components are available only for one day at month-end with about a two-week lag. For this reason, bank credit has frequently been replaced as a target by the bank credit proxy.

Figure 11-3 **Alternative Measures of Money Move Similarly**

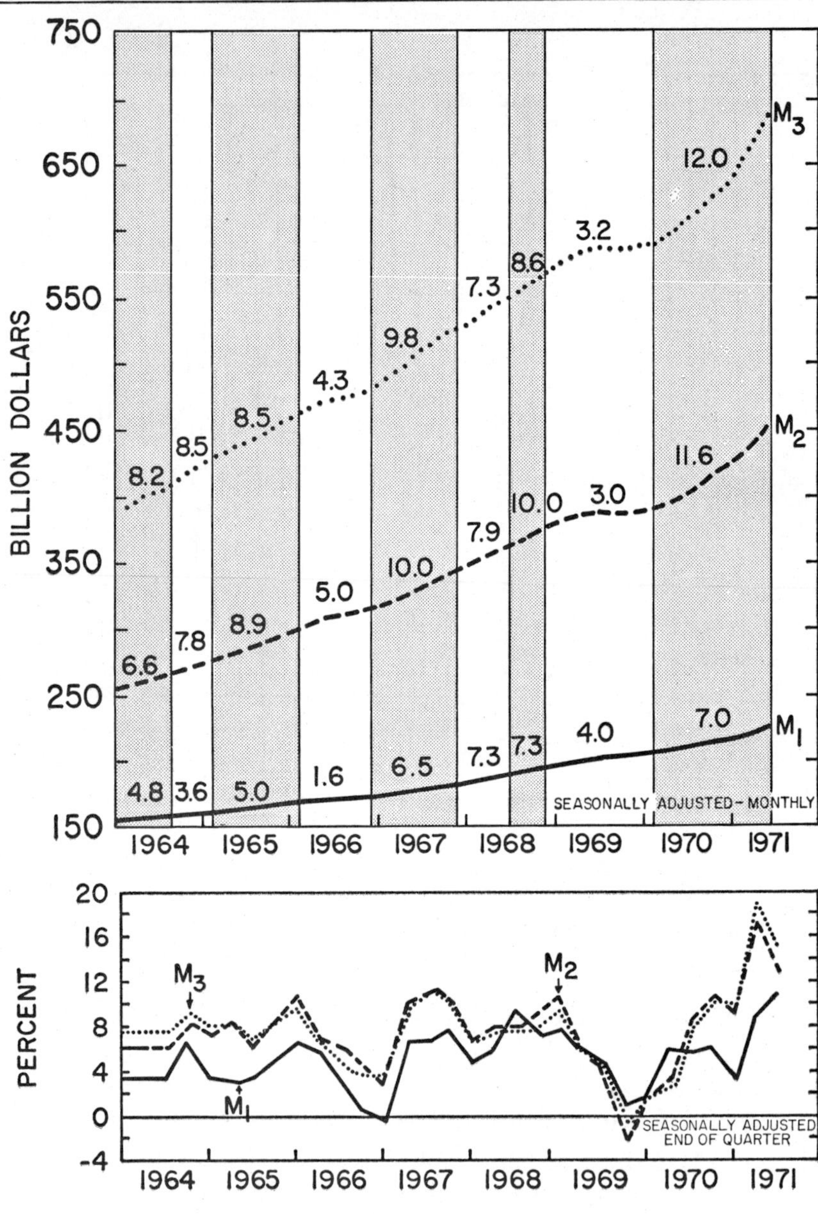

Source: *Economic Review* (Federal Reserve Bank of Cleveland), October, 1971, pp. 8-9.

Bank Credit Proxy. This is an estimate of total bank credit derived from daily deposit reports adjusted for balance sheet differences between deposits and earning assets. Because it is derived from deposit estimates, observations of the bank credit proxy are similar in timing and reliability to those of the various money supply measures.

Reserves Available to Support Private Nonbank Deposits. This measure focuses on deposits owned primarily by households and business firms. It is the newest intermediate target, being adopted by the Federal Open Market Committee at its February, 1972 meeting to express its reserve objective. The committee viewed these reserves, which exclude reserves required to support government and interbank deposits, "preferable to total reserves because short-run fluctuations in Government and interbank deposits are sometimes large and difficult to predict and usually are not of major significance for policy. It was deemed appropriate for System open market operations normally to accommodate such changes in Government and interbank deposits."[2] Similar to other aggregate measures, reserves available to support private nonbank deposits are volatile on a short-term basis, but are subject to less significant reporting delays and revisions.

References

Board of Governors of the Federal Reserve System, *The Federal Reserve System: Purposes and Functions,* Fifth edition (Washington, D.C.: 1963).

----, *Reappraisal of the Federal Reserve Discount Mechanism, Volumes 1, 2, and 3* (Washington, D.C.: 1971, 1972).

Commission on Money and Credit, *Monetary Management* (Englewood Cliffs, N.J.: Prentice-Hall, 1963).

Davis, Richard G., "An Analysis of Quantitative Credit Controls and Related Devices," *Brookings Papers on Economic Activity,* No. 1 (Washington, D.C.: The Brookings Institution, 1971). Pp. 65-96.

Guttentag, Jack M., "The Strategy of Open Market Operations," *The Quarterly Journal of Economics,* 80 (1), February, 1966, 1-30.

Hodgman, Donald R., "Selective Credit Controls," *Journal of Money, Credit, and Banking,* 4 (2), May, 1972, 342-359.

Holmes, Alan, "A Day at the Trading Desk," *Monthly Review* (Federal Reserve Bank of New York), 52 (10), October, 1970, 234-238.

Mayer, Thomas, *Monetary Policy in the United States* (New York: Random House, 1968).

Meek, Paul, *Open Market Operations* (New York: Federal Reserve Bank of New York, 1969).

Moore, Thomas, "Stock Market Margin Requirements," *Journal of Political Economy,* 74 (2), April, 1966, 158-167.

Roosa, Robert V., *Federal Reserve Operations in the Money and Government Securities Markets* (New York: Federal Reserve Bank of New York, 1956).

2. "Record of Policy Actions," *Federal Reserve Bulletin,* 58 (5), May, 1972, p. 459.

PART V

Monetary Theory

The Demand for and Supply of Money

12

We seek knowledge in order to better understand and control the phenomena we observe around us. These phenomena may or may not be systematically related to other phenomena. If a particular phenomenon is not related systematically to other phenomena, we can understand its randomness but cannot predict its behavior. If it is systematically related to one or more other variables, then by identifying the precise nature of the relationship, we can predict its behavior from observing the behavior of the other phenomena. Moreover, if the behavior of one or more of the related phenomena is controllable, then the behavior of the particular phenomenon may, at minimum, be affected, and, at best, be controlled.

Economic Theory and Method

A theory is a statement about the behavior of a phenomenon. It is possible to make an infinite number of statements about almost any phenomenon. However, to be useful in advancing knowledge, a theory must explain the observed behavior of the particular phenomenon at a reasonably low cost. Thus, all theories are not equally useful. The process by which we evaluate and differentiate among alternative theories of the behavior of the same phenomenon is called *method.*

A number of methods are used in deriving an explanation of the behavior of a phenomenon. Some methods involve esthetics, some involve intuition and "gut" feelings, some appeal to authority, others to unknown forces such as astrology, and some make comparisons of the behavior predicted by the hypothesis with the observed behavior. The last method is called *scientific method* and will be used in the balance of this book.

Scientific method is not a simple process. It involves:

constructing a hypothesis about a phenomenon on the basis of everything we have observed, read, or imagined;

checking the hypothesis for internal consistency in the logic of the argument;

simplifying the hypothesis to the point where it can explain the largest number of observations with the smallest number of inputs;

transforming the hypothesis into testable form;

generating quantitative predictions of the phenomenon being explained;

comparing the predicted outcomes with the observed outcomes;

summarizing the relationship of the predicted and observed outcomes in a meaningful statistic relevant to the hypothesis;

contrasting the statistical measure of explanation with others generated by alternative hypotheses; and,

if necessary, revising the construction of the hypothesis to improve its performance.

Although generally accepted in the physical sciences, scientific method is more controversial in economics. It is not easy to apply. In economics, experimenters generally cannot control the experiments to isolate the relationships being examined and must make do with data containing varying degrees of measurement error. In addition, the results attained typically leave considerable room for doubt, particularly with respect to causal relationships, and the experimenters have a difficult time avoiding the introduction of subjective decisions or biases into the design and interpretation of the experiment. Nevertheless, economic decisions are made, both personal and policy decisions, and only through the application of scientific method can objective evaluations of the decisions be reached or autopsies be performed and the action modified or repeated unchanged in subsequent use.

Simplicity

The most useful hypotheses are not only those which explain or predict best by whatever statistical criterion is selected, but also those that do so at the least cost. This requires that the theories focus on the elements common to the greatest number of observations. That is, the most useful theories are generalizations describing many observations of the same phenomenon, even if only approximately, rather than precise statements about individual observations. Thus, by their very nature, theories abstract from the complexities of the "real" world to construct a simplified "conceptual" world.

The importance of simplification can be demonstrated by the use of an example from physics. It has been observed that all unconstrained bodies in the earth's atmosphere fall towards the center of the earth. But they do so at different speeds. Analysis has shown that there is a force common to all the bodies which can describe their velocity or speed of fall as the product of only two variables, gravity (g) and time (t), thus:

$$v = gt.$$

However, this equation predicts accurately the observed velocity of only a small number of falling bodies, namely, those observed in a vacuum. Thus, the theory is "unrealistic." Yet, with some minor modifications for the specifics of the relevant atmosphere and the observed body, the equation can improve its predictive ability greatly and become "realistic." It can predict that a feather dropped in New York City falls more slowly than a brick. On the other hand, a theory designed specifically to predict the velocity of a feather dropped in New York City on a calm day would be of little value in predicting the velocity of a brick also dropped in New York City, or of a feather dropped in Mexico City, or probably even of a feather dropped in New York City on another, say, windy, day. All these would require completely different hypotheses.

A theory is a very practical concept. It should help us predict or explain what we observe. If it cannot do so, it is of little good to anyone and should be revised or replaced. As the old adage indicates, the test of the pudding is in the eating. I would hate to travel in an airplane that looks great on the blueprints but has failed to fly successfully. A statement that is fine in theory but not in practice is, in fact, not fine in theory either.

If a decision is to be made, scientific method does not permit the rejection of a particular course of action because the hypothesis upon which it is built does not perform well absolutely. The underlying hypothesis must perform more poorly than its competitors. Turning this statement around, a particular decision may be made even if the underlying hypothesis does not predict perfectly as long as it predicts better than all alternative hypotheses. This requires a testing of all competing hypotheses before a decision is made. Among two hypotheses equal in all respects but prediction, one should choose the one that predicts better by whatever statistical criterion is applied. Among two hypotheses equal in all respects but complexity, one should choose that which is simpler. Among two hypotheses equal in all respects but intuitive appeal, one should choose that one which is more appealing to the experimenter.

Economic Models

Monetary theory explains the relationship both among financial variables and between financial- and real-sector variables. The history of monetary theory has been to continuously improve the explanatory powers of statements describing these relationships. The following pages will describe briefly the more important monetary hypotheses advanced through the course of economic history and evaluate their ability to explain the observed relationships. In the next three chapters we will use one of the theories to construct a very simple model, first of a number of important sectors and then, by aggregation, of the economy as a whole.

A model is a representation or imitation of the real thing. For purposes of analysis, *a model is a transformation of theory into a testable form.* In some experiments, it is possible to construct a physical model or prototype, such as a model automobile, airplane, or environment. For many experiments, constructing a physical model is too costly or inappropriate for the tests to be conducted. Instead, the underlying relationships can be specified in quantitative form in a set of equations. The physical model automobile, airplane, and environment can all be alternately specified in equation form. A system of equations is no less a representation of the phenomenon described than is the physical model. In economics the costs of constructing physical models are often prohibitive and, even if feasible, they would be generally less useful for experimentation than the underlying equations.

Tracing the history of economic doctrine and classifying the "schools" of thought can be treacherous. A careful reading of most economists reveals that they have generally recognized the complexities of the relationships described, noted them briefly, and then focused on those they considered most important. In addition, hardly any two members of the same school of economic thought have articulated precisely the same hypotheses. Classification difficulties are particularly acute for economists who wrote before the introduction of mathematics into economics, which forced writers to specify their models more precisely. As a result, we will delineate schools or groups by their predictions or policy recommendations, which we can assume reflect their priorities.

The Quantity Theory of Money

The oldest monetary theory is the quantity theory of money. Its origins have been traced to before Adam Smith, the generally accepted "father" of economics as a distinct discipline. Basically, the quantity theory postulates that changes in the quantity of money generate proportionate changes in the price level in the same direction. That is, a 10 percent increase in the stock of money, ceteris paribus, would, in time, result in a 10 percent increase in prices and induce no other changes in the economy. In this system, money affects only the nominal value of items in the economy and has no effect on their relative value with respect to each other. Thus, it can induce only superficial changes.

Although clear statements of the quantity theory appear in the writings of most major economists of the seventeenth through the early twentieth centuries, the most rigorous statement of the argument was articulated by Irving Fisher at the turn of this century. Fisher started his analysis at the level of the individual. He observed that an individual at some time paid for every purchase he made. Assuming that he paid for all purchases immediately, then on the day of purchase:

$$M_{jk} = p_{1jk}q_{1jk} + p_{2jk}q_{2jk} + \cdots + p_{njk}q_{njk}, \tag{12-1}$$

where:

M = money spent by person j on day k
p = price of item i on day k
q = quantity of item i purchased by j on day k.

All the purchases of items i by person j on day k can be summed and written:

$$\sum_{i=1}^{n} p_{ijk}q_{ijk} = E_{jk}, \tag{12-2}$$

where:

E = the total expenditures on day k by person j.

The expenditures by individual j can also be summed for a period, say one year:

$$\sum_{k=1}^{365} \sum_{i=1}^{n} p_{ijk}q_{ijk} = E_j. \tag{12-3}$$

Unlike expenditures for any one day, it is improbable that the purchaser would have had a sufficient stock of money at the beginning of the year to finance all his expenditures during the year. Rather, he probably received money income payments regularly through the year, or sold assets. Thus, his average stock of money for the year would be less than the amount of his total expenditures. He would, in effect, be using each dollar more than once. Let us define the turnover or velocity of money by:

$$V'_j = E_j / M_j, \tag{12-4}$$

where:

M_j = average money stock held by person j during year.

One can now aggregate expenditures for all members of society:

$$\sum_{j=1}^{m} \sum_{k=1}^{365} \sum_{i=1}^{n} p_{ijk} q_{ijk} = P'Q' = E, \tag{12-5}$$

where:

P' = weighted average price of all quantities purchased
Q' = sum of the quantities of all items purchased.

Aggregating E in equation 12-4 and substituting into equation 12-5:

$$MV' = P'Q'. \tag{12-6}$$

This is Fisher's equation of exchange. The equation states that total money flows equal total expenditures. Money is viewed entirely as a medium of exchange.

Many other economists have found it useful to focus on national income rather than total expenditures. This specification of the quantity theory would include only the prices and quantities of final goods and services produced during the year and omits expenditures on previously produced items and on purely financial transactions. Because it is more closely related to national welfare, the income version of the quantity theory is the more frequently used of the two and can be written:

$$MV = PQ. \tag{12-7}$$

Q now equals national income in constant dollars and P the national income price index.

Both equations 12-6 and 12-7 are mathematical tautologies or truisms. If any two of the variables are held constant, then changes in one of the remaining two will, of necessity, result in proportionate changes in the other. If M and V are held constant, a 50 percent increase in Q would be accompanied by a 50 percent reduction in P, and vice versa. If M and Q are held constant, a 50 percent increase in V would be accompanied by a 50 percent increase in P, and so on. Although indicating association between two variables, the equations by themselves do not imply causation. Nor can they be used for prediction without additional information.

The equations can be made operational by assigning behavioral characteristics to the variables. The quantity theorists imposed three basic assumptions:

1. changes in V and Q are independent of changes in M,
2. V and Q change only slowly through time and can be assumed constant in the short run, and
3. M causes changes in P.

The first assumption states that changes in money do not affect velocity or real income. Thus, changes in M are reflected only in P. Moreover, by assumption 3,

Table 12-1 **Levels and Changes in Quantity Theory Variables, 1929–70**

Year	Level					
	M^a	P^b	Q^c	PQ^d	V	K
1929	26	51	204	103	4.0	.25
1950	114	80	355	285	2.5	.40
1960	142	104	488	504	3.5	.29
1970	210	135	724	977	4.7	.21

Period	Percent Increases			
	M	P	Q	V
1929–1970	708	165	255	18
1950–1970	84	69	104	88
1960–1970	48	30	48	34
1950–1960	25	30	37	40

[a] Billion dollars.
[b] Implicit price deflator for gross national product, 1958 = 100.
[c] Gross national product in constant (1958) dollars, billion dollars.
[d] Gross national product in current dollars, billion dollars.

the direction of causation between M and P runs from M to P. The second assumption is frequently misinterpreted as the fundamental characteristic of the quantity theory. It is nothing of the sort. Rather, it is a simplifying assumption, which permits the equation to be used for prediction. Only under all three assumptions does an increase in money generate a proportionate increase in prices. While changes in money were assumed to be reflected only in changes in prices, changes in prices were not limited only to being aftereffects of changes in money. Prices could also change because of changes in V and Q.

All three assumptions have been challenged. Data for the four variables in equation 12-7 for selected years are shown in Table 12-1. It should be noted at this point that one cannot derive independent estimates of income velocity. Estimates of income velocity can only be obtained by dividing observations of prices and real income by observations of the money stock for the same period. In contrast, it is possible to obtain independent estimates of Fisher's transactions velocity of equation 12-6. The turnover of demand deposits can be computed by dividing the dollar total of bank debits to demand deposits in a period by the average stock of demand deposits in that period. Such a series is published monthly in the *Federal Reserve Bulletin.* While income velocity and transactions velocity generally change in the same direction, they do include different elements and the correlation is not perfect.

The top panel of Table 12-1 shows that neither velocity nor real income were constant or even changed only slowly in the period since 1929. As a result, money and prices did not change proportionately. Between 1929 and 1970, the stock of money increased eightfold. In contrast, prices increased only 2½ times, velocity increased slightly, and real income increased 3½ times. In all but one period, prices increased more slowly than money supply. The relationships among the four variables also changed from period to period. For example, prices increased 30 percent both between 1950 and 1960 and between 1960 and 1970 even though money supply increased twice as rapidly in the second period as in the first. Rather than either being constant or changing slowly, both velocity and real income not only increased, but increased faster in both postwar decades than did prices.

The quantity theory would have been a poor predictor in this period. If velocity and real income were assumed to have remained at their 1960 levels in 1970, the actual money stock in 1970 would have generated a price level of 151, an increase from 1960 50 percent faster than the actual rate of increase. If velocity in 1970 had remained at its 1960 level, it would have been necessary to have had a money stock of $279 billion rather than the actual $210 billion in order to have generated the observed gross national product for that year.

As will be seen in subsequent chapters, it is evident why the quantity theory has predicted poorly in the periods examined. Not only did real income and velocity not remain constant nor change slowly, but both were affected by changes in the money supply. The relationship between changes in money and changes in prices has been found to be related to the differences between actual income and full employment income at the time. The further the economy is from full employment, the smaller the impact of a given change in money supply on prices and the greater the impact on real output. As the economy frequently operated below full employment levels in the postwar period, prices tended to rise somewhat less rapidly than money supply. Velocity has been found to be strongly affected by interest rates which, as we observed earlier, are affected, in turn, by each of the other three variables in the quantity equation. The higher interest rates are, the greater the velocity, and vice versa. In the postwar period, money expanded more slowly than the combined expansion in prices and real output and upward pressures were exerted on interest rates, encouraging the public to minimize its holdings of demand deposits and causing velocity to increase. The assumptions of the independence of velocity and real income from money and of the slow change in both variables have both proven inappropriate.

Why, then, did the quantity theory have so much appeal for so long? Because it had predicted considerably better in the periods during which it was developed. Until almost the twentieth century, the economies of most countries were basically rural. The industrial labor force was a minor percentage of total employment. The implications of business fluctuations were less widespread and had proportionately smaller effects on aggregate levels of income and employment. Real income advanced slowly, primarily at full employment levels, in proportion to increases in the labor force, which, in turn, increased slowly with increases in population. The assumption that real income could be viewed as constant in the short run did not differ greatly from actual experience.

In addition, financial institutions were in their infancy and were not used by a very large portion of the population. Indeed, significant portions of the population were relatively self-sufficient and did not participate greatly in the money economy. Money was considered only a medium of exchange. Savings were held primarily in real capital, such as land and buildings, rather than in financial assets, and interest rates significantly affected the portfolio decisions of only a few individuals and firms. For these reasons, velocity did not change much from year to year and again the assumption of constancy in the short run helped to generate useful predictions.

The conditions of the period also explain the other two assumptions. Because velocity changed slowly, and the changes that did occur appeared to depend mostly on changes in the proportion of the population entering the money economy and in payment patterns for these individuals, and because changes in real income closely reflected population changes, there was little reason to consider the relationship of either velocity or real income to money. Likewise, because money was, in large measure, either metal specie or closely linked to specie, it could not be changed quickly in response to forces within the economy. Thus, economists believed it more likely that prices responded to money than the other way.

This is not to suggest that every quantity theorist accepted all three assumptions in equal strengths. Indeed, few held to them rigidly. John Stuart Mill recognized the occasional inverse dependence of velocity on money. Henry Simons, at the University of Chicago, attributed severe business downturns to independent declines in velocity, which fed back on the money supply. Irving Fisher discussed the temporary transitional effects of money on real income, albeit only briefly. Richard Cantillon, a French banker, writing in about 1730 during the early development of the quantity theory, may have preempted all the doubts later raised about the theory when he wrote:

> I conclude that an increase of money circulating in a State always causes there an increase of consumption and a higher standard of expense. But the dearness caused by this money does not affect equally all the kinds of products and merchandise, proportionably to the quantity of money, unless what is added continues in the same circulation as the money before, that is to say unless those who offer in the Market one ounce of silver be the same and only ones who now offer two ounces when the amount of money in circulation is doubled in quantity, and that is hardly ever the case. I conceive that when a large surplus of money is brought into a State the new money gives a new turn to consumption and even a new speed to circulation. But it is not possible to say exactly to what extent.[1]

1. Richard Cantillon, *Essay on the Nature of Trade*, reprinted in Dean, *The Controversy Over the Quantity Theory of Money*, p. 8.

Nevertheless, the quantity theory was a useful theory for its times. It was simple and predicted reasonably well. Like all theories, it predicted the usual better than the unusual. It stopped being useful when it stopped predicting well. In large measure, as we have seen, this was not because it was a poor theory, but because the world it attempted to explain had changed greatly.

The Cambridge School

The first concerted attack on the quantity theory was mounted by a group of economists at Cambridge University in England around World War I. Like many first movements, this school emphasized reform more than revolution and viewed its proposals primarily as evolutionary.

Unlike the quantity theorists, who considered money strictly as a medium of exchange, the Cambridge school viewed money in a broader context as a financial asset. As an asset, the public had an ongoing demand for it. Money was no longer a hot potato that the public wanted to spend as soon as it was received. The focus of monetary analysis was shifted from the supply of money to the demand for money. The Cambridge school postulated that the public desired to hold cash balances in some proportion, K, to its real income. This can be written:

$$M = PKQ, \qquad (12\text{-}8)$$

where:

$0 < K < 1.$

If real income increased, so did the amount of money people demanded, and if the supply of money did not increase correspondingly, prices declined. If money increased independently, the public held more money balances than it desired, K increased, and, in the process of spending the money to reduce its holdings to desired levels, prices increased. But the public could also alter the amount of money it desired to hold as a result of changes in expectations. Unless offset by changes in money, changes in K resulted in changes in both prices and output and could be a major independent cause of business fluctuations.

The resemblance of the Cambridge equation to the quantity theory can be seen by comparing equations 12-7 and 12-8. Solving both equations for PQ and substituting one equation into the other yields:

$$MV = M(1/K),$$

and

$$V = 1/K. \qquad (12\text{-}9)$$

Thus, mathematically the Cambridge K is the reciprocal of the quantity theory V. In behavioral properties, as noted, it differs greatly. This again serves to emphasize the difference between an equation as a tautology and as an operational behavioral statement.

Although the Cambridge school focused on the demand for money and changes in the demand, it did not articulate a theory of how shifts in demand were related to economic factors. Shifts were primarily the result of changes in expectations. Similar to the quantity theorists and the independence of V from M, the Cambridge school did not relate K to M. Values of K for select years are shown in Table 12-1. The downward drift in the postwar period suggests that, unless one can explain changes in K, the theory is not very useful in predicting the effects of money on income.

The Keynesian Demand for Money

It remained for Lord John Maynard Keynes to mount the revolutionary attack on the quantity theory by questioning its most fundamental premise, the independence of V and Q from M. This, however, he did not undertake until after he had already made major contributions to traditional theory as a member of the Cambridge school. Expanding on the contribution of the Cambridge school, Keynes viewed money as an asset linking the present and the future and concentrated on explaining the reasons underlying its demand. He postulated that individuals and business firms desire to hold money balances for three distinct motives:

1. transactions,
2. precaution, and
3. speculation.

Transactions Demand. This motive views money strictly as a medium of exchange to finance transactions. Keynes speculated that the public demands to hold money balances for this purpose in a fixed relationship to the amount of its expenditures:

$$DM_T = f(\overset{+}{E}), \qquad \textbf{(12-10)}$$

where:

DM_T = demand for money for transactions purposes.

Assuming that total transaction expenditures in the economy are related to aggregate income, this equation can be rewritten to make the demand for money for transactions purposes a positive function of income:

$$DM_T = f(\overset{+}{Y}). \qquad \textbf{(12-11)}$$

Figure 12-1 **Keynesian Transactions Demand for Money**

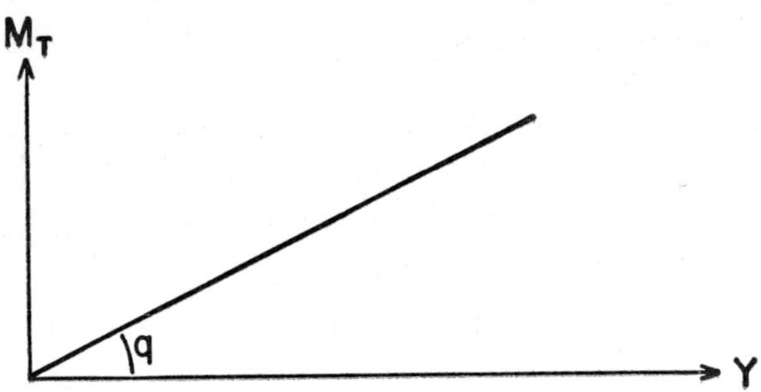

Keynes hypothesized further that the relationship was linear and passed through the origin. Hence:

$$DM_T = qY, \tag{12-12}$$

where:

q = slope of the schedule.

That is, the public demands transactions balances in some fixed proportion to its national income. This specification resembles the Cambridge *K*, except that it encompasses only money held to finance expenditures. The relationship is plotted in Figure 12-1.

Precautionary Demand. This motive focuses on the ability of money to yield immediate purchasing power on demand in case of emergency. Except for immediate availability and zero transactions costs, money balances would be an inferior form of emergency savings to fixed value or very short-term marketable interest-bearing securities. To the extent that the amount that might be needed in emergencies is directly related to income and that the amount held in cash balances for such purposes is inversely related to the interest rate on alternative forms of savings:

$$DM_P = f(\overset{+}{Y}, \overset{-}{i}), \tag{12-13}$$

where:

DM_P = demand for money for precautionary purposes.

However, the demand for precautionary money balances may be expected to vary only little as income and, particularly, interest rates change.

Speculative Demand. This the crux of Keynes's contribution to the demand for money. The speculative motive broadens the functions of money to include not only its functions as a medium of exchange and as a transactions-cost-free asset, but also its use as an income-generating asset in a world of uncertainty.

As money typically does not bear explicit interest, it can generate explicit income for the holder only if the price of what can be purchased with it declines, that is, if the price of money increases and it is sold at a later date at more than the price at which it was purchased. Remember the price of money is the value of what can be bought with it. The holding period yield of money can be computed by:

$$i_M = -\left(\frac{P_{t+1} - P_t}{P_t}\right), \qquad (12\text{-}14)$$

where:

i_M = holding period yield on money balances
P = price of item or items traded.

If the price of an item is expected to decline and expectations are realized, the sale of the item and subsequent repurchase at the lower price would generate a positive effective rate of return on money for the period it is being held. Imputing this return to money implies that price expectations have to be formed and, to the extent they may not be realized, involve the holder in speculation. The imputed yield on money in any current period is, therefore, an expected yield and may or may not be realized. Nevertheless, decisions are made on such yields.

Once a positive rate of return is imputed to money, an investor will hold money balances in his wealth portfolio for reasons other than financing expenditures and precaution. The higher the imputed yield, ceteris paribus, the more balances he would want to hold in relation to the other financial and nonfinancial assets in his portfolio.

Unlike the yield on other assets, the yield on money cannot be observed directly. It can only be computed by measuring the estimated change in the price of the items to be sold and repurchased. Keynes emphasized the return on money in relation to Treasury bonds, the asset he considered to be the closest substitute for money. He hypothesized that when investors expected the price of bonds to decline, they would sell bonds and increase their holdings of money balances. When investors expected bonds to rise, they would decrease their cash holdings. Remembering that bond prices are inversely related to interest yields on the bonds, investors would increase their money balances when interest rates were expected to rise and decrease them when they were expected to fall.

Keynes hypothesized further that investors hold expectations of a long-run average or "normal" level of interest rates. The more market rates rose above this normal level, the greater was the probability that they would soon decline, and the more market rates declined below the normal rate, the greater the probability that they would soon rise. Thus, bond rate expectations are inversely related to the existing level of bond rates and the speculative demand for money can be written in terms of the current level of interest rates as:

$$DM_S = f(\bar{i}), \tag{12-15}$$

where:

DM_S = demand for money for speculative purposes.

The higher interest rates are, the greater the probability of a decline in rates and a rise in bond prices, the lower the imputed yield on money, and the smaller the demand for speculative money balances. The analysis can easily be broadened to include stocks, other financial assets, nonfinancial assets, and goods and services. Money can be demanded for speculation on future declines in a particular price or in a broad spectrum of prices.

The speculative demand was postulated to be asymmetrical. Because nominal interest rates cannot decline below zero, the further interest rates decline, the smaller the probabilities of continued declines, the greater the probabilities of increases in rates, and the greater the increase in the demand for money for any given continued decline in interest rates. That is, the demand for money becomes increasingly more elastic with respect to interest rates as interest rates decline. For example, a decline in interest rates of one percentage point will be associated with a greater increase in the demand for money at 3 percent than at 6 percent. Finally, at some low level, the probability of a rise in interest rates becomes 100 percent and the demand becomes perfectly elastic. No one is willing to exchange money for bonds, and interest rates on bonds can fall no lower. At this level also, the transactions cost of purchasing bonds equals the yield on the bonds. Keynes designated this part of the demand schedule, where it runs parallel to the horizontal axis, as the *liquidity trap*. The speculative demand-for-money schedule is plotted in Figure 12-2. Note that the lower the interest rate, the more elastic the demand schedule.

Similar to the earlier Cambridge school, Keynes also placed considerable weight on the importance of expectations other than price or interest rate expectations in affecting the demand to hold money balances. He hypothesized that the speculative demand function was highly sensitive to changes in general economic expectations. Expectations of economic crises would cause the public to hold larger money balances at every interest rate, that is, would shift the function up and to the right from L_0 to L_1. Optimistic economic expectations would reduce the demand for money at every rate and shift the schedule to the left. Because

Figure 12-2 **Keynesian Speculative Demand for Money**

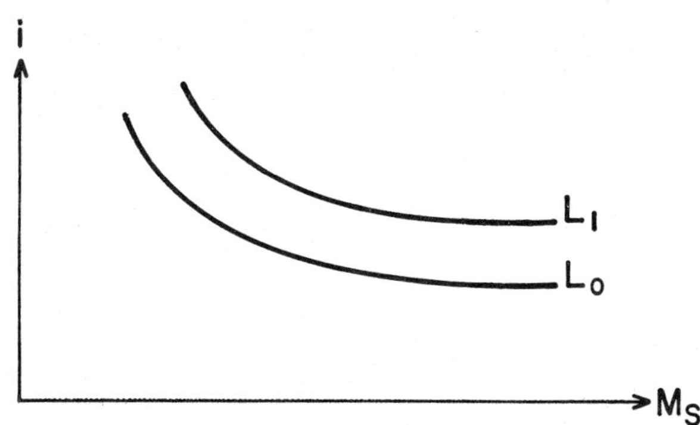

expectations are volatile, Keynes postulated that the demand for speculative balances was also volatile and that the function was unstable through time.

The implications of the speculative demand for money are most important for monetary policy. Increases in the quantity of money, ceteris paribus, beyond the amounts people demand for transactions and precautionary purposes lower the rate of interest without, at first, raising income. If the speculative demand is very interest elastic, as postulated by Keynes, increases in money will reduce interest rates less than proportionately and increase income also less than proportionately. Increases in money balances without a proportionate increase in income lower velocity. Thus, velocity is an explicit, inverse function of money supply. Ceteris paribus, the greater the stock of money, the lower the velocity. The implications of changes in the stock of money may now be distributed among variables on both sides of the quantity equation. An increase in M that would lower V would have less than the full proportionate effect on P and Q. Moreover, the lower the interest rates, the less a given increase in money would lower interest rates further, the more it would reduce velocity, and the less it would affect income. Finally, at the absolute liquidity trap, all the effects of an increase in money are offset by a reduction in velocity and none are transmitted to income. At this point on the demand for speculative money balances schedule, monetary policy becomes impotent. No matter how much money is injected into the economy, income is not affected.

Keynes believed the absolute liquidity trap would exist only during the troughs of severe business downturns. Many persons concluded that these conditions were satisfied in the United States during the early 1930s, concurrent with the times when Keynes was formulating his concepts, and accepted the view that monetary policy was not capable of generating relief. The sharp decline in velocity during this period was explained by the presence of a liquidity trap that caused households and business firms alike to absorb all the money balances provided by the Federal Reserve. This belief reduced confidence in the ability of the quantity theory to predict income satisfactorily and to underlie successful policy recommendations. As a result, the quantity theory was abandoned by many. Today, however, the existence of liquidity traps and their consequent implications for economic policy have become highly controversial parts of Keynes's reformulation of the demand for money.

Reformulation of the Quantity Theory

A small number of economists did not accept the theory of the impotency of money during the depression and in the immediate post-World War II period. They believed that, rather than money being impotent, the monetary authorities had been impotent and had not truly tried to increase the money supply in this period. To them, the high level of bank excess reserves and the very low interest rates that existed during the 1930s were not evidence of the failure of banks to use the reserves provided them and were insufficient reason for not providing banks with additional reserves. These economists argued that there had been an outward shift in the banks' demand for excess reserves in consequence of the large number of bank failures and the need to protect themselves against runs. After satisfying this demand, the banks would have used additional reserves, if they had been provided, to expand credit.

Moreover, they doubted that the demand for money became highly interest elastic at low interest rates and believed that increases in the supply of money could have lowered rates further and not been fully absorbed by offsetting reductions in velocity. The rapid increase in both money and prices during and immediately after World War II reinforced their faith in the potency of monetary policy.

Led by Milton Friedman at the University of Chicago, these economists rejected parts of Keynes's reformulation and effectively grafted other parts on to the lingering skeleton of the quantity theory. In particular, they rejected Keynes's tripartite demand for money, the concept that interest elasticities increased sharply as interest rates declined, and that the demand for money was unstable. They accepted that money was an asset and that its demand was sensitive to interest rates. In addition, they viewed the demand for money as an asset to be related more to wealth or some long-run average of income than to annual income, which could vary considerably from year to year. This school, which has become known as the *monetarists*, specified a single demand-for-money equation capturing all the motives for holding money balances. In simplified form, this function can be written:

$$DM = f(\overset{+}{W}, \overset{-}{i}). \tag{12-16}$$

They also preferred to separate wealth into price and real components and viewed the demand for money in terms of the real quantity of balances:

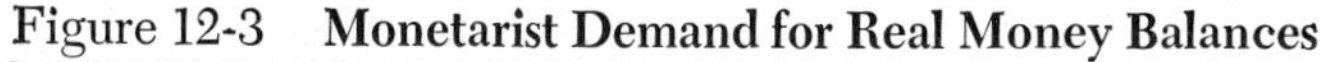
Figure 12-3 **Monetarist Demand for Real Money Balances**

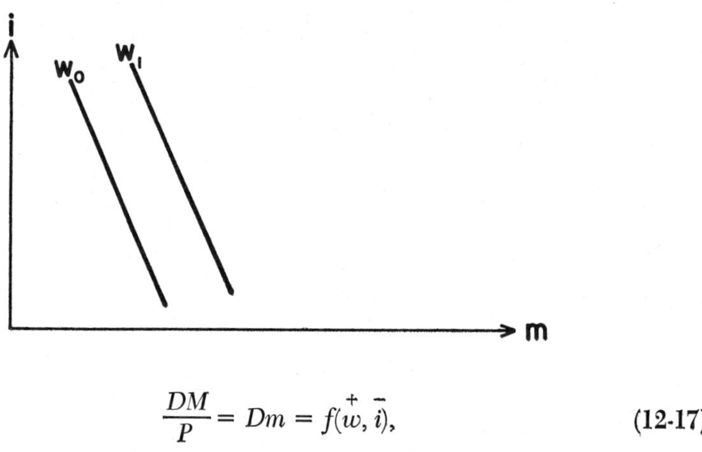

$$\frac{DM}{P} = Dm = f(\overset{+}{w}, \overset{-}{i}), \qquad (12\text{-}17)$$

where:

$m = M/P$

$w = W/P.$

The implications of this transformation are more than arithmetic. Now, the monetary authorities are assumed to have control over only the nominal quantity of money. The real quantity is determined by the public. If the monetary authorities provide a quantity of money different than the quantity the public wishes to hold, the public adjusts by either increasing or decreasing its spending, thereby affecting prices, until prices change sufficiently to produce the desired quantity of real money balances. The relationship between real money balances and interest rates is shown in Figure 12-3. The greater real wealth is, the more money balances are demanded at each interest rate. Note the lack of a liquidity trap and the smaller interest elasticity than in the Keynes specification (Figure 12-2).

The monetarists place great emphasis on scientific method and empirical testing. In the process of developing their theory, they have estimated a large number of alternative demand functions for money. For example, equation 12-18 was estimated by Professor Allan Meltzer for annual observations from 1900 through 1958 and resembles the formulation derived in equation 12-17.

$$\ln m = a + \underset{(42)}{1.11 \ln w} - \underset{(22)}{0.95 \ln i},$$

$$R^2 = .99 \qquad (12\text{-}18)$$

The figures in parentheses are t statistics and measure the reliability of the coefficients. The greater the value of the *t* statistic above 2, the more reliable the value of the coefficient. The equation is estimated linearly in natural logarithms, and the coefficients may be read as constant elasticities. The signs of the coefficients are as hypothesized in equation 12-17. The values of the coefficients indicate that for every 1 percent increase in wealth, ceteris paribus, the quantity of money balances demanded increases slightly more than 1 percent, and for every 1 percent rise in long-term interest rates, the quantity demanded declines by about 1 percent. The high values of the R^2 and t statistics suggest that the function is stable in the sense that it is possible to predict, at least in the time period sampled, the annual quantities of money balances demanded from observations of wealth and long-term interest rates with only small errors. A stable demand-for-money function also implies a stable velocity function.

While equation 12-18 is representative of the demand-for-money equations estimated by monetarists, it has a higher interest rate elasticity than many other equations and considerably higher than that estimated by Friedman, who finds little empirical evidence of any relationship between money and interest rates. A near unitary long-run wealth or income elasticity has been estimated in most long-run equations developed by the monetarists, again except by Friedman.

Similar to their quantity theory predecessors, the monetarists accept a close relationship between money and prices. Unlike the quantity theorists, however, they view money as more than a medium of exchange and accept the idea that its demand is sensitive to interest rates. They have also shifted emphasis from the supply of money to the demand for money. While they reject a constant velocity, they postulate that velocity is a stable function of, among other things, interest rates and can be predicted. Thus, velocity will not offset appropriate changes in money supply on income and will not reduce the potency of monetary policy. Last, and most important, they accept the belief that money can, at least in the short run and for policy purposes, affect real income and they have expanded the quantity theory from a theory of strictly prices to a theory of nominal income. Combined, these changes represent a denial of the independence of velocity and real income from money, the basic premise of the old quantity theory. It has, on occasion, been argued that the monetarists have accepted more from Keynes than from their proclaimed predecessors.

Economists in the Keynes tradition have also reformulated Keynes's demand for money. In particular, they have unified the three separate motives into one single demand function and expanded the concept of income to which money is related from concurrent observations to some longer-run average, which more closely approximates wealth. In essence, the modern neo-Keynesian and monetarist demand functions for money differ only slightly. However, the monetarists postulate a more stable function with lower interest elasticity. Hence, they envision a greater and more predictable impact for monetary policy.

Figure 12-4 Interest Rate Determination

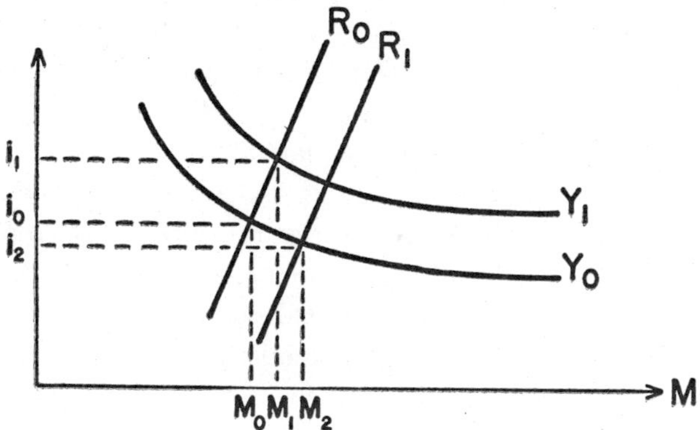

Money and Interest Rate Determination

As discussed earlier, the nominal level of interest rates is determined by the demand for and supply of money. In equilibrium, the demand for money equals the supply of money and it is possible to derive the interest rate by equating the demand and supply functions. For the sake of simplicity, the demand for money is specified as a function of income rather than wealth and in nominal, rather than real, terms as follows:

$$DM = f(\overset{+}{Y}, \overset{-}{i}). \tag{12-19}$$

For purposes of analysis, the interest elasticity is assumed to vary inversely with the level of interest rates in Keynesian fashion. From Chapter 8, the supply of nominal money balances is assumed to result from the joint actions of the Federal Reserve and the commercial banks:

$$SM = f(\overset{+}{R}, \overset{+}{i}). \tag{12-20}$$

Equating the demand for money with the supply of money and solving for interest rates:

$$\begin{aligned} DM &= SM, \\ f(\overset{+}{Y}, \overset{-}{i}) &= f(\overset{+}{R}, \overset{+}{i}), \\ i &= f(\overset{-}{R}, \overset{+}{Y}). \end{aligned} \tag{12-21}$$

Interest rates are negatively related with reserves and positively related with income. The demand and supply schedules are both plotted in Figure 12-4. At income level Y_0 and reserve level R_0, the equilibrium money stock is M_0 and equilibrium interest rate i_0. If income increases from Y_0 to Y_1 when reserves are R_0, the public wishes to hold greater balances and interest rates climb from i_0 to i_1. The money stock increases only slightly from M_0 to M_1 as banks reduce excess reserves. If, when income is Y_0, the Federal Reserve increases total reserves from R_0 to R_1, the money supply increases from M_0 to M_2 and interest rates decline from i_0 to i_2. It follows that expansionary actions by the Federal Reserve increase the stock of money and lower interest rates, ceteris paribus, and restrictive actions reduce the stock of money and raise interest rates. Note that if reserves are increased on the highly elastic section of the money demand schedule, interest rates decline only slightly, if at all. As we shall see, because monetary policy is transmitted to other sectors, either directly or indirectly, through changes in interest rates, if the Federal Reserve cannot reduce rates, its expansionary impacts are severely blunted.

As will be discussed in later chapters, the changes in interest rates in response to changes in reserves generated by equation 12-21 and illustrated in Figure 12-4 are only temporary solutions. The solutions will change as the impact of monetary policy is transmitted to other sectors and affects the demand for credit.

Equation 12-21 differs from equation 8-12 derived earlier by excluding price expectations. As discussed, price expectations importantly affect nominal interest rates. Inclusion of price expectations into the equation would shift the locations of the demand and supply functions in Figure 12-4 and generate different market rates of interest for the same quantity of money. Expectations of an acceleration in the rate of price increase would shift both schedules upward by equal amounts and generate a higher interest rate, and expectations of a deceleration would shift both schedules downward equally and generate a lower interest rate. The equilibrium amount of money would remain unchanged. Because we are primarily interested in analyzing the effects of a change in the stock of money, we will temporarily abstract from changes in price expectations and the schedules in Figure 12-4 may be viewed as holding for a given set of price expectations.

The next three chapters will trace the impact of changes in money and interest rates through the economy to the ultimate targets of monetary policy.

References

Brunner, Karl, and Allan H. Meltzer, "The Uses of Money: Money in the Theory of an Exchange Economy," *American Economic Review,* 61 (5), December, 1971, 784-805.

Dean, Edwin, ed., *The Controversy Over the Quantity Theory of Money* (Boston: Heath, 1965).

Fisher, Irving, *The Theory of Interest* (New York: Macmillan, 1930).

Friedman, Milton, *The Optimal Quantity of Money and Other Essays* (Chicago: Aldine, 1969).

———, "The Methodology of Positive Economics," in *Essays in Positive Economics* (Chicago: University of Chicago Press, 1953). Pp. 3-43.

Garvy, George, and Martin Blyn, *The Velocity of Money* (New York: Federal Reserve Bank of New York, 1969).

Keynes, John Maynard, *The General Theory of Employment, Interest and Money* (New York: Harcourt, Brace, n.d.).

Laidler, David E. W., *The Demand for Money: Theories and Evidence* (Scranton, Pa.: International Textbook Co., 1969).

Meltzer, Allan H., "The Demand for Money: The Evidence from the Time Series," *Journal of Political Economy,* 71 (3), June, 1963, 219-246.

Mill, John Stuart, *Principles of Political Economy* (London: Longmans, Green, 1926).

Patinkin, Don, "The Chicago Tradition, The Quantity Theory, and Friedman," *Journal of Money, Credit, and Banking,* 1 (1), February, 1969, 46-70.

13 A Model of Income Determination: 1–Measures and Consumption

This chapter and the two which follow will develop a simple four-sector model of the economy that will permit us to trace the impact of monetary policy actions through the economy to their ultimate effect on the aggregate levels of income, employment, and prices. The model encompasses the financial sector described in the previous chapter and three spending sectors—consumption, investment, and government.

No one model of the operation of the economy is universally accepted by all economists. Rather, a number of alternative models are favored by different economists, reflecting their particular theories of the functioning of the economy or their particular objectives for the economy. For purposes of pedagogy, we are interested in a model that emphasizes the structure of the economy. The model developed is a composite incorporating parts of both the neo-Keynesian and the monetarist theories. However, it differs in one important respect from the basic monetarist model: total economic activity is considered to result from the aggregation of activity in each of the three sectors considered. A pure monetarist model, as we will see later, constrains total economic activity by changes in the money supply and then allocates the activity among the sectors.

Measures of Aggregate Economic Activity

We shall focus on three of the many measures of overall economic activity in the country—prices, employment, and income. Measures of prices have already been discussed in Chapter 3.

Employment

Data on the characteristics of the labor force are collected monthly by the Bureau of Labor Statistics of the U.S. Department of Labor, frequently in cooperation with state employment agencies. Many of these data are obtained by sampling labor force participants and employers. Others are obtained from employers' Social Security and other tax returns. These data provide information on employment and unemployment by such major characteristics as industry, sex, age, race, marital status, and eligibility for unemployment compensation. The most interesting statistic for the purposes of aggregate analysis is the percent of the labor force unemployed. This reflects the underutilization of our labor resources. As noted earlier, many economists and policy-makers consider the United States economy to be at full employment when the unemployment rate is 4 percent or less. At rates above 4 percent, labor is considered underutilized.

The aggregate unemployment rate disguises wide differences in unemployment among sectors. Table 13-1 shows that unemployment tends to be permanently higher among teen-agers than adults, nonwhites than whites, blue-collar workers than white-collar workers, and construction workers than manufacturing workers. The differences reflect a number of factors. Teen-agers are generally less skilled than adults, nonwhites and females less educated and more discriminated against than whites and males, and construction workers subject to greater seasonal fluctuations in availability of employment than manufacturing workers. Structural shifts in the composition of the labor force may produce changes in the overall employment data independent of any change in the strength of economic activity. In recent years, the rapid increase in the proportion of teen-agers in the labor force has incorporated an upward bias in the aggregate unemployment series.

Income

Estimates of aggregate income generated by the economy are compiled by the U.S. Department of Commerce. The most inclusive income measured is *gross national product.* GNP is a measure of the total output of goods and services produced in a period valued at that period's market prices. It is computed quarterly and reported on an annual, seasonally adjusted basis. Because, for the economy as a whole, one person's expenditures on output are another's receipts or income, GNP can be measured either from the expenditures side or from the receipts side.

Table 13-1 **Selected Unemployment Rates, 1961-70**
(Percent)[1]

Group of workers	1961–65 average	1966	1967	1968	1969	1970
All workers	5.5	3.8	3.8	3.6	3.5	4.9
Sex and age:						
Both sexes 16–19 years	15.9	12.8	12.8	12.7	12.2	15.3
Men 20 years and over	4.4	2.5	2.3	2.2	2.1	3.5
Women 20 years and over	5.4	3.8	4.2	3.8	3.7	4.8
Race:						
White	4.9	3.4	3.4	3.2	3.1	4.5
Negro and other races	10.4	7.3	7.4	6.7	6.4	8.2
Selected groups:						
White-collar workers	2.8	2.0	2.2	2.0	2.1	2.8
Blue-collar workers	7.1	4.2	4.4	4.1	3.9	6.2
Craftsmen and foremen	4.8	2.8	2.5	2.4	2.2	3.8
Operatives	7.3	4.3	5.0	4.5	4.4	7.1
Nonfarm laborers	11.8	7.4	7.6	7.2	6.7	9.5
Private wage and salary workers in nonagricultural industries	5.9	3.8	3.9	3.6	3.5	5.2
Construction	12.8	8.1	7.4	6.9	6.0	9.7
Manufacturing	5.6	3.2	3.7	3.3	3.3	5.6

[1] Number of unemployed in each group as percent of civilian labor force in that group.
Source: Council of Economic Advisers, *Annual Report, 1971*, p. 40.

On the expenditures side, GNP (Y) is the sum of expenditures in four sectors:
1. personal private domestic consumption expenditures (C),
2. private domestic investment expenditures (I),
3. government expenditures on goods and services (G), and
4. net foreign expenditures on domestic goods and services ($X-M$).

This aggregation can be written:

$$Y = C + I + G + (X - M), \tag{13-1}$$

where:

X = exports of goods and services
M = imports of goods and services.

The values of each expenditure component and overall GNP in 1950 and 1970 are shown in Table 13-2.

Table 13-2 Gross National Product by Expenditure Sector, 1950 and 1970

	(Billion Dollars) 1950	1970	Percent Increase
Consumption	191	616	223
Investment	54	135	150
Government	38	219	476
Net Exports	2	4	100
Total GNP	285	974	242
GNP in 1958 Dollars	355	720	103
GNP Price Deflator (1958 = 100)	80	135	69

Source: Council of Economic Advisers, *Annual Report, 1972*, pp. 195–196.

On the receipts or income side, GNP may be viewed as the sum of all incomes accruing to households, businesses, and governments in payment for current services rendered. Of the income components of GNP, personal income, or the total income from all sources accruing to households and individuals, is by far the largest and, from the point of view of economic welfare, also the most important. Personal income encompasses not only the sources of household income included in GNP, but also some forms of income, such as transfer payments, which are not received for current services and, therefore, not included in GNP. Personal income is defined as:

$$PY = W + Q + D + R + P + N, \qquad (13\text{-}2)$$

where:

W = wages, salaries, and other labor income
Q = interest income
D = dividends
R = rental income
P = profits of unincorporated business firms
N = transfer payments.

To measure the purchasing power of consumers, it is necessary to first deduct personal income tax payments (T). The result is disposable personal income (DPY):

$$DPY = PY - T. \qquad (13\text{-}3)$$

Disposable income can be divided between consumption expenditures (C) and expenditures on capital assets or saving (S). Thus:

$$S = DPY - C. \qquad (13\text{-}4)$$

Table 13-3 **Personal Income by Components, 1971**

	Billion Dollars	Percent of Total Personal Income
Wages, salary, and other labor income	608	71
Rent	24	3
Dividends	26	3
Interest	68	8
Profits of unincorporated businesses	68	8
Transfer payments	95	11
Less Personal contributions for social security	31	4
TOTAL PERSONAL INCOME	857	100
Less Personal tax payments	116	14
TOTAL DISPOSABLE PERSONAL INCOME	741	86
Less Consumption expenditures	681	79
TOTAL PERSONAL SAVING	61	7

Source: *Federal Reserve Bulletin*, 58 (5), May, 1972, p. A 71.

The values of the principal components of personal income in 1971 are shown in Table 13-3. Wages and salaries account for 70 percent of total personal income payments.

Lastly, gross national product also is equal to the sum of the immediate uses to which income is put. Very broadly, income can be either spent on consumption goods or saved, including the purchase of investment goods. Consumption and investment goods, in turn, may be purchased either from the private sector or the public sector. The latter purchases are paid for by taxes. Thus:

$$Y = C + S + T, \tag{13-5}$$

where:

S = personal and business saving
T = government taxes.

Changes in GNP or other measures of national income are composed of two parts, changes in physical output and changes in the prices of the physical output. Thus, it is possible to have an increase in GNP attributed solely to an increase in prices without an increase, or possibly even with a decrease, in physical output. To evaluate the performance of the economy it is necessary to distinguish between the two causes of a change. An increase in GNP due entirely to price increases indicates poor performance and calls for different policy strategies than the same dollar or percentage increase attributed totally to increases in physical output

To distinguish between the two causes, the Department of Commerce values the physical output of goods and services included in GNP not only at current market value but also at the market value at some designated past year. Such a measure shows GNP in "constant" dollars and changes reflect only changes in physical output. In recent years, 1958 has been the base for constant dollar measures of GNP. The base year is changed periodically to remain current. A measure of changes in prices for the goods and services included in GNP is obtained by dividing GNP in current dollars for any period by the same goods and services valued in base year prices. The quotient is the GNP price deflator. As noted earlier, unlike the consumer and wholesale price indexes, the GNP price deflator series is not a pure price index. From year to year, the deflator does not value the same bundle of goods. Rather, it values two different bundles of goods in any two periods and thereby includes changes in tastes and substitution effects as well as changes in prices. If, for example, individuals through time substitute margarine for butter because the price of butter has increased more sharply than that for margarine, the GNP deflator would show a smaller price rise than an index measuring the price change of the initial mix of margarine and butter.

Table 13-2 shows that the increase in GNP between 1950 and 1970 reflected increases in both physical output and prices. As a result, GNP in constant dollars increased considerably less than GNP in current dollars. Because prices in 1950 were only 80 percent of those in 1958, converting nominal GNP in 1950 to GNP in constant 1958 dollars results in an increase in the value of GNP for that year, while it results in a decrease in GNP for 1970.

Because monetary policy operates primarily on spending, we will concentrate on the expenditures side of GNP. For the time being we will abstract from foreign trade and not consider exports (which will be discussed in two later chapters).

The basic equation we will consider is:

$$Y = C + I + G. \tag{13-6}$$

The following pages will examine the major forces affecting expenditures in each of the three sectors, explain how they are affected by monetary policy, and delineate the effects of changes in any one sector on the other two sectors and on GNP. While the explicit emphasis of the analyses will be on income, employment is considered implicitly. As will be discussed later, the two measures are closely related; the higher income is, the higher employment and the lower unemployment.

Consumption

Consumption expenditures are expenditures on goods and services consumed for their own use by the private sector. For any individual or family unit, the amounts

Table 13-4 **Gross National Product, Disposable Personal Income, and Consumption Expenditures, 1929–70**

Year	GNP	*DPY* (Billion dollars)	*C*	*C*/GNP	*C*/*DPY* (Percent)
1929	103.1	83.3	77.2	74.9	92.7
1930	90.4	74.5	69.9	77.3	93.8
1931	75.8	64.0	60.5	79.8	94.5
1932	58.0	48.7	48.6	83.8	99.8
1933	55.6	45.5	45.8	82.3	100.7
1934	65.1	52.4	51.3	78.8	98.9
1935	72.2	58.5	55.7	77.1	95.2
1936	82.5	66.3	61.9	75.0	93.4
1937	90.4	71.2	66.5	73.6	93.4
1938	84.7	65.5	63.9	75.4	97.6
1939	90.5	70.3	66.8	73.8	95.0
1940	99.7	75.7	70.8	71.0	93.5
1941	124.5	92.7	80.6	64.7	86.9
1942	157.9	116.9	88.5	56.0	75.7
1943	191.6	133.5	99.3	51.8	73.6
1944	210.1	146.3	108.3	51.5	74.0
1945	211.9	150.2	119.7	56.6	79.7
1946	208.5	160.0	143.4	68.8	89.6
1947	231.3	169.8	160.7	69.5	94.6
1948	257.6	189.1	173.6	67.4	91.8

and types of consumption expenditures are a function of a large number of factors. Among the more important are:

1. current personal income
2. savings from past income (wealth)
3. expected personal income
4. prices
5. interest rates on savings and borrowings
6. personal and family requirements
7. education
8. personal tastes.

Consumption expenditures for individuals can be aggregated to obtain overall consumption expenditures for the private sector. The same determinants that influence individual spending decisions may reasonably be expected to also influence aggregate spending decisions, although the precise nature of the individual relationships will be altered in the aggregation process to average relationships. All the determinants are not equally important nor equally sensitive to monetary policy actions. We will focus on only three determinants of consumption—income, interest rates, and wealth.

Table 13-4 (Continued)

Year	GNP	DPY (Billion dollars)	C	C/GNP (Percent)	C/DPY
1949	256.5	188.6	176.8	68.9	93.7
1950	284.8	206.9	191.0	67.1	92.3
1951	328.4	226.6	206.3	62.8	91.0
1952	345.5	238.3	216.7	62.7	90.9
1953	364.6	252.6	230.0	63.1	91.1
1954	364.8	257.4	236.5	64.8	91.9
1955	398.0	275.3	254.4	63.9	92.4
1956	419.2	293.2	266.7	63.6	91.0
1957	441.1	308.5	281.4	63.8	91.2
1958	447.3	318.8	290.1	64.9	91.0
1959	483.7	337.3	311.2	64.3	92.3
1960	503.7	350.0	325.2	64.6	92.9
1961	520.1	364.4	335.2	64.4	92.0
1962	560.3	385.3	355.1	63.4	92.2
1963	590.5	404.6	375.0	63.5	92.7
1964	632.4	438.1	400.2	63.4	91.6
1965	684.9	473.2	432.8	63.2	91.5
1966	749.9	511.9	466.3	62.2	91.1
1967	793.9	546.3	492.1	62.0	90.1
1968	864.2	591.0	536.2	62.0	90.7
1969	929.1	634.2	579.6	62.4	91.4
1970	974.1	687.8	615.7	63.2	89.5
1971	1,046.8	741.2	662.2	63.3	89.3

Source: Council of Economic Advisers, *Annual Report, 1972*, pp. 202–203.

Income

One of the more stable relationships in economics is the relationship between consumption expenditures and income. Annual values of consumption expenditures and both GNP and disposable personal income since 1929 are shown in Table 13-4. Because of measurement problems, the Department of Commerce includes all consumer durable purchases, except houses, in consumption expenditures. A few observations can be quickly made. Consumption expenditures are both greater and more stable as a percentage of disposable personal income than as a percentage of GNP. The first part of this observation is not surprising as disposable personal income is smaller than GNP. The greater stability is derived from two factors. First, business income, which is included in GNP but not in *DPY*, is more volatile over the business cycle than personal income. Second, the progressive nature of the federal income tax structure acts as an automatic stabilizer absorbing a larger proportion of income during expansions and a smaller proportion during contrac-

Figure 13-1 **Income and Consumption, 1900–71**

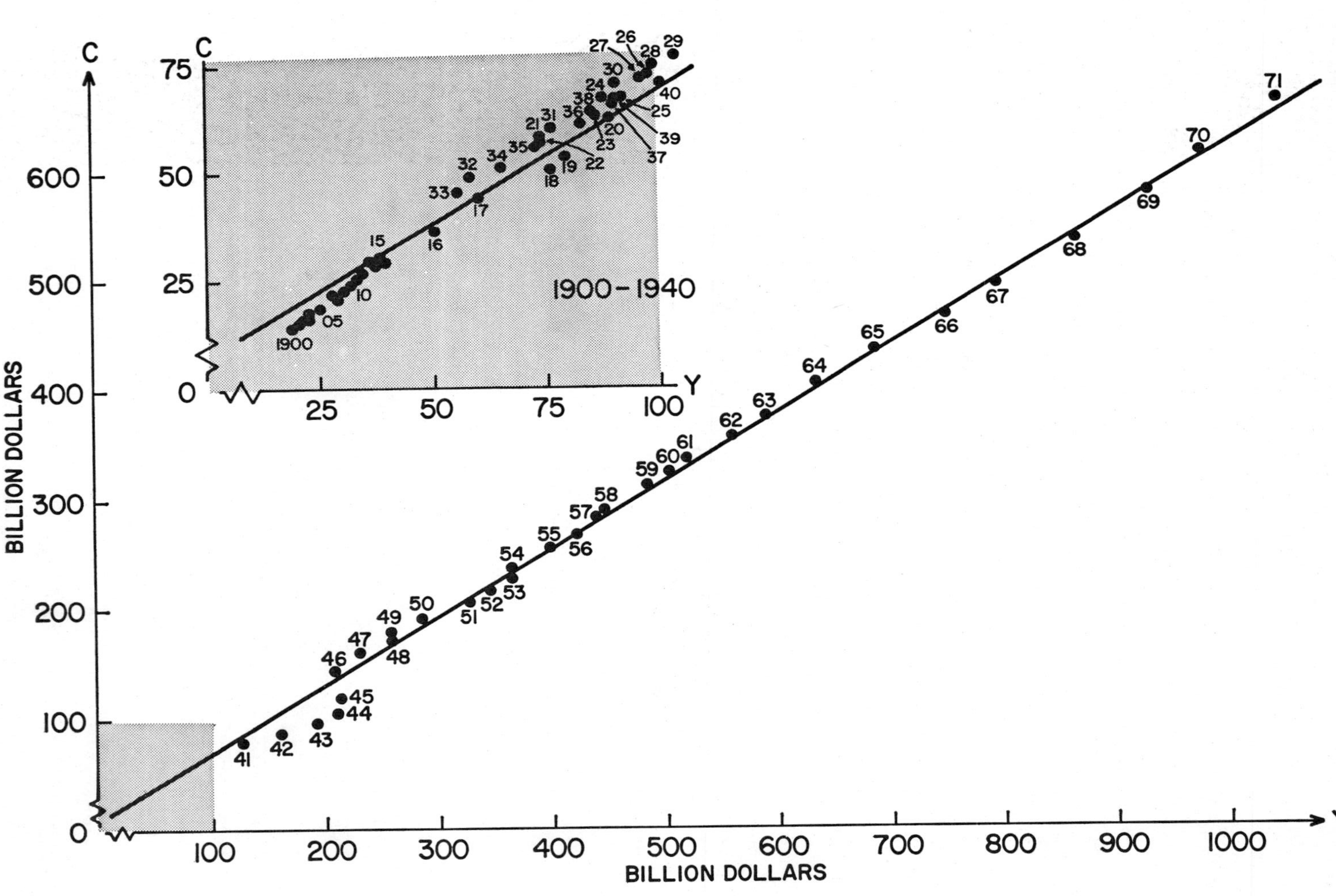

Source: U.S. Department of Commerce, *Long-Term Economic Growth, 1860–1965*, pp. 168–171; Council of Economic Advisers, *Annual Report, 1972*, p. 195.

tions, thereby reducing the impact of the business cycle on after-tax personal income.

The percentage of consumption expenditures to GNP has declined from around 80 percent in the early 1930s to slightly over 60 percent in the late 1960s. The decline reflects the relative growth in importance of the government sector in the economy. The percentage declined even lower during World War II years when consumption was deliberately restricted by economic policy to divert resources to war use. Contrary to the sharp continuous decline in the percentage of consumption to GNP, except for the war years, the percentage of consumption to disposable personal income declined only slightly. Consumption as a percentage of disposable income rose sharply during the depression years and exceeded 100 percent in 1933, the trough of the depression. In that year, the private sector as a whole dissaved, spending more for consumption than its after-tax income for the year.

The annual values of consumption and GNP since 1900 are plotted in a scatter diagram in Figure 13-1. Income is measured along the horizontal axis and consumption along the vertical axis. Observation suggests that the relationship between consumption and GNP can be approximated by a straight line. A straight line is fitted statistically to the points by regression analysis. While all points do not lie on the line, most lie only slightly off it. As might be expected, except for the early years of the period, the major deviations occur primarily during unusual periods. Consumption expenditures in dollars were lower than predicted by their long-run average relationship with income during war years—1918–19, 1942–45, 1951–53, and 1966–69. On the other hand, consumption expenditures were considerably greater than predicted by income during the depression of the 1930s and immediately following World War II.

The relationship between consumption and gross national product is written in functional notation as:

$$C = f(\overset{+}{Y}). \qquad (13\text{-}7)$$

If it is assumed that the relationship is linear, it can be described by a straight line:

$$C = a + cY. \qquad (13\text{-}8)$$

As Figure 13-1 shows, if the consumption line were extended to the left, it would intersect the vertical or consumption axis at a positive value, i.e., a in equation 13-8 is greater than zero. This implies that consumption exceeds income at some low levels of income and is positive even when income is zero. While this may be true for individual consumers and for all consumers briefly, it cannot exist for the entire economy for very long. Savings would soon be exhausted. Thus, it is unlikely that such a line reflects the true relationship over long periods of time. Rather, the true consumption-income relationship is probably shorter run and shifts through time as conditions change. Nevertheless, since 1900, changes in income alone statistically explain almost all of the annual changes in consumption expenditures ($R^2=0.999$). The straight line fitted to the observations in Figure 13-1 is described by the following equation:

$$C=6.82 + 0.62Y.$$

The relationship between consumption and income is referred to as *the propensity to consume out of income* or just *the propensity to consume.* The ratio of consumption to income at any time—C/Y—is referred to as *the average propensity to consume* (APC). The APC indicates the percent of income which is consumed at any income level. When the consumption-income function is plotted, the APC at any income level can be represented by the slope of a radial line going from the origin to the relevant point on the consumption function.

The evidence suggests that consumption as a proportion of income (APC) tends to decrease as income increases. This is even more true for households than for the economy as a whole. At some point on the consumption schedule, consumption is exactly equal to income and the APC is equal to 1. At this point, the consumption schedule intersects with a radial line extending at 45 degrees from the origin. Consumption and income are equal at all income levels along this radial line. In Figure 13-2, consumption equals income at Y_0. To the right of Y_0, consumption is less than income and the APC is less than 1. To the left of Y_0, the APC is greater than 1 and consumption exceeds income. As noted, this is an unlikely equilibrium for the economy as a whole for very long. The difference between an APC of 1, which is indicated by the 45-degree dotted line in the figure, and any other APC represents saving. The average propensity to save (APS) is defined as *the percent of income saved or not spent on consumption—S/Y*. As income is either consumed or saved, $Y=C+S$ and $S/Y=1-C/Y$. In the figure, the higher income is, the smaller the APC (C/Y) and the higher APS (S/Y).

The marginal propensity to consume (MPC) is defined as *the change in consumption associated with every change in income,* or $\Delta C/\Delta Y$. Because the APC declines as income increases, the MPC must be smaller than the APC; that is, as income increases, the economy consumes a smaller proportion of the additional income. This relationship can be seen in Figure 13-2. The consumption schedule intersects the vertical axis at a. The value of a—the constant term in equation 13-8—is included in the computation of APC, but not of MPC. In the extreme case, if income increases from 0 to Y_1, $\text{MPC}=(C_1-a)/(Y_1-0)$. At this point, $\text{APC}=(C_1-0)/(Y_1-0)$, and exceeds the MPC by the value of the distance $(a-0)$ in the numerator. As a straight line has constant slope, the MPC remains the same

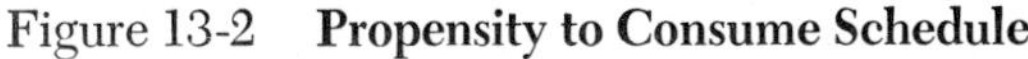

Figure 13-2 **Propensity to Consume Schedule**

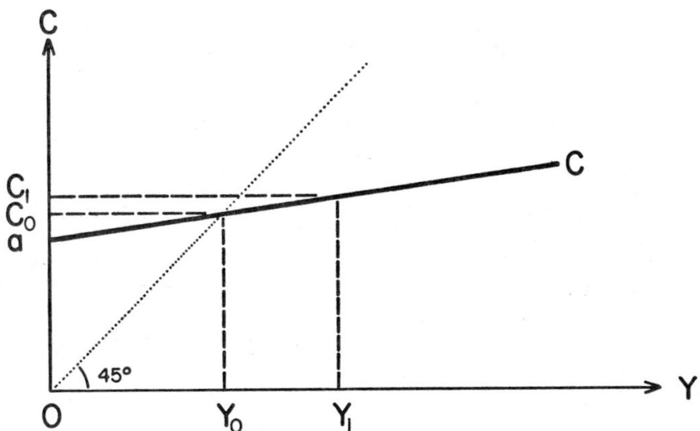

at all points along the schedule. The APC approaches the MPC as Y approaches infinity and the distance $(a-0)$ becomes very small in comparison to $(C-a)$.

In consumption functions of the general form shown by equation 13-8, the MPC is equal to c, the coefficient of the income term. For the linear function fitted to the observations from 1900 to 1971 plotted in Figure 13-1, the MPC is 0.62. That is, for every dollar increase in GNP, consumption expenditures increased, on the average, 62 cents. The importance of the MPC is discussed later.

The relationship between consumption and income is not perfect for a number of reasons. The other variables identified earlier as also influencing consumption are not included, GNP is used rather than *DPY*, which, as Table 13-4 shows, is more closely related to consumption and which we will use later when we introduce the government sector, and consumption patterns do not change quickly even if income does. When income declines abruptly, households will attempt to maintain their standard of living for some time by reducing savings before cutting back on consumption expenditures. When income rises abruptly, households will increase expenditures only cautiously until they are confident that the higher incomes are permanent. Thus, income varies more widely than consumption, with savings acting as the buffer. It follows that improved relationships between consumption and income may be obtained by averaging income over a number of periods to give some weight to past income and, to the extent a trend of past incomes is an indication of expected incomes, also to future income, in addition to current income. The propensity to consume out of some average income can be rewritten:

$$C_t = f\left(\sum_{n=0}^{m} q_n Y_{t-n}\right), \qquad (13\text{-}9)$$

where:

$$0<q<1 \text{ and } \sum_{n=0}^{m} q_n = 1,$$

in which the weights, q, decline the more distant the income observation, that is, $q \to 0$ as $n \to m$. Professor Friedman has reported considerable success in explaining consumption statistically by using a weighted sum of past incomes. Friedman refers to this concept as permanent income. It also follows that the propensity to consume is more stable the longer the measurement period. Income measures are more successful in explaining biennial consumption expenditures than annual expenditures, and the latter are more successfully explained than are quarterly expenditures.

Interest Rate

Decisions to undertake consumption expenditures are affected by interest rates, both directly and indirectly. Consumption is affected directly by the cost of credit and the return on savings, and indirectly by the effects of interest rate changes on the market value of asset portfolios (which will be discussed in the next section).

The effective cost of credit is not only determined by the nominal interest rate but also by the terms of the credit such as maturity and down payment. The longer the term to maturity and the lower the down payment, the lower the effective interest rate. In addition, to the extent that nominal interest rates reflect price expectations, the true cost of consumer credit or the reward for saving is the real rate of interest, or the observed rate less an adjustment for price expectations. It is likely, however, that except at times of very rapid inflation, most consumers would find the cost of making such an adjustment in the observed rate, including the cost of making price predictions, greater than the benefits derived from making the adjustment. In most periods, then, the observed interest rates may be substituted for the real interest rate. Ceteris paribus, consumption expenditures are inversely related to the nominal effective interest rate, both because the lower the rate, the cheaper it is to borrow and consume future income, and because the smaller the reward is for postponing current consumption and saving. In functional notation:

$$C = f(\bar{i}). \tag{13-10}$$

This function is shown in Figure 13-3. Empirical evidence suggests that the interest elasticity of consumption is not very high. The demand for consumer credit appears to be only moderately affected by interest rates. Nevertheless, to the

Figure 13-3 **Consumption-Interest Rate Schedule**

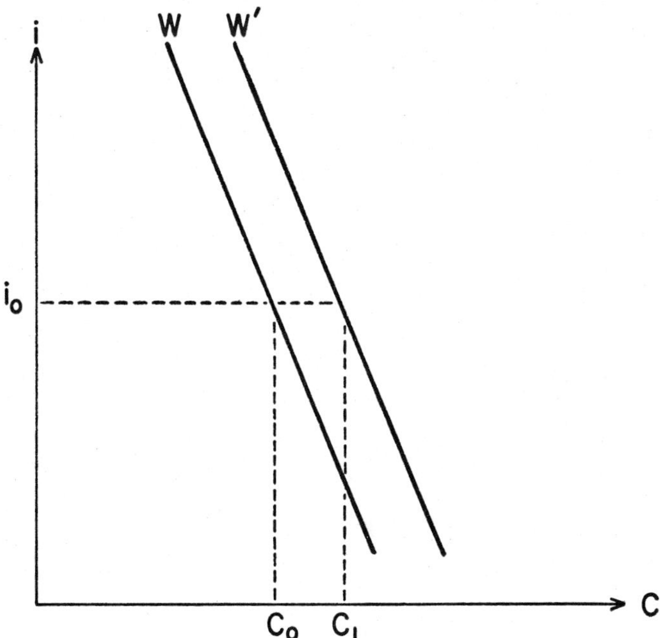

extent that monetary policy actions affect interest rates, they influence the amount of consumption. Expansionary actions that reduce interest rates increase consumption and restrictive actions that raise interest rates reduce consumption.

Wealth

Consumption expenditures are directly related to wealth or the accumulation of past savings in financial or nonfinancial assets. The greater is the value of wealth (W), the greater are consumption expenditures. Thus:

$$C=f(\overset{+}{W}). \tag{13-11}$$

To the extent that wealth is held in the form of marketable assets, the dollar value of wealth at any time is determined not only by current and past savings patterns, but also by current interest rates. As the market value of both financial and nonfinancial assets varies inversely with interest rates, the lower the rates, the higher the market value of wealth, and the higher the rates, the lower the market value. In the short run, changes in wealth may be attributed more to changes in interest rates than to changes in accumulated savings.

Recent empirical studies have tended to find evidence in support of both a strong effect of wealth on consumption and a strong effect of interest rates on short-run changes in wealth. The interest rate effect is transmitted to wealth primarily through changes in the market value of equities, which account for a large proportion of short-run changes in wealth. Because bonds and equities are substitutes, changes in interest rates not only will change bond prices but also stock prices by equalizing the earnings-to-price ratio on equities to the bond rate adjusted upward for an allowance for the greater risks on equities and downward for the effects of price expectations. Protection against changes in the rate of price increase is implicitly included in equities through the effect of expected price changes on the nominal amount of expected earnings. Thus, to the extent that monetary policy affects interest rates, it affects changes in wealth and consumption expenditures. In Figure 13-3, changes in wealth as a consequence of changes in interest rates are shown by shifts in the schedule. A reduction in interest rates increases the market value of wealth and shifts the schedule outward from W to W' so that consumption expenditures are greater for every level of interest rates. The evidence suggests that the indirect effects of monetary policy on consumption expenditures through wealth are proportionately stronger than the more direct effects through interest rates on the cost of consumer credit.

A Composite Consumption Function

The three determinants of consumption described above can be collapsed into one function:

$$C = f(\overset{+}{Y}, \overset{-}{i}, \overset{+}{W}). \qquad (13\text{-}12)$$

Monetary policy affects consumption expenditures through two of the three determinants—interest rates and wealth.

The impact of monetary policy on consumption can be demonstrated in Figure 13-4. Assume the introduction of an expansionary monetary policy reducing interest rates and increasing the market value of wealth. This can be shown by an upward shift in the propensity to consume out of income schedule from C to C'. Assume further that in equilibrium consumption equals income, that is, savings are zero. In the figure this is indicated by the intersection of the propensity to consume schedule with the 45-degree dotted line. At this point, APC = 1. At initial income Y_0, equilibrium consumption is C_0. The monetary policy action increases consumption at this income level to C_1. Now persons are consuming more than their income, or APC > 1. The deficit is financed by dissaving. The increased spending, however, will increase income to the point where income again equals consumption, or APC = 1. This occurs at Y_2. At this income level, consumption

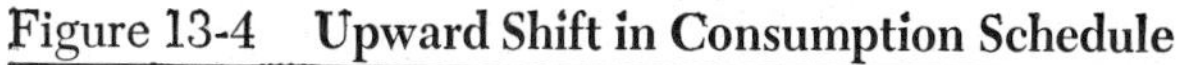
Figure 13-4 **Upward Shift in Consumption Schedule**

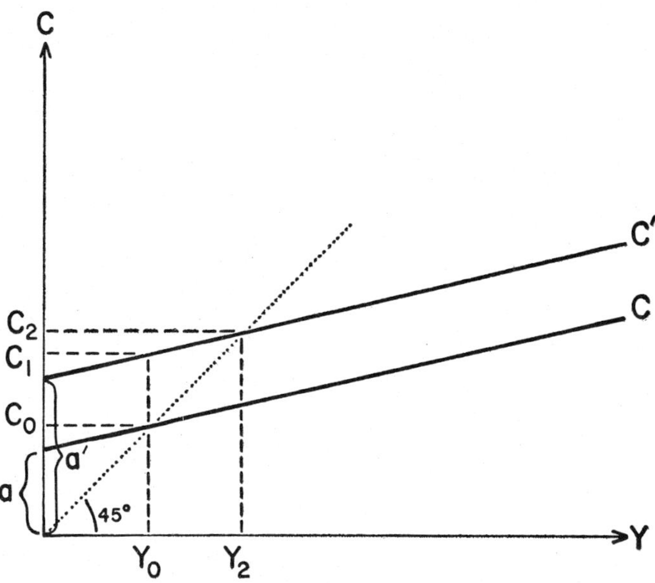

has increased further from C_1 to C_2. As the increase in income represented by $Y_2 - Y_0$ is equal to $C_2 - C_0$, income is seen to have increased by more than the initial increase in consumption, $C_1 - C_0$.

The amount of the ultimate increase in income in consequence of the initial policy-induced increase in consumption is related to the initial increase in consumption by the reciprocal of the MPS. This relationship can be seen from the following system of equations for our simple one-sector consumption model:

$$Y = C. \qquad (13\text{-}13)$$

$$C = a + cY. \qquad (13\text{-}14)$$

Substituting the consumption function (equation 13-14) into the equilibrium condition (equation 13-13) yields:

$$Y = a + cY. \qquad (13\text{-}15)$$

Designate the initial income and consumption equilibrium by the subscript 0 and, to be consistent with Figure 13-4, the final equilibrium position after the expansionary monetary shock by the subscript 2. The effect of the shock can be measured by subtracting the initial equilibrium values from the final equilibrium values:

$$(Y_2 = a_2 + cY_2) - (Y_0 = a_0 + cY_0).$$

Or

$$Y_2 - Y_0 = (a_2 - a_0) + c(Y_2 - Y_0).$$

Letting Δ represent change, collecting terms, and solving for ΔY:

$$\Delta Y = \Delta a / 1 - c, \qquad (13\text{-}16)$$

where Δa represents the initial increase in consumption induced by any factor other than an increase in income (the upward shift from a to a' in Figure 13-4). Since from before, $1 - c =$ MPS or s, equation 13-16 can be written:

$$\Delta Y = \Delta a / s,$$

and letting $1/s = K$:

$$\Delta Y = K\,\Delta a. \qquad (13\text{-}17)$$

As in the usual range of observation both c and s are less than 1, K is greater than 1, and income increases by a multiple of the initial policy-induced increase in consumption. The greater the marginal propensity to consume or the smaller the marginal propensity to save, the greater the income multiplier, K. The multiplier will be examined in greater detail in the next chapter in connection with investment expenditures, with which it is generally more closely associated.

The consumption function just developed is a deliberate oversimplification and may not be expected to predict actually observed consumption expenditures very well. It does, however, capture the essence of the better predictive functions in actual use. One of these functions is described in Exhibit 13-1.

Exhibit 13-1 **An Empirical Consumption Function**

While most empirical consumption functions are complex, they are structured on the relationship specified in equation 13-12. Some functions explain consumption in constant dollars and deflate consumption expenditures by prices. Others explain the ratio of consumption to income rather than the dollar amount of consumption.

The consumption function shown below was developed for the large scale FRB-MIT econometric model of the U.S. economy. This model of more than 100 equations was jointly constructed by the staff of the Board of Governors of the Federal Reserve System and a number of academic economists under the leadership of professors at the Massachusetts Institute of Technology at the time. The equation was estimated for quarterly observations from 1953 through 1966.

$$\frac{C(P)}{Y_D} = .0334\left(\frac{NW}{Y_D}\right) - 1.1739\left(\frac{\Delta K_{AR}(P)}{Y_D}\right)$$

$$-1.5318\left(\frac{\Delta K_{DR}(P)}{Y_D}\right) + \sum_{i=0}^{11} w_i \left(\frac{Y_{D-i}}{Y_D}\right) + \mu$$

$$(R^2 = .93;\ \text{standard error} = .0032;\ \sum_{i=0}^{11} w_i = .80),$$

where:

C = consumption expenditures including the services produced by durable goods but excluding expenditures on durables, 1958 dollars
P = price index for consumption goods
Y_D = disposable personal income
NW = consumer net worth (in which stock prices account for the major short-run changes)
K_{AR} = stock of consumer automobiles, 1958 dollars
K_{DR} = stock of other consumer durables, 1958 dollars
μ = residual error.

This equation indicates that consumption increases as a proportion of disposable income in any one quarter by .03 percentage points for every 1 percentage point increase in the ratio of net worth to disposable income in that quarter. Consumption decreases as a proportion of disposable income when the rate of saving in the form of purchases of new automobiles and other consumer durables increases. The last term in the equation indicates that current consumption as a percent of current disposable income is also affected by past values of disposable income. That is, the impact of disposable income on consumption occurs slowly through time and with diminishing strength. An increase of 1 percentage point in disposable income increases consumption as a proportion of income by .22 percentage points in the same quarter and by .80 percentage after three years.

References

See references at the end of Chapter 14.

14 A Model of Income Determination: 2—Investment, Government, and the Price Level

This chapter completes the construction of our simple four-sector model of the economy by introducing investments and government spending and examining the distribution of aggregate spending between real income and prices.

Investment

Capital goods are defined as *goods used to produce other goods and services and not consumed for their own consumption value.* Capital goods are consumed through time as they are used to produce other goods and services and their value declines. The consumption of capital goods is referred to as *depreciation.* Changes in the stock of capital goods are referred to as *investment.* Gross investment measures the change in capital stock before adjusting for depreciation, that is, including increases in capital goods used to replace depreciated goods. Net investment measures the change in capital stock after adjusting for depreciation, that is, changes in capital goods other than replacement goods. For the sake of expediency, we shall assume depreciation to be zero and gross investment equivalent to net investment. Then:

$$I = K_t - K_{t-1}, \tag{14-1}$$

Table 14-1 **Investment Expenditures, 1950 and 1971**
(Billion dollars)

	1950	1971
Business		
Plant	9	38
Equipment	19	70
Change in inventory	7	2
Consumer		
Residential construction	19	41
Total	54	151

Source: Council of Economic Advisers, *Annual Report, 1972*, p. 208.

or

$$I = \Delta K, \tag{14-2}$$

where:

I = investment
K = capital stock.

Although investment spending is considerably smaller than consumption expenditures (Table 13-2), it is much more volatile and accounts for a considerably larger proportion of changes in income. Investment expenditures are generally divided into four categories:

1. business expenditures on new plant and equipment,
2. business expenditures on changes in inventory,
3. consumer expenditures on residential construction, and
4. consumer expenditures on other durables.

The dollar amount of expenditures in each of these categories except consumer durables, which the Department of Commerce includes in consumption expenditures, is shown in Table 14-1. Changes in business inventories, which are the smallest component, are the most volatile. Annual changes in each of the three investment components in the postwar period are plotted in Figure 14-1.

The decision by business firms to purchase capital goods and which type to purchase is a function of a number of determinants including:

1. expected profit,
2. interest cost,
3. prices, and
4. technological change.

We shall examine the first two determinants in greater detail.

Figure 14-1 Investment Expenditures Are Highly Volatile

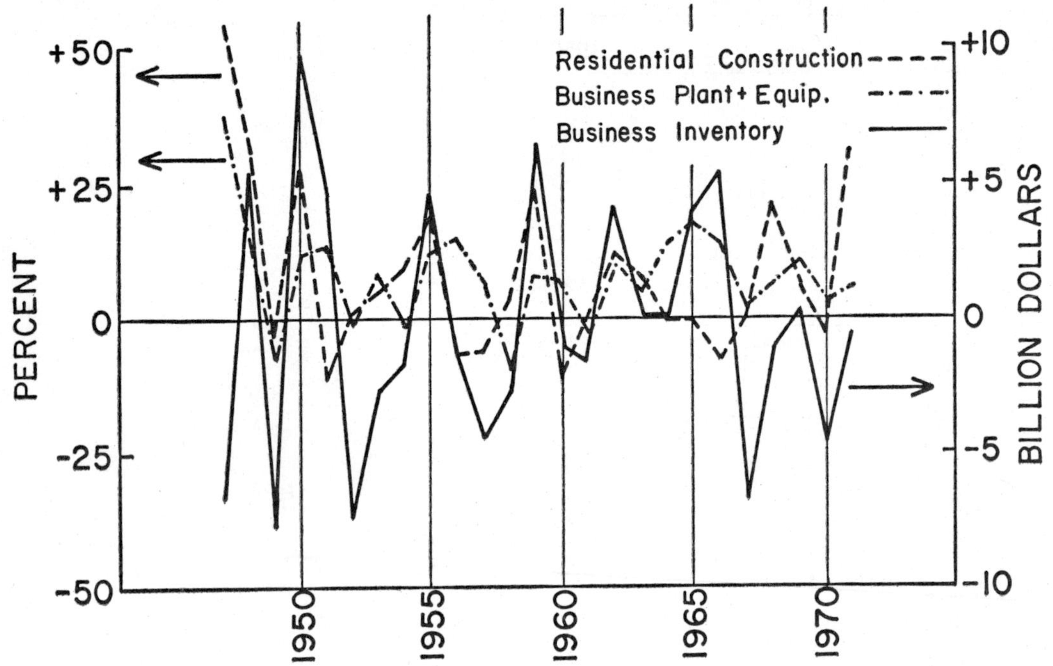

Source: Council of Economic Advisers, *Annual Report, 1972*, p. 208.

Expected Profit

Investment expenditures are undertaken for their net return after all costs. Ceteris paribus, the greater the return, the greater is the amount of investment expenditures. At any time with a given capital stock, there are a large number of individual investment opportunities. All of them, however, do not yield the same net return. It follows that the most profitable investments will be undertaken first. As aggregate investment expenditures are increased, a greater number of less-profitable individual investment projects are undertaken. The relationship between aggregate investment expenditures and the return on investments is referred to as the *marginal efficiency of investment* (MEI) and is shown in Figure 14-2, where λ is the profit rate or rate of return. The downward slope of the line reflects the diminishing marginal efficiency of investment, that is, the lower return associated with each additional investment venture.

Abstracting from costs, the profit rate for any individual investment project varies directly with the factors affecting the demand for the product or products generated by the investment project. To a considerable extent, these factors can be captured in aggregate income and the change in aggregate income. It follows

Figure 14-2 Marginal Efficiency of Investment

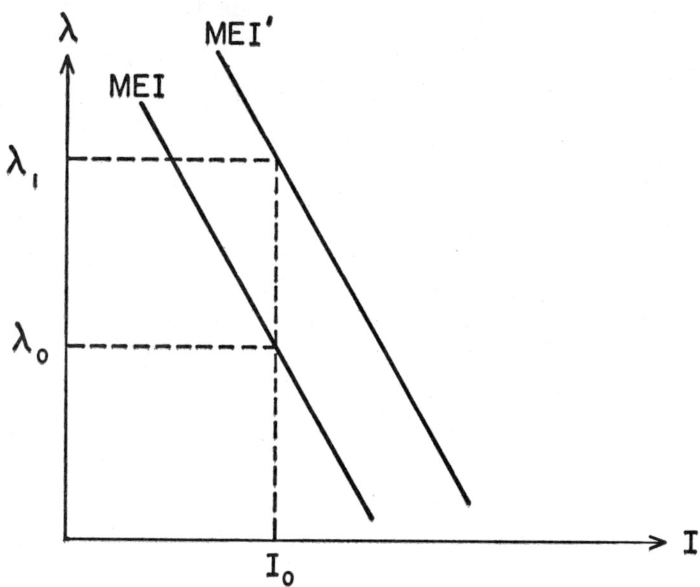

that aggregate investment expenditures are also affected by these two variables. The higher aggregate income, ceteris paribus, the higher profits and the greater aggregate investment. Higher income is represented by an outward shift in the MEI function to MEI′. After an increase in income, investment projects I_0 will yield a return of λ_1 rather than λ_0. Hence:

$$I = f(\overset{+}{Y}). \qquad (14\text{-}3)$$

The relation between investment and the change in income is referred to as *the accelerator effect.* Assume, in equilibrium, a given capital stock K and a given output (income) Y. The ratio of capital stock to output, K/Y, can be designated α. That is, α indicates the output a given capital stock is capable of producing. Assuming no technological changes so that α remains unchanged, a given increase in output (ΔY) will generate an accompanying increase in capital requirements equal to $\alpha\Delta Y$. The increase in capital represents investment and is governed by the following relationship:

$$I = K_1 - K_0 = \alpha Y_1 - \alpha Y_0 = \alpha(Y_1 - Y_0) = \alpha\Delta Y. \qquad (14\text{-}4)$$

As long as Y changes by the same amount through time, capital stock will also change by equal amounts and investment will not change. Only when income changes by different amounts will investment change. An increase in the amount of change in income in a period will generate a need for additional capital goods to produce the output, and investment will increase. Likewise, if the amount of increase in income falls, there is a smaller need for additional capital goods, and investment declines. This implies that expenditures on investment will increase only if the amount of the change in income increases. If income continues to increase but at a slower rate, investment will decline. If income declines in absolute value, then there is a surplus of capital goods, and the stock will be reduced; that is, investment becomes negative and capital is consumed on net. The dependence of I on ΔY rather than Y is, in part, responsible for the greater volatility in I than in Y.

The position of the MEI schedule in Figure 14-2 is thus a function of both Y and ΔY:

$$I = f(\overset{+}{Y}, \Delta \overset{+}{Y}). \tag{14-5}$$

The greater Y and ΔY, the further out to the right is the MEI and the greater is the return on any one individual investment project.

Interest Cost

Investment in capital goods is financed by withholding, or abstaining from purchasing, consumption goods. That is, investment expenditures are financed out of savings. The cost of using savings, either one's own or others, is the interest rate. When using one's own savings, the relevant cost is the opportunity cost of investing elsewhere. When using others savings, the relevant cost is the cost of borrowing. These costs are referred to as *the cost of capital.*

Unlike consumers, investors are likely to calculate both the estimated return on capital investments and the cost of capital carefully. If they expect prices to change between the time the investment is to be made and the period in which the returns are to be generated, appropriate allowances will be incorporated in the calculations. It is generally easier to make the adjustment for expected price changes in the current cost of capital—which is a single number—rather than in the projected rate of return—which involves numerous estimates. This suggests that the relevant cost of capital for investment decisions is the nominal interest rate adjusted for changes in price expectations, that is, the real rate of interest. To the extent that all investors do not hold the same price expectations, the anticipated real cost of capital associated with a particular observed cost will differ among investors.

A firm or household considering an investment expenditure can compare the expected rate of return on the investment project, which is typically computed in constant dollars and therefore equivalent to a real rate, with the real cost of

Figure 14-3 **The Lower the Interest Rate, the Greater Investment**

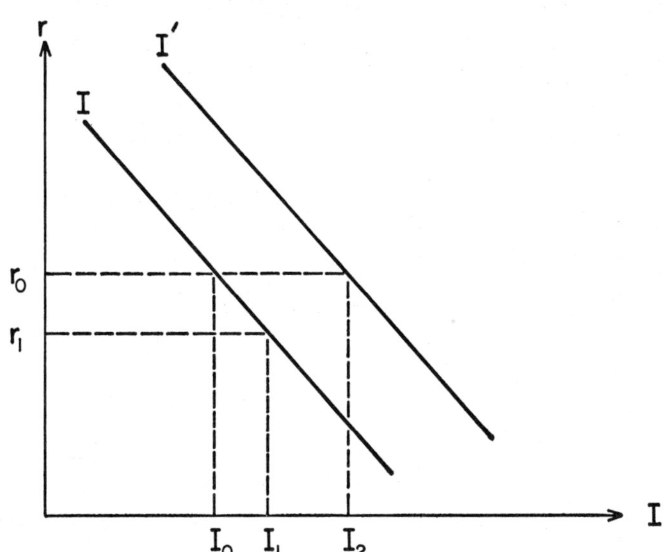

capital. If λ exceeds the real cost of capital, the investment is profitable. The economy as a whole will undertake all investment projects for which $\lambda > r$, where r is the real cost of capital. Equilibrium investment occurs where $\lambda = r$. It follows that, given λ, the lower r is, the larger the number of profitable investment projects that can be made and the greater aggregate investment, or

$$I = f(\overset{-}{r}). \tag{14-6}$$

This relationship is plotted in Figure 14-3. Interest rates are effectively superimposed on the previously developed MEI relationship. With MEI schedule I, an interest rate or cost of capital of r_0 will generate aggregate investment of I_0. A decline in the cost of capital to r_1 will increase the number of profitable investment projects and increase aggregate investment to I_1. An outward shift in the MEI to I', say, as the result of an increase in ΔY or a technological improvement, will increase the aggregate amount of investment at r_0 from I_0 to I_2. Investment will occur as long as $\lambda > r$.

A Composite Investment Function

Collapsing all three determinants into one investment function yields:

$$I = f(\overset{+}{Y}, \overset{+}{\Delta Y}, \overset{-}{r}). \tag{14-7}$$

Again, this is a greatly simplified functional relationship. An actually used investment function is described in Exhibit 14-1.

Monetary policy directly affects investment spending primarily through interest rates. To the extent that expansionary monetary policy actions lower real interest rates, more investment projects become profitable and aggregate investment expenditures increase.

The impact of monetary policy on income through investment expenditures can be delineated easiest by assuming investment to be temporarily independent

Exhibit 14-1 **An Empirical Investment Function**

The investment sector in the FRB-MIT model is highly complex and divided into a number of building-block equations and equations describing different components of investment. Only one of these equations is reproduced here and the remainder are discussed in skeleton form. The quarterly cost of capital for business plants is shown as:

$$R_s = (1 - .2t_c)(-1.833 + .0264\, R_{CBI} + .7258\, R_D),$$

where:

R_s = cost of capital
t_c = federal corporate tax rate
R_{CBI} = long-term bond yield
R_D = dividend-price ratio on common stock.

That is, the cost of capital for plants is directly related to the after-tax return on long-term marketable debt and equity securities. From the cost of capital and the price of new plant, which is determined elsewhere in the model, the annual rental value of business plant is derived by assuming that rental is an alternative to purchase and that the ratio of rental value to plant asset value must, in equilibrium, equal the cost of capital. If not, it pays either to rent or to buy depending on the relationship. The greater the rental value to the price of new plant, the higher is the cost of capital. Expenditures on new plants are then related inversely to the rental value of plants, related directly to current and past values of business income, and related inversely to the existing stock of plant. As, given the price of new plants, rental value reflects the cost of capital, this equation resembles our composite investment function, equation 14-7. The model also includes similar equations for deriving the cost of capital for business equipment and residential construction and, thereby, expenditures in these sectors.

Figure 14-4 **Equilibrium Where Saving Equals Investment**

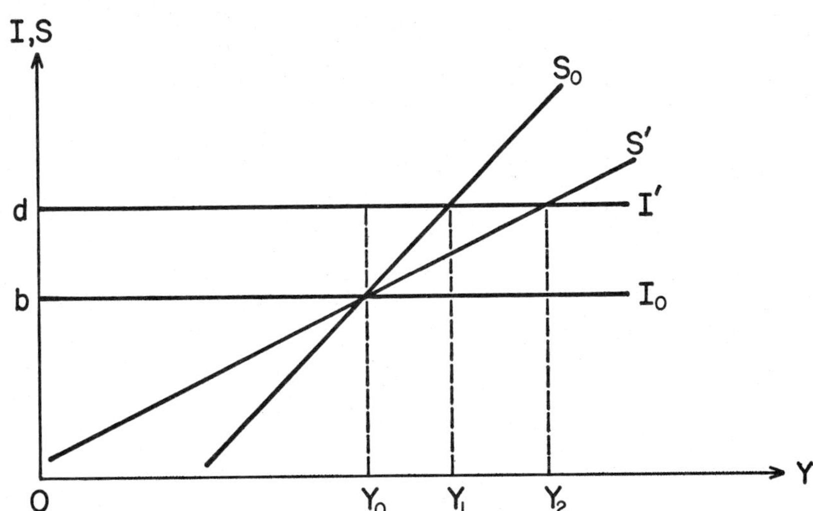

of income, i.e., $I=f(\bar{r}, X)$, where X represents all other autonomous forces. Investment expenditures can only be financed out of saving. Saving (S) is defined as $Y-C$ and, as $C=f(Y)$, S also is a positive function of Y; the higher income, the higher saving. The S schedule is computed by taking the vertical difference between every value of consumption on the C schedule and the 45-degree line in Figure 13-2. The resulting S schedule is plotted in Figure 14-4. It intersects the horizontal Y axis at the same income level at which the C schedule in Figure 13-2 intersects the 45-degree line. At this income level all income is consumed and saving is zero. If I is assumed equal to b, the investment schedule, I_0, representing the amount of desired investment, can be drawn parallel to the Y axis. Assume a saving schedule S_0 with a slope of less than 1. For points along the I_0 and S_0 schedules, equilibrium exists only at Y_0, where desired saving is equal to desired investment, that is, where $S=I$.

At income levels below and to the left of Y_0, the amount decision units wish to spend on investment exceeds the amount the same and other units wish to save. The resulting net addition to spending will increase income to the point where the enlarged amounts spending units wish to save out of the higher income are precisely equal to the amounts spending units wish to invest, that is, to Y_0. At income levels greater than Y_0, desired saving exceeds desired investment and the resulting withdrawal of expenditures from the income stream decreases income to Y_0, at which point desired saving out of the lower income is equal to desired investment.

During the transition to equilibrium, at any time actual saving, although not desired saving, will always be equal to actual, although not desired, investment at that moment in time. At income levels greater than Y_0, actual investment is brought into momentary equilibrium with the high level of saving through, say, involuntary buildups in inventories so the actual investment exceeds the desired investment temporarily. As inventories are eventually run down, actual investment approaches desired investment. Only at Y_0, where desired saving equals desired investment, will the equilibrium be more than momentary.

Assume now that, as a result of a decline in the real cost of capital in consequence of an expansionary monetary policy action, investment expenditures increase from b to d and the investment schedule is shifted straight upward to I'. On I', investment at every income level is equal to d. At Y_0, the level of desired investment exceeds desired saving and the resulting increases in expenditures exert upward pressures on income. The new stable equilibrium will be at Y_1 where intended saving and investment are again equal. Because the slope of the saving schedule is less than 1, the increase in income $(Y_1 - Y_0)$ is greater than the initial increase in investment $(d-b)$. Geometrically, the slope shows the marginal propensity to save or the change in saving, and, thus, also in investment, per unit change in income:

$$s = \frac{a - b}{Y_1 - Y_0} = \frac{\Delta I}{\Delta Y}.$$

Solving for ΔY,

$$\Delta Y = \frac{\Delta I}{s} = K \Delta I, \tag{14-8}$$

where:

$K = 1/s.$

K is the investment multiplier and can be seen to be equal to the consumption multiplier derived in equation 13-17.

The investment multiplier can also be derived algebraically. Equilibrium in a two-sector model is indicated by:

$$Y = C + I.$$

Assuming for the sake of expediency that only consumption is a function of income and solely of income, the consumption and investment functions are, respectively:

$$C = a + cY,$$

$$I = q,$$

where q is exogenously determined. Substituting the two spending functions into the equilibrium condition and collecting terms:

$$Y = \frac{a + q}{1 - c} = \frac{a + q}{s}.$$

If, initially, $q = I_0 = b$, then Y_0 is given by:

$$Y_0 = \frac{a + b}{s}.$$

Now let investment increase to $I' = d$. Substituting d for q above and solving for the new equilibrium income level yields:

$$Y_1 = \frac{a + d}{s}.$$

Subtracting Y_0 from Y_1:

$$\Delta Y = \frac{d - b}{s} = \frac{\Delta I}{s},$$

or

$$\Delta Y = K \Delta I.$$

The greater the marginal propensity to consume, the smaller the marginal propensity to save and the greater the multiplier or change in income for every change in expenditures—consumption, investment, and, as we will see also, government—not induced by a change in income. Such changes in expenditures are referred to as *autonomous* or *exogenous* changes with respect to income. The effect of changes in s on the multiplier can be seen from Figure 14-4. If the saving schedule were S', which has a smaller slope than S_0, the increase in investment from I_0 to I' would have increased income by $Y_2 - Y_0$, greater than $Y_1 - Y_0$.

In words, autonomous changes in expenditures result in a multiple change in income because the expenditures are someone else's income and, if $c > 0$, induce a chain of subsequent expenditures. Thus, expenditures on a new factory in response to a reduction in the real cost of capital become income for the engineers and construction workers employed on the project. These workers save a proportion of this income equal to s and consume the remainder. This, in turn, becomes income to the sellers of the consumption goods who, in turn, save a proportion,

Table 14-2 **Government Expenditures Included in GNP, 1950 and 1971**

	1950	1971	Percent increase
	(Billion dollars)		
Federal	18	98	445
State and Local	20	135	575
Total	38	233	513

Source: *Ibid.*, p. 195.

s, and consume a proportion, *c*. This process continues until all the increase is absorbed in saving, which, then, will sum to an aggregate amount exactly equal to the initial increase in investment. It can be readily seen that the smaller the *s*, the longer the spending process continues and the greater the induced increase in consumption and income for any given increase in investment.

Because a greater proportion of total investment expenditures are stimulated by forces other than income and because the multiplier applies only to such autonomous changes in expenditures, the multiplier has been associated with investment expenditures more frequently than with consumption expenditures.

Government Expenditures

Government expenditures on goods and services include expenditures by state and local governments as well as by the federal government. As is shown in Table 14-2, expenditures by the former currently exceed federal government expenditures and have also been increasing faster than federal expenditures. These data omit transfer payments and interest, which are not included in GNP. Because we are interested primarily in government expenditures undertaken for purposes of economic policy, we will limit our analysis to expenditures of the federal government and assume that these expenditures comprise total government expenditures. We will assume further that all federal tax revenues are derived from income taxes, although in reality these taxes account for only some 60 percent of total receipts.

Unlike private expenditures, federal government expenditures are generally not primarily related to economic determinants. Because the government can print money, it is not subject to the usual budget constraints. Governments have the responsibility of providing for the peace, security, and economic welfare of their citizens. Their expenditures may be divided into three types:

1. expenditures for social and political goals,
2. interest on the public debt, and
3. expenditures for economic goals.

The three categories are interrelated. If total expenditures necessary to satisfy economic objectives are smaller than the sum of the other two, cutbacks must be made in expenditures for social and political goals. Given the size of the public debt, interest on the public debt is a fixed obligation and cannot be changed. Social and political projects are generally ranked according to priority. If cutbacks have to be made, the lowest priority projects are eliminated or reduced in amount.

The amount of expenditures for economic objectives is determined in relation to the financing of the expenditures. The government finances its expenditures with funds raised either by taxation or by the sale of bonds. This relationship is summarized by the budget constraint:

$$G = T + \Delta B, \tag{14-9}$$

where:

G = government expenditures
T = tax revenues
B = government bonds.

It should be noted that only two of the three variables in this equation are independent at any one time. The third is a residual. If the government sets its expenditures and tax revenues, the amount of new bonds it has to sell is determined. If the government sets expenditures and the amount of bonds it wishes to sell or to retire, the amount of tax revenues is determined. Hence, the almost annual debate in the Congress on whether to increase the federal debt ceiling to permit the sale of new debt coming, as it does, after Congress has already approved the year's budget expenditures and tax rates seems to be economically, although not politically, superfluous. If expenditures equal tax revenues, the government budget is in balance. If expenditures exceed tax revenues, the budget is in deficit. If expenditures are less than tax revenues, the budget is in surplus. Government manipulation of its budget to affect economic activity is called *fiscal policy*.

When the government spends, it injects purchasing power into the economy; when it taxes, it withdraws purchasing power. Sales of bonds also withdraw purchasing power, but as the purchases are voluntary and result in a corresponding increase in financial assets, they are believed to affect primarily savings and to have a less restrictive impact on spending than an equal dollar amount of taxes. Typically, a budget deficit is considered stimulative to the economy and a budget surplus, restrictive. (A more complete discussion of the measurement of fiscal policy is presented in Chapter 21.) Similar to non-income-induced increases in consumption or investment expenditures, an autonomous increase in government spending increases income by a multiple of itself. The multiplier is again equal to the reciprocal of the marginal propensity to save, s. This can be seen from the following equations describing our expanded three-sector economy. For the sake of simplicity, only consumption is specified as an endogenous function and, then, only of income. Total expenditures now equal the sum of the expenditures in all three sectors. In initial equilibrium:

$$Y = C + I + G.$$

$$C = a_0 + cY.$$

$$I = I_0.$$

$$G = G_0.$$

G_0 as well as I_0 is determined exogenously. Substituting the three spending functions into the income equilibrium equation and solving for Y yields:

$$Y_0 = \frac{a_0 + I_0 + G_0}{1 - c} = \frac{a_0 + I_0 + G_0}{s}. \quad (14\text{-}10)$$

Now increase G from G_0 to G', while C and I are maintained unchanged. The resulting increase in income is given by:

$$\Delta Y = \frac{G' - G_0}{s} = \frac{\Delta G}{s}. \quad (14\text{-}11)$$

To the extent that an increase in G is accompanied by an increase in T or B, the increase in income given by equation 14-11 is overstated. Assume that the increase in G is matched by an equal increase in T. Substituting T for G in equation 14-11, and remembering that income is inversely related to tax revenues:

$$\Delta Y = \frac{-\Delta T}{s}. \quad (14\text{-}12)$$

Thus, the upward pressure on income in consequence of the increase in G is exactly offset by the downward pressure of the like increase in T. Equation 14-12 can be specified more precisely as:

$$\Delta Y = \frac{\Delta(G - T)}{s}. \quad (14\text{-}13)$$

However, as will be shown in the following section, even this is an oversimplification of the effects of government spending and taxing.

A Digression on the Balanced Budget Multiplier

As noted earlier, consumption is more closely related to disposable income than to GNP. Likewise after-tax income appears to be a better surrogate for profits than pretax income. Hence, the income variables in the consumption and investment functions can be rewritten.

$$C = a + c(Y - T). \tag{14-14}$$

$$I = b + d(Y - T) + e\Delta(Y - T). \tag{14-15}$$

It can be shown from these two equations that equal changes in government spending and taxing do not have equal effects on income. Assume again that only consumption is a function of income. Then in initial equilibrium:

$$Y = C + I + G.$$

$$C = a_0 + c(Y - T_0) = a_0 + cY - cT_0.$$

$$I = I_0.$$

$$G = G_0.$$

Substituting the spending functions in the income equilibrium equation and collecting terms:

$$Y = \frac{a_0 - cT_0 + I_0 + G_0}{1 - c}. \tag{14-16}$$

A balanced budget is defined as $G = T$. But equation 14-16 indicates that a change in G has a greater effect on income than an equal change in T in the opposite direction: $\Delta Y = 0$, if $\Delta G = \Delta cT$, but not if $\Delta G = \Delta T$.

Let G increase from G_0 to G' financed by an equal increase in taxes from T_0 to T' so that $G = T$. From equation 14-16:

$$\Delta Y = \frac{-c\Delta T + \Delta G}{1 - c}.$$

Substituting ΔG for ΔT:

$$\Delta Y = \frac{-c\Delta G + \Delta G}{1 - c} = \frac{\Delta G(1 - c)}{1 - c} = \Delta G. \tag{14-17}$$

Income increases by the amount of the increase in government expenditures. This is referred to as *the balanced budget multiplier*. In words, the balanced budget multiplier occurs because the government consumes all its income, while consumers consume only a fraction, c, of their income. Thus, a reduction in taxes increases consumption initially by an amount smaller than the reduction by $(1 - c)$, while an increase in government expenditures increases income initially by the full amount of the increase.

More realistically, the government controls the tax rate, t, rather than total tax revenues. The tax rate is typically applied to income, so:

$$T = tY. \qquad (14\text{-}18)$$

Substituting equation 14-18 into equations 14-14 and 14-15 and collecting terms:

$$C = a + c(1 - t)Y. \qquad (14\text{-}19)$$

$$I = b + d(1 - t)Y + e(1 - t)\Delta Y. \qquad (14\text{-}20)$$

An increase in the tax rate reduces both consumption and investment expenditures. Moreover, the application of taxes to income also affects the value of the autonomous expenditure multiplier as part of the change in income is siphoned off the expenditure process. The effect of taxes on the multiplier can be observed by again assuming that only consumption is a function of income. Replacing the earlier consumption function by equation 14-19 transforms equation 14-16 to:

$$Y = \frac{a_0 + I_0 + G_0}{1 - c(1 - t)} = \frac{a_0 + I_0 + G_0}{1 - c + ct}. \qquad (14\text{-}21)$$

The higher the tax rate is, the lower the income multiplier, and vice versa.

The Price Level

The aggregate price level is a weighted sum of all individual prices. It is affected by a number of factors. The early quantity theorists argued that changes in the price level were proportional to changes in the money supply. This relationship was based on the dual assumptions of independence of velocity and real income from money and of slow changes in velocity and real income. The evidence from the twentieth century to date suggests that neither of these assumptions has been very useful in explaining the relationship between prices and money.

Keynes hypothesized that the price level is a function of the scale of output of the economy as a whole. The closer the economy is to full employment, the lower the level of unemployment, the greater the price pressures, and the faster the rise in prices. This occurs for a number of reasons:

1. When there are considerable unused resources in the economy, they can be called back into employment to provide for an increase in output without bidding up either wages or prices. As the scale of output is increased and unemployment

declines, it takes continually greater increases in wages and prices to induce equal additional resources into production. Finally, as full employment is approached, firms begin bidding against each other for the resources, and wages and prices are driven up further, while employment and output are increased only slightly.

2. As output is increased from a level of high unemployment, the first resources to be recalled tend to be the most efficient available. Later, as less-efficient resources are employed, costs per unit of output increase and additional output is achieved only at more rapidly rising prices. At full employment, even the least-efficient resources are utilized and cost pressures increase in intensity.

3. It is unlikely that, as output is increased, all firms will experience proportional growth. As firms are interrelated, shortages will develop at some points along the supply pipeline and surpluses will accumulate at other points. Such misallocations tend to cause delays in production, further increasing costs and exerting upward price pressures. The probabilities and severities of bottlenecks increase the nearer the economy approaches full employment.

This analysis can be used to formulate an aggregate supply schedule for the economy. The schedule relates changes in the price level with real output–income. Price changes are measured by the rate of change: $\dot{P}=\Delta P/P$. Full-employment income, defined at some minimum level of unutilized resources which cannot easily be further reduced in the short run, is designated by y_F. The aggregate supply schedule slopes increasingly upward to the right reflecting the interaction between the increasingly higher prices required on the demand side to utilize additional resources and the higher costs on the supply side of utilizing the increasingly less-efficient resources. The supply schedule approaches full employment income asymptotically.

In functional form:

$$\dot{P}=f(\bar{y}_F - y)^m, \tag{14-22}$$

where:

m = some power: 1, 2, 3, ...

An aggregate supply schedule of this form is plotted in Figure 14-5.

While movements along the aggregate supply schedule affect prices, they provide an incomplete explanation of price changes. Experience has shown that changes in the scale of output affect prices only slowly, but once they are affected, price changes tend to linger and die out only slowly. The explanation appears to be that changes in the rate of price increase generate expectations of future price changes which, through affecting current spending decisions, feed back onto the current rate of price change. Thus, the current rate of price change is related both to the scale of output and to price expectations. Incorporating price expectations in equation 14-22:

Figure 14-5 **Aggregate Supply Schedule**

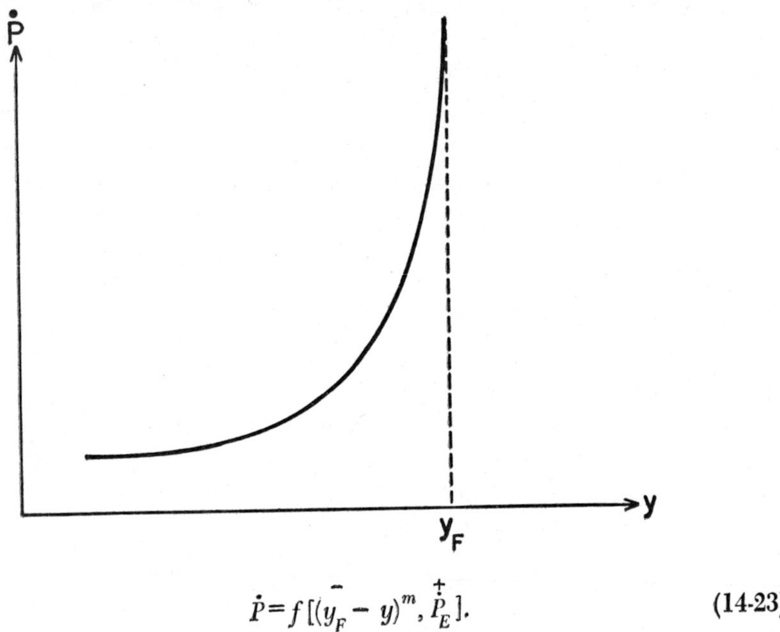

$$\dot{P} = f[(\overset{-}{y_F - y})^m, \overset{+}{\dot{P}_E}]. \tag{14-23}$$

To the extent expectations of future price changes are based on past price changes:

$$\dot{P} = f[(\overset{-}{y_F - y})^m, \sum_{n=1}^{\alpha} w_n \overset{+}{\dot{P}_{t-n}}], \tag{14-24}$$

and substituting for past price changes from equation 14-22:

$$\dot{P} = f[\sum_{n=0}^{\alpha} w'_n (\overset{-}{y_F - y})^m{}_{t-n}], \tag{14-25}$$

where:

$w'_n \rightarrow 0$ as $n \rightarrow \alpha$.

That is, the rate of change in the price level is directly related to current and past differences between full and actual income. The closer and longer the economy has operated at full capacity, the greater the rate of price increase.

Equations 14-23 through 14-25 indicate that if the economy is entering a period of rapid economic expansion after a period of considerable economic slack and little upward price pressures, prices will begin to rise only slowly as price expectations have not had time to change. After some period of continued expansion at or near full employment, prices rise rapidly pressured both by the proximity to full employment and by now widely held expectations of continued rising prices. If, thereafter, economic activity slackens and falls away from full employment, prices may not respond quickly as expectations of rising prices are dampened slowly. This price level equation has important implications for the successful use of traditional economic policies which will be examined in later chapters.

Phillips Curve

In the 1950s, Professor A. W. Phillips of the London School of Economics estimated an empirical relationship between the rate of unemployment in Great Britain and the rate of increase in money wages. On the basis of annual observations for an almost one-hundred-year period from 1861 through 1957, Phillips derived an inverse relationship approximating a convex hyperbola. High rates of unemployment were associated with low rates of money wage increases and low rates of unemployment were associated with high rates of money wage increases. Moreover, the nearer to full employment, the greater is the rate of money wage increases. Because money wage increases are closely associated with price level increases, most subsequent economists have preferred to specify this relationship between unemployment and the rate of price increase. The general form of the resulting Phillips curve is shown in Figure 14-6 and is plotted from postwar data for the United States. When unemployment is low, price increases are high and the greater the decline in unemployment the faster the rate of price increase.

The Phillips curve is suggestive of policy tradeoffs between unemployment and price stability. For example, lower rates of unemployment are consistent with faster rates of price increase, and slower rates of price increase or price stability with higher rates of unemployment. It follows that to decrease unemployment, greater price inflation must be accepted and to reduce inflation, greater unemployment must be accepted.

The stability of the Phillips curve through time and thereby the meaningfulness of its implications has been subject to considerable debate. Critics of the usefulness of the curve argue that price changes should not affect employment. Both employers and employees make employment decisions on the basis of real wages (W/P). Employers will hire additional employees only if the real wage declines and unemployed workers will accept employment only if the real wage rises. If prices change, employment will change only if nominal wages are not adjusted proportionately to the change in prices to maintain real wages constant.

We noted in Chapter 3 that it appears reasonable that business firms, who are accustomed to sharp-pencil computations, are likely to adjust for price changes faster than employees. Thus, if prices begin to increase, nominal wages may not

Figure 14-6 The Phillips Curve for the United States

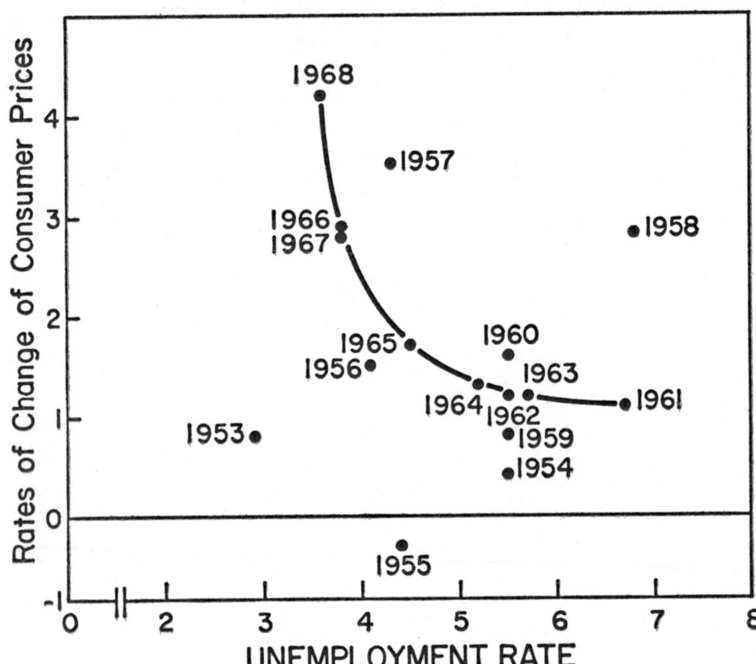

Data shown are in percentages. Curve has been arbitrarily fitted to 1961–68 data.
Source: Federal Reserve Bank of St. Louis, *Review*, March, 1969, p. 17.

increase proportionately and the real wage falls. Employers aware of this decline would employ additional workers. Employees are more likely to view the initial rise in nominal wages independently of the concurrent acceleration in the rate of price increases and to interpret the rise as an increase in real wages. As a result, they increase the supply of their services. This can be shown in Figure 14-7. As price increases accelerate from $\dot{P}_1$ to $\dot{P}_2$, the unemployment rate declines from U_1 to U_2. This suggests that, by observing only nominal magnitudes, employees are operating under money illusion.

After some time of continued price accelerations, employees recognize the slower rise in their nominal wages and the decline in their real wages, and demand proportional increases in wages. At this point, say $\dot{P}_3$ at U_3 on Phillips curve *H*, the real wage stops falling and unemployment stops declining. U_3 is lower than U_1 because real wages have declined. However, additional price accelerations will not reduce unemployment further. If, at this time, employees also attempt to compensate for past losses in real wages by demanding more than currently proportional increases in nominal wages, the real wage increases and employment declines. Because price expectations have already been formed at $\dot{P}_3U_3$, prices

Figure 14-7 A Phillips Curve Theory of the Business Cycle

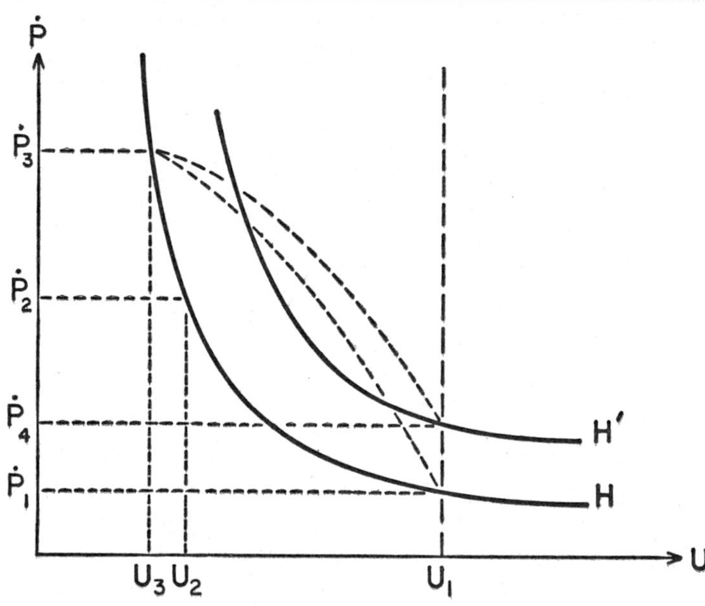

will not decelerate rapidly (equation 14-23). It is likely that the increase in unemployment and deceleration in prices will not proceed down along the same Phillips curve *H*, but will follow the dotted concave path back to the initial rate of unemployment, U_1.

Some economists argue further that both employees and employers will adjust fully to the price increases at $\dot{P}_3$. As a result, both see the same real wage at a level again equal to the initial real wage. As labor withdraws its services in response to the now-perceived lower real wage, unemployment rises. However, the rate of price increase will not decline to $\dot{P}_1$, but, if at all, only to, say, $\dot{P}_4$. At this point, the initial unemployment rate is reobtained but at a higher rate of inflation. The Phillips curve has shifted upward to *H′* and the process can begin all over again. These economists postulate an "explosive" Phillips curve and suggest that once inflation has begun, the original price rate can only be restored at a higher unemployment rate than initially.

Most critics of the Phillips curve recognize its existence for the short run as long as employees labor under money illusion. In the longer run, once money illusion is dissipated, the relationship between unemployment and price increases is assumed to be vertical. That is, unemployment is unaffected by changes in the price level. However, to the extent the Phillips curve exists, even only in the short run, it generates important policy implications, which will be discussed in the following chapters.

References

Ackley, Gardner, *Macroeconomic Theory* (New York: Macmillan, 1961).

Andersen, Leonall, and Keith M. Carlson, "A Monetarist Model for Economic Stabilization," *Review* (Federal Reserve Bank of St. Louis), 52 (4), April, 1970, 7-25.

deLeeuw, Frank, and Edward M. Gramlich, "The Channels of Monetary Policy," *Federal Reserve Bulletin*, 55 (6), June, 1969, 472-491.

Musgrave, Richard A., *The Theory of Public Finance* (New York: McGraw-Hill, 1959).

Perry, George L., "Inflation and Unemployment," in *Savings and Residential Financing, 1970 Conference Proceedings* (Chicago: U.S. Savings and Loan League, 1970).

Phelps, Edmund S., et al., *Microeconomic Foundations of Employment and Inflation Theory* (New York: Norton, 1970).

Rapping, Leonard A., "The Trade-Off Between Employment and Prices," in *Savings and Residential Financing, 1970 Conference Proceedings* (Chicago: U.S. Savings and Loan League, 1970).

Siegel, Barry N., *Aggregate Economic Analysis and Public Policy* (Homewood, Ill.: Irwin, 1970).

Spencer, Roger W., "The Relationship Between Prices and Employment: Two Views,' *Review* (Federal Reserve Bank of St. Louis), 51 (3), March, 1969, 15-21.

———, "High Employment Without Inflation: On the Attainment of Admirable Goals,' *Review* (Federal Reserve Bank of St. Louis), 53 (9), September, 1971, 12-26.

Tobin, James, "Inflation and Unemployment," *American Economic Review*, 62 (1), March, 1972, 1-18.

15

A Model of Income Determination: 3 – The Complete Model and Policy Implications

The major determinants operating in each of the four sectors into which we have divided the economy were analyzed in the previous three chapters. In this chapter, we sum the four sectors and identify the conditions necessary for stable equilibrium income. This level of income is then compared with the level of target or full employment income. If the two are not coincident, economic policies designed to achieve equilibrium at full employment are examined. In the process, the linkages in the transmission of monetary policy to income are explored in detail.

The Model

The simple model of the economy developed in Chapters 12, 13 and 14 is summarized in the equations in Exhibit 15-1. For the sake of simplicity, all the functional relationships are assumed linear.

Although this model already reflects a highly simplified view of the economy, it is not sufficiently simple for us to solve diagrammatically as well as algebraically. As a result, the model is reduced further to a form which is amenable to solution in two-dimensional diagrams. This permits us to trace the operation of the model more clearly. The reduced model:

$$C = a + c(Y - T). \tag{15-1}$$

$$I = b. \tag{15-2}$$

$$G = q. \tag{15-3}$$

$$T = u. \tag{15-4}$$

$$Y = C + I + G. \tag{15-5}$$

$$Y = C + T + S. \tag{15-6}$$

The model now has six equations and six unknowns (C, I, G, Y, T, and S). However, three of the unknowns—I, G, and T—are predetermined. Thus, the model is effectively only a three-equation model generating solution values for C, S, and Y. Of the three equations, one (15-1) is behavioral and the other two (15-5 and 15-6) are definitional. Of the three spending sectors, only C is determined by variables in the model and it only by disposable income. The other determinants of spending in each sector have to be introduced indirectly through the constant terms which incorporate the net effects of all the variables affecting the dependent variable, or the variable on the left side of the equations, except those that are explicitly specified on the right side of the equations. As the financial sector is omitted altogether, monetary policy effects on C and I, which operate through r and W in the larger model, are introduced in the reduced model through the constant terms a and b in equations 15-1 and 15-2, respectively.

The reduced model omits the important government budget constraint equation. As a result, the model does not consider the effects on interest rates of financing a government deficit. In effect, the model assumes that the private sector purchases any new bonds sold by the government to finance a deficit at existing interest rates. As this is unlikely and interest rates may be expected to rise somewhat, the model tends to overestimate the ultimate impact on income of changes in government spending financed through the sale or retirement of bonds. The implications of alternative ways of financing government deficits are examined more thoroughly later in this chapter.

By setting $b = I_0$; $q = G_0$; $u = T_0$; $a = a_0$; and $c = c_0$, the reduced model can be solved for equilibrium income by substituting equations 15-1, 15-2, and 15-3 into equation 15-5. This results in one equation with only one unknown (Y). After collecting and rearranging terms, the following solution value for equilibrium income is obtained:

$$Y_0 = \frac{a_0 - c_0 T_0 + I_0 + G_0}{1 - c_0}. \tag{15-7}$$

This value of Y can be substituted back into equation 15-1 to solve for C:

Exhibit 15-1 The Model of the Economy

$$C = a + c(Y - T) + dW^* - er.$$

$$I = b + f(Y - T) + g\Delta(Y - T) - hr.$$

$$T = t^* Y.$$

$$Y = C + I + G^*.$$

$$Y = C + S + T.$$

$$G^* = T + \Delta B.$$

$$\dot{P} = j - m(y_F{}^* - y) + n\dot{P}_E.$$

$$y = Y/P.$$

$$DM = a' + b'Y - c'i.$$

$$SM = d' + e'R^* + f'i.$$

$$DM = SM.$$

$$i = r + \dot{P}_E.$$

$$\dot{P}_E = g' + \sum_{n=1}^{m} w_n \dot{P}_{t-n}.$$

This model contains 13 unknowns—C, Y, T, I, S, M, i, r, y, B, P, $\dot{P}$, and $\dot{P}_E$—and 13 equations and can be solved algebraically. Values for the other variables specified, such as R, G, t, and y_F, are exogenously determined outside the system and are noted by an asterisk. The value of R is assumed to be established by the Federal Reserve in its monetary policy operations. The values of G and t are assumed to be predetermined by the government in its fiscal policy operations.

$$C_0 = a + c(Y_0 - T_0).$$

Knowing both Y and C, S is a residual given by equation 15-6:

$$S_0 = Y_0 - T_0 - C_0.$$

In equilibrium, intended total expenditures must equal intended total receipts. This implies that equation 15-5 must equal equation 15-6:

$$C + I + G = C + S + T,$$

or

$$I + G = S + T. \tag{15-8}$$

Equation 15-8 is referred to as *the equilibrium condition.* Unlike the previously derived implications of the analysis of individual sectors, the three-sector model does not require saving to equal investment for equilibrium. Instead, the sum of saving in the private sector *(S)* plus saving in the public sector *(T)* must be sufficient to finance the sum of investment by the private sector *(I)* plus government expenditures *(G)*. The interrelationship of the private and public sectors can be seen clearly by rearranging equation 15-8 so that the private and public sectors are on different sides:

$$\underbrace{G - T}_{\substack{\text{Public} \\ \text{Sector}}} = -\underbrace{(I - S)}_{\substack{\text{Private} \\ \text{Sector}}}. \tag{15-9}$$

For equilibrium, the deficit in the public sector must be equal to the surplus in the private sector, and vice versa. Thus, investment spending may exceed saving without disturbing equilibrium as long as tax revenues exceed government spending by an equal dollar amount. From another perspective, this equation suggests that the government can achieve equilibrium by exactly offsetting a disequilibrium in the private sector or generate a movement away from equilibrium in either direction by failing to offset or by more than offsetting a disequilibrium in the private sector. As we will see in the next section, this equation summarizes the operation of fiscal policy.

Algebraic Solution

A numerical example may be used to illustrate the solution of the model.

Let: $I = \$15$ billion
$G = \$30$ billion
$T = \$25$ billion
$a = \$20$ billion
$c = 3/5$.

These values are substituted into equation 15-7 to obtain the equilibrium level of income:

$$Y = \frac{a - cT + I + G}{1 - c} = \frac{20 - 3/5\,(25) + 15 + 30}{1 - 3/5} = \frac{50}{2/5} = \$125 \text{ billion.}$$

Solving next for C by equation 15-1:

$$C = a + c(Y - T),$$
$$= 20 + 3/5\,(125 - 25) = \$80 \text{ billion.}$$

And for S by equation 15-6:

$$S = Y - (C + T) = 125 - (80 + 25) = \$20 \text{ billion.}$$

These solution values can be checked to see whether they satisfy the equilibrium conditions specified by equation 15-8:

$$I + G = S + T,$$
$$15 + 30 = 20 + 25,$$
$$45 = 45.$$

They do.

The model can also solve for the implications of changes in any of the predetermined variables or parameters. Assume investment increases by $10 billion, from $15 billion to $25 billion. From equation 15-7 the new equilibrium income is:

$$Y = \frac{20 - 3/5(25) + 25 + 30}{1 - 3/5} = \frac{60}{2/5} = \$150 \text{ billion.}$$

And from equations 15-1 and 15-6:

$$C = 20 + 3/5\,(150 - 25) = \$95 \text{ billion.}$$
$$S = 150 - (95 + 25) = \$30 \text{ billion.}$$

These values satisfy the equilibrium condition:

$$I + G = S + T,$$
$$25 + 30 = 30 + 25,$$
$$55 = 55.$$

As a result of the $10 billion increase in investment, equilibrium income increases by $25 billion from $125 billion to $150 billion. This is consistent with the multiplier developed in Chapter 14. Substituting in equation 14-8:

$$\Delta Y = \frac{\Delta I}{1 - c} = \frac{10}{1 - 3/5} = \frac{10}{2/5} = \$25 \text{ billion.}$$

Figure 15-1 **Increase in Income as a Result of Increase in Investment**

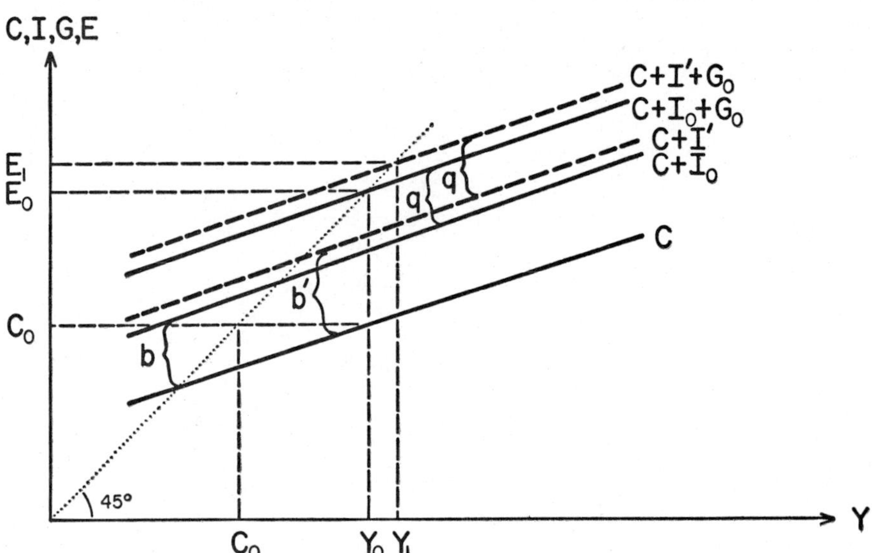

As neither investment nor government spending is specified as a function of income, all the increase in income above the initial increase in investment is generated by increases in consumption from \$80 billion to \$95 billion. The implications of changes in other predetermined variables for Y, C, and S may be solved for in this same way.

Graphic Solution

The determination of equilibrium income in the reduced model can also be obtained graphically in one diagram. In Figure 15-1, consumption, investment, government, and total expenditures (E) are measured on the vertical axis. Income received is measured on the horizontal axis. To simplify the plotting of the consumption schedule, equation 15-1 is rewritten:

$$C = a + cY - cT.$$

As T is determined exogenously, it can be combined with a in a new constant term, z, defined as $(a - cT)$. Thus:

$$C = z + cY. \tag{15-10}$$

Consumption can now be drawn as an upward-sloping function of Y with a vertical intercept of z, shown by the solid line C. Both investment and government spending are independent of income and can be drawn parallel to, but above, the C schedule by b and $b + q$, respectively. The middle solid line identified as $C + I_0$ represents total private spending and the top solid line $C + I_0 + G_0$ represents total private and public spending.

Equilibrium occurs only where intended total spending is equal to intended total income, or where the total spending function intersects the 45-degree line. In Figure 15-1 this occurs at Y_0. At all other points on the aggregate spending schedule, intended spending is either greater or smaller than income. At points to the left of Y_0, intended spending is greater than income at every income level and the additions to the income stream from involuntary dissavings, e.g., rundowns of inventory, increase income to Y_0. At points to the right of Y_0, intended spending is less than income, savings increase involuntarily, e.g., buildups in inventories, reducing inflows into the spending stream and lowering income to Y_0. Only at Y_0 is the equilibrium condition of $G + I = S + T$ satisfied. On the diagram these values are represented by the distances $(E_0 - C_0)$ and $(Y_0 - C_0)$, respectively, which can be seen to be equal by inspection. Note again that with introduction of the government sector, desired savings need no longer equal desired investment for equilibrium to exist. Instead, the sum of the receipts of income not intended to be spent on private consumption by any sector must equal the sum of the amount of intended government and investment spending.

Now let I increase from b to b'. This is shown in Figure 15-1 by shifting the private spending schedule from $C + I_0$ to the broken line $C + I'$. As government spending remains unchanged at q, aggregate spending also shifts up by $b' - b$ to the broken line $C + I' + G_0$. Equilibrium income increases to Y_1. The increase in income from Y_0 to Y_1 exceeds the increase in investment from b to b' as would be expected from the multiplier. Similar increases in income are generated when government spending is increased or the consumption schedule is shifted upward by increasing z. As $z = a - cT$, the schedule can be shifted upward either by an increase in a or by decreases in T. Multiple declines in income are generated by decreases in investment, government spending, and the consumption schedule through either a decrease in a or an increase in c or T.

Full Employment Income

The equilibrium level of income at which intended total spending equals intended total receipts may or may not be consistent with target or full employment income. In Figure 15-2, full employment income is defined as income at Y_F. This level of income represents a stable equilibrium only for aggregate spending lying on schedule E. Aggregate spending on higher schedules generates equilibrium incomes in excess of full employment levels. Aggregate spending on lower schedules generates equilibrium income below full employment levels. Equilibrium incomes in excess of full employment are possible because income is measured

Figure 15-2 **Inflationary and Deflationary Gaps**

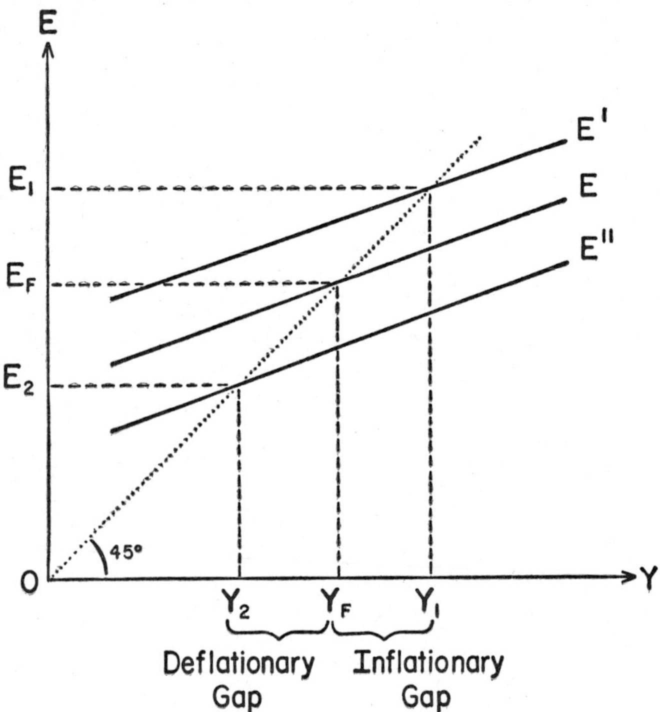

in nominal or dollar magnitudes. When income is measured in real or constant dollar magnitudes, it is difficult, by definition, to exceed full employment levels. The difference between full employment income (Y_F) and an equilibrium income level greater than full employment, say Y_1, generated by spending along schedule E', is referred to as *the inflationary gap.* All of the gap represents price increases. The difference between full employment income (Y_F) and an equilibrium income level below full employment, say Y_2, generated by spending along schedule E'', is referred to as *the deflationary gap.* This gap represents income that could be generated if the economy were at full employment. Only when equilibrium income coincides with full employment income is there neither an inflationary nor a deflationary gap. The function of economic policy may be viewed as preventing these gaps from arising and eliminating those that may have arisen as quickly as possible.

Fiscal Policy

The implications of both fiscal and monetary policy actions directed at eliminating inflationary and deflationary gaps can be traced diagrammatically in Figure 15-3.

Figure 15-3 Elimination of Inflationary Gap Through Restrictive Fiscal Policy Reducing Government Spending

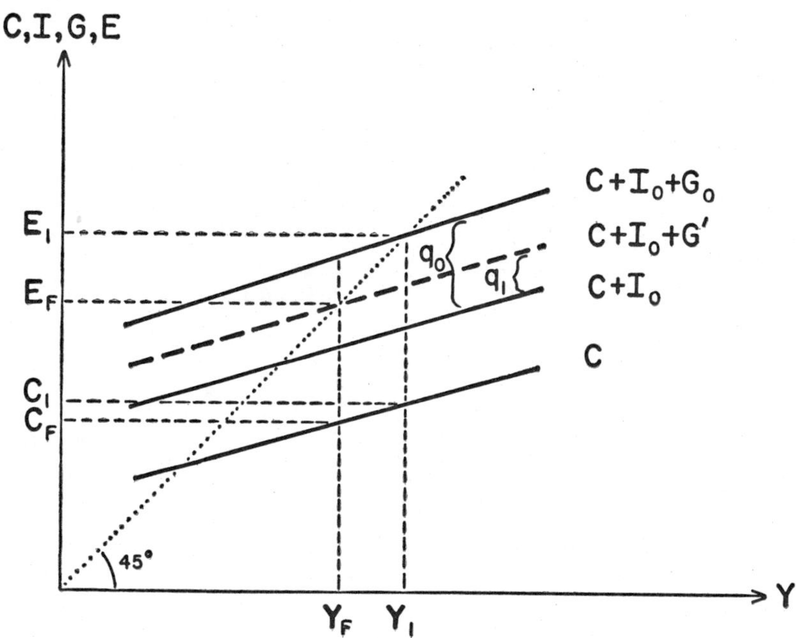

Assume that equilibrium income is Y_1, greater than full employment income Y_F. To attain full employment equilibrium, spending has to be reduced from E_1 to E_F. Fiscal policy can eliminate the gap by curtailing spending either through decreasing G or through increasing T. In our model an increase in T reduces consumption at every income level by lowering z and causing a downward shift in the C schedule. Because of the multiplier, the decrease in G or the increase in T required to eliminate the inflationary gap is less than the full amount of the gap. The dollar magnitudes of the necessary changes are obtained by rearranging the terms in the multiplier equations:

$$\Delta G = (1 - c)\,\Delta Y. \qquad (15\text{-}11)$$

$$\Delta T = -\left(\frac{1-c}{c}\right)\Delta Y. \qquad (15\text{-}12)$$

To achieve the same reduction in spending, tax revenues need to be increased by more than government expenditures need be reduced to compensate for the payment of some of the additional taxes out of savings rather than expenditures. This is the balanced budget multiplier effect discussed in Chapter 14. For example, if $c = 0.8$, the above equations indicate that government spending must be reduced by 20 percent of the target decline in income while tax revenue must be increased by 25 percent of this amount. The reduction in income in consequence of a reduction in government spending is shown in Figure 15-3. The equilibrium income generated by the spending schedule $C + I_0 + G_0$ is Y_1, which is to the right of Y_F and is indicative of an inflationary gap. By reducing G from q_0 to q_1, equilibrium full employment income is attained on spending schedule $C + I_0 + G'$ at Y_F. The reduction in income is greater than the reduction in government spending. The difference represents a decline in consumption expenditures from C_1 to C_F.

Likewise the new expenditure schedule could have been generated by maintaining G at q_0 and increasing T by an amount equal to $(q_0 - q_1)/c$. This would shift the C schedule down by the appropriate amount from C to C' (not shown). The resulting aggregate spending schedule $(C' + I_0 + G_0)$ is equal to $C + I_0 + G'$. With this strategy, all the decline occurs in consumption. Precisely the reverse strategy would be necessary to eliminate a deflationary gap through fiscal policy. Aggregate spending would be stimulated by increasing G or by reducing T and increasing private consumption spending. In more complete models, the effects of tax changes are felt on investment spending as well as on consumption.

In addition, as noted earlier, the model omits the implications of the use of debt financing on interest rates. In larger models, the demand for money is specified not only as a function of income and interest rates but also of wealth. If the government sells bonds to finance additional expenditures or tax reductions, public holdings of financial assets increase, increasing wealth and thereby the demand for money balances. Interest rates rise and the stimulative effects of the fiscal action are smaller than the solution generated by the simple multiplier analysis used above. How much smaller depends on the interest impact of the change in Treasury bonds outstanding.

Monetary Policy

Monetary policy actions can eliminate the inflationary gap $Y_1 - Y_F$ by shifting either or both the C and I schedules. Restrictive monetary actions initially raise interest rates and decrease the market value of financial and nonfinancial assets in wealth portfolios. The increase in rates and decrease in wealth reduce the value of the constant term a in the consumption schedule and thereby z and shift the schedule downward. The increase in rates also causes the investment schedule to shift down. As a result, the combined C and I schedule shifts down by $(\Delta z + \Delta b)$. The inflationary gap is eliminated when the restrictive monetary policy actions reduce consumption and investment spending by a combined amount which when multiplied by the multiplier is equivalent to the dollar size of the gap. The correct amount is given by:

$$\Delta(C + I) = (1 - c)\,\Delta Y.$$

Fiscal and monetary policy are not mutually exclusive and inflationary and deflationary gaps are generally combated by combined monetary and fiscal actions. A decrease in consumption in consequence of an increase in taxes may be reinforced by further restriction on consumption through monetary policy actions, which increase interest rates and reduce the market value of wealth.

A More Complete Monetary Model

It is now possible to expand our model somewhat to reintroduce the monetary sector and give explicit recognition to interest rates and wealth in affecting consumption and investment expenditures. This will permit us to trace more comprehensively the path by which monetary policy is transmitted to income. The model is shown diagrammatically in the first four sections of Figure 15-4. The interaction of the demand for and supply of money balances is shown in Figure 15-4 (*a*) for a given level of income, *L*, and of reserves, *R*. These two schedules determine r_0 and M_0. For the sake of simplicity, the nominal and real rates of interest are assumed to be equal. The consumption–interest rate schedule, *W*, for a given level of income and wealth is plotted in (*b*). The schedule is shown to slope out only moderately, indicating that consumption expenditures are not very sensitive to interest rates. At r_0, consumption spending is C_0.

The MEI schedule for a given level and change in income, Y_0 and ΔY_0, respectively, is shown in (*c*). The MEI schedule slopes outward more than the consumption schedule reflecting the greater sensitivity of investment expenditures to the cost of capital. At r_0, investment is equal to I_0.

The familiar aggregate spending-income function is shown in (*d*). Postulating an autonomously determined level of government spending, G_0, aggregate spending is $C + I_0 + G_0$ and equilibrium income is Y_0.

Assume that $Y_0 < Y_F$. To eliminate the deflationary gap, the Federal Reserve will increase reserves through the use of one or more of its tools—open market purchases, a reduction in the discount rate, or a reduction in reserve requirements. These actions will shift the supply of money schedule outward to R', increase the money supply from M_0 to M_1, and lower interest rates to r_1 as shown in (*a*). The lower rates will not only increase consumption expenditures by reducing the cost of consumer credit—a movement down and to the right on the consumption schedule in Figure 15-4 (*b*)—but by increasing wealth will shift the schedule out to W'. The combined effects increase consumption spending from C_0 to C_1. The lower interest rates will also increase investment from I_0 to I_1 as shown in (*c*). The greater *C* and *I*, together with unchanged *G*, shift the aggregate spending schedule upward to $C' + I_1 + G_0$, and, if increased by the correct amount, increase Y_0 to Y_F as shown in (*d*). The appropriate increases in *C* and *I* are given by:

Figure 15-4 Transmission of Monetary Policy

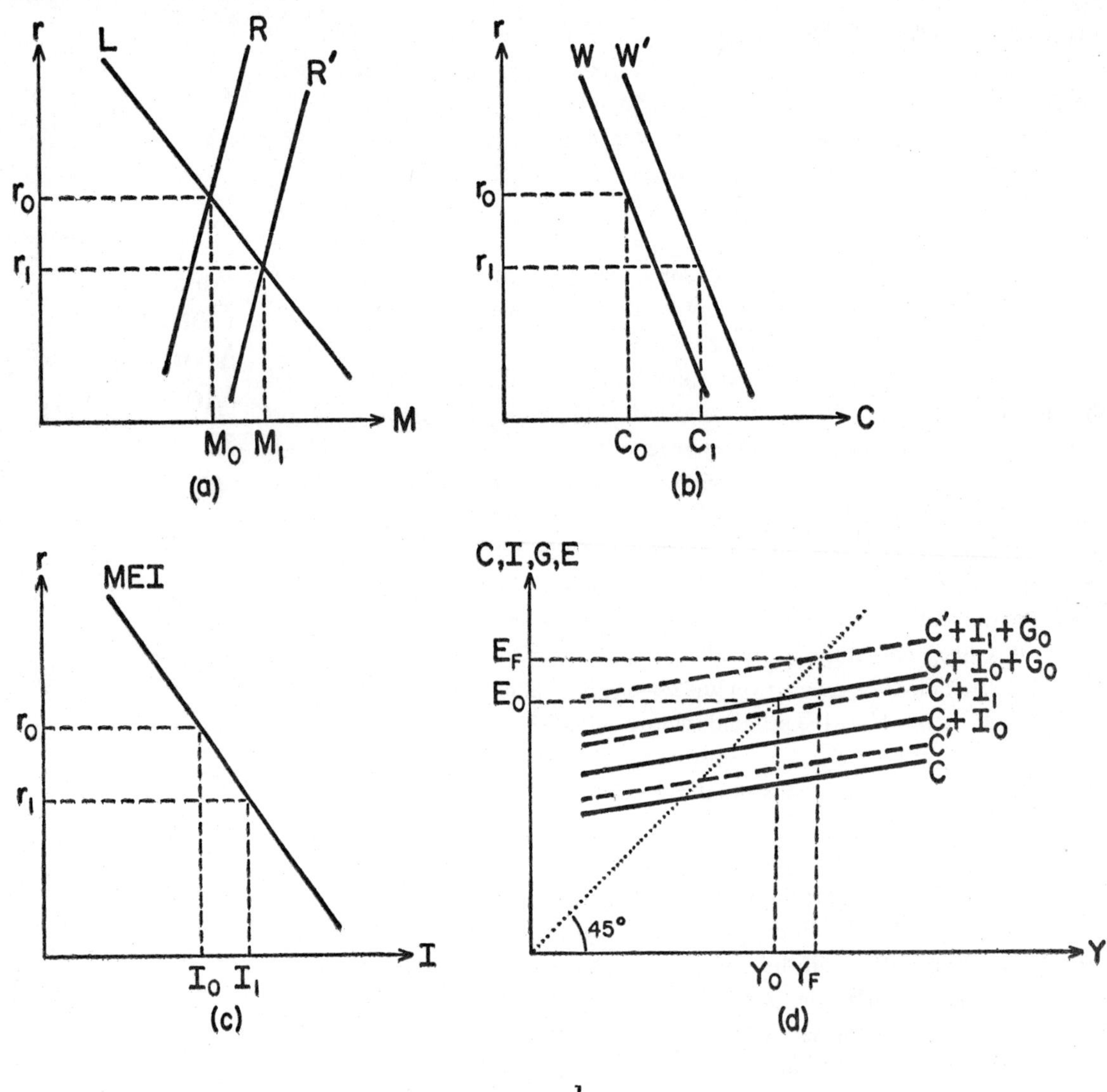

$$\Delta Y = \frac{1}{1-c}[(C_1 - C_0) + (I_1 - I_0)],$$

or simpler:

$$\Delta Y = K(M_1 - M_0).$$

A restrictive monetary policy action would generate precisely the reverse pro-

Figure 15-4 (Continued)

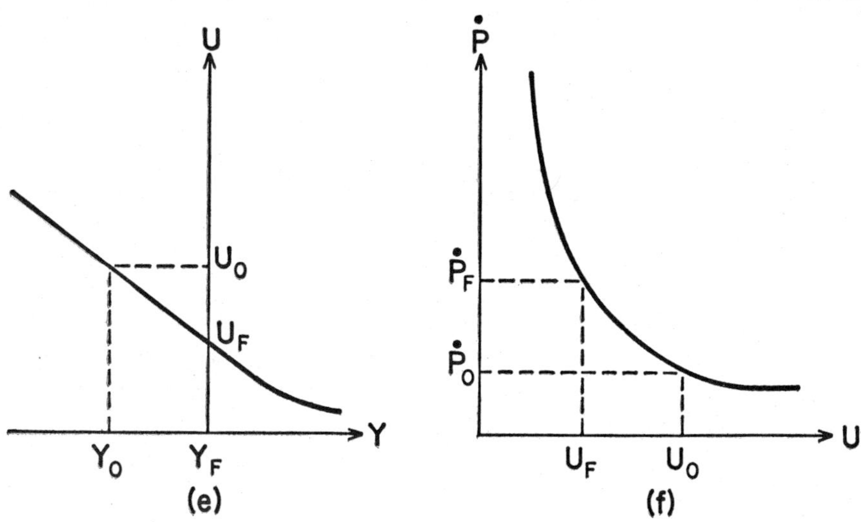

cess. The Federal Reserve absorbs reserves through open market sales, an increase in the discount rate, and/or an increase in reserve requirements. The supply schedule for money shifts inward to the left decreasing the stock of money and increasing interest rates. The higher rates reduce consumption expenditures, both by increasing the cost of consumer credit and by reducing the market value of wealth, thereby shifting the consumption schedule to the left. The higher rates also reduce investment expenditures. The reduction in spending generates a multiple reduction in income.

The Strength of Monetary Policy

The potency of monetary policy actions in either direction is shown in Figure 15-4 to depend on the shape or elasticity of the schedules in each step along the transmission of the monetary action from the time the Federal Reserve initiates the action to the ultimate impact on income. As the elasticities change, so does the effect of monetary actions per dollar of reserves.

The Demand for Money Schedule (Figure 15-4a). The more interest-elastic the demand for money (the flatter schedule *L*), the smaller will be the change in interest rates for any given shift in the supply of money function. Put another way, the more interest-elastic the schedule, the greater would have to be the shift in the supply schedule (the greater the strength of the monetary action) to obtain a given change in interest rates.

The Supply of Money Schedule (Figure 15-4a). Shifts in schedule R represent monetary policy actions. The larger the change in reserves brought about by open market operations, changes in the discount rate, and changes in reserve requirements, the greater is the shift in the schedule. The greater the role of the commercial banks in determining the stock of money through changes in their excess reserves not offset by the Federal Reserve, the more interest-elastic is the schedule. The greater the interest-elasticity of the schedule, the smaller is the impact of any given change in reserves on interest rates or the greater is the change in reserves necessary to generate a given change in interest rates.

The Interest Rate–Consumption Schedule (Figure 15-4b). The more interest-elastic the consumption schedule, the greater the change in consumption expenditures associated with a given change in interest rates. Although not explicit in the diagram, the greater the wealth elasticity, the greater is the shift in the interest-consumption schedule for any given change in interest rates and the larger the resulting change in consumption expenditures.

The Marginal Efficiency of Investment Schedule (Figure 15-4c). The more interest-elastic is investment, the greater the change in investment spending generated by a given change in interest rates.

The Aggregate Spending–Income Schedule (Figure 15-4d). The steeper the aggregate spending schedule $(C+I_0+G_0)$ is, the greater the marginal propensity to consume, the greater the multiplier, and the greater the impact of a given change in consumption and investment spending on income.

It follows from this analysis that monetary policy is most potent per dollar change in reserves the more interest-*inelastic* the demand for and the supply of money, the more interest-*elastic* the consumption and investment schedules, and the more income-*elastic* the aggregate spending function.

The Transmission of Monetary Policy

The sequence of steps by which monetary policy is transmitted through the economy until it affects income is traced schematically in Figure 15-5(a). Only "first round" effects are considered; that is, feedback from the change in income onto other sectors is omitted. The implications of expansionary actions are shown in (b) and of restrictive actions in (c).

Although they represent simplifications, these schematic diagrams do reintroduce a factor we did not introduce in the previous expenditure-income analyses, namely, that changes in nominal income consist of both changes in real income and changes in prices. As discussed in Chapter 14, the division of any changes

Figure 15-5 **Schematic Representation of Transmission Mechanism for Monetary Policy**

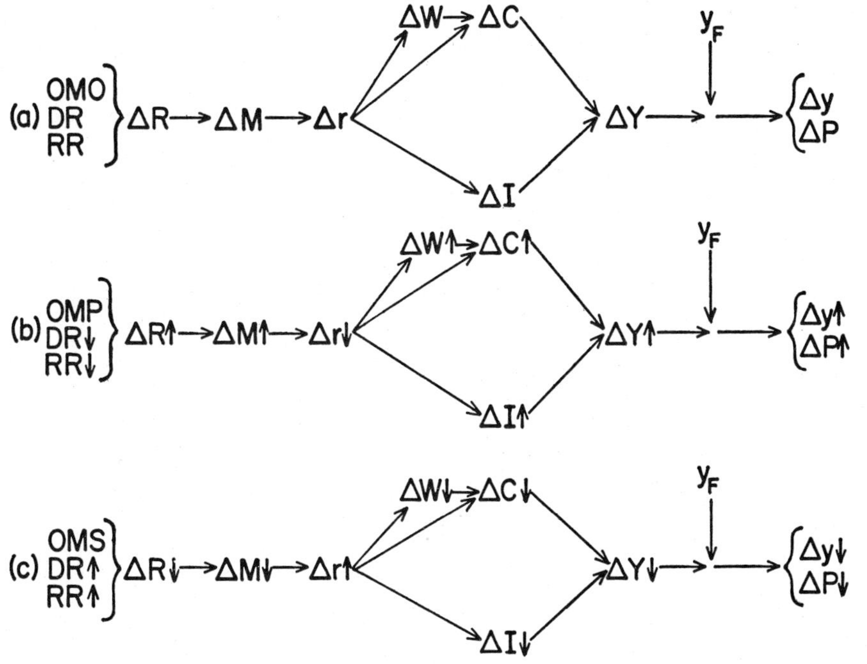

in nominal income into changes in real income and changes in prices depends in large part on the nearness of the economy to full employment at the time. The nearer to full employment, the more likely is any given change in nominal income to reflect changes in prices rather than changes in real output. In the schematic diagrams, full employment income (y_F) is introduced as an exogenous variable.

The interrelationship among monetary policy, price level changes, and actual income relative to full employment income is plotted in Figure 15-6. The steeper line traces the price consequences of monetary policy actions that expand the money supply when the economy is at or close to full employment. The less-steep line traces the price consequences of expansionary monetary actions when the economy is operating with considerable unused labor and capital resources. As is implicit in the previous discussion of the Phillips curve, curtailment of the money supply may not generate a slowing in price increases along the same path as previous expansions in money generated accelerations in the rates of price increases.

It is also possible to incorporate the price level into the four-sector model shown in (*a*) through (*d*) of Figure 15-4 by expanding the model slightly. The difference between actual income and full employment income at any moment of time may

Figure 15-6 **An Increase in Money Leads to a Faster Increase of Prices When Economy Is Near Full Employment**

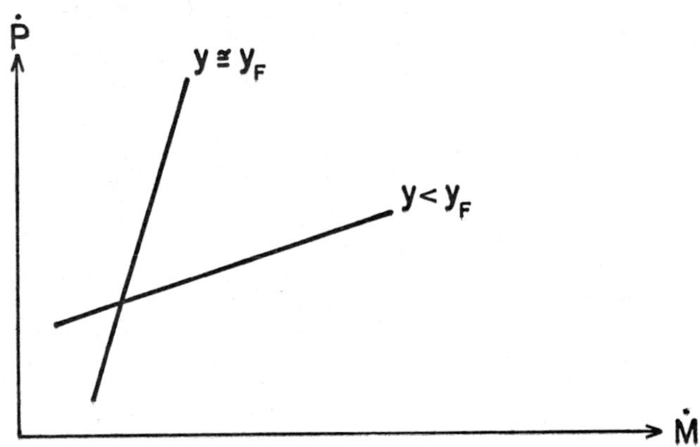

be translated into a corresponding unemployment rate. The further actual income is below full employment income, the greater is unemployment. This relationship is shown in Figure 15-4 (*e*). (Because *nominal* income is specified, while unemployment may reasonably be expected to be related to the spread between full employment and actual *real* income, the income-unemployment relationship is only approximated.) Full employment income is defined as the level of income that is consistent with an unemployment rate considered economically and socially acceptable. Income levels to the left of full employment income indicate deflationary gaps; to the right, inflationary gaps. Because of the increasing impracticalities involved in employing the very last members of the labor force, the schedule is drawn so that continued declines in unemployment require ever larger increases in the inflationary gap and unemployment never reaches zero. For every rate of unemployment, the previously developed Phillips curve shows the accompanying rate of price increase, as shown in Figure 15-4 (*f*).

At income Y_0, unemployment is U_0 and the rate of price increase $\dot{P}_0$. After the expansionary monetary policy action designed to eliminate the deflationary gap, unemployment declines to U_F and the rate of price increase accelerates to $\dot{P}_F$.

So far we have traced only the initial effects of monetary policy on income and prices. But this is not the entire story; income and prices feed back onto the financial sector and generate changes, which, in turn, affect the real sector again. Final equilibrium is only achieved after all the disturbances, primary and secondary, have been eliminated. This may require substantial time.

Consider a stimulative monetary policy action designed to reduce a deflationary gap. The resulting increases in income and prices feed back on the demand for money producing an upward shift to the right in the schedule. Interest rates rise

Figure 15-7 **Increases in Money First Lower, Then Raise, Interest Rates**

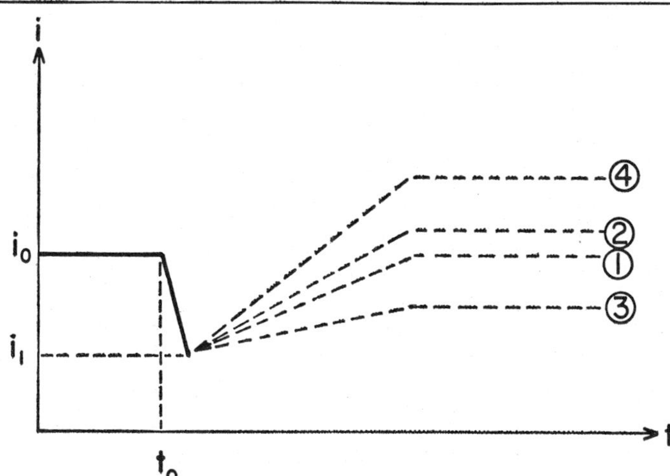

from their initially depressed levels and act to offset to some degree the increases in spending. Thus, the final increase in spending will be somewhat lower than it would have been in the absence of the rise in interest rates. The distribution of the increase in income between increases in real income and price increases depends on the nearness of the economy to full employment at the time the monetary policy action is taken. The closer the economy is to full employment, the more will a given outward shift in the supply of money schedule be reflected in price increases and the less in real income increases. It follows that as the economy approaches full employment it will require continuously stronger monetary actions to close the remaining real deflationary gap by equal amounts, since an increasing part of the stimulative effect is drained by price increases. As the rate of price increases accelerates, it is likely that price expectations will be revised upward. This will exert additional upward pressure on nominal interest.

The Impact on Interest Rates

The net effect of monetary policy actions on market rates of interest is complex. One possible scenario is traced on Figure 15-7. Time is measured on the horizontal axis and nominal interest rates on the vertical axis. In initial equilibrium, the market rate of interest is i_0. At some time, t_0, the Federal Reserve increases its open market purchases of securities.

The outward shift in the supply of money schedule in consequence of the stepped-up open market purchases reduces the rate sharply to i_1. At this level, the interest rate will generate increased consumption and investment expenditures, and nominal income rises. The higher income increases the demand for money balances, increasing interest rates through time along one of the solid lines. While interest rates rise, their final level depends on the response of income and prices.

In the absence of changed price expectations, if nominal income increases are proportional to the increase in the money supply, interest rates will rise along path 1 and eventually return to their initial level, i_0. If, as may be likely under the circumstances promoting expansionary monetary actions, nominal income rises proportionally more as underutilized resources are used more fully and some price increases occur, interest rates will rise along path 2 and climb above their initial value. If the increase in money generates a compensating increase in the demand for money balances so velocity declines and little of the effects are transmitted to consumption and investment spending, interest rates will climb slowly along path 3 and fail to return to their initial levels.

If the monetary expansion leads to an acceleration in the rate of price increase, it is likely that price expectations will be revised upward. To some extent, this will be reflected in market interest rates and interest rates will climb more sharply, say, along path 4. Ultimate interest rates will exceed the rates attained in the absence of changed price expectations by an amount proportional to the upward revision in expectations but, as discussed in Chapter 8, probably less than in a one-to-one proportion.

Thus, while expansionary monetary actions generate initially lower market rates of interest, the ultimate interest rate will be higher than the level to which rates decline immediately. The final rates may even exceed the initial level of rates.

The same analysis applies to restrictive monetary policy actions. Reductions in reserves in consequence of open market sales, increases in the discount rate, and/or increases in reserve requirements will initially generate higher market rates of interest. In time, however, as income and price increases are curtailed and price expectations are revised downward, interest rates will decline and most likely regain equilibrium at a level lower than before the restrictive action.

Complete consideration of the impact of monetary policy actions, therefore, indicates a different set of relations between money and interest rates than shown by the previous partial analysis. Accelerations in the money supply are now likely to be followed in time by higher, as well as by lower, market rates of interest. Decelerations in the supply of money are likely to be followed by higher, as well as by lower, interest rates. Empirically, the highest interest rates in the twentieth century have occurred during periods of full employment and rapidly rising prices preceded by rapid monetary expansion, such as in 1966 and 1969. The lowest rates of interest have been recorded during periods of substantial unemployment and stable or declining prices preceded by slow or negative monetary expansion, such as during the 1930s and to a lesser extent in the postwar recessions of 1958, 1961, and 1971.

Financing the Deficit: Mixed Fiscal and Monetary Policies

All government expenditures are financed through revenues raised either by taxation or by the sale of Treasury bonds. This equality is explicit in the government budget constraint previously developed:

$$G = T + \Delta B.$$

The impact of an exogenous change in government spending or tax revenue on aggregate income, ceteris paribus, depends not only on the size of the initial deficit (or surplus), but also on how the accompanying bonds are financed (or retired). Given the size of a proposed deficit, the financing decision is divided between the Treasury and the Federal Reserve. The Treasury determines the maturities and initial market yields of the new bonds to be sold. These decisions encompass debt management. The Federal Reserve determines the initial impact the bonds will have on market rates of interest by changing the money supply.

Ceteris paribus, sales of new bonds exert upward pressures on interest rates. This is represented in the earlier diagrams by an upward shift in the demand for money schedule in Figure 15-4 (*a*). The Federal Reserve can offset these pressures by providing additional reserves and shifting the supply of money schedule outward. The greater the provision of reserves, the smaller will be any increase in interest rates in consequence of the sale of new bonds. Changes in the money stock designed to offset changes in the stock of Treasury bonds affect aggregate levels of income through the rate of interest. This impact is in addition to the direct impact of the fiscal action on income. To the extent that changes in the stock of money accompany changes in government spending and taxing, the resulting change in income is attributed to both fiscal and monetary policies. The net impact on aggregate income of both policies can be summarized by:

$$\Delta Y = K\Delta(G - T) + K'\Delta M. \quad (15\text{-}13)$$

This equation permits the effects of the two policies to be distinguished. The multiplier, K, is defined as an empirical relationship. Thus, it incorporates the effects of higher interest in consequence of the sale of new bonds and is smaller than the multipliers derived earlier from only the reciprocal of the marginal propensity to save. Similarly, K' represents an empirically determined income-money multiplier.

Let us define a "pure" fiscal action as *a change in government spending and/or taxing without an accompanying change in money supply.* If we consider only a deficit produced by an increase in government spending without a change in tax revenues, the pure fiscal effect on income would be:

$$\Delta Y = K\Delta G.$$

Four alternative deficit-financing strategies can be distinguished. Assume an increase in government spending, ΔG, financed by the sale of an equivalent amount of bonds, ΔB.

Case 1. Pure Fiscal Policy. All the bonds are effectively purchased by the private sector ($\Delta R = 0$). Income increases by:

$$\Delta Y_1 = K\Delta G.$$

Interest rates rise initially as the new bonds are marketed, and thereafter rise slightly further as income and prices increase.

Case 2. Mixed Fiscal–Monetary Policy A. Concurrent with the sale of the bonds, the Federal Reserve increases total reserves by an amount equal to the dollar amount of the bonds ($\Delta R = \Delta B$). In effect, the Federal Reserve purchases the bonds directly or indirectly. The resulting increase in money supply will be a multiple of the increase in bonds:

$$\Delta M_2 = k\Delta R_2 = k\Delta B.$$

Income increases by:

$$\Delta Y_2 = K\Delta G + K'\Delta M_2.$$

Interest rates will decline initially as the increase in money supply is greater than the increase in bonds. Through time, the combined effects of the budget deficit and lower interest rates will increase income and prices, and interest rates will rise. As the stimulative pressures are great, the rate of price increases is likely to accelerate and interest rates would rise above their initial levels.

Case 3. Mixed Fiscal–Monetary Policy B. Concurrent with the sale of bonds, the Federal Reserve increases reserves by an amount that would increase the money stock by exactly the amount of the new bonds ($\Delta R < \Delta B$):

$$\Delta M_3 = k\Delta R_3 = \Delta B.$$

Income would increase:

$$\Delta Y_3 = K\Delta G + K'\Delta M_3.$$

Interest rates would initially remain unchanged as money increases to absorb all the bonds. Subsequently, as the stimulative effects of the deficit increase income and prices, interest rates rise.

Case 4. Mixed Fiscal–Monetary Policy C. Concurrent with the sale of bonds, the Federal Reserve increases reserves by an amount smaller than would be necessary for an increase in the money stock to absorb all the additional bonds ($\Delta R << \Delta B$):

$$\Delta M_4 = k\Delta R_4 < \Delta B.$$

Income increases by:

$$\Delta Y_4 = K\Delta G + K'\Delta M_4.$$

Interest rates would rise initially as the increase in bonds is greater than the increase in money stock. Thereafter, there is continued upward rate pressures through income from the fiscal action.

Summary. The comparative impact of the four financing strategies can be summarized as follows:

ΔG is the same for all four strategies,
$\Delta R_2 > \Delta R_3 > \Delta R_4 > \Delta R_1 = 0.$

As a result:

$\Delta M_2 > \Delta M_3 > \Delta M_4 > \Delta M_1 = 0$, and
$\Delta Y_2 > \Delta Y_3 > \Delta Y_4 > \Delta Y_1.$

The increases in interest rates need to be examined at two points in time, initially and ultimately:

Initially: $\Delta i_1 > \Delta i_4 > \Delta i_3 > \Delta i_2.$

Final: $\Delta i_2 > \Delta i_3 > \Delta i_4 > \Delta i_1.$

These examples demonstrate that the way a fiscal deficit is financed has important implications for income and interest rates. For a given deficit, a pure fiscal action generates the smallest increase in income and, although initially the greatest rise in interest rates, through time the smallest ultimate increase in interest rates. The greater the monetization of the debt is, the greater the increase in income, prices, and interest rates, although initial changes in interest rates are small and may even be negative.

References

Ackley, Gardner, *Macroeconomic Theory* (New York: Macmillan, 1961).

Friedman, Milton, and Walter W. Heller, *Monetary vs. Fiscal Policy* (New York: Norton, 1969).

Kaufman, George G., and Robert D. Laurent, "Simulating Policy Strategies Under Two Alternative Monetary Policy Regimes," *Quarterly Review of Economics and Business*, 10 (4), Winter, 1970, 51-64.

Samuelson, Paul A., "Money, Interest Rates and Economic Activity: Their Interrelationship in a Market Economy," in *Money, Interest Rates, and Economic Activity* (New York: American Bankers Association, 1967). Reprinted in William E. Gibson and George G. Kaufman, *Monetary Economics: Readings on Current Issues* (New York: McGraw-Hill, 1971).

Siegel, Barry N., *Aggregate Economics and Public Policy* (Homewood, Ill.: Irwin, 1970).

Yohe, William P., and Roger W. Spencer, "The Crowding Out of Private Expenditures by Fiscal Actions," *Review* (Federal Reserve Bank of St. Louis), 52 (10), October, 1970, 12-24.

Channels of Monetary Policy 16

The previous four chapters have developed and analyzed a simple theoretical model of the economy emphasizing the transmission of economic policy, particularly monetary policy. The potency of monetary policy on various sectors of the economy as well as on aggregate income and prices was seen to depend both on the magnitude of the particular action and on the interest, income, and wealth elasticities of the different sectors. The value of such an analysis would be greatly enhanced if we could quantify the implications of policy actions and predict actual outcomes.

Recent advances in the application of statistical and mathematical techniques to economics, referred to as *econometrics,* and in the development of the computer to quickly and accurately manipulate large quantities of data have expedited the construction, testing, and simulation of large and complex empirical models of the United States economy. These models permit us to trace the path of monetary policy through the economy more thoroughly and to generate empirical evidence with regard to the theoretical statements developed to date. For example, does money affect aggregate income and, if so, through interest rates, wealth, or some other variables; do interest rates decline in response to expansionary monetary actions; what are the values of the important elasticities in the transmission process; and so on.

As noted, models are theories quantified. Two of the more important models recently constructed incorporate opposing theories of the operation of the economy. The very large FRB-MIT model, to which we have already referred, reflects primarily neo-Keynesian thought. A smaller model developed by the research staff at the Federal Reserve Bank of St. Louis reflects the monetarist or neo-quantity theory view. The size of a model is a function of a number of factors such as objectives and costs, but also reflects differences in theoretical approach. Neo-Keynesians, as we have seen, view aggregate income as an aggregation of income in various individual sectors. Thus, their models incorporate at least the more important sectors. Monetarists, on the other hand, view aggregate spending as determined directly by monetary policy and other exogenous factors, and the distribution of income—both between prices and output and among industrial sectors—as determined by the price system. Thus, these models need not incorporate individual sectors in order to generate predictions about aggregate income.

In large measure, the size of a model is a function of the objective of the model builders. If one is interested only in explaining, say, aggregate income or residential construction, then there would be little reason to incorporate equations explaining variables only remotely related to these. If, however, one is interested in interrelating major sectors of the economy, then one would include as many equations as there are sectors proposed to be explained.

While empirical models can attach numbers to outcomes, this property by itself does not make models useful, although quantification per se is not infrequently substituted for authoritativeness. For the model to be useful, the numbers generated must approximate those observed in the world being explained, often, but incorrectly, referred to as the "real" world. The "real" world is frequently only the observer's personal impression of the real "real" world. To date, most empirical models have had, at best, only moderate success in generating accurate outcomes. Nevertheless, the outcomes of the two models discussed compare favorably with the outcomes generated by less quantitative forecasting techniques. With these words of caution, it appears that, at minimum, the direction and relative magnitudes, if not the absolute magnitudes, of the solutions will provide us with meaningful and fairly reliable insights into the operation of the economy. The solutions, however, reflect only the information that is built into the model.

The FRB-MIT Model

This section describes a series of monetary policy experiments conducted on an early version of the FRB-MIT model. The model incorporated almost 200 variables in some 110 equations. For the model to generate unique solutions for each and every variable, the number of unknown or endogenous variables must equal the number of equations. Thus, this model contains 110 endogenous variables. The values of the remaining exogenous variables are predetermined outside the model. The 110 equations collapse the economy into ten major spending, pricing, and employment sectors.

After theoretical construction, an empirical model is fitted to the data to obtain values for the coefficients and constant terms. Thereafter, solution values for the endogenous variables may be generated from the values of the exogenous variables introduced into the model. The parameters of the FRB-MIT model were estimated one equation at a time by linear regression techniques from quarterly observations made from 1950 through the mid-1960s. Generating solution values for the endogenous variables is somewhat more complex. Many of the endogenous variables appear in more than one equation. For the solution values of these variables to satisfy each equation in which they are specified, all equations in the model must be solved simultaneously. The model is dynamic and can generate a continuous stream of solution values through time concomitant with the simultaneous introduction of current values of the exogenous variables.

As discussed earlier, models attempt to reproduce the conditions found in the observed world. Experiments may thus be conducted at lower costs than under actual conditions. Experiments that attempt to identify the consequences of changes in the environment are called *simulations.* In the model, simulations of economic policy actions are conducted by changing the values of one or more of the policy variables and recording the resulting changes in the values of the endogenous variables. This involves a two-step procedure. In the first step, a temporal stream of solution values is generated for one set of values of the exogenous variables, frequently the actually observed values. This solution is called *the control solution.* In the second step, the values of one or more exogenous variables over the same period are changed, or "shocked," and another stream of solution values is generated for the endogenous variables. The differences between the two solution values for a particular endogenous variable at a particular point in time are attributed to the effect of the introduced shock.

This is demonstrated graphically in Figure 16-1. The solid line in (*a*) traces the observed values of exogenous variable X, say, reserve requirements, in time period t_0 through t_n. The solid line in (*b*) traces the corresponding solution values for endogenous variable Y, say, consumption expenditures. In the next step, the values of X are changed at time t_1. A step increase of z units is introduced and maintained for the remainder of the observation period. The broken line in (*a*) plots the new values of X at z units above the original values. The new solution values of Y, in consequence of the changed values of X, are traced by the broken line in (*b*). The differences between the broken and solid lines represent the change in Y attributed to the change in X and are the policy implications discussed in the following sections. In the simulation illustrated in Figure 16-1, the increase of z in reserve requirements (X) results in a decrease in consumption expenditures (Y) below the levels when reserve requirements were not shocked.

In the experiments to be described, monetary policy actions are restricted to open market operations and are introduced in the model as maintained step changes in unborrowed or total reserves, depending upon the particular experi-

Figure 16-1 **Measurement of the Implications of a Policy Shock in Simulation Experiments**

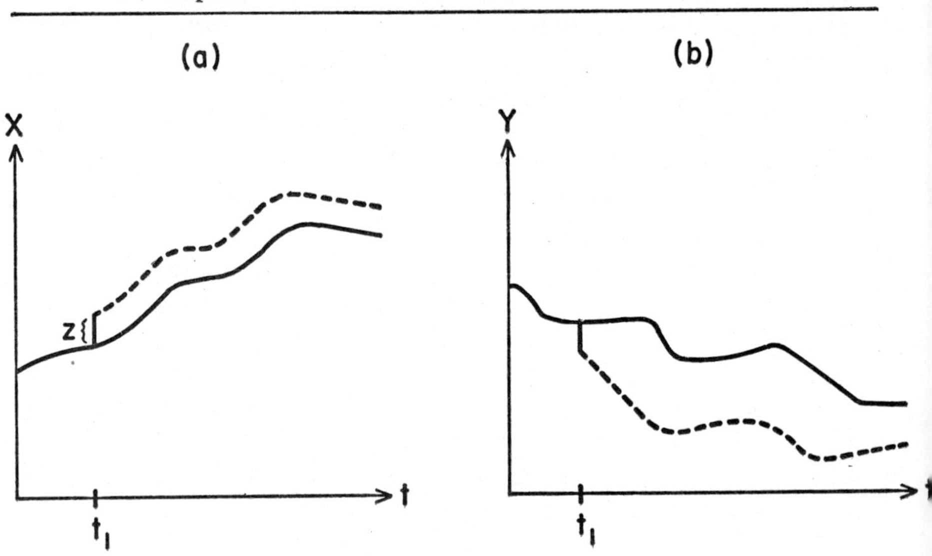

ment. The impact of monetary policy is transmitted to the real sector through three channels: cost of capital, wealth, and credit rationing. The first two channels have already been discussed. Credit rationing refers to the rationing or distribution of credit among borrowers by lenders by means other than nominal prices or interest rates alone.

Credit Rationing

Credit rationing occurs because financial institutions find it profitable to maintain ongoing and continuous relations with their customers and are reluctant to introduce abrupt, explicit changes in their prices, particularly upward, for fear of losing their customers. The greater short-run sensitivity of most spending units to changes in price rather than to changes in quantity has long been recognized by economists, and was assigned a strategic role by Keynes in his analysis. As a result, in periods of curtailment of reserves or heavy credit demands financial institutions prefer to allocate their available supply of credit, to an extent, by cutting back on individual loan requests through, say, increasing down payments or scaling back the amount of the requests, rather than by raising their explicit loan rates by the full amount of the increase necessary to bring demand into equality with supply. Some loan requests previously granted at the prevailing interest rate are denied altogether. While this procedure lessens increases in the explicit loan rate, the cutback in loan extensions increases the implicit cost of obtaining a loan of a given amount. Through time as the conditions of excess loan

Figure 16-2 **Flow Chart: First-Round Effects of Monetary Policy**

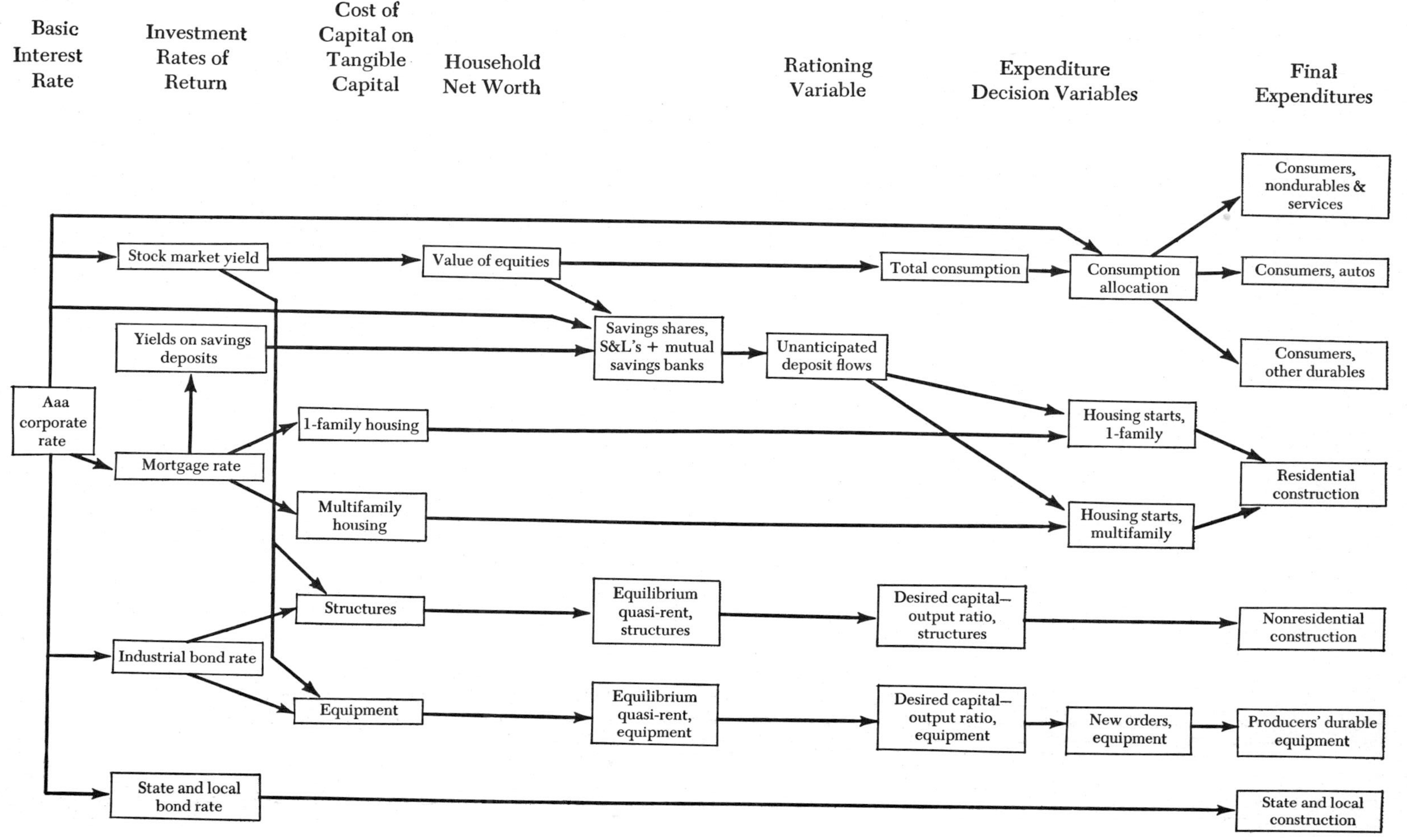

Source: deLeeuw and Gramlich, "Channels of Monetary Policy," p. 484.

demand continue, nominal loan rates are increased to levels at which they again equate supply and demand.

The reverse conditions hold when reserves are expanded sharply or loan demand declines sharply. Financial institutions will first liberalize lending terms, such as down payments, creditworthiness, and length of customer relationship, before lowering explicit loan rates.

The existence of credit rationing reduces the impact of monetary policy on nominal loan rates and consequently the strength of policy transmitted through this channel. Credit rationing does not affect interest rates on broadly traded securities for which personal relationships are not of primary concern. Nor does it reduce the potency of overall policy. Rather, the transmission of the impact is partially rechanneled. For example, thrift institutions may respond initially to curtailed deposit inflows by tightening mortgage loan terms rather than raising mortgage rates. The tighter terms increase the effective cost of mortgage funds and lead to a reduction in mortgage demand and residential construction. In time, if the pressures continue, it is likely that the thrift institution will raise explicit mortgage rates more sharply. The FRB-MIT model considers credit rationing to exist primarily at nonbank financial institutions in their lending for residential construction.

These institutions are assumed to increasingly tighten their nonprice loan terms the more their deposit inflows in a quarter drop below the average inflow for the previous three years, and to increasingly liberalize their nonprice terms the more current inflows climb above this average. Credit rationing supplements mortgage rates in the equations for single and multifamily housing starts.

The major channels through which monetary policy is transmitted in the FRB-MIT model are delineated schematically in Figure 16-2. The diagram shows only the initial effects from policy to the economy; feedback effects from the real sector to the financial sector and secondary effects of the policy action are not included. The corporate bond rate captures the immediate impact of monetary policy.

First-Round Policy Effects

The initial effects of an expansionary monetary policy and the proportion of the effect transmitted through each of the three channels are observed by simulating a step increase of $1 billion in unborrowed reserves. The reserve increase is introduced in the first quarter of 1964 and maintained for 16 quarters. The implications of this change for major sectors are summarized in Table 16-1. (This table, as well as Tables 16-2 and 16-3, shows the difference in values between the shocked and control solutions for the relevant variables.) Like the schematic diagram, the simulations in this experiment do not provide for feedback or secondary effects. Only the initial round of implications is considered. Both the table and figure show that all three channels do not affect all sectors. Personal consumption expenditures

Table 16-1 **Direct Effects of a Billion-Dollar Step Increase in Unborrowed Reserves**[a]
Initial conditions of 1964, Q1

a. Billions of current dollars

Quarter	Personal consumption expenditures			Residential construction expenditures			Plant and equipment	State and local construction	Total			
	Cost of capital	Wealth	Total	Cost of capital	Credit rationing	Total	Cost of capital	Cost of capital	Cost of capital	Wealth	Credit rationing	Total
4	.3	1.2	1.5	1.0	.6	1.6	.2	.2	1.7	1.2	.6	3.5
8	.4	2.3	2.7	1.3	.5	1.8	.6	.3	2.6	2.3	.5	5.4
12	.5	3.0	3.5	1.5	.3	1.8	1.1	.4	3.5	3.0	.3	6.8
16	.4	3.2	3.6	2.2	−.8	1.4	1.5	.5	4.6	3.2	−.8	7.0

b. Percentages of total effect

Quarter	Personal consumption	Residential construction	Plant and equipment	State and local	Channel		
					Cost of capital	Wealth	Credit rationing
4	43	45	6	6	49	34	17
8	50	33	11	6	48	43	9
12	51	26	16	7	51	44	5
16	51	20	21	8	66	45	−11

[a] Numbers are differences between the shocked and control solution values.

Note.—The results shown describe only the effect of unborrowed reserves in financial markets and, through financial markets, on final demand for goods and services. They do not include multiplier-accelerator interactions or feedbacks from goods markets to financial markets.

Source: *Federal Reserve Bulletin*, 55 (6), June, 1969, p. 487.

are affected by both the cost of capital and wealth but not by credit rationing, residential construction by cost of capital and credit rationing but not wealth, and other investment by only the cost of capital. Total spending is, of course, affected by all three sectors. The effects of the increase in reserves build up over time.

Wealth effects are seen to dominate the increase in consumption expenditures, accounting for between 80 and 90 percent of the total initial impact. The cost of capital is the major transmitter of monetary policy to residential construction in all periods, but its importance increases through time. In the early quarters after the reserve increase, thrift institutions increase their mortgage lending both by reducing rates and by liberalizing nonprice credit terms. The liberalization of terms is slowly reduced and, after a while, reversed as mortgage rates are lowered explicitly. This evidence supports the view that nonprice credit rationing applies only in the shorter run as lenders attempt to avoid introducing abrupt changes in nominal rates.

As a proportion of total spending, residential construction responds most quickly and plant and equipment most slowly. This may be attributed to the credit rationing effect on the former and suggests that credit rationing, rather than offsetting monetary policy intent, as is sometimes argued, accelerates its impact. One-half of the total first-round effects on total spending is generated by increased consumption. The cost of capital is the most important transmission channel, but wealth is almost as important.

Complete Policy Effects

The model also delineates the total effects of monetary policy actions including feedback and other secondary effects. As before, unborrowed bank reserves are increased by $1 billion starting in the first quarter of 1964. The resulting changes in nominal income, real income, prices, and interest rates from their control solution values are summarized in Table 16-2. The changes in income and prices are affected by the economic characteristics of the initial quarter in which the shock is introduced. The model incorporates a Phillips curve relation between unemployment and prices, in which the relative changes in each depend on the nearness of the economy to full employment in the initial quarter. The first quarter of 1964 was a period of considerable unemployment, about 5½ percent, and only slow price increases. As a result, the outcomes of this experiment are not perfectly transferable to other initial quarters for which the economic conditions differ.

Like the first-round effects, the total effects build up slowly. The peak in real income does not occur until ten quarters after the increase in reserves; 50 percent of the maximum income increase occurs after four quarters, and 75 percent after

Table 16-2 **Effects of a Billion-Dollar Step Increase in Unborrowed Reserves, Full Model Effects**[*]

Initial conditions of 1964, Q1 (in percentage points unless otherwise indicated)

Quarter	Real GNP (billions of 1958 dollars)	GNP deflator	Money GNP (billions of current dollars)	Corporate Aaa bond rate	Unemployment rate
1	.7		.8	−.27	
2	2.0		2.3	−.14	−.1
3	3.6	.1	4.3	−.12	−.2
4	5.4	.1	6.6	−.16	−.3
5	7.0	.2	8.9	−.19	−.4
6	8.3	.3	11.1	−.22	−.5
7	9.3	.4	13.2	−.22	−.6
8	10.0	.6	15.1	−.24	−.6
9	10.5	.8	16.9	−.25	−.7
10	10.7	.9	18.6	−.26	−.7
11	10.3	1.2	19.9	−.24	−.7
12	9.4	1.4	20.6	−.25	−.6
13	7.9	1.7	20.6	−.25	−.6
14	6.1	1.9	20.1	−.23	−.5
15	3.9	2.1	19.0	−.23	−.3
16	1.4	2.2	17.2	−.23	−.2

[*] Numbers are differences between the shocked and control solution values.

Source: *Ibid.*, p. 488.

six. After ten quarters, the increase in real income falls off and income approaches and eventually stabilizes at the level it would have attained in the absence of the policy shock. Prices also rise, but continue to remain above their control values. This supports the hypothesis that monetary policy is effective in changing real sector forces only in the short run as long as some spending units operate under money illusion. In the longer run, as money illusion wears off, monetary policy affects only prices. Changes in real income are determined by real factors such as population, resource endowment, education, and technology.

Long-term interest rates decline immediately upon the increase in reserves. Short-term rates, like long-term rates, decline immediately and, except for a brief period contemporaneous with the peaking in real income, remain below their control levels. This pattern is surprising in light of the theoretical analysis presented in earlier chapters, which predicts an eventual rise in rates and, in part, may be attributed to the absence of a price-expectations effect on interest rates in the version of the model described here.

Fiscal Policy

The implications of both fiscal policy and alternative financing of the government debt resulting from the fiscal policy actions are simulated on the model through two fiscal actions, one at a time. Again starting in the first quarter of 1964, government expenditures are increased by $5 billion without an accompanying change in tax rates, and the average personal income tax rate is reduced by two percentage points without a change in government spending. The latter action reduces tax revenues in that quarter by about $4.5 billion. The implications generated include the full feedback effects of higher income on both interest rates and tax revenues. When the initial deficit for each shock is financed totally by the private sector and there is no increase in the total reserves provided by the Federal Reserve in excess of any increases that appear in the control solution, real income increases to a maximum of almost $10 billion above its control solution in consequence of the increase in government spending. This is a "pure" fiscal policy shock. The increase in income is twice the dollar magnitude of the initial increase in government spending. Likewise, the $4.5 billion reduction in taxes generates a maximum increase in real income of more than $6 billion (Table 16-3). As discussed in Chapter 14, fiscal policy multipliers are obtained by dividing the dollar change in income by the dollar magnitude of the fiscal policy action. Thus the fiscal multiplier for the increase in government spending is about 2 and for the reduction in income taxes about 1.4. The greater relative increase in income in consequence of the spending change is consistent with the balanced budget multiplier effect.

Not only does income increase more in response to the increase in government spending than in response to the tax cut, but it increases markedly faster. The maximum increase in real income effectively occurs within one year and 75 percent of the maximum increase occurs after only one quarter. In contrast, the smaller maximum increase in income following the tax cut is not completed until the seventh quarter and is only 75 percent complete after two quarters.

The increases in income are enlarged when part of the initial deficit generated by each shock is financed by increases in reserves. These effects are obtained in the model by permitting the commercial banks to increase their reserve base through borrowing from the Federal Reserve Banks as interest rates rise in consequence of the initial sale of bonds by the Treasury. The increase is not completely offset by the Federal Reserve. This represents a "mixed" fiscal-monetary policy shock. In all, banks increase their reserves by less than 2 percent in response to the rise in interest rates. Nevertheless, the peak real income multiplier

Table 16-3 **Effects of $5 Billion Step Increase in Government Spending and of $4½ Billion Step Decrease in Personal Income Taxes***
Initial conditions of 1964, Q1

	Real GNP (billion dollars)			
	Spending Increase		Tax Cut	
Quarter	Pure Fiscal Policy	Mixed Fiscal Policy	Pure Fiscal Policy	Mixed Fiscal Policy
1	6.9	7.0	1.7	1.7
2	8.8	9.0	3.6	3.7
3	9.3	9.9	4.8	5.1
4	9.7	10.7	5.5	6.0
5	9.8	11.4	6.0	6.8
6	9.2	11.3	6.2	7.3
7	7.8	10.5	6.3	7.8
8	7.7	10.9	6.3	8.2
9	6.9	10.5	6.3	8.5
10	5.8	9.6	6.3	8.8
11	4.9	8.8	6.3	8.9
12	4.9	8.8	6.2	8.8

* Numbers are differences between the shocked and control solution values.

Source: Kaufman and Laurent, "Simulating Policy Strategies Under Two Alternative Monetary Policy Regimes," p. 54.

for the spending increase rises from 2.0 to 2.3 and for the tax cut from 1.4 to 2.0. These results are again consistent with our earlier theorizing about the impact of monetary actions in support of fiscal policy. Because the time lags by which monetary policy affects income are somewhat longer than for fiscal policy, the income effects in consequence of the mixed fiscal-monetary action, while larger, build up more slowly than for the pure fiscal action.

A Monetarist Model

Econometric models tend to differ greatly in size and form, even if they adhere to the same economic theories. The differences are even greater if they reflect opposing theories. While the FRB-MIT model traced monetary actions through individual sectors to aggregate income, the monetarist model has monetary policy affect aggregate income directly. The monetarist model described here was constructed by the Federal Reserve Bank of St. Louis and is considerably smaller than the FRB-MIT model, containing only eight equations. Therefore, it can solve for only eight unknowns and two of these only serve as inputs for other equations. Further reflecting its simplicity, the model has only three exogenous variables, two representing economic policy and one the potential full employment growth rate of the economy.

Unlike the FRB-MIT model, the St. Louis model is not solved simultaneously.

Figure 16-3 **Flow Chart of Monetarist Model**

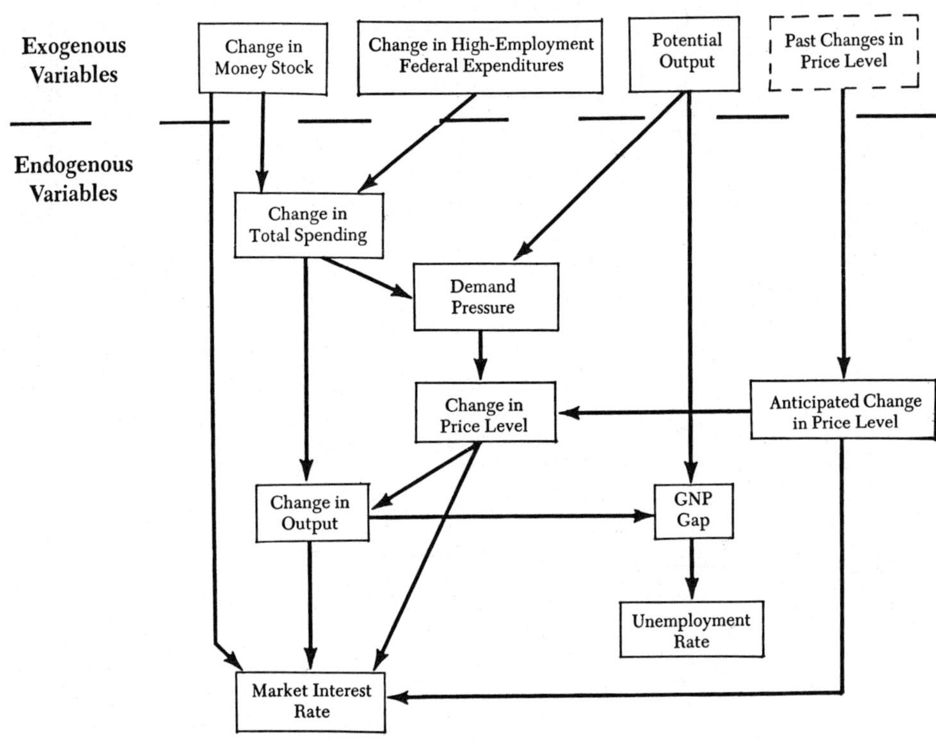

Source: Andersen and Carlson, "A Monetarist Model for Economic Stabilization," p. 10.

Each endogenous variable for any particular period appears in only one equation and is related to exogenous variables and to endogenous variables for earlier periods whose values are already known. Such a system of equations represents a recursive model in which one equation is solved at a time and the solutions, in turn, are used in solving other equations for variables in a later time period. The operation of the model is traced in Figure 16-3 and shown in algebraic form in Table 16-4.

The fundamental equation in the model relates dollar changes in nominal income to dollar changes in current and past monetary policy changes (*MP*) and to dollar changes in current and past fiscal policy changes (*FP*):

$$\Delta Y = f(\Delta MP_t \ldots \Delta MP_{t-n}, \Delta FP_t \ldots \Delta FP_{t-n}). \qquad (16\text{-}1)$$

The best empirical estimates of equation 16-1 are obtained when the conventional money supply is used to represent monetary policy and fiscal policy is represented by government expenditures and revenues standardized for differences in income

Table 16-4 Monetarist Model in Algebraic Form

(1) Total Spending Equation
$\Delta Y_t = f_1(\Delta M_t \ldots \Delta M_{t-n}, \Delta E_t \ldots \Delta E_{t-n})$

(2) Price Equation
$\Delta P_t = f_2(D_t \ldots D_{t-n}, \Delta PA_t)$

(3) Demand Pressure Identity
$D_t = \Delta Y_t - (XF_t - X_{t-1})$

(4) Total Spending Identity
$\Delta Y_t = \Delta P_t + \Delta X_t$

(5) Interest Rate Equation
$R_t = f_3(\Delta M_t, \Delta X_t \ldots \Delta X_{t-n}, \Delta P_t, \Delta PA_t)$

(6) Anticipated Price Equation
$\Delta PA_t = f_4(\Delta P_{t-1} \ldots \Delta P_{t-n})$

(7) Unemployment Rate Equation
$U_t = f_5(G_t, G_{t-1})$

(8) GNP Gap Identity
$G_t = \frac{XF_t - X_t}{XF_t}$

Endogenous Variables

ΔY_t = change in total spending (nominal GNP)
ΔP_t = change in price level (GNP price deflator)
D_t = demand pressure
ΔX_t = change in output (real GNP)
R_t = market interest rate
ΔPA_t = anticipated change in price level
U_t = unemployment rate
G_t = GNP gap

Exogenous Variables*

ΔM_t = change in money stock
ΔE_t = change in high-employment Federal expenditures
XF_t = potential (full-employment) output

* Other than lagged variables.
Source: Andersen and Carlson, "A Monetarist Model for Economic Stabilization," p. 9.

levels relative to full employment income. The results of the equation are surprising. The equation suggests that the major and lasting changes in nominal income are generated only by changes in money supply. Changes in government spending have weak and quickly reversed effects on income, while changes in tax revenues have no statistical effects on aggregate income. Because the monetary and fiscal actions involve different magnitudes and have occurred with different frequencies,

Figure 16-4 **Effects of Equally Likely Unit Policy Changes on Aggregate Income in Monetarist Model**

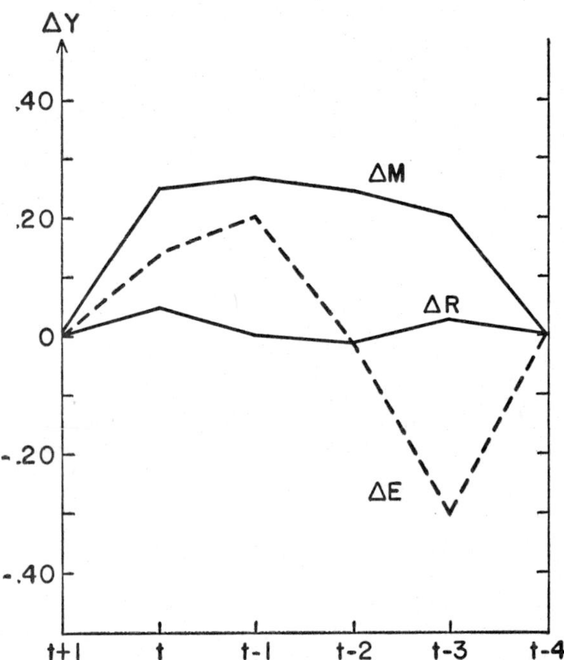

Source: Andersen and Jordan, "Monetary and Fiscal Actions: A Test of Their Relative Importance in Economic Stabilization," p. 21.

evaluation of their relative importance on income requires that they first be transformed to a common scale. This is accomplished by stating the change in each policy in terms of its standard deviation, a statistic whose probability of occurring is known. The results are plotted on Figure 16-4. The horizontal axis shows the time periods in which the policy actions are undertaken. Period t represents the current period. Progressively earlier periods are measured to the right and identified as $t - n$. This scale may also be viewed as showing the progressively later impacts of a policy action undertaken in period t. Periods $t + 1$ and $t - 4$ are the initial and final equilibrium positions. The vertical axis measures the change in aggregate income (Y) generated by an equally likely unit change in money stock (M), government spending (E), and tax revenues (R) in the current (t) and three earlier quarters ($t - 1, t - 2, t - 3$). The effect of money is seen to be quick, strong, and lasting. Increases in government expenditures increase income in the same and the following quarters, but then reduce income in the next two quarters, and have no lasting effect. Because of the continuous insignificant effect of changes

Figure 16-5 **Ex Post Predictions of Monetarist Model**
(Annual rates of change)

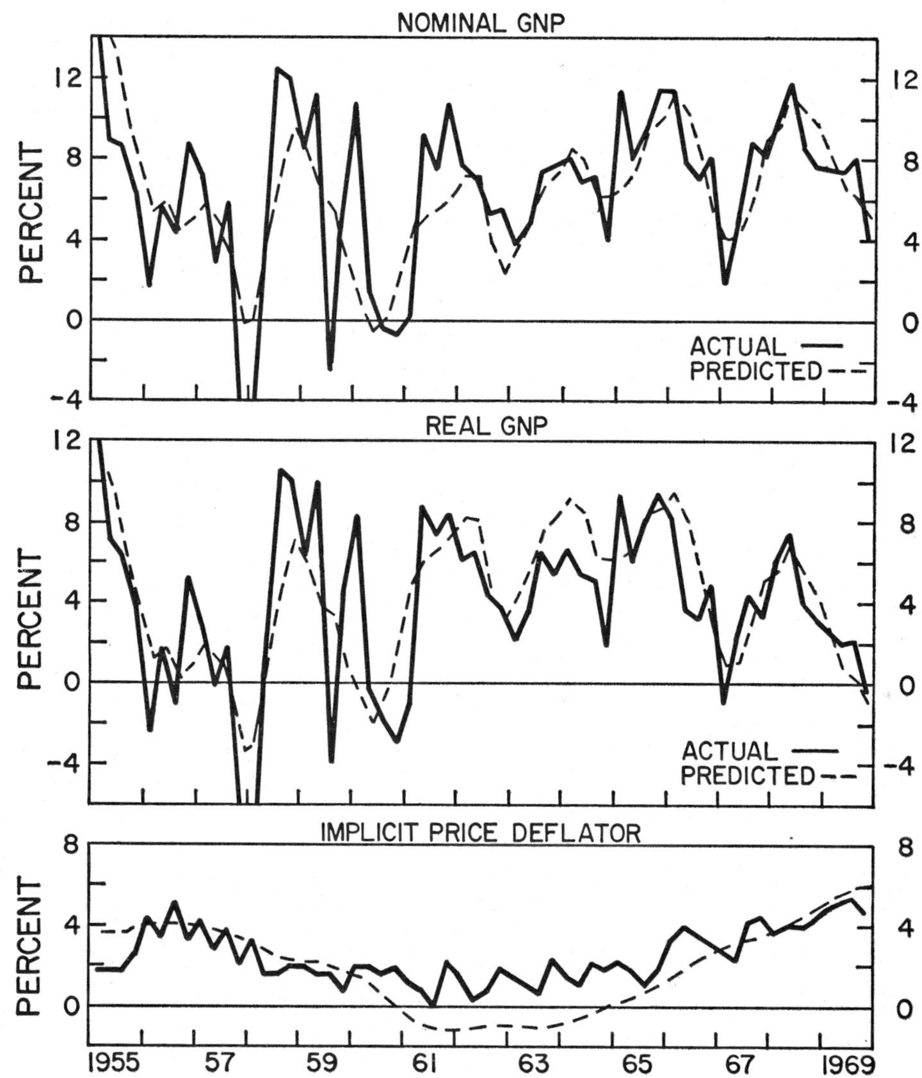

Source: Andersen and Carlson, "A Monetarist Model for Economic Stabilization," p. 17.

in tax revenues on aggregate income, equation 16-1 is generally shown with government expenditures as the only fiscal variable (see Figure 16-3 and Table 16-4).

If this equation is reliable, fiscal policy has no lasting effect on income independent of any accompanying changes in monetary policy. That is, the sale of bonds to finance government expenditures reduces private spending by almost the same amount as an equal increase in tax revenues. In addition, the equation denies the balanced budget multiplier. These results contrast sharply with those generated by the FRB-MIT model, which shows both monetary and fiscal policies to have strong independent effects on income; and with traditional Keynesian analysis, which, because it believes the demand for money to be both unstable and highly interest-elastic and the investment and consumption schedules to be highly interest-inelastic, emphasizes fiscal policy over monetary policy.

Because the St. Louis model is of limited size, we can quickly trace through the remaining equations. After determining the change in nominal income, the model distinguishes between the changes in real income and in prices (Figure 16-3 and Table 16-4). Price changes are derived jointly from the difference between the change in current nominal income and the gap between actual and full employment real income, and from price expectations. Thus, similar to the FRB-MIT model, price changes are generated by a Phillips curve construct, but reinforced in this model by past price experiences. After adjusting for price changes, the residual change in nominal income is assumed to represent the change in real income. This differs significantly from the FRB-MIT model in which monetary effects act on real variables directly. Unemployment is related to the gap between actual and full employment real income. Interest rates, the last endogenous variable in the model, are explained by money balances, real output, and price expectations.

All these equations but the first are consistent with the theory developed earlier in this book. The nominal income equation, however, is the heart of the monetarist model. In this model, the major effects of monetary policy are on the price component of nominal income. As fiscal policy has only insignificant effects, the real sectors of the economy are affected primarily by nonpolicy forces that affect the productive capacity of the economy. These, as noted earlier, would include technology, population, resource endowment, and education.

The model can generate solution values for income, output, unemployment, prices, and interest rates on the basis of values for only money supply, government expenditures, and potential full employment growth. Actual and predicted quarterly changes in nominal income, real income, and prices are plotted in Figure 16-5 for the period 1955 through 1969. Because the "predictions" are for periods in the past when actual observations of the exogenous variables were available, the errors measure only the imperfections incorporated in the model.

The model is also relatively simple to use to predict future values. For such purposes, the model, as all models, may err not only because of model imperfections, but because the values of the imposed exogenous variables are unknown, must be predicted, and may be predicted incorrectly. The need to predict values of some inputs is common to all forecasting techniques and models. Because the

Figure 16-6 **Ex Ante Predictions of Monetarist Model for Alternative Rates of Monetary Expansion***

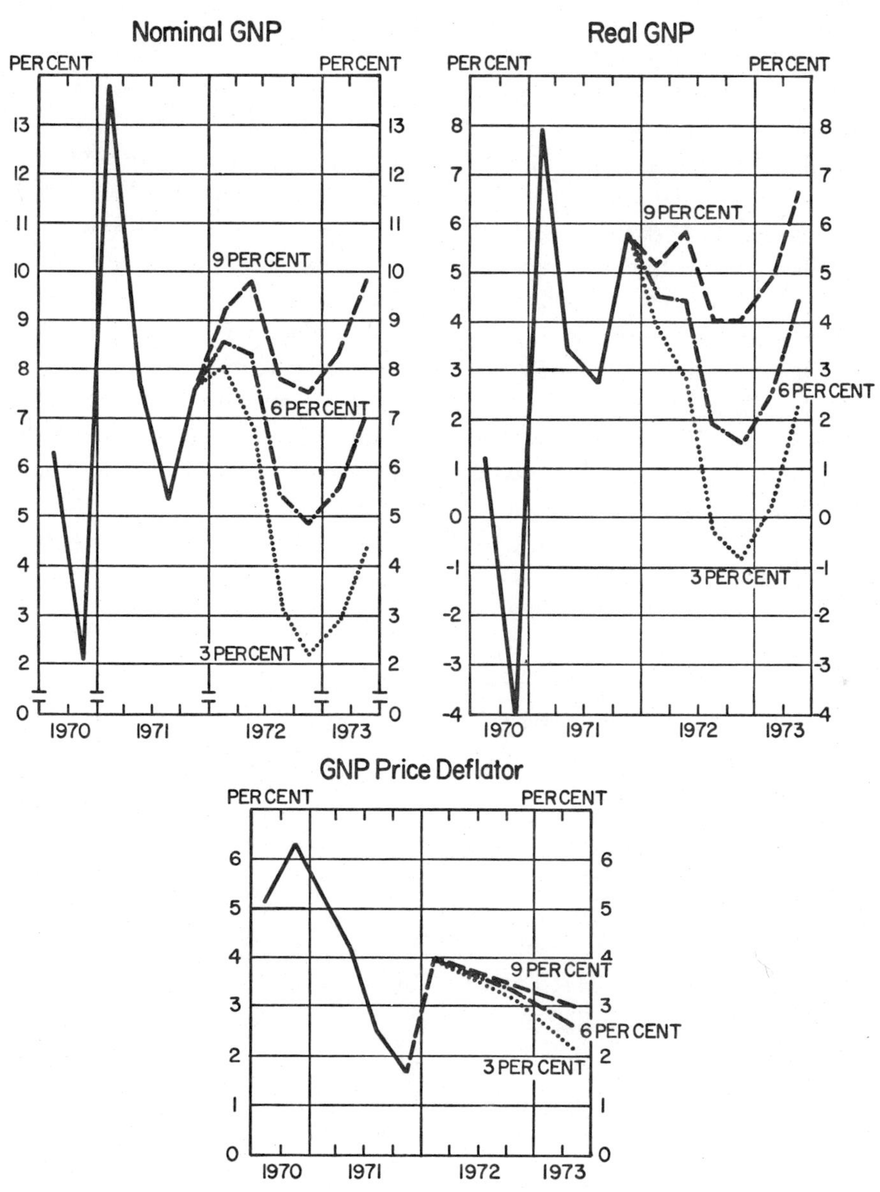

*Annual rates of change in the money stock. IV/1971 rates of change are based on actual data. Projected rates of change start in I/1972.

Source: *Quarterly Economic Trends* (Federal Reserve Bank of St. Louis), February 29, 1972, p. 7.

St. Louis model uses only three exogenous variables, this problem is less severe for this model than for most models.

In addition to forecasts on the basis of predicted values for the exogenous variables, the model can generate the implications of alternative assumptions about the future course of monetary policy as reflected in changes in the money supply. A set of alternative projections of nominal income for alternative rates of growth of money of 3, 6, and 9 percent, annual rate, from the first quarter of 1972 through the middle of 1973 is shown in Figure 16-6. These projections were computed early in 1972 on the basis of the best estimates of government spending and full employment growth for the period. Not surprisingly, the faster the assumed growth in money, the more rapid the growth in nominal and real income and the less rapid the slowing in the rate of increase in prices.

The relationship between monetary growth and the three predicted variables is neither constant nor simple. By the end of 1972, a 9 percent expansion in money supply generates increases in nominal income less than three times as rapid as a 3 percent rate of money growth, increases in real income about three times as rapid as the slower monetary growth, and price increases less than twice as rapid. These results reflect the more complex relationships between money and economic activity specified by the monetarists in comparison to the simpler views of their quantity theory predecessors.

References

Andersen, Leonall C., and Keith M. Carlson, "A Monetarist Model for Economic Stabilization," *Review* (Federal Reserve Bank of St. Louis), 52 (4), April, 1970, 7-25.

Andersen, Leonall C., and Jerry L. Jordan, "Monetary and Fiscal Actions: A Test of Their Relative Importance in Economic Stabilization," *Review* (Federal Reserve Bank of St. Louis), 50 (11), November, 1968, 11-24. Reprinted in William E. Gibson and George G. Kaufman, *Monetary Economics: Readings on Current Issues* (New York: McGraw-Hill, 1971).

Carlson, Keith M., "Projecting with the St. Louis Model: A Progress Report," *Review* (Federal Reserve Bank of St. Louis), 54 (2), February, 1972, 20-27.

deLeeuw, Frank, and Edward M. Gramlich, "The Channels of Monetary Policy," *Federal Reserve Bulletin*, 55 (6), June, 1969, 472-491. Reprinted in William E. Gibson and George G. Kaufman, *Monetary Economics: Readings on Current Issues* (New York: McGraw-Hill, 1971).

Friedman, Benjamin M., *Credit Rationing: A Review* (Washington, D.C.: Board of Governors of the Federal Reserve System, 1972).

Kaufman, George G., and Robert D. Laurent, "Simulating Policy Strategies Under Two Alternative Monetary Policy Regimes," *Quarterly Review of Economics and Business*, 10 (4), Winter, 1970, 51-64.

Klein, Lawrence R., "Empirical Evidence on Fiscal and Monetary Models," in *Issues in Fiscal and Monetary Policy*, James J. Diamond, ed. (Chicago: De Paul University, 1971).

PART VI

The International Economy

International Trade

17

We have concentrated so far on the determinants of domestic business activity and the effects of alternative economic policies under the assumption that the economy is closed and that all trading occurs among domestic residents. While such an assumption is a reasonable first approximation for the United States and permits us to analyze its primary economic structure more readily, it is useful neither for a more careful analysis of the United States economy nor for even a preliminary analysis of most other economies in which international trade accounts for a substantially greater proportion of economic activity. For example, while the value of exports is only equivalent to 5 percent of GNP in the United States, it is equal to 25 percent of GNP in the United Kingdom, and almost 50 percent in the Netherlands. Nevertheless, in some sectors of the U.S. economy, exports and imports account for a sizable proportion of total activity. In 1968, exports represented 30 percent or more of the total domestic output of leaf tobacco, oil-field machinery, construction equipment, and cotton farm products. Imports represented a like share of the total new supply of fish, bicycles and motorcycles, pulp-mill products, and distilled liquors. In addition, the entire supply of a number of agricultural products such as coffee, tea, cocoa, and bananas is imported. Although international trade does not loom very large in the U.S. economy, U.S. trade does account for a sizable portion of world trade. U.S. merchandise exports to other countries represent almost 15 percent of total world

Table 17-1 **World Exports by Origin and Destination, 1970**

Exports From \ To	United States	Canada	Latin America	EEC	EFTA	Other Free World Europe	Soviet Bloc Europe
United States	–	20.7 8,810 70.6	13.3 5,650 37.4	19.6 8,330 9.8	10.1 4,300 9.6	3.8 1,640 11.4	0.8 350 1.2
Canada	65.3 10,920 28.1	–	3.3 560 3.7	7.1 1,190 1.4	10.7 1,790 4.0	1.0 163 1.1	0.8 135 0.5
Latin America	30.1 4,440 11.4	3.4 500 4.0	11.5 1,700 11.2	21.2 3,130 3.7	8.8 1,300 2.9	3.8 560 3.9	4.7 690 2.4
EEC	7.5 6,630 17.0	0.8 730 5.8	3.2 2,810 18.6	48.9 43,300 50.9	16.8 14,840 33.1	5.6 4,920 34.3	3.4 3,050 10.7
EFTA	9.1 3,730 9.6	2.3 960 7.7	3.4 1,400 9.3	26.4 10,770 12.7	24.6 10,050 22.4	8.5 3,490 24.3	4.2 1,720 6.0
Other Free World Europe	9.0 785 2.0	0.9 79 0.6	4.6 403 2.7	29.9 2,620 3.1	29.3 2,560 5.7	3.1 268 1.9	13.7 1,195 4.2
Soviet Bloc Europe	0.7 220 0.6	0.2 65 0.5	3.1 960 6.4	7.1 2,186 2.6	7.2 2,190 4.9	4.9 1,490 10.4	60.4 18,480 65.1
Africa & S. Africa	5.9 880 2.3	0.8 123 1.0	0.7 106 0.7	42.5 6,285 7.4	19.8 2,930 6.5	3.7 546 3.8	5.1 753 2.6
Japan	31.2 6,020 15.5	2.9 560 4.5	5.1 990 6.5	6.7 1,300 1.5	5.5 1,060 2.4	2.9 563 3.9	2.3 445 1.6

exports and the U.S. is the largest single importer for most major countries (Table 17-1).

Nations trade for the same reasons individuals, households, cities, and regions trade—to obtain goods and services comparatively more cheaply than if they were produced internally. Like individuals, nations cannot profitably be self-sufficient. A wag once defined international trade as interpersonal or interregional trade made difficult. International trading is more complex because the trading partners frequently have:

1. different languages,

Africa & S. Africa	Japan	Asian Mid-East	Other Asia	CPE Communist Asia	Oceania	Rest of World	Total[1] World
3.7 1,560 10.0	10.8 4,610 29.4	3.1 1,330 18.1	9.4 4,000 21.3	—	2.6 1,120 21.4	2.1 900 19.8	42,590 13.7
1.3 220 1.4	4.7 790 5.0	0.4 61 0.8	2.0 340 1.8	0.9 145 5.1	1.5 245 4.7	0.9 155 3.4	16,710 5.4
0.8 114 0.7	6.9 1,020 6.5	0.4 58 0.8	1.0 155 0.8	0.7 105 3.7	0.1 15 0.3	6.6 970 21.4	14,750 4.7
6.0 5,310 34.2	1.1 990 6.3	2.1 1,830 24.9	2.2 1,910 10.1	0.4 360 12.8	0.7 640 12.2	0.9 780 17.2	88,500 28.4
7.3 2,970 19.1	1.6 650 4.1	3.3 1,360 18.5	3.8 1,550 8.2	0.4 175 6.2	3.3 1,340 25.6	1.3 550 12.1	40,820 13.1
3.8 334 2.1	0.8 70 0.4	2.0 173 2.3	1.3 115 0.6	0.2 19 0.7	0.6 54 1.0	0.5 45 1.0	8,750 2.8
3.1 954 6.1	1.5 465 3.0	2.4 730 9.9	1.8 550 2.9	3.2 990 35.1	0.1 25 0.5	0.0 2 0.0	30,590 9.8
8.5 1,265 8.1	5.9 875 5.6	1.0 146 2.0	2.0 293 1.6	0.6 88 3.1	0.4 53 1.0	0.7 98 2.2	14,790 4.7
7.2 1,400 9.0	—	2.8 540 7.3	25.2 4,870 25.9	3.1 600 21.3	3.8 740 14.1	1.1 215 4.7	19,320 6.2

(Table continued)

2. different customs,
3. different legal systems,
4. different currencies, and
5. different national economic policies that restrict the free flow of goods, services, labor, and capital among trading partners.

These difficulties serve to increase the cost of conducting trade among nations relative to that of conducting trade within nations.

A transcript of all transactions between one trading partner and all other trading partners is referred to as *the balance of payments*. The balance of payments is

Table 17-1 (Continued)

Exports From \ To	United States	Canada	Latin America	EEC	EFTA	Other Free World Europe	Soviet Bloc Europe
Asian Mid-East	3.6 355 0.9	0.8 81 0.6	1.6 165 1.1	28.8 2,870 3.4	14.4 1,440 3.2	4.3 426 3.0	1.6 160 0.6
Other Asia	23.7 3,370 8.7	1.7 245 2.0	0.9 135 0.9	9.4 1,340 1.6	8.3 1,180 2.6	1.3 186 1.3	5.5 780 2.7
CPE Communist Asia	0.0 1 0.0	0.8 19 0.1	3.6 85 0.6	10.2 245 0.3	5.9 140 0.3	0.5 13 0.1	20.9 500 1.8
Oceania	13.5 790 2.0	3.0 175 1.4	0.7 44 0.3	9.9 580 0.7	17.3 1,010 2.2	1.6 94 0.6	2.3 135 0.5
Rest of World	44.4 1,150 2.9	5.6 145 1.2	4.2 110 0.7	9.8 255 0.3	15.8 410 0.9	0.8 22 0.1	0.0 1 0.0
Total[1] World	12.5 38,910	4.0 12,480	4.8 15,109	27.3 85,030	14.4 44,930	4.6 14,350	9.1 28,390

Note: Center figures are F.O.B. values in millions of U.S. dollars. Figure in upper left corner is percent of row total; figure in lower right corner is percent of column total.

[1]May not equal the sum of the corresponding row and column figures because of approximation error and statistical discrepancy.

Source: Thomas M. Humphrey, "The World Trade Matrix," *Monthly Review* (Federal Reserve Bank of Richmond), 58 (6), June, 1972, p. 9.

a double-entry bookkeeping account of the type and value of all such transactions during a specified period of time, say, one year. Every transaction involves a receipt and a payment, or, in accounting terms, a credit and a debit. Increases in assets and decreases in liabilities are debits, and decreases in assets and increases in liabilities are credits. When one trading partner sells or exports a good to another partner, the value of the good is recorded as a credit (a reduction in an asset) and the resulting receipt as a debit (an increase in an asset or a reduction in a liability). When a trading partner buys or imports a good, the value of the good is debited (an increase in an asset) and the payment credited (a reduction in an asset or an increase in a liability). Transactions that involve purely financial dealings, such as borrowing, lending, and investing, are treated similarly except that the financial instrument is considered the offsetting item to the transfer of funds. A loan to a foreigner is evidenced by the import of an IOU and is recorded in the balance of payments similar to the import of merchandise. Credit entries are frequently referred to as receipts because they accent the receipt of payment

Africa & S. Africa	Japan	Asian Mid-East	Other Asia	CPE Communist Asia	Oceania	Rest of World	Total[1] World
6.4 635 4.1	20.8 2,080 13.3	6.2 620 8.4	6.7 670 3.6	0.2 24 0.8	1.9 195 3.7	0.4 43 0.9	9,980 3.2
3.2 450 2.9	16.7 2,370 15.1	2.3 325 4.4	21.7 3,080 16.4	1.3 185 6.6	2.7 385 7.3	0.8 110 2.4	14,190 4.6
6.3 150 1.0	12.5 300 1.9	3.8 90 1.2	33.5 800 4.2	—	1.7 40 0.8	0.2 6 0.1	2,390 0.8
2.7 159 1.0	23.4 1,370 8.7	1.4 82 1.1	13.2 770 4.1	2.4 140 5.0	5.6 330 6.3	2.4 140 3.1	5,850 1.9
1.2 31 0.2	4.6 120 0.8	0.1 2 0.0	1.5 39 0.2	—	2.9 74 1.4	7.3 190 4.2	2,590 0.8
5.0 15,530	5.0 15,670	2.4 7,360	6.0 18,810	0.9 2,820	1.7 5,240	1.4 4,540	311,260

accompanying a reduction in assets. Likewise, debit entries are referred to as payments because they accent the payment involved in financing an increase in assets.

Because every transaction is entered on both sides of the ledger, the balance of payments is technically always in balance. Total debits (payments) always equal total credits (receipts) for all trading partners. Nevertheless, all partners may not be equally well off. One may be in debt to another and under pressure to repay in the near future. Likewise, one may have financed some, if not all, of his purchases by "involuntarily" selling some of his assets. To differentiate the longer-run implications of the transactions on the financial strength of the trading partners, the entries are divided into those describing transactions motivated by their own sake for the gains from trade, and those describing transactions motivated by the need to finance other transactions. The latter transactions reduce the future international trading options open to the trading partner and reveal an underlying weakness in his trading position. The first type of entry (transactions motivated by gains from trade) is frequently referred to as an *above-the-line entry* and the second type (transactions to finance other transactions) as a *below-the-line entry*.

While the algebraic sum of all entries in the balance of payments must balance, the entries above and below the line need not. It is only necessary that the net total or balance (debits minus credits or payments minus receipts) above the line be equal in magnitude and opposite in sign to the balance below the line. The state of the balance of payments is described by the state of the items above the line. If receipts exceed payments in this part, the balance of payments is said to be in surplus; if receipts fall short of payments, the balance of payments is in deficit. The items below the line indicate the financing of the balance above the line. If the algebraic sum of the items above the line shows a surplus, the items below the line identify the means by which the surplus is financed, e.g., by the net import of claims on the trading partners and on oneself—which had been exported in earlier deficit periods—and of international reserve assets, such as the currencies of leading trading countries and gold. If there is a net deficit above the line, the items below the line identify the means by which the deficit is financed, e.g., by net exports of claims on oneself or on trading partners—which had been imported in earlier surplus periods—and of international reserve assets. Where the line is drawn is an unresolved question. The positioning of the line varies with the ability to determine the motivation of the transactions, the economic characteristics of the trading partner, and the time horizon over which its trading strength is to be analyzed.

As international trade is basically interpersonal trade made difficult, the operation of international trade can best be introduced by first describing interpersonal trade.

Interpersonal Trade

Individuals buy goods and services which they desire and which they prefer not to produce themselves. They will finance the purchases of these goods or imports by selling or exporting goods and services which they produce. Thus, individuals export in order to finance imports. Most individuals generate the greater part of their revenues by selling their labor services for wages and salaries. In addition, individuals may, on the one hand, invest or buy equities, lend, or provide aid (gifts) and, on the other hand, sell new equities, borrow, or receive aid (gifts). Aid transactions involve the transfer of funds for a thank-you note. If, after these transactions, an individual's receipts are insufficient to finance his desired purchases, he will need to sell liquid assets from his wealth portfolio. If his receipts exceed his desired purchases, he will add liquid claims on future imports to his wealth portfolio. The latter transactions represent below-the-line entries. This description of interpersonal trade provides a more complete framework in which to analyze the behavior of deficit and surplus spending units than was developed in Chapter 4.

A schematic balance of payments statement for an individual summarizing his

Table 17-2 Schematic Balance of Payments, Individual A

Receipts	Payments
1. Wages and salary	1. Goods and services
2. Interest, dividends, and rent	2. Interest, dividends, and rent
3. Sale of equity	3. Purchase of equity (investment)
4. Aid (gifts)	4. Aid (gifts)
5. Borrowing	5. Lending
a. Long term	a. Long term
b. Short term	b. Short term
6. Sale of liquid assets (dissavings)	6. Purchase of liquid assets (savings)

transactions with all other individuals is shown in Table 17-2. In the long run, purchases must be financed from earnings. For briefer periods, purchases may be financed from short-term borrowing, sale of liquid assets, and gifts. It is thus possible to distinguish between transactions undertaken for their own sake and those undertaken primarily to obtain financing. If one assumes that all short-term borrowing and sale of liquid assets represent temporary financing, then the line between normal and financing transactions can be drawn below item 5a. That is, an individual's balance of payments is in surplus if his receipts from the sale of his labor; interest, dividends, and rent; sale of equity; long-term borrowing; and aid exceed his expenditures for these same items. The surplus is financed by short-term lending and purchases of liquid assets, including money balances, which represent claims on the future output of his trading partners. Likewise, a deficit in transactions above the line is financed by receipts from short-term borrowing and/or the sale of liquid assets below the line. A balance of payments surplus is experienced by SSUs and a deficit by DSUs.

An individual's balance of payments need not be in equilibrium each and every year nor with each and every trading partner. Deficits in some years may be financed by the proceeds of surpluses experienced in past years—savings—or by the expected proceeds from future surpluses through short-term borrowing. Savings are thus a buffer against planned or unexpected balance of payments deficits. Through his lifetime, an individual may expect to switch a number of times from experiencing balance of payments surpluses to balance of payment deficits.

It is unlikely that an individual can continue to experience either a surplus or a deficit for a prolonged period of time. Because the end product of economic strategy is consumption, unless he receives psychological pleasure from the act of saving itself, an individual experiencing balance of payment surpluses will eventually either increase his purchases or decrease his sale of services. On the other side, a deficit spending unit will eventually exhaust his savings and other marketable assets and be forced to finance his purchases by creating additional IOUs. However, as the amount of IOUs issued increases, creditors will become increasingly concerned over the ability of the DSU to redeem the obligations and may hesitate to accept additional amounts. At such a time, if not before, the deficit unit is forced to make an adjustment. He may curtail his expenditures, increase his sale of labor services, or both. These alternatives all result in a reduction in his standard of living, reflecting the fact that he has been living beyond his means during the period the deficit existed.

To increase the sale of his labor services it may be necessary for the individual to work longer hours, possibly at a reduction in his asking price. This will increase his total receipts as long as the demand schedule for his services is sufficiently elastic so that the revenues gained from working additional hours more than offset any revenues lost from a lower hourly wage. If he voluntarily reduces his asking price, he is devaluing the cost of his services, making them more attractive to potential buyers.

Because the adjustment to eliminate a deficit in the balance of payments entails a reduced standard of living and is painful, deficit units are tempted to postpone the adjustment as long as possible. If the deficit is eliminated as a result of other forces, such as an increase in the demand for his services or a decrease in his demand for goods and services, the adjustment cost is avoided. However, if the deficit is not reversed, the longer the postponement, the greater are the eventual size and cost of the adjustment. During the period when the adjustment is postponed, the deficit unit will be both accruing interest liabilities on his outstanding IOUs and issuing additional IOUs at increasing interest rates to compensate the creditor for the increased risk of default. These payments increase the deficit and, thereby, also the size of the subsequent adjustment. In addition, the longer an individual operates at a particular standard of living, the more psychologically painful it is for him to accept a lower standard of living and the more reluctant he is to do so.

The *adjustment* problem should be distinguished from the *liquidity* problem, which may be defined as the problem of insufficient savings or reserves, in the language of the balance of payments. As noted, reserves permit an individual to finance deficits. The larger the reserves, the larger or longer deficits can be maintained. Reserves are the product of past surpluses. Thus, it is unlikely that chronic deficit units will possess reserves. In addition, it is likely that, in the absence of necessary adjustments to increase earnings or reduce expenditures, grants of reserves to such units will quickly be dissipated to finance the deficit. Reserves are not an alternative to adjustment; they only permit a postponement of the adjustment. A simultaneous increase in reserves to all trading partners or a one-time redistribution of reserves from surplus to deficit units will, by themselves, not permanently eliminate deficits.

International Trade

The description of interpersonal trade applies equally well to international trade before the introduction of the complicating factors cited earlier. Perhaps the most important of these factors, at least from the point of finance, is the use of different currencies. In the case of interpersonal finance, it was implicitly assumed that all payments and receipts were conducted in a common currency. In international trade, this is no longer the case. Almost every country has its own currency and, even in countries which use the same name for their currencies, they may not have the same value. Thus, the dollar is the domestic currency in both the United States and Canada, although not the same dollar, the pound in the United Kingdom and Israel, although not the same pound, the franc in France and Switzerland, although not the same franc, the peso in Spain, the mark in Germany, the guilder in the Netherlands, and so on. Each currency may have a different value in terms of domestic purchasing power and, thereby, also in terms of other currencies. The value of any one currency in terms of the others is determined by how much of one currency can be bought by one unit of the other currency.

The price of one unit of foreign currency in terms of the domestic currency is referred to as *the exchange rate.* At year-end 1971, the exchange rate for the British pound sterling (£) in terms of U.S. dollars ($) was about $2.60, and for the German mark about $.31. Inversely, the exchange rate for the U.S. dollar in terms of British pounds was about £.38 and in terms of German marks, DM 3.2. The names and foreign exchange rates of the currencies of major foreign countries at year-end 1971 are shown in Table 17-3. Trading partners have to convert costs and prices from their own currencies into those of their partners either explicitly or implicitly. Moreover, as is discussed in the next chapter, exchange rates among currencies may not be constant but may change through time, increasing further the complexity of using more than one currency.

Different legal systems and customs result in different payment and receipt patterns; different packaging, labeling, and disclosure; different weights and measures; etc. Different languages increase the costs of communication among trading partners. Different national policies result in different tax treatments, different costs of credit, and quantitative and qualitative restrictions on the free flow of goods, services, and capital among trading partners.

International Balance of Payments

A simplified schematic balance of payments for a country is shown in Table 17-4. Similar to an individual, a country's largest foreign expenditures are for the pur-

Table 17-3 Par Value of Selected Foreign Currencies, December 31, 1971

Country	Currency unit	Par values expressed in terms of units per U. S. dollar		Par values expressed in terms of U. S. cents per unit		Percent change of currency against U. S. dollar
		Old*	New	Old*	New	
Belgium	franc	50.0000	44.8159	2.0000	2.2313	11.5675
Canada	dollar	1.0811**	floating	92.5000**	floating	—
France	franc	5.5542	5.1157	18.0044	19.5476	8.5714
Italy	lira	625.0000	581.5000	0.1600	0.1719	7.4806
Japan	yen	360.0000	308.0000	0.2777	0.3246	16.8831
Netherlands	guilder	3.6200	3.2447	27.6243	30.8194	11.5665
Sweden	krona	5.1732	4.8129	19.3304	20.7774	7.4863
Switzerland	franc	4.0841	3.8400	22.8685	26.0416	6.3567
United Kingdom	pound sterling	0.4166	0.3837	240.0000	260.5727	8.5744
West Germany	mark	3.6600	3.2225	27.3224	31.0318	13.5764
Austria	schilling	24.7500	23.3000	3.8461	4.2918	6.2231
Denmark	krone	7.5000	6.9800	13.3333	14.3266	7.4498
Finland	markka	4.1999	4.1000	23.8097	24.3902	2.4383
Greece	drachma	30.0000	30.0000	3.3333	3.3333	0.0000
Norway	krone	7.1428	6.6454	14.0000	15.0480	7.4859
Portugal	escudo	28.7500	27.2500	3.4782	3.6697	5.5045
Spain	peseta	70.0000	64.4737	1.4285	1.5510	8.5714
Australia	dollar	0.8928	0.8396	112.0000	119.1000	6.3392
New Zealand	dollar	0.8928	0.8366	112.0000	119.5200	6.7143
India	rupee	7.5000	7.2700	13.3333	13.7551	3.1637
Iraq	dinar	0.3571	0.3264	280.0000	306.3725	8.5714
Israel	pound	3.5000	3.9900	28.5714	25.0626	−14.0000
Kuwait	dinar	0.3571	0.3264	280.0000	306.3725	8.5714
Malaysia	dollar	3.0612	2.8195	32.6667	35.4672	8.5724
Pakistan	rupee	4.7619	4.7619	21.0000	21.0000	0.0000
Saudi Arabia	riyal	4.5000	4.1143	22.2222	24.3054	8.5714
Singapore	dollar	3.0612	2.8195	32.6667	35.4672	8.5724
Ethiopia	dollar	2.5000	2.2857	40.0000	43.7502	8.5714
Ghana	new cedi	1.0204	1.8162	98.0000	55.0600	−84.0000
Malawi	pound	0.4166	0.3808	240.0000	262.6050	8.5714
South Africa	rand	0.7143	0.7652	140.0000	130.6847	− 6.6530
Uganda	schilling	7.1428	7.1428	14.0000	14.0000	0.0000
Czechoslovakia	crown	7.2000	6.5500	13.8888	15.2671	9.9236
Poland	zloty	24.0000	22.0800	4.1666	4.5289	8.6956
Soviet Union	rouble	0.9000	0.8290	111.1110	120.6272	8.5640
Yugoslavia	dinar	15.0000	17.0000	8.0000	5.8823	−11.7647
Mexico	peso	12.5000	12.5000	8.0000	8.0000	0.0000

*As of April 30, 1971.

**As of May 31, 1970.

Note: Latin American countries which are various multiple exchange rate systems and have no stated par value have employed various methods to devalue their currencies against the dollar. Brazilian devaluation, in a series of mini-devaluations since May [1971], amounts to 8.7 percent.

Chile devalued the escuda used for trade by about 25 percent. Colombia reduced the dollar value of its pesa by 4 percent, and Uruguay devalued its peso by imposing a surcharge of P 120 on certain trade transactions. The Dutch Antilles and Surinam revalued their currencies against the dollar by 5 percent. Venezuela revalued the bolivar by 2.3 percent.

Source: *International Letter* (Federal Reserve Bank of Chicago), No. 46, December 31, 1971, p. 2.

Table 17-4 **Schematic Balance of Payments, Country A**

Receipts	Payments
Exports	Imports
1. Merchandise	1. Merchandise
2. Services	2. Services
3. Private and government aid	3. Private and government aid
Capital	Capital
4. Investment	4. Investment
5. Government borrowing	5. Government lending
6. Private borrowing	6. Private lending
a. Long term	a. Long term
b. Short term	b. Short term
1. Nonliquid private	1. Nonliquid private
2. Liquid private	2. Liquid private
3. Official	3. Official
Sale of reserves	Purchase of reserves

chase of goods it cannot efficiently produce at home. Unlike an individual, it generates the funds to finance the imports from earnings from the sale of the output of its labor resources rather than the sale of the labor resources themselves. It exports those goods it can produce relatively most efficiently. Nations also invest in each other's economies, loan funds to each other, and provide financial assistance of various sorts.

Balances can be drawn at various points along the balance of payments accounts to analyze the trading strength of a country. Among the more frequently drawn balances are the following:

Balance of Trade (after item 1). This balance focuses on earnings from and expenditures on physical output. Many consider merchandise trade both the fundamental reason for trade and a reflection of the long-run earnings potential and trading strength of a country. Comparative advantages and disadvantages in physical production typically do not change abruptly.

Balance on Goods and Services (after item 2). This balance recognizes that in the normal course of business countries trade in more than merchandise and that services, such as transportation, tourism, and earnings on investments, also generate basic and lasting earnings and expenditure patterns. This balance serves as the net export component of GNP.

Balance on Current Account (after item 3). This measure identifies the balance on the trade of items generated by current production. It includes private and government aid, which may be considered a reward or payment for current activities not usually traded on the market place. These transactions are, on the whole, less permanent than trade in goods and services, but still not as volatile as capital flows, which, like domestic investment expenditures, are subject to large vagaries as profit potentials are continuously reevaluated.

Balance on Current and Long-Term Capital Account (after item 6a). International capital transactions occur in the normal course of business for a number of motivations. At minimum, long-term capital responds to international differences in profit potentials. While long-term capital movements may, on the average, not be as stable as trade in goods and services, they do reflect basic trends in the climate of investment and are indicative of the likelihood of continued flows. Thus, this balance isolates intermediate-term stability in the sources and uses of international exchange.

Net Liquidity Balance (after item 6b-1). This balance separates all transactions into liquid and nonliquid. Transactions involving financially nonliquid assets are recorded above the line. Liquid transactions are defined as changes in reserve assets and in all liquid short-term capital transactions and are recorded below the line. The balance reflects the unique role, although decreasingly so, of the United States as the banker for the world and its consequent need to protect its reserves. Thus, it includes liquid short-term capital transactions among private parties, which are motivated by interest rate and profit differentials, as well as official short-term capital transactions. While not financing transactions at the time, because of their volatile nature, private claims have the potential for being sold to foreign official agencies and thereby becoming a direct claim on reserves.

Official Settlements Balance (after item 6b-2). This measure attempts to delineate purely financing transactions. These are defined as changes in reserve assets and in short-term capital movements among governments. The latter transactions are considered the consequences of actions by these governments to maintain near-par levels of exchange rates by buying or selling foreign currencies. In contrast, private liquid short-term capital flows are assumed to be motivated by profit considerations.

Which of these balances is most meaningful depends on the objective of the analyst. If he wished to identify long-term tendencies in a country's balance of payments, he may prefer the balance on goods and services or on current account. If he wished to gauge the potential pressures on reserves from both purely financing transactions and the most volatile of other transactions, he may prefer the net liquidity balance; while if he wanted to identify purely financing transactions and immediate pressures on reserves requiring corrective adjustment, he may use the official settlements balance.

The International Sector and Economic Activity

When we constructed our simple model of the economy previously, we assumed away the existence of an international sector. This simplifying assumption is now removed. Although not included in total domestic spending, the production of export goods increases overall domestic production and employment and adds to GNP. On the other hand, imported foreign-produced goods and services are included in total domestic spending but do not increase domestic production or employment. Thus, they are excluded from GNP. GNP may be adjusted to include the contribution of the international sector by adding to the value of domestic spending on goods and services the value of the net surplus of the export of goods and services over the import. Hence:

$$Y = C + I + G + (X - M), \qquad (17\text{-}1)$$

where:

X = exports of goods and services
M = imports of goods and services.

The demand for both exports and imports can be specified in functional form. The quantity of goods and services exported is directly related to aggregate real income in the importing countries and to the exchange rate, and inversely related to the ratio of domestic prices to prices in the rest of the world. The greater the income abroad, the greater is the demand for all goods, including imports. Countries, like individuals, buy where the cost is lowest. The higher are foreign prices and the exchange values of foreign currencies, the cheaper are imports to residents of foreign countries and the greater are domestic exports to these countries.

$$x = f(\overset{+}{y}_{row}, \overset{-}{\frac{P}{P_{row}}}, \overset{+}{E}), \qquad (17\text{-}2)$$

where:

x = quantity of goods and services exported
y_{row} = real income in rest of world
E = foreign exchange rate (domestic price of foreign currency)
P = domestic prices
P_{row} = prices in rest of world.

Likewise, the quantity of imports is directly related to domestic real income and the ratio of domestic prices to prices in other countries and inversely related to the exchange rate. The higher are domestic income and prices and the lower is the cost of foreign currencies in terms of domestic currency, the greater is the domestic demand for imports:

$$m = f(\overset{+}{y}, \overset{+}{\frac{P}{P_{row}}}, \overset{-}{E}), \tag{17-3}$$

where:

m = quantity of goods and services imported.

Equations 17-1 through 17-3 indicate that no country is an economic island. Its international trade position affects domestic income and, thereby, prices, and these two variables, relative to their counterparts in other countries, in turn, affect the trade position. Thus, for example, the faster prices rise domestically relative to abroad, the smaller exports will be, the greater imports, and the smaller real overall domestic activity. Vice versa, the slower domestic prices increase in comparison to the rest of the world, the greater exports, the smaller imports, and the greater real domestic economic activity. It should be remembered, however, that while exports increase income and employment, in the absence of an approximately equal amount of imports, they do not provide the workers with the ultimate reward for their labors—consumption. As noted, in the long run, a country, like an individual, exports in order to import.

Countries trade in financial or capital claims as well as in goods and services. A net gain in foreign currencies obtained through these transactions provides a country with claims against the output of other countries, while a net drain of domestic currency through financial transactions provides other countries with claims on domestic production. Continuous and nonoffsetting imbalances in either current and capital accounts, or both, will eventually precipitate an adjustment. Because deficit trading partners are typically under more immediate pressure to undertake corrective adjustments, we will examine primarily the alternative adjustment strategies available to such countries. Generally, the adjustment possibilities open to surplus countries are the reverse of those available to deficit countries.

Balance of Payments Adjustment

Adjustments to restore equilibrium in the balance of payments can be made in the current account, the capital account, or both. Adjustments affecting capital transactions are examined in the next chapter. Adjustments affecting the trading of goods and services may be of six basic types:

1. general monetary and fiscal policies,
2. change in exchange rate,
3. tariffs,
4. quotas,

Figure 17-1 Impact of Restrictive Domestic Economic Policy

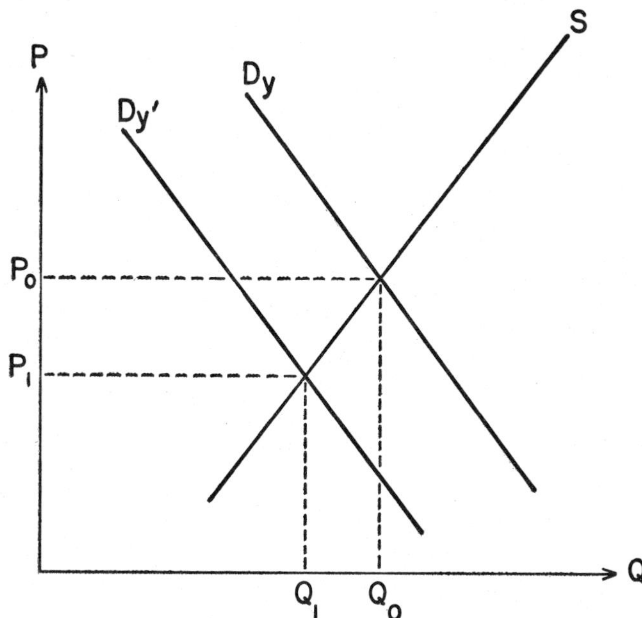

5. exchange controls, and
6. domestic price preferences, or "Buy American."

We shall examine each of these adjustment strategies, albeit only cursorily.

General Economic Policies

As exports and imports are functions of domestic income and prices, they are amenable to influence by general monetary and fiscal policies. A deficit in the current account may be reduced through restrictive economic policies curbing expansion in domestic purchasing power and slowing increases in domestic prices relative to those abroad. Both effects would stimulate exports while reducing imports. The effects of restrictive general economic policies on imports can be observed from Figure 17-1. Domestic prices of imports are measured along the vertical axis and quantities imported along the horizontal axis. For any level of domestic income, domestic demand for imports is assumed to be an inverse function of domestic import prices, and foreign supply a positive function of domestic prices. In equilibrium, Q_0 units of goods are imported at an average price, P_0. If restrictive monetary policies are imposed decreasing real income from y to y', import demand declines from Dy to Dy'. At this income level, only Q_1 units of goods are imported at average price P_1, lower then P_0.

A disadvantage of the use of general economic measures to correct a balance of payments imbalance is the possibility of conflict with domestic goals. If, for example, a country is experiencing a deficit on current account concomitant with domestic unemployment, it may be undesirable to direct monetary and fiscal policies toward increasing unemployment further in order to dampen imports. This would be particularly true for a country such as the United States in which international trade affects only a small proportion of total income and employment. As noted earlier, however, in most foreign countries, international trade is a considerably more important sector.

Change in Exchange Rate

Prices of goods sold in countries other than the ones in which they are produced are a product of both their domestic price and the exchange rate. The foreign price of U.S. goods is given by the following equation:

$$P_A = P_{US}\left(\frac{1}{E_{A,US}}\right), \tag{17-4}$$

where:

P_A = price of U.S. goods in country A
P_{US} = price of U.S. goods in U.S.
$E_{A,US}$ = exchange rate (price of A's currency in terms of U.S. dollars).

Assume that the currency in country A is the wheel and designated by the symbol #. The dollar exchange rate for wheels is $0.25, or each dollar is equivalent to four wheels. The price of a $10.00 U.S. good (*G*) in country A is:

$$P_{A_G} = \$10.00\left(\frac{1}{0.25}\right) = \$10.00\,(4) = \#40.00.$$

Likewise the U.S. price of goods imported from country A is given by:

$$P_{US} = P_A\,(E_{A,US}). \tag{17-5}$$

Hence, the U.S. price of good *H* which sells for #20.00 in A is:

$$P_{US_H} = \#20.00\,(0.25) = \$5.00.$$

It follows from these conversion equations that the lower the domestic cost of foreign currency is, the higher are the prices of domestic products in foreign markets and the cheaper are foreign products in domestic markets, and vice versa.

To the extent that the demand for products is price-elastic, a country may both stimulate the quantity of exports by reducing their foreign prices and curb the quantity of imports by increasing their domestic prices through reducing the exchange value of its currency and making foreign currency more expensive. For example, if the exchange rate of the wheel increased from $.25 to $.33 (the exchange rate of the U.S. dollar were depreciated from #4 to #3) the price of the $10.00 U.S. export in A would decline from #40.00 to #30.00, stimulating the quantity demanded, and the U.S. price of the #20.00 export from A would increase from $5.00 to $6.66, dampening the quantity demanded. Likewise, an appreciation in the exchange rate of a local currency making foreign currency cheaper would encourage imports and dampen exports.

Establishing and maintaining the desired values of exchange rates is not always possible for prolonged periods of time. Similar to all prices, exchange rates are a product of the forces of demand and supply and, unless these change concurrently and alike, any particular two-country exchange rate can be maintained only as long as one of the nations prefers to support an *overvalued* rate by running down its reserves or an *undervalued* rate by building up its reserves. A currency is overvalued when its exchange rate in terms of other currencies is higher than that which would clear the market where demand equaled supply. At an overvalued rate, trading units are willing to supply larger quantities of the overvalued currency than other units are willing to purchase and the excess supply must be absorbed by the government of the overvalued currency at this rate through sales from its holdings of the undervalued currency. Similarly, an undervalued exchange rate is a rate at which the demand for the undervalued currency exceeds supply. To prevent a runup in the rate, the government of the undervalued currency must accommodate the excess demand by buying the other currency and increasing its reserves. If one currency is overvalued in terms of another, the latter is undervalued in terms of the first.

Moreover, the other trading partner also has influence over the exchange rate. As changes in the exchange rate affect a country's economic welfare, it is unlikely to permit changes that would reduce its welfare. The relative strength of the influence of each country over the rate is approximately proportional to its international reserve position. Thus, unilateral changes in exchange rates to correct balance of payments imbalances must be part of a wider corrective package concurrently affecting domestic income and prices.

Tariff

A tariff is a tax levied on all or select merchandise imports. Like any tax, it is, in the first instance, either shifted forward, increasing the price of the product imported to the consumer, or shifted backward, reducing the profitability of imports to the importer. In either case, imports are reduced. The effect of the

Figure 17-2 **Impact of a Tariff**

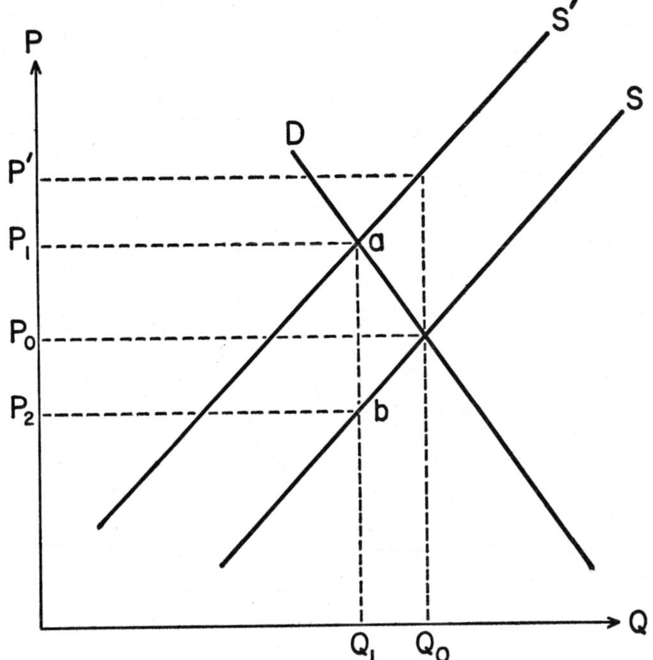

imposition of a tariff can be traced in Figure 17-2. The demand schedule for the imported good is assumed to slope downward. Before the tariff, quantity Q_0 of good A is imported at price P_0. A tariff equivalent to $P' - P_0$ per unit imported is imposed. Importers view this as an increase in their costs and shift the supply schedule upward by a like amount from S to S′. As a result, the quantity of product A imported declines to Q_1 and the equilibrium price rises to P_1. Note that the per unit price rise from P_0 to P_1 is less than the amount of the tariff because the quantity of good A demanded declines. Although the consumer pays P_1, the importer receives only P_2. The difference, equivalent to $P' - P_0$ per unit imported, is paid to the government. Thus, not only are imports reduced, but the government generates revenues equivalent to the rectangle P_1abP_2. Through time, consumers may substitute other goods for good A, shifting the demand schedule down and reducing the price.

The more price-inelastic the demand schedule for the import, the less effective is a given tariff in reducing imports. Ironically, the less effective a tariff is in reducing imports, the greater are the tax revenues it generates, and the more effective the tariff in reducing imports, the smaller are the tax revenues it generates.

Figure 17-3 **Impact of a Quota**

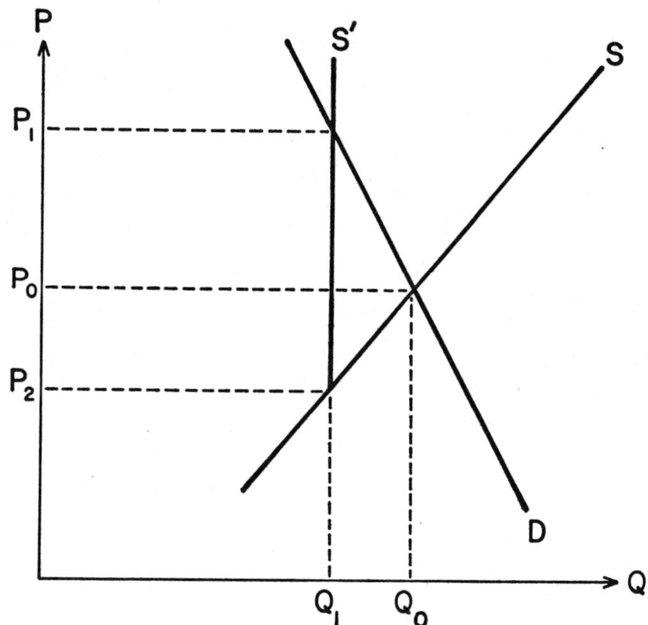

By increasing the domestic price of foreign products, at least initially, and reducing supply, tariffs tend to reduce overall domestic efficiency and welfare, particularly if the products on which tariffs are imposed compete with domestically produced goods. In addition, the price level increases. Lastly, exporting countries affected by the tariff will receive less foreign exchange and may introduce retaliatory tariffs, further reducing international trade and worldwide economic welfare. On the other hand, tariffs are frequently favored by firms producing goods in competition with imported goods and by new or "infant" firms who argue that a temporary shelter from foreign competition would permit them to expand to the point where they would be able to produce, at a minimum, as efficiently as the foreign producers. At such a time, the tariff would be removed. However, experience suggests that once imposed, for whatever reason, tariffs generate additional welfare for those protected and become difficult to remove. Infant industries rarely mature!

Quotas

Quotas impose specific limits on the value or quantity of particular imported goods. The impact of quotas is shown by Figure 17-3. Before the imposition of quotas, Q_0 units of good A were imported, selling at price P_0. A quota is imposed limiting the quantity of A imported to no more than Q_1 units. To the right of Q_1, the supply schedule is effectively shifted from S to the vertical line S′. At this quantity, the price to consumers rises to P_1. The supply price to importers declines to P_2. However, unlike the case of a tariff, the difference between the selling and buying prices ($P_1 - P_2$) does not accrue to the government but to the importers. This represents a windfall to them at the expense of the consumers.

Because of this profit, a large number of importers will request to import the affected goods. The government must allocate subquotas to each importer. The bidding for these subquotas is intense and, in the absence of an explicit price-bidding system, is marked by sub rosa payments, bribes, influence peddling, and favoritism. One need only observe the antics of importers and exporting countries at times when the U.S. sugar quotas are subject to congressional and presidential review to conclude that quotas encompass all that is inefficient and inequitable in a distribution system. The welfare of everyone, save the politicians and winning importers, is reduced, as is the level of world trade. Similar to tariffs, quotas are likely to lead to retaliatory actions by affected countries.

Exchange Controls

Exchange controls restrict the domestic purchase and sale of foreign currency and are imposed both to maintain exchange rates different from those the market may determine and to allocate foreign currency among users according to purpose rather than to price. Exchange controls can be used to affect current transactions, capital transactions, or both. Under exchange controls the domestic currency is not freely convertible into foreign currencies at the market rate. One or more exchange rates are established by the government according to the type of transaction. The imposed exchange rates may be either above or below the free market rate, but are most frequently below, that is, the domestic currency is overvalued and the foreign currency is undervalued. Recipients of foreign exchange are generally required to sell some or all of their exchange to the government at the specified price. Demanders of foreign currency must purchase the currency from the government at a price established according to the use to which the funds are to be put. If the controls maintain the price of the foreign currency at below its equilibrium rate, the demand for foreign currency will exceed supply, and the government needs to allocate the available supply among potential users. Such allocation generates problems similar to those applicable to quotas.

The implications of exchange controls are shown in Figure 17-4. The exchange rate, or the price of a unit of foreign currency in terms of the domestic currency, is measured on the vertical axis. The higher the exchange rate, the more expensive the foreign currency and the cheaper the domestic currency. The quantity of foreign exchange is measured on the horizontal axis. As for any import good, a domestic demand schedule and a foreign supply schedule exist for foreign cur

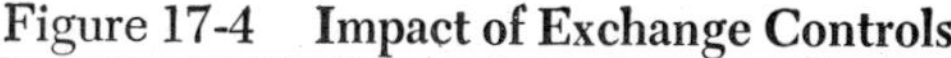

Figure 17-4 **Impact of Exchange Controls**

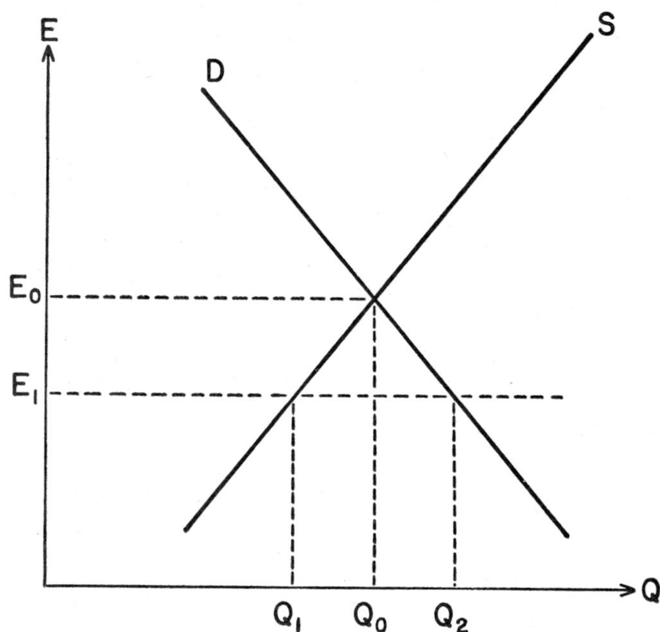

rency. Without exchange controls, the equilibrium exchange rate for wheels of country A is E_0 at which Q_0 units are traded. Assume that the domestic government wishes to maintain the exchange rate at E_1 and imposes controls to prevent a deterioration in this rate. At E_1, the domestic currency is overvalued with respect to wheels and the demand for wheels exceeds the supply, $Q_2 - Q_1$. Recipients of wheels may sell their wheels only to the government at below the equilibrium market price. This amount of wheels, Q_1, is then allocated in some fashion among the demanders. Imports are limited to the amount of wheels obtained or Q_1, which is less than Q_0.

The government may also establish a number of different or multiple exchange rates to encourage certain exports, imports, or capital transactions over other exports, imports, or capital transactions. Similar to the other types of non-market-induced reductions in imports, exchange controls are likely to reduce aggregate welfare and efficiency.

"Buy American"

"Buy American" measures restrict imports by requiring the consumer to purchase domestic goods rather than imported goods unless the price differential in favor of the imported good is greater than a specified amount, say, 50 percent. Thus

Figure 17-5 **Impact of "Buy American"**

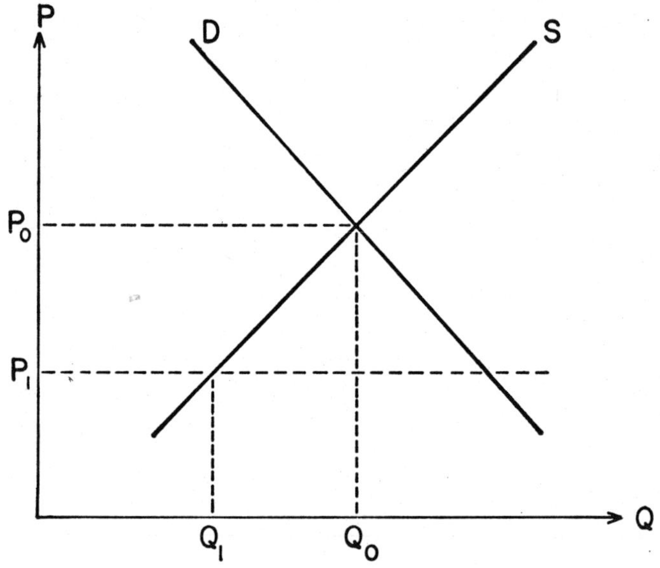

purchases are not made at lowest cost. Such requirements are commonly imposed by governments, both federal and local, on their own purchases and on the purchases of firms engaged in contract work for them, such as on military production. Assume that in the absence of "Buy American" restrictions, consumers would purchase Q_0 of foreign goods at domestic price P_0 (Figure 17-5). This price is equal to that on comparable domestic goods. Now impose a provision that foreign goods can only be purchased if their price is no more than 50 percent of the price of comparable goods produced domestically, or at most P_1. The volume of imports is thereby reduced from Q_0 to Q_1. Assuming no change in overall demand for these goods, the shortfall is shifted to the domestic market at the higher prices. Moreover, to the extent that the increased demand for domestic goods cannot be accommodated at the previous prices, the price of these goods will increase further. By promoting and protecting inefficiencies, general domestic economic welfare is again reduced to the benefit of the protected sector.

A recent study estimated that the "Buy American" practices of the U.S. Department of Defense during 1963 and 1964 were successful in reducing the United States balance of payments by $26 million in each year. However, this reduction was accompanied by an annual loss of $14 million in welfare costs to all countries affected, with the lion's share of this amount borne by U.S. residents.[1] As the reduction in the deficit may be expected to generate a gain in aggregate welfare

1. Fieleke, "The Buy-American Policy of the United States Government," pp. 2-18.

equal to only a small fraction of the reduction at best, the loss in welfare resulting from the "Buy American" restrictions may reasonably be expected to have greatly exceeded the gain. Some individual persons and/or groups, however, did benefit.

The United States Balance of Payments

An abbreviated balance of payments for the United States for the year 1970 is shown in Table 17-5. By most measures, the United States experienced a sizable deficit in its international transactions. (This does not imply, of course, that the U.S. had a deficit with each and every country; with some it experienced sizable surpluses.) Only in trade and services transactions did the U.S. generate overall receipts in excess of overall expenditures. In 1970, the U.S. exported $2 billion more merchandise than it imported.

In the remainder of the current account, a large surplus on income from investments abroad was almost offset by large military expenditures abroad and a sizable deficit in tourist expenditures. It is important to note that while capital investments abroad have a negative impact on the balance of payments at the time they are made, the subsequent return of earnings makes a positive contribution. The surplus on services added to the trade surplus generated a surplus on goods and services of some $3.5 billion, larger than any other balance on the accounts. However, large outflows resulting from remittances, pensions, and transfers, including Social Security payments to former residents living abroad, and from government grants almost wiped out this surplus and left only a negligible surplus on the overall current account.

The United States experienced large deficits on capital transactions. Domestic firms invested heavily in overseas operations for a variety of reasons, including to be nearer to foreign markets, to escape restrictive tariffs on products shipped from the U.S., and to realize lower production costs. Direct investments by U.S. firms in either overseas subsidiaries or foreign-owned firms were more than four times the dollar amount of foreign direct investment in the U.S. To some extent, such investment replaces exports. However, unlike exports, for which the favorable effect on the balance of payments is immediate, the favorable effect from investments is delayed until earnings are generated and repatriated to the U.S. In contrast, foreigners purchased a larger amount of U.S. portfolio securities (investments not accompanied by control) than Americans purchased foreign portfolio securities. The federal government extended a far larger amount of loans overseas than it was repaid. The overall deficit on the long-term capital account totaled nearly $3.5 billion, offsetting all of the previously cited surpluses.

As a direct outgrowth of its large and continuous deficits on long-term capital transactions, the United States has acquired a substantial surplus in long-term claims on foreigners. At year-end 1970, private long-term U.S. claims on foreign countries were more than double the dollar amount of private long-term foreign claims on the U.S. The excess was even greater for private direct investments, in

Table 17-5 **United States Balance of Payments, 1970**
(Billions of dollars)

	Receipts	Payments
Current Account		
1. Merchandise	$42.1	$39.9
2. Services		
a. Military	1.5	4.9
b. Investment Income	11.4	5.1
c. Travel	2.3	4.0
d. Other	5.7	5.4
3. Remittances, Pensions, and Transfers		1.4
4. U.S. Government Grants		1.8
Capital Account (Long-term)		
5. Private		
a. Direct	1.0	4.5
b. Portfolio	3.0	0.9
6. Government		2.0
Other		
7. Private Nonliquid Short-term Capital	0.8	1.4
8. Errors and Omissions		1.1
9. SDR Allocation	0.9	
10. Change in Reserve Assets	2.5	
11. Liquid Short-term Capital		
a. Private	0.3	6.2
b. Official	7.3	
Total	78.7	78.7

Balances	
Trade (Line 1)	$2.1
Goods and Services (Lines 1+2)	3.6
Current Account (Lines 1+2+3+4)	0.4
Current Account and Long-Term Capital (Lines 1+2+3+4+5+6)	−3.0
Net Liquidity (Lines 10+11)	−3.9
Official Reserve Transactions (Lines 10+11b)	−9.8

Note: Balances may not equal the sum of the individual accounts because of rounding.
Source: U.S. Department of Commerce.

which U.S. assets abroad were sixfold foreign investments in the U.S. Almost one-half of total U.S. claims abroad were equity investments compared to only 15 percent of total foreign claims on the U.S. On the other hand, foreign liquid investments in the U.S. were almost three times the amount of U.S. liquid investments abroad. Thus, to an extent, the United States has been acting as an international financial intermediary borrowing abroad short term and investing abroad long term in equity. However, some 40 percent of total U.S. claims on foreigners have been financed by domestic funds.

The U.S. also experienced an outflow of nonliquid short-term capital. Recorded outflows exceeded inflows by $0.6 billion. In addition, another $1 billion of payments could not be accounted for and were recorded under errors and omissions. Past analyses have suggested that the larger part of these transactions tend to be short-term capital movements. The U.S., along with all other member countries of the International Monetary Fund, was allocated additional special drawing rights (SDRs) in 1970 by the IMF. As will be discussed in the next chapter, SDRs are a form of international currency and additional distributions may be viewed as a grant to the recipient country, which are recorded as a receipt on the balance of payments.

The deficits were financed by sales of reserve assets and increases in short-term liquid liabilities to foreigners in excess of liquid claims on them. Sales of gold and other reserve assets totaled $2.5 billion. Liabilities to official foreign governments increased by more than $7 billion. Thus, the official settlements balance, which encompasses purely financing transactions, registered a deficit of some $10 billion. A large portion of the increase in official foreign holdings of short-term liquid claims reflected purchases of already outstanding claims from private foreign holders rather than of new U.S. liabilities. The latter totaled only about $1 billion. As a result, the deficit on net liquidity account was less than half as great. Both deficits would have been larger in the absence of the SDR allocation.

The private foreign holdings of dollar claims, which were sold to European central banks, were primarily in the form of Eurodollars, which are dollar-denominated balances at European banks including European branches of American commercial banks. (The mechanics of these dollars are discussed in the next chapter.) In previous years, U.S. banks had tapped the European money market through this channel to offset the restrictive impact of Federal Reserve policy, particularly the inability to market CDs because of the ceilings imposed by Regulation Q. In the process, they bid up the interest rates on Eurodollars inducing private foreigners to purchase dollars to loan to the U.S. banks. These dollars were provided to a large extent by foreign central banks who sold the dollars to maintain the dollar exchange rate. In the process, official liquid claims on the U.S. were reduced. As a result, the U.S. experienced surpluses in the official settlements balance in both 1968 and 1969. In 1970, as interest rates declined in the U.S., American banks sharply curtailed their borrowings of Eurodollars and private foreigners sold their dollars back to the foreign central banks. The sharp rise in the official settlements deficit in 1970 therefore reflects an unwinding of the Eurodollar transactions and is in part an offset to the surpluses of the previous two years.

The net liquidity deficit in 1970 was the thirteenth consecutive such deficit in the U.S. balance of payments. Since 1950, the U.S. has experienced a surplus on this account in only one year. The causes of the deficits have tended to vary from year to year, sometimes originating primarily in the current accounts and other times in the capital accounts.

Through the years the United States has attempted to correct the deficit through a number of adjustment strategies affecting the current account. "Buy American" restrictions and restrictions tying government aid to purchases from the United States were imposed in the 1950s and intensified in the 1960s. Official or voluntary quotas were imposed on a number of goods for which imports were accounting for a large and increasing proportion of domestic consumption such as petroleum, textiles, shoes, and steel. After reducing tariffs on many items in the Kennedy round of negotiations with other major trading countries in 1962, a temporary surcharge was imposed on all dutiable imports as part of the emergency economic measures of mid-1971. This duty was removed at year-end. Also as a part of this latter package of actions, the value of the dollar was depreciated with respect to most major foreign currencies, reducing the price of American goods in foreign markets and increasing the price of imports in domestic markets (see Table 17-3). In addition, as is discussed in greater detail in later chapters, the outflow of capital has been subjected to taxes and other restrictions, and general monetary and fiscal policies were frequently designed with the balance of payments in mind to be more restrictive than required by domestic considerations alone. None of these measures, either alone or combined, has been sufficiently successful to date to eliminate the deficit or even to reduce it significantly.

References

Devlin, David T., "The International Investment Position of the United States: Developments in 1970," *Survey of Current Business*, 51 (10), October, 1971, 19-25.

Federal Reserve Bank of Boston, *The International Adjustment Mechanism* (Boston: 1969).

Fieleke, Norman S., "The Buy-American Policy of the United States Government," *New England Economic Review* (Federal Reserve Bank of Boston), July/August, 1969, 2-18.

———, "Accounting for the Balance of Payments," *New England Economic Review* (Federal Reserve Bank of Boston), May/June, 1971, 2-15.

———, "The Cost of Tariffs to Consumers," *New England Economic Review* (Federal Reserve Bank of Boston), September/October, 1971, 13-19.

Goldstein, Henry N., "The U.S. Deficit—Who Cares," *Quarterly Review* (National Westminster Bank, London), May, 1970, 2-13.

U.S. Department of Commerce, "Balance of Payments Review," *Survey of Current Business*, various issues.

Walter, Ingo, *International Economics* (New York: Ronald Press, 1968).

Yeager, Leland B., *International Monetary Relations* (New York: Harper & Row, 1966).

International Finance

18

As with domestic finance, international finance involves the form, timing, and other provisions of receipts and payments for the sale and purchase, respectively, of goods, services, and financial claims. International finance differs from domestic finance in that the transfers of funds cross national boundaries and generally involve more than one currency. Except for any difficulties induced by the use of multiple currencies, restrictions on the free flow of capital among countries, and differences associated with transacting business in more than one country, the principles of international finance are similar to those of domestic finance.

Exchange Rates

As discussed in Chapter 17, exchange rates are the conversion price of one currency into another, that is, they are the price of one currency in terms of another. An increase in the exchange rate or price of one currency implies decrease in the price of the other. Because each country has its own currency, for any one country there are as many exchange rates as there are foreign countries. For all countries, the overall number of exchange rates is given by:

$$N = \frac{n(n-1)}{2}.$$

where:

N = number of exchange rates
n = number of countries.

Thus, in a world of 100 countries, there are a total of 4,950 different exchange rates.

The exchange rate of any particular foreign currency relative to a particular domestic currency is defined as the domestic price of one unit of the foreign currency. Thus, a rise in the rate represents a depreciation of the domestic currency and a fall in the rate, an appreciation. Like any price, in a free market the exchange rate is determined by the demand for and supply of the respective currencies.

The supply of a foreign currency in another country is the sum of the payments received in that country for exports to the foreign country and of the proceeds of borrowings, investments, and aid from that country. The domestic supply of all foreign currencies is equal to:

$$FC_S = X + KI, \qquad (18\text{-}1)$$

where:

FC_S = supply of foreign currencies
X = payment value of exports of goods and services
KI = capital and other inflows.

Abstracting from aid, both exports and capital inflows may be related to fundamental determinants. In Chapter 17, the foreign demand for exports was specified as:

$$x = f(\overset{+}{y}_{row}, \overset{-}{\frac{P}{P_{row}}}, \overset{+}{E}).$$

To obtain the amount of foreign currency acquired, the quantity of exports must be multiplied by the average foreign price paid. Thus:

$$X = xP_{row} = f(\overset{+}{y}_{row}, \overset{-}{\frac{P}{P_{row}}}, \overset{+}{E}, \overset{+}{P}_{row}). \qquad (18\text{-}2)$$

Like their domestic counterparts, international capital movements may be expected to flow, when unencumbered, to where the returns are the highest. Debt capital flows across national boundaries in response to interest rates and equity capital in response to profits. Specifying the rate of change in real income—the investment accelerator—as a surrogate for profit potential, the inflow of capital may be written in functional notation as:

$$KI = f(\overset{+}{\frac{i}{i_{row}}}, \overset{+}{\frac{\dot{y}}{\dot{y}_{row}}}), \qquad (18\text{-}3)$$

where:

$\dot{y}$ = rate of change in real GNP.

Substituting equations 18-2 and 18-3 into equation 18-1 yields:

$$FC_S = f(\overset{+}{y_{row}}, \overset{-}{\frac{P}{P_{row}}}, \overset{+}{\frac{i}{i_{row}}}, \overset{+}{\frac{\dot{y}}{\dot{y}_{row}}}, \overset{+}{E}, \overset{+}{P_{row}}). \qquad (18\text{-}4)$$

Domestic demand for foreign currency is dependent upon the need to finance imports and capital outflows, or loans, investments, and aid abroad. The total amount of foreign currencies demanded is:

$$FC_D = M + KO, \qquad (18\text{-}5)$$

where:

FC_D = demand for foreign currencies
M = payment value of imports of goods and services
KO = capital and other outflows.

Domestic demand for imports was developed in the preceding chapter as:

$$m = f(\overset{+}{y}, \overset{+}{\frac{P}{P_{row}}}, \overset{-}{E}).$$

The demand for foreign currency generated by the demand for imports is obtained from the gross domestic revenues derived from the sale of the imports:

$$M = mP = f(\overset{+}{y}, \overset{+}{\frac{P}{P_{row}}}, \overset{-}{E}, \overset{+}{P}). \qquad (18\text{-}6)$$

Again abstracting from aid, capital inflows are determined by the same factors affecting capital outflows with the signs of the relationships reversed. Thus:

$$KO = f(\overset{-}{\frac{i}{i_{row}}} \overset{-}{\frac{\dot{y}}{\dot{y}_{row}}}). \qquad (18\text{-}7)$$

Substituting equations 18-6 and 18-7 into equation 18-5 yields:

$$FC_D = f(\overset{+}{y}, \overset{-}{\frac{\dot{y}}{\dot{y}_{row}}}, \overset{-}{\frac{i}{i_{row}}}, \overset{+}{\frac{P}{P_{row}}}, \overset{-}{E}, \overset{+}{P}). \qquad (18\text{-}8)$$

Figure 18-1 **The Price of Foreign Exchange**

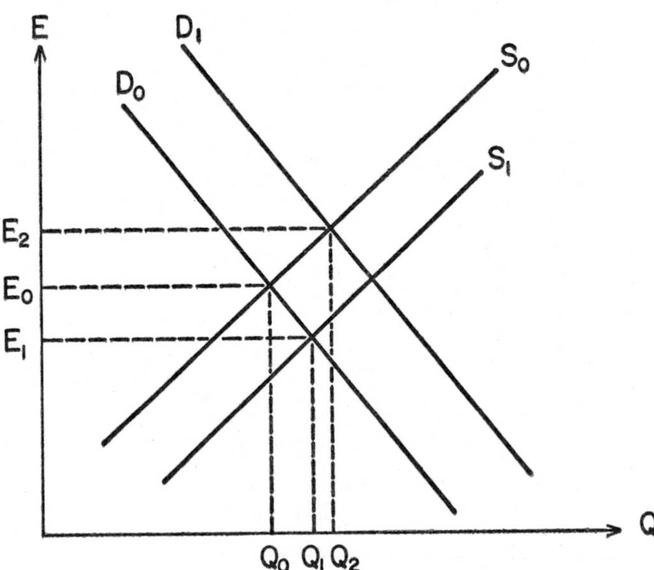

The domestic demand for (D_0) and foreign supply of (S_0) a particular foreign currency are drawn as functions of the exchange rate (the domestic price of one unit of foreign currency) in Figure 18-1. The equilibrium exchange rate is E_0, at which rate, holding all the other factors specified in equations 18-4 and 18-8 constant, the demand for the foreign currency is exactly equal to the supply of the foreign currency. At this rate, Q_0 units of the foreign currency will be traded. Increases in the value of exports or capital inflows, generated by higher real income in the foreign country, an acceleration in real domestic growth, a slowing in domestic price pressures, higher domestic interest rates, or higher foreign prices for the exports, will increase the domestic supply of the foreign currency and shift the supply schedule out to the right to S_1 and reduce the exchange rate to E_1. Increases in the value of imports or capital outflows, generated by higher domestic real income, a slowing of real domestic growth, an acceleration in domestic price pressures, lower domestic interest rates, or higher domestic prices for the imports, will increase domestic demand for the foreign currency and shift the demand schedule to D_1 and increase the exchange rate to E_2.

Like any price, the exchange rate may be expected to fluctuate through time as the determinants specified in equations 18-4 and 18-8 change. All the determinants are not equally volatile. Interest rates tend to fluctuate more in the short run than either income or prices and, by inducing capital flows, are responsible for instilling considerable short-term volatility in exchange rates. Countries may pursue two basic alternative policies with respect to movements in exchange rates.

They may attempt to offset the changes and establish fixed exchange rates or they may permit the rates to vary unencumbered under a system of flexible exchange rates. The next sections will examine the advantages and disadvantages of each exchange rate structure.

Fixed Exchange Rates

Under fixed exchange rates, exchange rates are established between the domestic currency and each foreign currency and, except for minor fluctuations within predesignated limits, are maintained at that rate. As nonoffsetting changes in the supply of and demand for foreign currency threaten to push a particular exchange rate beyond the permissible range, one or both of the governments of the two countries involved are forced to intervene in the foreign exchange market. If pressures threaten to increase the exchange rate of the foreign currency above the upper limit (the domestic currency depreciates), the domestic government must provide foreign currency by repurchasing its own currency on the exchange markets. If the pressures act to depress the exchange rate of the foreign currency below the lower limit (the domestic currency appreciates), the domestic government must absorb the excess supply of foreign currency by selling domestic currency. The provision and absorption of foreign currencies in consequence of operations to stabilize the exchange rate necessitates the governments maintaining reserves of foreign currencies. In most instances, countries establish their exchange rate with respect to the U.S. dollar and conduct the majority of their stabilizing operations in dollars. Thus, foreign countries hold dollars as reserves for use as an intervention currency. By fixing the rates against the dollar, the nondollar cross-exchange rates for these countries are also fixed.

Proponents of fixed exchange rates cite two major advantages over flexible rates. One, they contend that fixed exchange rates encourage maximum international trade, and, thereby, maximize worldwide efficiency and economic welfare. This is achieved by providing maximum certainty in the exchange rate relationships. Converting from one currency to another is considered difficult enough without introducing concern about the value of the exchange rate at the time payments are made or received. Increases in the volatility of exchange rates add to uncertainty and the cost of conducting international trade, thereby reducing the volume of trade. In addition, increases in exchange rate volatility are believed to encourage speculation in the future value of the rates and to induce speculative capital flows, which both amplify the volatility and may produce changes in the rates that are unwarranted by underlying trends in basic trade and longer-term capital movements.

Two, the proponents believe that fixed exchange rates provide conditions conducive to the formulation of optimal domestic economic policies, particularly with respect to curbing inflationary pressures. If exchange rates are fixed, in the absence of changes in tastes, imports and exports are seen from equations 18-2 and 18-6 to be determined by changes in domestic aggregate income and price levels relative to foreign aggregate income and price levels. If domestic income and prices increase faster than those abroad, exports decline, imports increase, and, abstracting from capital flows, surpluses in the balance of payments are reduced or deficits are enlarged, upward pressure is exerted on the exchange rate, and reserves are run down. As a consequence, in time policy-makers will be required to formulate economic policies to restore international competitiveness. It is argued that the constraint induced by the fixed exchange rate is frequently necessary to ensure that policy-makers give sufficiently high priority to maintaining domestic price stability.

As noted, reserves provide the ammunition with which governments are able to offset, at least temporarily, pressures which threaten to force exchange rates away from their established levels. When a country experiences a surplus in its balance of payments, the supply of most foreign currencies at the established exchange rate exceeds the demand, and by purchasing the excess stock, a country augments its reserves. When a country experiences a deficit in its balance of payments, the supply of domestic currency at the established exchange rate exceeds the demand by most foreign countries and, by purchasing the excess supply through selling foreign currencies, a country diminishes its reserves. Thus reserves act as a buffer for financing occasional deficits. It follows that the maintenance of exchange rates at an established level is possible only as long as a deficit country has reserves or unused borrowing power and a surplus country prefers to increase reserves or extend additional loans.

International reserves are an integral part of the fixed reserve rate system. They permit a postponement of more fundamental adjustments to correct imbalances. Under fixed exchange rates, lasting adjustments are brought about through general economic policies acting on aggregate income and prices or through selective policies reducing the volume of international trade. Selected implications of fixed exchange rates are itemized in Table 18-1. In the absence of effective stabilization policies in all countries, fixed exchange rates accelerate the transmission of economic difficulties in one country to its trading partners and impel countries to pursue similar economic policies. Assume country A inflates relative to country B. A's exports decline and imports rise. Downward pressures will be generated on A's exchange rate. To maintain the exchange rate, A will sell B's currency out of its reserves. With the exchange rate thereby unchanged, A's import demand will continue strong. The resulting expansion of export production in B will eventually generate domestic price pressures, effectively transmitting the inflation from A to B. Restrictive policies in B will decrease import demand, increase exports, further increase the surplus, build up B's reserves and, in the absence of corrective policy actions in A, only postpone the price pressures in B. Thus, in the long run all countries march to the beat of the most inflationary drummer, and the ability

Table 18-1 **Implications of Fixed and Flexible Exchange Rates**

	Fixed	Flexible
Spot rate certainty	Great in short run	Small in short run
Forward rate certainty	Small	Small
Adjustment primarily in	Income and prices	Exchange rates
Reserves necessary	Yes	No (except to moderate fluctuations)
Independent domestic economic policy	Not in long run	Yes
Require international economic cooperation	Yes	No

to pursue independent domestic economic policies is impaired. Pursuit of optimal domestic policies requires international economic cooperation to deter individual countries from pursuing less optimal policies.

Most major countries have operated on a fixed exchange rate standard throughout the greater part of their modern history. Following World War II, Western nations, through the auspices of the newly created International Monetary Fund (IMF), established exchange rates with respect to the U.S. dollar. The U.S. dollar, in turn, was tied to gold at $35.00 an ounce by the promise of the U.S. government to buy and sell gold freely at this rate in transactions with foreign governments. Changes in exchange rates outside a narrow band of 1 percent on either side of par value were discouraged. Countries were obligated to offset wider exchange rate swings through reserves and eventually to undertake more basic adjustments in income and prices.

Fixed exchange rates are not equivalent to constant exchange rates. Rates are free to fluctuate within prescribed limits. More importantly, if forces persistently operate to edge an exchange rate away from its established par, the deficit country would eventually exhaust its reserves in stabilizing transactions while the surplus country would build up its reserves to levels costly in terms of foregone consumption. At such times, a change will be made in the rate and a new par value established. The currency of the deficit country will be devalued in terms of the currency of the surplus country and the latter's currency will be appreciated in terms of the deficit country's currency. As the next section shows, fixed exchange rates have been changed quite frequently.

The system of fixed exchange rates established by the International Monetary Fund at the end of World War II operated with periodic modifications through mid-1971. At that time, the cumulative effects of many years of differential changes in income and prices in the various countries, particularly vis-à-vis the United States, forced a breakdown of the established par values. After a four-month period of operating without fixed exchange rates, par values were reestablished at year-end 1971, with most foreign currencies revalued upward with respect to the U.S. dollar (see Table 17-3). The amount of the revaluations in terms of the dollar varied from country to country so that the par values of the foreign currencies were also changed in terms of each other. In addition, the width of the band around the par value within which the rates were free to fluctuate was more than doubled to 2¼ percent on either side. As this band is drawn with respect to the U.S. dollar, its width permits fluctuations of up to 9 percent among non-dollar countries vis-à-vis each other.[1] This widening was expected to permit the impact of minor and self-reversing disturbances on exchange rates to be corrected without the need either to absorb or sell off reserves or to initiate major corrective policies.

Flexible Exchange Rates

Proponents of flexible exchange rates argue that it is impossible to successfully offset basic changes in supply and demand for any extended period of time either on exchange rates or on any other commodity. As the determinants underlying international trade and capital flows change, and not necessarily in offsetting directions, attempts to protect the exchange rate are costly in terms of reductions in economic efficiency and welfare and, at least as often as not, must usually be abandoned. As evidence, they point out that, even before the major currency realignments in 1971, fixed exchange rates had been anything but fixed. An IMF study shows that between 1948 and 1967, 97 of the 109 member countries had changed their exchange rates with respect to the dollar at least once.[2] Only 12 countries, including the United States, Switzerland, Japan, and 9 less-developed countries, did not change their exchange rate in this period. Lebanon appreciated its currency slightly once. A small number of other countries, such as Germany and the Netherlands in 1961, also appreciated their currencies but the amount of the appreciation did not offset earlier devaluations. Twenty-one countries devalued their currencies four or more times. More than one-half of the countries, including the United Kingdom, France, and Spain, devalued their currencies cumulatively in excess of 40 percent. Less-developed countries have tended to devalue their currencies more often and by larger amounts than more-developed countries. These changes are summarized in Tables 18-2 and 18-3. Since 1967, the number of changes in exchange rates has increased greatly.

1. For example, if country A's currency was at the ceiling vis-à-vis the U.S. dollar and B's was at the floor, the spread between the two currencies would be 4½ percent. If B's currency now rose to the dollar ceiling, it would rise 4½ percent relative to both the dollar and A's currency. If, at the same time, A's currency declined to the dollar floor, it would also decline 4½ percent relative to the dollar, but 9 percent relative to the initial value of B's currency.

2. Margaret G. deVries, "The Magnitude of Exchange Devaluation," *Finance and Development,* 5 (2), Second Quarter, 1968, 8-12.

Table 18-2 **Cumulative Percentage Devaluations, 1948-67**
(Number of countries)

	Total	Europe and Major Powers	Africa	Asia	Latin America	Middle East
No devaluation*	13	2	2	1	7	1
Less than 30%	12	7	0	0	3	2
30–39%	22	4	10	4	1	3
40–75%	38	6	18	6	5	3
More than 75%	24	5	6	4	7	2
Total	109	24	36	15	23	11

* One appreciation.

Source: deVries, "The Magnitude of Exchange Devaluation," p. 10.

Table 18-3 **Magnitude of Devaluations, 1948-67**

Region	Number of Countries	Average Weighted Devaluation* (percent)
Australia, Canada, New Zealand and the United States	4	5.2
Europe	20	23.5
Middle East	12	38.4
Asia (excluding Japan)	14	46.1
Africa	36	47.6
Latin America	23	62.2
Total	109	22.8

* Weighted by share of country's exports in 1966 to total world exports.

Source: *Ibid.*

It is argued further that participants in international trade are generally not fooled by the term "fixed," particularly in their dealings with less-developed nations. They act to protect themselves against unfavorable exchange rate movements by demanding payment in currencies with small probabilities of devaluation and offering payment in weaker currencies. In addition, they frequently hedge against exchange rate risks by offsetting their transactions in weaker currencies on the forward market.

The proponents of flexibile exchange rates also contend that, rather than discouraging destabilizing speculation on exchange rates, fixed exchange rates actually encourage such speculation. Exchange rates under continued pressure can only change in one direction and, by the time a change is made, generally by a relatively large amount. Speculators are thereby presented with an almost riskless proposition—heads you win big, tails you lose, at most, small. If the rate changes as speculated, the speculator profits. If it does not, he can sell the currency at near his purchase price, protected on the other side of the exchange rate range by the limit established by the fixed rate structure.

Flexible exchange rates need not imply volatile exchange rates any more than fixed rates imply constant rates. A country may stabilize its exchange rate through appropriate economic policies. In addition, since speculation in exchange rate changes now involves the possibility of equal-sized losses and gains, such speculation may be reduced in intensity. Before 1971, among the major trading countries, only Canada had experimented with flexible exchange rates for any meaningful length of time. Studies of this experience have failed to find evidence of greater short-term volatility in its exchange rate in this period than under fixed exchange rates. In addition, price volatility by itself may not reduce trade. It is doubtful whether exchange rate markets for major currencies would be any more volatile under flexible exchange rates than commodity or stock markets are currently. Recent evidence hardly suggests any diminution of trade on these markets. Also, as noted earlier, risk averters are able to hedge their transactions on the forward markets.

Lastly, if fixed exchange rates indirectly pressure countries into pursuing less-inflationary policies, it may be argued that the pressures must not be too great in light of the inflationary experiences of most major countries in the postwar era.

Flexible exchange rates require little or no government intervention to offset the influence of changing supply and demand conditions on exchange rates. Rather, exchange rates are allowed to fluctuate in response to these forces. As a result, the exchange rate always clears the foreign exchange market and balance of payments imbalances are automatically corrected rather than requiring changes in aggregate income and prices or the imposition of trade-reducing measures such as tariffs, quotas, and exchange controls. Countries are, thereby, able to pursue independent economic policies.

Likewise, flexible exchange rates do not transmit economic disturbance from country to country as readily as fixed exchange rates. Instead, the disturbances are absorbed by the exchange rate. Consider the previous example in which country A inflated faster than country B. A's exports decline, imports rise, and the cost of foreign exchange increases. By permitting the foreign exchange rate to increase, the effect of the rise in domestic prices on the foreign price of exports is offset, and exports do not decline. Concurrently, the domestic price of imports is increased to near the domestic price level by the rise in the price of foreign exchange, and imports do not increase. Countries are thus freer to pursue policies they view to be in their own best interests without either concern for or pressure from other countries.

The International Monetary Fund

The International Monetary Fund is an international, quasi-central bank owned and operated by its member countries. At year-end 1971, 120 countries were members of the Fund. Only the Communist bloc of countries has remained outside. The IMF was organized at a conference of leading trading nations at Bretton Woods, New Hampshire, in 1944, near the end of World War II. The participants to the conference were charged to devise a stable international monetary system for the postwar period which would be conducive to maximum international trade and economic welfare. Such a conference and assignment were a natural outgrowth of the chaotic international financial conditions of the 1930s, which resulted in massive restrictions on the international transfer of goods, services, and capital, accompanied by sharp reductions in trade and economic welfare.

The IMF engages in four major activities:

1. provision of facilities for establishing exchange rates and determining conditions under which international payments may be restricted,
2. provision of facilities for augmenting owned and borrowed reserves,
3. provision of technical, statistical, and research assistance, and
4. provision of facilities for international consultation.

Exchange Rates and Payment Restrictions

Largely in reaction to the conditions of the 1930s, the representatives at Bretton Woods concluded that international monetary stability and maximum levels of international trade and investment would be achieved most effectively through fixed exchange rates. Member countries were required to establish par values with respect to either gold or the U.S. dollar. All countries but the United States established par values with respect to the dollar. The U.S. dollar was priced at $35.00 per ounce of gold, its gold price since 1934. Thus all currencies were indirectly tied to gold. Spot exchange rates were permitted to fluctuate within 1 percent of either side of parity. In practice, most major countries permitted only smaller fluctuations. Any subsequent change in par value, beyond an initial cumulative 10 percent, requires the approval of the IMF and is permitted only to correct "fundamental" payments disequilibriums of a secular nature. Shorter payment disequilibriums are to be financed through reserves.

This system was to be reinforced by the removal of all restrictions which hamper international trade. Countries were encouraged to permit free convertibility of their currency into other currencies at the market rate, at a minimum, for financing current transactions.

In the immediate postwar period, most countries severely restricted the convertibility of their currencies into other currencies for both current and capital transactions. After unsuccessful attempts early in the postwar period and subsequent gradual freeing of currency transfers, the major European countries effectively adopted full convertibility on current account at year-end 1958. Restrictions with respect to capital account have been maintained in varying degrees by these countries and effectively adopted by the United States in the 1960s through measures such as the foreign credit restraint program. Most less-developed countries have maintained some type of restrictions on the use of foreign currency on both current and capital accounts.

Throughout this period international trade expanded rapidly and most member countries experienced record levels of economic welfare. Nevertheless, periodic strains developed as domestic economic objectives and policies clashed with the external constraints imposed by fixed exchange rates. At these times, the flow of capital was increasingly constrained and exchange rates increasingly changed.

Reserves

As discussed earlier, reserves are required to assist countries in maintaining fixed exchange rates. Reserves of an individual country may be either owned or borrowed. Owned reserves include gold, convertible foreign currencies of major trading partners, and, more recently, IMF sponsored special drawing rights (SDRs). The mix of these reserve assets within the total reserve holdings of any country reflects the preferences of the country. Foreign currencies carry the risk of depreciation. On the other hand, such reserves can be invested in interest-yielding liquid financial instruments. The resulting interest income serves to augment the amount of reserves. In the postwar period, the U.S. dollar supplanted the British pound sterling as the major national currency used to finance international transactions worldwide. Consequently, the dollar was also used as the major reserve currency.

Gold has served a unique financial role throughout the history of the world. Its domestic history has already been discussed. Its international appeal stems from much the same property as its domestic appeal—scarcity. Throughout modern history, whenever people feared a devaluation of domestic currencies, they hoarded gold. Nations have proved no exception. As a hedge against devaluation of other currencies, a portion of reserves has been held in gold. How much has varied from country to country and in large measure has reflected the country's own currency experience. Thus France, which has had a history of inflation and currency depreciation, maintains the larger share of its international reserves in gold, while Japan maintains only a small proportion of its reserves in gold. The greater the gold holdings are, the greater the interest income foregone to the country.

In the postwar period, the stock of gold has increased only slowly as rising costs of mining and, until 1972, no increase in the official price have held back production. Although gold production almost doubled between the end of World War

Figure 18-2 **Gold: Estimated New Supplies and Absorption, 1958–71**

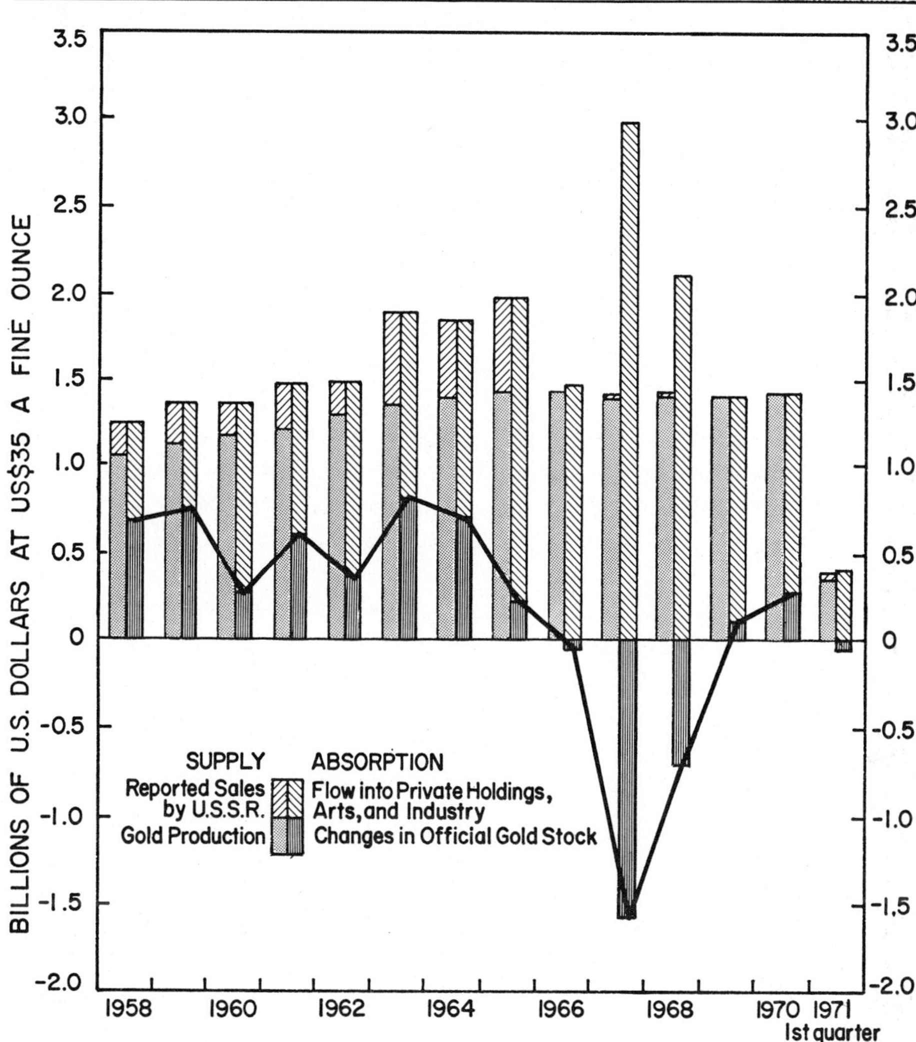

Source: International Monetary Fund, *Annual Report, 1971,* p. 145.

II and 1971, annual production was small, measuring only about 4 percent of official gold holdings and less of total gold holdings. At mid-1971, before the upward revaluation in the price of gold, total gold holdings of central banks and governments were less than one-third higher than at the end of World War II and about the same as in 1960. As Figure 18-2 shows, an increasing share of both new production and the total world stock has been absorbed by industrial use and private hoarding in countries where gold ownership is legal. This absorption occurred despite periodic increases in the free market price of gold to well above the official price. In mid-1972, the free market price hovered near $60 an ounce, considerably above the new official price of $38 an ounce established in May, 1972.

As long as there was little doubt about the ability of the United States to maintain the gold value of the dollar, the slow growth of gold was not overly important. Indeed, most countries preferred to hold the greater part of their reserves in liquid dollar investments in the U.S. and earn interest income. However, as the continued deficits in the U.S. balance of payments increased and the amount of foreign-owned dollar balances rose sharply from $8 billion in 1950 to more than $50 billion in 1971, doubts increased about the ability of the U.S. to maintain free convertibility at the official dollar-gold exchange rate and countries became increasingly reluctant to hold dollars as reserves. Countries across-the-board stepped up their purchases of gold from the U.S. at the promised $35.00 price and the U.S. gold stock declined from $23 billion in 1950 to nearly $10 billion in 1971. At the same time, no other national currency had all the characteristics necessary to be widely accepted as a reserve currency. As a result, there was a danger that the inability to increase world reserves would slow the expansion in trade. The provision of supplementary reserves, both owned and borrowed, to assure continued high levels of international trade is the Fund's most important operation.

After many years of investigation and negotiation, the IMF created a new reserve currency—SDRs, an international paper currency. In 1969, the members of the Fund voted to distribute almost $10 billion of SDRs over the next three years to supplement gold. The SDRs were to be allocated among member countries in the same proportion as each country's quota in the fund. (The quotas are described in the next section.) The first $3.5 billion allocation was made January 1, 1970, and two subsequent allocations of $3 billion each were made January 1 of each of the following two years. The U.S.'s share was $867 million in the first round and about $715 million in each of the next two rounds.

To increase the acceptability of SDRs to member countries, the IMF tied their value to gold, pays a small 1½ percent annual rate of interest on them, and requires countries, after a stipulated period of time, to repurchase at the fixed gold price the SDRs they sold in excess of 70 percent of their allocation. This last provision limits the ability of countries to use the SDRs to finance extended deficits. In addition, countries allocated SDRs pay 1½ percent interest on their allocation to the Fund. As this is the same rate as is paid on SDRs, it effectively represents a 1½ percent payment from countries holding less than their allocated amount of SDRs to countries holding more than their allocated amount, or a payment from debtor countries to creditor countries.

Total reserves of IMF member countries at year-end 1960 and at mid-1971 are shown in Table 18-4. Aggregate reserves of all member countries increased about

Table 18-4 **International Reserves**
(Billion U.S. dollars)

	December, 1960	June, 1971
Total IMF members	60.5	104.9
Gold	38.0	36.5
SDRs	–	5.9
IMF position	3.6	6.9
Foreign currency	18.9	55.6
United States	19.4	13.5
United Kingdom	3.7	3.6
Canada	2.0	4.9
Japan	1.9	7.8
Industrial Europe	20.1	44.5
Other developed areas	3.7	10.2
Latin America	3.0	6.0
Middle East	1.4	3.8
Other Asia	3.1	5.4
Other Africa	1.9	5.1

Source: International Monetary Fund, *International Financial Statistics*, 23 (12), December, 1970, p. 20; and 25 (6), June, 1972, p. 19.

75 percent in this period. All of the increase occurred in reserve assets other than gold. Increases in foreign currency holdings accounted for three-fourths of the increase, the newly created SDRs for 15 percent, and increases in the net Fund position of member countries the remainder. The net IMF position represents automatic drawing rights on the Fund by member countries and, in the aggregate, is equivalent to aggregate gold subscription to the Fund. With the exception of the United States and the United Kingdom, all major industrial countries and most less-developed areas increased their aggregate reserve position, many quite sharply.

Countries may also borrow reserves from each other or the IMF. Intercountry borrowing can either be bilateral or multilateral. Immediately after World War II, the United States extended a large loan to the United Kingdom to finance an unsuccessful return to convertibility at the old prewar par value. In the early 1960s, the United States, through the Federal Reserve System, entered into agreements with a number of foreign central banks to exchange or swap currencies to offset temporary reserve losses. In mid-1972, standby credit arrangements under these swap agreements totaled some $12 billion with 14 countries. At the same time, the United States Treasury borrowed foreign currency from foreign countries through the sale of special Treasury securities having gold guarantees or denominated in foreign currencies. Also at the beginning of the 1960s, ten major industrial countries, including the United States, pledged to make their currencies

Table 18-5 **IMF Position of Member Countries, June 30, 1971**
(Billion dollars)

	Quota	Borrowing	Fund Currency Holding As Percent of Quota
Total	28.5	3.8	
United States	6.7	0.2	79
United Kingdom	2.8	1.6	140
Canada	1.1	–	59
Japan	1.2	–	63
Industrial Europe	6.4	0.6	62
Other developed areas	2.4	0.2	81
Latin America	2.6	0.3	NA
Middle East	1.0	0.2	NA
Other Asia	2.8	0.5	104
Other Africa	1.4	0.2	97

Source: *International Financial Statistics*, 24 (8), August, 1971, pp. 8-9.

available in an overall amount up to $6 billion through the Fund to supplement the Fund's holdings of these currencies. This standby credit pool is referred to as the General Arrangement to Borrow (GAB).

Reserve borrowing facilities are also provided member countries by the IMF. Individual country access to this facility is tied to its quota. Quotas are established by the Fund according to a country's domestic economic strength, foreign reserve strength, and share in world trade. The original quotas established in 1946 totaled about $8 billion. Subsequent increases in the quotas in 1958, 1966, and 1970, plus the increase in the number of member countries, have raised the total quotas to $28.5 billion at midyear 1971. The U.S. has the largest quota by far, $6.7 billion, accounting for 23 percent of all quotas. The quotas of major countries are shown in Table 18-5. Subscription payments, voting rights, and SDR allocations, as well as borrowing rights, are tied to the quota.

Member countries are required to subscribe to an amount equal to their quota. Twenty-five percent of this amount—called *the gold tranche*—must be paid in gold, the remainder in domestic currency. Subscription payments account for almost all of the Fund's financial resources. Members may borrow foreign currencies up to an amount equal to 25 percent of their quota, that is, up to the amount collateralized by their gold tranche, essentially without question. Countries may borrow beyond 25 percent of their quota after consultation with and approval of the Fund. Approval is tied to the country's agreement to initiate appropriate corrective policy measures to close the payments deficit. The loans are generally for periods not in excess of three to five years. Interest charges are scaled to the amount and duration of the loan. Technically, countries borrow by purchasing the desired currencies with their own currency and repay by repurchasing their own currency with the purchased currency or an acceptable substitute currency.

Through mid-1971, the Fund had loaned $22 billion. Repayments had effectively totaled $18 billion, so that only $4 billion remained outstanding. Almost all of these loans had been outstanding for less than three years (Figure 18-3). To finance its lending activities through the years, the Fund occasionally has made use of its standby borrowing arrangement under the GAB, but almost all of these loans had been repaid by 1971.

Fund holdings of a particular currency as a percentage of the country's quota reflect the reserve strength of the country. As, in the absence of transactions, the Fund's holdings of a currency are equal to 75 percent of the country's quota, Fund holdings in excess of 75 percent indicate the country has borrowed other currencies, and Fund holdings below 75 percent that other countries have borrowed its currency. The greater the Fund's holdings of a particular currency relative to that country's quota, the weaker the overall international payments position of the country is likely to be (see Table 18-5).

Technical Assistance and Consultation

The Fund provides technical assistance to member countries in the areas of fiscal and monetary affairs. Representatives of the Fund are assigned to applicant countries to offer advice on the development and execution of appropriate economic policies; on institutional reforms in central banking, commercial banking, financial markets, and fiscal systems; and on improvements in statistical reporting and the analysis of economic intelligence. The Fund also maintains an economic research staff at its headquarters in Washington, D.C., which collects and analyzes data on international and domestic trade, finance, employment, and prices in each member country. Staff missions are periodically assigned to survey member countries to obtain a more complete analysis of financial conditions and problems in the country. Such missions have been particularly active in the less-developed nations. The findings of these reports are shared with the country and, when necessary, used to design mutually acceptable corrective measures. Under the charter of the IMF, all countries maintaining controls on current account are required to consult annually with the Fund on their need to maintain the restrictions. Countries are also required to consult with the Fund before any borrowings or changes in exchange rates.

The IMF also provides facilities for all, or groups of, member countries to meet together to discuss problems of mutual concern. Such sessions are regularly scheduled at the annual meetings of the Fund. These meetings are generally held in conjunction with the comparable meetings of the International Bank for Reconstruction and Development, a sister international institution that makes longer-

Figure 18-3 **Length of Time for Which IMF Loans Have Been Outstanding, 1962–71**
(Year ending April 30)

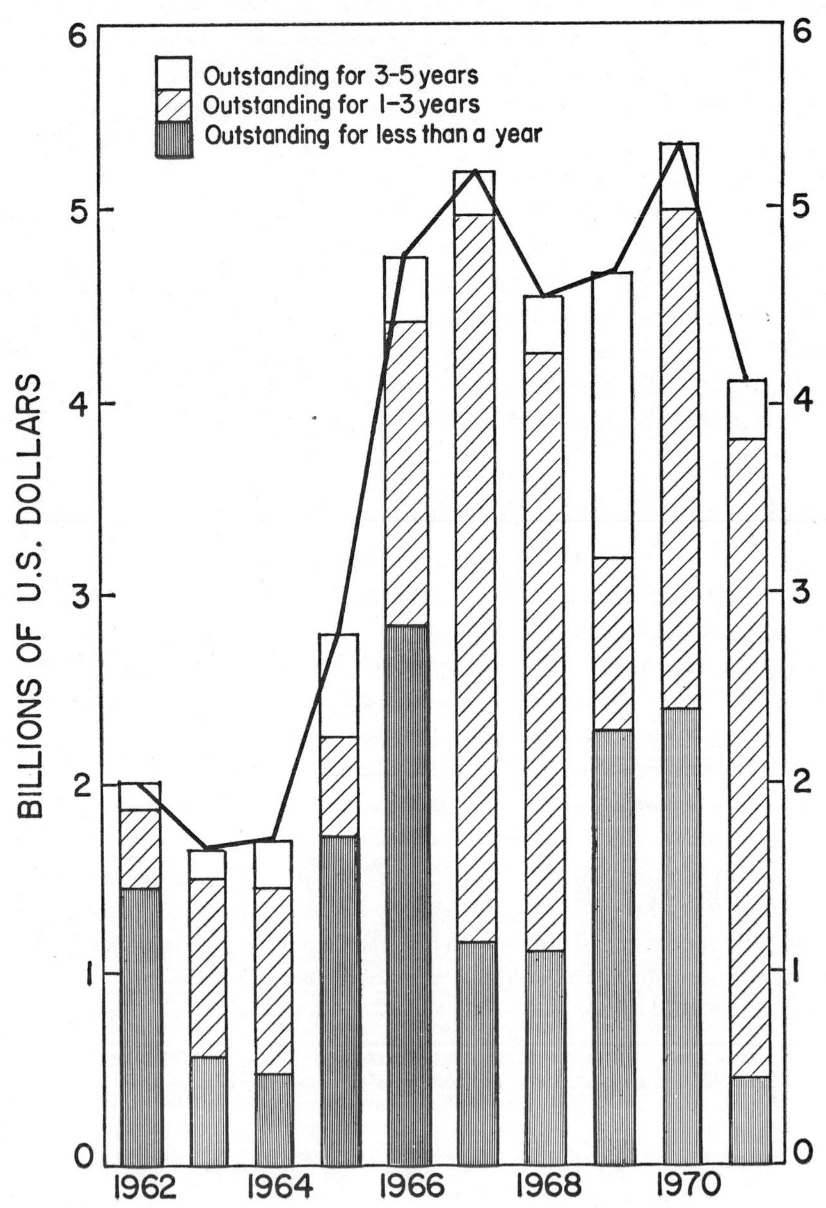

Source: *Ibid.*, p. 165.

term development funds available, primarily to less-developed countries. The meetings are attended by representatives of each member country, usually including the country's minister of finance, governor of the central bank, or both. Less regularly scheduled meetings are also held to discuss general economic and financial problems of common interest to a limited group of countries.

Not a Central Bank

The IMF is not a central bank in the usual meaning of the term as applied to, say, the Federal Reserve System. It cannot determine or influence domestic money supply, although the introduction of SDRs provides it with limited powers to influence the international money stock. There is no single worldwide financial policy. Member countries remain free to pursue their own domestic economic policies, subject to the exchange rate and borrowing provisions of the Fund. All major policy actions must be voted on by members of the Fund. Additional allocation of SDRs, for example, require approval by 85 percent of the voting power. Sanctions that may be applied to countries that disregard recommendations are weak. Frequently, the Fund is notified only at the last minute of a pending change in exchange rates. Nevertheless, its large membership and, more importantly, control over its borrowing facilities serve to make its advice more than gratuitous.

Adjustment and Liquidity

Differences between adjustment and liquidity have already been discussed in the previous chapter with respect to interpersonal trade. The same differences apply to international trade. Under fixed exchange rates, adjustment refers to basic changes in the economy to correct a balance of payments imbalance. As a lasting correction of a payments deficit typically involves a reduction in the standard of living, such an adjustment involves considerable cost. The adjustment problem involves the design and reluctant implementation of such painful measures.

Liquidity refers to the ability of a country to finance a postponement of costly adjustment measures, that is, liquidity buys time. The liquidity problem involves the search for sufficient liquidity either to postpone adjustment measures temporarily or to impose effective but slow-acting measures rather than harsher measures that have stronger and less-desirable impacts on world trade. Liquidity is not a substitute for adjustment. Additional allocation of owned reserves to chronic deficit countries, such as most less-developed countries, will not permanently correct their imbalances. These countries tend to generate continuous deficits because their demands for imports vastly exceed their ability to generate sufficient foreign exchange to finance these imports. They are short of reserves and experience continuous liquidity problems, primarily because they are poor but have expensive tastes and aspirations. Additional grants of liquidity would be quickly exhausted. The solution lies in adjustment actions to increase the export base, if possible, or to increase self-reliance and cut import demand. In the absence of such actions, increased reserve allocations permanently transfer resources from surplus to deficit countries and should be viewed as a form of international welfare, not as a contribution to a lasting adjustment solution.

Forward Exchange Rates

Similar to many commodities, foreign currency may be purchased for future delivery, say 30, 90, 180, or 360 days hence, as well as for immediate delivery. Currency for immediate delivery is traded on the spot exchange market, while that for future delivery is traded on the forward exchange market. In both markets, payment is concurrent with delivery. As a result, trading in the forward market is in contracts promising future delivery or payment of a particular amount of a particular currency at a particular price on a particular date. Except for possible small margin payments, no funds change hands until the delivery date.

There are a number of reasons why some traders may prefer to buy or sell foreign currency for future delivery. They may wish to reduce uncertainty. Transportation time in international trade is typically longer than for domestic trade and exchange rates may fluctuate between the dates of order and delivery, even under fixed exchange rates. Importers may prefer to eliminate the risk of unfavorable rate fluctuations by contracting at the time of the order to purchase the foreign currency for delivery on the payment date. Likewise, exporters expecting payment in foreign currency may wish to hedge against the risk of the foreign currency declining in value before the payment date by contracting to sell the currency for delivery on the payment date at a predetermined price. Through such transactions importers know with certainty the domestic cost of the goods ordered and exporters the domestic revenues from their sales. Similar transactions may be undertaken by importers and exporters in instances when credit is involved in the transaction and payment is not scheduled until some time after the delivery of the goods. Thus, importers are important buyers of foreign currencies on the forward market and exporters, important sellers.

The participation of exporters and importers in the forward market is augmented by that of traders in financial claims. Borrowers facing repayment of foreign currency loans or interest and dividend payments may prefer to contract for the purchase of the foreign currency before the payment date in order to take advantage of a favorable exchange rate or to reduce the uncertainty of rate fluctuations until the payment date. Investors and lenders scheduled to receive loan repayments or interest and dividend payments in foreign currencies may wish to contract to sell the currency before receipt for the same reasons. The use of the forward market by these participants may be expected to be directly proportional to the volatility of exchange rates: the greater the probability of changes in exchange rates, the greater the overall use of the forward market. Uncertainty about future exchange rates exists under both fixed and flexible rates and forward markets operate under both systems. However, to the extent that participants may consider short-run exchange rate volatility to be greater under flexible than fixed exchange rates, the forward market may be expected to be used more heavily under flexible rates (see Table 18-1).

Use of the forward market is not costless. Apart from transactions costs, the decision to use the forward market depends, on first consideration, on the relationship between the spot rate expected at the payment date and the current forward rate. If the forward rate is above the expected comparable spot rate, the potential expense of the purchase of the forward currency must be compared to the nominal value of any benefit derived from the increase in certainty. If the potential cost exceeds the value of the certainty gain, the forward market will not be used. If the forward rate is below the expected comparable spot rate, the transaction is potentially profitable.

Of course, expectations may not be realized. If the actual spot rate at the time of payment is below both the expected spot rate and the previous forward rate, the purchase of the forward currency was costly. If, on the other hand, the actual spot rate is above the expected rate, any profit is greater than expected. Thus, while use of the forward market in the transactions described reduces the uncertainty of not knowing the exchange rate and thereby costs or revenues, it does not reduce the uncertainty associated with selecting the most profitable strategy. Indeed, it increases the number of alternative strategies to consider. For example, potential users of the forward market must also consider the alternative of purchasing or selling the currency on the spot market to achieve rate certainty and simultaneously lending or borrowing the proceeds, respectively, until the payment date. An importer can purchase the foreign currency on the spot market at the time of his order and invest the proceeds until the payment date. Likewise, an exporter can borrow foreign currency on the sale date, sell it spot, invest the domestic currency until the payment date, and repay the foreign currency loan with his proceeds from the sale. Hence, the forward rate is not only related to the spot rate expected at the future time, but also to the current spot rate and to prevailing interest rates, both domestically and abroad.

The forward exchange rate, like the spot rate, is determined by demand and supply. We have already identified two important participants on each side—international traders in goods and services and international traders in financial claims. A third important participant also operates in the forward market and must be considered in order to identify all the demand and supply pressures. This participant is the pure speculator who expects to profit from buying and selling assets without consideration for the usual consumption or income services the asset may yield. Speculators operate on the foreign exchange markets on both the spot market by, say, buying a currency whose exchange rate they expect to rise, expecting to sell it later at the higher price, and on the forward market by, say, buying a currency forward whose forward price is lower than the spot price they expect at maturity, or selling a currency forward whose forward rate is higher than the spot rate they expect at maturity. As funds do not change hands on the forward market until delivery, although a small security deposit is often required, this is a more favorable market for speculators than the spot market, in which costly capital may be tied up. If, in the first example above, the speculator is correct and the spot rate in the future exceeds the forward price paid for the currency, the difference is profit effectively on no investment. It follows that spot and forward exchange rates are interconnected in both directions.

In sum, the demand for forward foreign currency arises from importers and borrowers of foreign currency who wish to hedge against unfavorable changes in the exchange rate or to speculate that the spot exchange rate will be higher at the payment time than the current forward rate, and from pure speculators who likewise speculate that the future spot rate will exceed the current forward rate. The supply of forward foreign currency arises from exporters and lenders of domestic currency to foreign borrowers who hedge against a fall in the foreign exchange rate or speculate that the current forward rate will exceed the spot rate at the payment time, and from pure speculators who also engage in the latter speculation. The greater the amount of hedging against, and speculation on, increases in spot rates, the higher the current forward rate will be. The greater the amount of hedging against, and speculation on, decreases in the spot rate, the lower the current forward rate will be. It appears evident that hedging is differentiated from speculation only by the apparent motive of the trader. Hedging is ostensibly undertaken to avoid a loss and speculation to produce a gain. Markets for forward currency as well as spot currency are operated by most large commercial banks. In addition, the International Monetary Market, a central market for forward foreign currency, was recently established in Chicago by the Chicago Mercantile Exchange, which also operates central markets for commodities.

Interest Arbitrage

A convenient measure of the cost of forward exchange is to relate it to the cost of concurrent spot exchange. Let E_s designate the present spot exchange rate for a foreign currency and E_f the present forward rate for that currency for delivery at time *t*. If $E_s > E_f$, the forward rate is said to be selling at a discount; if $E_s < E_f$, the forward rate is selling at a premium. The purchase of forward currency is frequently referred to as *forward cover*, emphasizing its use to hedge future payments. The cost of cover *(C)* is defined as:

$$C = E_s - E_f. \tag{18-9}$$

If the forward rate is at a premium, the cost of forward cover is negative and, in the absence of interest rate differentials, a profit may be realized by simultaneously buying the foreign currency spot and selling it forward.

Because the decision whether to purchase forward or spot foreign currency is dependent upon the prevailing interest rates in the respective countries, it is useful to transform the cost of forward cover into comparable percentage terms:

$$C = \frac{E_s - E_f}{E_s}. \tag{18-10}$$

If, for example, the current spot exchange rate for country A's wheels is $0.25 and the current one-year forward rate $0.24, the forward wheel is said to be selling at a discount with respect to the dollar of .01/.25, or 4 percent. Frequently, forward contracts are for periods of less than one year. In these instances, the cost of forward exchange is generally converted to an annual rate percentage basis. If, in the above example, the forward rate applied to a 90-day contract, the annual rate discount or cost of forward wheels would be about 16 percent.

When interest rates on two comparable investments differ, arbitragers may reasonably be expected to attempt to eliminate the rate difference by shifting funds from the lower-yielding security to the higher-yielding security. In international investment transactions in which different currencies are involved, such interest rate arbitrage is complicated by the possibility of an unfavorable change in exchange rates during the investment period, which could make it more expensive to repurchase the domestic currency and could reduce or even eliminate the gain from the initial shift of funds. As a result, many investors will not transfer funds into other currencies to take advantage of interest rate differentials without, at the same time, protecting themselves against an unfavorable shift in exchange rates. Thus, a U.S. investor wanting to invest in country A for a one-year period without assuming an exchange rate risk would simultaneously purchase wheels spot to make the investment and sell an equal amount of wheels (buy dollars) forward for delivery one year hence when the investment matures. It stands to reason that investment in A's securities will be made only if the interest return less the cost of forward dollars exceeds the interest return on comparable securities in the U.S. In the first example above, this would mean that the annual interest return in A must exceed that in the United States by at least 4 percent.

A useful statistic relating the interest rate differential between comparable securities in two countries and the cost of forward cover is the net incentive, which is defined as:

$$NI_o = i_g - C = (i_o - i_d) - \frac{(E_s - E_f)}{E_s}, \tag{18-11}$$

where:

NI_o = net incentive to invest abroad
i_o = foreign interest rate
i_d = domestic interest rate
$i_g = (i_o - i_d)$
E_s = domestic price of one unit of foreign currency for spot delivery
E_f = domestic price of one unit of foreign currency for future delivery.

Capital will flow, on a covered basis, to the country for which the net incentive is positive. Equation 18-11 shows that a country may have a positive net incentive (1) because its interest rates are higher than in the other country and its forward currency is selling at spot value, (2) because the interest rate spread in favor of the country is greater than the discount on the forward sale of the country's currency, or (3) because its interest rates are lower than in the other country but its currency is selling at a forward premium greater than the unfavorable interest rate spread. These relationships can be illustrated best by the use of simple numerical examples.

Assume that the spot dollar price of wheels is \$0.25, that the one-year forward price is \$0.24, and that the interest rate on one-year securities—the intended investment period—in country A is 10 percent. Transaction and search costs are assumed to be zero.

Case 1.

Let: $i_{US} = 5\%$.

$$NI_A = (i_A - i_{US}) - \frac{(E_s - E_f)}{E_s} = (10 - 5) - \frac{(.25 - .24)}{.25} = (5 - 4) = 1\%.$$

In this case, the interest spread in favor of A is greater than the cost of the forward sale of wheels for dollars and capital will flow on a covered basis from the U.S. to A.

Case 2.

Let: $i_{US} = 7\%$.

$$NI_A = (10 - 7) - \frac{(.25 - .24)}{.25} = (3 - 4) = -1\%.$$

In this case the interest rate spread in favor of A is smaller than the cost of forward dollar cover and U.S. investors will not transfer funds to A on a covered basis. Moreover, investors in A will transfer funds to the U.S., since for them the spread in favor of domestic interest rates is less than the discount on forward wheels or the premium on forward dollars. That is, their gain from buying spot dollars and simultaneously selling them for forward delivery one year hence is 4 percent, which, when added to the 7 percent interest available in the U.S., exceeds the 10 percent interest return available on domestic securities.

Case 3.

Let: $i_{US} = 6\%$.

$$NI_A = (10-6) - \frac{(.25-.24)}{.25} = (4-4) = 0\%.$$

In this case the interest rate gain from investing in A rather than in the U.S. is exactly equal to the discount on future wheels and there would be no incentive to transfer covered funds either from the U.S. to A or from A to the U.S.

Case 4.

Let: $i_{US} = 7\%$,
and the forward dollar price of wheels rise from \$0.24 to \$0.26.

$$NI_A = (10-7) - \frac{(.25-.26)}{.25} = (3+4) = 7\%.$$

Funds will flow to country A both because of the higher interest rates and the gain that can be made by simultaneously buying its currency spot and selling it forward.

Case 5.

Let: $i_{US} = 12\%$
$E_f = \$0.26$.

$$NI_A = (10-12) - \frac{(.25-.26)}{.25} = (-2+4) = 2\%.$$

In this case funds will flow to country A even though it has lower interest rates than the U.S. because the rate differential is smaller than the gain from buying wheels spot and selling them forward. Such a situation is likely primarily when the market expects A's currency to be revalued upward.

A number of conclusions can be derived from these examples:

1. In equilibrium, the *NI* will be zero and the country experiencing the higher interest rate also experiences a discount on its forward currency exactly equal to the interest rate spread:

$$(i_A > i_{US}) = \frac{(E_s > E_f)}{E_s};$$

$$(i_A < i_{US}) = \frac{(E_s < E_f)}{E_s}.$$

2. When $NI \neq 0$, interest arbitrage will occur and covered funds will move to the country for which the favorable (unfavorable) interest rate spread exceeds (falls short of) the forward discount (premium) on its currency until the inflow of funds lowers the interest rate in that country and raises the forward discount on its currency to the point where $NI = 0$.

3. Given interest rate differentials between countries, the direction and magnitude of international capital flows are affected by the relationship between spot and forward exchange rates. Capital may not always flow to the country that has the highest interest rates. At times, countries have attempted to regulate international capital flows by acting on the cost of forward cover rather than on domestic interest rates. Some evidence has been generated to indicate that, on the average, short-term capital is more sensitive to covered interest rate differentials, while long-term capital is more sensitive to uncovered rate differentials.

The existence of an inverse relationship between the interest rate spread and the cost of forward cover can be seen from the data. The spread in interest rates on three-month Treasury bills between the U.S. and the United Kingdom is plotted in Figure 18-4 (top section) from 1969 through 1971. Throughout almost the entire period, rates were higher in London. Also throughout most of this period, the three-month forward British pound sold at a discount relative to its spot rate. In the first third of the period, the forward discount was greater than the interest rate spread and the net incentive was negative and away from the high interest rate center, London, and in favor of New York (bottom section). In the middle third of the period, the cost of forward sterling cover declined sharply and almost exactly offset the favorable interest rate. The net incentive to transfer capital between New York and London on a covered basis was zero. In the final third, the premium on forward pounds reinforced the higher interest rates in the U.K. and there was a net incentive for covered short-term capital to flow from the U.S. to the U.K.

Eurodollars

Eurodollars are deposits, generally time deposits, at European banks or branches of U.S. banks denominated in U.S. dollars. In contrast, the large majority of deposits at these banks are denominated in the respective local currency. Banks accepting Eurodollars maintain dollar reserves against these deposits at U.S. banks. Except for currency transfers, which loom small in the overall scope of international money transfers, U.S. dollars never leave domestic U.S. banks. Transfers of Eurodollars from one European bank to another result only in transfers of corresponding dollar balances from one U.S. bank to another, depending on where the paying and receiving European banks maintain their dollar reserves. The

Figure 18-4 **Interest Arbitrage: United States and United Kingdom**

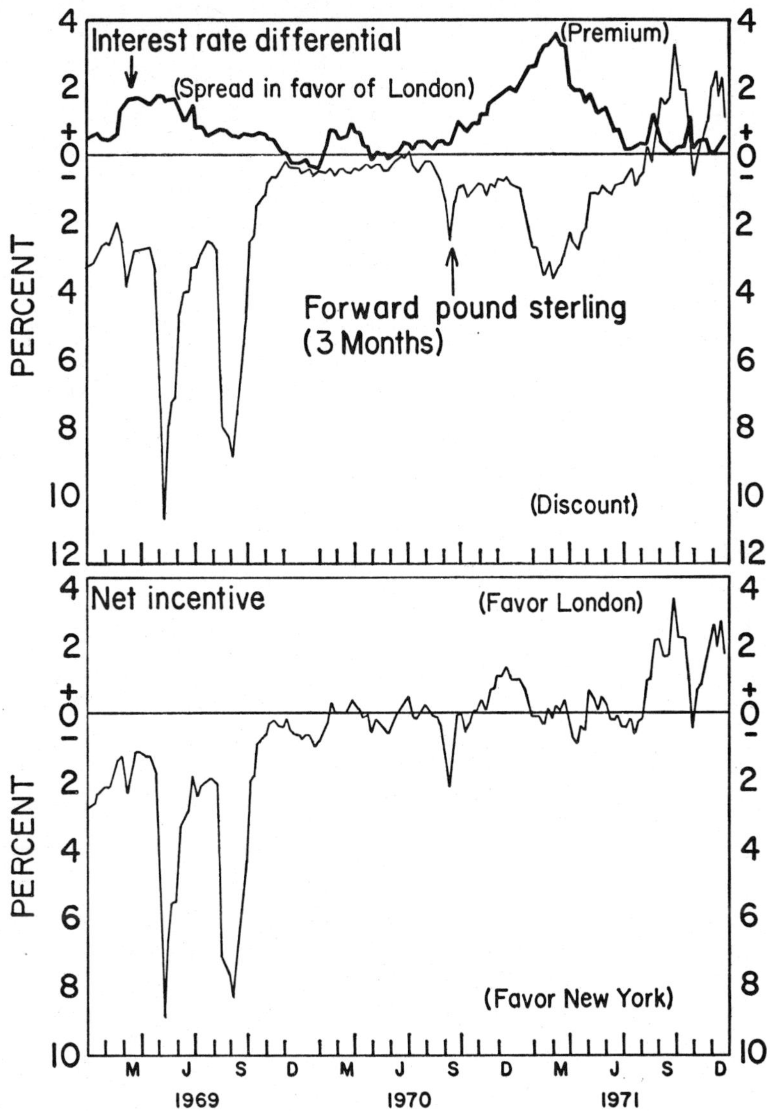

Source: Board of Governors of the Federal Reserve System, "Selected Interest and Exchange Rates for Major Countries and the U.S.," August 9, 1972.

funds may even remain at the same bank, if both European banks maintain their dollar accounts there.

Similar to the policies of U.S. banks, European banks will hold dollar reserves at U.S. banks equal to only a fraction of their dollar denominated deposits. Thus aggregate Eurodollar deposits may be a multiple of the amount of dollar reserves

Table 18-6 T-Accounts for Eurodollars

New York National Bank (U.S.)

Assets	Liabilities
Reserves	Deposits
Loans	London Bank
	All Others
	Capital

London Imperial Bank (U.K.)

Assets	Liabilities
Reserves	Deposits
Sterling at Bank of England	Sterling
Dollars at N.Y. National Bank	Dollars (Eurodollars)
Loans	Capital
Sterling	
Dollars (Eurodollars)	

the European banks have at U.S. banks. The T-accounts for a typical Eurodollar deposit are shown in Table 18-6. Eurodollars, similar to U.S. dollars, are related to U.S. bank reserves, but more indirectly through the dollar reserve balance the European bank maintains at its correspondent U.S. bank. The latter is required to maintain legal reserves against this deposit. Eurodollars are not part of the U.S. money supply.

Eurodollars have expanded rapidly since 1960 to become a major international currency for two main reasons. One, by conducting international transactions in the same currency, the costs of exchange transactions are reduced. Frequently, recipients of Eurodollars will maintain their proceeds in this form in anticipation of making payments abroad or of investing either domestically or abroad. Even if the funds are eventually converted into domestic currency, users need only consider a single dollar–domestic currency exchange rate rather than numerous exchange rates with different foreign currencies. Eurodollars are particularly amenable for use in searching out the optimum short-term investment opportunities among countries. Through their use, investors reduce spot exchange costs and bypass forward exchange costs and at least some of the restrictions on the convertibility of some currencies for capital transactions. Eurodollars have expedited the creation of an integrated world capital market in which borrowing occurs in countries with the lowest interest rates and lending in countries with the highest interest rates. Abstracting from search and transactions costs, uncovered international capital movements are induced until the rate differentials are

Table 18-7 **Eurodollars**
(Billion U.S. dollars)

	Year-end				
	1966	1967	1968	1969	1970
Sources					
United States	1.1	1.7	3.2	3.8	4.2
Western Europe	8.4	9.6	13.2	18.3	21.0
Rest of world	5.0	6.2	8.6	15.4	20.8
Uses					
United States	4.4	5.2	9.5	16.5	12.7
Western Europe	6.3	6.9	7.9	11.6	17.4
Rest of world	3.8	5.4	7.6	9.4	15.9
Total	14.5	17.5	25.0	37.5	46.0

Source: Bank for International Settlements, *Annual Report,* 1968/69, June, 1969, p. 149; and 1970/71, June, 1971, p. 164.

eliminated. In the process, the development of Eurodollars has added an additional constraint on the ability of countries to pursue independent domestic monetary policies under fixed exchange rates without experiencing payment imbalances.

Two, Eurodollars have been periodically used by U.S. banks to obtain funds in circumvention of Regulation Q ceilings on deposit rates. Deposits due overseas branches and foreign banks have been classified as borrowings by the Federal Reserve and exempted from Regulation Q and, until mid-1969, also from reserve requirements. At times when Q ceilings prevented U.S. banks from successfully bidding for domestic deposits, the banks increased their borrowings from abroad. This induced European banks and branches of U.S. banks, which are not constrained by Q ceilings, to offer higher interest rates on dollar deposits in order to attract dollars to rechannel to U.S. banks, creating Eurodollars in the process. Domestically, this resulted primarily in a reshuffling of reserves among U.S. banks. To the extent that the high rates offered by the European banks or branches attracted funds from the U.S., it increased the volume of Eurodollars outstanding.

The Eurodollar market has expanded rapidly in recent years. At year-end 1970, the amount of Eurodollars outstanding was triple the level of four years earlier and almost double that of two years earlier. The influence exerted by U.S. banks can be clearly identified from Table 18-7. Borrowings from European banks, shown as a use of Eurodollars, increased sharply during the two periods of high interest rates in the United States—1966, and again in 1968-69. In the latter period, U.S. bank use of Eurodollars accounted for more than 40 percent of the total use of these funds. U.S. takings of Eurodollars declined sharply in 1970, concurrent with the ability of U.S. banks to successfully market CDs again. Although all Eurodollars ultimately are derived from the U.S., the table identifies the source by the country of the immediate lender, say, a French exporter to the United States. In contrast to the substantial use made of the funds by U.S. residents, they supplied only about 10 percent of all Eurodollars. Europeans are the net suppliers of Eurodollars in recent years, lending more dollars to their banks than they borrow from them.

Eurodollars affect the U.S. balance of payments in two ways. First, high interest rates on Eurodollars may attract funds from the U.S. to European banks. Thus, the market increases U.S. short-term liabilities abroad, which, however, are offset by short-term claims abroad. To the extent that these dollar liabilities remain in private hands, the U.S. balance of payments is not affected. Second, the high interest rates may lead to a shift of dollar balances already owned by foreign countries from official government hands to private ownership as these governments intervene in the exchange markets to dampen the upward pressures on the dollar. As a result, reserves of foreign central banks decline, pressures on the U.S. gold stock are eased, and the official settlements account of the U.S. balance of payments becomes more favorable. As Eurodollar rates decline, private holdings would be unwound, the dollars would again be absorbed by the central banks, pressure on the U.S. gold stock would increase, and the surpluses on the official settlements balance regress into offsetting deficits. As already noted in Chapter 17, surpluses in the official settlements account were recorded in 1966, 1968, and 1969, when interest rates on Eurodollars were high, and deficits were recorded in 1967 and 1970, when the rates declined sharply.

References

Clark, Peter B., and Herbert G. Grubel, "National Monetary Sovereignty Under Different Exchange Rate Regimes," *The Bulletin* (New York University, Institute of Finance), Nos. 78-79, January, 1972.

Crump, Norman, *The ABC of the Foreign Exchanges* (London: Macmillan, 1958).

Federal Reserve Bank of Boston, *The International Adjustment Mechanism* (Boston: 1969).

Fleming, J. Marcus, *The International Monetary Fund* (Washington, D.C.: International Monetary Fund, 1964).

Friedman, Milton, "The Euro-Dollar Market: Some First Principles," *The Morgan Guaranty Survey*, October, 1969, 4-14.

———, et al., *The Futures Market in Foreign Currencies* (Chicago: International Monetary Market, 1972).

Gold, Joseph, *Special Drawing Rights, Character and Uses*, Second edition (Washington, D.C.: International Monetary Fund, 1970).

Holmes, Alan R., and Francis H. Schott, *The New York Foreign Exchange Market* (New York: Federal Reserve Bank of New York, 1965).

International Monetary Fund, *Annual Report* (Washington, D.C.: various years).

Johnson, Harry G., "The Case for Flexible Exchange Rates, 1969," *Review* (Federal Reserve Bank of St. Louis), 51 (6), June, 1969, 12-24.

Katz, Samuel I., *The Case for the Par-Value System, 1972* (Princeton University, Essays in International Finance), No. 92, March, 1972.

Kvasnicka, Joseph G., "Eurodollars—An Important Source of Funds for American Banks," *Business Conditions* (Federal Reserve Bank of Chicago), June, 1969, 9-20.

League of Nations, *International Currency Experience* (New York: United Nations, 1947).

Machlup, Fritz, and Burton G. Malkiel, *International Monetary Arrangements: The Problem of Choice* (Princeton: Princeton University Press, International Finance Section, 1967).

Mundell, Robert, "Towards a Better International Monetary System," *Journal of Money, Banking, and Credit,* 1 (3), August, 1969, 625-648.

Sarsoun, Lawrence C., *The Foreign Currency Futures Handbook* (Chicago: Heinhold Commodities, Inc., 1972).

Yeager, Leland B., *International Monetary Relations* (New York: Harper & Row, 1966).

PART VII

Monetary Policy

Controversies in Monetary Policy—1

19

Until now, we have emphasized what we know about the economy and monetary policy. In this chapter and the next, we will discuss some of the areas we do not know and in which there are disagreements and controversies. Controversy exists because the empirical evidence to date, some of which has been reviewed in the preceding chapters, has been insufficient to differentiate among competing theories to everyone's satisfaction. Thus, there is more than one explanation for many economic problems.

Conflicts in Goals

As has become evident throughout this book, economic policy attempts to achieve a large number of different objectives. For monetary policy, these objectives can be classified into three major groups:

1. Ultimate Objectives
   a. Full employment
   b. Price stability
   c. Economic growth
   d. Equilibrium in balance of payments
2. Sectoral Objectives
   a. High level of residential construction
   b. High level of state and local spending
   c. Solvency of financial thrift institutions

3. Short-Term Objectives
   a. Stability in financial markets
   b. Accommodation of Treasury financings.

The specific objectives cited under each major category are only illustrative and do not represent an exhaustive listing. The ultimate objectives of policy were discussed in Chapter 1. Here we will discuss briefly the other objectives and then explore the problems involved in achieving all objectives simultaneously.

Sectoral Objectives

Primarily for social reasons, all sectors in the economy are not equal. High levels of performance in some sectors are deemed more socially desirable than high levels of performance in others. Among sectors commonly assigned high social priority are:

Residential Construction. Adequate housing for all citizens has been explicitly recognized as a national goal in this country since the Housing Act of 1949. The Housing Act of 1968 extended this general objective and established annual targets for the number of houses to be constructed and rehabilitated over the subsequent decade. Residential construction is of particular concern to the monetary authorities because it is financed almost totally through borrowed funds. Curtailment of flows into mortgages will be reflected almost proportionately in curtailed housing starts.

Municipal Expenditures. Many of the expenditures of state and local governments, such as on education, health, welfare, and safety, are generally assigned high social priority. To the extent that these expenditures are financed through borrowed funds, the cost and availability of funds to state and local governments is of concern to the Federal Reserve.

Thrift Institutions. The well-being of thrift institutions is of concern to the Federal Reserve for three reasons. First, these institutions hold a large portion of the liquid savings of the economy and large-scale failures would result in severe contractions in national spending and income. Second, these institutions provide a majority of all mortgage funds in the country. Curtailment of inflows into thrift institutions is thereby reflected in curtailment of mortgage loans and the number of new housing starts.

Lastly, by borrowing short and lending long, thrift institutions encounter financial problems when short-term rates increase more than had been expected by the institutions. Because, as discussed in Chapter 9, long-term rates are, in part, an average of current and expected short-term rates, underestimation of future deposit rates results in charging lower than break-even long-term mortgage loan rates, in losses, and in an inability to finance competitive deposit rates. This, in turn, leads, at a minimum, to a slowdown in deposit inflows and threatens the continued operation of the institutions. However, the failure to correctly predict future interest rates is not always evidenced by, and should be distinguished from, the narrowing and even reversal of the spread between mortgage loan rates and deposit rates paid by these institutions near peaks in economic expansions. For the most part, such a pattern is perfectly normal and not of major concern. If the institution predicted rates correctly, any losses it might experience at these times are offset by the gains it experienced earlier, when deposit rates were further below mortgage rates, and should cause the institution, at most, only temporary problems. But, as mortgage loans are long term and accuracy in predicting is inversely related to the length of the period to be predicted, the probabilities of thrift institutions incorrectly predicting deposit rates is relatively high.

A high level of inflows into thrift institutions is generally considered desirable both to maintain high mortgage flows and to permit continued viable operations of the institutions.

Short-Term Objectives

Ultimate and sectoral objectives are important for their own sakes. Short-term objectives are typically for the sake of achieving other—ultimate and sectoral—objectives.

Stability in Financial Markets. Wide and abrupt short-term swings in interest rates tend to introduce uncertainties, confuse expectations, and limit the use of financial markets and, thereby, reduce and interrupt the flow of funds from DSUs to SSUs. In addition, wide short-term variability in interest rates may induce temporary, and therefore inefficient and costly, movements of real resources.

Accommodation of Treasury Financings. Central banks in almost every country have the ultimate responsibility of assuring the successful marketing of new issues of government securities and maintaining continuity in the market for outstanding issues. It is widely believed that permitting a Treasury financing to fail, in terms of insufficient bids to absorb the entire issue, would have detrimental implications both at home and abroad for the credit rating of the federal government and for the success of future debt marketings.

Conflicts

Experience indicates that, while it may be possible to achieve all the objectives of policy in the long run, they may not be mutually consistent in the shorter run. We have already noted inconsistencies among some of the major ultimate objectives, which make it difficult to achieve them at the same time. If the Phillips curve is accepted, at least in the short run, improvements in employment may only be achieved at the cost of additional price pressures and, vice versa, improvements in price stability may only be achieved at the cost of a deterioration in employment. Likewise, to the extent that international capital flows are sensitive to interest rates, countries experiencing price stability and surpluses in current account may still experience deficits in the overall balance of payments, if sufficient funds flow abroad in response to inflation-generated higher rates of interest. Full employment may also conflict with rapid economic growth, which is dependent on the acceptance of innovation and change, if maintenance of full employment encourages reliance on the status quo.

The difficulties of formulating monetary policy strategy when all the ultimate objectives are not mutually consistent can be seen from the following reaction function or function describing the forces to which the policy-makers respond. Assume that monetary policy actions can be summarized by the money supply (M_S), and that the stock of money is changed by the Federal Reserve both to accommodate the needs of trade, represented by Y, and to achieve target levels of real income, y_T, unemployment, U_T, prices, P_T, and balance of payments surplus, B_T. This can be written:

$$M_S = f[\overset{+}{Y}, (y_T \overset{+}{-} y), (U_T \overset{-}{-} U), (P_T \overset{+}{-} P), (B_T \overset{-}{-} B)]. \tag{19-1}$$

The Federal Reserve increases the stock of money whenever Y increases, y and P decline below their target values, and U and B rise above their target values. Vice versa, the Federal Reserve decreases the stock of money when Y declines, y and P rise above their target values, and U and B fall below. Values of P below P_T and B above B_T are not so much positive reasons for expanding the money supply as for the removal of constraints on the expansion of the money supply. It is obvious that, if the goal variables do not all change in a consistent direction, there is no change in the money supply that can simultaneously generate target values for all the variables.

Aggregate goals may also be inconsistent with sectoral goals. Attainment of sectoral goals requires promoting conditions conducive to large flows of funds into the desired sectors. Ceteris paribus, the demand for expenditures in these sectors is greater, the lower interest rates are. Full employment, however, is generally accompanied by cyclically high interest rates. Both residential construction and municipal government borrowing tend to be particularly sensitive to interest rates, primarily because they are for long-lived assets, which are considered postponable by the individual buyers for some time. High interest rates also work hardships on thrift institutions, either temporarily from their maturity intermediation function or more permanently because of underestimates of the rate increases.

Thus, full employment in the economy as a whole is frequently accompanied by less than desired levels of spending in some sectors, such as residential construction and municipal governments, and by financial difficulties for thrift institutions. Conversely, when the economy is operating at less than overall full employment, other than in an outright depression, activity in residential construction and municipal government spending is usually relatively high and thrift institutions apparently profitable and expanding rapidly. Moreover, policy actions to achieve high levels of residential construction and local government spending by maintaining low interest rates may result in unsatisfactory overall price performance arising out of the continually faster rate of monetary expansion required to maintain interest rates at these levels. By inducing expectations of faster price increases on interest rates, such policies may also ultimately generate higher nominal interest rates and lower levels of performance in these sectors than otherwise.

Conflicts may also arise between the concurrent achievement of full employment and of the short-term objectives of financial market stability and accommodating Treasury financings. High interest rates in consequence of full employment depress bond prices and may discourage some market participants from continuing in the markets. These rates also increase the cost of new or refinanced Treasury debt, a change no more popular with the Treasury than with private debtors.

Proposed Conflict Resolutions

If all the objectives of monetary policy are not mutually attainable, tradeoffs among the goals must be considered and each objective must be ranked with respect to its relative importance. The rankings are the responsibility of the Board of Governors and the Federal Open Market Committee. Because rankings are, by necessity, value judgments, the relative ordering is generally highly controversial. The problem is further complicated by the lack of widely accepted definitions for the goals. Is full employment equivalent to an unemployment rate of 3, 4, or 5 percent? Does price stability mean 0, 2, or 4 percent annual rates of increases in prices? Is stability in financial markets achieved only if there are no fluctuations whatsoever in interest rates? Does adequate housing for all citizens imply 2 million, 3 million, or more housing starts annually? A trade of a one percentage point increase in unemployment from 3 to 4 percent for greater stability in prices may be more acceptable if full employment is defined as 5 percent unemployment rather than as 2 percent.

Dissatisfaction with monetary policy may arise for two different reasons: dissatisfaction with the priority ranking of goals by the policy-makers and dissatisfaction with the policy strategy formulated to achieve a particular ordering of goals. The latter dissatisfaction reflects differences in the underlying theory describing the transmission mechanism and can be resolved only through additional empirical testing of competing hypotheses. The first dissatisfaction reflects disagreement over value judgments and can be resolved only by changing the identity and organization of the policy-makers.

Critics of the goal-ordering employed by the Federal Reserve have suggested that the System be made both more and less independent of the administration. Those that believe it should be less independent argue that the president alone has the full responsibility for the economic welfare of the country and is evaluated by how well the economy performs. Yet he does not have direct control over one of the two major instruments of economic policy. Among other proposals, these individuals recommend that the Federal Reserve be transferred to the Treasury Department, that the members of the Board of Governors serve for shorter terms and at the pleasure of the president, that the System obtain appropriations from Congress, that the presidents of the reserve banks be removed from policy-making committees, and that the vestiges of private bank ownership of the district reserve banks be terminated.

On the other hand, proponents of greater independence for the Federal Reserve System have recommended increasing the policy powers of the reserve bank presidents, decreasing the role of Congress and the president in appointing members of the Board of Governors, and moving the headquarters of the System out of Washington, D.C.

In addition, numerous recommendations have been proposed over the years emphasizing changes in the organization of the System directed not at limiting its independence but at increasing its policy efficiency. Such proposals call for reducing the size of the Board of Governors from seven to five, three, and even one; collapsing the duties of the Board and the Open Market Committee; and transferring nonmonetary policy functions, such as bank regulation and supervision, to other bank supervisory agencies, such as the Federal Deposit Insurance Corporation, the Comptroller of the Currency, or a newly created agency charged solely with bank regulation and supervision.

Although many changes have been proposed, no change of great importance in the organization or structure of the Federal Reserve System has been adopted since the Banking Act of 1935. As all changes have to be enacted by the Congress, this suggests, at minimum, general satisfaction with the performance of the System, lack of agreement as to the type of structure and reorganization that would generate the desired changes in goal priorities, or lack of agreement on the rankings of the goal priorities.

Figure 19-1 Elasticities Depicting Impotent Monetary Policy

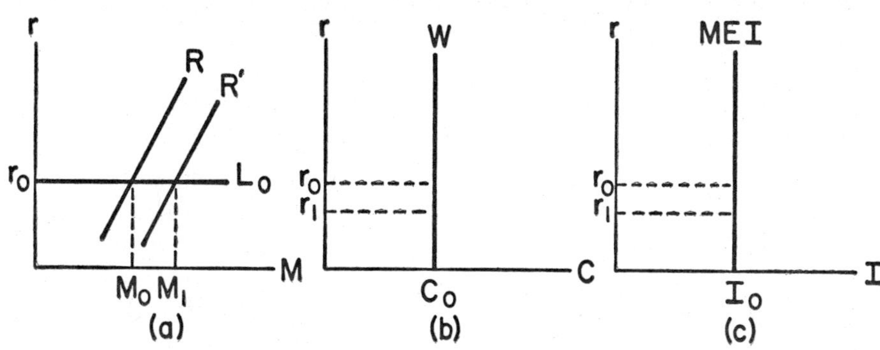

The Strength of Monetary Policy

The efficacy of monetary policy depends on the strength and speed with which the initial impact of the policy actions is transmitted throughout the economy to the ultimate policy objectives. In the simple model of the economy developed in Chapter 15, monetary policy actions pass through three sectors before affecting aggregate income and prices—the financial sector, the consumption sector, and the investment sector. As discussed at the time, the strength of a monetary policy action is affected by the elasticities in each of these sectors. Economists who doubt the potency of monetary policy postulate a series of elasticities that absorb almost the entire impact of a policy action before it can reach the ultimate targets. In the extreme, such a series of elasticities is shown in Figure 19-1. The demand for money is perfectly interest-elastic, while both consumption and investment spending are perfectly interest-inelastic. Although not shown, consumption is also assumed to be perfectly wealth-inelastic. Under these conditions, changes in the supply of money in consequence of Federal Reserve actions on reserves, as evidenced by shifts in the supply schedule in (*a*) from *R* to *R′*, have no effect whatsoever on interest rates. Even if they did, interest rate changes would have no effect on consumption and investment spending, as shown in (*b*) and (*c*), and thereby have no effect on income.

Obviously, those who postulate a significant influence to monetary policy assume a different set of elasticities. They view the demand for money to be relatively interest-inelastic and the consumption and investment schedules to be relatively interest- and wealth-elastic. The more interest-inelastic the demand for money and the more interest-elastic consumption and investment spending, the stronger the impact of a given monetary policy action on aggregate income will be. Because they view the impact of changes in the money supply on aggregate income as occurring through each and every sector, monetarists are primarily concerned with the properties of the demand for money schedule rather than those of the spending schedules. The following sections briefly review the empirical evidence with respect to the interest elasticity of each of these schedules.

The Demand for Money

While the Keynesian concept of an absolute liquidity trap or perfect interest elasticity at low levels of interest rates had considerable appeal during the depression and immediate postdepression period, such low interest rates have occurred only rarely in American history and the observations have been too few to generate convincing evidence in favor of such a property of the money demand function. At least equally convincing evidence exists in support of a competing hypothesis that banks and the public became increasingly cautious in the 1930s and continuously increased their demands for money in consequence of the threat of, and recent experiences with, the failure of banks and nonbanking firms. At least one reason for the difficulties in distinguishing between the two hypotheses is shown in Figure 19-2. At any point in time, only the intersection of the demand and supply schedules is observable, not the schedules themselves. If the intertemporal equilibrium points—where progressively farther out demand for money schedules intersect progressively farther out supply of money schedules—suggested by the latter hypothesis are connected, the result resembles a single demand schedule with a liquidity trap, as suggested by the Keynesian hypothesis. In the absence of additional evidence, points along a stable demand schedule are indistinguishable from points generated by shifts in the schedules. If the observed equilibrium points reflect shifting schedules, the Federal Reserve could have decreased interest rates further in the 1930s by increasing reserves further. If the points represent a stable demand schedule, lower interest rates could not have been achieved by such a policy.

Most recent research on the demand for money has been directed at generating evidence for the range of interest rates experienced in the postwar period. With the primary exception of studies by Professor Friedman, these studies have found the demand for money to be significantly affected by interest rates in an inverse direction. The interest elasticities have generally been found to be less than 1. A recent survey by the Bank of England of some 25 empirical studies of the demand for money in both the U.S. and U.K. reported that only a small minority of the studies estimated interest elasticities either greater than -1.0 or less than -0.1. This evidence suggests that the demand for money is sufficiently interest-inelastic to generate marked interest rate changes in response to moderate changes in the money supply.

The postulated interest elasticity also has significant implications for the efficacy of fiscal policy. If the demand for and supply of money are both perfectly interest-elastic, increases in income generated by expansive fiscal actions would have no effect on interest rates. Income would also be perfectly interest-elastic.

Figure 19-2 **Alternative Explanations of the "Liquidity Trap" of the 1930s**

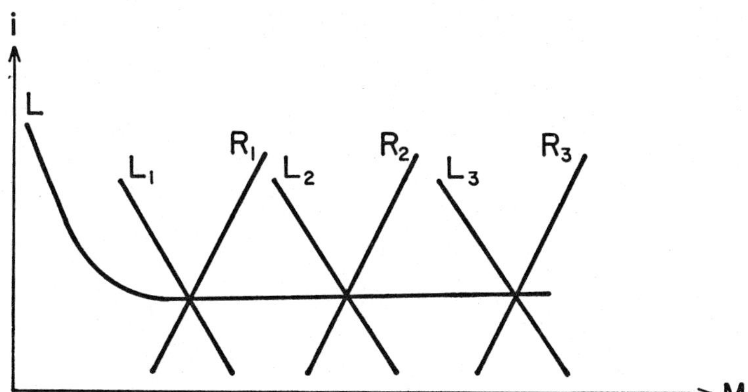

As there would be no dampening secondary effects, fiscal policy would be highly effective in raising nominal income. If, on the other hand, the demand for, as well as the supply of, money were perfectly interest-inelastic, then income is constrained by the existing stock of money. Any increase in spending generated by expansive fiscal actions, without a concurrent increase in the money supply, would only raise interest rates to the level where other private spending is curtailed by a like amount.

Consumption

Most single equation estimates of the consumption function have reported little or no effect of observed interest rates on consumption expenditures. These studies have generated somewhat greater evidence of a significant effect on consumption expenditures, particularly on durable goods, such as automobiles, by the terms of credit, which importantly affect the implicit price of credit. A more recent study has also found a significant but long-delayed effect of interest rates on consumer expenditures for durable goods. The FRB-MIT model does not specify interest rates directly in its overall consumption function, although rates do enter in allocating total consumption among the different components.

Evidence in favor of a strong wealth effect on consumption expenditures, particularly on nondurable expenditures, is recent. Until the FRB-MIT model, the link between wealth and interest rates was not incorporated explicitly. Thus, the previous studies failed to delineate an important channel through which monetary policy actions affect consumption. The FRB-MIT model suggests that the larger part of the impact of monetary policy on consumption is transmitted through changes in wealth.

In sum, the empirical evidence supports the view that the consumption function is sufficiently interest-elastic and particularly wealth-elastic to respond to and transmit the effects of monetary policy.

Investment

Evidence of significant interest rate effects on investment spending has also been uncovered only recently. Early studies primarily surveyed businessmen and found that, on the whole, interest rates were represented as only a small part of the cost of plant and equipment and were not considered to play an instrumental role in the investment decision. These findings were supported by statistical studies that were unable to identify a significant relationship between rates and investment spending. More recent studies, however, have tended to confirm the interest sensitivity of investment spending.

The success of these studies, in contrast to the earlier ones, may be attributed to three factors: (1) advances in statistical techniques, (2) the theoretical and empirical introduction of time lags in the estimating equations, and (3) differentiation between observed and real interest rates. Because interest rates are closely correlated with aggregate income and sales, early studies experienced difficulties in differentiating between these effects. Often the interest rate effect was statistically disguised in the income or sales effects. It appears reasonable that changes in financial conditions will affect investment decisions only slowly through time. Except for inventory and small-ticket durable purchases, investment decisions involve considerable time from the point of initial consideration to the point of final expenditures. Thus, the effects of changes in interest rates on investment spending should be observed in later, not concurrent, periods. Evidence of such lagged relationships have been found in those studies that have specified them. Lastly, the inflation of recent years, accompanied in its early years by increasing investment spending, has reemphasized that most business firms consider real, not observed, interest rates in their investment strategy.

A continuing inability of survey studies to find interest rates important probably reflects the preoccupation of the respondents with other, more important and obvious, factors affecting investment spending, such as changes in sales and in the availability of capital goods from suppliers. Moreover, many respondents emphasize that expected price increases outweigh interest rates in their investment decisions, suggesting that they are discussing their reactions to nominal and not real rates. To the extent that monetary policy affects sales through influencing consumption expenditures, investment spending is indirectly affected.

Economic theory suggests that the effects of interest rates are not the same for all types of investment. Interest rates should have greater effects the longer the expected life of the investment project. This appears to be borne out by the evidence, which suggests less definite effects on business inventory spending than on business or residential construction.

Investment was considered the key sector in the early Keynesian models, which did not view consumption as highly interest-elastic. However, the early evidence of an interest-inelastic investment function also convinced many Keynesians that, even if the demand for money were not highly interest-elastic and monetary policy could affect interest rates, policy actions would only have a small effect on investment. Nevertheless, because they considered investment the driving force in the economy and, while possibly interest-inelastic, more interest-elastic and responsive to monetary policy than consumption, Keynesians installed the interest rate as a key variable in their models. Monetarists, on the other hand, view the transmission process as affecting all sectors through changes in relative prices and consider interest rate effects on investment as no more or less significant than any other price effect.

Lags in the Effect of Monetary Policy

Monetary policy may be used to achieve both cyclical and secular goals. However, to be effective for cyclical or stabilization use, monetary policy must not only be potent, it must also affect economic activity within a time period shorter than the period within which the economy would reverse course in the absence of policy actions. That is, the time delay between the time the need for policy action is recognized and the time the effects of the resulting action are felt by the economy must be short in comparison with the length of the phase of the cycle. Expansionary monetary actions contribute to stabilization only if the major portion of the policy effects are absorbed when the economy is operating at less than full employment and restrictive monetary actions contribute only at times the economy is operating at inflationary levels. At all other times, the policy action would reinforce rather than offset the destabilizing forces. Besides being short, the lag must also be predictable so that the appropriate type and strength of action may be selected.

The overall lag in monetary policy may be divided into three components:

1. the *recognition lag,* or the time lag between the need for economic policy action and the recognition of this need by the policy-makers,
2. the *action lag,* or the time between the recognition of the need for policy action by the policy-makers and the taking of action, and
3. the *impact lag,* or the time lag between the taking of a policy action and the subsequent impact of the action on the ultimate goals of economic policy.

The lags are shown schematically in Figure 19-3. The first two lags are frequently combined and referred to as the *inside lag,* reflecting their involvement with the policy-making process rather than with the structure of the economy, while the third lag is referred to as the *outside lag.*

The recognition lag relates to the ability of policy-makers to accurately interpret or predict economic developments in need of correction by economic policy actions. The longer the time required for policy-makers to become aware of unde-

Figure 19-3 **Schematic of the Lags of Monetary and Fiscal Policy**

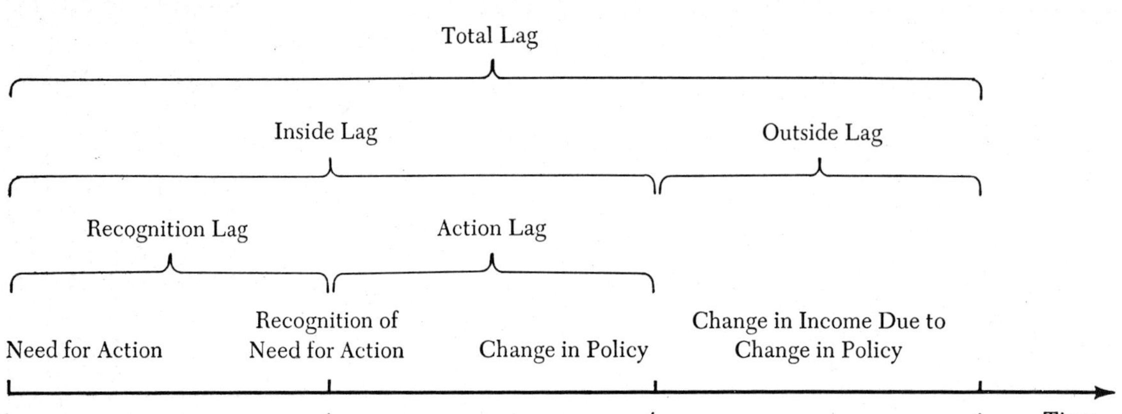

Source: Willes, "Lags in Monetary and Fiscal Policies," p. 3.

sirable economic trends, the longer the time slippage in initiating action. The greater the ability of policy-makers to predict developments, the faster can action be initiated. Prediction is the key to the length of this lag. With sufficient ability to predict, the need for corrective action can be identified before the developments themselves occur and the lag would be negative. Because much data on economic developments are available only with some delay, even interpretation of ongoing developments frequently requires some forecasting.

The action lag relates to the ability of policy-makers to select and implement a course of action or policy strategy after recognizing the need for such action. The length of this lag is affected by such factors as the number of policy-makers, the frequency of meetings, the nature of the decision-making process, and other competing duties and responsibilities of the policy-makers. The length of the impact or outside lag is determined by the transmission linkages described earlier and is a function of the speed with which a policy action is transmitted along this mechanism. Thus, it reflects the structure of the economy.

Estimates of the length of the three lags, either individually or combined, differ widely. A summary of representative estimates of a number of empirical studies is shown in Table 19-1. The recognition lag is generally considered to be quite short, at most about three months. As data collection and accuracy improve, this lag may approach zero. Further shortening is possible through improved forecasting techniques. The action lag is also generally estimated to be quite short for monetary policy. Once the Board of Governors or the Federal Open Market Committee recognized the need for action, it typically has responded within the same month. It should be noted, however, that the taking of action does not imply that

Table 19-1 **Range of Estimates of the Average Lags of Monetary and Fiscal Policy**
(Months)

Policy	Inside Lag		Outside Lag	Total Lag
	Recognition Lag	Action Lag		
Monetary Policy	3	0	1-20	4-23
Fiscal Policy	3	1-15	1-3	5-21

Source: Willes, "Lags in Monetary and Fiscal Policy," p. 7.

the action taken was either correct or effective. As we will see later, some economists believe that, while possibly acting quickly, the Federal Reserve has frequently acted incorrectly.

Estimates of the impact or outside lag are the most tenuous and controversial. The empirical estimates are hampered by a number of factors. Unlike the recognition and action lags, the impact lag is not a discrete lag in the sense that action is taken in time periot t and the entire impact felt on, say, aggregate income n periods later in period $t+n$. Rather the impact is distributed through time. Some of the effects may be immediate, while others may not be felt until considerably later. This makes the lag difficult to quantify. Statistical measures of the lag generally rely on single-valued summary measures. For example, these measures provide estimates of the period between the time of the action and the time the strongest subsequent impact on a policy objective is observed, or of the time lapse between the action and the subsequent observation of a specified proportion of the ultimate impact on an objective, say 50 or 75 percent.

Second, as discussed earlier, the process by which the effects of policy actions are transmitted has not been mapped to everyone's complete satisfaction. Thus, at times, it is treacherous to associate a particular change in an objective variable with a particular policy action taken some time before and in some sector removed from the final effect. Third, the duration of the impact lag may be related to the magnitude of the policy action. Stronger actions may be transmitted through the economy faster than weaker actions. Lastly, the relationship between monetary policy action and impact may not be stable and may change through time. Averages of past lags may then be poor clues to the length of any particular future lag.

The earliest investigations of the impact lag simply related changes in either the money supply or interest rates with changes in national income in single equations. Changes in the money supply were found to be most closely correlated

Table 19-2 **Business Cycle Expansions and Contractions, 1854-1972**
(Months)

Complete Cycles	Contraction (trough from previous peak)	Expansion (trough to peak)
Average 27 cycles	19	33
Average 5 postwar cycles	11	49
Longest Expansion: Feb. 1961–Nov. 1969		105

Source: U.S. Department of Commerce, *Business Conditions Digest,* June, 1972, p. 114.

with changes in nominal income some six to nine months afterwards. By relating changes in the rate of growth of money with turning points in the business cycle, Friedman estimated longer lags of about 15 months. Moreover, he found the lag to be highly variable and considered the estimates too unreliable to be useful for policy formulation. Later studies obtained estimates of the impact lag on larger econometric models. The monetarist Federal Reserve Bank of St. Louis model estimated reasonably short time lags of six to nine months. The FRB-MIT model generated somewhat longer lags. Fifty percent of the ultimate effect on real income of an increase in total reserves or a decrease in the discount rate was found to occur only after nine months, and 75 percent after 15 months. The model also indicates that the length of the lag is related to the variable on which the Federal Reserve operates. Somewhat longer lags are obtained when the Federal Reserve operates on unborrowed reserves rather than on total reserves.

Summing the estimates of the three individual lags yields estimates of the overall lag in monetary policy of some 8 to 20 months from the occurrence of the event requiring corrective action to the time when the major strength of the impact of the action accumulates.

This estimate of the length of the overall lag can be evaluated with respect to the effectiveness of monetary policy for stabilization by comparing it with the length of economic expansions and contractions. Between 1854, the year data on business cycles was first recorded, and 1972, the United States experienced 27 complete business cycles of varying durations. The average length of the periods of expansion was 33 months and of the periods of contraction 19 months (Table 19-2). In the postwar period, the average expansion was lengthened by nearly 50 percent over the prewar average and the average contraction almost cut by half to 11 months. A considerable part of the substantial lengthening of the average period of expansion, however, is attributed to the record 105-months period of continued economic growth encompassing the greater part of the 1960s, a period three times the duration of the average period of expansion.

These data would suggest that the lag in monetary policy is sufficiently short for monetary policy to be used effectively in curtailing overly exuberant expansions, but that policy must be used much more carefully in offsetting economic contractions, particularly if recessions continue to become briefer. The fact that the average postwar recession appears to be considerably shorter than the lag in monetary policy does not, by itself, rule out antirecessionary monetary policy. Some of the effects will be felt quickly. In addition, unless the subsequent expansion is very rapid, the tail-end effects of the stimulative policies will continue to make a positive contribution. If the expansion is rapid, the Federal Reserve could take quick restrictive actions to offset the remaining expansionary effects of the earlier policy.

It may also be possible to reduce the length of the inside lag. As discussed previously, improved forecasting could generate a negative recognition lag. If it were possible to accurately forecast six months in advance, the overall lag could be reduced by about nine months or almost one-half.

Nevertheless, at least some economists believe that the overall lag is too long for monetary policy to be effective as a stabilization control. The leading proponent of this minority view is Professor Friedman, who reinforces his argument by citing his evidence that the lag is also highly variable, making accurate prediction of the impact of policy difficult, and that the linkages are not sufficiently understood to permit policy-makers to formulate appropriate policy strategy.

While monetary policy operates with reasonably long lags, fiscal policy appears to have at least equally long overall lags. However, the relative distribution of the overall lag among the three component lags differs significantly for the two policies. In contrast to monetary policy, which has short inside lags and long outside lags, fiscal policy is estimated to have long inside lags and short outside lags, although some economists question the briefness of the outside lag. The major delay in fiscal policy is the action lag reflecting the inherently slow political process through which proposals for changes in government tax rates and spending must pass. For example, the reduction in personal and corporate income taxes enacted by Congress in mid-1968 was first recommended by the president in early 1967 and reiterated in midyear. The long delay in enacting this legislation appears to have substantially reduced the anti-inflationary effectiveness of the action. Thus, unless the action lag can be reduced significantly, fiscal policy appears to be less effective in combating short cycles than monetary policy.

The Effects of Near-Monies on Monetary Policy

In earlier chapters, we discussed some of the difficulties of delineating the set of financial assets to be included in the definition of money supply. Most commonly, only assets that serve as a medium of exchange are considered money. However, many financial assets have some of the attributes of money and, if they can be readily and cheaply converted into money, are fairly good substitutes both for money and for each other in wealth portfolios. These include savings deposits at thrift institutions, U.S. Treasury savings bonds, cash value of life insurance policies, and possibly short-term marketable high-quality debt securities and mutual fund shares. Similar to changes in money, changes in the amount and composition of near-monies may be expected to affect aggregate spending and income.

In the postwar period, most near-monies have expanded considerably faster than the money supply (Figure 19-4). Because Federal Reserve operations are directed primarily at commercial bank reserves and deposits, the rapid growth of near-monies has caused some economists to be concerned about the effectiveness of restrictive monetary policy. These economists argue that, at the times when the Federal Reserve curtails bank reserve expansion and interest rates rise, the private capital market and nonbank financial intermediaries can quickly bid deposits away from commercial banks, which are frequently constrained by interest rate ceilings, and provide the credit the banks are not able to extend. In short, the Federal Reserve can affect primarily only the mix of total credit between bank and nonbank credit but cannot greatly affect the total amount of credit. At the time this hypothesis was initially introduced, only commercial banks were subject to interest rate ceilings on deposits.

An analogous argument focused on changes in velocity. As the Federal Reserve curtails reserves, and therefore the money supply, interest rates rise and spending units increasingly substitute higher-yielding liquid assets for either non-interest-bearing demand deposits or for lower-yielding bank time deposits. At the same time, they do not cut back on their overall spending. As a result, the average dollar is used more intensively and velocity rises. The increase in velocity was postulated to partially or completely offset the restrictive impact of the curtailment of the money supply and thereby the potency of monetary policy.

While theoretically appealing, the evidence in support of these hypotheses is not very convincing. Contrary to the hypotheses, near-banks have tended to expand faster in periods of recession and expansionary monetary policy than in periods of prosperity and more restrictive policy. Moreover, the credit extended by nonbank institutions differs in many respects from that extended by banks. A large steel company could hardly expect to replace a bank loan at a savings and loan association, which specializes in residential mortgage lending. In the above example, however, the steel company may obtain a loan from an insurance company or eventually raise funds by selling its own commercial paper on the private capital market. While all financial assets are substitutes, they are not perfect substitutes and do not have like effects on spending. This conclusion is supported by studies that found that the addition of liquid assets to bank deposits does not greatly increase the correlation between these financial assets and aggregate income.

Nor does the evidence suggest that, in the absence of interest rate ceilings, the flow of funds among competing types of financial institutions would be abrupt

Figure 19-4 Near-Monies Have Grown Faster Than the Money Supply

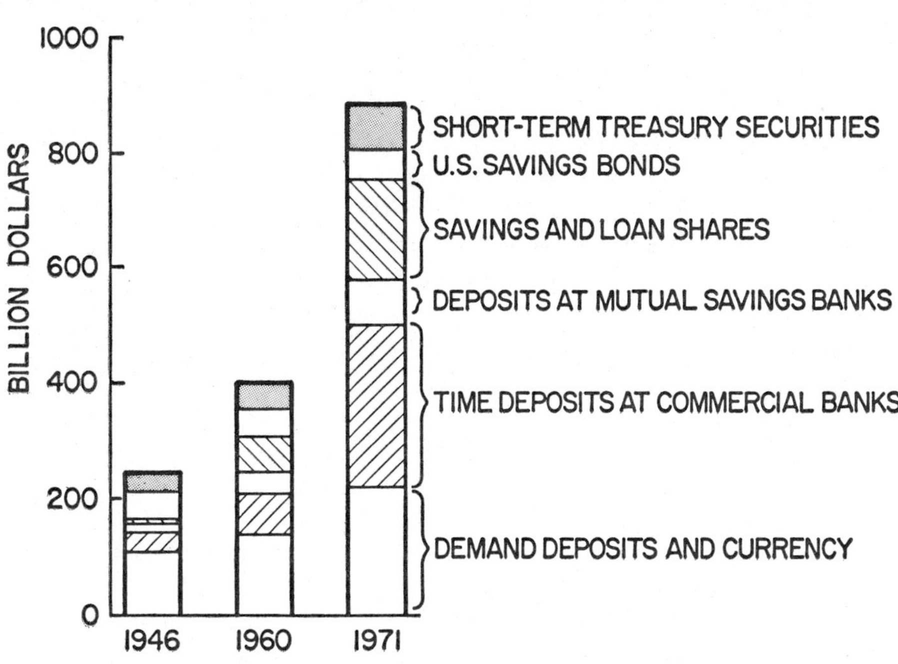

Source: Council of Economic Advisers, *Annual Report*, 1972, p. 260.

and unpredictable and greatly complicate the task of policy formulation. As noted earlier, in the mid-1960s rate ceilings on deposits were extended to thrift institutions, which had been depicted as the major avenue of escape. The experience since then suggests that the effects of the ceilings have been much more restrictive on these institutions than on the commercial banks. Rather than putting restrictive monetary policy out of business, the thrift institutions were themselves almost put out of business by restrictive monetary policy!

The evidence also does not suggest that velocity increased sufficiently to offset the effectiveness of monetary policy. This argument assumes both that money and velocity move in opposite directions and that the functions describing each are unstable. However, money and velocity have changed in the same direction at least as often as in opposite directions. In addition, although far from overwhelming, the weight of recent empirical studies indicates that the demand for money is sufficiently stable to permit the Federal Reserve to predict and take into account changes in velocity in consequence of changes in interest rates resulting from policy-induced changes in the stock of money.

To summarize, the evidence indicates that at times of restrictive monetary policy, funds do shift from banks and now also from thrift institutions to financial institutions not subject to interest rate ceilings and to the private capital market. Such shifts are enlarged if qualitative instruments of monetary control, such as Regulation Q, are activated concomitantly with restrictive changes in quantitative instruments. However, in the late 1960s, as already discussed, commercial banks offset nearly the full amount of their CD losses through greater use of funds not subject to these ceilings, primarily Eurodollars, thereby maintaining their share of the market. At the same time, business firms whose loan demands were not accommodated by the banks intensified their sale of commercial paper on the private capital market. Nevertheless, there is little evidence that these shifts have been either sufficiently large or sufficiently abrupt to seriously reduce the effectiveness of monetary policy. In addition, while velocity also tends to change procyclically with interest rates, to date these changes have also not been sufficiently large or unpredictable to offset the thrust of monetary policy.

Inflation and Incomes Policy

Inflation has been defined as a rapid rise in the overall price level. Inflation is economically undesirable for two reasons. One, unless all spending units adjust at equal speeds, income will be arbitrarily distributed from the more slowly adjusting sectors to the more rapidly adjusting sectors. Two, under a system of fixed exchange rates, unless all countries experience the same rate of inflation, exports will decline in countries experiencing faster price increases, imports will rise, and real income will decline.

Inflation is always ignited by some exogenous shock to the economy that drives nominal demand to or above full employment supply. Prices rise from competitive bidding for the limited supply of goods and services. The exogenous shock can act on demand, such as overly stimulative monetary and fiscal policies and changes in expectations accelerating current spending because of possible higher prices later. Or it can act on supply, such as poor weather reducing agricultural and nonagricultural output, import or domestic restrictions on supply, and changes in the product mix in favor of the production of goods not included in the usual market basket priced in the price index, e.g., war goods and national prestige.

Inflation does not appear to start from purely endogenous forces, such as sudden, autonomous price increases by business firms or increased wage demands by labor unions. As with given incomes, buyers resist higher prices, unless basic supply (including the degree of monopoly influence) or demand conditions change, these attempts will be self-defeating and only result in temporary unused resources. United States economic history reveals no instance in which a serious inflation has begun at levels substantially below full employment without accompanying supportive policy actions or other exogenous shocks. The first stage of inflation is thus dominated by price increases to allocate the limited supply of resources among competing demanders of the resources. This stage is referred to as *demand-pull.* If diagnosed quickly, demand-pull inflation may be curtailed quickly by appropriate policy actions reducing demand or increasing supply.

If, however, demand-pull inflation is not quickly curbed, expectations of continued inflation develop and the inflation moves into a second stage referred to as *cost-push.* Cost-push inflations are considerably more difficult and time-consuming to bring to a halt. As inflation persists, price expectations, which are to a large extent built on past price experience, are revised upward. If the intial stage of the inflation was accompanied by a reduction in unemployment, as labor operated under money illusion, the subsequent stage, which is characterized by a dispelling of money illusion, is accompanied by no further reduction in unemployment and not infrequently even by a rise in unemployment as real wages increase. The higher wages push prices up, replacing excessive demand as the driving force behind the price rise. If, as may be, labor bargains not only to return to the intial real wage but also for compensation for the period during which it worked below this wage, cost pressures would be intensified further and reflected in still higher prices.

Expectations of continually higher prices encourage business firms and households alike to accelerate their purchases to avoid paying higher prices later. Expenditures increase not because of increased incomes but because of a decrease in the demand for savings. This exerts additional price pressures. Firms and households also incorporate their price expectations into contracts for future delivery of services and are less likely to resist price increases incorporated by others in their contracts. As a result, expectations of higher prices become a self-fulfilling prophecy.

In such a setting, monetary and fiscal policies directed at slowing demand are likely, at first, primarily to reinforce increases in unemployment and to curtail price increases only negligibly. This can be seen from equation 14-23 developed earlier to explain changes in the price level:

$$\dot{P}=f[\overset{-}{(y_F - y)}, \overset{+}{\dot{P}_E}].$$

Changes in the price level are determined both by the relation of actual income to full employment income and by price expectations. In the demand-pull stage of inflation, price expectations have only begun to be revised upward and a slowing of real income below full employment levels would result in a prompt curtailment in the rate of price increase. The more price expectations are revised upward, however, the smaller will be the dampening effect on the rate of increase in prices of a given gap between actual and full employment income. To curtail a cost-push inflation, therefore, requires either greater unemployment than otherwise or additional time.

As higher levels of employment are increasingly considered intolerable, traditional monetary and fiscal policies, which operate to curtail demand, produce results only slowly. To many, the slow speed of response is interpreted as indicating that the traditional instruments of economic policy have become incapable of curtailing cost-push inflation and should be abandoned. In addition, the longer period of unemployment required also causes individuals, particularly the unemployed, to question whether the cure may not be worse than the disease. Ordinary citizens, as well as economists and policy-makers, search for alternative anti-inflation policies.

One type of economic policy that receives considerable attention and support at these times is wage, price, and profit controls, more generally referred to as *incomes policy*. Unlike monetary and fiscal policies, incomes policy bypasses the market mechanism. Instead, prices, wages, and profits are established by fiat by a central government agency. Every or, at minimum, important price or wage change must be approved by this agency. In effect, inflation as evidenced by nominal prices is outlawed. In terms of equation 14-23, incomes policy is directed at breaking price expectations rather than at increasing unemployment.

As appealing as incomes policy may appear at first blush, further analysis tends to reveal some rather serious shortcomings and potential long-term disadvantages. It is readily evident that an incomes policy would not be effective in curtailing a demand-pull inflation. The policy does not reduce demand to full employment levels and, by preventing the price increases necessary to ration the available goods, encourages the use of shadow prices, which do not appear in the reported price indexes. That is, incomes policy tends to disguise rather than eliminate demand-pull inflation. During World War II, an incomes policy was employed in the United States. Although reasonably successful, the policy was supplemented by ration stamps, which effectively represented the introduction of a new form of money and wealth in quantities designed to curtail demand pressures. Nevertheless, evidence of black markets, under-the-counter payments, and tied pricing was ample.

Incomes policy is somewhat more effective in curbing cost-push inflations. But even here, unless the penalties for violation are severe, experience has shown that the controls tend to be effective primarily for groups with little bargaining power. Groups with significant bargaining power are generally in a position to lobby to have the rules changed and/or are willing to risk penalties for exceeding the allowable price and wage increases. Political forces tend to dominate the distribution process.

Moreover, assuming incomes policy to be reasonably effective in curtailing price pressures, its desirability may be questioned on other grounds. The prices and wages initially imposed generally are tied to the prevailing price and wage patterns. Thus, the imposed price structure reinforces the status quo. As time passes, such a price pattern will interfere with continued, efficient allocation of resources. Changed consumer and business demands will not be reflected in changed relative prices and, thereby, in changed production patterns. If business profits are not subject to control, changed production patterns in consequence of innovations resulting in lower production costs will very likely be reflected in increased business profits rather than in changed price patterns. If business profits are controlled, innovation would be stifled as the incentive to adopt them in order to generate higher profits would have been removed. Old products will continue to be produced in old ways. At the same time, in the absence of changes in relative prices, surpluses will pile up in goods for which there is little demand and shortages will develop in goods heavily in demand but not priced sufficiently high to equate demand with supply.

Incomes policy may strengthen economic and social rigidities. The free market rewards success and penalizes failure. The poor man has an opportunity to become rich and, just as important, the rich man to become poor. While one may question the equity of its operation, the free market is impersonal. More than under any alternative system of distribution, an individual is evaluated and advanced on what he accomplishes rather than on who he is and whom he knows. This results in mobility and continuous churning as individuals move up or down from one economic stratum to another. Under an incomes policy, the controls affecting mobility are applied by the authorities in power who may reasonably be expected to operate to maintain their own authority by reducing both upward and downward mobility.

The rigidity is not only economic. As economic and social power are intertwined, individuals will find it more difficult to penetrate higher social strata, while members of these strata will operate to ensure their continued residence and protect themselves against ouster.

The experiences of the United States, as well as those of Canada and many West-European countries, suggest that, except for brief periods of national emergency, incomes policy does not work effectively in curbing inflation. Canada abandoned an incomes policy in 1970 after less than two years in operation because of noncooperation from the strong bargaining sectors in the economy. The U.S. imposed such controls in mid-1971 to combat a stubborn cost-push inflation. Although it was too early to draw definitive conclusions at the time this chapter was written, preliminary indications give little evidence of quicker and more lasting anti-inflationary results than would have occurred in the absence of the controls.

To the extent that incomes policies do succeed in reducing price pressures, they do so only at a substantial cost. Rigidities are strengthened, reducing economic and social mobility, inefficiencies are tolerated, initiative is stifled, and economic progress, however measured, is slowed. To the extent that the costs of both traditional monetary and fiscal policies and income policies in curbing cost-push inflation appear great, the necessity of slowing inflation early while still in the demand-pull stage increases in importance.

Coordination of Monetary and Fiscal Policies

Monetary policy shares with fiscal policy the responsibility for achieving the economic goals of the economy. As both policies are basically directed at the same goals, although some differences may arise from the comparative advantage one policy may have over the other for certain objectives, coordination between the two strategies is necessary to achieve the objectives most efficiently. In this country coordination is complicated somewhat because the responsibility for each policy is housed in a separate agency. While the quasi-independent Federal Reserve System has responsibility for monetary policy, the administration, through the Treasury Department, has primary responsibility for fiscal policy. This responsibility, however, is shared with Congress, which must pass on all federal government spending and taxing programs.

The historical record of coordination between the two policies has been spotty. In large part, the poor record of coordination reflects the differing sets of pressures on the two policy-making bodies. While the Federal Reserve was deliberately organized to minimize its day-to-day responsiveness to political pressures and thereby permit it to concentrate more on longer-term objectives, the administration is subjected to intense day-to-day pressures that cause it to give greater emphasis than otherwise to expedient and short-run solutions. Conflicts between the two policy-making groups are generally most pronounced, at least in the popular press, at times when there is a new president and an incumbent Chairman of the Board of Governors.

Frequently, one policy has dominated the other. For example, in the immediate post–World War II period, monetary policy was directed at maintaining the market value of the Treasury debt, which had been enlarged greatly during the war. This was achieved by resisting any tendency for interest rates to rise. The administration did this to avoid the sharp fall in Treasury bond prices that had occurred after the end of World War I. This had resulted in much resentment and disillusionment on the part of persons who had patriotically purchased bonds during the war. At the same time, this policy contributed little to curtailing ongoing price increases. After the outbreak of the Korean War in 1950, the price pressures intensified. The Federal Reserve was constrained in its operations by its commitment to not allow interest rates to rise. Instead, reliance was placed on qualitative credit controls on consumer durables and real estate. These controls soon proved unpopular and ineffective. In time, it became evident that the benefit of maintaining the market value of the Treasury debt was less than the cost of handcuffing monetary policy in its attempts to restrain price pressures. Finally, in 1951, after considerable discussion, at times quite heated, the Treasury and the Federal

Reserve entered into an accord that freed the Federal Reserve to direct its operations toward curtailing prices.

Thereafter, for a decade coordination between monetary and fiscal policy became minimal. Rarely did representatives of the two policy-making groups meet to evaluate economic developments and to discuss strategies. As a result, each policy was formulated in almost total disregard of the other. Coordination increased again during the 1960s, spurred by the large income tax reduction in 1964, which raised questions of the appropriate degree of Federal Reserve financing of the resulting deficit. Formal channels of communications were established and regular meetings were held between the Chairman of the Board of Governors, the Chairman of the President's Council of Economic Advisers, and the Secretary of the Treasury.

At times this group was enlarged to include the Secretary of Commerce, the old Budget Director and, more recently, the Director of the new Office of Management and Budget. Depending on the number participating, this group is often referred to as the Troika or Quadriad. Concurrently and more frequently, meetings are also held between senior staff members of these organizations.

The increased communication did not always result in coordinated economic policies. At year-end 1965, for example, the Federal Reserve shifted to a policy of intended greater restraint, signaled by an increase in the discount rate, before the administration considered such a policy necessary. The result was a heated public debate, which served to generate confusion over both the state of the economy and the direction of overall economic policy. In contrast, and perhaps as a result of the earlier clash, the Federal Reserve cooperated with the administration in 1967 and 1968 to finance large deficits in the federal budget at only slowly rising interest rates. As the economy was operating at close to full employment levels at these times, the combined monetary and fiscal stimuli contributed to promoting inflationary pressures.

Thus, while coordination is a prerequisite for efficient general economic policy, it does not by itself guarantee the formulation of correct policies. At times, a lack of coordination may, by chance, generate better economic policies than coordinated incorrect policies. This, however, should not be viewed as a desirable strategy. Optimum economic policy can only be achieved through coordinated use of correct monetary and fiscal measures by the Federal Reserve, the administration, and the Congress.

References

Ackley, Gardner, *Macroeconomic Activity* (New York: Macmillan, 1961).

Commission on Money and Credit, *Money and Credit: Their Influence on Jobs, Prices, and Growth* (Englewood Cliffs, N.J.: Prentice-Hall, 1961).

Diamond, James J., ed., *Issues on Fiscal and Monetary Policy* (Chicago: De Paul University, 1971).

Federal Reserve Bank of Boston, *Consumer Spending and Monetary Policy: the Linkages* (Boston: 1971).

Frances, Darryl R., "Proposed Solutions to Inflation," *Review* (Federal Reserve Bank of St. Louis), 53 (7), July, 1971, 25-30.

Gibson, William E., and George G. Kaufman, *Monetary Economics: Readings on Current Issues* (New York: McGraw-Hill, 1971).

Goodhart, C. A. E., "The Importance of Money," *Quarterly Review* (Bank of England), 10 (2), June, 1970, 159-198.

Hamburger, Michael J., *The Impact of Monetary Variables: A Selected Survey of the Empirical Literature, Staff Economic Studies* (Washington, D.C.: Board of Governors of the Federal Reserve System, 1967).

Hansen, Alvin E., *Monetary Theory and Fiscal Policy* (New York: McGraw-Hill, 1949).

Kardouche, George K., *The Competition for Savings* (New York: National Industrial Conference Board, 1969).

Kaufman, George G., "Current Issues in Monetary Economics and Policy: A Review," *The Bulletin* (New York University, Institute of Finance), No. 57, May, 1969.

Laidler, David E., *The Demand for Money: Theories and Evidence* (Scranton, Pa.: International Textbook Co., 1969).

Mayer, Thomas, *Monetary Policy in the United States* (New York: Random House, 1968).

Morley, Samuel A., *The Economics of Inflation* (Hinsdale, Ill.: Dryden Press, 1971).

Phelps, Edmund S., et al., *Microeconomic Foundations of Employment and Inflation Theory* (New York: Norton, 1970).

Tobin, James, "Inflation and Unemployment," *American Economic Review*, 62 (1), March, 1972, 1-18.

Willes, Mark H., "Lags in Monetary and Fiscal Policy," *Business Review* (Federal Reserve Bank of Philadelphia), March, 1968, 3-10.

Controversies in Monetary Policy—2

20

Indicators of Monetary Policy

Because the impact of monetary policy is all pervasive and in some way impinges on every spending unit in the economy, a description of current policy is an important input for both private and public decision-makers. In a world of perfect knowledge and complete certainty, the problem of describing policy would be trivial. All linkages between the variables in the transmission mechanism would be known and all variables along this chain would indicate the same policy and serve equally well in describing policy. Moreover, in such a world, one would only need to ask the policy-maker his intent.

Unfortunately, we do not live in a world of perfect knowledge and complete certainty. The linkages along the transmission chain are not mapped precisely and readings of changes in the linkage variables may yield little policy information or be subject to varying policy interpretations. An increase in interest rates, for example, may be interpreted as indicating a restrictive monetary policy by some observers, an expansionary policy by others, and no information about policy by a third group. In addition, the intent of the policy-makers may not be realized by their actions.

A policy indicator may be defined as *a variable that quantifies the relative strength of the contribution of policy actions on the ultimate objective of policy.* That is, an indicator of monetary policy would describe a particular policy as more or less expansionary than an alternative policy or another earlier or later policy. At first glance, it would appear that either the ultimate objective or the policy instruments themselves would provide such information. For example, increases in income and reductions in reserve requirements would both indicate expansionary policy. But income could increase for a large number of reasons apart from an expansionary monetary policy or even despite a restrictive monetary policy, while the reduction in reserve requirements could offset or be offset by open market security purchases. Likewise, all variables on the transmission chain are also subject to influences besides monetary policy. To be meaningful, a policy indicator needs to distinguish policy influence from the other influences and describe only the contribution of policy. As no variable can do this perfectly, the most useful indicator variable is one that describes reliably at least the relative direction of a policy—expansionary or restrictive, more expansionary or less expansionary.

Indicator variables may be selected by either of two methods. By the first method, directly observable variables can be evaluated for their usefulness as indicators of monetary policy by how well they satisfy five criteria:

1. an important link in the transmission mechanism,
2. positioned close to Federal Reserve control,
3. permit frequent, timely, and accurate readings,
4. influenced primarily by the central bank, and
5. influenced only minimally by other forces.

Alternatively, a variable may be statistically adjusted for nonpolicy changes by isolating monetary policy from the other forces impinging on it either through peeling off changes in its value that are not induced by monetary policy or through standardizing the nonpolicy influence through time. An example of an indicator constructed in this manner is the full employment federal government budget surplus, which specifies expenditures and receipts at full employment whether or not the economy is actually operating at that level at the time. Thus, changes in its value reflect only fiscal policy actions. (This indicator will be discussed in the next chapter which reviews postwar monetary and fiscal policy.) For a number of reasons, not the least being simplicity and ability to observe directly, indicators of monetary policy have generally been selected by the first method, which will be the only one discussed here.

The first criterion of the first method specifies both that the variable is responsive to monetary policy actions and itself affects economic activity. The second criterion specifies that the variable is conducive to policy readings shortly after the policy actions are taken. The last three criteria are self-explanatory.

Nonfinancial variables do not satisfy criteria two and three and are generally not used as indicators of monetary policy. Among financial variables, those most commonly used as indicators are measures of the price of credit (interest rates), the quantity of money and credit (monetary aggregates), and the relative availabil-

Table 20-1 **Popular Indicators of Monetary Policy**

Interest Rates	Reserve Positions	Monetary Aggregates
Federal funds rate	Excess reserves	Narrow money supply (M1)
3-month Treasury bill rate	Borrowed reserves	Broad money supply (M2)
Dealer loan rate	Free reserves	M2 plus deposits at thrift institutions (M3)
Treasury bond rate		Total liquid assets (M4)
		Bank credit (M5)
		Total credit (M6)

Table 20-2 **Ranking of Ability of Selected Variables to Satisfy Indicator Criteria**

	Indicator		
Criterion	Interest Rates	Reserve Positions	Monetary Aggregates
Important link	1	2	1
Close to Fed	1	1	1
Quick, accurate readings	1	2	3
Primary affect by Fed	3	3	2
Weak other effects	3	3	2

Ranking Code: 1—satisfies well, 2—satisfies moderately, 3—satisfies poorly.

ity of credit (bank reserve positions). Table 20-1 lists the variables in each of these categories most frequently chosen as indicators. The relative ability of each of the three categories to satisfy the five criteria is ranked in Table 20-2.

The relationship of interest rates and monetary aggregates to both monetary policy actions and the ultimate targets is well documented in the economic theory reviewed in previous chapters. Ceteris paribus, expansionary monetary policy actions on bank reserves reduce interest rates and increase monetary aggregates. Lower interest rates and larger monetary aggregates, in turn, stimulate economic activity, ceteris paribus. While the relationship between monetary policy actions and reserve positions is also well documented, the relationship between reserve positions and the ultimate policy objectives is more tenuous. As will be discussed in a later section, this is particularly true for borrowed and free reserves, changes in which may not affect the ultimate objectives in a consistent direction. Thus, measures of reserve position are less meaningful links in the policy transmission mechanism than either interest rates or monetary aggregates.

Financial variables in all three categories are located sufficiently close to the policy action on the linkage chain to be affected by monetary policy actions with no significant time delays. All three, however, do not yield equally accurate and reliable readings. Accurate readings of market rates of interest on broadly traded securities are available almost minute by minute throughout each working day. Because banks may average their reserves over the reserve period, data on bank reserve positions and money supply are meaningful only for complete reserve weeks. While data on daily average reserve positions of member banks for the week are published the day after the close of a reserve period, excess reserves are subject to substantial revision. In addition, as banks may carry limited amounts of excess reserves either forward or backward to adjacent reserve periods, the published data on excess reserves, which apply only to the current week, are not accurate measures of bank absorption of reserves.

Data on monetary aggregates are, at best, published weekly with about a one-week delay. Conventional money supply data are available weekly, broader liquid assets and bank credit monthly, and total credit quarterly. Reporting lags for each series are more or less proportional to the length of the time period encompassed. All data are subject to substantial revision because of inadequacies of the reporting samples. Unlike data on reserve positions, which apply only to member commercial banks and thus require information from only a segment of the financial sector, monetary aggregates apply, at minimum, to all commercial banks and expand to all financial institutions. Weekly estimates, however, are based primarily on member bank data. While data for money supply are daily averages, liquid assets, bank credit, and total credit are only one-day month-end figures. Because of the substantial daily volatility in aggregate series, one-day data may not be representative of the period and a number of monthly observations must be averaged. All series must also be adjusted for regularly recurring seasonal patterns. In addition, to reflect changing modes of operation on the part of both financial institutions and the public, the definitions of the monetary aggregates are subject to periodic revision with respect to what are or are not legal deposits.

Although monetary aggregate data are subject to revisions in seasonal patterns, this does not lengthen the reporting lag relative to that of interest rates. Interest rates also experience seasonal variations, but are typically not seasonally adjusted. Thus, a reporting lag does not exist in practice. As a result, however, changes in interest rates are subject to misinterpretation. Increases in short-term rates near year-end may be read as indicating a change in stabilization policy rather than totally or in part as an annually recurring seasonal pattern. Nevertheless, both monetary aggregates and reserve positions must be ranked as providing accurate readings more slowly and less frequently than interest rates.

The last two criteria—primary influence by the central bank and minimal influence by other forces—can be analyzed together. Satisfaction of these two criteria are of greatest importance if the indicator variable is to minimize the probability of misrepresenting the thrust of monetary policy. The relative ability of the alternative indicator variables to satisfy these two criteria is determinable only through empirical tests that attempt to separate changes in the values of the variables between those in response to monetary policy and those in response to all other forces. While, as in most areas in economics, the evidence in this area is not airtight, it does suggest that changes in monetary aggregates tend to be more strongly affected by monetary policy actions and less strongly affected by nonpolicy forces than either interest rates or reserve positions. As discussed in earlier chapters, interest rates are influenced most by credit demands and changes in price expectations. The separation of influences is not complete, however. Monetary aggregates respond to more than monetary policy influences alone. Nevertheless, these measures permit observers to describe policy with the greater confidence of at least having identified the direction of policy correctly. Acceleration in the rate of growth of monetary aggregates is more likely to indicate a more expansionary monetary policy with its accompanying implications for income and prices than any other factor. In contrast, higher interest rates reflect a higher cost of credit, but not necessarily a more restrictive monetary policy in terms of the consequences for aggregate income and prices.

Because somewhat greater weight can be given in the evaluation process to the satisfaction of the last two criteria than of the first three, the analysis suggests that changes in measures of monetary aggregates, such as narrow or broad definitions of money supply, are more useful in correctly identifying and describing monetary policy than are changes in short- or long-term interest rates or in excess, borrowed, or free reserves. While monetary aggregates may be used to describe the direction and relative strength of monetary policy, by themselves they provide insufficient information to evaluate the appropriateness of the policy.

Intermediate Targets

As discussed in Chapter 11, the Federal Reserve uses intermediate targets to direct its daily policy operations because the chain of causation from its actions to the ultimate impact is long and the speed of transmission of policy along this chain is slow. Thus, the Federal Reserve directs its actions toward variables on the linkage chain closer in timing to its operations in order to obtain quicker readings of the impact of its use of its policy instruments. Unlike a policy indicator, an intermediate target need not be affected solely, or even primarily, by monetary policy actions. Rather, target variables are selected both because their values can be closely controlled despite other forces simultaneously impinging on them and because changes in their values are closely and predictably related to variables further out on the transmission chain and eventually to policy objectives. Whether the appropriate value of the target variable is brought about primarily through monetary actions or through other forces is not of great importance. While indicators are of importance to both the policy-maker and market participant, intermediate targets are of concern primarily to the policy-maker.

An intermediate target must satisfy two criteria. It must be controllable by the Federal Reserve and it must be closely related to the objectives of policy. As there are a number of short-run, sectoral, and ultimate goals of monetary policy, it is possible for different variables to best satisfy the second criterion for different policy objectives. Target variables are generally selected from the same three categories of financial variables as indicator variables—interest rates, reserve position, and monetary aggregates.

For the Federal Reserve to control a variable as an intermediate target, its value must be quickly established and quick, continuous, and accurate readings must be obtainable. A variable under Federal Reserve control but for which readings are available only with a considerable lag and little reliability would make a poor target, as would a variable yielding quick and accurate readings but which is not under Federal Reserve control. Both the ability to establish the value of a variable and the ability to obtain accurate readings of a variable are a function of time. While it may not be possible for the value of a particular variable to be established daily, it may be established weekly, monthly, or quarterly. Likewise, while accurate readings of a particular variable may not be available daily, they may be obtainable weekly, monthly, or quarterly. The selection of a variable as a target is therefore dependent on the desired time horizon.

As noted in the previous section, accurate, although not seasonally adjusted, readings of interest rates are obtainable throughout the working day. Preliminary readings of reserve positions are obtainable for a reserve week the day after the close of the period. These figures are subject to moderate revision within the next week. Accurate readings of monetary aggregates are available only with longer delays. (Readings of aggregate reserve series are available more quickly.)

Because, if conducted through open market operations, all Federal Reserve operations directly affect short-term interest rates, the Federal Reserve can effectively control short-term interest daily. It can also more or less control reserve positions weekly. While precise control of excess reserve was reduced by the introduction of lagged reserve requirements, the ability to establish desired levels of borrowed reserves over the reserve week was increased. Banks cannot change their amount of required reserves after the reporting week, while the Federal Reserve can change unborrowed reserves through open market operations, thereby determining the amount of reserves the banking system needs to borrow to satisfy its reserve requirements.

Measures of money supply can effectively be controlled only for longer periods, say, at minimum, one month. To establish target levels of money, it is necessary to predict the magnitudes of the leakages in the reserve-deposit multiplier, such as Treasury deposits, currency, time deposits, and shifts in deposits among banks subject to different reserve requirements. While the evidence suggests that these leakages can be predicted for periods of one month or longer, large day-to-day volatility makes it difficult to predict their values for periods much shorter than one month. In sum, on the basis of control, market rates of interest qualify best as daily targets, reserve positions as weekly or biweekly targets, and monetary aggregates as monthly to quarterly targets.

Different intermediate targets may be optimum for different policy objectives. Most frequently, these targets have been associated with short-run goals. In the short run, the Federal Reserve conducts defensive operations to achieve stability in the financial debt markets and to promote successful Treasury financing. Stability is defined as minimum fluctuations in interest rates. At any one time, it is possible to establish either the price or quantity of any commodity but not both. Thus, the Federal Reserve can control either the quantity of money or the interest rate. If it establishes the stock of money, the accompanying interest rate will be determined by the demand for money. If it establishes the interest rate, the accompanying stock of money is determined by the demand for money.

The short-run demand for money tends to be lumpy, as needs for money and credit do not flow evenly from day to day or even from week to week. Large borrowers market their new securities only periodically and a greater amount of outstanding securities mature on certain days than others. Likewise, the volume of transactions is not the same on every day. If the Federal Reserve operated to control money supply day to day along paths determined by longer-run considerations, the result would be abruptly rising interest rates on days of large Treasury or corporate security offerings or of large payments due, and abruptly declining rates on days of slack demands. These fluctuations in rate could be offset by controlling rates and letting the stock of money accommodate changes in demand. The cost would be greater short-run fluctuations in monetary aggregates. Because movements in reserve positions are highly correlated with interest rates, short-run interest rate stability may also be achieved by controlling reserve positions. (A discussion of the properties of free reserves as an intermediate target is postponed until the next section.)

Because of the greater association of interest rates with stability in the financial markets, interest rates would appear to be a more appropriate intermediate target to achieve this goal than money supply. Both because the market for short-term securities is larger and attracts many more participants, so that Federal Reserve operations are less dominating, and because even large interest rate changes on short-term securities result in only small price changes, the Federal Reserve conducts most of its defensive operations in the money market sector of the financial market. Interest rate stability in this sector is also conducive to the successful marketing of Treasury securities. The Federal Reserve acts to maintain an "even keel" during such operations to prevent the formation of interest rate expectations that may threaten the success of the financing.

Some economists argue that, by reinforcing short-run volatility in the money supply, defensive operations to offset short-run interest rate movements set the stage for longer-term instability in other sectors. These economists contend that if the stock of money were changed at a publicly announced, smooth pace, demanders of money and credit would smooth the congestion in their demands in order to avoid high interest rate periods and take advantage of low interest rate periods. Thus, the Federal Reserve could achieve both stability in short-run interest rates and in monetary expansion.

Considerably greater controversy exists about the association of alternative target variables with the sectoral and ultimate objectives of monetary policy. As discussed in previous chapters, Keynesians and neo-Keynesians focus on investment as the driving force in the economy and view the interest rate, particularly the long-term rate, as the key monetary variable affecting investment expenditures. Monetarists, on the other hand, view a monetary action as being transmitted through all sectors with no one sector dominant. To them, interest rates are of no more or less importance than any other relative price. Moreover, it is the real rate of interest, not the market rate, that affects spending. As this rate is unobserved, it would be difficult to use it as a target. To them, the overall impact of monetary policy is best summarized in the money supply, which they claim bears a close and predictable relationship with income in subsequent periods and thus serves as the logical target at which to direct policy actions. Changes in the stock of money will be followed by predictable changes in nominal income.

In addition, monetarists view the relation between money and income as closer than between income and either investment alone or investment and government spending combined. The monetarists buttress their arguments with empirical evidence generated by models, such as the previously analyzed St. Louis Federal Reserve Bank model, that show money supply to have a stronger, faster, and more predictable impact on aggregate income than other economic policies and policy-affected variables.

As monetarists believe that monetary policy generates changes primarily in aggregate income and that the distribution of changes among sectors is affected by relative prices not policy actions, they view with skepticism attempts to achieve sectoral objectives through monetary policy. To them, undue concern with sectors in the formulation of monetary policy strategy will only result in poorer aggregate performance as well as poorer sector performance in the long run. For example, continued offsetting of upward pressures on mortgage rates to maintain a high level of demand for residential construction would result in ever-expanding monetary growth, increased inflationary pressures, upward revisions in price expectations, increased pressures on mortgage rates, and eventually higher mortgage rates and lower construction demand than otherwise.

Neo-Keynesians, in turn, grant the significant statistical correlation between money and aggregate income but argue that the correlation still leaves a substantial proportion of income unexplained, that the direction of causation between the two variables runs primarily from income to money and not the other way around, and that the relationship is too unstable through time to be of great policy assistance. Money is important only to the extent that it can be used to affect interest rates. To them, the economic process it too complex to be summarized in one variable from now to forever, particularly in a variable whose definition is uncertain and subject to periodic revision. Moreover, as long-term interest rates regulate the flow of funds into mortgages and municipal securities and affect the financial fortunes of thrift institutions, they are the appropriate target for sectoral goals as well.

Throughout most of its history, the Federal Reserve has tended to use interest rates or reserve positions as its intermediate target for three reasons: (1) it could achieve greater technical short-term control, (2) it wished to promote stability in the money markets, and (3) it believed that interest rates were most closely related to the more important sectors in the economy and, thereby, the ultimate policy objectives. Contrary to the target recommendation of the Keynesians, however, the Federal Reserve operated primarily in the money market to lessen its impact on interest rates and prices.

During the 1950s, the almost total reliance in open market operations on short-term rates, referred to as "bills only," was challenged from both within and without the Federal Reserve System. The critics preferred at least some operations on long-term rates to influence expenditures on long-term investment projects more directly. During the period of monetary expansion at the beginning of the 1960s, the Federal Reserve came under increasing pressure to reduce long-term interest rates in order to stimulate housing and business investment without, at the same time, generating declines in short-term rates, which would induce capital outflows abroad. In response, the Federal Reserve increased its operations in the capital market.

In the second half of the 1960s, the Federal Reserve began to conduct open market operations with a view toward affecting monetary aggregates as well as interest rates. This change in strategy was the result of increasing inflationary pressures and of alternate periods of overly rapid and overly restrictive expansions in monetary aggregates. Under its old money market strategy, the Federal Reserve frequently acted first to offset rising demand pressures on interest rates—in part fueled by large government budget deficits—through rapid monetary expansion. It then acted to reinforce the subsequent rise in interest rates to curtail the economic expansion through curbing monetary expansion. The periods of rapid and slow monetary growth were followed by unsatisfactory periods of rapid and slow economic growth, accompanied by equally unsatisfactory performance in most high priority sectors, such as housing. This outcome stimulated reconsideration of the relationship between interest rates and monetary aggregates, on the one side, and money and aggregate income on the other.

In 1966, the Federal Reserve added monetary aggregates to the intermediate targets specified in the open market policy directive. This was accomplished through a "proviso" clause, which maintained the primary emphasis of operations on interest rates provided, however, that the resulting changes in monetary aggregates were within predetermined tolerance limits. At the same time, the Federal Reserve improved its collection and preparation of money supply data to ease the task of control, although it continued to emphasize its technical inability to control the money stock in the short run. This disclaimer has been vigorously challenged by critics.

As a result of the change in emphasis, the Federal Reserve viewed money market rates and reserve positions not only as targets for their associated short-run objectives, but also as short-run intermediate targets to achieve desired changes in monetary aggregates, which, in turn, were used as longer-run intermediate targets for more distant objectives. The use of dual intermediate targets frequently resulted in conflicts in operation to attain desired levels of both targets. These were generally reconciled in favor of interest rates. When interest rates threatened to rise or fall sharply, the tolerance limits on monetary aggregates were widened. At times, however, the Federal Reserve has experimented with operating primarily on monetary aggregates, most recently, for example, on reserves available to support private nonbank deposits. Nevertheless, for technical reasons, in day-to-day operations the emphasis remained on money market rates or reserve positions, but at levels consistent with the desired changes in monetary aggregates.

This increased emphasis on monetary aggregates as intermediate targets in Federal Reserve operations reflected the increasing empirical evidence of a close causal relation between money and aggregate income generated by the monetarists, and increasing dissatisfaction with the performance of the economy under interest rate targets. In 1968, the majority of both Democratic and Republican members of the Joint Economic Committee of the Congress recommended that the Federal Reserve restrict quarterly expansions in the money supply to between a 2 and 6 percent annual rate. Simulations on the FRB-MIT model have indicated that, for periods of one quarter or longer, steady rates of monetary growth would have generated better performance in most sectors of concern than policy directed at money market conditions. Nevertheless, Congress and the administration, as well as the Federal Reserve, continue intuitively to favor reducing pressures on rising interest rates at times when conflicts between the two intermediate targets arise. For example, in its 1972 report, the Joint Economic Committee of Congress recommended that

> monetary actions should be sufficient to accommodate an expansionary fiscal policy. Certainly, if we have any hope to achieve the 9-plus percent growth in money GNP

> in 1972 predicted by the Administration, the money supply growth target should be at the upper limit of the 2–6 percent range recommended by this Committee for more normal circumstances. Equally important is the necessity that the monetary authorities have regard for the impact—or lack thereof—of monetary policy on interest rates. Long-term interest rates are still too high for sustained economic growth. The Federal Reserve should develop appropriate policy tools to achieve lower long-term interest rates, particularly those on home mortgages and on State and local bonds.[1]

Free Reserves

Of all financial variables, none is as controversial with respect to its significance, interpretation, and use as free reserves. The concept of free reserves was developed by the Federal Reserve in its early years of operation and has been closely associated with the System since. Technically, free reserves are the algebraic difference between excess and borrowed reserves:

$$FR = ER - BR. \qquad (20\text{-}1)$$

The significance of free reserves is derived from the postulated significance of its two components. Excess reserves are postulated to reflect the degree of reserve absorption by the banking system. The greater the absorption of total reserves in the form of required reserves is, the smaller the potential additional bank deposit and credit expansion; and the smaller the reserve absorption is, the greater the potential additional deposit and credit expansion. Higher levels of excess reserves are considered to reflect less actual reserve absorption and greater potential absorption and, thereby, greater potential increases in money and credit. This argument assumes that excess reserves are true surplus reserves, that is, reserves unwanted by the banks. However, we have seen earlier that banks have a demand for excess reserves as part of their overall demand for reserves, related to, among other factors, the return on earning assets and the cost of making reserves adjustments to accommodate deposit withdrawals. The lower the interest return or the greater the cost of making reserve adjustments are, the greater the amount of excess reserves demanded. Excess reserves are excess only in a legal sense, not in an economic sense. Thus, high continuing levels of excess reserves most likely reflect a desire by banks to hold reserves in this form rather than to use them to expand credit and deposits.

Borrowed reserves reflect bank indebtedness to the Federal Reserve Banks and, as one of the items on the asset side of the Federal Reserve balance sheet, are a source of reserves to the banking system as a whole. The Federal Reserve postulates that borrowed reserves affect banks differently than an equal dollar amount

1. Joint Economic Committee, *1972 Joint Economic Report* (92nd U.S. Congress, Second session, March 23, 1972), p. 18.

of reserves obtained by the banking system as a whole through, say, increases in Federal Reserve float, gold, or security purchases, and by individual banks through deposit inflows, Fed funds purchases, etc. On the one side, the Federal Reserve exerts pressures on the borrowing banks to repay their borrowings promptly and not to substitute these funds for deposits or capital. On the other side, many banks have traditionally been reluctant to borrow substantially at the discount window for fear of Federal Reserve interference in their daily operations. As a result, increases in borrowed reserves are viewed as only temporary to support temporary credit expansion or to temporarily postpone reductions in credit in consequence of an unexpected decline in deposits. A dollar increase in borrowed reserves is thus considered more restrictive or less expansionary than a dollar increase in unborrowed reserves, or reserves provided to the banking system by any means other than the discount window.

Critics have argued that this view reflects tunnel vision. What may be true for one bank may not be true for the banking system as a whole. Even if one bank views borrowed reserves as temporary and curtails credit upon repayment, the act of credit curtailment exerts pressures on other banks who may then increase their borrowings from the Federal Reserve. Such a game of musical banks is almost guaranteed under the existing system of lagged reserve requirements in which banks cannot adjust their requirements by contracting deposits but must acquire the necessary reserves. The Federal Reserve is obligated to provide the difference between the aggregate amount of required reserves and the amount of unborrowed reserves in the banking system through the discount window. In the absence of either changes in the discount rate or discount administration, a continued level of borrowed reserves will change only the mix of borrowing banks, rather than contracting the reserve base, which is set by the amount of deposits two weeks earlier. Moreover, it is unlikely that many larger individual banks view borrowed reserves as any more temporary than Federal funds, Eurodollars, or other short-term funds, and rearrange either the size or mix of their asset portfolio differently. The growth of liability management has served to remove the onus from bank use of short-term funds.

To support their case, the critics note that increases in borrowed reserves have been consistent with both periods of expansion and periods of contraction in money and credit, and vice versa. Simulations on the FRB-MIT model also fail to indicate any significant changes in money supply or income as a result of a change in mix between borrowed and unborrowed reserves, independent of changes in total reserves or the discount rate.

By combining an indicator of ease with an indicator of restraint, free reserves are widely believed to serve as a more sensitive indicator of both pressures. The higher free reserves are, the less the pressure on the banking system and the greater the potential for deposit and credit expansion are. The lower or more negative

Figure 20-1 **Free Reserves Vary Inversely with Interest Rates**

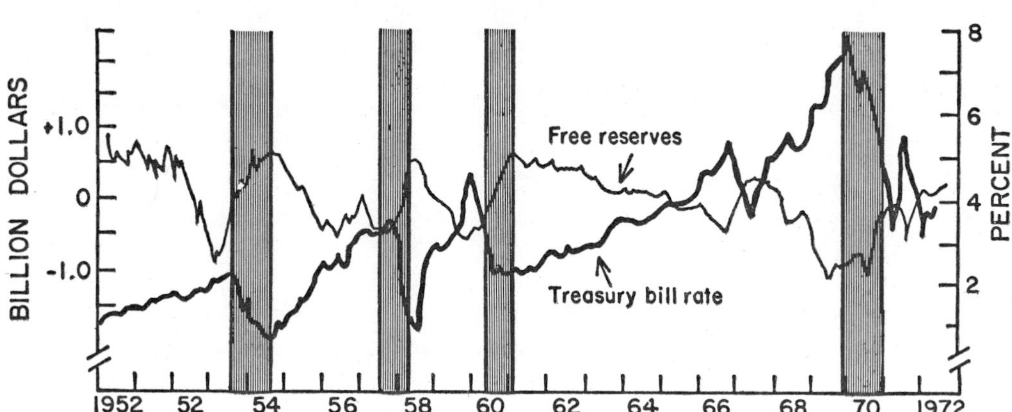

Shaded areas represent periods of economic recession.
Source: U.S. Department of Commerce, *Business Conditions Digest*, June, 1972, p. 35.

free reserves are, the greater the pressure on the banking system and the greater the potential for contraction are. Because excess reserves and borrowed reserves are reinforcing functions of interest rates, free reserves are also a function of interest rates. As Figure 20-1 shows, free reserves trace a cyclical pattern through time inverse to that of income and interest rates. The combination of the intuitive interpretation of the components and the appealing contracyclical pattern in the direction policy may be expected to operate has made free reserves a popular and widely used indicator of monetary policy.

However, as discussed earlier, free reserves are an unreliable indicator of the thrust of monetary policy. They are subject to considerable influence by forces other than monetary policy. Indeed, in the absence of open market operations or other factors affecting unborrowed reserves, free reserves describe precisely the reverse policy from that described by money supply. This can be seen from the following set of equations relating total reserves (TR) to its components: required reserves (RR), unborrowed reserves (UR), excess reserves (ER), and borrowed reserves (BR):

$$TR = RR + ER. \qquad (20\text{-}2)$$

$$TR = UR + BR. \qquad (20\text{-}3)$$

Equating 20-2 and 20-3 and solving for required reserves:

$$RR = UR + BR - ER. \qquad (20\text{-}4)$$

Remembering that $FR = ER - BR$, equation 20-4 can be written:

$$RR = UR - FR. \tag{20-5}$$

The relationship between free reserves and money stock can be derived by making use of the previously derived required reserves–money multiplier, $M = kRR$. Substituting for RR from equation 20-5:

$$M = k(UR - FR). \tag{20-6}$$

This equation indicates that, ceteris paribus, increases in free reserves are associated with declines in money supply and decreases in free reserves with increases in money. As money stock is positively related to income, free reserves incorrectly identify the contribution of monetary policy on income.

However, under certain conditions, free reserves would indicate monetary policy correctly. These conditions exist when the Federal Reserve acts to change unborrowed reserves. Assume an increase in unborrowed reserves through, say, open market purchases. Ceteris paribus, market rates of interest decline. The lower rates encourage banks to repay their borrowings at the discount window, increasing free reserves. Because of bank reluctance to borrow, the interest elasticity of borrowed reserves may reasonably be expected to be less than 1. Thus the reduction in borrowed reserves will be less than the increase in unborrowed reserves and the money supply will increase. Free reserves and money stock now generate the same policy signal.

It follows that free reserves are a reliable policy indicator when, and only when, changes are the result of Federal Reserve open market operations on unborrowed reserves either directly or indirectly by not offsetting changes in other factors affecting reserves. While this information is readily available to the Federal Reserve, it is far less available to the public. Free reserves, thus, can provide much more useful policy feedback to the Federal Reserve than policy information to others.

This analysis is predicated on an unchanged relationship between the discount rate and market rates of interest. If this relationship changes, so does the interpretation of changes in free reserves. A decline in free reserves in consequence of an increase in the discount rate, ceteris paribus, is no more indicative of increased monetary restraint than an increase in free reserves in consequence of a reduction in the discount rate is of increased monetary ease.

The Federal Reserve also uses free reserves as an intermediate target for its daily defensive operations. As noted, in the short run, day to day and week to week, the demand for money is lumpy. In addition, the factors affecting reserves such as Federal Reserve float and currency are also lumpy so that changes in the supply of money are not smooth. Large short-run swings in the supply of or demand for bank reserves can generate large fluctuations in short-term interest rates and interfere with the objective of market stability. Some of the causes of such shifts can be predicted, such as new debt financings by the Treasury or corporations and currency flows over holidays, and offsetting strategy planned. Many others are random and cannot be predicted. However, abrupt changes in loan demand or reserve supply are typically reflected almost immediately in member bank borrowings at the discount window as the banks try to accommodate their loan customers. Changes in pressure on the banks are, thereby, quickly recognized by the open market desk, which can take action to accommodate all, part, or none of the pressures. In the absence of changes in the discount rate, the use of free reserves as an intermediate target provides the desk with a partial offset to the inadequacies of projections of short-term reserve pressures. By maintaining the prevailing level of free reserves, the Federal Reserve automatically accommodates all increases—projected or unexpected—in bank credit demands or shortfalls in reserve provisions. By permitting free reserves to decline somewhat, the Federal Reserve accommodates part of the increased pressures.

During certain periods in its history, the Federal Reserve has also used free reserves as an intermediate target for its longer-range ultimate objectives. At times when credit demands increased cyclically, the Federal Reserve would reduce its free reserve target. Borrowings, and, thereby, also total reserves, would be permitted to rise but by an amount less than necessary to accommodate all of the demand at unchanged interest rates. Interest rates would rise but by less than if the reserves had not been provided. At the same time, the increase in the proportion of total reserves in the form of borrowing was believed to transmit the restrictive intent of the Federal Reserve to the banks. Likewise, at times of cyclical declines in credit demands, the free reserve target would be raised. As interest rates declined, the concurrent reduction in borrowings would typically exceed any increase in unborrowed reserves and total reserves would decline, curtailing the rate decline. However, the replacement of borrowed reserves with unborrowed reserves would remove a restraining factor on the banks. Such a policy strategy was commonly referred to as "leaning against the wind." This use of free reserves results in the accommodation of some but not all of the cyclical changes in credit demands. The money stock would vary procyclically but less procyclically than if the free reserve target had not been changed.

Critics of the use of free reserves as an intermediate target for ultimate objectives charge that, although the money stock could have fluctuated more procyclically, it was permitted to fluctuate sufficiently procyclically to destabilize the economy more than stabilize it. In addition, the Federal Reserve would frequently fail to distinguish between free reserves as a short-run target and free reserves as a longer-run target and permit actions accommodating short-term, random or seasonal pressures to extend into accommodating cyclical pressures. Within technical limits, these critics would prefer to have the Federal Reserve operate directly on monetary aggregates at all times.

Incidence of Monetary Policy

When restricted to quantitative controls, monetary policy is a general policy instrument. Only bank reserves and, at times, Treasury bill rates are affected directly. The impact on aggregate income and on different sectors is determined by the marketplace. Unlike fiscal policy, which can affect different sectors directly through altering government spending aimed at a particular sector or tax rates levied on a sector, monetary policy influences sectors only indirectly through affecting variables that, in turn, change demand and supply conditions in the sector.

The incidence of economic policy pertains to the relative impact of policy actions on different sectors of the economy, or the redistribution effects, as well as to the impact on aggregate levels of income, prices, and employment. It is unlikely that any economic policy affects all sectors equally. Some sectors are affected more than others. Because restrictive policies are directed at curtailing or reducing spending, sectors that are affected more than others are generally considered to bear an unproportionate amount of the burden, while other sectors escape. To the extent that these are sectors assigned high social priority, the cost of the overall policy is sometimes questioned. Incidence is frequently symmetrical. Sectors curtailed most severely by restrictive policies are also stimulated most by expansive policies. Nevertheless, because expansive policies stimulate most types of spending, relative benefits at such times are typically not viewed as favorably as relative costs are viewed unfavorably at times spending is cut back.

Because monetary policy acts on individual sectors, either directly or indirectly, through interest rates, it affects most those sectors most sensitive to changes in interest rates or to changes in variables, which are, in turn, directly affected by interest rates, such as wealth. Spending in such sectors is curbed more than in less interest-sensitive sectors in consequence of restrictive actions and is stimulated more than in other sectors in consequence of expansionary actions. Although monetary policy affects interest rates, it is not the only force affecting rates, as we have seen, nor is it, on average, even the most important. Therefore, all changes in a particular sector attributed to interest rate changes are not attributable to monetary policy. Because many observers describe monetary policy in terms of interest rates, they frequently tend to confuse the incidence of monetary policy with the incidence of interest rates.

A number of sectors are widely considered to bear an unduly heavy burden from restrictive monetary policies. These sectors include residential construction, state and local government spending, small business, and thrift institutions. In addition, it is often claimed that restrictive policies bear hardest on the lower income groups. While the incidence of policy actions on particular sectors may be measured, it cannot be evaluated unless the incidence of the conditions the policy was directed to offset is also known. Thus, to properly evaluate the impact of restrictive monetary policy on, say, residential construction, it is also necessary to know the incidence of unchecked inflation on residential construction.

Incidence on Residential Construction

As Figure 20-2 indicates, residential housing starts trace a distinctly cyclical pattern. When this pattern is superimposed on the cycles in aggregate economic activity and interest rates, residential construction is seen to decline in periods when income and interest rates are in the later stages of their cyclical expansions and to increase in periods when income and interest rates are declining and in the early stages of a cyclical recovery. This contracyclical pattern has suggested to many that residential construction is extremely sensitive to restrictive monetary policies evidenced by high and rising interest rates. The cycle in housing starts is frequently contrasted to that in business capital expenditures to emphasize the heavy incidence borne by residential construction. As is evident from the figure, capital expenditures tend to increase when interest rates increase and decrease when interest rates decrease.

The fluctuations in residential construction can be explained by examining the demand for and supply of housing. As almost all housing is financed by mortgage debt, an important additional consideration is the supply of mortgage funds. The demand for new housing can be summarized as:

$$RH_D = f(\overset{+}{N}, \overset{+}{F}, \overset{+}{W}, \overset{-}{i}, \overset{-}{P_H}), \tag{20-7}$$

where:

RH_D = demand for residential housing starts
N = population
F = family formation
W = wealth
i = market rate of interest
P_H = price of housing.

As neither population nor the rate of family formation may be expected to vary greatly over the cycle, the cyclical demand for new housing is sensitive primarily to changes in interest rates, wealth, and the price of new houses. Because, as noted earlier, households are unlikely to differentiate quickly between changes in observed and real rates of interest, short-term housing demand is sensitive to

Figure 20-2 **Housing Starts, Business Fixed Investment, and Interest Rates**

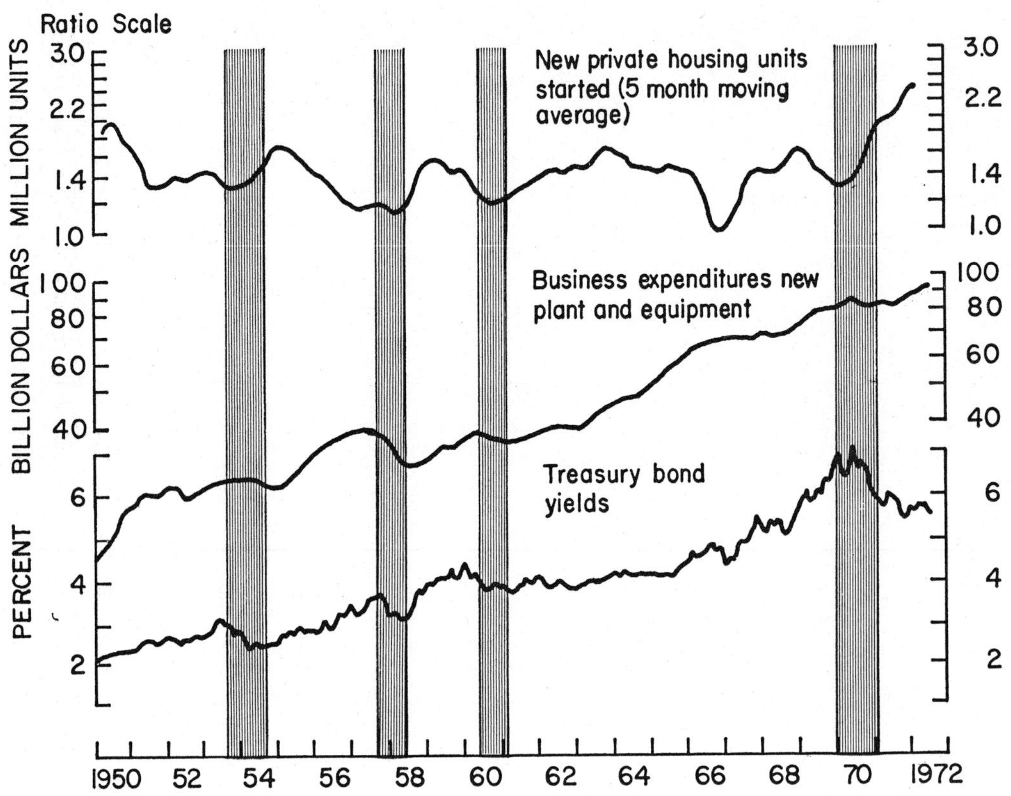

Shaded areas represent periods of economic recession.
Source: *Ibid.*, pp. 26, 27, 35.

changes in observed interest rates. The market value of wealth, of course, varies inversely with interest rates. As both interest rates and the price of new houses vary procyclically, the overall demand for housing varies contracyclically. Because the purchase of a house is a large long-term investment to the buyer and potential buyers are almost always currently housed, the purchase of housing **is** readily postponable, which explains the high sensitivity to market rates of interest.

In contrast, the demand for business capital expenditures on plant and equipment is procyclical. The demand for business investment may be specified as:

$$BI_D = f(\overset{+}{Y}, \Delta\overset{+}{Y}, \overset{-}{r}, \overset{-}{P_P}), \tag{20-8}$$

where:

BI_D = demand for business investment
Y = aggregate income
r = real rate of interest
P_P = price of plant and equipment.

While interest rates and prices vary cyclically and affect the demand for business capital expenditures inversely, their impact is smaller than on residential construction for two reasons. First, business firms tend to adjust to inflation more quickly than households and are more sensitive to real rates of interest, which fluctuate less over the cycle than nominal rates. Second, the contracyclical effects are frequently more than offset by the procyclical effects of income and, particularly, of changes in income, or the accelerator. If, as demand and profits increase, a firm does not expand its output, it may lose its share of the market to competing firms. Unlike housing, business investment is frequently not postponable. On the other hand, for the same reasons, at times when aggregate income contracts, the accompanying decline in interest rates is insufficient to prevent a sharp decline in business investment. Over the cycle, the ratio of expenditures on residential construction to business investment will decline as income rises, and rise as income declines.

The contrasting patterns in housing and in business investment are also explained by factors affecting the supply of funds. As business firms are both less sensitive to nominal interest rates than consumers and less willing to postpone capital expenditures, they are generally willing to pay higher nominal interest rates, if necessary. Consequently, in periods of rising income, profit-maximizing lenders will redirect funds from residential mortgage loans to business loans. This effect is reinforced by rigidities and structural defects in the financial markets. Many states impose usury ceilings on interest rates that lenders are permitted to charge households, but not business firms. As a consequence, in periods when market rates of interest exceed these ceilings, the proportion of funds directed into residential mortgages will diminish. Rate ceilings are also imposed on federally insured or guaranteed mortgages, such as FHA and VA. Although these ceilings are flexible, they are generally changed only after market rates have risen above the ceiling and have intensified the cutback in the flow of funds to residential construction. Administrative reluctance to change ceiling rates frequently results from fears that the increase will be interpreted by the public as causing the increase in mortgage rates, rather than as being necessitated by the rise in market interest rates.

Moreover, in periods of rising interest rates, thrift institutions, which are the major suppliers of residential mortgage funds, experience either temporary or

Figure 20-3 **Housing Starts Vary with Thrift Institution Activity**

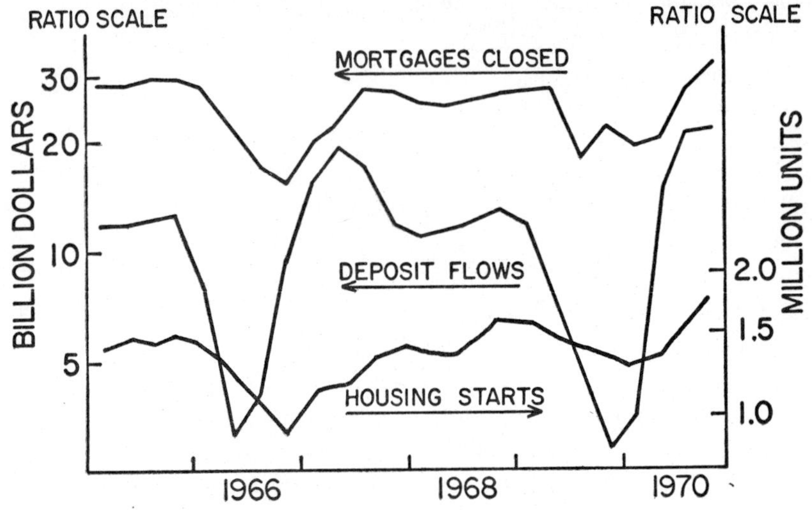

Source: Board of Governors of the Federal Reserve System, *Annual Report, 1970*, p. 39.

more fundamental financial difficulties. In an attempt to ease their plight, regulatory agencies have imposed deposit rate ceilings, which, as we have seen, have frequently functioned in periods of high rates to slow deposit inflows and reduce the participation of these institutions in the mortgage markets (Figure 20-3). As market rates of interest decline below usury, FHA, VA, and deposit ceiling rates, lenders redirect funds into residential mortgages and the supply of funds increases sharply.

This analysis indicates that residential housing is sensitive to interest rate fluctuations. However, by itself, this is insufficient to indicate that it is also sensitive in the same direction to monetary policy. A recent study has shown that while housing starts are negatively correlated with interest rates, they are also negatively correlated with money supply. That is, housing starts tend to be greatest when monetary expansion is slowest, and vice versa. This suggests that residential construction is stimulated, not curtailed, by a restrictive monetary policy. To the extent that rising interest rates are more the result of rising income and upward revisions in price expectations than of monetary restraint, the two pieces of evidence are not contradictory. In addition, at least in recent years, prices on new homes have risen considerably faster than average prices, reflecting rapidly rising land and labor costs. This further suggests that it is inflation at high levels of employment, possibly the result of overly rapid previous expansions in monetary aggregates, rather than restrictive monetary actions that accounts for the curtailment in residential construction near cyclical peaks. With respect to the flow of

Figure 20-4 **State and Local Government Security Issues, 1947-71**

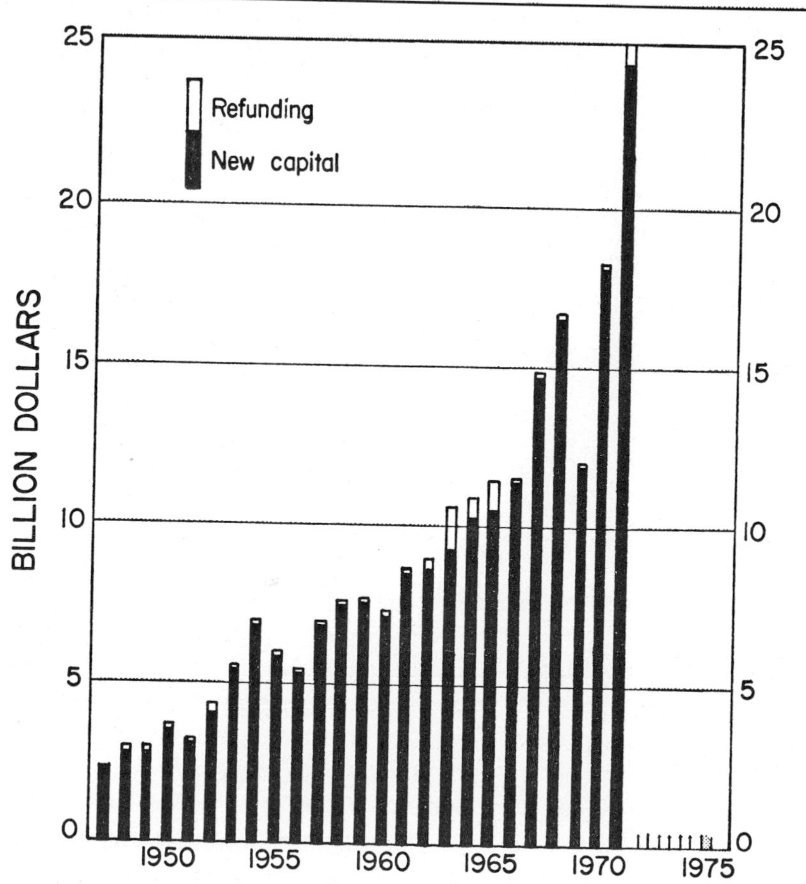

Source: Board of Governors of the Federal Reserve System, *Historical Chart Book, 1972*, p. 45.

mortgage funds, the evidence suggests that ceilings on deposit and mortgage rates have contributed more to reducing the flow of funds into mortgage loans than any other factor.

Incidence on State and Local Government Expenditures

Expenditures by state and local governments have also been considered by some to bear an unjustly heavy proportion of restrictive Federal Reserve policies. The evidence for this argument is developed from the distinct contracyclical pattern in the sales of new municipal obligations. As is evident from Figure 20-4, sales of long-term municipal securities vary inversely with interest rates, rising sharply in periods in which interest rates have declined and increasing less or declining in periods in which interest rates have risen. The effect of interest rates on municipal financing was quantified by a recent survey of state and local governments conducted by the Federal Reserve. In 1966, a year of high and rising interest rates, state and local governments reduced planned long-term borrowing by about 25 percent. By far the major reason for abandoning or postponing borrowing was the high level of interest rates and expectation of lower rates later. A subsequent survey in 1969–70, another period of high and rising interest rates, found that long-term borrowing by state and local governments in this period was almost 40 percent below planned long-term borrowing. About one-half of the shortfall in borrowing could be attributed to high interest rates. Borrowing was reduced both in anticipation of lower rates and because of statutory ceilings in many states on the rates that state and local governmental units may pay on bonds.

Although long-term borrowing by state and local governments varies inversely with, and apparently in response to, interest rates, actual expenditures by these units are less volatile. Rather, they show a strong and almost continuous upward trend even during periods when borrowing plans were substantially reduced. The smaller volatility in expenditures than in long-term borrowing was achieved by financing more expenditures out of current revenues, liquid asset holdings, and short-term borrowing during periods in which long-term borrowing was curtailed, and by shortening the lag between borrowing and disbursements. The surveys also found that smaller municipal government units had less flexibility than larger units and experienced greater cyclical volatility in expenditures concurrent with volatility in long-term borrowing.

Similar to residential construction, ceilings on interest rates and upward pressures on rates from rising income and inflationary expectations appear to be at least as important in curtailing long-term borrowing by municipal governments as is any slowing in monetary expansion. Moreover, while the incidence of high interest rates and possibly monetary policy on borrowing is marked, the incidence on actual spending by municipal governments is less adverse, if not almost nonexistent. Through most of these periods, state and local governments increased their share of total spending in the economy.

Incidence on Thrift Institutions

The difficulties savings and loan associations and mutual savings banks experience in periods of high and rising interest rates have already been discussed. These problems can be put in their proper perspective by means of a simple analysis. Like all financial intermediaries, thrift institutions sell secondary securities that have a wider range of denominations than primary securities and, through asset pooling and greater lender expertise, also carry lower risks of default. However, unlike some financial intermediaries, they sell primarily short-term secondary

Figure 20-5 **Mechanics of Maturity Intermediation**

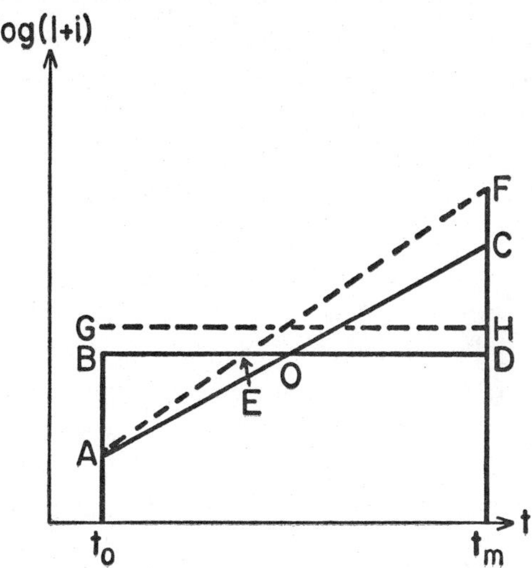

securities, while purchasing long-term primary securities. They lend long and borrow short, or engage heavily in maturity intermediation.

The expectations theories of the term structure of interest rates suggest that, except for risk and liquidity premiums, long-term rates are a geometric average of the current and expected short-term rates Thus, thrift institutions must continuously predict short-term deposit rates in order to know what long-term mortgage loan rates to charge. Abstracting from operating costs, if they predict correctly, the returns on their loans will equal the cost of their deposits plus any profits from other than pure maturity intermediation. Nevertheless, at times, pure maturity intermediation may appear unprofitable.

Consider a period for which short-term deposit rates are expected to rise from their current levels. Assume that expected rates increase along line *AC* in Figure 20-5, and that expectations are realized. Abstracting from risk differences, funds obtained at the beginning of the period at rate *A* will be loaned by the institution at rate *B*, which is the geometric average of the rates along line *AC*. As deposit rates begin to rise, the institution's profit margin begins to decline and eventually turns negative when short-term rates exceed *B*. However, for the period as a whole, the institution breaks even on its pure maturity intermediation operations. The initial profit represented by triangle *ABO* is equal in area to the later loss represented by triangle *DCO*. In the latter period, however, the institution experiences temporary liquidity problems as reserves built up in the first period are run down. To some market participants, the second period, particularly in isolation, may appear more serious than it actually is.

Now assume that the thrift institutions have underpredicted the rise in short-term rates. Actual short-term rates rise smoothly along path *AF* rather than along *AC*. The correct long-term rate is *G*, higher than *B*, the rate the institution is charging. The institution will now experience a loss on its pure maturity intermediation operations. The profit triangle *ABE* is smaller than the loss triangle *DEF*. Unlike the earlier case, this results in a lasting loss to the institution and impairs its ability to continue to pay competitive deposit rates. It is now apparent that the fundamental difficulties of the thrift institutions occur not when short-term rates rise relative to long-term rates, but when the institution underpredicts the actual increase in short-term rates. These two causes are frequently confused by the institutions and policy-makers alike. Of course, the fact that the problem arises from poor forecasts rather than from fundamental structural weaknesses does not reduce its seriousness. Rather, it suggests a different set of solutions.

In recent years it appears that thrift institutions have frequently underpredicted the increase in short-term rates and have charged lower mortgage rates than necessary to remain profitable. To hold costs down and relieve the resulting pressures on profits, the Federal Home Loan Bank Board imposed ceilings on the rates the institutions may pay on deposits. As we noted, on occasions when the ceiling rates were below comparable market rates, the institutions experienced curtailed deposit inflows, which, in turn, curtailed their investments in mortgages at the higher loan rates.

Again, the evidence is not clear-cut on whether the financial difficulties of the thrift institutions in periods of high and rising interest rates can be attributed to restrictive monetary policies. It appears unlikely, however, that the institutions, most of which have experienced many successful years of operation, would suddenly begin underpredicting the restrictiveness of monetary policy, particularly, as a number of economists had postulated that their successful operations during previous periods of monetary stringency were a threat to the effectiveness of restrictive policy. It appears much more likely that, like almost everyone else in the late 1960s, the thrift institutions underestimated the rate of inflation and the accompanying response of interest rates to the upward revisions in price expectations. Thus, the difficulties of the institutions appear to be primarily the result of overly expansive rather than overly restrictive monetary policies.

Incidence on Income Distribution

The incidence of monetary policy on income groups is particularly difficult to analyze. If monetary policy were optimal and its objective of full employment at stable prices were achieved, the greatest benefits would accrue to those income groups that would have been unemployed in the absence of full employment. The incidence of below-optimum monetary policies would depend on the nature of the objectives not achieved. The incidence of excessive unemployment is clearly on the unemployed. The incidence of inflation was discussed in Chapter 3. It bears heaviest on those groups slowest to adjust their real income to the acceleration in prices. In the absence of a Phillips curve relationship between inflation and unemployment, the evidence suggests that the less educated and lower income groups are likely to operate under money illusion longest and be disadvantaged the most.

Moreover, the surveys of household wealth cited in Chapter 3 have also indicated that the lower income groups are both relatively larger net creditors, after the allocation of government and corporate debt liabilities to spending groups, and hold proportionately fewer investment-type securities and more fixed-value-type securities in their asset portfolios than do higher income groups. As a result, low income units experience a decline in the real value of their assets as prices rise, ceteris paribus, in relation to higher income units, and benefit proportionately less from declines in the real value of their outstanding debt. Overall, the redistribution effects of inflation per se while apparently regressive are also apparently modest.

Ceteris paribus, rising interest rates tend to favor new creditors at the expense of new debtors. If one assumes that new creditors and debtors have the same income characteristics as existing creditors and debtors, then on the basis of full allocation of government and corporate debt, lower income groups will benefit from high and rising interest rates relative to higher income groups. At the same time, rising interest rates reduce the market value of investment-type assets, also benefiting lower income groups proportionately more. To the extent that the rising interest rates are generated by and accompany inflation, the regressive income and wealth incidence of inflation is offset in part or in total. To the extent that the rising interest rates reflect restrictive monetary policies successfully directed at slowing inflation without increasing unemployment, the net incidence of restrictive monetary policy is most likely modestly progressive. To the extent that monetary policy is directed at holding down interest rates and in the process generates inflation, its incidence is most likely modestly regressive.

References

Board of Governors of the Federal Reserve System, *Open Market Policies and Operating Procedures—Staff Studies* (Washington, D.C.: 1971).

Brimmer, Andrew F., "The Political Economy of Money: Evolution and Impact of Monetarism in the Federal Reserve System," *American Economic Review*, 62 (2), May, 1972, 344-362.

Brunner, Karl, ed., *Targets and Indicators of Monetary Policy* (San Francisco: Chandler, 1969).

Committee on Banking and Currency, *Compendium on Monetary Policy Guidelines and Federal Reserve Structure* (90th U.S. Congress, Second session, 1968).

Federal Reserve Bank of Boston, *Controlling Monetary Aggregates* (Boston: 1969).

———, *Housing and Monetary Policy* (Boston: 1970).

Gibson, William E., and George G. Kaufman, *Monetary Economics: Readings on Current Issues* (New York: McGraw-Hill, 1971).

Holmes, Alan R., "A Day at the Trading Desk," *Monthly Review* (Federal Reserve Bank of New York), 52 (10), October, 1970, 234-238.

Joint Economic Committee, *Standards for Guiding Monetary Action: Report* (90th U.S. Congress, Second session, 1968).

Kaufman, George G., "Current Issues in Monetary Economics and Policy: A Review," *The Bulletin* (New York University, Institute of Finance), No. 57, May, 1969.

———, Anne Marie Laporte, and Robert D. Laurent, "Implications of Federal Reserve Operations on Monetary Aggregates," *Nebraska Journal of Economics and Business,* 9 (4), Autumn, 1970, 47-65.

Mayer, Thomas, *Monetary Policy in the United States* (New York: Random House, 1968).

Meek, Paul, and Rudolf Thunberg, "Monetary Aggregates and Federal Reserve Open Market Operations," *Monthly Review* (Federal Reserve Bank of New York), 53 (4), April, 1971, 80-89.

Meigs, A. James, *Money Matters* (New York: Harper & Row, 1972).

Petersen, John E., "Response of State and Local Governments to Varying Credit Conditions," *Federal Reserve Bulletin,* 57 (3), March, 1971, 209-232.

Sprinkel, Beryl W., *Money and Markets* (Homewood, Ill.: Irwin, 1971).

Monetary Policy in The Postwar Period

21

The course of economic activity in the United States since the end of World War II is the concern of this chapter. The performance of the economy is evaluated in relation to commonly accepted standards of optimal performance for the major objectives of the economy. The strategy and impact of economic policy, in particular monetary policy, are described and evaluated. The first part of the chapter provides a broad general sweep of economic activity in the period, while the second part describes activity and policy in briefer subperiods.

Overview

On the whole, the U.S. economy experienced substantial growth and prosperity in the postwar period. Between the end of World War II in 1945 and 1971, GNP increased fivefold. All this growth did not represent real expansion. Prices more than doubled. Nevertheless, real GNP also more than doubled and, even after allowing for a 50 percent increase in population in this period, real per capita personal income rose more than 50 percent. As Figure 21-1 shows, the secular expansion in this period was not without its cyclical ups and downs. The economy experienced five downturns in business activity in 1948, 1953, 1957, 1960, and 1969 (see Table 21-3, p. 481, following the text of this chapter). The average length of the recessions, however, was only half that of the average prewar recessions, while the average period of expansion was some 70 percent longer than prewar expansions. As noted earlier, the lengthening of the average expansion is, in great

Figure 21-1 **Income Expanded in Postwar Period**

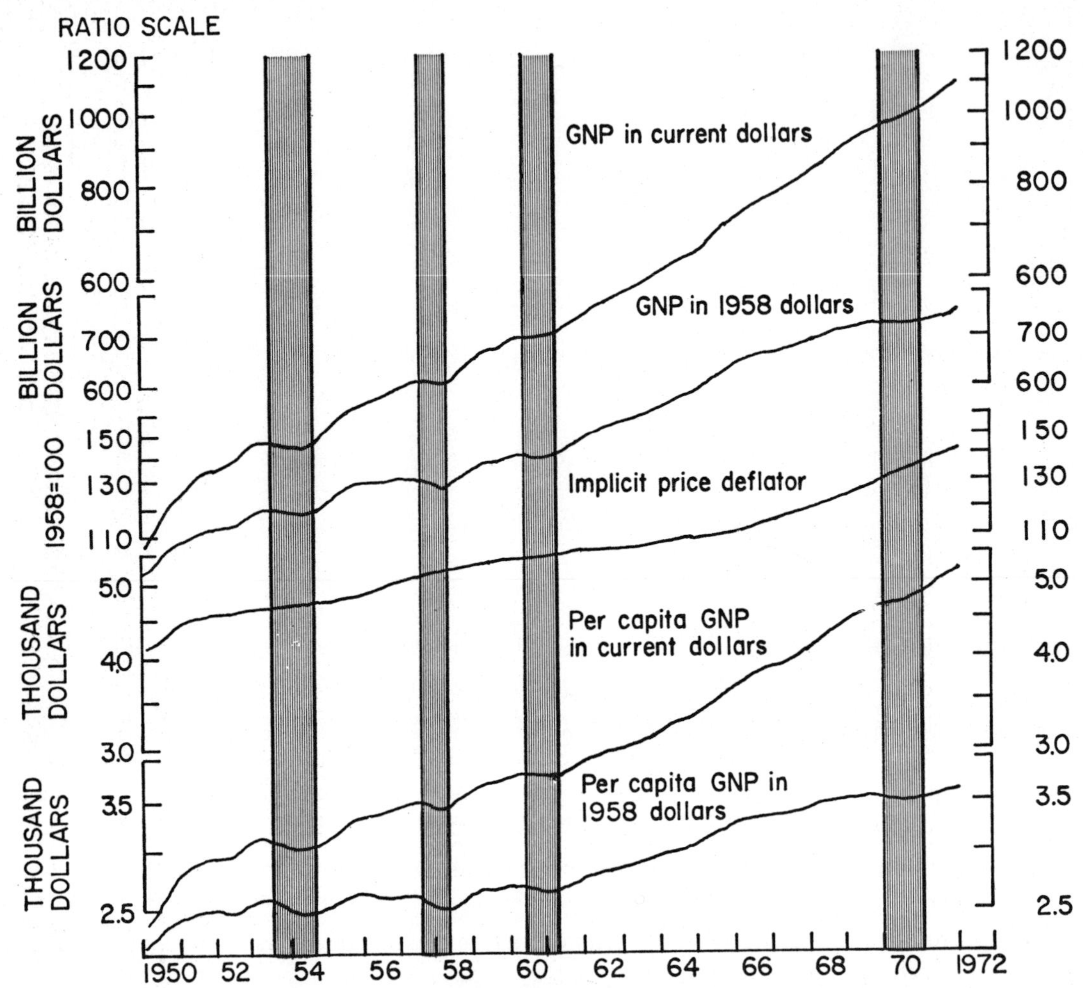

Shaded areas represent periods of economic recession.

Source: Department of Commerce, *Business Conditions Digest,* June, 1972, p. 9.

part, attributable to the record 105-month expansion stretching almost the entire decade of the 1960s. In its absence, the postwar expansions would have averaged only slightly longer than the prewar expansions.

In addition to being briefer, none of the postwar recessions approached the severity of some of the earlier economic downturns in American history. Between 1931 and 1940, for example, unemployment did not dip below 14 percent of the labor force and reached 25 percent in 1933. Unemployment also topped 10 percent from 1893 through 1898 and again in 1921. Although the performance of

Figure 21-2 **Unemployment Varies Cyclically**

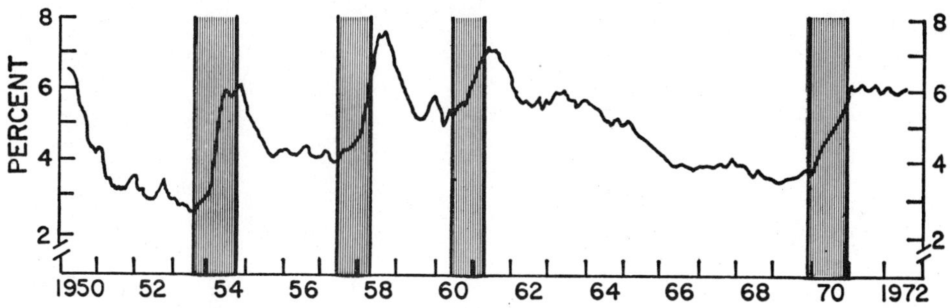

Shaded areas represent periods of economic recession.
Source: *Ibid.*, p. 22.

the economy in the postwar period may be rated successful by pre–World War II standards, it did not live up to the high expectations of both policy-makers and the public founded on the increasingly greater knowledge of the economic processes at our disposal.

Full Employment

The U.S. economy is generally considered to be operating at full employment when the number of unemployed persons seeking employment is no greater than 4 percent of the labor force. Some persons would favor a somewhat lower rate and others a somewhat higher one. In addition, the aggregate target may be changed in response to changes in the composition of the labor force toward or away from groups with above- or below-average rates of unemployment.

The rate of unemployment in the postwar period is plotted in Figure 21-2. Unemployment rose in periods of general economic recession and contracted in periods of general economic expansion. As may be noted, downturns in unemployment tend to lag slightly behind lower turning points in aggregate economic activity. This occurs because, as demands for labor increase, workers reenter the labor force to seek employment and temporarily offset the impact of employment increases.

The economy operated at or above full employment in only a minority of the years, basically during the Korean and Vietnam conflicts. Unemployment climbed above 7 percent during the 1949, 1958, and 1961 recessions and exceeded 6 percent at times in both 1954 and 1970. To some extent, the increases in unemployment in the two latter periods resulted from cutbacks in military expenditures, reflecting the "winding down" of periods of armed conflict. Although unemployment declined from the peak levels of 1958 in the subsequent expansion, the recovery was aborted before full employment could be attained and unemployment remained at high levels for almost a decade. From 1966 through 1969, unemployment was at its lowest levels since the early 1950s. Concurrent with the downturn in economic activity near year-end 1969, unemployment increased to about 6 percent within a year and stabilized at near that level through the early part of the subsequent slow recovery.

Economic Growth

The economy grew rapidly in the postwar period. Per capita real GNP and real disposable personal income both increased by more than 50 percent. Output per man-hour more than doubled, and almost quadrupled in agriculture. The average spendable weekly earnings of a worker with three dependents employed in manufacturing industries increased by more than one-third in constant dollars.

The growth performance of an economy may be evaluated best by comparing its actual growth with its maximum potential growth. The potential growth rate of the economy may be estimated by computing output at full employment and adjusting for natural and cyclical increases in the labor force and increases in productivity. Such a growth rate has been estimated by the President's Council of Economic Advisers for the period since 1952 and is plotted in Figure 21-3. The potential real growth of the economy is estimated to have accelerated in this period from an annual rate of 3½ percent from 1952 through 1962, to 3¾ percent from 1963 through 1965, to 4 percent from 1966 through 1969, and to 4⅓ percent since. Also shown is the actual level of real GNP.

The difference between the potential GNP and the actual GNP is considered an inflationary gap, if actual income exceeds potential income, and a deflationary or full employment gap, if actual income falls short of potential income. The deflationary gap measures the cost to the economy of operating below potential output in terms of output permanently lost. As the capacity of the economy generally continues to rise during downturns, the cost of a decline in real output is not only the output lost from the previous peak but also the output lost from that level to the potential level.

For the greater part of the period since 1952, the economy operated below its potential. At the trough of the 1958 recession, the economy was operating at a full 10 percent below its potential levels. The abortive recovery from that recession is clearly evident in the figure and by early 1961 actual output was again 10 percent below potential output. In part, this low starting base may help account for the longevity of the subsequent record 105-month expansion as strong anti-inflationary economic policies were not required as long as the economy was performing substantially below its capacity. It is also clear from the diagram that

Figure 21-3 **Actual and Potential Gross National Product**

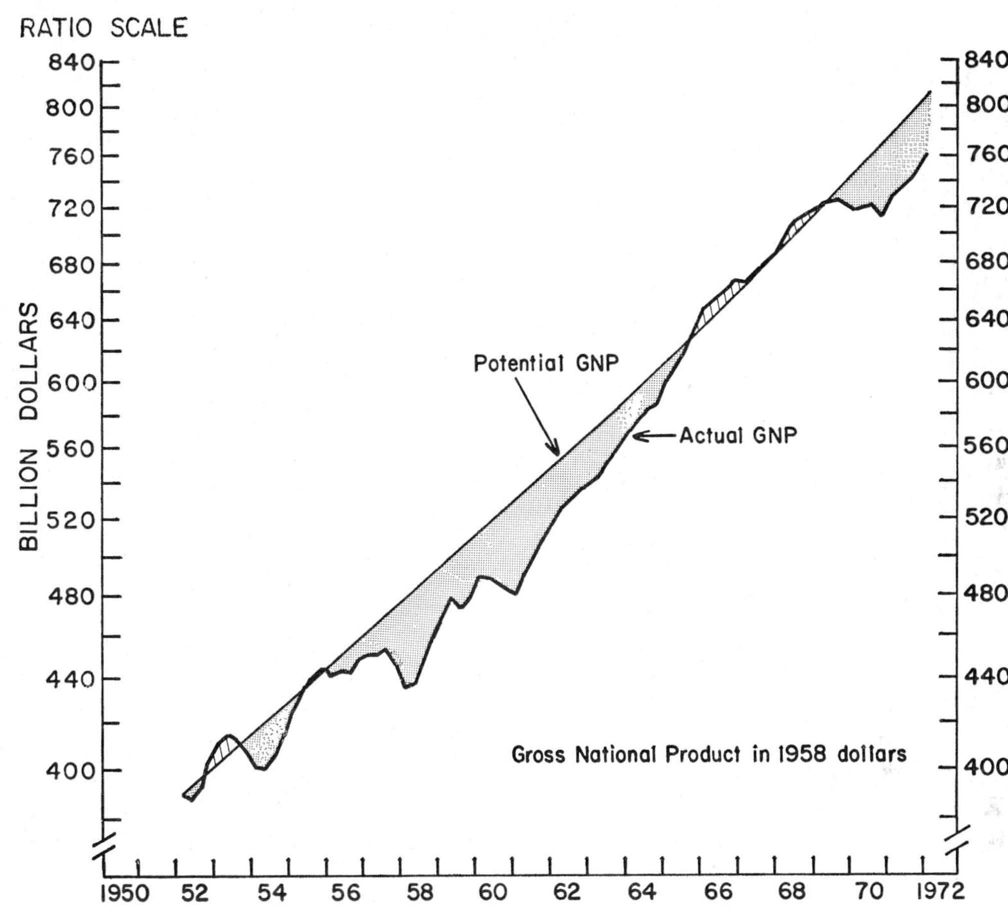

Source: *Ibid.*, p. 61.

the economy can expand at faster rates when operating below potential than when operating at or above potential, where it is constrained by the growth in the labor force.

Cyclical phases of expansion and contraction are seen to enclose briefer subperiods in which output grows at different rates and even in different directions. For example, slight declines in output are noticeable in 1959 during the brief 1958–60 period of expansion and in 1967 during the lengthy 1961–69 expansion. The first period is attributed to a lengthy steel strike, while the latter period is, in part, the response to an earlier restrictive monetary policy that was reversed before the slowing in economic activity could develop into a recession. Thus, economic policy need not be constant nor even consistent within a cyclical phase.

Figure 21-4 Increases in Consumer Prices Accelerated in the 1960s

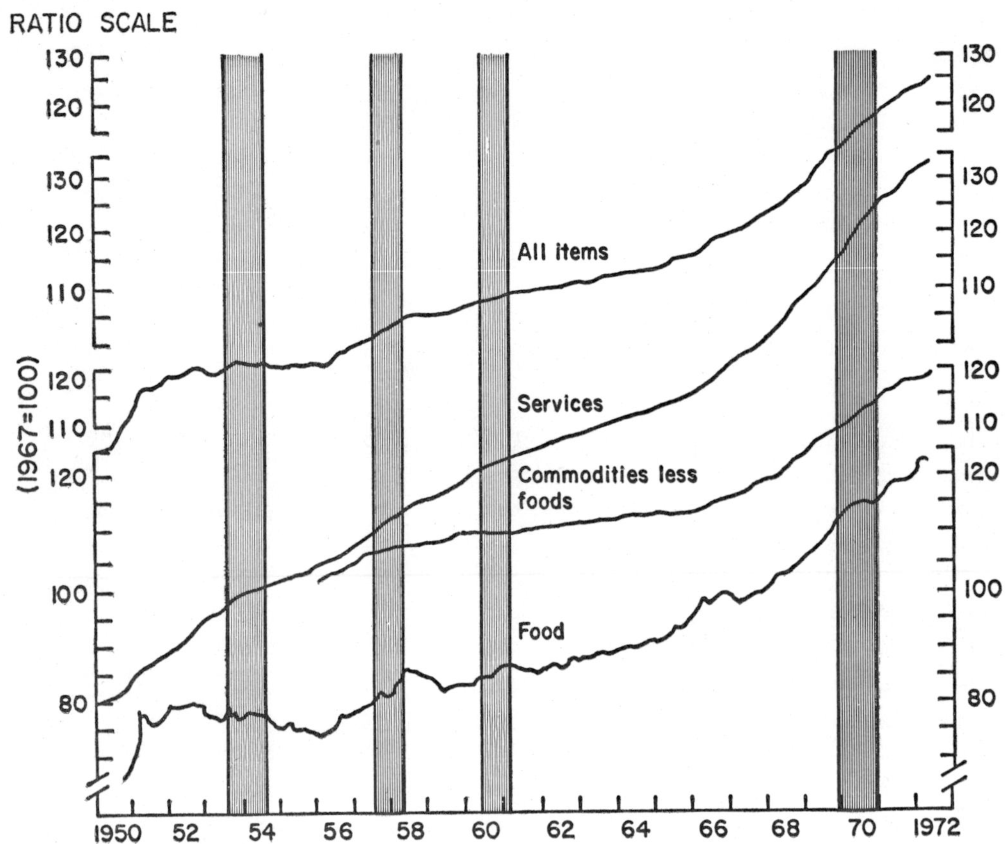

Shaded areas represent periods of economic recession.
Source: *Ibid.*, p. 56.

Prices

The price level has trended upward throughout the postwar period, but at differing rates (Figure 21-4). At the end of 1971, the consumer price index stood at 123 (with 1967 as 100), more than twice the reading of 54 in 1945. This increase represents an average annual increase of about 3.2 percent. All prices did not increase equally. Since 1950, the largest increases were recorded for services, particularly medical services (Table 21-1). Rents increased substantially less than other services and even less than the average of all items. Commodity prices increased less than food prices. Prices on household durables increased only 10 percent in the 20-year period.

The price rise was also not steady through time. Prices tended to rise faster as the economy approached and surpassed full employment capacity and more

Table 21-1 **Percent Increase in Consumer Prices, 1950 to 1970**

Item	Increase
All items	61
All commodities	44
All food	54
All services	107
Durable goods	26
Household durables	10
Nondurable goods	48
Rent	56
Medical services	124

Source: Council of Economic Advisers, *Annual Report, 1972*, pp. 248–249.

slowly at times of substantial excess capacity. Only rarely did prices decline. The close relationship between changes in the rate of price increase and the spread between actual and potential output is evident from a comparison of Figures 21-3 and 21-4. On occasion, prices did not slow greatly at times that output declined, as in 1957–58 and 1969–70. On these occasions the pressure of expectations of further price increases, based on observations of past price increases, temporarily outweighed the impact of increased unemployment and excess capacity. Prices did slow subsequently as price expectations were revised downward. On two occasions, in 1951 and 1971, price controls were imposed. In the former instance, the controls were to help ration reduced consumer supplies, as production was shifted to military output for the Korean war, and in the latter instance, to help curb upward price expectations in a period of substantial, but not sufficient, unemployment for price stability.

The effects of price increases on the growth in GNP are shown in Figure 21-5. In the years of downturns in real activity, GNP still increased, but all the increase was attributed to price increases. In the 20 years from 1951 to 1971, price increases accounted for at least one-half of the annual increases in GNP in almost one-half of the years. All of these years were near the end of an expansion phase. Prices accounted for more than one-half the annual growth in GNP in every year from 1967 through 1971. In contrast, from 1962 through 1966, real growth accounted for the greater part of the annual increase in GNP.

Balance of Payments

The U.S. balance of payments has been in deficit almost continually since 1950 (Figure 21-6). In the immediate postwar period through 1949, the balance of payments was in surplus, as the U.S. was the primary source of supply to a wartorn

Figure 21-5 **Price Increases Account for Larger Proportion of GNP Increases in Recent Years**

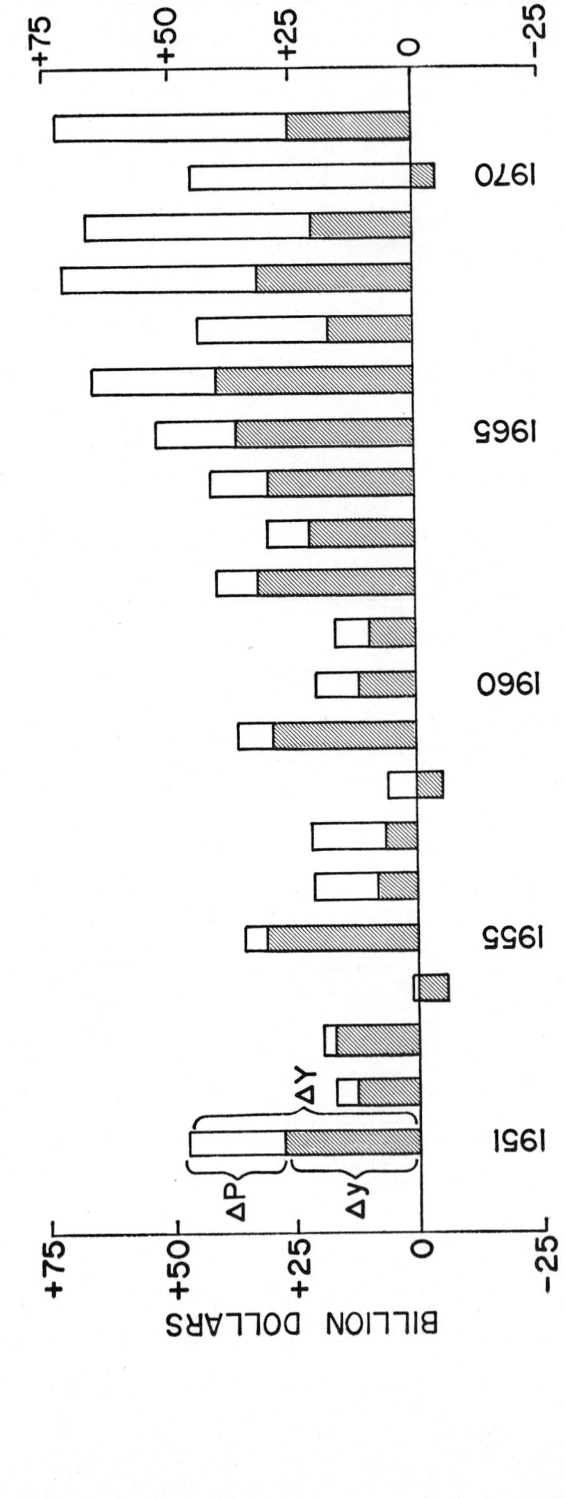

Source: Council of Economic Advisers, *Annual Report, 1972*, pp. 195–196.

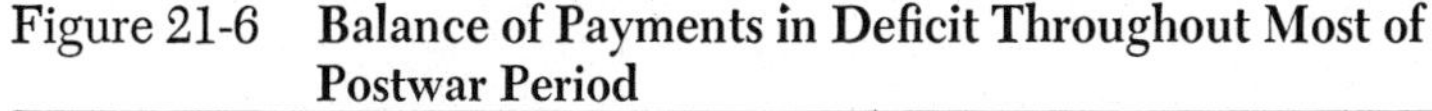

Figure 21-6 **Balance of Payments in Deficit Throughout Most of Postwar Period**

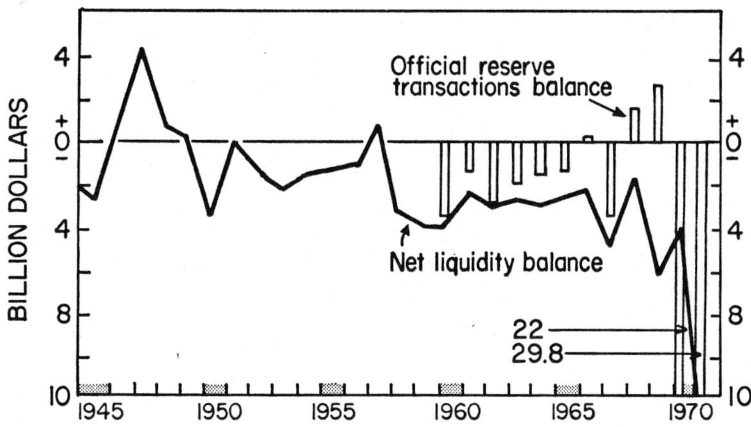

Source: Board of Governors of the Federal Reserve System, *Historical Chart Book, 1971*, p. 106.

world whose productive capabilities had been substantially reduced. The rebuilding of these productive facilities combined with the greater imports and overseas military expenditures associated with the Korean war and the intensification of the Western defense alliances spelled an end to the surpluses. U.S. merchandise exports did not exceed 1947 levels again until 1956. The deficits, however, did not cause policy concern, as they were readily financed by the large gold reserves accumulated before, during, and immediately after World War II. U.S. gold holdings did not decline below their war-end levels until 1958.

During the 1950s, the European economies experienced rapid economic gains crystallized by the formation of the European Common Market in 1957. In 1958, as a result of a sharp decline in exports and increased capital outflows, the U.S. deficit jumped sharply to the highest level since 1950 and the gold loss was the largest in the postwar period. One year later, the balance of trade, a usual strong point in the U.S. balance of payments, almost disappeared. By the end of the 1950s, U.S. military expenditures abroad were sixfold the levels of a decade earlier and U.S. private investment overseas more than twice as great. For the first time since the onset of the Great Depression, the U.S. balance of payments became a domestic policy concern.

The deficits continued into the 1960s. In the first half of the decade, the trade balance improved sharply. At least partially attributed to slower price increases here than abroad, exports expanded 50 percent more than imports (Figure 21-7). At the same time, however, short- and long-term portfolio investments abroad, in search of higher yields, increased sharply and combined with a rise in govern-

Figure 21-7 **International Consumer Price Movements**

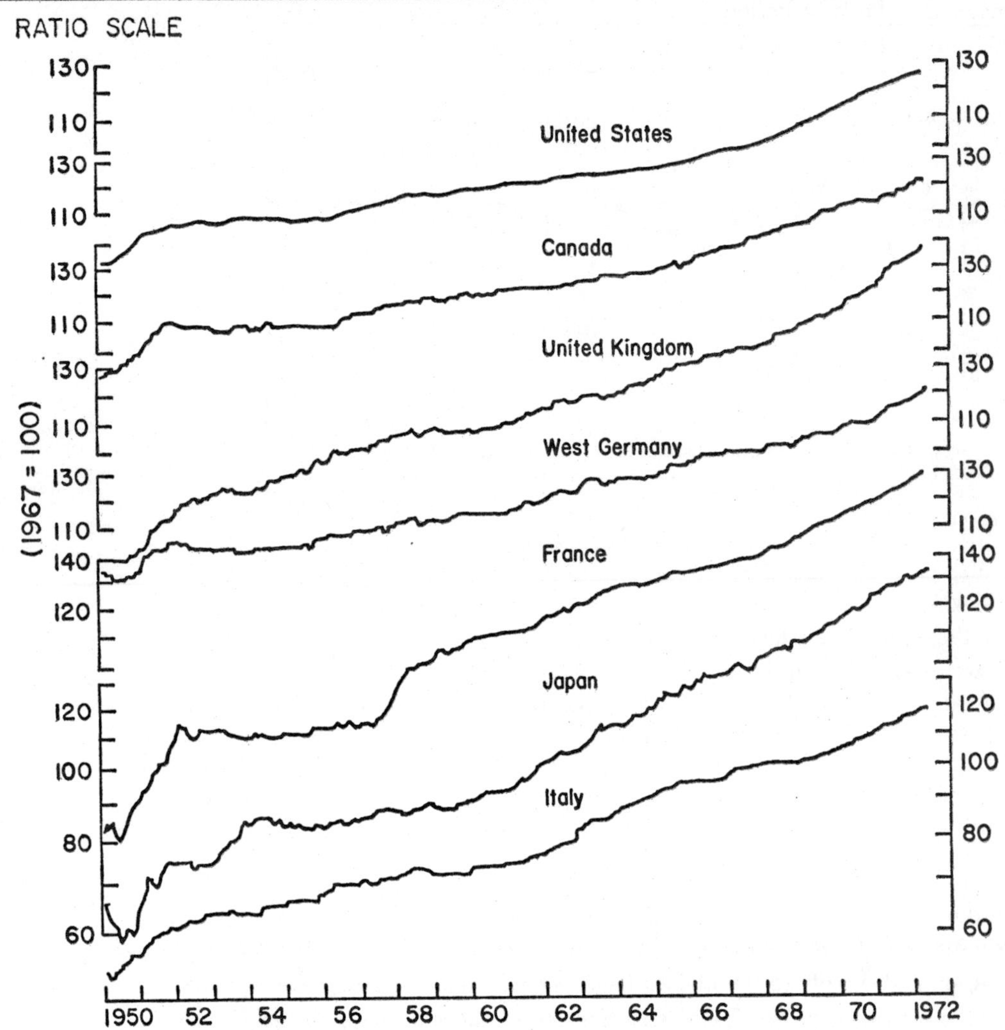

Source: Department of Commerce, *Business Conditions Digest*, June, 1972, p. 66.

ment foreign aid to offset much of the favorable impact of the trade surplus. Although somewhat smaller than the deficit at the end of the 1950s, the deficit in the first half of the 1960s was accompanied by accelerated gold outflows. By year-end 1965, the U.S. gold stock was one-third lower than at year-end 1959, while U.S. dollar liabilities to foreigners increased 50 percent.

In the second half of the 1960s, the deficit worsened, although temporary capital inflows connected with attempts by U.S. commercial banks to circumvent Regulation Q through the use of Eurodollars made it appear favorable at times. Long-term capital outflows increased and the trade balance deteriorated sharply concurrent with the acceleration in domestic prices. Reserves continued to be run down and by the end of 1971 were 40 percent below the levels of 1959 despite large increases in SDRs and IMF quotas (as shown in Figure 21-12). Gold holdings were reduced to almost half of the amount held in 1959 despite a halt in the official sale of gold, first on the world's private markets, abandoning the attempt to maintain the free market price near $35 an ounce, and then in mid-1971 to foreign governments. In early 1972, the official value of gold was increased to $38 an ounce but gold sales were not resumed.

Economic Policy

This section describes and evaluates the fiscal and monetary policy actions undertaken in the postwar period.

Full Employment Budget

As is the case with monetary policy, all measures of federal government spending and taxing do not describe fiscal policy equally accurately. Government spending and, in particular, tax revenues are affected not only by government decisions but also by changes in aggregate income. Unemployment benefit payments vary automatically with the level of unemployment: the higher the unemployment, the greater the aggregate expenditures on unemployment benefits. Tax revenues are a joint product of the tax rate established by the government and the prevailing level of aggregate income. Changes in the former are a policy action, changes in the latter are not. Changes in tax revenues commingle the effects of both types of changes and are an unreliable indicator of fiscal policy.

As discussed previously, a deficit in the budget is generally considered expansionary and a surplus, contractionary. Ceteris paribus, as aggregate income declines, tax revenues fall off and a deficit results. But, in the absence of reductions in tax rates or increases in government spending, an increase in the deficit in consequence of a decline in revenues concomitant with a decline in economic activity is no more expansionary than is a continuation of personal spending in the face of a decline in household income. At best, it is more expansionary than if tax revenues had been maintained constant by increasing the tax rate.

The full employment budget developed in the early 1960s is an attempt to separate the policy or exogenous impact on government spending and revenue from the feedback or endogenous impact of economic activity and to construct a more meaningful indicator of fiscal policy. This is accomplished by computing what expenditures and revenues would be at full employment. Endogenous effects are thereby neutralized. Any combination of expenditures and tax rates that produces the same computed dollar surplus or deficit if the economy were operating

Figure 21-8 **Full Employment Budget Surplus**

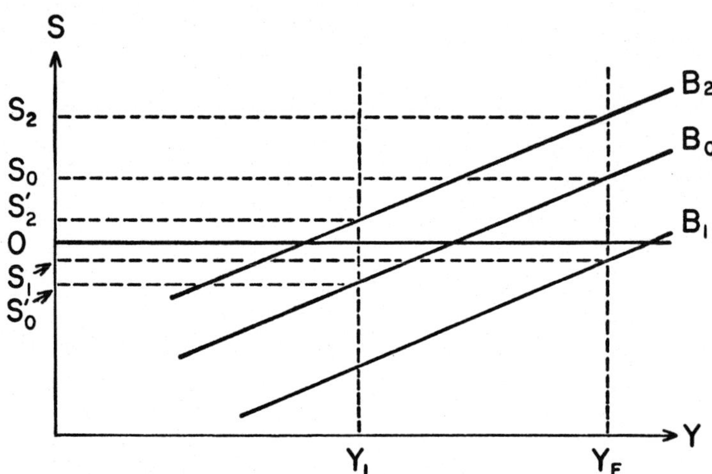

at full employment, whether the economy is actually operating at that level at the time or not, is considered as generating the same impact on the economy, and would be described as policies of equal force. Alternative fiscal policies would differ only if the surpluses at full employment differed. The greater the surplus at full employment or the smaller the deficit at full employment, the less expansionary is the contribution of fiscal policy to economic activity. The smaller the surplus at full employment or the larger the deficit at full employment, the more expansionary is the fiscal policy.

The construct of the full employment budget surplus concept is shown clearly in Figure 21-8. The major feedback from the economy on levels of government spending and revenues is on revenues. On first approximation, the magnitude of the actual budget surplus varies directly with income, being greatest when income is highest. Assume a given level of expenditures and a given tax rate. The resulting budget surplus or deficit for any income level up to full employment is shown by budget schedule B_0. (Values above zero are surpluses and below zero, deficits.) The surplus that such a fiscal strategy generates at full employment (Y_F) is given by the value of B_0 at Y_F, or S_0. All points along B_0 describe the same strength of fiscal policy. Although this set of expenditures and tax rates generates a smaller surplus when income declines from Y_F to Y_1, equal to S'_0 (actually a deficit), the smaller surplus does not indicate a more stimulative fiscal policy. All the decline in government revenue is attributed to the endogenous decline in aggregate income.

Sets of expenditures and tax rates will generate different impacts on economic activity only if they generate different surpluses at full employment. If the tax rate is reduced and/or expenditures increased, the surplus at all income levels would decrease, as shown by schedule B_1. At full employment, the resulting surplus would be S_1, less than S_0, and policy B_1 can be identified as more expansionary than B_0. Similarly, if tax rates are increased and/or expenditures reduced, the resulting surpluses fall along B_2 and indicate a less expansionary policy than B_0. Contrary to the regular budget, the full employment budget indicates that, although the actual surplus S'_2 generated by policy strategy B_2 at Y_1 is smaller than the surplus S_0 generated by B_0 at Y_F, policy B_0 is a less restrictive policy than B_2.

1945 to 1950

The immediate postwar period was dominated by the conversion from a wartime to a peacetime economy. Based on the experiences after previous wars, the standard economic forecasts predicted a severe economic downturn accompanied by falling prices.

Wartime price, wage, profit, and credit controls and rationing were quickly removed. Because of pent-up demands and purchasing power on the one side and shortages of supplies on the other, prices increased sharply. By 1948, consumer prices averaged one-third higher than three years earlier. The observed price increases probably overstated the real increases. Under rationing and price controls, many items were available only under-the-counter with the purchase of additional items or on the grey and black markets. Thus, the actual price of these items was understated. On the other hand, after being freed, the price of some items, such as automobiles, did not rise sufficiently to clear the market and waiting queues developed.

Although private consumption and investment spending increased in this period, they did not increase sufficiently to offset all the decline in government spending. As a result, real GNP declined from a postwar peak in 1944 through the first quarter of 1947. Unemployment increased from the extraordinary low wartime levels of less than 2 percent to nearly 4 percent. This compared with an unemployment rate of 15 percent in 1940 and 10 percent in 1941, the last two prewar years. Despite an accompanying decline in real disposable personal income, real private consumption expenditures increased, financed out of the large liquid savings built up during the war.

At the end of 1948, the heavy consumer demands subsided and inventories built up. Production was cut back to permit inventories to run off. Although many believed this to be the beginning of the much heralded postwar depression, activity declined only moderately. Gross national product in constant dollars declined only 2 percent from peak to trough and, on an annual basis, was actually slightly higher in 1949 than in 1948. Industrial production declined more sharply and prices dropped slightly. Unemployment climbed from less than 4 percent in 1948 to nearly 7 percent by late 1949. The economy troughed in October, 1949, and by the next June had recovered its losses in income and production, although unemployment remained somewhat higher.

Fiscal Policy

Fiscal policy played a major role in this period. In 1944, federal government spending on national income account was $89 billion and represented fully 42 percent of GNP. Less than $2 billion of this was for nondefense purposes. By 1946, federal government spending had declined to $17 billion and accounted for less than 10 percent of GNP. At the same time, tax revenues declined only slightly, despite broad tax reductions as soon as the war ended. As a result, the government experienced large surpluses after 15 years of continuous deficits. In mid-1948, Congress enacted small tax cuts over a presidential veto. At the same time, government spending increased as a result of higher overseas economic aid and higher payments to farmers. These changes coincided with the slowing in economic activity and the full employment surplus declined sharply by more than $10 billion on a $30 billion spending base between the first and fourth quarters of 1948. The surplus continued to decline slowly and developed into a small deficit in the first quarter of 1950, $7 billion below the year-end 1948 surplus. Although not designed as contracycle, fiscal policy contributed to stabilization in this period (Figure 21-9).

Monetary Policy

Monetary policy was directed primarily at maintaining low interest rates on the Treasury debt. During the war years, rates had been pegged at ⅜ of 1 percent on short-term Treasury securities and graduated up to 2½ percent on long-term bonds (Figure 21-10). Although the rate ceilings were gradually removed from short-term rates, these rates climbed only moderately. Believing that they were handicapped in curbing inflation through quantitative controls, the Federal Reserve requested and received congressional approval in 1948 to reimpose controls on consumer credit and to raise reserve requirements on demand deposits above their statutory ceilings. Minimum down payments of 33 percent were established on automobile credit and of 20 percent on credit for other consumer durables. Maturities were restricted to from 15 to 18 months. Reserve requirements on demand deposits were raised from 20 to 26 percent at larger banks and by lesser amounts at other banks. In 1948, also, the discount rate was increased in two steps from 1 to 1½ percent. Earlier, margin requirements had been raised from 50 to 100 percent between 1945 and 1946, but were lowered again to 75 percent in 1947. Postwar changes in reserve requirements, the discount rate, and

Figure 21-9 **Fiscal Measures, 1947–72**
(+, surplus; −, deficit; quarterly, seasonally adjusted)

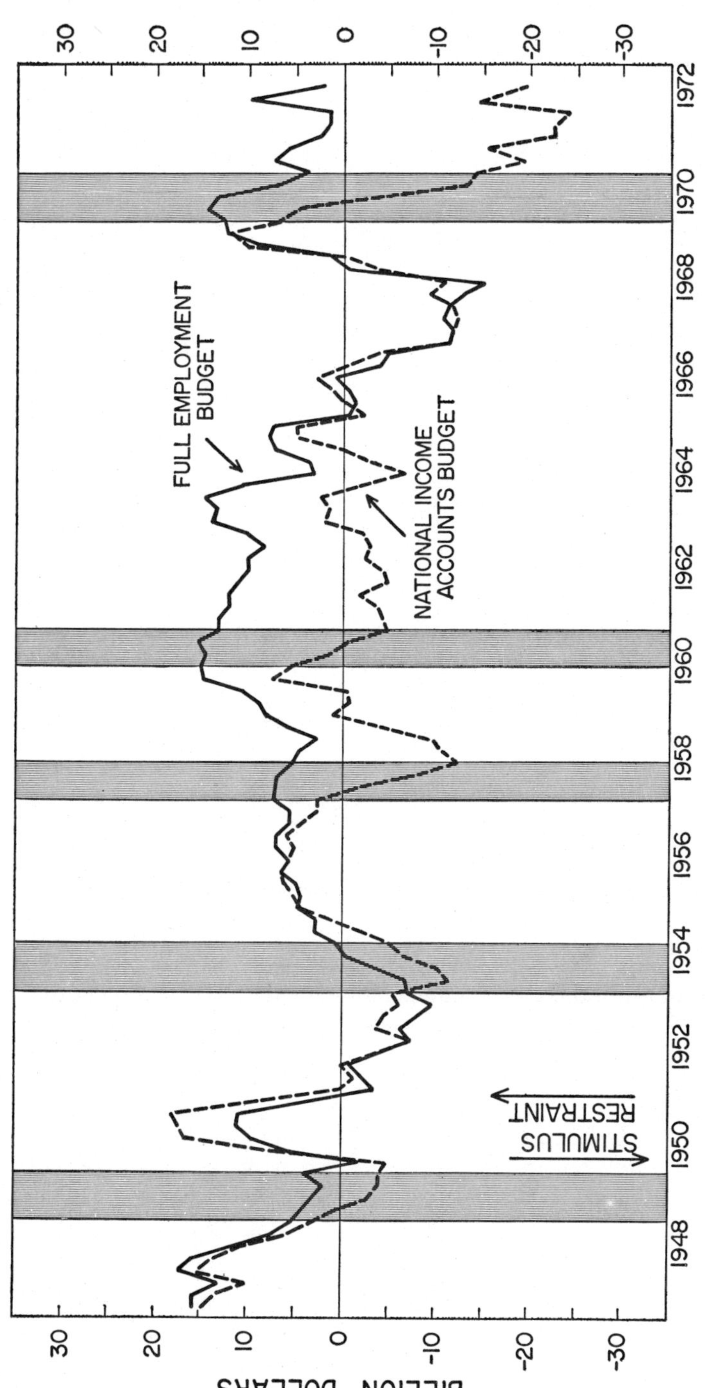

Shaded areas represent periods of economic recession.

Source: Federal Reserve Bank of St. Louis, 1972, preliminary figures.

Figure 21-10 **Yields on U.S. Government Securities, 1944–72**
(Monthly averages of daily figures)

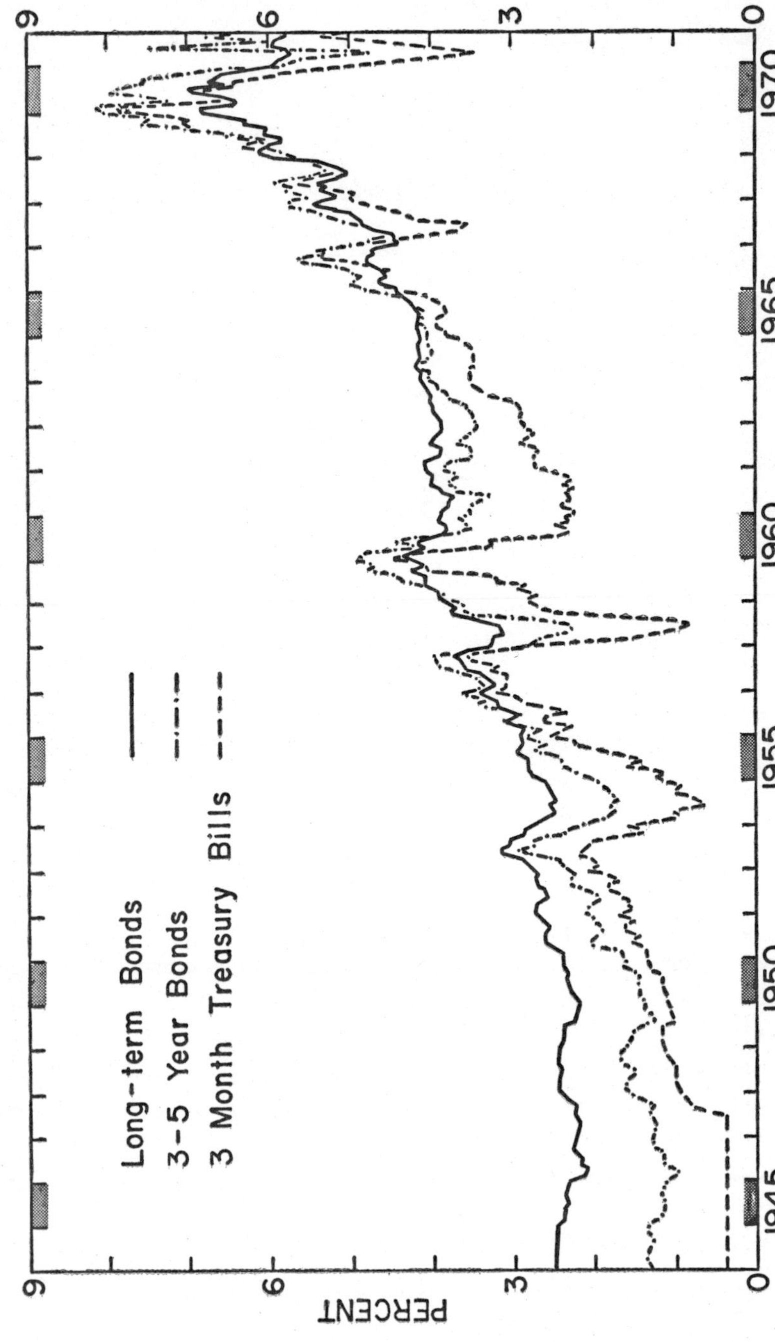

Source: Board of Governors of the Federal Reserve System, *Historical Chart Book, 1971*, p. 25.

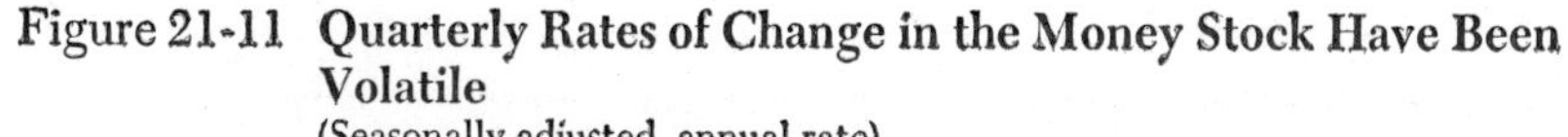

Figure 21-11 Quarterly Rates of Change in the Money Stock Have Been Volatile
(Seasonally adjusted, annual rate)

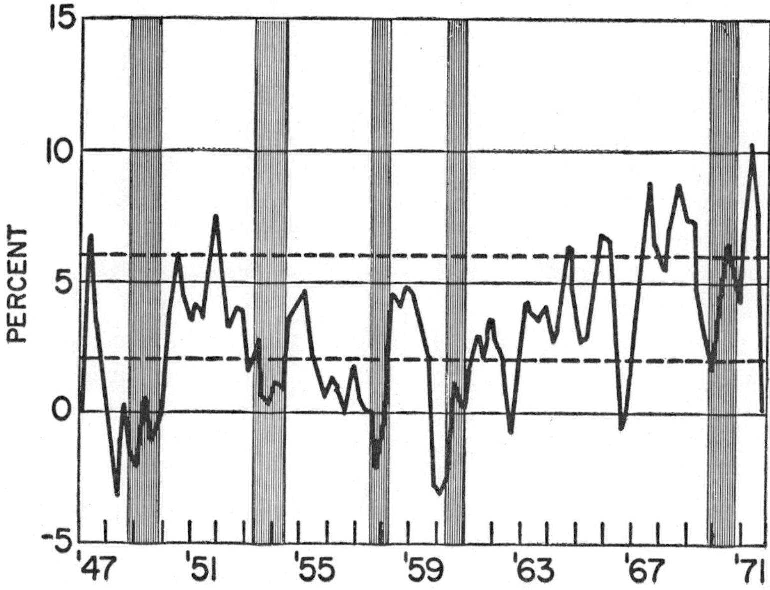

Shaded areas represent periods of economic recession. Dotted lines represent the 2–6 percent guidelines recommended by the Joint Economic Committee in 1969.

Source: *Monthly Economic Letter* (First National City Bank of New York), January, 1972, p. 5. Used by permission.

margin requirements are shown in Tables 21-4, 21-5, and 21-6 (on pp. 482-485), respectively. In 1949, reserve and margin requirements were lowered and Congress permitted the consumer credit controls to lapse.

Although short-term interest rates rose only moderately and long-term rates hardly at all, the money supply did not expand rapidly (Figure 21-11). From early 1946 to early 1948, the stock of money expanded at only about 2 percent annually. Thereafter, the money stock declined until late in 1949, when it reversed direction. During this period the Federal Reserve found it necessary to let interest rates drift below the previous support levels in order to provide sufficient reserves to prevent additional contraction of the money supply. Monetary policy appears to have followed a slightly procyclical course in this period and, surprisingly, appears to have been hampered more by a reluctance to let interest rates sink than to avoid an increase. This suggests that expectations of a recession and decelerating prices acted to keep nominal interest rates low, independent of monetary policy, particularly in the early part of the period.

1950 to 1954

In June, 1950, concurrent with the return of the economy to prerecession levels of activity, North Korea invaded South Korea and the United States quickly mobilized. Spurred by government orders for military equipment and by private spending in anticipation of wartime shortages similar to those experienced during World War II, production increased sharply. Unemployment declined from more than 6 percent in the first half of 1950 to less than 4 percent in the second half. GNP in real terms increased by more than 10 percent in the six months. Prices started rising almost immediately. Between June, 1950, and January, 1951, when price and wage controls were imposed, consumer prices increased 8 percent and wholesale prices, 16 percent. Wholesale prices on textiles and leather products increased more than 30 percent.

The economic impact of the military buildup continued into 1951 and 1952. Unemployment declined to nearly 2½ percent by mid-1953. Real output was at or above capacity levels throughout 1951, 1952, and the first nine months of 1953. After the imposition of price controls, consumer prices continued to increase, but at a considerably slower rate, while wholesale prices declined. Consumer prices increased only 2 percent in 1952 and less than 1 percent in 1953 and 1954. Wholesale prices declined 3 percent in 1952, 1 percent in 1953, and remained stable in 1954. Price controls were slowly phased out starting early in 1952 and were completely removed one year later.

The phasing out of the Korean war, beginning in 1953, lead to a period of reduced government expenditures and reduced private investment expenditures, primarily in the form of smaller inventory buildups. Reflecting these changes, aggregate business activity peaked in midyear 1953 and retreated for the next year. Real GNP declined almost 5 percent in this period and unemployment increased to near 6 percent.

Fiscal Policy

Fiscal policy dominated the period. Although military expenditures increased immediately after the outbreak of the Korean war, tax revenues increased even faster for some time in response both to rising incomes and to an increase in tax rates. In the first quarter of 1951, the full employment budget registered a surplus of $11 billion, up sharply from a deficit of $2 billion one year earlier. Thereafter, despite another increase in tax rates, increases in government expenditures outpaced revenues and the full employment surplus declined through mid-1953. Between 1950 and 1952 government purchases of goods and services doubled as a proportion of GNP from 6 to 15 percent. In the same period, military expenditures tripled.

Full employment government expenditures stabilized in 1953 and declined in 1954, while full employment tax revenues remained stable in both years despite a reduction in tax rates effective January 1, 1954. Although concurrent with the slowing in economic activity, the tax reduction was motivated more by a belief that tax rates were too high in principle and by anticipation of declining needs for government revenues to finance declining expenditures than by stabilization needs. While the tax reductions and the downturn in income resulted in a large immediate increase in the actual deficit on national income account, the full employment surplus increased from a near $10 billion deficit in mid-1953 to a balanced budget one year later.

Thus, after starting contracyclically, fiscal policy turned procyclical midway through the period. This reflected congressional reluctance to accept the president's strategy of financing the increased military expenditures almost entirely through taxation. The procyclical posture of fiscal policy was maintained during the recession when the tax reductions were both too late and too little to offset the restrictive effects of slowing and then declining government expenditures.

Monetary Policy

The outbreak of the Korean war found the Federal Reserve still committed to maintaining a low level of interest rates. After declining since mid-1948, the money supply increased at an annual rate of more than 5 percent during the economic recovery in the first half of 1950 while interest rates held steady. Rates rose only moderately in the second half of the year even though the rate of increase in the money supply slowed somewhat and economic activity and prices both soared. The rate of increase in the money stock accelerated again in the first quarter of 1951.

From the time of the outbreak of the Korean conflict, the Federal Reserve System requested the administration to be relieved of its responsibility of maintaining interest rates at low levels. The System argued that this policy reinforced the swelling price pressures. Such a policy change, however, was strenuously opposed by the Treasury Department, which feared both a disorderly market for Treasury securities from sudden massive selling pressures and higher interest costs on the public debt. After considerable private and public controversy, which encompassed both Congress and the president, the Federal Reserve and Treasury reached an accord in March, 1951. The Federal Reserve was permitted to allow interest rates to rise, if necessary to curb inflation, consistent with maintaining orderly conditions in the financial markets. William McChesney Martin, who as Assistant Secretary of the Treasury conducted the negotiations for the Treasury, was appointed Chairman of the Board of Governors.

After the accord, short-term rates continued to drift upward and by year-end 1951 reached 2 percent, double their level of two years earlier. Long-term Treasury bond rates climbed above 2½ percent for the first time since before World War II and closed the year at 2¾ percent.

The Federal Reserve increased the discount rate promptly at the outbreak of the war and again in early 1951. Reserve requirements and margin requirements, which had been lowered from 100 percent to 50 percent, were also increased at that time. The Federal Reserve also requested the banks and other lending institutions to voluntarily curb their loan expansion and organized national and regional credit restraint committees of bankers to oversee both the program and each other. In addition to its quantitative controls, the Federal Reserve was authorized by Congress to reimpose minimum down payments and maximum maturities on real estate and consumer credit. These controls were imposed in September, 1950, and permitted to lapse two years later.

In 1952, short-term rates continued to drift up, while longer-term rates stabilized. The money stock expanded some 3 percent. In the first half of 1953, long-term rates climbed sharply as the Treasury floated its first long-term bond at a coupon rate in excess of 3 percent since the 1920s. Both long- and short-term rates peaked in midyear and declined sharply in the second half. By mid-1954, Treasury bill rates had declined to 0.6 percent, the lowest level since World War II. Bond rates declined to 2½ percent. After continuing to expand in the first months of 1953, the money supply remained level for the remainder of the year and increased only slightly in the first half of 1954. Reserve requirements were reduced in mid-1953 and again in mid-1954, while the discount rate was lowered twice in the first months of 1954.

Although freed from pegging interest rates at low levels, the Federal Reserve did not pursue a vigorous contracyclical policy. The money supply accelerated during the period of fastest expansion and stabilized during the contraction. Nevertheless, policy was not greatly destabilizing and probably was as good as could be expected after a decade and a half of disuse. The money stock in all likelihood would have expanded even further from 1950 through 1953 if attempts had been made to offset the rise in interest rates, and the sharp decline in interest rates in 1953–1954 could have been offset by contracting the money stock. In retrospect, many policy-makers at the time believed that the last action would have been the more appropriate course.

1955 to 1960

Between mid-1954 and year-end 1960, the economy experienced two complete cycles in economic activity. Although the economy recovered quickly from the 1954 recession, unemployment did not decline to prerecession levels. Rather, unemployment stabilized near 4 percent through mid-1957. After briefly regaining full employment output in 1955, the economy expanded at less than capacity for the next two years, opening a full employment gap. The recovery was fueled by large capital expenditures on business plant and equipment. In 1955, gross investment increased in real terms by 12 percent over 1954 and was 10 percent higher than in 1952. As a percent of GNP, investment expanded from 14 percent to 17 percent, a level not matched since. The rise in investment helped offset the decline in federal government spending from 15 percent of GNP in 1953 to 10 percent two years later.

The spurt in investment also increased substantially the productive capacity brought on-line during the next few years, and the utilization rate in manufacturing declined from about 95 percent during the Korean war to about 85 percent in the second half of the decade. The high level of capital expenditures in 1955 was not continued and by 1958 such expenditures had declined to 14 percent of GNP again. Running out of investment and government spending steam, the economy turned down sharply in mid-1957. Unemployment increased from 4 percent to 7½ percent over the next 12 months, the highest level in the postwar period. The gap between actual and potential output doubled from 5 percent to 10 percent in six months. The subsequent recovery, which started strongly in April, 1958, was aborted before unemployment could be reduced below 5 percent, in part, as a result of a four-month steel strike in mid-1959. Despite glowing economic predictions for the 1960s, the economy soon lapsed into its fourth postwar recession starting in May, 1960.

After having been stabilized following the abrupt runup at the beginning of the Korean war, prices began to rise again. Consumer prices climbed 1½ percent in 1956 after showing no net increase over the two previous years, and gained almost 4 percent in 1957, igniting widespread fears of inflation. The rate of price increase slowed to 3 percent in 1958 and only 1 percent in 1959, but accelerated slightly in 1960. Wholesale prices followed a similar pattern. Because of the concurrent existence of both rising prices and substantial underutilization of both labor and capital, concern was expressed that the economy was experiencing a new type of inflation in which the primary pressures originated not from excess demands but from increases in wages and other costs. It was feared that traditional economic strategies would be ineffective and that inflation could be restrained only through more direct economic controls.

The balance of payments experienced sizable deficits from 1958 through 1960, but was not yet a major policy concern.

Fiscal Policy

The tax cuts effective January 1, 1954, were the only major change in tax rates in this period. Despite the tax reductions, the full employment surplus increased steadily from year-end 1953 through year-end 1957. In 1958, the surplus declined by a moderate $4 billion on an expenditure base of nearly $90 billion. Nevertheless, this compared favorably with an increase of $7 billion on a spending base of $70 billion during the recession year 1954. In contrast, the actual budget switched from a $6 billion surplus on national income account in the fourth quarter, 1956, to a $12 billion deficit by the second quarter of 1958. All of the fiscal stimulation in this period reflected increased spending.

The full employment surplus turned sharply upward through 1959 and 1960 increasing by $12.5 billion from $2.5 billion in the fourth quarter of 1958 to $15 billion by the second quarter of 1960 on a base of $90 billion in expenditures. After 1958, federal expenditures expanded only slowly and the increase in the surplus represented sharply increasing revenues.

Fiscal policy only rarely contributed to economic stabilization in this period. The sharp recovery in 1955 occurred despite fiscal stringency. Policy was more stabilizing during the next year and a half, although possibly somewhat overly restrictive in light of the failure of the economy to expand at its potential rate. Fiscal policy overstayed its restrictive posture during the 1957 downturn and contributed only moderately to the subsequent recovery. From year-end 1958 through 1960, excess fiscal restrictiveness contributed importantly to aborting the recovery and stimulating a downturn in activity. In all fairness, these policy strategies were formulated before the development of the full employment budget concept. Changes in the actual budget reflect, inaccurately, a substantially more contracyclical policy.

Monetary Policy

The Federal Reserve accelerated the growth in the money supply sharply in the second half of 1954 to nearly 5 percent annual rate. As a result, interest rates remained at low levels despite the rapid expansion in income. Monetary growth was sharply curtailed thereafter, expanding only about 1 percent annually in each of the next three years. The slowing in monetary expansion was reinforced by public announcements of restraint accompanying seven increases in the discount rate from 1½ percent in 1954 to 3½ percent in 1957, the final increase occurring simultaneously with the peaking of business activity.

Interest rates increased smartly throughout this period. Treasury bill rates rose from 0.65 percent in mid-1954 to 2.6 percent by year-end 1955 and 3.5 percent by mid-1957. Long-term bond rates increased from 2.3 percent in mid-1954 to 3.7 percent in 1957. These increases reflected the combined effects of slow monetary expansion, heavy credit demands, and inflationary expectations.

Concurrent with the peaking in economic activity in mid-1957, the money supply began to contract and declined through early 1958. Thereafter, money increased at a rate of 5 percent through mid-1959. The discount rate was reduced four times between November, 1957, and April, 1958; reserve requirements were also reduced in four steps on the largest banks and somewhat less on other banks, and margin requirements were lowered once. Three-month Treasury bill rates declined abruptly from 3.6 percent in mid-1957 to less than 1 percent one year later. Likewise Treasury bond yields declined from 3.7 percent to 3.1 percent.

The sharp declines encouraged substantial speculation in long-term bonds during the first half of 1958.

The sharp recovery starting in midyear 1958, combined with an increase in uncertainty resulting from a landing of U.S. Armed Forces in Lebanon, caused interest rates to reverse direction abruptly. The swiftness of the turnabout caught many bond investors by surprise and selling pressure mounted quickly as speculators acted to obtain sufficient margin cover. For a brief period sellers greatly outnumbered buyers and transactions were consummated only at continuously rapidly falling prices. The Federal Reserve considered conditions on the bond market inconsistent with an orderly channeling of funds from savers to borrowers and for a while acted directly to defuse the situation and slow the rise in rates through large-scale purchases of longer-term bonds. At the same time, margin requirements on stocks were raised to 70 percent and then 90 percent. By year-end, bill rates had returned to 2.75 percent and bond rates to 3.8 percent, above their previous 1957 peak. The discount rate was increased twice to 2½ percent.

The restrictive policy intent was continued into 1959 and the discount rate was raised another three times to 4 percent. Starting in midyear, the money supply began to contract and declined for the next 12 months at a 2 percent annual rate. Interest rates continued to rise briskly. By year-end 1959, Treasury bill rates reached 4½ percent, sixfold their 1958 lows, and bond rates peaked at almost the same level.

In mid-1960, monetary policy was reversed again. Money supply increased slightly during the remainder of the year and the discount rate, reserve requirements, and margin requirements were all reduced. Interest rates again declined steeply from their year-end 1959 peaks, although not to the low levels of previous recessions.

Monetary policy made only a slight contribution to overall economic stability in this period. Increases in the money supply occurred only after economic declines. After initial sharp turnarounds, which accelerated the recoveries, the continuing rates of monetary expansion were insufficient to provide for growth at capacity potentials, while the restrictive policies resulted in two prolonged declines in the money stock and contributed to the two economic downturns experienced in the six years. The evidence suggests that the Federal Reserve assigned substantially higher priority to price stability in this period than to full employment.

1961 to 1972

From the trough of the recession in February, 1961, the economy entered its longest period of uninterrupted expansion on record—105 months, three times the average period of expansion and one-third longer than the previous record expansion of 80 months during World War II. The expansion may be divided into two parts. The first part from 1961 through 1965 witnessed slow recovery to full employment at only slightly rising prices. The second part from 1966 through the downturn at year-end 1969 saw economic activity at its highest levels relative to capacity since the early 1950s, but accompanied by the fastest sustained acceleration in prices in the postwar period. The expansion ended in the final months of 1969 and was followed by a mild downturn in economic activity, which lasted about one year. Thereafter the economy recovered slowly. Both the downturn and the early part of the subsequent recovery were accompanied by rapidly rising prices.

Between early 1961 and late 1965, unemployment declined slowly from 7 percent to 4 percent. Real income expanded slowly, but somewhat faster than the capacity of the economy, and by year-end 1965 the 10 percent gap between actual and potential output existing in 1961 had been eliminated. The increase was financed by all sectors but the federal government. Federal government expenditures declined from 11 percent to less than 10 percent of GNP. Throughout this period, prices increased slowly, rising less than 1½ percent annually.

In 1966, spurred by sharply higher military expenditures to support the intensification of the war in Vietnam, aggregate demand increased sharply. Federal government spending on national defense, which had declined slowly from $52 billion in 1962 to $50 billion in 1965 and even more so in real terms, jumped to $61 billion in 1966, $72 billion in 1967, and $78 billion in 1968. As unemployment was already only 4 percent, the increase in aggregate demand caused a reduction below that level and pushed the economy above desired capacity for the first time since 1953. After slowing briefly in the first half of 1967, demand surged forward again in the second half. Unemployment declined to below 3½ percent and real output was again above capacity. Consumer prices accelerated rapidly from 1½ percent in 1965 to 3 percent in 1966 and 1967, 4 percent in 1968, and 5 percent in 1969. Although economic activity peaked at year-end 1969 and declined until year-end 1970, consumer prices continued to accelerate and increased 6 percent in 1970. Unemployment increased from 3½ percent to 6 percent. Unlike the previous postwar recoveries, the expansion from the 1970 recession was slow, and by early 1972 aggregate output was still more than 6 percent below capacity and unemployment had declined only slightly from 6 percent. Also unlike the previous recoveries, the rate of price increase did not slow rapidly. In response, in August, 1971, President Nixon introduced a two-phase economic program. Phase 1 froze all prices and wages for three months. This was followed by Phase 2 in which most price and wage increases were restricted to predetermined ceilings and important price and wage increases were subject to individual government review and approval.

Throughout this entire period the balance of payments was unfavorable. From 1961 through 1964, there was some improvement in the overall deficit as the surplus on current account increased to $8 billion from about zero in 1959. Capital outflows, however, increased across-the-board offsetting much of this improve-

Figure 21-12 **U.S. Gold Sales to Other Countries Accelerated in the 1960s**

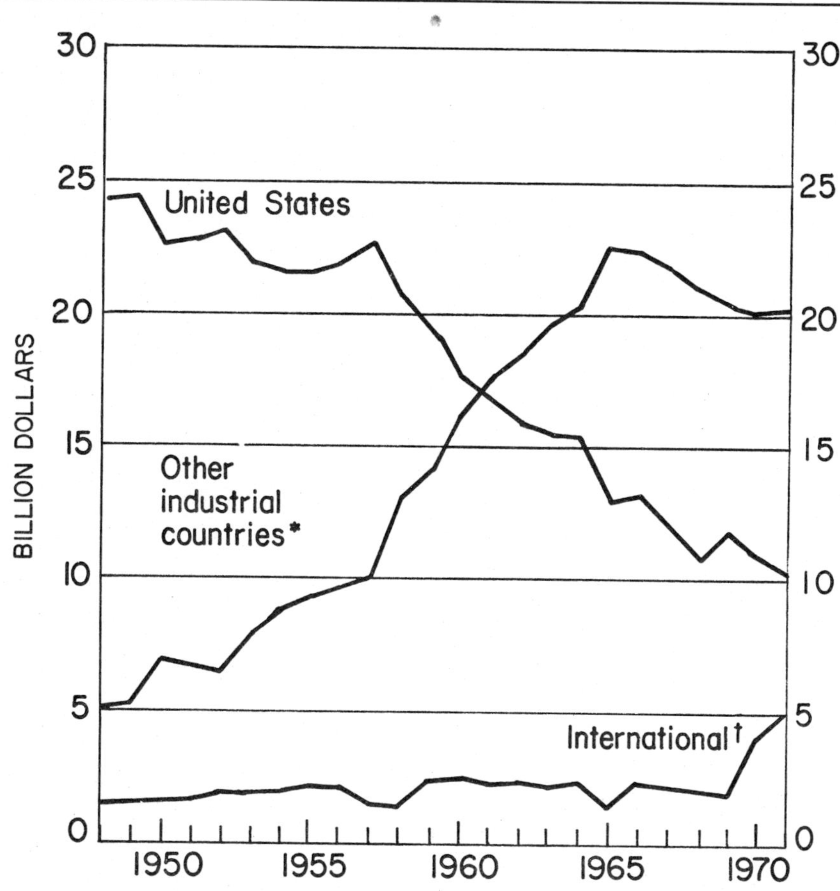

*Excluding the U.S.S.R., other countries of Eastern Europe, China, etc.
†International Monetary Fund, Bank for International Settlements, etc.
Source: *Ibid.*, p. 9. Used by permission.

ment. Starting in 1965, the surplus on current account began to deteriorate and, combined with continued large capital outflows, generated a further deterioration in the overall balance. By 1971, the surplus on current account had withered away altogether. The accompanying large gold reserve losses forced the United States, first in 1968, to halt its attempts to maintain the price of gold on the world's private markets near the official $35 per ounce by selling gold on these markets and then, three years later, to separate the dollar from the price of gold and devalue the dollar to $38 per ounce. By year-end 1971, the U.S. gold stock was only $10 billion, some $5 billion less than at year-end 1965 and only half as great as it was in 1959 (Figure 21-12). Despite the creation of SDRs on January 1, 1970, total foreign reserves continued to decline. At the same time, U.S. dollar liabilities to foreigners

Figure 21-13 **Major Currencies Increased in Value Against the U.S. Dollar in 1971**

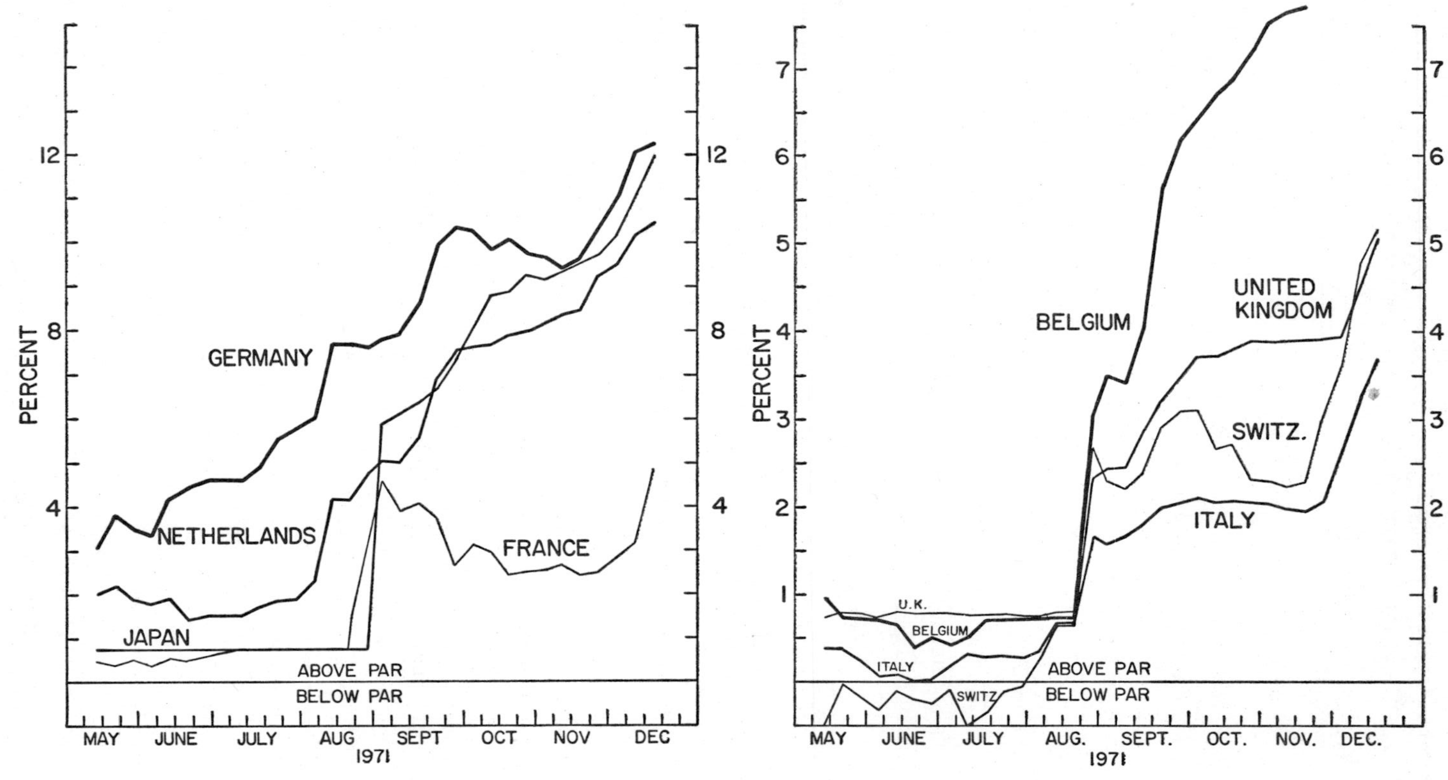

Source: Board of Governors of the Federal Reserve System, "Selected Interest and Exchange Rates for Major Countries and the U.S.," June 28, 1972.

increased 50 percent from 1965 to $45 billion, more than twice the 1959 level. Although Germany and a limited number of other West-European economies appreciated their currencies relative to the dollar in this period, pressures continued to build on the dollar exchange rate through the time the fixed exchange rate was temporarily abandoned in midyear 1971. Thereafter, almost all currencies were permitted to float upward relative to the dollar until December when fixed exchange rates were reestablished at an international monetary conference held at the Smithsonian Institution in Washington, D.C. The new rate structure did not remain unaltered long and the British pound was permitted to float down again only six months later.

Fiscal Policy

Fiscal policy had a strategic role in the events of this period. The large full employment surplus declined only fractionally during the recession in 1961. To stimulate expansion, Congress enacted a 7 percent tax credit on business investment in 1962, and liberalized depreciation regulations. The president also recommended to Congress large across-the-board reductions in personal and corporate income taxes and announced a program of voluntary price-wage guidelines tying wage increases to average productivity gains. Congress failed to enact the tax recommendations and the full employment surplus increased in 1963. To remove this fiscal "drag," Congress approved the tax reductions in early 1964 to be effective over the next two years. As a result of the initial reductions, the full employment surplus declined abruptly from $14 billion in the fourth quarter of 1963 to $2 billion in the second quarter of 1964, on a base of $115 billion of expenditures.

This was the largest stimulative fiscal shock since the Korean war and also the first time stimulative fiscal actions had been taken to accelerate an already well-developed expansion and to produce a planned deficit in the budget. The subsequent acceleration in income expanded full employment revenues quickly and, by the first quarter of 1965, the full employment surplus had increased by some $5 billion. The national income accounts budget registered a $7 billion deficit in the second quarter of 1964 as the full immediate effects of the tax reductions were recorded. However, by the fourth quarter, revenues already matched the pretax revenue intake and by the first quarter of 1965, only one year after the tax reductions, the national income budget registered its largest quarterly surplus since 1960. The expanding full employment surplus was once more reduced in mid-1965 as a result of the final stages of the 1964 reduction in income taxes, large reductions in excise taxes, and a sharp jump in government expenditures on social programs.

The full employment surplus again expanded shortly after these tax reductions and a small deficit was turned into a small surplus within three quarters. However, this time the increase in the surplus was halted by steeply rising expenditures as the full impact of the increased military spending was felt. The full employment surplus declined more than $12 billion to a large deficit between the second quarter, 1966, and first quarter, 1967, at a time the economy was operating at above capacity levels. In October, 1966, the investment credit was suspended and scheduled further excise tax reductions were postponed. At the beginning of 1967, the president requested Congress to enact a temporary surtax on personal and corporate incomes.

The slowdown in economic activity in the first half of the year generated second thoughts about introducing additional restraint and Congress postponed action on the president's request. Indeed, the investment credit was restored in the spring. However, after the pace of economic activity accelerated sharply in the second half of the year, the president renewed his request for a surtax, and in mid-1968, by which time the full employment deficit had increased to $16 billion, Congress enacted the tax hikes. In response, the deficit declined by $15 billion in the next quarter and by $28 billion over the next year to a surplus of $12 billion. Expenditures increased only slightly as specified in the surtax agreement, Social Security taxes were increased, and the investment credit was suspended again.

The full employment surplus continued to rise through the fourth quarter of 1969 and then declined sharply in consequence of a two-step elimination of the surtax. The surplus stabilized near $5 billion until mid-1971 when the president recommended a package of fiscal measures, including the elimination of the excise tax on automobiles, reductions in income taxes, the reimposition of the investment tax credit, and a temporary surtax on imports. Congress enacted these measures later in the year.

Fiscal actions were also undertaken to aid the balance of payments. Effective in mid-1963, a tax was imposed on foreign borrowing in this country to equalize the effective interest rates at home and abroad. In mid-1971, a temporary surtax was imposed on dutiable imports. In the intervening years, overseas aid was curtailed. The impact of these reductions, however, was offset by increased military purchases abroad.

In sum, after a slow start, fiscal policy contributed to the balanced recovery and expansion through 1965. From 1966 through 1968, fiscal policy was strongly destabilizing. The surtax in 1968, although too late and too little to undo the previous damage, did put fiscal policy back on a contracyclical track. Simulations on the FRB-MIT model indicate considerably greater overheating in the absence of this tax, although it has been considered ineffective by a large group of analysts. As in 1958 and 1961, the reduction in the full employment surplus in 1970 was relatively small and again insufficient to quickly reverse the downturn in aggregate activity. Unlike the earlier declines, however, the increase in fiscal stimulus occurred despite no noticeable slowing in prices.

Monetary Policy

Through the first part of the 1961–69 expansion, monetary policy strategy was directed primarily at balance of payments considerations. The money supply expanded at a slow, but accelerating, rate—2 percent in 1961 and 1962, 3 percent in 1963, and 4 percent in 1964 and 1965. Except for some slowing in 1962, the rate of monetary expansion was relatively steady. Reflecting the moderate rate of recovery, short-term interest rates increased gradually from near 2 percent to 3½ percent in mid-1965. Long-term Treasury bond yields were only slightly higher in 1965 than at the trough in 1961. The discount rate was increased one-half of a percentage point in mid-1963 and again by the same amount in mid-1964. Both increases were designed to exert upward pressure on short-term rates and discourage short-term capital outflows abroad.

The same considerations also induced a shift in policy away from restricting open market operations to the Treasury bill sector. In an attempt to exert downward pressure on long-term rates, while minimizing the effect on short-term rates, reserves were provided in increasing amounts through open market purchases of longer-term securities. Lower long-term rates were desired to stimulate domestic investment. This strategy also led to a reduction in reserve requirements in 1962 on less-variable time deposits rather than on more-variable demand deposits. It was hoped that the banks would use the reserves thereby released to invest in longer-term securities, particularly in residential mortgages. The acceleration of the growth of the money stock in 1964 and 1965 may be attributed, in part, to a desire to minimize upward pressures on longer-term interest rates resulting from the financing of the budget deficits associated with the major tax reductions of those years.

This period also saw record sustained expansions in time deposits. From 1961 through 1965, time deposits at commercial banks increased at an average annual rate of 15 percent. This was twice the rate of expansion during the 1950s. The acceleration can be attributed to the introduction in 1961 of the large negotiable certificates of deposit (CDs), the continuous liberalization of Regulation Q ceilings as market rates of interest rose, and renewed interest by commercial banks in both interest-bearing deposits and mortgage loans. Bank credit and money supply, defined to include time deposits at commercial banks (M2), also expanded at record rates during this period reflecting the rapid expansion in time deposits.

At year-end 1965, rapidly building inflationary pressures caused the Federal Reserve to clarify publicly its intentions to pursue a more restrictive policy by raising the discount rate to 4½ percent. The action was explained as being directed primarily at curbing existing and potential inflationary tendencies fueled, in part, by larger than expected federal military expenditures. The increase received wider than usual attention because of the publicity surrounding the narrow one-vote margin of the four to three vote on the Board of Governors and public murmurs of displeasure by the administration, which argued that the action was premature and should have awaited the annual budget message at the beginning of 1966. To many, the Fed's action reinforced their own fears of accelerated inflation, and the demand for credit strengthened sharply. Interest rates jumped abruptly across-the-board and continued to increase throughout the first half of 1966. The president's subsequent budget message did little to allay fears of sharply increased government spending, and, by midyear, Treasury bill rates had climbed to 5½ percent and bond rates to almost 5 percent, the highest levels since the 1920s.

Concurrent with the increase in the discount rate, Regulation Q ceilings were raised to permit banks to continue to attract interest-bearing deposits. To moderate the effects of the sudden spurt in credit demands on interest rates, the Federal Reserve accelerated its reserve provision. As a result, in the first few months of 1966, money supply expanded at about 7 percent, annual rate, and time deposit growth accelerated slightly to 17 percent.

The rapid expansions were halted near midyear and the money supply showed no further increase from April, 1966, through January, 1967. Reserve requirements were raised on time deposits in excess of $5 million, that is, on banks relying heavily on CDs, in two steps from 4 to 6 percent. Unlike previous periods of rising market rates, Regulation Q ceilings on time deposit rates were not raised (see Table 21-7, p. 486). By mid-1966, many banks were unable to turn over their maturing CDs and the amount outstanding declined. In addition, to slow the flow of funds out of thrift institutions after rate ceilings had been extended to these institutions in September, ceiling rates on some types of small time deposits at commercial banks were rolled back. At the same time, the Federal Reserve urged the banks to curb business loans and accommodate municipal credit needs, and that "this objective will be kept in mind by the Federal Reserve banks in their extensions of credit to member banks through the discount window."

At the beginning of 1967, monetary policy was sharply reversed. Monetary expansion was renewed vigorously and the money supply increased at an annual rate of about 8 percent over the next two years. The discount rate and reserve requirements on savings and the first $5 million of time deposits were lowered. Treasury bill rates declined briskly from 5½ percent to 3½ percent between late 1966 and early 1967. Longer-term rates also declined. Banks took this opportunity to rebuild their CD volume. However, as economic expansion resumed in mid-1967, interest rates turned around and rose as steeply as they had declined. By year-end, short-term rates had recouped most of their decline and long-term rates surged well above their previous peaks. Short-term rates continued to rise in the first half of 1968, while long-term rates stabilized. Between mid-1967 and mid-1968, the discount rate was increased three times to 5½ percent, the highest level since 1930. Reserve requirements on demand deposits in excess of $5 million and margin requirements were also both raised in this period.

In mid-1968, acting in anticipation of the restrictive impact of the long awaited income surtax, the Board of Governors reduced the discount rate to 5¼ percent. Interest rates dipped across-the-board. When it became evident shortly thereafter that the surtax would not impose the restraint necessary to curtail demand and price accelerations, interest rates reversed and climbed steeply. By year-end 1968, Treasury bills and bonds both yielded near 6 percent.

In 1969, the Federal Reserve intensified its restraint and policy mirrored that of 1966. Money supply was slowed by almost two-thirds to near 3 percent, and even more if the data before later revision are used. Interest rates climbed to record levels. At times during the year, the Federal funds rate exceeded 10 percent, the three-month Treasury bill rate 8 percent, and the bond rate 7 percent.

CDs declined abruptly as market rates of interest climbed well above unchanged Q ceiling rates and made it difficult for banks to turn over maturing certificates on a purely interest rate basis. By year-end, large CDs had declined to $11 billion, less than one-half their levels of one year earlier (see Figure 6-3 and Table 6-6, pp. 101, 102). The banks attempted to offset CD losses by attracting funds through means not restricted by Regulation Q. Banks more than doubled Eurodollar borrowings from their overseas branches and foreign banks to $15 billion. Banks owned by one-bank holding companies, an increasingly popular form of ownership at the time, obtained another $6 billion by borrowing from or selling loans to their parent companies who, in turn, obtained the necessary funds by issuing commercial paper secured by the name of the bank. As a result, the decline in time deposits was not reflected in bank credit, which increased 4 percent during 1969 and averaged 7 percent above 1968.

Thrift institutions did not fare much better than banks and experienced only small increases in deposits, although savings and loan associations increased their borrowings from the Federal Home Loan Banks to an extent that their total asset growth moderated only slightly. The Federal Reserve reinforced its restraint by increasing the discount rate to 6 percent and reserve requirements on demand deposits across-the-board. Reserve requirements were also imposed on Eurodollars in excess of the bank's holdings at midyear.

Attempts to circumvent the restrictive impact of Regulation Q were not limited to financial institutions. Savers who were unable to obtain a competitive market rate of return at financial institutions withdrew their funds and reinvested in the private capital markets. Particular interest was shown by small savers in Treasury bills and, until the Treasury and Federal Reserve made life difficult for these investors by increasing the minimum denomination of bills at time of issue to $10,000 and tightening the payment procedures, small bids for Treasury bills at the weekly auctions increased substantially to record levels. Large corporate borrowers rejected by banks turned to the commercial paper market where their IOUs were readily accepted by holders of maturing CDs. While CDs declined from

$24 billion to $11 billion, commercial paper increased from $20 billion to almost $40 billion. The increase included about $7 billion issued by bank holding companies. The net effect of the failure to raise Q ceilings was to slow the expansion of financial institution credit substantially, the expansion of total credit considerably less, and to increase inefficiency in the capital market significantly.

In 1970, Federal Reserve policy reversed direction again. Money supply increased about 5 percent during the year despite a marked slowing in the fourth quarter as credit demands fell in response to a prolonged automobile strike. In 1971, growth in the money supply accelerated sharply. In the first seven months, money supply expanded at an annual rate of 10 percent. Between November, 1970, and February, 1971, the discount rate was reduced five times in one-fourth percentage point steps to 4¾ percent, and then it was increased one-fourth point. The apparently greater flexibility was designed to maintain the discount rate in closer harmony with short-term market rates. Also in late 1970, reserve requirements were reduced on time deposits in excess of $5 million, although about one-half of the reserves freed were simultaneously absorbed by the imposition of reserve requirements on funds obtained from affiliated bank holding companies. Margin requirements had been reduced somewhat earlier.

After declining significantly at the beginning of 1970, short-term rates continued to drift downward while long-term rates backed up sharply to or above their earlier levels. Rates turned down again in the second half of the year and declined steeply into 1971. By the end of the first quarter of 1971, Treasury bill rates had declined to below 3½ percent, down more than four and one-half percentage points from their early 1970 highs, while bond rates dropped from 7 percent to 5½ percent.

As market rates dropped below Q ceiling rates, banks were once again able to sell CDs. By year-end 1970, the banks had not only recouped their previous losses but increased their amount of CDs outstanding to a record level. The amount of CDs outstanding continued to increase, but at a considerably slower pace in 1971. As a result of the sale of CDs and strong inflows of savings funds, time deposits as a whole increased in excess of 15 percent between the beginning of 1970 and mid-1971. Inflows into thrift institutions were also heavy in this period.

The increase in CDs negated bank needs for Eurodollars and other nondeposit funds. By mid-1971, bank holdings of Eurodollars had declined from $15 billion to less than $2 billion despite an attempt by the Federal Reserve to moderate the downflow by doubling reserve requirements on amounts in excess of the minimum levels attained. Thus, any later rebuilding of these balances would entail a higher cost. Bank-related commercial paper also declined from $7.5 billion to under $2 billion in the year ending mid-1971.

In mid-1970, the Penn Central Railroad filed bankruptcy procedures. This action sent quivers throughout the money market as the railroad had in excess of $80 million of commercial paper outstanding. At the same time, the credit rating of a large automobile firm was being questioned. To ease any potential problems of refinancing maturing commercial paper, the Federal Reserve suspended the rate ceilings on CDs of 30- to 89-days maturity. This served to increase the ability of banks to obtain funds to meet demands from firms experiencing difficulties in rolling over their paper and explained part of the rapid rise in CDs in the second half of 1970. At the same time, the Fed reminded the banks of the availability of the discount window for appropriate borrowing.

The speedy action is consistent with the Federal Reserve's concern with stability in the financial markets. The Vice-Chairman of the Board of Governors considered the crisis sufficiently serious to conclude, "I think it's not extreme to say that we avoided another 1933."[1] On the other hand, the Council of Economic Advisers in its *Annual Report* for 1970 concluded that it could find no evidence of a serious liquidity crisis. It is of interest to speculate whether the rapid buildup of commercial paper with undoubtedly some deterioration in quality may not, at least in part, have been a direct consequence of earlier Federal Reserve actions maintaining the Q ceiling and forcing corporations to bypass the more experienced credit scrutiny of the commercial banks.

Following the announcement of Phase 1 of President Nixon's price-wage program in mid-August, 1971, monetary policy changed again. After expanding rapidly in the first half of the year, the narrow money stock remained stable in the second half, while broader measures expanded at more moderate rates. Short-term interest rates declined sharply, after having risen equally sharply in the second quarter. Long-term rates showed similar but less volatile changes. The discount rate, which had been increased just shortly before the introduction of the new economic program, was reduced twice to 4½ by year-end.

The decline in interest rates concurrent with the slowing in monetary expansion most likely reflected downward revisions in price expectations, consistent with the objectives of the new incomes policy. Vigorous monetary expansion was renewed in the first nine months of 1972. Short-term rates continued to decline into the first quarter, but then turned up.

International Monetary Policy

The continuing balance of payments problems and the accompanying strains on the dollar exchange rate occupied a considerable portion of Federal Reserve concern. As noted earlier, the discount rate increases in 1963 and 1964 were both executed for balance of payments reasons. In 1962, the Federal Reserve com-

1. J. L. Robertson, quoted in Lawrence Malkin, "A Practical Politician at the Fed," *Fortune*, May, 1971, p. 151.

Table 21-2 **Federal Reserve Swap Arrangements by Foreign Bank, September 8, 1972**
(Millions of U.S. dollars)

Foreign bank	Amount of arrangement
Austrian National Bank	200
National Bank of Belgium	600
Bank of Canada	1,000
National Bank of Denmark	200
Bank of England	2,000
Bank of France	1,000
German Federal Bank	1,000
Bank of Italy	1,250
Bank of Japan	1,000
Bank of Mexico	130
Netherlands Bank	300
Bank of Norway	200
Bank of Sweden	250
Swiss National Bank	1,000
Bank for International Settlements:	
Swiss francs/dollars	600
Other authorized European currencies/ dollars	1,000
Total	11,730

Source: *Federal Reserve Bulletin*, 58 (9), September, 1972, p. 758.

menced operations in foreign currencies, primarily through currency swap operations with foreign central banks. These operations paralleled domestic open market operations, except that foreign currencies were traded to affect spot and forward exchange rates and, thereby, influence international capital flows. A special manager was appointed to supervise these operations.

From a modest beginning, these operations expanded rapidly. By 1972, the Federal Reserve had entered into swap arrangements with central banks in 14 countries and the Bank of International Settlements in Switzerland in an aggregate amount of almost $12 billion (Table 21-2). In March, 1972, about $3 billion of foreign currency debts were outstanding on these agreements. Repayment of swap debts, at times, has involved complex arrangements and included Treasury issuance of special securities to foreign countries and IMF drawings.

The Federal Reserve also has responsibility for the Voluntary Foreign Credit Restraint Program for financial institutions, initiated in 1965. Under this program, banks and nonbanks are restricted in their lending and investing abroad. At year-end 1971, bank loans abroad were at about the same level as five years earlier and well under their ceiling levels. Nonbanks also operated at considerably below their ceiling limits.

In 1969, reserve requirements were imposed on U.S. bank holdings of Eurodollars above a base level, increasing their effective cost to the banks, in order to reduce the pressures on the Eurodollar market and curb the outflows of short-term capital from European countries to the U.S. In 1970, when banks began to repay their Eurodollar borrowings, the requirements were increased and the requirement-free base effectively lowered, in order to discourage banks from repaying these loans and reduce outflows of capital from the U.S. to European countries, by increasing the potential costs to the banks of tapping this market again. Balance of payments considerations also influenced monetary policy indirectly. In 1967, restraint was postponed, at least partially, in order to avoid exerting additional pressures on the British pound, which was devalued later in the year, by inducing capital outflows to the U.S. in search of higher interest rates.

At best, these actions postponed the eventual crises in the balance of payments. As noted, gold reserves continued to decline. In 1968, the U.S. stopped selling gold to maintain the world price at parity with the official dollar price. In 1971, all gold sales were halted. The dollar became inconvertible into gold in official transactions for the first time since 1934. In 1972, the official price of gold was raised to $38 an ounce, but gold sales were not renewed.

Evaluation

The record of monetary policy in this period is mixed. Many have argued that monetary policy was not sufficiently aggressive in the first part of the expansion. Monetarists argue that it was not until the acceleration in the growth of the money stock in 1964 and 1965 that monetary policy became actively expansionary and that it was this change in policy, rather than the concurrent tax reductions, that generated the acceleration in economic activity. On the other hand, however, they view this as the only subperiod within the overall expansion period in which monetary expansion was relatively steady and contributed to overall economic stability.

From 1966 through 1971, monetary policy became more active. However, it would be difficult to argue that it contributed greatly to stability.[2] To the extent that changes in money supply generate later changes in the same direction in nominal income, the abrupt shifts between monetary expansion and constraint contributed to instability. In large part, Federal Reserve policy in this period was

2. One critic of monetary policy attributes its performance to characteristics inherent in central bankers: "Being a central banker generates a certain respect for the potentialities of monetary policy, but also a certain reluctance to accept primary responsibility for achieving basic objectives by monetary means" (Stein, *The Fiscal Revolution in America*, p. 278).

conducted to permit the exceedingly large deficits in the federal budget to be financed without raising interest rates sharply. Yet two times, in 1966 and in 1969, interest rates climbed to record levels. These runups must, at least in part, be attributed to preceding sharp accelerations in monetary growth. Likewise, the abruptness of the curbing of monetary expansion appears to have contributed to the subsequent slowing of aggregate activity. While stabilizing, these periods of severe monetary restraint might not have been necessary if monetary expansion had been more moderate in the preceding periods.

The reduction in the discount rate in mid-1968 on the heels of the surtax is of particular significance. It marks the first time the Federal Reserve executed policy on the basis of an economic forecast. This was an attempt to shorten the length of the inside time lag in the impact of monetary policy. Unfortunately, the forecast was incorrect and the action, in retrospect, destabilizing. Nevertheless, the action represented an important experiment, which may reasonably be expected to be repeated, hopefully with better results.

The sharp acceleration in monetary expansion in the first half of 1971 can also be questioned, although it occurred during a period of substantial unemployment. Apparently undertaken to moderate long-term interest rate increases, the acceleration was followed by increases, not decreases, in interest rates and only insignificant moderation in price pressures. In midyear, price and wage controls were imposed. The abrupt swings in the rate of monetary expansion did not stop, however. The sharp slowing in monetary growth in the last half of 1971 was followed by an equally sharp acceleration in the next six months.

The continued pursuit of such highly criticized policies by the Federal Reserve reflects not so much either a lack of knowledge of the monetary processes or a disregard for the arguments of the critics as it does an inability to reconcile the conflict in the short run between low and stable interest rates and longer-term objectives. Improved monetary policies, as well as fiscal policies, await not only continued gains in our knowledge of the economic processes but also a downgrading of interest rates as an important objective of economic policy.

References

Anderson, Clay J., *A Half-Century of Federal Reserve Policymaking, 1914–1964* (Philadelphia: Federal Reserve Bank of Philadelphia, 1965).

Board of Governors of the Federal Reserve System, *Annual Report* (Washington, D.C.: 1945 through 1972).

Cagan, Phillip, *Recent Monetary Policy* (Washington, D.C.: American Enterprise Institute, 1971).

Carlson, Keith M., "Estimates of the High Employment Budget: 1947–1967," *Review* (Federal Reserve Bank of St. Louis), 49 (6), June, 1967, 6-14.

Council of Economic Advisers, *Annual Report* (Washington, D.C.: 1950 through 1972).

Heller, Walter W., *New Dimensions of Political Economy* (New York: Norton, 1967).

Meigs, A. James, *Money Matters* (New York: Harper & Row, 1972).

Okun, Arthur M., *The Political Economy of Prosperity* (Washington, D.C.: The Brookings Institution, 1970).

———, and Nancy H. Teeters, "The Full Employment Surplus Revisited," *Brookings Papers on Economic Activity*, No. 1 (Washington, D.C.: The Brookings Institution, 1970). Pp. 77-110.

Stein, Herbert, *The Fiscal Revolution in America* (Chicago: University of Chicago Press, 1969).

Appendix to Chapter 21

Table 21-3 **Business Cycle Expansions and Contractions in the United States: 1854 to 1972**

Business cycle reference dates		Duration in months			
		Contraction (trough from previous peak)	Expansion (trough to peak)	Cycle	
				Trough from previous trough	Peak from previous peak
Trough	Peak				
December 1854	June 1857	(X)	30	(X)	(X)
December 1858	October 1860	18	22	48	40
June 1861	April 1865	8	46	30	54
December 1867	June 1869	32	18	78	50
December 1870	October 1873	18	34	36	52
March 1879	March 1882	65	36	99	101
May 1885	March 1887	38	22	74	60
April 1888	July 1890	13	27	35	40
May 1891	January 1893	10	20	37	30
June 1894	December 1895	17	18	37	35
June 1897	June 1899	18	24	36	42
December 1900	September 1902	18	21	42	39
August 1904	May 1907	23	33	44	56
June 1908	January 1910	13	19	46	32
January 1912	January 1913	24	12	43	36
December 1914	August 1918	23	44	35	67
March 1919	January 1920	7	10	51	7
July 1921	May 1923	18	22	28	40
July 1924	October 1926	14	27	36	41
November 1927	August 1929	13	21	40	34
March 1933	May 1937	43	50	64	93
June 1938	February 1945	13	80	63	93
October 1945	November 1948	8	37	88	45
October 1949	July 1953	11	45	48	56
August 1954	July 1957	13	35	58	48
April 1958	May 1960	9	25	44	34
February 1961	*November 1969	9	105	34	114
*November 1970		12	(X)	117	(X)
Average, all cycles:					
27 cycles, 1854–1970		19	33	52	[1]52
11 cycles, 1919–1970		15	42	56	[2]60
5 cycles, 1945–1970		11	49	60	[3]59
Average, peacetime cycles:					
22 cycles, 1854–1961		20	26	45	[4]46
8 cycles, 1919–1961		16	28	45	[5]58
3 cycles, 1945–1961		10	32	42	[6]42

Note: Underscored figures are the wartime expansions (Civil War, World Wars I and II, Korean War, and Vietnam War), the postwar contractions and the full cycles that include the wartime expansions.

*Tentative and subject to revision as more information becomes available.

[1]26 cycles, 1857–1969.
[2]10 cycles, 1920–1969.
[3]5 cycles, 1945–1969.
[4]21 cycles, 1857–1960.
[5]7 cycles, 1920–1960.
[6]3 cycles, 1945–1960.

Source: Department of Commerce, *Business Conditions Digest*, June, 1972, p. 114.

Table 21-4 Reserve Requirements of Member Banks
(Percent of deposits)

Through July 13, 1966

Effective date	Net demand deposits			Time deposits (all classes of banks)
	Central reserve city banks	Reserve city banks	Country banks	
1917—June 21	13	10	7	3
1936—Aug. 16	19½	15	10½	4½
1937—Mar. 1	22¾	17½	12¼	5¼
May 1	26	20	14	6
1938—Apr. 16	22¾	17½	12	5
1941—Nov. 1	26	20	14	6
1942—Aug. 20	24			
Sept. 14	22			
Oct. 3	20			
1948—Feb. 27	22			
June 11	24			
Sept. 24, 16	26	22	16	7½
1949—May 5, 1	24	21	15	7
June 30, July 1		20	14	6
Aug. 1			13	
Aug. 11, 16	23½	19½	12	5
Aug. 18	23	19		
Aug. 25	22½	18½		
Sept. 1	22	18		
1951—Jan. 11, 16	23	19	13	6
Jan. 25, Feb. 1	24	20	14	
1953—July 9, 1	22	19	13	
1954—June 24, 16	21			5
July 29, Aug. 1	20	18	12	
1958—Feb. 27, Mar. 1	19½	17½	11½	
Mar. 20, Apr. 1	19	17	11	
Apr. 17	18½			
Apr. 24	18	16½		
1960—Sept. 1	17½			
Nov. 24			12	
Dec. 1	16½			
1962—July 28				
Oct. 25, Nov. 1				4

Table 21-4 (Continued)

Beginning July 14, 1966

Effective date	Net demand deposits				Time deposits (all classes of banks)		
	Reserve city banks		Country banks		Savings deposits	Other time deposits	
	Under $5 million	Over $5 million	Under $5 million	Over $5 million		Under $5 million	Over $5 million
1966—July 14, 21	16½		12		4	4	5
Sept. 8, 15							6
1967—Mar. 2					3½	3½	
Mar. 16					3	3	
1968—Jan. 11, 18	16½	17	12	12½			
1969—Apr. 17	17	17½	12½	13			
1970—Oct. 1							5

Effective date	Net demand deposits (Million dollars)					Time deposits (all classes of banks)		
	First 2 or less	Over 2 to 10	Over 10 to 100	Over 100 to 400	Over 400	Savings deposits	Other time deposits	
							Under $5 million	Over $5 million
1972—Nov. 9, 16	8	10	12	13	17½	3	3	5
In effect—Dec. 31, 1972	8	10	12	13	17½	3	3	5

Source: Board of Governors of the Federal Reserve System, *Annual Report, 1971,* p. 258; *Federal Reserve Bulletin,* July, 1972, p. 680.

Table 21-5 Federal Reserve Discount Rate, 1946 to 1972
(Percent per annum)

Effective date		Range (or level) All F.R. Banks	F.R. Bank of N.Y.	Effective date		Range (or level) All F.R. Banks	F.R. Bank of N.Y.	Effective date		Range (or level) All F.R. Banks	F.R. Bank of N.Y.
In effect 1946			1	Apr.	18	1¾–2¼	1¾	Apr.	19	5 –5½	5½
1948—Jan.			1¼	May	9	1¾	1¾		26	5½	5½
Aug.			1½	Aug.	15	1¾–2	1¾	Aug.	16	5¼–5½	5½
1950—Aug.			1¾	Sept.	12	1¾–2	2		30	5¼	5¼
1953—Jan			2		23	2	2	Dec.	18	5¼–5½	5½
1954—Feb.			1¾	Oct.	24	2 –2½	2		20	5½	5½
Apr.			1½	Nov.	7	2½	2½	1969—Apr.	4	5½–6	6
1955—Apr.	14	1½–1¾	1½	1959—Mar.	6	2½–3	3		8	6	6
	15	1½–1¾	1¾		16	3	3	1970—Nov.	11	5¾–6	6
May	2	1¾	1¾	May	29	3 –3½	3½		13	5¾–6	5¾
Aug.	4	1¾–2¼	1¾	June	12	3½	3½		16	5¾	5¾
	5	1¾–2¼	2	Sept.	11	3½–4	4	Dec.	1	5½–5¾	5¾
	12	2 –2¼	2		18	4	4		4	5½–5¾	5½
Sept.	9	2 –2¼	2¼	1960—June	3	3½–4	4		11	5½	5½
	13	2¼	2¼		10	3½–4	3½	1971—Jan.	8	5¼–5½	5¼
Nov.	18	2¼–2½	2½		14	3½	3½		15	5¼	5¼
	23	2½	2½	Aug.	12	3 –3½	3		19	5 –5¼	5¼
1956—Apr.	13	2½–3	2¾	Sept.	9	3	3		22	5 –5¼	5
	20	2¾–3	2¾	1963—July	17	3 –3½	3½		29	5	5
Aug.	24	2¾–3	3		26	3½	3½	Feb.	13	4¾–5	5
	31	3	3	1964—Nov.	24	3½–4	4		19	4¾	4¾
1957—Aug.	9	3 –3½	3		30	4	4	July	16	4¾–5	5
	23	3½	3½	1965—Dec.	6	4 –4½	4½		23	5	5
Nov.	15	3 –3½	3		13	4½	4½	Nov.	11	4¾–5	5
Dec.	2	3	3	1967—Apr.	7	4 –4½	4		19	4¾	4¾
1958—Jan.	22	2¾–3	3		14	4	4	Dec.	13	4½–4¾	4¾
	24	2¾–3	2¾	Nov.	20	4 –4½	4½		17	4½–4¾	4½
Mar.	7	2¼–3	2¼		27	4½	4½		24	4½	4½
	13	2¼–2¾	2¼	1968—Mar.	15	4½–5	4½	In effect			
	21	2¼	2¼		22	5	5	June 30, 1972		4½	4½

Source: Board of Governors of the Federal Reserve System, *Supplement to Banking and Monetary Statistics* (Section 12), p. 31; *Federal Reserve Bulletin*, July, 1972, p. A 9.

Table 21-6 **Margin Requirements**
(Percent of market value)

<table>
<tr><th colspan="2">Period</th><th colspan="7">For credit extended under Regulations T (brokers and dealers), U (banks), and G (others than brokers, dealers, or banks)</th></tr>
<tr><th rowspan="2">Beginning date</th><th rowspan="2">Ending date</th><th colspan="3">On margin stocks</th><th colspan="3">On convertible bonds</th><th rowspan="2">On short sales (T)</th></tr>
<tr><th>T</th><th>U</th><th>G</th><th>T</th><th>U</th><th>G</th></tr>
<tr><td>1937–Nov. 1</td><td>1945–Feb. 4</td><td colspan="2">40</td><td></td><td colspan="3"></td><td>50</td></tr>
<tr><td>1945–Feb. 5</td><td>July 4</td><td colspan="2">50</td><td></td><td colspan="3"></td><td>50</td></tr>
<tr><td>July 5</td><td>1946–Jan. 20</td><td colspan="2">75</td><td></td><td colspan="3"></td><td>75</td></tr>
<tr><td>1946–Jan. 21</td><td>1947–Jan. 31</td><td colspan="2">100</td><td></td><td colspan="3"></td><td>100</td></tr>
<tr><td>1947–Feb. 1</td><td>1949–Mar. 29</td><td colspan="2">75</td><td></td><td colspan="3"></td><td>75</td></tr>
<tr><td>1949–Mar. 30</td><td>1951–Jan. 16</td><td colspan="2">50</td><td></td><td colspan="3"></td><td>50</td></tr>
<tr><td>1951–Jan. 17</td><td>1953–Feb. 19</td><td colspan="2">75</td><td></td><td colspan="3"></td><td>75</td></tr>
<tr><td>1953–Feb. 20</td><td>1955–Jan. 3</td><td colspan="2">50</td><td></td><td colspan="3"></td><td>50</td></tr>
<tr><td>1955–Jan. 4</td><td>Apr. 22</td><td colspan="2">60</td><td></td><td colspan="3"></td><td>60</td></tr>
<tr><td>Apr. 23</td><td>1958–Jan. 15</td><td colspan="2">70</td><td></td><td colspan="3"></td><td>70</td></tr>
<tr><td>1958–Jan. 16</td><td>Aug. 4</td><td colspan="2">50</td><td></td><td colspan="3"></td><td>50</td></tr>
<tr><td>Aug. 5</td><td>Oct. 15</td><td colspan="2">70</td><td></td><td colspan="3"></td><td>70</td></tr>
<tr><td>Oct. 16</td><td>1960–July 27</td><td colspan="2">90</td><td></td><td colspan="3"></td><td>90</td></tr>
<tr><td>1960–July 28</td><td>1962–July 9</td><td colspan="2">70</td><td></td><td colspan="3"></td><td>70</td></tr>
<tr><td>1962–July 10</td><td>1963–Nov. 5</td><td colspan="2">50</td><td></td><td colspan="3"></td><td>50</td></tr>
<tr><td>1963–Nov. 6</td><td>1968–Mar. 10</td><td colspan="2">70</td><td></td><td colspan="3"></td><td>70</td></tr>
<tr><td>1968–Mar. 11</td><td>June 7</td><td colspan="3">70</td><td colspan="3">50</td><td>70</td></tr>
<tr><td>June 8</td><td>1970–May 5</td><td colspan="3">80</td><td colspan="3">60</td><td>80</td></tr>
<tr><td>1970–May 6</td><td>1971–Dec. 3</td><td colspan="3">65</td><td colspan="3">50</td><td>65</td></tr>
<tr><td colspan="2">In effect Sept. 30, 1972</td><td colspan="3">55</td><td colspan="3">50</td><td>55</td></tr>
</table>

NOTE:—Regulations G, T, and U, prescribed in accordance with the Securities Exchange Act of 1934, limit the amount of credit to purchase and carry margin stocks that may be extended on securities as collateral by prescribing a maximum loan value, which is a specified percentage of the market value of the collateral at the time the credit is extended; margin requirements are the difference between the market value (100 percent) and the maximum loan value. The term margin stocks is defined in the corresponding regulation.

Regulation G and special margin requirements for bonds convertible into stocks were adopted by the Board of Governors effective Mar. 11, 1968.

Source: *Federal Reserve Bulletin*, July, 1972, p. A 10.

Table 21-7 Maximum Interest Rates Payable on Time and Savings Deposits, 1933-72
(Percent per annum)

Rates Nov. 1, 1933–July 19, 1966

Type of deposit	Effective date							
	Nov. 1, 1933	Feb. 1, 1935	Jan. 1, 1936	Jan. 1, 1957	Jan. 1, 1962	July 17, 1963	Nov. 24, 1964	Dec. 6, 1965
Saving deposits:								
12 months or more	3	2½	2½	3	4	4	4	4
Less than 12 months					3½	3½		
Postal savings deposits:[1]								
12 months or more	3	2½	2½	3	4	4	4	4
Less than 12 months					3½	3½		
Other time deposits:[2]								
12 months or more	3	2½	2½	3	4	4	4½	5½
6 months to 12 months					3½			
90 days to 6 months	3	2½	2	2½	2½			
Less than 90 days (30–89 days)	3	2½	1	1	1	1	4	

Rates beginning July 20, 1966

Type of deposit	Effective date			
	July 20, 1966	Sept. 26, 1966	Apr. 19, 1968	Jan. 21, 1970*
Savings deposits	4	4	4	4½
Other time deposits:[2]				
Multiple maturity:[3]				
30–89 days	4	4	4	4½
90 days–1 year	5	5	5	5
1 year to 2 years				5½
2 years and over				5¾
Single maturity:				
Less than $100,000:				
30 days to 1 year	5½	5	5	5
1 year to 2 years				5½
2 years and over				5¾
$100,000 and over:				
30–59 days	5½	5½	5½	[4]
60–89 days			5¾	[4]
90–179 days			6	6¾
180 days to 1 year			6¼	7
1 year or more				7½

Table 21-7 (Continued)

[1]Closing date for the Postal Savings System was Mar. 28, 1966.

[2]For exceptions with respect to foreign time deposits, see ANNUAL REPORTS for 1962, p. 129; 1965, p. 233; and 1968, p. 69.

[3]Multiple-maturity time deposits include deposits that are automatically renewable at maturity without action by the depositor and deposits that are payable after written notice of withdrawal.

[4]The rates in effect beginning Jan. 21 through June 23, 1970, were 6¼ per cent on maturities of 30–59 days and 6½ per cent on maturities of 60–89 days. Effective June 24, 1970, maximum interest rates on these maturities were suspended until further notice.

[°]In effect June 30, 1972.

NOTE.—Maximum rates that may be paid by member banks as established by the Board of Governors under provisions of Regulation Q; however, a member bank may not pay a rate in excess of the maximum rate payable by State banks or trust companies on like deposits under the laws of the State in which the member bank is located. Beginning Feb. 1, 1936, maximum rates that may be paid by nonmember insured commercial banks, as established by the FDIC, have been the same as those in effect for member banks.

Source: Board of Governors of the Federal Reserve System, *Annual Report, 1971*, p. 260.

Index

Printed in U.S.A.